When should I travel to get the best airfare?
Where do I go for answers to my travel questions?
What's the best and easiest way to plan and book my trip?

frommers.travelocity.com

Frommer's, the travel guide leader, has teamed up with **Travelocity.com**, the leader in online travel, to bring you an in-depth, easy-to-use resource designed to help you plan and book your trip online.

At **frommers.travelocity.com**, you'll find free online updates about your destination from the experts at Frommer's plus the outstanding travel planning and purchasing features of Travelocity.com. Travelocity.com provides reservations capabilities for 95 percent of all airline seats sold, more than 47,000 hotels, and over 50 car rental companies. In addition, Travelocity.com offers more than 2,000 exciting vacation and cruise packages. Travelocity.com puts you in complete control of your travel planning with these and other great features:

Expert travel guidance from Frommer's - over 150 writers reporting from around the world!

Best Fare Finder - an interactive calendar tells you when to travel to get the best airfare

Fare Watcher - we'll track airfare changes to your favorite destinations

Dream Maps - a mapping feature that suggests travel opportunities based on your budget

Shop Safe Guarantee - 24 hours a day / 7 days a week live customer service, and more!

Whether traveling on a tight budget, looking for a quick weekend getaway, or planning the trip of a lifetime, Frommer's guides and Travelocity.com will make your travel dreams a reality. You've bought the book, now book the trip!

Travelocity.com
A Sabre Company

Frommer's®

Other Great Guides for Your Trip:

Frommer's New York City

Frommer's Portable New York City

Frommer's New York from $80 a Day

Frommer's Irreverent Guide to Manhattan

New York City For Dummies

The Unofficial Guide to New York City

Frommer's Memorable Walks in New York

Frommer's Wonderful Weekends from New York City

Here's what the critics say about Frommer's:

"Amazingly easy to use. Very portable, very complete."
—*Booklist*

♦

"The only mainstream guide to list specific prices. The Walter Cronkite of guidebooks—with all that implies."
—*Travel & Leisure*

♦

"Complete, concise, and filled wih useful information."
—*New York Daily News*

♦

"Hotel information is close to encyclopedic."
—*Des Moines Sunday Register*

♦

"The best series for travelers who want one easy-to-use guidebook."
—*US Airways Magazine*

new york city
with kids

7th Edition

by Holly Hughes

IDG Books Worldwide, Inc.
An International Data Group Company
Foster City, CA • Chicago, IL • Indianapolis, IN • New York, NY

ABOUT THE AUTHORS

Holly Hughes is a freelance writer and editor who lives on the Upper West Side of Manhattan with her husband and three children. She has been the editor of Pocket Books' *Nancy Drew Mysteries,* a contributing editor to Scholastic's *Literary Cavalcade* magazine, and an executive editor of Fodor's Travel Guides. For Frommer's, she has been series editor for Frommer's Irreverent Guides and Frommer's By Night guides. **Meredith Horton** assisted Holly in fact-checking this edition.

Mercer Warriner is an editor and writer living in SoHo with her husband and two sons. She has been editor and writer on various Nancy Drew and Hardy Boys series; as a senior editor at Berkley Books, she acquired and edited romances and mysteries. She has also worked at William Morrow and Pocket Books.

IDG BOOKS WORLDWIDE, INC.

An International Data Group Company
909 Third Ave.
New York, NY 10022

Find us online at **www.frommers.com**

ISBN 0-7645-6285-1
ISSN 1060-3719

Editor: Kitty Wilson Jarrett
Production Editor: Tammy Ahrens
Photo Editor: Richard Fox
Design by Michele Laseau
Cartographer: John Decamillis
Production by IDG Books Indianapolis Production Department

SPECIAL SALES

For general information on IDG Books Worldwide's books in the U.S., please call our Consumer Customer Service Department at 1-800-762-2974. For reseller information, including discounts, bulk sales, customized editions, and premium sales, please call our Reseller Consumer Service Department at 1-800-434-3422.

Manufactured in the United States of America.

5 4 3 2 1

Contents

List of Maps

An Invitation to the Reader

In researching this book, we discovered many wonderful places—hotels, restaurants, shops, and more. We're sure you'll find others. Please tell us about them, so we can share the information with your fellow travelers in upcoming editions. If you were disappointed with a recommendation, we'd love to know that too. Please write to:

Frommer's New York City with Kids, 7th Edition
IDG Books Worldwide, Inc.
909 Third Avenue
New York, NY 10022

An Additional Note

Please be advised that travel information is subject to change at any time—and this is especially true of prices. We therefore suggest that you write or call ahead for confirmation when making your travel plans. The authors, editors, and publisher cannot be held responsible for the experiences of readers while traveling. Your safety is important to us, however, so we encourage you to stay alert and be aware of your surroundings. Keep a close eye on cameras, purses, and wallets, all favorite targets of thieves and pickpockets.

What the Symbols Mean

✪ Frommer's Favorites

Our favorite places and experiences—outstanding for quality, value, or both.

The following abbreviations are used for credit cards:

AE	American Express	DISC	Discover
CB	Carte Blanche	MC	MasterCard
DC	Diners Club	V	Visa

Find Frommer's Online

www.frommers.com offers up-to-the-minute listings on almost 200 cities around the globe—including the latest bargains and candid, personal articles updated daily by Arthur Frommer himself. No other Web site offers such comprehensive and timely coverage of the world of travel.

How to Feel Like a New York Family

My first 9 New York years BC—Before Children—I did all the things folks think Manhattanites do. I went downtown to CBGBs to hear head-banging new bands; I did the standing-room thing at the Met and Carnegie Hall; I saw experimental theater pieces in dingy alternative spaces way downtown; I stood in line all day to get free tickets to Shakespeare in the Park. I checked out every art museum and shopped at Barneys and Bloomingdale's. I never made it to Times Square on New Year's Eve (somehow or other, there was always a party I had to go to instead), but on Thanksgiving eve I joined the throngs on the Upper West Side to watch the giant helium balloons being blown up for the Macy's parade. I ate at hole-in-the-wall ethnic restaurants and sought out atmospheric bars straight out of *The Lost Weekend*. I rode the subway everywhere and at all hours; I walked from one end of Manhattan to the other.

After my husband and I had our first baby, I felt initially as though my life as a Manhattanite was over. If ever we wanted to stay out late, we'd end up paying a fortune to a baby-sitter, and if we ordered tickets to anything in advance, most likely we'd have to give away our seats when the baby came down with an ear infection or roseola at the last minute. We made an effort to go out to eat as a family, but we stuck close to pizza, Chinese, and burger joints, where baby wails and spilled Cheerios would be tolerated. Drinking? Forget about it—if I wasn't either pregnant or nursing, I was so exhausted that one sip of alcohol would send me straight to sleep.

Well, we've got three kids now and I've come full circle. In fact, I feel as though I never really got to know Manhattan until I began exploring it with children. We actually talk to passersby now—there's no better way to strike up conversations with New Yorkers than by the simple virtue of having a baby strapped to your chest in a Snugli. (Alec Baldwin actually stopped *me* to have a chat when he spotted my week-old daughter, Grace.) Taxi drivers, most of them immigrants from far-flung foreign lands, teach us about their native countries and coach us to speak words in their own languages. Deli clerks slip us tidbits; greengrocers pop extra strawberries into our pint cartons. When we pass fire stations, we're allowed to go inside and climb all over the hook-and-ladder truck, not to mention pat the firehouse dog. Shopping with kids, you can really have a ball in this city—you're handed free popcorn and balloons with your shoes and lollipops with your haircuts.

I used to rush around the city underground, crammed into the subway cars at rush hour; now we take buses at off-peak hours, peering out the windows as the city rolls past, or we take the stroller across Central Park, stopping frequently to feed pigeons or watch the horses on the bridle trail. On weekends we do take the kids on subways—they love them, actually; what's not to love about whooshing through a dark underground tunnel in an air-conditioned stainless-steel bullet?—because that's the best way to get out to the other boroughs, where there are some awesome attractions: the Bronx Zoo and the New York Botanical Garden, Brooklyn's Prospect Park sights, the zoo and museums in Queens's Flushing Meadows–Corona Park.

I spend my weekends in the local playground now, getting to know neighborhood parents, instead of browsing beside strangers through stuffy museums. Of course, we still go to museums, but we go to the same ones over and over—I've been to the American Museum of Natural History at least 100 times, and I'm ready to go again today if the kids so choose. We make our ritual visits to favorite nooks of the Metropolitan Museum, the Museum of Modern Art, and the Museum of the City of New York; the New York Fire Museum and the New York Transit Museum are also on our roster of beloved places to dawdle and hang out for an afternoon.

After much trial and error, our family has gradually discovered which restaurants are kid-friendly and still manage to have palatable food for adults. (Along the way, I've learned to accept the idea that a toddler will be just fine if he eats only bread or french fries for one night.) And with children's theater and puppet shows and dance concerts and classical concerts for kids, we're getting our children prepped for the time when we can take them with us to the Met or Carnegie Hall. (They'll have to see the head-banging bands at CBGBs on their own—and they'll probably be begging to do that all too soon.)

A lot of families we know ditch the city every weekend to flee to a country house in the Hamptons or Connecticut, but so far we haven't felt the need. Weekends, when kids are out of school, are particularly rich times for pee-wee culture, and even if you don't have tickets to a show or concert, from spring to fall you can always find a street fair to wander through. Central Park alone is loaded with activities on weekends—from nature workshops up by Harlem Meer to folk dancing beside Turtle Pond to the never-failing carousel rides. With kids, a simple excursion like a bike ride to the park's Belvedere Castle can be an adventure—you'll always find plenty to see along the way. And you can always find a cart selling ice cream or hot pretzels if your youngsters' energy starts to flag.

We're totally happy living in New York. More than that: We think it's the greatest city on earth and the greatest place to raise children.

The thing that really turned my perceptions around was realizing that Manhattan isn't one monolithic city but a strange amalgamation of different cities, all sharing the same space. And just as the Alternative Art New York is worlds apart from the Wall Street New York, so is New York with Kids a quite different place from Singles New York. It just takes time to scout out this new turf.

The chief requirements for enjoying life as a single Manhattanite are money, clothes sense, and an ability to stay up all night—but to make it as a New York parent you need time, patience, and a willingness to enjoy things on your child's level. So what if that SoHo art gallery has an installation of cutting-edge art? You'll learn more about the nature of art if you swing over to the nearby Children's Museum of the Arts afterward and help your youngster create his or her own whacked-out mask or mobile. So what if you protested against the Vietnam War when you were in college? Visiting the *Intrepid* Sea-Air-Space Museum, on its aircraft carrier anchored in the Hudson, may tap surprising wells of patriotic sentiment as your kids explore their innate fascination with guns and vehicles. So what if your idea of classic TV is vintage *Playhouse 90* segments? Go to the Museum of Television and Radio or the American Museum of the Moving Image with your child, and you may also get a nostalgic rush from reruns of *Sesame Street.* So what if the jokes in that magic show are as old as the hills? Watching your child giggle hysterically makes it seem funny all over again.

1   Frommer's Favorite New York City Family Experiences

- **Watching Sea Lion Feeding Time at the Central Park Wildlife Center:** Check out the feeding schedule as you walk in the front entrance—the Sea Lion Pool is the centerpiece of this tidily landscaped little gem of a zoo, and an audience starts to gather well in advance. Claim a spot on the top steps where short people can most easily view the frisky sea lions, though chances are you'll need to hoist toddlers to your shoulders once the crowds close in. Have snacks and juice on hand so the wait won't seem so long. Don't expect fancy tricks, but there'll be enough barking and diving and splashing to satisfy everybody.

- **Spending a Sunday Afternoon at the American Museum of Natural History:** Weekends are definitely family time at this magnificent big museum on the Upper West Side, but the more the merrier—these dim, cool, high-ceilinged halls never seem too crowded. Get there early to nab tickets to the sky show at the new Rose Planetarium; slot in some time for a special exhibit, a free tour, or an awesome IMAX film; cruise by the Natural Science Center in the early afternoon for hands-on puttering with plants and live animals (for age 4 and older).

- **Enjoying a Sunny Afternoon at a World-Famous Ballpark:** You've got two choices in New York: Yankee Stadium in the Bronx, where the Bronx Bombers play, and Shea Stadium in Flushing, Queens, where the Mets play. Both are handy to the subway, and unless there's a full-blown pennant race in swing, you can usually buy tickets that day, at least in the so-called nosebleed sections high up (prime territory for catching foul balls, so bring your mitts). Nobody minds if your kids make noise or if you get tired and leave early; and there's plenty of fast food available—especially the overpriced hot dogs that are so much a part of the experience.

- **Taking the Ferry Ride to the Statue of Liberty and Ellis Island:** In many ways, the boat ride over is the best thing about this de rigueur sightseeing excursion— out on the sparkling waters of New York Harbor, with the wind in your hair and the seagulls shrieking overhead, you'll see the Manhattan skyline in all its glory. Even if there's a bit of a wait for the ferry at Battery Park, there are usually street musicians on hand to entertain you. Ride on the upper deck if you really want a dose of salt air and sun.

- **Heading to a Playground on a Weekday Afternoon:** Choose a neighborhood playground (see chapter 6), pack a picnic lunch, and head for the sandpits, swings, and slides where New York kids hang out. Mornings are when parents with infants and toddlers congregate, preschoolers start to arrive right after lunch, and the big kids hit the ground at 3 or 4pm, when their schools let out. In summer, many playgrounds have sprinklers that are a perfect way for youngsters to cool off without getting all wet.

New York City Dateline

1524   Sailing under the French flag, Italian Giovanni da Verrazano is the first European to enter what's now New York Harbor.

1609   Henry Hudson sails up the Hudson River, exploring for the Dutch East India Company.

1626   The Dutch settle in Nieuw Amsterdam and make it a fur-trading post; Peter Minuit, governor of Nieuw Amsterdam, buys Manhattan Island from the Algonquin Indians for trinkets worth 60 florins (about $24).

1653   Dutch settlers build a wall as a fortification against the English and name the adjacent street Wall Street.

1664   English invaders take Nieuw Amsterdam from the Dutch (wooden-legged Peter Stuyvesant is the Dutch governor).

1673   The Dutch take back Manhattan.

1674   Under the Treaty of Westminster, the Dutch finally give Nieuw Amsterdam to the English, who rename it New York after James, duke of York.

1776   American colonists topple the statue of King George on Bowling Green on July 9, but by year's end New York becomes a British stronghold that remains during the Revolutionary War.

1783   Victorious Gen. George Washington bids farewell to his troops at Fraunces Tavern in Lower Manhattan.

1789   Washington is inaugurated as the first president at Federal Hall in New York City, the first capital of the new United States.

1790   Philadelphia deposes New York City as the nation's capital.

1792   The first U.S. stock exchange is founded in New York City, making it the country's financial capital.

1811   The city north of 14th Street is laid out, using an orderly grid system.

1825   The Erie Canal opens upstate, dramatically increasing New York City's role as a major port.

1853   The World's Fair is held in New York's Bryant Park.

1858–73   Central Park is laid out by Frederick Law Olmsted and Calvert Vaux, who won the design competition.

1870   The American Museum of Natural History is founded.

- **Checking Out the Front-Car Views in the Subway:** For some reason, kids tend to love making any ride as scary as possible, which on a New York subway means standing in the front car and looking out the window as the train hurtles down the dark track into the tunnel. Signal lights blink on and off, sparks flash from the third rail (the rail supplying electric power to the train), and you get the feeling of descending into a mysterious underworld. Creepy and totally cool.

- **Watching One of the Parades of All Nations:** Every one of the many nationalities that share New York City gets its own day in the sun—generally a national holiday celebrated with a parade down Fifth Avenue. St. Patrick's Day is the biggie—it's celebrated more festively here than it is even in Ireland—but there are scores of others, from the German Steuben Day Parade in September to the Italian Columbus Day Parade in October to the Mexican Cinco de Mayo Day Parade in early May and the Puerto Rican Day Parade in June; Greeks, Israelis, Poles, and more all have their own celebrations, complete with floats, marching

1880   The Metropolitan Museum of Art opens on the east side of Central Park.

1883   The Brooklyn Bridge is completed, spanning the East River and linking Manhattan and Brooklyn.

1885–86   The Statue of Liberty is delivered from France and erected in New York Harbor.

1887   Electric streetcars begin to run on elevated railways.

1892   Ellis Island opens as an immigration station.

1898   The newly consolidated New York City incorporates all five boroughs.

1904   Construction begins on the first line of the New York City subway system.

1920s   African-American literary culture flowers with the Harlem Renaissance.

1925   *New Yorker* magazine is founded.

1929   The stock market crashes on October 29th, sending not only Wall Street but the entire nation into an economic tailspin that results in the Great Depression.

1939   New York's second World's Fair is held in Flushing Meadows, Queens.

1964–65   New York's third World's Fair is held in Flushing Meadows, Queens.

1970s   New York nearly declares bankruptcy.

1973   The World Trade Center opens.

1976   The entire city experiences a power blackout.

1983   The restoration of South Street Seaport takes wing with the opening of the Seaport Museum and a festival marketplace.

1986   The Statue of Liberty's centennial is celebrated with a fireworks extravaganza.

1990   Ellis Island reopens as a museum after a spectacular 6-year renovation.

1993   Terrorists bomb the World Trade Center.

1996   The city endures the heaviest winter of snowfall in its history.

1997   The restored New Amsterdam Theater opens, a milestone in the rehabilitation of West 42nd Street.

1998   The restoration of Grand Central Terminal is completed.

1999–2000   Proclaiming itself "The Millennium Capital of the World," New York City hosts its hugest-ever New Year's Eve celebration in Times Square.

---

bands, and loads of costumes from the old country. Scout out the uptown parts of the parade route, as some parades—notably those on St. Patrick's Day and Puerto Rican Day—get uncomfortably rowdy once they near Midtown. If crosstown traffic seems tied up on a fair-weather Saturday, hurry on over to Fifth—chances are there's a parade in progress. See "Kids' Favorite New York City Events" in chapter 2 to check out who marches when.

- **Hanging Out at Rockefeller Plaza:** The sunken plaza beneath the golden Prometheus statue truly is a locale for all seasons: In winter it's a tiny ice rink lively with the clash of blades and the tinny blare of piped-in music; in summer it's an open-air cafe with big umbrellas. In December it's an especially thrilling holiday sight, with the city's biggest Christmas tree (a real doozy) twinkling with lights. A railing surrounds the plaza at street level, where onlookers hang over and take in the scene; overhead, colorful flags flap from a rank of tall flagpoles. You really feel at the heart of the Big City.

- **Eating a Piece of New York Pizza:** Thin-crust pizza may have been invented in Naples, but New Yorkers know it was brought to perfection right here: oversized triangles with flat, crisp bread crusts, dripping with tangy tomato sauce and sloppy melted mozzarella. Even the most basic corner pizza stands usually have a couple of tables where you can sit down, and the open glass counters let kids watch the pizza being made—toss the dough, smear the sauce, scatter on some cheese, fling on a few rounds of pepperoni, and presto! For some suggestions, see chapter 9.
- **Shopping on Fifth Avenue:** With kids? Yes, indeed, because it's not all Tiffany's and Bergdorf's anymore. FAO Schwarz, the top-end toy store, has long been at 58th and Fifth, but in the mid-1990s the huge, glitzy Warner Bros. Studio Store opened a block south at the corner of 57th Street; a spectacular Disney Store, the largest in the chain, soon arrived at 55th Street, followed soon after by Nike-Town, around the corner on 57th Street between Fifth and Madison avenues, and a big NBA Store at 55th Street and Fifth. See chapter 7 for details.

2 The Best Dining Bets

For the full descriptions of the restaurants below, see chapter 9.

- **Best Views:** The **Rock Center Café,** 20 W. 50th St. (☎ 212/332-7620), features a movie—perfect view of Rockefeller Plaza's lower plaza—in winter you can watch ice-skaters through the windows, and in summer you can dine at tables set out on the plaza. Uptown, the **79th Street Boat Basin Café,** West 79th Street at the Hudson River in Riverside Park (☎ 212/496-5542), gives you much the same glorious horizon, along with houseboats bobbing charmingly in the foreground. Get a table by the windows at **Café SFA** in Saks Fifth Avenue, 611 Fifth Ave., 8th floor (☎ 212/940-4080), and you'll have a pigeon's-eye view of Rockefeller Center and the spires of St. Patrick's.
- **Prettiest Decor:** The famous **Tavern on the Green,** in Central Park at West 67th Street (☎ 212/873-3200), looks positively enchanting day or night, with its lushly planted Garden Room, its many windows overlooking the park, and its surrounding thicket of tiny white lights. The Plaza Hotel's **Palm Court,** 768 Fifth Ave. (☎ 212/546-5350), dazzles with its rococo setting of marble, mirrors, and gilt. The two **Ruby Foo's** restaurants, 2182 Broadway (☎ 212/724-6700), and 1626 Broadway (☎ 212/489-5600), have stunning Asian-themed decor, with lots of precisely placed, spotlit art objects. For a dreamy sort of California casual look, **Petaluma,** 1356 First Ave. (☎ 212/772-8800), is very handsome indeed.
- **Funniest Decor:** Among the theme restaurants, the standout is **Mars 2112,** 1633 Broadway (☎ 212/582-2112), with its *Star Trek*-meets-*Star Wars* space-station look. The East Village's funky **Two Boots,** 37 Avenue A (☎ 212/505-2276), litters the dining room with a goofy collection of cowboy boots in every shape, color, and size; the Western motif at **Cowgirl Hall of Fame,** 519 Hudson St. (☎ 212/633-1133), is lively too, though a little more packaged. The roadhouse/frat-house clutter of the three **Brother Jimmy's** restaurants, 428 Amsterdam Ave. (☎ 212/501-7515), 1461 First Ave. (☎ 212/288-0999), and 1644 Third Ave. (☎ 212/426-2020), makes for lively fun as well, but it's outmatched by the West Village's **Hog Pit,** 22 Ninth Ave. (☎ 212/604-0092), populated by stuffed boars' heads and a divey decor that looks straight out of backwoods Georgia.

- **Best Outdoor Eating:** At the **79th Street Boat Basin Café,** in Riverside Park on West 79th Street at the Hudson River (☎ **212/496-5542**), you can sit on a terrace overlooking the marina, with wide-open river vistas and no nearby car traffic. The **Cloister Café,** 238 E. 9th St. (☎ **212/777-9128**), has a charming courtyard off a quiet East Village side street.
- **Most Kid-Friendly Service:** Kudos to these four family favorites, where every waiter and waitress I've ever encountered is friendly, uncloying, and unflappable: **Trattoria Sambucca,** on the West Side at 20 W. 72nd St. (☎ **212/787-5656**); **Bubby's,** in TriBeCa at 120 Hudson St. (☎ **212/219-0666**); **Two Boots,** in the East Village at 37 Avenue A (☎ **212/505-2276**); and **Ellen's Stardust Diner,** just north of Times Square at 1650 Broadway (☎ **212/956-5151**).
- **Best Kids' Menu:** To most Manhattan restaurants, a kids' menu means burgers, chicken fingers, and spaghetti and meatballs, with maybe a hot dog or a grilled cheese sandwich thrown in. But **Gabriela's,** 685 Amsterdam Ave. (☎ **212/961-0574**), or 311 Amsterdam Ave. (☎ **212/875-8532**), makes kids' tacos and roast chicken that are wonderfully savory and free of spicy sauces; **Go Fish,** 1675 Third Ave. (☎ **212/410-4900**), urges kids to try a little fish-and-chips; **Friend of a Farmer,** near Gramercy Park at 77 Irving Place (☎ **212/477-2188**), adds some comfort foods like macaroni and cheese and chicken with pasta; and the publike **Telephone Bar & Grill,** at 142 Second Ave. (☎ **212/529-5000**), includes such English-nanny favorites as shepherd's pie.
- **Best Burgers:** My top favorite just might be the perfectly grilled burgers at the Upper East Side's **Luke's Bar and Grill,** 1394 Third Ave. (☎ **212/249-7070**), though a close runner-up would be the succulent O'Neal burger served not only at **O'Neal's,** 49 W. 64th St. (☎ **212/787-4663**), but at its fair-weather park satellites including **79th Street Boat Basin Café,** W. 79th Street at the Hudson River (☎ **212/496-5542**). Then there's the fabulous Moroccan-spiced Kefta burger at **Cookies & Couscous,** 230 Thompson St. (☎ **212/477-6562**). If you're partial to "sliders," those moist miniburgers steamed with onions, know that **Sassy's Sliders,** 1530 Third Ave. (☎ **212/828-6900**), put the White Castle version to shame.
- **Best Barbecue:** Whether it's the thick cuts of meat, the hickory smoke, the sauce, or just the divey roadhouse atmosphere, **Brother Jimmy's BBQ,** 1461 First Ave. (☎ **212/288-0999**), and its two branches, **Brother Jimmy's Bait Shack,** 1644 Third Ave. (☎ **212/428-2020**), and the **West Side's Brother Jimmy's BBQ & Booze,** 428 Amsterdam Ave. (☎ **212/501-7515**), score big with transplanted Southerners. In the Theater District, **Virgil's Real Barbecue,** 152 W. 44th St. (☎ **212/921-9494**), does a meticulous imitation of a down-home barbecue joint, only on a bigger, cleaner, brassier scale—and the food more than lives up to the stage set. A longtime SoHo favorite, **Tennessee Mountain,** 143 Spring St. (☎ **212/431-3993**), has brought its savory barbecue to the Theater District at 121 W. 45th St. (☎ **212/869-4545**), to give Virgil's a run for its money.
- **Best Retro Diners:** The TV-era kitsch at **Ellen's Stardust Diner,** 1650 Broadway (☎ **212/956-5151**), is a hoot. **EJ's Luncheonette** bustles at three locations—on the Upper West Side at 447 Amsterdam Ave. (☎ **212/873-3444**), on the Upper East Side at 1271 Third Ave. (☎ **212/472-0600**), and in the Village at 432 Sixth Ave. (☎ **212/473-5555**). In the same vein is the **Black Sheep Luncheonette,** 1725 Second Ave. (☎ **212/348-1144**). But I prefer the chrome-trimmed **Comfort Diner,** in Midtown at 214 E. 45th St. (☎ **212/867-4555**), and on the

Upper East Side at 142 E. 86th St. (☎ **212/426-8600**), for their cheerful attention to kids.

- **Best Breakfast:** TriBeCa's **Bubby's,** 120 Hudson St. (☎ **212/219-0666**), welcomes kids for breakfast until 4pm daily; the weekend brunches are especially popular. At **NoHo Star,** 330 Lafayette St. (☎ **212/925-0070**), breakfasts are blissfully relaxed and uncrowded. If it's lox and bagels you're after, the place to go is the famous **Barney Greengrass,** 541 Amsterdam Ave. (☎ **212/724-4707**); for country breakfasts, southern style, dig into the grits at **Emily's,** 1325 Fifth Ave. (☎ **212/996-1212**), or **Old Devil Moon,** 511 E. 12th St. (☎ **212/475-4357**).
- **Best Brunches:** Cookie baking is part of the brunchtime fun at the leafy **Treehouse,** in the west Village at 436 Hudson St. (☎ **212/989-1471**). Brunch is a popular time for kids at **Ernie's,** 2150 Broadway (☎ **212/496-1588**)—try to snag a table in the garden room in the back. **Elephant and Castle,** 68 Greenwich Ave. (☎ **212/243-1400**), is a longtime Village favorite for leisurely weekend brunches that won't break the bank.
- **Tops for Tea Parties:** The **T Salon,** in the Flatiron District at 11 E. 20th St. (☎ **212/358-0506**), feels very artsy, grown-up, and restrained—no one in your party will suffer a sugar overload. And if you're in Midtown, try **Café SFA** at Saks Fifth Avenue, 611 Fifth Ave. (☎ **212/940-4080**), which has a harpist playing and serves real scones and Devonshire cream.
- **Best Ice Cream:** For sheer old-fashioned soda shoppe ambience, my vote has to go to the East Side's **Peppermint Park,** 1225 First Ave. (☎ **212/288-5054**), but the ice-cream sundaes are truly amazing at **Serendipity,** 225 E. 60th St. (☎ **212/838-3531**).
- **Best Milk Shakes:** The **Barking Dog Luncheonette,** 1678 Third Ave. (☎ **212/831-1800**), way up on the Upper East Side, has a great retro soda fountain, and the sodas, sundaes, and shakes to go with it. The **Lexington Candy Shop,** 1226 Lexington Ave. (☎ **212/288-0057**), has shakes that are nearly as good, in an authentic vintage coffee-shop setting.
- **Best Chinese:** Taking into account factors like cleanliness, service, and kid-friendliness, as well as the flavors of its food, Chinatown's **New York Noodletown,** 28½ Bowery (☎ **212/349-0923**), is supremely authentic, as is **Lin's Dumpling House,** 25 Pell St. (☎ **212/577-2777**).
- **Best Dim Sum Chinese:** While many Chinatowners roll out the dim sum carts only on Sunday, **HSF,** at 46 Bowery (☎ **212/374-1319**), makes every day a dim sum day: Waiters offer a selection of small servings of dumplings, skewers, rolls, and other delectables right at your table.
- **Best Chinese Outside Chinatown:** That reliable Uptowner, **Hunan Balcony,** on the Upper West Side at 2596 Broadway (☎ **212/865-0400**), presents a menu much like all the Chinese restaurants in New York, but adds noodles and grilled seafood and steamed dishes as well. My kids are great fans of the noodle dishes and roast meats at the East Side's **LiLi's,** 1500 Third Ave. (☎ **212/639-1313**).
- **Best Pizzas:** I'm treading on controversial ground here, in this pizza-loving city, but I'll have to give the nod to **John's Pizza;** the original Greenwich Village location, at 278 Bleecker St. (☎ **212/243-1680**), is still the best, but the three other branches at 408 E. 64th St. (☎ **212/935-2895**), 48 W. 65th St. (☎ **212/721-7001**), and 260 W. 44th St. (☎ **212/391-7560**) serve up thin-crust brick-oven pies that are pretty darn close to perfection. John's longtime rival is **Patsy's Pizzeria,** with four locations: 67 University Place (☎ **212/533-3500**),

509 Third Ave. (☎ 212/689-7500), 1312 Second Ave. (☎ 212/639-1000), and 64 W. 74th St. (☎ 212/579-3000).

- **Best Pastas:** Forget Little Italy: The best Italian pastas I've found, outside of a couple of expensive places I could never take kids, are at **Presto's,** up near Columbia University at 2770 Broadway (☎ 212/222-1760), and **Mangia e Bevi,** 800 Ninth Ave. (☎ 212/956-3976). Pizza at both places is also superb. Sleek **Bella Luna,** 584 Columbus Ave. (☎ 212/877-2267), is in a more sophisticated class, but for friendliness to kids it beats all other designer pasta restaurants hands-down.

- **Best Mexican: Gabriela's,** 685 Amsterdam Ave. (☎ 212/961-0574)—also at 311 Amsterdam Ave. (☎ 212/875-8532)—has to be tasted to be believed, and the staff is lovely to kids. If you like Mexican, pick a time when you can beat the weekend-night lines.

- **Grandma's Favorites:** For a very dressed-up special meal, linen and china and all, I'd pick **Petaluma,** 1356 First Ave. (☎ 212/772-8800); if you want to go more casual, **Miss Elle's Homesick Bar & Grill,** 226 W. 79th St. (☎ 212/595-4350), has a sort of *Fried Green Tomatoes* ambience that grandmothers tend to adore. Or do afternoon tea Downtown, either in the West Village at **Anglers and Writers,** 420 Hudson St. (☎ 212/675-0810), or in the Flatiron District at the **T Salon,** 11 E. 20th St. (☎ 212/358-0506).

- **Grandpa's Favorite:** At 42 Central Park South, **Mickey Mantle's** (☎ 212/688-7777) celebrates the sports stars Granddad has actually heard of—plus, it's handsome, the food's pretty darn good, and there are lots of big TVs so you won't miss the big game. A granddad who loves seafood may enjoy the catch of the day at **Go Fish,** 1675 Third Ave. (☎ 212/410-4900). Or he can take the progeny for an ice-cream pig-out at fun and friendly **Serendipity,** 225 E. 60th St. (☎ 212/838-3531).

- **Jock Heaven:** While some kids, especially collectors of vintage baseball cards, may get a kick out of the sports lore at **Mickey Mantle's,** 42 Central Park South (☎ 212/688-7777), young fans and wanna-be athletes are more likely to fall for the pro-name glitz of the **Official All Star Café** theme restaurant on Times Square at 1540 Broadway (☎ 212/840-8326), or the **ESPN ZONE,** at 1472 Broadway (☎ 212/921-3776).

- **Cyber Geek Heaven:** In the East Village, seek out the friendly online ambience of the **Internet Café,** 82 E. 3rd St. (☎ 212/614-0747).

- **Most Fun Menu:** At **America,** 9 E. 18th St. (☎ 212/505-2110), you'll find a gargantuan menu that links every one of its regional dishes with a different town in the U.S.A. For sheer goofy tongue-in-cheek menu descriptions, I get a kick out of the card at **Chat 'n' Chew,** 10 E. 16th St. (☎ 212/243-1616). **Mars 2112,** 1633 Broadway (☎ 212/582-2112), has a big and very amusing menu; every dish has a spaced-out name that packs a pun.

- **Best Floor Show:** If most waiters in Manhattan are really actors waiting for their break, the guys and gals at **Ellen's Stardust Diner,** 1650 Broadway (☎ 212/956-5151), at least get to belt out their favorites to a karaoke machine in this Times Square cafe's weekend dinner shows.

- **Best Cooking Show:** The flying knives of the teppanyaki chefs at **Benihana West,** 47 W. 56th St. (☎ 212/581-0930), are pretty hard to beat. (Another branch is located at 120 E. 56th St.; ☎ 212/593-1627.) But for some do-it-yourself cooking action, try the Korean tableside barbecuing at **Won Jo,** 23 W. 32nd St. (☎ 212/695-5815).

3 The Best Hotel Bets

For the full descriptions of the hotels below, see chapter 10.

- **Most Family Friendly:** The **Doubletree Guest Suites,** 1568 Broadway (☎ **800/ 222-8733** or 212/719-1600), not only provides standard two-room accommodations sleeping four or six, but also kitchenettes, baby equipment, childproof rooms, and a super toddler playroom. The hotel is busy developing an activities program as well, and you can just tell when you walk in that the staff is happy to see children. The **Loews New York,** 569 Lexington Ave. (☎ **800/ 836-6471** or 212/752-7000), and **Le Parker Meridien,** 118 W. 57th St. (☎ **800/543-4300** or 212/245-5000), are two more friendly Midtown hotels, both with essential child equipment on hand and welcoming packets for young guests.

- **Best Suite Deals:** The **Doubletree Guest Suites,** 1568 Broadway (☎ **800/ 222-8733** or 212/719-1600), is a sensible family option, sleeping the whole crew in one unit for a relatively easy price. If you need a lot of space, any of the Manhattan East Suite hotels—the **Surrey Hotel,** 20 E. 76th St. (☎ **800/ME-SUITE** or 212/288-3700); the **Lyden Gardens Suite Hotel,** 215 E. 64th St. (☎ **800/ ME-SUITE** or 212/320-8022); the **Beekman Tower,** 3 Mitchell Place (First Avenue at 49th Street; ☎ **800/ME-SUITE** or 212/355-7300); and six other Midtown properties listed in the Beekman Tower's write-up in chapter 10— deliver a small apartment with a full kitchen for a reasonable amount of cash. In Midtown, the **Roger Smith,** 501 Lexington Ave. (☎ **800/445-0277** or 212/755-1400), has some homey country-decor suites with lots of room for a fair price. The **Embassy Suites,** 102 North End Ave. (☎ **800/EMBASSY** or 212/945-0100), offers some very favorable rates on weekends for its roomy, sleek suites.

- **Most Peace & Quiet:** It's all relative in New York, of course, but the **Stanhope,** 995 Fifth Ave. (☎ **800/233-1234** or 212/774-1234), sits right on the cultured serenity of Museum Mile, and the **Gracie Inn,** 502 E. 81st St. (☎ **212/ 628-1700**), is tucked away on an Upper East Side street near the East River. The **Crowne Plaza at the United Nations,** 304 E. 42nd St. (☎ **212/ 986-8800**), is your most serene bet in Midtown, sitting near the United Nations and residential Tudor City.

- **Best Views:** While several hotels boast Central Park views on higher floors, you'll often pay a good deal for them, with the notable exception of the pleasantly down-to-earth **Mayflower,** 15 Central Park West (☎ **800/223-4164** or 212/265-0060). Go instead for river views, which are rarities in Manhattan: The **Regal U.N. Plaza Hotel,** 44th Street and First Avenue (☎ **800/222-8888** or 212/758-1234), dazzles with its high-rise East River vistas (other rooms have equally dazzling skyline views), while the **New York Marriott Financial Center,** 85 West St. (☎ **800/228-9290** or 212/385-4900), features panoramas of Battery Park, the Hudson River, and New York Harbor from most of its rooms. The **Embassy Suites,** 102 North End Ave. (☎ **800/EMBASSY** or 212/ 945-0100), has those great Downtown views, too, though partially blocked by its Battery Park City neighbors.

- **When Price Is No Object:** My vote goes to the **Carlyle,** 35 E. 76th St. (☎ **800/ 227-5737** or 212/744-1600), for its dignified East Side calm, its well-nigh perfect service, and the spaciousness of its designer-decorated rooms, which really deserve to be called apartments. And since money is no object, make sure you get a suite with a Central Park view and a grand piano. The **Four Seasons,** 57 E. 57th St. (☎ **800/332-3442** or 212/758-5700), has a stylish Midtown address, sleek if somewhat small rooms (but then you're springing for a suite, right?), fabulous service, and a surprisingly kid-friendly gourmet restaurant. And then there's the **Plaza,** 768 Fifth Ave. (☎ **800/759-3000** or 212/759-3000), which overlooks Central Park and FAO Schwarz and has several gilded-to-the-max suites that are straight out of an Eloise fantasy.

- **When Price Is Your Main Object:** You can't go wrong with the **Travel Inn,** 515 W. 42nd St. (☎ **800/869-4630** or 212/695-7171), which delivers roomy, clean, fairly quiet motel rooms, plus a huge pool and free parking, for around $150 a night. Unfortunately, despite its unprepossessing location far to the west of the Theater District, it's booked up way in advance—the desk clerk laughingly told me people should call a year ahead to make a reservation. Families willing to sleep in bunk beds and forego ensuite bathrooms should pounce on the very clean and safe, if somewhat spare, **Vanderbilt YMCA,** 224 E. 47th St. (☎ **212/756-9600**).

- **Best Lobby:** You've gotta love the classic art deco lobby of the **Waldorf-Astoria,** 301 Park Ave. (☎ **800/WALDORF,** 800/HILTONS, or 212/355-3000), with its marble-faced pillars, deep red–patterned carpeting, ornamental plasterwork touched with gilt and silver accents, and parade of neoclassical figures on the cornice frieze. Guests ensconce themselves in the plush armchairs, and Peacock Alley and Sir Harry's Bar open off to the sides; budding Eloises will be tempted to wander around all sorts of corridors trailing off to elevator lobbies, ballrooms and banquet halls, and classy shops with venerable names like Sulka, H. Stern, and Cellini. For hushed elegance and big-city buzz, it can't be beat. The **Plaza,** 768 Fifth Ave. (☎ **800/759-3000** or 212/759-3000), rivals it in architectural detail, but the Plaza's lobby has one fatal flaw. There's absolutely no place to sit and drink it all in, unless you want to pay through the nose for a table at the Palm Court cafe.

- **Best Pool:** The pool at the **Regal U.N. Plaza Hotel,** 44th Street and First Avenue (☎ **800/222-8888** or 212/758-1234), has it all: views, cleanliness, handsome tile work, and not much of a crowd.

- **Best Fitness Center:** The three largest and best-equipped, without a doubt, are the health clubs at **Le Parker Meridien,** 118 W. 57th St. (☎ **800/543-4300** or 212/245-5000); the **Crowne Plaza Manhattan,** 1605 Broadway (☎ **800/ 2-CROWNE** or 212/977-4000); and the **Marriott World Trade Center,** 3 World Trade Center (☎ **800/228-9290** or 212/938-9100). All three also sell membership to nonguests, so people staying in the hotel don't have exclusive use of the facilities. If you do take your kids with you into the fitness center, don't let young children "play" on the exercise equipment; if they want to try to work out with you, make sure equipment is adjusted properly to their size and strength levels.

- **Best Bathrooms:** The **Four Seasons,** 57 E. 57th St. (☎ **800/332-3442** or 212/758-5700), has absolutely stunning huge bathrooms with the finest fixtures, and the water pressure's so good the bathtubs reputedly fill in 60 seconds. The **Mark,** 25 E. 77th St., at Madison Ave. (☎ **800/843-6275** or 212/744-4300), has large, beautifully outfitted marble baths too, with soaking tubs and bidets and separate shower stalls, depending on various layouts.

- **Best Room Service:** The **Surrey Hotel,** 20 E. 76th St. (☎ **800/ME-SUITE** or 212/288-3700), has room service provided by Café Boulud, headed by master chef Daniel Boulud—many foodies claim his Restaurant Daniel, now moved nearby to 65th and Park Avenue, is the best restaurant in Manhattan these days.

- **Best Coffee Shop:** I'm kind of partial to Raffles, the bright and cheery coffee shop attached to the **Radisson Hotel New York East Side,** 511 Lexington Ave. (☎ **800/448-4471** or 212/755-4400), but the **Crowne Plaza Manhattan,** 1605 Broadway (☎ **800/2-CROWNE** or 212/977-4000), comes in a close second with its skylit Balcony Cafe, offering a hearty breakfast and lunch buffet.
- **Best Hotel Restaurant for Kids:** At the **Marriott World Trade Center,** 3 World Trade Center (☎ **800/228-9290** or 212/938-9100), the Greenhouse Café has a kids' menu and a placemat to color. The **Doubletree Guest Suites,** 1568 Broadway (☎ **800/222-8733** or 212/719-1600), is runner-up, with its kid-friendly Center Stage Cafe.
- **Tops for Toddlers:** When all is said and done, the **Hotel Wales,** 1295 Madison Ave. (☎ **212/876-6000**), wins for its Carnegie Hill location, friendly staff, residential calm, and Puss-in-Boots theme. The complimentary continental breakfast buffet is another big plus when you've got a fidgety youngster. The **Doubletree Guest Suites,** 1568 Broadway (☎ **800/222-8733** or 212/719-1600), scores big here, too, for its suite convenience and toddler playroom.
- **Tops for Teens:** Budding bohemians may want to be in Greenwich Village at the **Washington Square Hotel,** 103 Waverly Place (☎ **800/222-0418** or 212/777-9515), while the athletically minded are likely to appreciate the fitness options at **Le Parker Meridien,** 118 W. 57th St. (☎ **800/543-4300** or 212/245-5000), which also puts you spot in the middle of Theme Restaurant Row. Trendsetters will gravitate to the way-cool decor and hipster cachet of the **Paramount,** 235 W. 46th St. (☎ **800/225-7474** or 212/764-5500), or the Zen-like minimalism of **On the Ave,** 2178 Broadway (☎ **800/509-7598** or 212/362-1100).

4 A Few Practical Words of Wisdom

I can understand how intimidating it must be to families who come here as tourists, not knowing a single local soul, trying to navigate and negotiate around the sights. In New York's heavy tourist areas, the prices are high, the traffic is dense, and the crowds are pushy and rude. Outside those areas, certain pockets of town may be dingy and even downright scary. And when you're traveling with kids, one bad experience can send you home to Nashville or Indianapolis or Dubuque shaking your head and wondering why anybody would live in a place like New York City.

So let's deal with some of the negatives head-on. First of all: Yes, there's crime in New York. It's by no means America's crime capital, however—perhaps the biggest coup of Rudolph Giuliani's mayorship has been the city's plummeting crime rate in all categories. TV cop shows and gritty action movies may paint New York as a town of mean streets, but face it—the real reason they set their stories here is that so many producers, directors, and actors love this city and live here themselves.

Of course, it's possible to get mugged at night on the sidewalks of New York—to avoid such an incident, stay on well-lighted, well-populated streets as much as possible and know where you're going. If you're in dense crowds—rush-hour buses or subways, the pre- and postcurtain crush in the Theater District—be on the alert for pickpockets. Keep your wallet in a front pocket and hold your purse in front of you; tell your kids to zip up their backpacks and keep a grasp on one of the shoulder straps. Keep a firm grip on your cameras, too. Don't leave purses or backpacks or cameras hanging on the backs of your chairs in restaurants. With kids in tow, you may not stay out all that late, but it's wise after dark to take taxis if you're going any distance. All this is just plain common sense.

Three Invaluable Tips

- **Eat outdoors whenever you can.** If a restaurant has tables in a courtyard or on the sidewalk, grab them (your fellow diners won't hear your kids' racket, and the passing show will distract your restless offspring). If the weather's decent, pick up food from a deli or hot-dog stand and eat in a park—you'll save money and have fun.

- **Never be shy about asking directions.** New Yorkers may look like they're in a rush, but most are such incurable know-it-alls they're always happy to tell you where to go. Even lifelong Manhattanites can get disoriented when emerging from a subway station, so verifying that you're headed the right way doesn't brand you as a tourist. Don't wear your kids out with needless walking—ask.

- **Don't spend all your time in Midtown.** Granted, most visitors' hotels are in Midtown, and there are some boffo attractions for kids here—the Empire State Building, the Sony Wonder Technology Lab, the Museum of Modern Art, the New Victory Theater, FAO Schwarz—but you can't really understand New York City unless you get out to the neighborhoods. They're quieter, safer, cheaper, and more kid-friendly. The Upper West Side, the Upper East Side, Greenwich Village, Chelsea, and Brooklyn Heights—this is where New Yorkers with children live. Go thou and do likewise.

Traffic is another problem, which is why I heartily advise you not to drive in the city if you don't have to. New York pedestrians get pretty cocky about darting off the curb into traffic, but don't let your kids follow their example: My under-6s know they have to hold my hands when crossing a street, and we don't step into the intersection until we get a white "Walk" signal. (We hold hands even in midblock in congested pedestrian areas like Midtown. My kids know this isn't even a negotiable point.) Just about all intersections have traffic lights and most streets are one-way, which means it's fairly straightforward even for a kid to see where traffic is coming from and to know when it's safe to cross.

Yet another reality of life in New York is the street people. The number of beggars, homeless people, and scruffy loiterers has fallen drastically since the late 1980s; panhandlers aren't allowed to hassle people on the subways anymore (though a few still do). Nevertheless, you and your kids may spot a die-hard vagrant or two sleeping in doorways or pawing through corner trash bins. What do you say to your children when you see a wino relieving himself against a building wall or when a red-eyed junkie weaves past you on a subway platform? My husband and I try to steer our kids away from such individuals, though we've had our share of earnest talks about how people can end up so marginalized in modern society. Keep your wits about you to anticipate such scenes.

The reason folks are more likely to run into desperate characters like this in New York is really not because New York has such a high percentage of weirdos, wackos, and wastrels. It's simply because you're always out walking on the streets here, not whizzing around in the isolation of your car. And with so many million human beings coexisting in a relatively small area, you're bound to come into contact with lots of people in the course of a day, and the law of averages dictates that some of those people will have more of an edge to them than you'd like. But to my mind that's just the flip side of one of this city's great pluses: Everybody, from the Wall

Street banker to the greengrocer to the starving actor waiting tables, shares the streets. The rich can't ignore the poor, the young can't ignore the old, the Republicans can't ignore the Democrats, and vice versa. My kids are well aware of how tough it is for people in wheelchairs to get around, because they often have to sit and wait on a city bus while such folks doggedly haul themselves aboard. They know that not everyone in the world speaks English, because there's a constant counterpoint of French, Greek, Urdu, or Japanese swirling around them. My fourth-grader has no questions about why he should study Spanish in school; he *knows* it's a useful language, because he hears it spoken every day.

A million different agendas clash every day in the Manhattan melee, and it keeps us all honest; it keeps us all in touch with reality. Kids who grow up in New York City tend to have street smarts—not a bad thing to have, in my opinion. If you want a sanitized version of America, you go to Walt Disney World.

Now that I've gotten the negatives out of the way, I'll go back to the positives. The pulse and tempo of New York City can be dizzying at first if you're not used to it—I'll grant you that—but once you attune yourself, you'll find it tremendously exciting, even for youngsters. When my kiddos return to the city after an idyllic 2-week vacation at the beach, I've seen them stride down the sidewalks and look around eagerly, glad to be back in a place where there's something happening every few yards. They love the fact that when they go to a playground there's always someone else to play with. Driving through Times Square, they don't see the traffic jams—they just ooh and aah at the neon gaudiness. The West Side subway is their own homegrown thrill ride, racketing through tunnels and running races with the trains on neighboring tracks. World-class museums are their after-school classrooms, where they encounter more art, science, and history than I'd been exposed to by the time I graduated from college. Central Park is their backyard, all 840 acres of it, and it provides them with nature ponds, tennis courts, horseback riding, ice-skating, and on and on and on.

Let me tell you about one Sunday we spent a while ago. Right after breakfast, from our own apartment windows, we heard via loudspeakers the pope—*the pope!*—saying mass in Central Park. Walking outside afterward, we saw legions of the faithful trooping home, festooned with pope pennants and badges and memorabilia. As we rode the subway downtown, we had an earnest conversation about who the pope is and why so many people wanted to see him—that is, until we changed trains and got distracted by the Asian guy who plays electric harmonica on the N/R platform in Times Square. We went on to a SoHo furniture store where we saw performance artist Eric Bogosian busy trying out the rocking chairs (my kids weren't impressed, but my 5-year-old admitted that Bogosian's young son's leather jacket was pretty cool). When we ran into Bogosian and Bogosian Jr. minutes later down the street at the Fire Museum, we all smiled at one another with recognition. ("Your kids bugging you to buy souvenir fire engines, too?" Bogosian's weary chuckle seemed to say to us.) Then on the subway ride home we sat next to actress Sarah Jessica Parker, who kept sneaking eye contact with our baby. By the time we got home, it was too late to cook, so we ordered in Chinese food; my older son, who we've nicknamed the Bok Choy Boy, snarfed down Buddhist Delight with his chopsticks like an old pro, while our toddler delicately dismantled an egg roll on her plate and smeared her face with cold sesame noodles. A whole family of satisfied customers.

And that wasn't even an unusual day—we hadn't planned anything more glamorous than furniture shopping. Serendipity is the name of the game in New York

City, all the more so if you've got kids. So many things are coming at you all the time, you can't help but stumble onto something interesting.

At a luncheon for new mothers I went to shortly after my youngest was born, one young mom wistfully said to me that she felt shut out of Manhattan life. "This city is totally oriented toward singles," she sighed. "That's what Manhattan is all about. People in Manhattan think babies should be kept in a closet until they reach the age of 21." I nodded my head, but even though there's a kernel of truth to what she was saying, I couldn't really agree with her. I thought of her complaint constantly while writing this book. I made it my mission to help people like her get up and running. I do know how she felt—I've been there. But, like the kids in *A Wrinkle in Time* or the Narnia Chronicles, I've discovered a parallel universe: New York City with Kids. It's a grand, goofy, glorious place. And there isn't anywhere else on the planet I'd rather live.

2

Planning a Family Trip to New York City

New York City is much more kid-friendly than most visitors anticipate—the trick lies in planning your trip to take advantage of it. Timing is everything, as is fortifying yourself with all the printed information you can snare.

1 Visitor Information

Once you decide to visit Manhattan, write to the **New York Convention & Visitors Bureau's Visitors Information Center,** 810 Seventh Ave., 3rd floor, New York, NY 10019, for maps, hotel lists, brochures, and sightseeing suggestions. The bureau's 24-hour information hotline at ☎ **800/NYC-VISIT** or 212/397-8222 offers similar info by phone; via the Internet, contact the bureau at **www.nycvisit.com**.

You may want to send away for the local parents' monthlies: the $35-per-year *Big Apple Parent,* 9 E. 38th St., 4th floor, New York, NY 10016 (☎ **212/889-6400;** fax 212/689-4958; www. parentsknow.com); or the $22-per-year *New York Family,* 141 Halstead Ave., Suite 3D, Mamaroneck, NY 10543 (☎ **914/ 381-7474;** www.parenthoodweb.com). Once you're here, you can pick up free copies of these publications and the *ParentGuide* (published by Parent Guide Network Corp., 419 Park Ave. S., New York, NY 10016 (☎ **212/213-8840;** www.parentguidenews.com), at toy stores, bookstores, children's clothing and shoe stores, and indoor playgrounds all around town. Parents of infants may want to go online to check out **newyork.urbanbaby.com**, which zeros in on topics such as maternity clothing stores, nursery furnishings, havens for nursing mothers, and baby-friendly playgrounds.

2 When to Go

New York buzzes every day, with pretty much everything open year-round. All school vacation seasons—late December, spring vacation, and summer—tend to be busy times; lots of museums schedule special programs then, since New York schoolchildren are looking for something to do, too. December is particularly jam-packed, with lots of annual holiday entertainment (*The Nutcracker,* the Big Apple Circus, the Radio City Christmas Spectacular, a musical version of *A Christmas Carol*). Fall is traditionally the prime season for culture, with new plays opening on Broadway and

What Things Cost in New York City	U.S.$
Hot dog at corner umbrella cart	1.00–1.25
Hot pretzel at corner umbrella cart	1.25–1.50
16-oz. soft drink in a deli	1.00
16-oz. apple juice in a deli	1.25
Take-out bagel with cream cheese	75¢–1.50
Slice of plain pizza	1.00–2.00
McDonald's Happy Meal with Chicken McNuggets	3.50
Weekday *New York Times*	75¢
Weekday *Daily News* or *New York Post*	50¢
Local telephone call	25¢
Movie ticket	9.00–10.00 adult, 6.00 child
Taxi ride from the Empire State Building to FAO Schwarz	4.00 (plus $1.00 tip)
Taxi ride from the World Trade Center to Rockefeller Center	10.00, depending on traffic (plus $2.00 tip)
Package of Pampers	10.00
Package of Luvs	7.00
32 oz. can prepared Similac formula	4.60

classical music venues booked solid, but even in summer, music series at Lincoln Center and star-studded limited-run plays fill the boards. Spring and summer weekends really bustle, with street fairs all over town and what seems like an endless succession of parades, one for every ethnic group in the city, filing down Fifth Avenue.

There's no "high" or "low" season as far as hotel rates go, though it may be a little harder than usual to get a reservation around Christmas or Labor Day (when the U.S. Open is in town) or during the fall and spring fashion shows. Hotels are slightly less crowded on weekends, when business travelers clear out of town; many even offer weekend package rates.

In terms of weather, winter tends to be cold but not intolerably so, whereas July and August can be sweltering and muggy—but that never stops hordes of visitors from descending on the city every summer.

Kids' Favorite New York City Events

February
- **Black History Month** is observed with some very good programs for kids at museums around town.
- The **Chinese New Year** rattles the streets of Lower Manhattan with dragon parades, firecrackers, and fun.
- The **Westminster Kennel Club Dog Show** at Madison Square Garden (☎ 212/465-MSG1) brings champion pooches of every breed to the city. Besides watching the judging, it's fun just to walk around outside the ring, where the dogs and handlers hang out.

March

- The **International Cat Show** at Madison Square Garden (☎ 212/465-MSG1) draws hosts of cat fanciers and their felines to a world-class competition.
- The **St. Patrick's Day Parade** rolls down Fifth Avenue on March 17.
- The **Ringling Bros. and Barnum & Bailey Circus** begins its annual month-long run at Madison Square Garden (☎ 212/465-MSG1).

April

- The annual **Central Park Easter egg hunt** is held on Easter Sunday near the Bandshell, with activities, giveaways, and visiting celebrities.
- The **Easter Parade** on Easter Sunday morning is a stroll down Fifth Avenue that anyone can join—the bigger the bonnet, the better.

May

- The Brooklyn Botanic Garden's annual **Cherry Blossom Festival** (☎ 718/623-7200) takes a cue from Japanese tradition in celebrating the flowering pink trees around its pond.
- The **Ninth Avenue International Food Festival** lines the avenue from 37th to 57th streets, with open-air stalls selling an amazing array of snacks, nibbles, and noshes.
- **Fleet Week** (☎ 212/245-0072) welcomes a host of U.S. and foreign naval ships to the Hudson River piers, highlighted by a parade of ships.

July

- ✪ **Macy's July 4 Fireworks Extravaganza** explodes in the skies over the East River.

August

- The **Lincoln Center Out-of-Doors Festival** (☎ 212/875-5108) turns the plaza around the arts complex into one big street fair, with crafts and food stalls and loads of free performances.

September

- The **U.S. Open Tennis Championships** (☎ 718/760-6200) are played in Flushing Meadows, Queens, for 2 weeks starting just before Labor Day.
- The **San Gennaro festival** fills the streets of Little Italy with carnival booths and Italian food stands for a week around the saint's day, September 19.

October

- ✪ The Cathedral of St. John the Divine overruns with animals for its **Blessing of the Animals** on the Feast of St. Francis, the first Sunday of the month.
- ✪ The **Big Apple Circus** (☎ 212/268-2500) settles in for its annual 3-month run at Lincoln Center's Damrosch Park.
- Halloween activities include the outrageous **Greenwich Village Halloween Parade** up lower Sixth Avenue.

November

- ✪ The **Christmas Spectacular** at Radio City Music Hall (☎ 212/247-4777) ushers in the holiday season early, beginning a 2-month run.
- ✪ The **Big Apple Circus** (☎ 212/268-2500) continues at Lincoln Center's Damrosch Park.
- ✪ The **Macy's Thanksgiving Day Parade** runs from 77th Street and Central Park West down to Broadway and 34th Street; sidewalk viewing along the route is first-come, first-served. The evening before, the parade's mighty balloons are blown up on 77th and 81st streets, around the Museum of Natural History, but it's a mob scene; come by at 8am Thanksgiving morning and you can view the whole parade lying in wait, with no one else around but Macy's elves and Santa.

December
- The **Christmas Tree Lighting** at Rockefeller Center is in early December.
- ✪ The **Christmas Spectacular** continues at Radio City Music Hall (☎ 212/247-4777), bringing music, dancing, Santa, and the Rockettes together on one enormous stage.
- ✪ More **Big Apple Circus** (☎ 212/268-2500) at Lincoln Center's Damrosch Park.
- A live musical version of *A Christmas Carol* (☎ 212/465-MSG1) takes the stage at the Theater at Madison Square Garden.
- ✪ The New York City Ballet's annual *The Nutcracker* (☎ 212/870-5570) is a perpetual delight at Lincoln Center.
- The **Lighting of the Giant Hanukkah Menorah** at Grand Army Plaza (Fifth Avenue and 59th Street) is on the first night of Hanukkah.
- **New Year's Eve** is celebrated famously in Times Square; though this is hardly an event for kids (or for parents who aren't crazy about lunatic crowds), several other events around town capitalize on the holiday. The New York Convention & Visitors Bureau should have a schedule of these by the fall of 2000.

3 What to Pack

If you plan to go out to a fancy dinner or the theater, you'll want at least one dressy outfit, which means a jacket and tie for men (boys may be able to get by without the tie). Most restaurants have no dress code, though.

It's important to remember that this is preeminently a walking city. There's almost always a bit of a walk from the subway to wherever you're going, and even if you intend to cab it everywhere, you'll have to sprint for a taxi or two or trudge a few blocks when no cabs are in sight—which will happen. So bring sturdy low heeled shoes and don't skip socks unless you're wearing well-broken-in sneakers. Sandals, however, aren't smart, since the streets can be dirty and your bare toes are vulnerable to being run over by a kamikaze bicycle messenger, a rolling dress rack or hot-dog cart, or any of a dozen other urban vehicles.

Walking a lot also makes strollers a must for any young children who can't hike at least a mile without complaining. Strollers can be a hassle, though, when getting in and out of cabs or up and down subway stairs; make sure you've got one that folds easily. If you have an infant, a soft carrier is a better idea.

July and August can be miserably hot and sticky, conditions worsened by the fact that subway platforms are like saunas, thanks to the heat thrown off by the subway trains' air-conditioning (subway cars are glacially cool, by the way). Short-sleeved T-shirts and shorts are best—the baggier the better. Sun hats are helpful, and a folding hand fan is a great idea—if nothing else, it could distract the kids from how hot it is. If you don't own such a thing, buy one in Chinatown while you're here.

January and February may be cold, but all the buildings around you in Manhattan retain heat, so it's never as cold here as it is outside the city. Still, this is the Northeast, so gloves, hats, and scarves are advisable if you come from November to March. If it does snow, the streets are plowed swiftly and sidewalks get shoveled fast: It takes a really big blizzard to stop Manhattan in its tracks—like the Blizzard of '96. Plowed banks of snow can stand for weeks, getting filthier and filthier. Boots are a good idea in winter, just in case, because sewers quickly back up and lake-sized puddles form at curbs—too big for kids to jump over.

If you're bringing an infant, call ahead to your hotel to check what baby equipment it can provide—besides a crib, it may help to have a bathing ring and a high

Top Kids' Books Set in New York City

Picture Books

- *The Adventures of Taxi Dog* by Debra and Sal Barracca (Dial; ages 2–6). This, or any of the Barraccas' books about Maxi the Taxi Dog, is a lovable look at the city from the seat of a yellow cab.
- *Tar Beach* by Faith Ringgold (Crown; ages 2–5). Evocative memories of a Harlem childhood and hot summer nights up on the roof.
- *The Little Red Lighthouse and the Great Gray Bridge* by Hildegarde H. Swift and Lynd Ward (Harcourt Brace; ages 4–7). A Hudson River lighthouse feels superceded by the new George Washington Bridge, until one dark and stormy night. . . . Kids can still see both landmarks today.
- *Eloise* by Kay Thompson (Simon & Schuster; ages 4–8). This irrepressible 6-year-old growing up in the Plaza Hotel definitely has an exotic view of life. Perfect for the precocious.

Chapter Books

- *The Cricket in Times Square* by George Selden (Farrar Straus Giroux or Yearling paperback; ages 6–10). A Connecticut cricket winds up in the Times Square subway station and becomes the toast of Manhattan.
- *Stuart Little* by E. B. White (Harper & Row; ages 7–10). The Little family's mouse-sized young son has adventures in and around Central Park.
- *The Pushcart War* by Jean Merrill (Dell Yearling; ages 7–10). Tongue-in-cheek chronicle of a prolonged fight between the city's pushcart vendors and delivery trucks.
- *All of a Kind Family* by Sydney Taylor (Dell Yearling; ages 7–10). Portrait of a Jewish family living on the Lower East Side is a window onto turn-of-the-century New York.
- *The Saturdays* by Elizabeth Enright (Puffin Books; ages 7–10). Four siblings pool their resources to explore New York City on weekends; set in the 1940s but not as dated as it may seem.
- *Harriet the Spy* by Louise Fitzhugh (HarperTrophy; ages 8–11). Spunky sixth-grader Harriet M. Welch keeps tabs on her East Side friends and neighbors.
- *From the Mixed-Up Files of Mrs. Basil E. Frankenweiler* by E. L. Konigsburg (Simon & Schuster or Aladdin paperback; ages 8–12). A 12-year-old Connecticut girl and her younger brother hole up in the Metropolitan Museum and become involved in an art mystery.
- *It's Like This, Cat* by Emily Neville (Harper; ages 8–12). Although somewhat dated, this coming-of-age novel paints a memorable picture of the Gramercy Park area of Manhattan during the late 1950s.
- *It's Okay If You Don't Love Me* by Norma Klein (Fawcett, young adult). Upper West Side teenagers deal with life, love, and sex.

chair in your room. You may want to pack a few outlet covers so you can childproof your room when you arrive. Of course, you can buy diapers, wipes, formula, and no-tears shampoo here, but it might be handier to bring your own bottles, spout cups, feeding dish, and infant spoon, which you can bring to restaurants. You don't want to waste your entire first day locating the right items in baby stores here.

Accidents do happen, so bring extra changes of clothes for your children—for infants and for toddlers who haven't mastered the fine art of using the potty, you should probably bring two or three changes of clothes for each day. You'll also want a tote bag full of toys, for travel time and for downtime in your hotel room. Toys without lots of separate pieces are best (imagine trying to pick up dozens of spilled Lego pieces off the floor of an airplane!). Older kids may want to carry their own backpacks with books, colored markers and pads, a deck of cards, handheld electronic games, personal CD player, or whatever keeps them happy.

4 Getting the Kids Interested

Send away in advance to the **New York Convention & Visitors Bureau** (see "Visitor Information," earlier in this chapter) for a Big Apple packet, which should include a city map with subway lines that kids can study. The very idea that Manhattan is an island may fascinate them.

Several corny old songs come in handy as memory guides for New York City geography: Start with "I'll take Manhattan / the Bronx and Staten Island too" to teach your kids about the city's five boroughs, the other two being Brooklyn and Queens. (Fun fact: Brooklyn on its own has a big enough population to be the sixth-largest city in the United States.) Then there's "New York, New York, a wonderful town / The Bronx is up and the Battery's down / The people ride in a hole in the ground." Discuss the subway lines—rendered in different colors on the map—and talk about the neighborhoods and sights they pass through. New York's subways have been cleaned up incredibly since the early 1980s, and it's perfectly safe to take your kids for rides on these underground trains.

Current TV shows tend to present New York either as a hangout for self-involved singles or as a gritty battlefield for cops and psycho killers. For a more fun image of Manhattan, let your kids view *Home Alone 2, Ghostbusters,* or *Big;* among vintage movies, *Miracle on 34th Street* is a winner. Older kids may like Woody Allen's *Everybody Says I Love You,* which interweaves the stories of several Upper East Side upscale teens; *Big Daddy,* in which Adam Sandler introduces a small boy to downtown New York's amusements; or *You've Got Mail,* a charming love story set on the Upper West Side; then there's the perennially lovely classic *Breakfast at Tiffany's.* For the younger set, Disney's animated *Oliver and Company* has a Manhattan setting, as do *The Cricket in Times Square, A Troll in Central Park,* and Jim Henson's *The Muppets Take Manhattan. Sesame Street,* of course, is more or less set in New York City, but don't promise your toddlers they'll actually meet Big Bird.

New York City's skyline is a famous sight—prime your youngsters for that first glimpse of it. Buildings to identify include the World Trade Center, twin rectangular towers at the southern tip of Manhattan, which the Dino de Laurentis King Kong scaled; the Empire State Building, with its tall antenna tower up which the original King Kong climbed; the Chrysler Building's chrome-tipped art deco spire, looking for all the world like a hood ornament; the riverside United Nations, a vertical plane of sheer glass anchored by the dome of the General Assembly; the slant-roofed white Citibank Building; the Chippendale-style crest on the Sony Building. The Statue of Liberty is another indelible New York landmark to show your kids pictures of ahead of time. Yet another is Rockefeller Plaza, where a giant gilded Prometheus statue overlooks an ice-skating rink in winter and an outdoor cafe in summer—and where the even-more-giant Rockefeller Center Christmas tree sparkles during the holiday season.

Older kids may be interested in New York's battery of sports teams—depending on the season, watch some innings of Yankees or Mets baseball, a Jets or Giants football game, a Rangers or Islanders hockey match, or a Knicks or Nets basketball game.

To give kids a taste of the city's sights ahead of time, the nifty guidebook *New York City* by Deborah Kent (Children's Press) offers a clear and comprehensive introduction to the city, written at a second-grade reading level. *Citybook* by Shelley Rotner and Ken Kreisler (Orchard Books) may be better for toddlers, with great color photos of the city and only a few well-chosen words per page. Also for preschoolers, *The Escape of Marvin the Ape* by Caralyn and Mark Buehner (Dial Books) portrays a fugitive gorilla happily losing himself in New York City's parks, museums, stores, and ballparks. *My New York* by Kathy Jakobsen (Little Brown), a great picture book for kids 3 to 7, is written in the form of a letter from a young New Yorker to a friend from the Midwest who's coming to visit. *You Can't Take a Balloon into the Metropolitan Museum of Art* (Dial Books) is a wordless picture book, almost like a delightful comic book, that juxtaposes a child's trip through the museum with the wild adventures of the yellow balloon she thought she'd left tethered to a tree outside. *Pamela's First Musical* by noted playwright Wendy Wasserstein (Hyperion, ages 4–8) depicts a 9-year-old's first thrilling evening at a Broadway theater. In *Amy Elizabeth Explores Bloomingdale's* by E. L. Konigsburg (Atheneum; ages 4–8), a little girl from Houston visits her grandmother in the city, setting out every day to visit the famous department store and always getting wonderfully sidetracked. *Be-Bop-a-Do-Walk* by Sheila Hamanaka (Simon & Schuster) works well for the same age group, illustrating a lively walk from the Lower East Side up to Central Park in 1950s New York. George Selden's *Chester Cricket's Pigeon Ride* may be hard to find, but this chapter book for young readers, by the author of the classic *The Cricket in Times Square,* gives a soaring bird's-eye view of Manhattan.

5 Getting There

BY PLANE

Almost every major domestic carrier serves the New York area. Here's a handy list of toll-free numbers and Web sites: **America West** (☎ **800/235-9292;** www.americawest.com), **American** (☎ **800/433-7300;** www.americanair.com), **Continental** (☎ **800/525-0280;** www.flycontinental.com), **Delta** (☎ **800/221-1212;** www.delta.com), **Northwest** (☎ **800/225-2525;** www.nwa.com), **TWA** (☎ **800/221-2000;** www2.twa.com), **US Airways** (☎ **800/428-4322;** www.usair.com), and **United** (☎ **800/241-6522;** www.ual.com).

In recent years there has been rapid growth in the number of no-frills airlines serving New York. These smaller, sometimes struggling airlines may offer lower fares—and all that that implies. You might check out **AirTran** (☎ **800/247-8726;** www.airtran.com), **Frontier** (☎ **800/432-1359;** www.frontierair.com), **Midway** (☎ **800/446-4392;** www.midwayair.com), and **Midwest Express** (☎ **800/452-2022;** www.midwestexpress.com).

Most of the major international carriers also fly into New York (see the appendix for details).

One way to find the lowest fare is to call a discount travel agency like **Travel Avenue** in Chicago at ☎ **800/333-3335.** Unlike most travel agencies, this one

Cyber Deals for Net Surfers

It's possible to get great information as well as great deals on airfare, hotels, and car rentals via the Internet. So grab your mouse and start surfing before you head to New York. A good place to start is **Arthur Frommer's Budget Travel Online** (www.frommers.com), where you'll find lots of up-to-the-minute information—including the latest bargains and candid articles updated daily by Arthur Frommer himself.

✪ **Travelocity** (www.travelocity.com; www.frommers.travelocity.com) now incorporates Preview Travel and is Frommer's online travel planning/booking partner. Travelocity uses the SABRE system to offer reservations and tickets for more than 400 airlines, plus reservations and purchase capabilities for more than 45,000 hotels and 50 car-rental companies. An exclusive feature of this system is its **Low Fare Search Engine,** which automatically searches for the three lowest-priced itineraries based on a traveler's criteria. Last-minute deals and consolidator fares are included in the search. If you book with Travelocity, you can select specific seats for your flights with online seat maps and also view diagrams of the most popular commercial aircraft. The **hotel finder** provides street-level location maps and photos of selected hotels. With the **Fare Watcher** e-mail feature, you can select up to five routes and receive e-mail notices when the fare changes by $25 or more. Travelocity's **Destination Guide** includes updated information on some 260 destinations worldwide—supplied by Frommer's.

Expedia (www.expedia.com) is Travelocity's major competitor. It offers several ways of obtaining the best possible fares: **Flight Price Matcher** service allows your preferred airline to match an available fare with a competitor; a comprehensive **Fare Compare** area shows the differences in fare categories and airlines; and **Fare Calendar** helps you plan your trip around the best possible fares. Its main limitation is that like many online databases, Expedia focuses on the major airlines and hotel chains, so don't expect to find too many budget airlines or one-of-a-kind B&Bs here.

TRIP.com began as a site geared toward business travelers, but its innovative features and highly personalized approach have broadened its appeal to leisure travelers as well. It is the leading travel site for those using mobile devices to access Internet travel information. TRIP.com includes a trip-planning function that provides the average and lowest fare for the route requested, in addition to the current available fare. An on-site **newsstand** features breaking news on airfare sales and other travel specials. Among its most popular features are **Flight TRACKER** and **intelliTRIP.** Flight TRACKER allows users to track any commercial flight en route to its destination anywhere in the United States, while accessing real-time FAA-based flight monitoring data. intelliTRIP is a travel search tool that allows users to identify the best airline, hotel, and car-rental rates in less than 90 seconds. In addition, the site offers e-mail notification of flight delays, plus city resource guides, currency converters, and a weekly e-mail newsletter of fare updates, travel tips, and traveler forums.

Yahoo! (www.travel.yahoo.com) is currently the most popular of the Internet information portals, and its travel site is a comprehensive mix of online booking, daily travel news, and destination information. The **Best Fares** area offers what it promises, plus provides feedback on refining your search if you have flexibility in travel dates or times. There is also an active section of **message boards** for discussions on travel in general and specific destinations.

doesn't offer advice or itinerary planning; it does, however, offer cash rebates on fares from major airlines (over $300) and hotels.

If you decide on a trip to New York at the last minute, give a call to **1-800/ FLY-ASAP,** a national reservation service that uses a new computer program to find the lowest fares available. You could realize substantial savings here.

A highly praised organization called **FreeFlier,** P.O. Box 844, Bowling Green Station, New York, NY 10274-0844 (☎ 212/727-9675), may be able to save you travel dollars—even if you're a relatively "infrequent flyer." For a small fee ($9.95 adults; $7.50 seniors, retirees, students, and groups of four or more), it forwards the applications of travelers to more than two dozen frequent-flyer, car-rental, and hotel-stay programs. Owner Robert Reiner points out that many programs provide instant benefits and don't require long-term loyalty. Frequent-flyer programs often offer insider discounts or advance notice of lower fares that only members may obtain. Many car-rental programs offer free upgrades or an extra day's usage. Several hotel-stay programs reward members with a free weekend night when they stay on a weekday night. Reiner advises that they often receive extra coupons for frequent-traveler bonuses that they'll pass on to anyone sending a stamped, self-addressed no. 10 envelope.

NEW YORK AREA AIRPORTS

New York City has three major airports: **La Guardia** (☎ 718/533-3400), **John F. Kennedy (JFK) International** (☎ 718/244-4444), and **Newark International** (☎ 973/961-6000) in New Jersey. JFK, in southeastern Queens about an hour's drive from Manhattan, is largely served by international flights, though some domestic flights are routed through. La Guardia, chiefly for domestic flights, is also in Queens, though not as far from Manhattan—it's a shorter ride (30–45 minutes) into Midtown. Newark Airport serves both domestic and international flights; it takes about 45 to 60 minutes to drive into Manhattan from Newark. If you need to make connections at another airport, you can contact **New York Airport Service** (☎ 718/875-8200), which shuttles travelers between La Guardia and JFK for $11 one-way.

With young kids in tow, it's best to take a **cab** from the airport into the city. All three airports have orderly taxi stands where you line up until it's your turn for the uniformed dispatcher to help you into a licensed cab (yellow cabs only from JFK and La Guardia; New Jersey cab companies work from Newark). Cab fares from JFK into Manhattan are set at $30, which comes to around $40 once you've added bridge and tunnel tolls and a 15% to 20% tip; the total from Newark, including tolls and tip, is also about $40, and from LaGuardia it's more like $25. There's no charge for extra people or for luggage, though yellow cabs add a 50¢ surcharge on weekends and from 8pm to 6am; New Jersey cabs are allowed to tack on a $10 fee for crossing the state line (stay alert, for New Jersey cab drivers have been known to get lost on the way to Midtown). Passengers are expected to pay bridge and tunnel tolls, though the driver may pay the toll and then add it to your fare.

If your kids are older and you don't have loads of luggage, you can save money by taking a **New York Airport Service** bus (☎ 718/875-8200), running from either JFK or La Guardia to Manhattan. Buses leave clearly marked stops at the terminals every 20 minutes. The trip in from JFK costs $13 and takes about an hour; from La Guardia to Midtown it costs $10 and takes 45 minutes. New York Airport Service buses stop at Grand Central Terminal (Park Avenue and 42nd Street), the Port Authority Bus Terminal (Eighth Avenue between 40th and 42nd streets), Pennsylvania Station (between Seventh and Eighth avenues and 31st and 33rd streets), and a number of Midtown hotels. If you hail a cab from Grand Central, Port Authority, or Penn Station, the fare should be $5 to $7 to most Midtown hotels, though catching a cab at these busy terminals can be stressful. All three have taxi stands; never let a local hustler get a cab for you—they can get abusive if you don't pay them as much as they feel they deserve for this illegal service.

From Newark Airport, **Olympia Trails Airport Express** (☎ 212/964-6233) operates a 30-minute bus ride to Pennsylvania Station, Port Authority Bus Terminal, Grand Central Terminal, or the World Trade Center downtown; the ride costs $11 one-way ($20 round-trip) and buses leave every 20 to 30 minutes. **Gray Line Air Shuttle** (☎ 212/315-3006) operates a minibus service between all three airports and a number of Manhattan hotels for $14 from JFK, $13 from La Guardia, and $14 from Newark.

To have a limousine (actually, a luxury sedan—don't promise the kids a stretch limo) pick you up, call before you fly (at least a day in advance) to arrange pickup from private car-service companies like **All State Car and Limo** (☎ 212/741-7440) and **Sabra** (☎ 212/777-7171); the cost is about $33 from La Guardia, $44 from JFK, and $45 from Newark, not counting tolls and tips. **Carmel** (☎ 212/666-6666) charges even lower rates, provided you book an ordinary car rather than a luxury sedan—$25 from La Guardia, $35 from JFK, and $34 from Newark, not counting tolls, parking, and tips.

If you're determined to save money and have lots of time, the cheapest way to get into the city from JFK is to take the free **Port Authority Shuttle Bus** to the Howard Beach subway station, where you can catch an **A train** into Manhattan. From La Guardia, you can take a local **Q33 bus** to the subway's Roosevelt Avenue station, where you can catch the no. 7 train to Midtown; or the local **Q48 bus** to the 111th Street station, also on the no. 7 line to Manhattan. The **M60 bus** goes directly from La Guardia to Manhattan, where it makes stops along 125th Street and then down Broadway, terminating at 106th Street; you can catch the no. 1 or 9 train at 116th or 110th Street and head down the Upper West Side from there. Any of these trips can take well over an hour, though the second two routes from La Guardia are generally quicker. Except for the JFK shuttle bus, which is free, you'll have to pay regular bus and subway fares, $1.50 per person (children under 44 inches ride free). Note that you can transfer free from a bus to the subway, but only if you use a MetroCard, sold at subway station fare booths; without a Metro-Card, you'll have to pay a second fare when you enter the subway.

If you take a weekday flight to La Guardia on Delta's Boston or Washington shuttle, the **Delta Water Shuttle** (☎ 800/53-FERRY) between La Guardia's Marine Air Terminal and Manhattan's East 90th Street (10 minutes from the airport), East 62nd Street (15–20 minutes), East 34th Street (25–30 minutes), and Wall Street's Pier 11 (40–45 minutes) can be a fun ride. It costs $15 one-way or $25 round-trip. To get to your hotel, you'll need to hail a cab once you disembark.

BY TRAIN

The major long-distance rail terminal in Manhattan is **Pennsylvania Station,** known to all as Penn Station, between Seventh and Eighth avenues and 31st to 33rd streets. **Amtrak** trains (☎ 800/872-7245) come through Penn Station from all across the country. Two commuter train lines, **New Jersey Transit** (☎ 973/762-5100) and the **Long Island Rail Road** (☎ 718/217-5477), also come into Penn Station, so it can be a madhouse at rush hour, especially on the lower-level LIRR platforms. **Grand Central Terminal,** at 42nd Street and Park Avenue, is the city's other train station, used today only by **Metro North** commuter trains

(☎ 212/532-4900), serving Connecticut and New York State. **Path** commuter trains (☎ 800/234-PATH) from New Jersey have their own underground stations in Manhattan: World Trade Center, Christopher Street, West 9th Street, West 14th Street, West 23rd Street, and 33rd Street and Eighth Avenue; fare is $1, free for children under 5. There are taxi stands at both Penn Station and Grand Central. Penn Station has subway stations on the A, C, E, 1, 2, 3, and 9 lines. Grand Central subway station serves the 4, 5, 6, and 7 lines, and the S shuttle to Times Square.

Even if you don't catch a train from Grand Central, take your kids to see the gloriously restored main hall, a grand marble cavern with a star-spangled ceiling. The old Penn Station was just as handsome, but it was torn down in the 1960s and replaced with the soulless modern pile detailed above. Plans are to convert the neoclassical main post office on Eighth Avenue between 31st and 33rd streets (across from the current Penn Station) into a new Penn Station. Stay tuned.

BY BUS

The **Port Authority Bus Terminal,** at Eighth Avenue between 40th and 42nd streets (☎ 212/564-8484), still has its grubby corners, despite the remarkable transformation of the nearby Times Square area. On the whole, however, this cheerless big station is well lit and well patrolled, with lots of discount shops and fast-food restaurants lining the main hall. In the great tradition of urban bus stations, it also has more than its share of derelicts and panhandlers. Greyhound, Trailways, and other long-distance bus lines stop here, along with various commuter bus lines. Upon arrival, head straight for the taxi stand on Eighth Avenue, where a dispatcher can get you a cab. The A, C, and E subways make a stop at Port Authority, and a long underground tunnel leads you to Times Square and the 1, 2, 3, 7, N, R, and S trains. But these are some of the city's dingiest subway stops—take a cab if you can. The fare won't be more than $5 or $6 to most Midtown hotels, barring traffic jams.

BY CAR

Having a car in Manhattan isn't an asset. Drive here only if you must. If you do, my best advice is to get to your destination, put your car in a garage, and keep it there. Yes, hotel and independent garages charge exorbitant rates, but street parking can be a nightmare and you don't want to deal with having your car broken into while you're on vacation.

North–south **I-95** runs up through New Jersey, jogs across the northern tip of Manhattan and the Bronx, and heads up to New England. From the south, you can exit I-95 (the New Jersey Turnpike) at I-78 in Jersey City, which takes you to the **Holland Tunnel** ($4 toll) into Downtown; at I-495 in Union City, which takes you to Midtown's **Lincoln Tunnel** ($4 toll); or after crossing the **George Washington Bridge** ($4 toll), where NY 9A (the **Henry Hudson Parkway**) goes down the West Side of Manhattan. I-278 branches off I-95 south of Elizabeth, New Jersey, crossing east to Staten Island, then into Brooklyn across the **Verrazano Narrows Bridge** ($7 toll westbound into Staten Island; no toll eastbound into Brooklyn).

From the north, I-95 connects with the **Bruckner Expressway** (I-278), which swings down to the **Triborough Bridge** ($3.50 toll), leading you into Manhattan on the East Side's **FDR Drive.** If you're going to the West Side of Manhattan, stay on I-95 as it becomes the **Cross Bronx Expressway** and take the last exit in Manhattan to the **Henry Hudson Parkway** (NY 9A). Other useful routes from the north include the **Merritt Parkway/Hutchinson Parkway/Cross County Expressway** from New England and the **Taconic Parkway** from upstate New York, both of which feed into the **Saw Mill Parkway,** which crosses into Manhattan at the **Henry Hudson Bridge** ($1.75 toll) and becomes the Henry Hudson Parkway (NY 9A). **I-87** also leads down from upstate New York; either exit south onto the **Palisades Parkway** into New Jersey and take that down to the George Washington Bridge, or stay on I-87/287 as it turns east and crosses the Hudson at Tarrytown, New York, then exit onto the Saw Mill Parkway and continue south across the Henry Hudson Bridge into Manhattan.

From the west, **I-80** feeds into the George Washington Bridge. **I-280** branches off I-80 out near Morris Plains, New Jersey, heading southeast to join **I-95;** from there, you can pick up **I-78** to the Holland Tunnel or **I-495** to the Lincoln Tunnel. **I-78** is another Interstate highway coming into New York from the west; it leads into the Holland Tunnel downtown.

Getting to Know New York City

3

At first glance New York can be a very intimidating town, especially when you have a flock of youngsters under your wing. Take time from the outset to get a grasp of the city's layout and the best navigating methods.

1 Orientation

VISITOR INFORMATION

New York City Visitor Centers are scattered around Manhattan; the most comprehensive one is at **Times Square** (Seventh Avenue between 46th and 47th streets), but there are also booths at **Grand Central Terminal** (42nd Street between Lexington and Vanderbilt avenues), **Macy's** department store (34th Street between Sixth and Seventh avenues), **Bloomingdale's** department store (Lexington Avenue between 59th and 60th streets), the **World Trade Center** (2 World Trade Center, the same building where the observation deck is located), and **JFK Airport.** Stop by to pick up maps, brochures, and sightseeing suggestions, along with "two-fers" for savings on Broadway and Off-Broadway plays.

The **New York Convention & Visitors Bureau**'s 24-hour information hotline at ☎ **800/NYC-VISIT** or 212/397-8222 offers similar information. Pick up info on the Internet at **www.nycvisit. com** or stop by the bureau's **public information office** at 810 Seventh Ave., between 52nd and 53rd streets (☎ **212/484-1222**), which is open Monday to Friday 8:30am to 6pm and Saturday and Sunday 9am to 5pm.

For recorded listings of **Lincoln Center** events, call ☎ **212/ 546-2656** or visit its Web site at **www.lincolncenter.org.** For upcoming events in **city parks,** call ☎ **888/NY-PARKS** or 212/360-3456.

CITY LAYOUT

MAJOR ARTERIES IN MANHATTAN The limited-access **FDR Drive** runs along Manhattan's East River shore, from the Brooklyn Battery Tunnel (which links to Brooklyn) north to the Triborough Bridge (which links to Queens and to I-95). The **West Side Highway** goes from Battery Park up along the Hudson, eventually becoming the limited-access **Henry Hudson Parkway** running all the way to Manhattan's northern tip and on through the Bronx (Riverdale), where it finally becomes the **Saw Mill Parkway.**

A Street by Any Other Name

When the Street Sign Says . . .	It's the Same as . . .
Amsterdam Avenue	Tenth Avenue (above 59th Street)
Avenue of the Americas	Sixth Avenue
Cathedral Parkway	West 110th Street (from Central Park West to Riverside Drive)
Central Park North	West 110th Street (between Fifth Avenue and Central Park West)
Central Park South	59th Street (between Fifth and Eighth avenues)
Central Park West	Eighth Avenue (from 59th to 110th streets)
Columbus Avenue	Ninth Avenue (above 59th Street)
Fashion Avenue	Seventh Avenue (from 34th to 42nd streets)
Park Avenue	Fourth Avenue (above 14th Street)
St. Luke's Place	Leroy Street (from Seventh Avenue to Hudson Street)
St. Mark's Place	8th Street (from Third Avenue to Avenue A)
West End Avenue	Eleventh Avenue (from 59th to 107th streets)

Broadway is Manhattan's spine, beginning at Battery Park and angling north all the way through Washington Heights (from there on, as U.S. 9, it continues all the way to Albany). Since Manhattan's axis is skewed to the northeast, Broadway—which runs due north—seems to run at an angle, and every time it crosses a major avenue in the Manhattan grid, there's a significant traffic junction: **Union Square** at 14th Street, **Madison Square** at 23rd Street, **Herald Square** at 34th Street, **Times Square** at 42nd Street, **Columbus Circle** at 59th Street, **Lincoln Square** at 66th Street, **Verdi Square** at 72nd Street, and **Straus Park** at 106th Street. Above 59th Street, where Central Park divides Manhattan, Broadway is the West Side's main drag.

The other big avenues in the grid are one-way, with the exception of the East Side's **Park Avenue,** which is mostly high-rent residential north of 57th Street (between 14th and 34th streets it's known as **Park Avenue South**). The avenues that run uptown (north) are **First Avenue, Third Avenue, Madison Avenue, Sixth Avenue** (also called **Avenue of the Americas**), **Eighth Avenue** (called **Central Park West** between 59th and 110th streets and **Frederick Douglass Boulevard** above 110th Street), and **Tenth Avenue** (called **Amsterdam Avenue** above 59th Street). To go downtown (south), take **Second Avenue, Lexington Avenue** (to 21st Street), **Fifth Avenue, Seventh Avenue, Ninth Avenue** (called **Columbus Avenue** above 59th Street), or **Eleventh Avenue** (called **West End Avenue** from 107th Street, where it begins, to 59th Street). In the older areas of town, below 8th Street, the grid doesn't apply and you'll need a map to navigate. **Hudson Street** is a major north-bound thoroughfare on the West Side; on the East Side it's **Fourth Avenue** (the southern section of Park Avenue South below 14th Street), which is created when the **Bowery** splits into Third and Fourth avenues.

Manhattan Neighborhoods

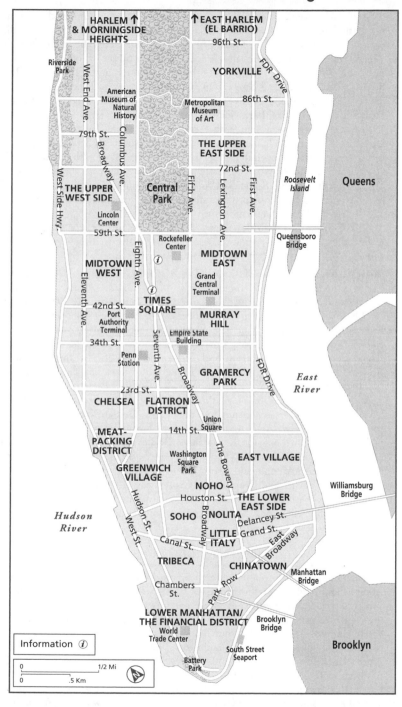

HARLEM ↑
& MORNINGSIDE
HEIGHTS

↑ EAST HARLEM
(EL BARRIO)

96th St.

Riverside
Park

West End Ave.

YORKVILLE

FDR Drive

American
Museum of
Natural
History

Metropolitan
Museum
of Art

86th St.

79th St.

Columbus Ave.

Broadway

THE UPPER
EAST SIDE

West Side Hwy.

THE UPPER
WEST SIDE

Central
Park

Fifth Ave.

72nd St.

Lexington Ave.

First Ave.

Roosevelt
Island

Queens

Lincoln
Center

59th St.

Eighth Ave.

Rockefeller
Center

ⓘ

MIDTOWN
EAST

Queensboro
Bridge

MIDTOWN
WEST

Eleventh Ave.

ⓘ

Grand
Central
Terminal

42nd St.
Port
Authority
Terminal

TIMES
SQUARE

MURRAY
HILL

34th St.

Seventh Ave.

Empire State
Building

Penn
Station

Broadway

FDR Drive

East
River

23rd St.

GRAMERCY
PARK

CHELSEA

FLATIRON
DISTRICT

Union
Square

MEAT-
PACKING
DISTRICT

14th St.

Washington
Square
Park

EAST VILLAGE

Williamsburg
Bridge

GREENWICH
VILLAGE

The Bowery

Hudson
River

NOHO

Houston St.

THE LOWER
EAST SIDE

SOHO

Hudson St.

West St.

NOLITA

Broadway

Delancey St.

Grand St.

East Broadway

LITTLE
ITALY

Canal St.

TRIBECA

CHINATOWN

Manhattan
Bridge

Chambers
St.

Park Row

LOWER MANHATTAN/
THE FINANCIAL DISTRICT

World
Trade Center

Brooklyn
Bridge

South Street
Seaport

Battery
Park

Brooklyn

Information ⓘ

0   1/2 Mi
0   .5 Km

Most cross streets in the grid are one-way; generally, even-numbered streets are east-bound and odd-numbered streets are west-bound. You'll find two-way traffic on a few major cross streets: **Canal Street,** which cuts across the island from the Manhattan Bridge to the Holland Tunnel; **Houston Street,** which funnels traffic from the Williamsburg Bridge to the Holland Tunnel; and **14th Street, 23rd Street, 34th Street, 42nd Street,** and **57th Street.** Central Park bisects the city between **59th Street** and **110th Street** (which are also called, respectively, **Central Park South** and **Central Park North**). You'll find two-way traffic on **72nd Street, 79th Street, 86th Street,** and **96th Street.** To cut across Central Park from the Upper East Side to the Upper West Side, choose either **66th Street, 72nd Street** (open weekday rush hours only), **79th Street, 85th Street,** or **97th Street.** If you're going from the Upper West Side to the Upper East Side, your options are **65th Street, 81st Street, 86th Street,** and **96th Street.** All other car entrances to the park feed into the circular drive, open only during weekday rush hours. Above the park, **125th Street** is Harlem's major two-way commercial street.

Note: Consult the front of a Yellow Pages telephone directory for details on how to find the cross street for an avenue address and/or the avenues between a street address.

MAJOR ARTERIES IN THE OUTER BOROUGHS   The **Grand Central Parkway** leads from the Triborough Bridge to La Guardia Airport, in northern Queens, and on to Long Island. The **Long Island Expressway** (I-495) goes from the Queens Midtown Tunnel across Queens, through Forest Hills and Flushing, and out to Long Island. The **Brooklyn–Queens Expressway**—known as the BQE—runs north–south linking Brooklyn and Queens; you can get on it from the Grand Central Parkway, from the 59th Street Bridge (also called the Queensboro Bridge), from the Queens–Midtown Tunnel, and from the three Brooklyn–Manhattan bridges—the Williamsburg, the Manhattan, and the Brooklyn.

At the southern end of Brooklyn, the BQE links with the **Verrazano Bridge** (toll $7 westbound only) from Staten Island, then (as the **Belt Parkway**) swings around the coast past Coney Island and the Rockaways, feeding into **Southern Parkway,** which heads out to Long Island. **Northern Boulevard** is one of Queens's major commercial thoroughfares. Radiating out from Brooklyn Heights, **Atlantic Avenue, Flatbush Avenue,** and (starting near Prospect Park) **Ocean Parkway** fan out across Brooklyn. The **Cross-Bronx Expressway** (I-95) is the major highway cutting across the Bronx; the Bronx River Parkway runs up through Bronx Park, where you'll find the Bronx Zoo and the Botanical Garden.

Manhattan Neighborhoods in Brief

Manhattan was settled from its southern tip northward, so the oldest area is **Lower Manhattan,** roughly everything south of Canal Street. Within this, the **Financial District,** centered around Wall Street and lower Broadway, has pretty much obscured traces of the early colonial settlement with its battery of skyscrapers, but you'll still find a few venerable churches tucked away, and some of the skyscrapers themselves are early 20th-century landmarks. The only really historic quarter left is on the East River waterfront at South Street Seaport, a 19th-century district that has been mall-ified, but not out of recognition. North of the Seaport, you'll find City Hall, other municipal buildings, and an imposing set of courthouses (clustered around Foley Square). Over on the Hudson side of the narrow island, you get some open green space at Battery Park, with its ferries and harbor views; the sleek planned community of Battery Park City just north of the park has a great riverside promenade and connects via walkway to the immense World Trade Center. The nickname **TriBeCa** derives from the *Tri*angle *Be*low *Ca*nal Street, but the label is used for only the northwestern chunk of that triangle, a hypercool neighborhood of converted industrial lofts dotted with trendy restaurants and a few galleries.

Above South Street Seaport and the courts, **Chinatown** occupies the East River side of the below-Canal area, but it burst its traditional boundaries long ago and now also spills north of Canal Street, engulfing the vestiges of **Little Italy,** which still clings to Mulberry Street as its main drag. The tenement buildings lining these streets should clue you in to the fact that these neighborhoods were the 19th century's immigrant slums. East of Little Italy lies the **Lower East Side,** for years the Jewish immigrant district, more recently a Hispanic area, and increasingly colonized by young urban bohemians. To the west of Little Italy, a derelict 19th-century industrial zone was converted in the 1970s to artsy **SoHo** (*So*uth of *Ho*uston Street—pronounced, by the way, "*how*-stun," never "*hew*-stun"). Its commercial streets are now lined with art galleries, boutiques, and restaurants, but some of the back streets still look grim and forbidding.

Above Houston Street, you enter the Villages—**Greenwich Village,** from Broadway west to the Hudson River; and the **East Village,** from Broadway on east, though the rougher neighborhoods along Avenues A, B, C, and D are sometimes set apart under the tag "Alphabet City." Greenwich Village still has a certain bohemian cachet, and its quiet side streets, with their red-brick town houses, make a good place to ramble when the city gets on your nerves. The East Village is funkier and grittier, just the place to bring teenagers who think their parents are so uncool they don't want to be seen with them. (Just walk five paces behind them, okay?) Teens may also want to hang out in the New York University area, which sprawls around the Village's focal point, Washington Square Park, and spills over into the fringes of the East Village.

Above 14th Street, the Manhattan grid falls into place, and the city starts to get more buttoned-down. Between 14th and 30th streets, **Chelsea** occupies the area from Sixth Avenue west. This is now a very hot area for art galleries, fashion industry types, and gays; at its far west end, the Chelsea Piers' sports complex on the river is a major draw for families. East of Sixth Avenue is what's called the **Flatiron District** (named after the famous Flatiron Building at 23rd Street and Broadway), a trendy area for restaurants and nightlife, and the quiet older neighborhoods around **Gramercy Park,** the city's only private park; north of Gramercy lies **Murray Hill,** a largely residential neighborhood of limited interest for families.

Midtown is the major business district, sprawling across the island from about 34th Street to 59th Street. Big department stores and elegant shops march up Fifth Avenue, with a handful of museums set on side streets; looming skyscrapers (notably the Empire State Building and the Rockefeller Center buildings) draw hundreds of thousands of workers every day. The **Theater District** clusters around Times Square (42nd Street and Broadway); the United Nations anchors 42nd Street at the East River. By far the greatest number of Manhattan hotels are in Midtown, and many restaurants as well. But with its crowded sidewalks and restaurants packed with impatient workaday New Yorkers, it's not necessarily where families want to concentrate their time. Come here to shop and to gawk at the tall buildings; at Christmastime, Rockefeller Center and the store windows are so magical they shouldn't be missed. But venture away from Midtown, and you'll get a better idea of how New York families experience the city.

Manhattan's Bridges & Tunnels

Manhattan's an island—to get on or off it you have to go over or under the water. Going clockwise around the island, starting from the northern tip, you can take the **Henry Hudson Bridge** (on the Henry Hudson Parkway; $1.75 toll); the **Triborough Bridge** ($3.50 toll); the **59th Street/Queensboro Bridge** (no toll); or the **Queens–Midtown Tunnel** (part of I-495; $3.50 toll). A trio of toll-free bridges into Brooklyn—the **Williamsburg,** the **Manhattan,** and the **Brooklyn**—all connect handily with the Brooklyn–Queens Expressway, as does the **Brooklyn Battery Tunnel** ($3.50 toll) at the island's southern tip. Two big tunnels cross the Hudson on Manhattan's West Side—the **Holland Tunnel** ($4 toll into Manhattan), which funnels into Canal or Houston Street; and the **Lincoln Tunnel** ($4 toll into Manhattan), which funnels into 40th Street—and the **George Washington Bridge** (part of I-95; $4 toll into Manhattan) crosses above the water up at 175th Street. Lines at bridge and tunnel toll booths have been significantly eased in the past few years with the introduction of **E-Z Pass,** a small device that drivers can post on their windshields to have tolls electronically deducted from a credit-card account. Certain lanes at toll stations are designated for E-Z Pass users only, so stay alert (there are no toll attendants at those booths). E-Z Pass lanes move much faster than toll-paying lanes, so anyone living in the metropolitan area would be well advised to use this service; to set up an account, call ☎ 800/333-TOLL or go online at **www. e-zpassny.com**.

The **Upper West Side** occupies the part of Manhattan directly west of Central Park—here you'll find the city's best museums for kids, lots of kid-friendly restaurants, toy stores, and playgrounds in both Central and Riverside parks. The **Upper East Side,** everything east of Central Park, is also very child-oriented but less casual; you'll see packs of uniformed kids from tony private schools gathering in pizza parlors and Gaps. The **East Side** is rich in museums, especially along the park on Fifth Avenue, but many of them are either too stuffy or too dull for children (the beautiful Frick Museum, in fact, won't even allow kids under 10 to enter).

Above Central Park to the west is **Morningside Heights,** dominated by Columbia University and two magnificent churches—Riverside Church and the Cathedral of St. John the Divine; it's a casual, friendly area with some good family restaurants. East of Morningside Park, **Harlem** takes over the island north of Central Park. Many tourists visit Harlem as part of a guided tour, though you can certainly check it out on your own. However, your kids' interest in the social-history aspects of a Harlem guided tour may lag if they're under 10. Unless you're visiting the Cloisters (the Metropolitan Museum's medieval art branch in Fort Tryon Park), there's not much reason for you to tour **Washington Heights,** which lies above Harlem.

The Outer Boroughs in Brief

New York City's other four boroughs surround the island of Manhattan. To the north and east lies the **Bronx,** which only partly deserves its bad rap as a crime-infested slum. Parts of the Bronx are rotten indeed, but the Bronx also includes suburban Riverdale, along the Hudson, and the middle-class Fordham area, anchored by Fordham University and Bronx Park (where the zoo and the botanical garden are). The New York Yankees are called the Bronx Bombers because Yankee Stadium is at

161st Street in the Bronx (though owner George Steinbrenner is forever threatening to move them elsewhere); it's a bad area, but crowds of baseball fans make it safe around game time, and the subway takes you directly to the stadium.

The landmass directly east of Manhattan—the western end of Long Island—contains the two most populous boroughs: Brooklyn and Queens. Immortalized (rightly or wrongly) as Archie Bunker territory, **Queens** is the city's great middle-class borough, where hardworking immigrant groups have colonized various neighborhoods from Astoria (Greek and Irish) to Flushing (various Asian nationalities). Directly across the river from Manhattan, Long Island City has become a haven for young artists, and Forest Hills in the middle of Queens is a manicured residential area. Further-out areas of Queens, like St. Albans, Little Neck, and Douglaston, are basically suburban neighborhoods.

Brooklyn on the whole is more urban and edgy, though it has some of the city's loveliest residential areas, notably brownstone-lined Brooklyn Heights, right across the Brooklyn Bridge from Manhattan, and nearby gentrified neighborhoods packed with 19th-century row houses, such as Cobble Hill, Carroll Gardens, and Park Slope (the last has the advantage of bordering Prospect Park, Central Park's Brooklyn cousin). Facing Staten Island across the Narrows, Bay Ridge is a vast middle-class enclave; Brighton Beach, on Brooklyn's southern shore, is a former Jewish area now heavily colonized by immigrant Russians. But other Brooklyn neighborhoods, like Bedford-Stuyvesant, Brownsville, and East New York, aren't for the uninitiated. If you visit Brooklyn, know where you're going.

That leaves **Staten Island**, the most suburban of the boroughs, the one that's always threatening to secede from the city—which actually makes sense, since Staten Island is geographically more like part of New Jersey. Staten Island's attractions for visitors—the restored historic village at Richmondtown, a zoo, a children's museum, a couple of historic houses—don't lure many New Yorkers across the water, which suits most Staten Islanders just fine. Still, the Staten Island Ferry ride is one of those classic New York things to do, a pleasant way to spend an hour or so crossing the harbor—and it's free.

2 Getting Around

BY SUBWAY

The **MTA—New York City Transit** (☎ 718/330-1234) operates the city's buses and subways, which run 24 hours. Even mildly adventurous visitors should feel comfortable underground from 7am to 8pm—however, the morning and evening rush hours (generally 8–9:30am and 5–6:30pm weekdays) make the trains so crowded you'd be better off not traveling then, especially with a family to squeeze in. The **fare** is $1.50, and for your buck and a half you can ride as long and far as you like, changing lines at any of more than 50 transfer points.

You can buy brass **tokens** at booths in each station for $1.50 each; you deposit them in the turnstiles to enter the train system, and once you exit the system you have to pay to get in again. But most New Yorkers use multiride **MetroCards,** with magnetic strips that automatically deduct one fare every time you slip them through a groove in a turnstile; each time you run your card through a turnstile, your remaining balance is displayed. MetroCards can be bought in various denominations from $3 to $80 and can be refilled at most token booths, with 10% discounts offered for buying $15 or more; unlimited-ride passes are also available, costing $63 for 30 days, $17 for 7 days, and $4 for 1 day (expires at 3am). All of these except

---

A Map Note

See the inside back cover of this guide for a full-color map of Manhattan's subway system.

---

the 1-day pass (the Fun Pass) are available at token booths and at vending machines in some stations; the Fun Pass can be bought only in the vending machines or at newsstands and shops around town (look for blue-and-yellow METROCARDS SOLD HERE signs). Up to four passengers traveling together can use the same Metro-Card—just slide it through the turnstile once for each rider. (Unlimited-ride passes cannot be used by more than one passenger.) Children under 44 inches tall ride free; in practice, kids under 6 can just duck under the turnstile bar and no one challenges them.

One big advantage of using a MetroCard is that the cards allow riders **free transfers** to and from city buses, whereas token users have to pay twice. If you're coming from a city bus, just slide your card through the groove and the machine should indicate that this is a transfer. Note that transfers do expire after a certain amount of time; sometimes you'll be pleasantly surprised when you reenter the system half an hour after one ride to find that your second ride registers as a transfer, but don't count on it.

Maps are posted inside stations (usually out by the token booths, so you can make sure where you're going before you enter) and in most cars. Near the token booths, many stations now also feature detailed street maps of the immediate area, so you can get oriented before you hit the street.

Many Manhattan stations were renovated in the 1990s, and more will be in the new century. The tile walls along waiting platforms often feature work by local artists or symbols appropriate for that particular neighborhood. Not only are stations brighter and better lit than they used to be, the trains themselves are now clean, graffiti-free, and blessedly air-conditioned in summer. Rush-hour crowds can still be pushy and testy, and derelicts, panhandlers, and thugs still disturb riders' peace from time to time. Trains don't run as often as they should, either. But the subway is truly a viable alternative, especially for long daytime rides, when you'll save time as well as money by gliding under the streets instead of getting mired in city traffic.

BY BUS

Buses require a **MetroCard** (the same one you use for the subway), a **token** (ditto), or $1.50 in exact change (no pennies). You can't buy tokens on board; you have to get them at a subway station. Children under 44 inches tall ride free (there's a line near the driver's seat against which to measure your child), but in practice kids under 6 are usually allowed to ride free, regardless of height.

To transfer to a second bus, if you're using coins or a token, request a transfer card from the driver of the first bus *when you pay your fare*. If you're using a Metro-Card, dip it into the fare box slot; if you've just come from the subway or another bus, the machine will register this as a transfer (reading "Xfer OK" or "2 Xfers OK" if two passengers are using the same card). Note that if more than one passenger is using the same card, *only dip once for the transfer*. (Dip a second time, and an additional fare will be deducted.) Transfers do expire after a certain amount of time, but you probably can slip into a shop or pick up a cup of coffee between buses and still have your second ride count as a transfer.

Each bus's destination is displayed above its front windshield; routes are posted at most bus stops. Look for blue-and-red bus stop signs along sidewalks; at transfer points, a glassed-in shelter often accompanies them. Within Manhattan, bus stops are stationed every 2 or 3 blocks along avenues or major crosstown streets. Once you're riding a bus, if you wish to get off at the next stop, press any one of several electronic strips posted around the bus. A sign at the front of the bus should light up, reading STOP REQUESTED, and the driver will then pull over at the next stop.

BY TAXI

The only taxis authorized to pick up passengers hailing them on the street are **yellow cabs,** which have an official taxi medallion screwed onto the hood. So-called gypsy cabs, working for car services, sometimes stop illegally for passengers on the street, but since they have no meter, you'll have to negotiate your own fare with the driver and you'll have no legal recourse if there's a problem (besides, some gypsy cabs are filthy rattletraps). To know whether a yellow taxi is available, look for the lit-up center sign on the roof of the cab; off-duty cabs (side sections of the roof sign lit) may pick up passengers at their own discretion.

Taxi meters calculate the fare: $2 when you get in, plus 30¢ for each one-fifth of a mile or 90 seconds of waiting time in traffic. The meter should "click" every 4 blocks in normal traffic or once every crosstown block. There's an extra 50¢ charge from 8pm to 6am, and passengers pay any bridge or tunnel tolls. A 15% to 20% tip is expected, unless the service is bad. For complaints or inquiries about lost property, call ☎ **212/302-TAXI.**

Technically, a taxi doesn't have to take more than four passengers (with adults, this is possible only if one sits in the front seat next to the driver). But if your kids are small, most cabbies will let you all squeeze in, which is good news for families of five. All New York yellow cabs are supposed to have working seat belts, though few locals actually use them when taking quick trips around town. If your kids are car-seat size, technically you could haul around a car seat and strap it in every time you get in a cab, but the only person I've ever known to do this did it only once, when cabbing her newborn home from the hospital. Most cabbies are cool about letting kids sit on laps or even kneel on the seat to look out the cab window. Occasionally you'll get one who'll hassle you about your 2-year-old getting his sneakers on the backseat upholstery. I never fight the cabbies on this one—hey, it's their cab.

BY FERRY

The free **Staten Island Ferry** (☎ 718/727-2508) at Battery Park remains the best way to enjoy views of the Manhattan skyline, New York Harbor, and the Statue of Liberty. The **Ellis Island and Statue of Liberty Ferry** (☎ 212/269-5755) leaves Battery Park every 30 to 40 minutes for two of the city's most popular tourist destinations, costing $7 round-trip for adults and $3 for kids 16 and under. The **New York Waterway Ferry System** (☎ 800/53-FERRY) runs a spiffy service between the World Financial Center (near the World Trade Center) and the Colgate Center in New Jersey, costing $2 each way.

BY CAR

Cars are the least efficient way to get around town, but if you must drive, keep in mind that car-rental rates at the airports are often lower than those in Midtown. All the big national chains operate several locations: **Avis** (☎ 800/831-2847; at all three airports and nine city locations), **Budget** (☎ 800/527-7000; at all three airports and five city locations), **Dollar** (☎ 800/800-4000; at all three airports and three city locations), **Enterprise** (☎ 800/325-8007; at JFK and La Guardia airports and nine city locations), **Hertz** (☎ 800/654-3131; at all three airports and 11 city locations), and **National** (☎ 800/227-7368; at all three airports and seven city locations).

Some local companies offer rates that might be lower. **Autorent** has four locations: 415 W. 45th St. (☎ 212/315-1555), 433 E. 76th St. (☎ 212/517-8900), 464 W. 18th St. (☎ 212/206-1900), and 307 E. 11th St. (☎ 212/477-6500). **New York Rent-a-Car** has eight locations throughout the city (call ☎ 212/799-1100 for locations and reservations).

PARKING   On the streets, look for parking signs stating what days or hours you can park curbside. In Midtown and other spots where police feel it's vital to keep traffic flowing, your illegally parked car will be towed in minutes, so don't even think of violating parking laws. In residential neighborhoods, "alternate side of the street parking" means that everybody's expected to shift their cars to the opposite curb once a day. Officers are required to complete any parking ticket they start to fill out, so pleading will do no good. If your car does get towed, call the **Borough Tow Pound** at ☎ 212/971-0770 to find out where it is; you'll have to pay $150 in cash to retrieve it.

Space is so tight in New York that some residents are willing to pay over $300 a month for parking garage spaces. Public garages dot Manhattan streets every 2 blocks or so, with rates averaging about $7 for less than 2 hours (more like $10 or $12 in Midtown, though), $15 for half a day, and $30 overnight. Prices are sometimes lower at night or on weekends in business districts and during the day in residential areas; outdoor lots are less expensive, when you can find them. Few hotels offer parking. Some Midtown hotels provide valet parking at about $35 per night, often with the requirement that guests not take their car from the garage between arrival and final departure. **Kinney System, Inc.,** has more than 150 garages (call ☎ 212/355-9210); **Rapid Park** has over 30 locations (call ☎ 212/866-1000, ext 203); and **GMC** has 55 locations (call ☎ 212/888-7400).

DRIVING RULES   Except for major crosstown streets and a few north–south avenues (Broadway, Park Avenue), most of Manhattan's streets are one-way, so sometimes you'll have to circle around a couple of blocks to get to a specific address. Right turns on red are not legal, and left-hand turns are prohibited in some major intersections (watch for signs). Several major avenues have designated bus lanes (marked on the pavement), which are off-limits to cars during rush hours. Midtown streets are prone to the phenomenon known as *gridlock*. Beware of edging into an intersection in slow-moving traffic—if you don't manage to get through the intersection before the light changes, you can get stranded in the path of oncoming cross-traffic, and if a police officer's watching, you may even be ticketed for "blocking the box." Every passenger is supposed to wear a seat belt, and all kids 5 and under should be in car seats of some kind.

3 Planning Your Outings

Everything is relatively close together in Manhattan, but if you're traveling by cab, traffic jams can make even a few blocks' travel take half an hour; waiting for frequent changes of buses or subways can add up to lots of wasted time; and plodding long distances on foot could tire out the kids (or yourself) before you get to the

A Museum Note

One thing to take into account is museum closing days—many are closed on Monday.

---

sights you want to see. Instead, plan carefully and you may be able to spend the entire day within a few blocks' radius, wasting little time on street travel. If you do have to hop from one part of town to another, don't underestimate travel time—snarled traffic or sluggish subways or buses can make a 40-block journey seem to take forever.

Prime areas for families are the **Upper West Side,** with the American Museum of Natural History and the Children's Museum of Manhattan; **SoHo,** with the Children's Museum of the Arts and the Fire Museum; **Midtown,** where you'll find the Sony Wonder Technology Lab, Rockefeller Center, the Empire State Building, the Museum of Modern Art, the Museum of Broadcasting, and the *Intrepid* Sea-Air-Space Museum; **Lower Manhattan,** with South Street Seaport and the World Trade Center; and the stretch of Fifth Avenue known as **Museum Mile.** If you're going to **Brooklyn** to see the Botanic Garden or Prospect Park Zoo, take in the Transit Museum and Brooklyn Heights on the same day. The same ferry goes to both the **Statue of Liberty** and **Ellis Island,** so it's a natural to do both the same day—but after waiting in all those lines, you probably won't have time to do much else that day. The **Bronx Zoo** and the **New York Botanical Garden** are right next to each other, but it'd be pretty exhausting to do both in a day.

FINDING A REST ROOM

If you've got a recently toilet-trained toddler in tow, better think ahead, because in Manhattan it's not easy to find a bathroom at sudden notice. Rest rooms do exist in **Central Park** (see chapter 6 for locations), as well as in **Bryant Park,** which is at 42nd Street and Sixth Avenue behind the **New York Public Library;** the library itself has nice large bathrooms. Another option may be to use the bathrooms at various skyscrapers' shopping atriums, notably those at the **Sony Building** (56th Street and Madison Avenue), **Trump Tower** (56th Street and Fifth Avenue), and the **CitiGroup Building** (between Lexington and Third avenues and 53rd and 54th streets). **Barnes & Noble** bookstores, which are all around the city (see chapter 7), usually have decent bathrooms available. Major hotel lobbies are other good bets. In a pinch, if your child looks very distressed, you may be able to talk sympathetic waiters or store owners into letting you use their facilities. (I even once got the manager of a D'Agostino's grocery store to let me take my 2-year-old down to the employees' john in the basement—a real adventure.)

Best advice: Always use the potty at your hotel before you leave, and stop in the rest room before you leave any museum or restaurant.

NURSING MOMS & INFANTS

New Yorkers are wonderfully unflappable; there are plenty of mothers who nurse in public—usually onlookers pretend not to look and everything is cool. Then, of course, there are some people who stare rudely and mutter disparagingly. Ignore them. You'll find a fairly receptive atmosphere in all playgrounds and some casual restaurants. Women's lounges in the large department stores (Lord & Taylor's is best) tend to be good havens for breast-feeding a squalling infant.

Fast Facts: New York City

Area Codes   The area codes for Manhattan are 212 and the less frequent 646. To call Brooklyn, Queens, Staten Island, or the Bronx (at no charge), dial 1, then the area code 718, then the phone number. (Area code 917 covers all of New York City, but it's primarily for beepers, cellular phones, and businesses.) For directory assistance, dial ☎ **411.**

ATMs   Walk-up cash machines can be found every few blocks at various bank branches and stores, all linked to the NYCE network, as well as to Cirrus or PLUS. Locked lobbies with electronic card access are preferable to on-street cash machines, for security reasons; some even have guards on duty after bank hours. In Times Square, which is notably short on ATMs, look for a battery of Fleet Bank ATMs in the street-level lobby of the Marriott Marquis, Broadway and 46th Street, and more across the street at the Times Square Visitor Center. Note that many ATMs now charge at least a $1 transaction fee over and above the fee your own bank charges you.

Business Hours   The city that never sleeps truly doesn't. Although Midtown and Downtown **stores** tend to close at 6pm, shops in residential areas often stay open to 7pm or so, with drugstores and groceries usually going strong until 9pm or later, and delis and corner produce markets lasting on into the wee hours. Most stores (except for Midtown and Upper East Side boutiques) are open on Sunday, though they may not open until noon. **Restaurants** stay open late, usually at least until 11pm, and most are open daily. Many **museums** are closed on Monday, but several have late hours—until 9 or 10pm—on Thursday, Friday, or Saturday. **Banks** tend to keep more standard hours—Monday to Friday 9am to 3pm.

Child Care   Many New York hotels provide baby-sitting services or keep a list of reliable sitters. If your hotel doesn't, call the **Baby Sitters Guild** (☎ 212/ 682-0227) or the **Frances Stewart Agency** (☎ 212/439-9222). Both services provide in-room child care as well as on-request trips to the playground, the Central Park Zoo, and so on, for children of all ages, with licensed, bonded, insured sitters (baby nurses are trained in CPR).

Dentists   You can get a list of dentists near you by calling the **Emergency Dental Service** (☎ 212/573-9502). Emergency dental care is available from **ABC Dental Care,** 242 E. 60th St. (☎ 212/888-0015).

Disability Services   The **Community Ambulette** (☎ 718/231-6666) provides ambulette service for the disabled. Note that the subway system remains largely inaccessible to the disabled, but 95% of the city's buses are equipped to carry wheelchairs.

Doctors   Dial-A-Doctor (☎ 212/971-9692) sends physicians on house calls 24 hours a day.

Drugstores   Some 24-hour **Duane Reade** stores are at Lexington and 47th Street (☎ 212/682-5338), 625 Eighth Ave. in the Port Authority Bus Terminal (☎ 212/967-8110), Broadway and 57th Street (☎ 212/541-9708), Broadway and 91st Street (☎ 212/799-3172), Third Avenue and 74th Street (☎ 212/ 744-2668), and Sixth Avenue at Waverly Place (☎ 212/674-5357). **Rite-Aid** drugstores open 24 hours a day include 408 Grand St. on the Lower East Side, a block above Delancey Street (☎ 212/529-7115); 282 Eighth Ave. at 24th Street

(☎ 212/727-3854); 2833 Broadway at 110th Street (☎ 212/663-3135); and 146 E. 86th St., between Lexington and Third avenues (☎ 212/876-0600).

Emergencies   Call ☎ 911 for police, fire, and ambulance service; there is TTY service for the deaf as well. Fires can also be reported in Manhattan by dialing ☎ 212/628-2900 or 212/999-2222. Other emergency numbers include **Animal Bites** (☎ 212/676-2483), **Park Emergencies** (☎ 800/201-PARK), **Poison Control** (☎ 212/340-4494), and **Travelers Aid** (☎ 212/758-4689).

Hospitals   The following hospitals have full-service emergency rooms: **New York University Medical Center,** 550 First Ave., at 33rd Street (☎ 212/263-7300); **New York Presbyterian Hospital,** 510 E. 70th St. (☎ 212/746-5454); **Beth Israel Medical Center,** First Avenue at 16th Street (☎ 212/420-2000); and **St. Luke's–Roosevelt Hospital,** 58th Street and Ninth Avenue or 113th St. and Amsterdam Ave. (☎ 212/523-4000). For eye, ear, or facial injuries, go to the **New York Eye and Ear Infirmary,** 310 E. 14th St. (☎ 212/979-4000).

Hotlines   For information on theater, music, and dance performances, call **NYC On Stage** (☎ 212/768-1818). Review current offerings at **Lincoln Center** (☎ 212/LINCOLN). The **City Parks Special Events Hotline** (☎ 888/NY-PARKS or 212/360-3456) gives details on outdoor concerts and performances and New York Roadrunner Club events. Listings of commercial films are available through **Moviefone** (☎ 212/777-FILM), which also allows you to prepurchase movie tickets via credit card. **Sports Scores** (☎ 212/976-1717) gives updates of the most recent pro sports events.

Libraries   At any branch of the **New York Public Library** you can pick up a monthly brochure listing all the kids' activities planned—films, story hours, puppet plays, and the like—at the system's many branches. These are usually wonderful programs, and they're absolutely free. The **Donnell Library,** 20 W. 53rd St. (☎ 212/621-0636), has the main children's room for the entire system, with lots of scheduled readings and events. Branches with good children's rooms include **Jefferson Market,** 425 Sixth Ave., at West 10th Street (☎ 212/243-4334); **Yorkville,** 222 E. 79th St. (☎ 212/744-5824); **Epiphany,** 228 E. 23rd St. (☎ 212/679-2645); and **St. Agnes,** 444 Amsterdam Ave., at 82nd Street (☎ 212/877-4380).

The Early **Childhood Resources & Information Center** at 66 Leroy St. (☎ 212/929-0815) has lots of parenting books as well as a big indoor play space for kids 5 and under. The **Riverside branch,** 127 Amsterdam Ave., at 65th Street, near Lincoln Center (☎ 212/870-1810), has listening stations in its children's room with lots of tapes and CDs. The **central research library** on Fifth Avenue at 41st Street is worth a stop to see its magnificent main reading room; there are frequent free guided tours and fascinating exhibits, but these are usually more interesting for parents than for kids, who prefer visiting the grand stone lions—named Patience and Fortitude by Mayor Fiorello La Guardia—guarding the sweeping front steps.

Newspapers/Magazines   Pick up free copies of the local parents' monthlies, the *Big Apple Parent,* 9 E. 38th St., 4th floor, New York, NY 10016 (☎ 212/889-6400; fax 212/689-4958); *ParentGuide,* Parent Guide Network Corp., 419 Park Ave. S., New York, NY 10016 (☎ 212/213-8840); or *New York Family,* 141 Halstead Ave., Suite 3D, Mamaroneck, NY 10543 (☎ 914/381-7474), at toy stores, children's clothing and shoe stores, and indoor playgrounds all around Manhattan. Every Friday, the *New York Times* runs a

"Family Fare" column in its Weekend leisure section, detailing special events in the upcoming week. The weekly magazines *Time Out* and *New York* and the *Village Voice* weekly newspaper have sections on children's events in their comprehensive events listings.

Post Offices   The **main post office** at Eighth Avenue between 31st and 33rd streets (☎ **212/967-8585**) is open daily 24 hours. There are many other branches around town. Call the **Postal Answer Line** at ☎ **800/725-2161** for information.

Rest Rooms   See "Finding a Rest Room," earlier in this chapter.

Safety   Panhandlers have been aggressively kept off the streets in Mayor Giuliani's New York City; still, they do appear here and there. Giving them hand-outs isn't a good idea—you may just be supporting someone's drug habit. Also beware of fast-talking con artists who prey on tourists around the bus and train terminals. They may be well dressed and have a very persuasive story, but don't give them any money, no matter how ardently they promise to repay you later.

Not to be paranoid, but I don't recommend letting your kids wear clothes with their names on them. If your child did get separated from you, it'd be easy for a non-well-meaning stranger to gain his or her confidence by seeming to know your kid's name. A small card with your name and hotel information on it could be slipped into your child's pocket, on the other hand, to help the authorities contact you if your child were lost. Since you'll often be in crowded places, if you've got a speedy, independent toddler who might dash away, consider getting a flexible cord or harness to keep your child within arm's reach.

Pickpockets like to work crowds (particularly jam-packed buses and subways), so always keep your purse or wallet in front where you can keep an eye on it. Don't let your kids carry valuables in a backpack, either. Areas to avoid after dark if you're not a local: the deserted after-hours Wall Street area, the Lower East Side, the East Village east of Second Avenue, Midtown west of Ninth Avenue, Uptown north of 96th Street (except for the corridor along Broadway up to 120th Street). With kids in tow, you might as well just use cabs at night.

Taxes   **Sales tax** is 8.25%, charged on everything except groceries, take-out food, and clothing and shoe purchases under $110. **Hotels** add a 13.25% hotel tax to room rates.

Telephones   There are public phones on every other street corner in Manhattan, though not all are in what you'd call working order; large hotels generally have a bank of public phones off the lobby, too. A local call costs 25¢.

Useful Telephone Numbers   For **directory assistance,** call ☎ **411** or 555-1212. For the **time,** call ☎ **212/976-6000.** For the **weather,** call ☎ **212/976-4111** (you'll also get current winning lottery numbers).

What Kids Like to See & Do

4

Considering what a world-class sightseeing destination New York City is, it's surprising to realize how limited its attractions for kids can be. In the first place, many of its top museums are classy art repositories not inherently suited for youngsters—the most extreme example being the Frick Museum, which won't even let in anyone under 10. Real estate is too tight here for anything like a theme park, and though there are three children's museums—one in Manhattan, one in Brooklyn, and one on Staten Island—none of them is as big and clean and stimulating as their counterparts in Boston, Chicago, and Indianapolis.

The other problem is that so much of what you can do here gets crowded, especially on weekends and school holidays. Waiting in line is inevitable for top attractions like the Statue of Liberty, the Sony Wonder Technology Lab, and the World Trade Center's observation deck. If you're visiting from out of town during the school year, try hitting the popular museums in the mornings, when the local kids are in school. On rainy weekends, it seems every family in town heads for the American Museum of Natural History—if you want peace and quiet, you'll be better off going there on the first glorious day of spring, when the hordes have deserted it for Central Park. The park, however, only gets better when it's full of people, as it usually is every weekend—see chapter 6 for the lowdown on this great green Manhattan haven.

When all is said and done, though, this metropolis is still a great place for kids, all the more so if you're willing to get on a subway and zip to the outer boroughs. Remember, kids love subway rides and on weekends especially it's the way to go. Spend a day out in Brooklyn's Prospect Park, dividing your time between the Wildlife Center and the Lefferts Homestead and the Carousel, or pop over to the Brooklyn Botanic Garden and the Brooklyn Museum—incredibly, these are all within a few minutes' walk of one another. Flushing Meadows is my destination of choice in Queens, where you can do both the New York Hall of Science and Queens Wildlife Center in one easy go. In the Bronx, the huge Bronx Zoo and the equally huge New York Botanical Garden are right across the road from each other. Getting to Staten Island is even more fun because you get to take a ferry ride, and the children's museum there is only a short bus ride from the ferry docks.

What's in a Name?

Here's a trivia quiz to test your kids' knowledge of New York City history:

1. Who was the Hudson River named after?
2. Who was the Verrazano Bridge named after?
3. Where does the downtown street name Wall Street come from?
4. Where does the name Harlem, for the uptown neighborhood, come from?
5. Why is the street leading down to South Street Seaport named Fulton Street?
6. What does the name of the New York Mets refer to? (*Hint:* Think of the opera and the big art museum.)
7. What other two area sports teams have names that rhyme with the Mets?
8. Why is Times Square called Times Square?
9. Carnegie Hall, the famous concert hall at 57th Street and Seventh Avenue, is named after whom? And how do you get there?
10. Who is buried in Grant's Tomb?

ANSWERS: 1. *English explorer Henry Hudson, who sailed up the river in 1609. 2. Italian explorer Giovanni da Verrazano, the first European to enter the Narrows, in 1524. 3. In the original Dutch settlement, a wall was built at that point to keep out invaders. 4. Nieuw Haarlem was a separate Dutch settlement in the mid-1600s, named after the Dutch city of Haarlem. 5. Ferry service, operated by steamship inventor Robert Fulton, crossed the river at that point, linking Manhattan to Brooklyn (until the completion of the Brooklyn Bridge in 1883). 6. It's short for Metropolitans. 7. The New York Jets football team and the New Jersey Nets basketball team. 8. Because the headquarters of the New York Times newspaper is there (an earlier paper, the New York Herald, lent its name to Herald Square a few blocks south at 34th Street). 9. It's named for the man who built it, industrialist/philanthropist Andrew Carnegie (his former mansion is now the Cooper–Hewitt Museum). How do you get there? Practice, practice, practice. 10. Grant, of course (that's Ulysses S. Grant, Civil War commander and U.S. president), as well as his wife, Julia.*

Many museums court families by designing weekend and holiday workshops for kids—these are detailed in chapter 6, where you'll also find everything you'll need to know about having fun outdoors in New York's great parks, playgrounds, and neighborhoods.

Sightseeing Suggestions

If you're trying to cram a lot of sightseeing into a short time, you may want to consider buying a **City Pass,** which gives you entry to six popular attractions—the **American Museum of Natural History,** the *Intrepid* **Sea-Air-Space Museum,** the **Museum of Modern Art,** the **Guggenheim Museum,** the **Empire State Building** observation deck, and the **Top of the World** (the World Trade Center's observation deck)—at a 50% savings. Good for a 9-day period, it can be bought at the admission desk of any of the attractions in the package. Passes cost $32 for adults, $24 for children ages 12 to 17, and $21.75 for seniors.

IF YOU HAVE ONLY 1 DAY   Talk to the animals at the **Central Park Zoo,** then swing over to take a spin on the **Carousel.** Grab a hot dog for lunch in the park, then head up Central Park West to the **American Museum of Natural History,** with its magnificent dinosaur bones and wildlife dioramas. If you've got enough stamina, wind up with a hour or so at the **Children's Museum of Manhattan,** a couple of blocks away on West 83rd Street.

IF YOU HAVE 2 DAYS   Spend Day 1 as above—unless the weather's gorgeous, in which case do the Day 2 itinerary, then pick up the above for your second day. On Day 2, get up early to be first in line for the ferry to the **Statue of Liberty** and **Ellis Island.** This should take most of the day, especially if your kids want to wait in line to climb to Lady Liberty's crown. And don't skip the stop at Ellis Island— my kids like it better than the Statue. After the ferry deposits you back on Manhattan, walk a few blocks to the World Trade Center's **Top of the World observation deck,** where you can see for miles and miles, then saunter east on Fulton Street to **South Street Seaport,** where you can shop, visit maritime-history exhibits, and maybe have a seafood dinner.

IF YOU HAVE 3 DAYS   Spend Days 1 and 2 as above. On Day 3, roam around **Rockefeller Center,** hanging over the railing at Rockefeller Plaza and delving into the concourse to see the underground city in action. Go up Fifth Avenue past St. Patrick's Cathedral, visiting the **Disney Store,** the **Warner Bros. Studio Store,** and **FAO Schwarz** (see chapter 7). Then swing over to Madison Avenue, where you can pick up a sandwich to eat while waiting in line for the **Sony Wonder Technology Lab.** (Optional Midtown alternatives, depending on your kids' tastes, are the **Museum of Television and Radio** and the **Museum of Modern Art.**) Then take the Fifth Avenue bus down to 34th Street, where you can ascend the **Empire State Building** for a late-afternoon vista.

IF YOU HAVE 4 DAYS   Spend Days 1 to 3 as above. With older kids, start out Day 4 by taking the 45-minute tour of the **United Nations,** have an early lunch in the Delegates' Dining Room, then cab it uptown for an afternoon at the **Metropolitan Museum of Art.** If you have younger kids, start out at the Metropolitan first thing in the morning (when the crowds are lighter and the guards a trifle more patient), have lunch at an East Side coffee shop, then repair to **Central Park playgrounds** so your youngsters can let off some steam. Work your way up Fifth Avenue to 103rd Street, where you can pop in to check out the toy gallery at the **Museum of the City of New York,** and end your day with a stroll through the **Conservatory Garden.**

IF THE WEATHER'S COLD   To cram the most into 1 day with a minimum of exposure to the elements, start out at the **American Museum of Natural History,** then scoot across Central Park on the 79th Street crosstown bus (just as quick as a taxi) and dive into the **Metropolitan Museum of Art.** Or do it the other way around, depending on which you think your child will want more time for. Both have reasonable on-site cafes, so you won't have to venture outside to eat.

IF THE WEATHER'S HOT   East River breezes make **South Street Seaport** a refreshing spot in summer, and you can always duck inside the air-conditioned shops and museums when the sun beats down too strongly. When that gets stale, cab it across town to **Battery Park City,** where you can shop and eat in the tony Winter Garden atrium, loll on the plaza by the yacht basin, or stroll down the breezy Esplanade along the Hudson. Another good warm-weather refuge is the **Cloisters,** the Metropolitan's medieval art annex located north, up in Fort Tryon

Park, where you can chill out amid the dim light and cool stone of transplanted European chapels.

Don't be tempted to do the **Statue of Liberty/Ellis Island** trip if the weather's insufferably hot. The ferry ride will be a pleasant break, it's true, but waiting in line for the boat (once in Battery Park, again on Liberty Island, and again on Ellis Island) will strain your family's temper, and the wait in line to climb the statue—an indoor wait in close quarters, often for 2 hours or more—will be cruel and unusual punishment. If you want a boat ride that badly, take the **Staten Island Ferry.**

IF YOU'VE GOT A SITTER   Take advantage of the opportunity to dawdle in one of the art museums kids aren't as happy in—like the **Frick,** the **Whitney Museum of American Art,** or the **Asia Society Galleries,** all on the Upper East Side. Then window-shop along tony **Madison Avenue,** where designer boutiques cluster from the 80s on down to 57th Street. Another child-free option may be to prowl around the Wall Street area: Visit the **New York Stock Exchange,** venerable **Trinity Church,** and the surprisingly small but ornate **City Hall.** Go out to dinner at an elegant restaurant, then catch either a **Broadway show** or a concert at **Carnegie Hall** or **Lincoln Center.** For complete details on all such grown-up activities, pick up a copy of *Frommer's New York City.*

1 Kids' Top 10 Attractions

☉ American Museum of Natural History. All ages. Central Park West at 79th St. **☎ 212/769-5100;** for reserved tickets to Space Show and other special exhibits, **☎** 212/769-5200. www.amnh.org. Suggested admission $10 adults, $7.50 students and seniors, $6 children 2–12, free for children under 2. Museum admission plus IMAX movie ticket $15 adults, $11 students and seniors, $9 children 2–12, free for children under 2. Museum admission plus Space Show $19 adults, $14 students and seniors, $11.50 children. Museum admission plus Space Show plus IMAX $25 adults, $18.50 students and seniors, $15 children. Members: admission free, additional fee for Space Show ($9.50 adults, $6 children) or IMAX ($7.50 adults, $4.50 children). Sun–Thurs 10am–5:45pm, Fri–Sat 10am–8:45pm. Closed Thanksgiving and Dec 25. Limited parking available on site (enter on W. 81st St. between Central Park West and Columbus Ave.). Subway: B/C to 81st St.; 1/9 to 79th St.

This one isn't listed first just because it comes first alphabetically—it's the city's one real don't-miss if you're with kids. When you enter the rotunda at the top of the Central Park West steps, a rearing skeleton of a mommy dinosaur protecting her baby from a small, fierce predator clues you in that the dazzling fourth-floor **dinosaur halls** are the perennial star attraction—brought up to speed in the early 1990s, they feature interactive consoles, glass-floored walkways that bring you up to the dino's eye level, and please-touch displays illustrating key points of evolution. The stunning **Rose Center for Earth and Space,** a 95-foot-high glass cube opened in early 2000, includes an interactive exhibit on the nature of the universe, where you can step on a scale that shows your weight on Saturn, see an eerie phosphorescent model of the expanding universe, and touch cosmic debris. The immense sphere in the middle of the cube is the new **Hayden Planetarium,** which shows a cutting-edge **space show** narrated by Tom Hanks. It was the hottest ticket in town for the first few months after it opened (you can call a couple of weeks in advance to order your tickets, though 600 same-day tickets are available at the door every morning). Let me go on record to say, though, that I was disappointed in it, especially at this price—even members pay the going feature-film rate to be treated to less than 30 minutes of Carl Sagan-ish wonder at how big the universe is and how tiny we are.

Natural History veterans like my kids know that's only the tip of the iceberg. The excitement begins even in the subway station below (B and C trains to West 81st Street), which has an entrance leading directly into the museum: The tiled walls feature wonderful ceramic bas reliefs of dinosaurs, insects, birds, and mammals. One of our favorite sights is the superb dioramas in the **North American Mammals** (first floor)—the grizzly bear raking open a freshly caught salmon, majestic elks lifting their massive antlers, wolves loping through eerie nighttime snow. Or, on the floor above, walk through the bilevel **African Mammals Hall** and you can circle around a lumbering herd of elephants, then check out the giraffes browsing by their water hole.

A circuit of the first floor alone could take a whole day. The PC-but-never-preachy **Hall of Biodiversity** features an immense multimedia re-creation of an African rain forest, one of the planet's most threatened ecosystems; nine other ecosystems, from tundra to coral reef to desert, are explored in a multiscreen video installation; and the Spectrum of Life displays the entire family tree of Earth's living creatures, with more than 1,500 specimens and models spread out along a 100-foot wall. We love the dimly lit **Ocean Life room,** where a gargantuan model of a blue whale swims overhead, with dioramas of walruses, dolphins, and sharks along the side walls; it has informally become known as the place where toddlers can stretch their legs, racing and twirling around the vast open space. Around the corner, the less-well-visited **North American Forest dioramas** are our family secret—a peaceful part of the museum where you can hunt for bluejays in oak trees and rattlesnakes behind the cactus. Most people hurry through here to get to the interactive **Human Biology and Evolution** exhibits, which seem always full of busy grade-schoolers. Past that lies the **Mineral and Gem room,** where little kids can thrust their hands into a huge geode while older kids gape in awe at the jewels on display.

The museum is not all animals, by any means (remember that Margaret Mead was only one of many brilliant anthropologists whose research was supported by this museum over the years). Studying Native Americans? On the first floor, by the 77th Street entrance, is the astounding collection of **Northwest Coast Indian** totem poles immortalized by J. D. Salinger in *Catcher in the Rye.* The haunting soundtracks in the African and Asian peoples sections (on the second floor) lull you into studying the precisely detailed displays there too.

The **IMAX theater** (additional ticket required—see above) is an important part of the experience; my sons' current favorite is *Dolphins.* (For more on IMAX, see "Films" in chapter 8.) Squirreled away in a back corner of the second floor is the **Natural Science Center,** a delightful hands-on workshop where kids 4 and older can explore the natural life of New York City (open Tuesday to Friday 2 to 4:30pm, Saturday and Sunday 1 to 4:30pm). There are several excellent gift shops, too; if your kid is bugging you for a souvenir, make a beeline for the **Junior Shop** by the restaurants and rest rooms on the lower level, which has 99¢ rubber dinosaurs.

Where to Eat: We used to avoid eating at the museum, until the old Dinersaurus was replaced by the excellent **Museum Food Court** (open Sunday to Thursday 11am to 4:45pm, Friday and Saturday 11am to 7:45pm). A wide range of sophisticated sandwiches, salads, fruit, and snacks are available, as well as hot food, including hamburgers and french fries. There's also the **Cafe on 4** (on the fourth floor by the 77th Street elevators) and **Cafe 77** (by the 77th Street entrance on the first floor). Since you can reenter the museum with your admission tag, consider popping out into the neighborhood to **Rain, Pizzeria Uno, Monsoon,** or **T & R Pizzeria** (see chapter 9), only a block or two away.

Uptown Attractions

Subway stop **Ⓜ**
Route of M5 Bus ········

E. 106th St.
E. 105th St.
E. 104th St.
E. 103rd St. Ⓜ
E. 102nd St.
E. 101st St.
E. 100th St.
E. 99th St.
E. 98th St.
E. 97th St. Ⓜ
E. 96th St.
E. 95th St.
E. 94th St.
E. 93rd St.
E. 92nd St.
E. 91st St.
E. 90th St.
E. 89th St.
E. 88th St.
E. 87th St.
E. 86th St. Ⓜ
E. 85th St.
E. 84th St.
E. 83rd St.
E. 82nd St.
E. 81st St.
E. 80th St.
E. 79th St.
E. 78th St.
E. 77th St. Ⓜ
E. 76th St.
E. 75th St.
E. 74th St.
E. 73rd St.
E. 72nd St.
E. 71st St.
E. 70th St.
E. 69th St.
E. 68th St. Ⓜ
E. 67th St.
E. 66th St.
E. 65th St.
E. 64th St.
E. 63rd St. Ⓜ
E. 62nd St.
E. 61st St.
E. 60th St.
E. 59th St.

Ward's Island Footbridge
Ward's Island Park
Ward's Island

Upper Manhattan

Uptown

Midtown

Downtown

Carl Schurz Park

MUSEUM MILE

Fifth Ave.
Madison Ave.
Park Ave.
Lexington Ave.
Third Ave.
Second Ave.
First Ave.
York Ave.
East End Ave.

The Reservoir

The Great Lawn
Metropolitan Museum of Art

UPPER EAST SIDE

FDR

FDR Dr.

East River

Roosevelt Island

Sheep Meadow

Central Park Zoo
Wollman Rink
Central Park South

Roosevelt Island Tram
Queensboro Bridge
Sutton Pl.
From Lower Level
To Upper Level

0   1/3 Mi
0   .3 Km

14
15
16
17
18
19
20
21
22
23
24

49

Natural History Museum Treasure Hunt

The American Museum of Natural History is so vast, kids can easily tire if you trudge from hall to hall with no organizing purpose. Here, then, is a treasure hunt designed by my sons, Hugh and Tom, to keep your kids busy exploring. Younger kids may get through only one floor in an afternoon, but persist— I swear, it's all here.

First Floor

1. **North American Mammals**—Where is the rabbit hiding from the lynx?
2. **Ocean Life**—Who's talking back to the orca? (*Hint: Orca* is another name for a killer whale.)
3. **New York State Environment**—How many baby chipmunks are sleeping in the spring burrow?
4. **Human Biology and Evolution**—Find the cave of mammoth bones.
5. **Minerals and Gems**—Where are the rocks that glow in the dark?

Second Floor

6. **African Peoples**—Find the xylophone.
7. **Birds of the World**—How many stuffed penguins are there?
8. **Asian Peoples**—Who's getting married?
9. **Rose Center**—How soon after the Big Bang did our solar system start to form?

Third Floor

10. **African Mammals**—Who's watching the ostriches fight the wart hogs?
11. **Reptiles and Amphibians**—Which is the crocodile and which is the alligator?

Fourth Floor

12. **Saurischian Dinosaurs**—Find the fossil dinosaur teeth.
13. **Ornithischian Dinosaurs**—Touch the triceratops horn.

ANSWERS: 1. *Behind the bush.* 2. *The leopard seal.* 3. *Four.* 4. *Toward the end of the exhibit, in the Earliest Architecture display.* 5. *In the first gem room, the southeast corner.* 6. *Midway through the hall, on the west wall, across from the guys in straw skirts who look like Cousin Itt from The Addams Family.* 7. *Twenty in all—16 adults, 4 babies.* 8. *In the Chinese section, a bride in her ornate ceremonial sedan chair.* 9. *Eight billion years.* 10. *The mouselike elephant shrew, behind a dead log.* 11. *Facing each other by the entrance at the north end of the hall—the gator (on your right) has the snub snout; the croc (on your left) has the pointy snout.* 12. *On the south wall.* 13. *On the east wall.*

⚫ **Bronx Zoo/Wildlife Conservation Park. All ages.** In Bronx Park, Bronx River Pkwy. and Fordham Rd. ☎ **718/367-1010.** www.wcs.org or www.bronxzoo.com. Admission: Apr–Oct $9 adults, $5 children 2–12 and seniors, free for children under 2; Nov–Dec $6 adults, $3 children 2–12 and seniors, free for children under 2; Jan–Mar, $4 adults, $2 children 2–12 and seniors, free for children under 2. Free for everyone on Wednesday, but separate charges apply to exhibits inside the park; see below. Apr–Oct Mon–Fri 10am–5pm, Sat–Sun and holidays 10am–5:30pm; Nov–Mar daily 10am–4:30pm. Stroller rental $5, with $10 deposit (inquire at park entrances). Parking $6. Transportation: See below.

The Big Kahuna of New York City's wildlife parks, the Bronx Zoo is a world-class facility in every way. It covers 265 acres and boasts more than 4,000 animals, from Siberian tigers and snow leopards to condors and vultures to naked mole-rats and meerkats. Though there's a scattered number of indoor exhibits, such as the deliciously creepy **World of Darkness** (nocturnal animals), the **World of Reptiles,** the **Monkey House,** the **Giraffe House,** and the **Mouse House,** most of the animals live outdoors in large enclosures re-creating as closely as possible the species' native environment. This is all laudably humane, but kids under 5 may get frustrated by the long walks between animals and the fact that certain creatures may be viewable only at a distance. This doesn't mean they won't love the zoo—it just means you've got to organize your visit sensibly.

My one beef with this zoo is all the added charges once you get inside the gates. From April to October, several rides are available to help you navigate the park— an **open-sided tram** that rattles in a big loop around the main part of the zoo, the **Skyfari** cable car that soars high over the middle of the park (handy for cutting across), and the narrated **Bengali Express monorail ride** (May to October only) in the Wild Asia section. All of these cost $2 a person. There's often a long line for the monorail, but of the three rides, it's the best deal—it's the only way you can see Wild Asia at all, and the guide en route helps you spot all the lions and antelopes patrolling their roomy open-air habitats. (My family still fondly remembers the guide we landed one time—his punchline for every anecdote was "Don't worry, be happy, because it's a happy day, and Jason is your driver.") There's also a $2-per-person charge for the good-sized **Children's Zoo,** open April to October only, which is surprisingly fun even for 8- or 9-year-olds, with lots of learn-by-doing exhibits (like a spider web rope climb and a prairie dog burrow that kids can climb through), and a petting zoo. The zoo also tacks on a special fee to visit its two star exhibits, the **Congo Gorilla Forest** ($3 per person April to October, $1 November to March) and the **Butterfly Zone** ($2 per person, free for children under 2, open June to September only). Both of them are fascinating—on a good day you can practically go snout-to-snout with our huge simian cousins through a wide glass window, or have immense tropical butterflies land on your outstretched hand—but it's wise to make your choices ahead of time, and even let your family split up to enjoy separate attractions. (Consider whether your younger kids may get skittish having butterflies swoop close to their heads, or be terrified of the Skyfari's heights.) Given all these extras, you could easily spend over $75 on a full day for a family of five. You might as well buy a 1-year family membership ($65), which nets you a number of free passes to various Bronx Zoo attractions as well as free admission to all other **Wildlife Conservation Parks.**

During winter, when many of the outdoor animals aren't on view, the park lures visitors with fanciful animal sculptures spangled with lights, as well as the indoor exhibits (still enough species on view to fill a smaller zoo); there's a certain pleasure in visiting during this uncrowded season.

The zoo has several entrances: I recommend the Southern Boulevard/Crotona entrance, which brings you in near the Children's Zoo and the elephants, or the Asia entrance (pedestrians only, closest to the subway station), which brings you in near Wild Asia, Jungle World, and the camel rides. In any case, study the zoo map as soon as you enter and plot which animals you want to visit and the simplest route to pass them. Operate on the assumption that you can't see everything in 1 day, even if your kids are good walkers. Relax, take your time, and enjoy yourselves.

Getting There: By **bus,** Liberty Lines BxM11 service (call ☎ **718/652-8400**) runs about every 15 minutes from stops along Madison Avenue in Manhattan: The fare is $3 per person one-way (free for a child under 45 inches riding on an adult's lap). By **train,** take Metro North from Grand Central Terminal to Fordham Road, change to the Bx9 bus, and ride to the zoo's Southern Boulevard entrance. By **subway,** take the no. 2 to the Pelham Parkway station; walk west 1 block to Boston Road, turn left and go to first traffic light, turn right and go straight to the zoo entrance. A **taxi** might cost $15 to $28 one-way, depending on your Manhattan starting point or destination. By **car,** take exit 6 off the Bronx River Parkway.

Where to Eat: The zoo's **Lakeside Cafe** is open year-round, and three open-air cafes operate seasonally. Expect fast-foodish menus, with slightly high (but not outrageous) prices. Pack a picnic lunch if you can—there are plenty of places to sit and eat outdoors.

Central Park Wildlife Center and Tisch Children's Zoo. All ages. In Central Park, near the park entrance at Fifth Ave. and 64th St. ☎ **212/861-6030.** Admission (includes both zoos) $3.50 adults, $1.25 seniors, 50¢ children 3–12, free for children 2 and under. Mon–Fri 10am–5pm, Sat–Sun and holidays 10am–5:30pm. Subway: N/R to Fifth Ave.; 6 to 68th St.

Beautifully landscaped, this pair of tiny zoos is perfect for young animal lovers—there's nothing bigger than a polar bear here, you can get pretty close to every species on display, and you don't have to walk very far to see everything. The centerpiece of the main zoo is the oval **Sea Lion Pool,** which has glass sides so everyone can watch the sea lions swimming underwater. A few steps to the west is **Monkey Island,** where a troop of snow monkeys scramble over the rocks and a few swans glide on the water. To the north lies the **Polar Circle,** with a big flock of penguins indoors and a trio of polar bears outside, cavorting in and out of their rock-edged pool (the obsessive-compulsive male that used to swim in the same frantic loop day after day has been responding very nicely to therapy, thank you). Up on the hill behind Monkey Island is the **Temperate Territory,** which stars an otter, some ducks, and a shy red panda; at the south end you can stand on the bridge over a mucky turtle pond and look for frogs sunning themselves. The greatest number of species in the zoo are inside the **Tropical Zone,** a two-story enclosed aviary with plenty of glass tanks arranged along the wall, featuring exciting creatures like piranhas and bats and snakes—not to mention our favorites, the golden lion tamarins, whose wizened faces look for all the world like those of the flying monkeys from *The Wizard of Oz.* Be sure to climb to the upper levels and stand out on the stairways, looking for the bright plumage of tropical birds flitting from tree to tree. Always warm and humid, the Tropical Zone is a great refuge on a chilly day. As soon as you go through the main zoo's gates, check signs near the entrance to see when the sea lion and penguin feedings are scheduled; there's often a crowd for these, but it's fun to see the animals scamper over to their keepers for their fish. (No, they don't do tricks—that wouldn't be PC.)

The **Tisch Children's Zoo** is a short stroll north, on the other side of the Delacorte Arch. Much of this friendly hilltop spot is a walk-through aviary, which my older son, the budding ornithologist, finds incredibly cool. My kids also love the waterfall they can stick their hands through, with a dusky little grotto full of fish tanks behind it. Wooden bridges cross over a tidy central pond, cedar-chip paths circle around (strollers are useless here—park yours by the gate), and at the back is a giant spider web kids can clamber over. Children can get right up close to most of the animals here, so who cares if none of them is an exotic species?

Where to Eat: If you can, pack a picnic lunch and eat it at outdoor tables in the cafeteria courtyard. Otherwise, you'll have to go with the **zoo cafeteria** (there aren't many choices in the park), which has a limited menu, with a few sandwiches, salads, and fast-food items. At least there's a special kids' meal that may include animal crackers. There's usually also a cart selling drinks and ice cream in the central courtyard. Note that drinks are served without straws, since a straw tossed into an animal's enclosure could be harmful.

Ellis Island Immigration Museum. Ages 4 & up. On Ellis Island in New York Harbor. ☎ 212/363-3200. Free admission (but you have to pay for the ferry—see "Getting There" in the Statue of Liberty listing). Daily 9am–5:30pm (extended hours in summer). Closed Dec 25. Subway: 4/5 to Bowling Green; 1/9 to South Ferry.

Our first time here, my son was 5 and we only got off the ferry on a whim after visiting the Statue of Liberty—and we discovered that Ellis Island was even *more* fun. We returned last spring on a third-grade class trip and discovered many more things that we hadn't even seen the first time. From the mountain of ragtag luggage stacked right inside the front doors, upstairs to the cramped dormitories and medical examination rooms (cough the wrong way and you could be sent right back to Europe), to the family heirlooms immigrants brought with them in the **Treasures from Home** collection—this place really brings history to life. The second-floor **Registry Hall** is awesome, with its soaring vaulted ceiling faced with white tile; this is where new arrivals waited in endless lines to be interviewed by immigration officials. My son lingered over the first-floor **Peopling of America** exhibit, with a life-sized "family tree" and huge three-dimensional bar graph tracking immigration patterns over the years. And the **Wall of Honor** outside, where some 420,000 immigrants' names are inscribed in steel, was fun even though no one in our family ever ponied up the dough to have a relative's name enshrined—we looked up two or three family names anyway. There's a self-guided audio tour, or you can pick up handsets at various displays to hear narration; the stirring documentary *Island of Hope, Island of Tears* runs frequently throughout the day, but we chose instead to watch a delightful little play with young actors reenacting the immigration experience. We stayed for nearly 2 hours this time and look forward to our next visit.

Getting There: See the Statue of Liberty entry, below.

Where to Eat: There's a big, clean **cafeteria** on the site, as well as a snack bar on the ferry. Bring a picnic lunch if you can—there are plenty of places to sit out and eat.

✪ Intrepid Sea-Air-Space Museum. Ages 3 & up. At Pier 86, the Hudson River at the foot of W. 46th St. ☎ 212/245-0072. www.intrepidmuseum.org. Admission $12 adults, $9 children 12–17, students, and seniors, $6 children 6–11, $2 children 2–5, free for children under 2. Mon–Fri 10am–5pm, Sat–Sun 10am–6pm. Bus: M42 westbound (to the last stop) or M50 (stops directly in front of the museum).

Now that my boys are older, this has rapidly become their favorite place to spend a day off from school. You don't even have to be a weapon-obsessed boy to be fascinated by this rambling museum set on a disused aircraft carrier. Many areas of the ship remain off-limits—don't expect a re-creation of life on board a carrier—but the cavernous hangar of the *Intrepid* has plenty of room to cover all the bases: audiovisual displays, uniforms, weapons, equipment, vintage aircraft, and memorabilia from all branches of the navy. For my kids, the biggest draw is the lineup of small planes, jets, and copters up on the landing deck, some of which you can climb up into. (The *Blackbird,* a black-coated stealth bomber with an eerie space-age silhouette, is my son Tom's favorite.) Belowdecks, the **fighter jet simulator** is a big draw for boys of a certain age; there's also a vintage bathysphere and the incredibly tiny capsule from an early space mission. Moored across the pier are the submarine *Growler* and the Vietnam-era destroyer *Edison,* which you can tour as part of your *Intrepid* admission. There are special free Saturday workshops once a month.

The *Intrepid* has a clear patriotic bias to all its exhibits, which could be annoying but instead comes across as refreshingly honest. (There always seem to be World War II veterans on hand as volunteers who are happy to bend your ear about their experiences in the war.) From time to time, **visiting aircraft and sea vessels** land here and you can tour them; during **Fleet Week** at the end of May, it's a beehive of activity. Call for an updated schedule of visiting ships.

Where to Eat: There's an on-site **cafe** serving predictable fast food, but you can bring your own lunch and eat at the tables on board the ship. My kids also like to cross the West Side Highway to pick up fresh-from-the-oven bagels at **H&H Bagels** (see chapter 9).

✪ **Metropolitan Museum of Art. All ages.** 1000 Fifth Ave. (at 82nd St.). ☎ **212/ 535-7710.** www.metmuseum.org. Suggested donation (includes same-day admission to the Cloisters, below) $10 adults, $5 students and seniors, free to children 11 and under. Tues–Thurs and Sun 9:30am–5:30pm, Fri–Sat 9:30am–9pm. Closed Jan 1, Thanksgiving, and Dec 25. Strollers not permitted Sun (back carriers available at 81st St. entrance). Subway: 4/5/6 to 86th St.

Even though this is the city's number-one tourist attraction, many families we know never take their young kids here. Big mistake. You can have a great time at the Metropolitan, even with toddlers, so long as you remember two rules: Go at their pace, not yours (forget about standing transfixed for 10 minutes in front of that wonderfully serene Vermeer), and don't let the gruff museum guards intimidate you. They're the city's most fervent believers that children should be seen and not heard—they'll level stern, disapproving glares if your child so much as skips for joy or exclaims above a whisper. Naturally, don't let youngsters touch the precious works of art or press their fingers against glass cases, but otherwise let your own common sense prevail.

The echoing marble-clad Great Hall tells you as you enter that this is a Serious Art Museum. If there's a long ticket line at the booths in front of the entrance, go to the right, past the cloakroom—the booth at the north end is generally quicker. My kids love to climb the awesome central stairway up to the European painting galleries, the museum's prize jewel, but we generally veer off and skip those galleries—they go on forever, boring the pants off most kids.

Here are the galleries kids are more likely to enjoy: the **arms and armor** (first floor), the extensive **Egyptian rooms** (also on the first floor—make a beeline for the glorious mummies), **musical instruments** (second floor, off the American Wing's courtyard), the **Costume Institute** (ground floor–rotating installations will be of varying interest to kids), and the **European** and **American period rooms** (all over the place). On the first floor of the **American Wing** is a side gallery displaying vintage baseball cards, and a whole gallery of grandfather clocks ticks away on the second floor. Older kids who are beginning to appreciate art may go for the **impressionist gallery** (second floor) or the **Lehman Pavilion,** set up like the town house of a wealthy collector—it's art in small enough doses that it doesn't overwhelm.

Our favorite corner, hands down, is the **courtyard of the American Wing,** a light-filled open space with plantings, benches, and statues kids can actually relate to (a mountain lion and her cubs, a pensive Indian brave). Bring lots of small change for them to throw into the pool here and in the pool in front of the Egyptian Wing's momentous **Temple of Dendur** (but not in the Chinese scholars' court goldfish pool in the second-floor Asian art galleries!). In the Japanese galleries, there's a little-known room overlooking the Temple of Dendur, a perspective my kids prefer. They also like the balcony off the musical instruments gallery overlooking the mounted knights in armor and a second-floor balcony overlooking a transplanted Spanish courtyard. Get the idea? Wander around this immense museum, keep your eyes open, and be willing to walk away from anything that interests you if it doesn't interest your children.

The huge **museum gift shop** up on the second floor, one of the world's best, has a lot of stuff for kids.

Where to Eat: The **museum cafe** is in a vast pink-columned salon that can be a thrill, but the cafeteria line is awfully long and the food is overpriced and not great. Since your museum badge allows reentry, with younger kids it's probably better just to go outside and sit on the splendid Fifth Avenue steps (one of the city's best impromptu grandstands) to eat a hot dog bought at a nearby pushcart. Or walk a block east to Madison and try **Nectar of 82nd Street,** 1090 Madison Ave. (☎ 212/772-0916)—clean, kid-friendly, and fairly priced for the usual coffee-shop menu.

✪ **Sony Wonder Technology Lab. Ages 4 & up.** 550 Madison Ave. (entrance on 56th St.). ☎ 212/833-8100. www.sonywondertechlab.com. Free admission. Tues–Sat 10am–6pm (until 8pm Thurs), Sun noon–6pm. Subway: E/F/N/R to Fifth Ave.

Though no doubt it helps sell Sony products, this wonderful interactive exploratorium isn't annoyingly self-serving. (Leave that to the Playstation and other Sony outlets arranged around the sleek atrium here at Sony's Manhattan headquarters.) Sony Wonder actually lets people experiment with all types of **high-tech equipment,** from TV cameras to industrial robots to ultrasound scanners; you can play at being a recording engineer, videotape editor, or computer designer or just mess around on the Internet.

When you first enter the lab, you get your own **personal card,** which becomes magnetically encoded with your name and photo; as you continue through three floors of activities, every time you slide the card through the scanner on a new terminal, your name and photo are inserted into whatever program is up. On your way out, you can print out a personalized certificate recording all the activities you tried. Kids love seeing their name and face everywhere, and the activities have been pretty well designed so that even 4- and 5-year-olds can work them (though older kids can explore them to greater depth and adults are bound to get hooked, too). Saturday and Sunday **workshops** (small fee charged, pre-registration advisable) help youngsters explore different aspects of technology in greater depth.

The staff is careful not to let too many people in at one time, so it's not unusual to wait in line in the lobby for up to an hour (an awesome robot, b.b.wonderbot, chats up the crowds as they wait). Don't let the wait daunt you—once you're inside, you should always be able to get your hands on equipment. Loads of friendly young Sony staffers are around to help you figure out how stuff works. I wanted to linger on the Communications Bridge—a long ramp between floors where terminals and displays tell the history of communications—but as I stood transfixed in front of a videotape of the Beatles arriving in New York in 1964, my son kept yanking on my arm to move on. Plan for at least 2 hours here, more if you've got a really high-tech kid.

Where to Eat: Buy something at food stalls in the sleek **Sony Plaza atrium,** or bring sandwiches to eat at the tiny metal tables in the atrium.

South Street Seaport and the Seaport Museum. All ages. 12 Fulton St. (between Water & South sts.). ☎ 212/748-8600. www.southstseaport.org. Admission $6 adults, $5 seniors, $4 students, $3 children. Apr–Sept daily 10am–6pm (until 8pm Thurs); Oct–Mar Wed–Mon 10am–5pm. Subway: 2/3/4/5 to Fulton St.; A/C to Broadway/Nassau St.

This collection of warehouses and maritime shops on the cobblestoned East River waterfront was a major shipping port in the days of clipper ships, but the spectacular renovation of these historic 19th-century buildings has often been overshadowed by

The While-Waiting-in-Line-at-Lady-Liberty Quiz

1. The Statue of Liberty weighs

   a. 225 tons.

   b. 25 tons.

   c. 225 pounds (when she's been to her step-aerobics class).

2. The statue's full official name is

   a. The Gatekeeper of Liberty.

   b. Liberty Enlightening the World.

   c. Liberty Looking for a Lost Contact Lens.

3. Sculptor Frédéric-Auguste Bartholdi is said to have modeled the statue after

   a. the Mona Lisa.

   b. Napoléon Bonaparte's girlfriend.

   c. his mommy.

4. Emma Lazarus's poem *The New Colossus* ("Give me your tired, your poor . . .") is engraved

   a. on the tablet Liberty cradles in her arm.

   b. on a plaque inside the base of the statue.

   c. on a tattoo on every park ranger's left bicep.

5. The engineer who designed the statue's tricky steel skeleton is also known for

   a. the Eiffel Tower in Paris.

   b. the Brooklyn Bridge.

   c. the Spaceship Earth sphere at Epcot.

6. The French intellectual who first proposed the idea for the statue was

   a. the marquis de Lafayette.

   b. Edouard René Lefebvre de Laboulaye.

   c. Pepe Le Pew.

the attendant development of much of the site as a "festival marketplace" (touristy urban shopping mall). You can spend a fun day here without ever paying admission to the Seaport Museum, what with all the shops and restaurants, pierside entertainers, and wide-open views of the East River and Brooklyn.

That said, when we finally forked over museum admission one steamy July afternoon, we discovered a whole new dimension to the Seaport that goes beyond the shopping-mall experience. There's a small but interesting hands-on **children's museum** at 165 John St., a 19th-century **printing shop** at 211 Water St., and a **boat-building shop** at the corner of John and South streets—each occupied us for 20 minutes or so. My sons' (and husband's) favorite part of the day was clambering all over the **historic ships** moored to the piers. There are always special exhibits, like the one we saw about tattoos (my kids thought it was gross, but older kids might've been totally fascinated); harbor cruises on the **Seaport Liberty Line** or the historic *Pioneer,* an 1885 schooner, also leave from here (see "Boat Tours," later in this chapter). Special children's workshops and storytelling hours are organized all

7. Once completed and shipped in sections to the United States, the statue almost wasn't erected because

a. Americans lost the instructions on how to put it together.

b. Americans hadn't raised enough money to build a pedestal for it.

c. everybody thought it was so ugly.

8. Lady Liberty looks green because

a. the statue's hammered-copper sheathing has oxidized as expected.

b. pollution from New York Harbor has corroded it.

c. she gets seasick from watching the ferries chug past all day.

9. The statue's nose is

a. $4\frac{1}{2}$ feet long.

b. 10 feet long.

c. 100 feet long (she could use some plastic surgery).

10. The Statue of Liberty was given to the people of the United States by the people of France

a. because there was no room for it in Paris.

b. in repayment of old war debts.

c. to symbolize a special friendship between the two countries.

ANSWERS: 1. *a*   2. *b*   3. *c*   4. *b*   5. *a*   6. *b*   7. *b*   8. *a*   9. *a*   10. *c*.

over the place—pick up a schedule at the visitor center. Because the various museum buildings are scattered all over the site, you'll be mingling with the tourist crowds of shoppers, but the museum sites themselves are usually pleasantly uncrowded. What with the ocean air whipping in off the estuary, you'll feel like old salts before the day is through.

Where to Eat: The Seaport is loaded with restaurants of varying quality. With kids, your best bet is to go to the top floor of the Seaport's **Pier 17,** where there's an excellent food court with a wide choice of fast foods (not all of the greasy variety), often live music, and great East River views.

Statue of Liberty. Ages 3 & up. On Liberty Island in New York Harbor. ☎ **212/ 269-5755.** Free admission (but you have to pay for the ferry—see "Getting There," below). Daily 9:30am–5pm (until 6pm in summer except July 8:30am–4:30pm). Closed Dec 25. Subway: 4/5 to Bowling Green; 1/9 to South Ferry.

The symbol of New York is impressive enough from across the harbor, but close up—man, this chick is BIG. It gives me vertigo just to look up at her. In fact,

Midtown Attractions

Information *(i)*

Subway stop Ⓜ

Route of M5 Bus ·········

younger kids may be frightened by the sheer scale of Lady Liberty, and they won't want to climb the 354 steps up to her crown for the prizewinning view. (And for the climb there's also a wearying wait in line that can last 2 or 3 hours in fair weather.)

Here are your alternatives: Take the elevator up to the 10th floor (the top of the statue's pedestal), where there's a pretty amazing view, or go out on the plaza around the base of the pedestal to gaze out over the harbor. The exhibit inside the base is more fun than you'd expect—full-scale models of her left foot and immense ear, videos of smiths hammering out copper sheathing, a cross-section to show how the copper skin was hung on her steel skeleton. Right inside the entrance, you can see her original torch (replaced at the statue's centennial in 1986). For some kids, the ferry ride over may be more fun than the statue itself, but the whole excursion is a blast, so long as you don't waste too much time waiting in line.

Getting There: The **ferryboats** make frequent trips, running a loop from Battery Park to Liberty Island to Ellis Island and back to Battery Park (from New Jersey you can board ferries in Liberty State Park). In Battery Park, you can buy tickets at Castle Clinton, where there are some interesting exhibits to help pass the time before your ferry. You can disembark at either island and board a later boat to continue your trip. Schedules vary, but the service generally runs daily starting at 9:30am (the last trip starts around 3:15pm, later in summer). Boats depart every 30 minutes, every 20 minutes on busy weekends; sailing time is about 15 minutes to Liberty Island, another 10 minutes to Ellis Island, and 10 minutes back to Manhattan. The fare is $7 for adults, $6 for seniors, and $3 for children 3 to 17. For information and current schedules, call ☎ **212/269-5755.**

Where to Eat: There's a **cafeteria** on the site, as well as a **snack bar** on the ferry. Bring a picnic lunch if you can—there are plenty of places to sit and eat. (Just watch out for marauding seagulls.)

United Nations. Ages 8 & up. On the East River from 42nd to 48th sts. (entrance at First Ave. and 46th St.). ☎ **212/963-TOUR.** www.un.org. Admission $7.50 adults, $5 students, $6 seniors, $4 grades 1–8; children under 5 not admitted on tours. Daily 9:30am–4:45pm (no tours Jan 1, Thanksgiving, or Dec 25; limited schedule Sept–Oct; no weekend tours Jan–Feb). Subway: 4/5/6/7/S to Grand Central. Bus: M15, M42, M104.

When I was 13 and on my first visit to New York, the United Nations made a very deep impression on me. The idea of a world peacekeeping organization may have lost a little of its luster since then, but it's still a pretty darn impressive sight. First of all, there's the location: a commanding East River site with serene lawns and gardens cantilevered cleverly over FDR Drive. Then there's that memorable architectural design: the low dome of the General Assembly building tucked in at the base of the sheer glass plinth of the Secretariat Building. Finally, the thing that struck me most as a kid was the place's international population, with African and Asian and Scandinavian and Middle Eastern and Latin American bureaucrats bustling around chattering in a babel of different tongues; it really brought home to me how big the world is and what an amazing feat it is to get all these people to agree on *anything.*

Stop by the booth near the 46th Street entrance to get on a **guided tour** in English; these run about every half hour and last 45 minutes (call to find out about tours in other languages). These information-loaded talks fill you in on the organization's history while you cruise around to the complex's major highlights—the General Assembly Hall, the Security Council chamber, and other major meeting halls—and take in lots of internationally donated art and sculpture en route. A sobering exhibit of relics from the 1945 bombing of Nagasaki and Hiroshima reminds us of why the U.N. was formed in the first place.

The various U.N. agencies operate year-round, so there's always plenty of activity on the grounds. But things heat up when the General Assembly is in session, from the third Tuesday in September until sometime near the end of December. The **Gift Center** downstairs is great for finding unusual international handcrafts.

Where to Eat: The **Delegates Dining Room** (reservations required—call ☎ **212/963-7625** and be sure to bring a photo I.D.) is open to the public Monday to Friday 11:30am to 2:30pm. Even if it's not exactly packed with high-level diplomats, the river views are great. If that's too sedate for your kids, head away from the U.N. to the **Comfort Diner** on East 45th Street (see chapter 9).

2 Best Views

Battery Park City Esplanade. All ages. On the Hudson River, between Chambers Street and Battery Place. Subway: A/C/E to World Trade Center.

The Statue of Liberty, Ellis Island, the Verrazano Bridge, and the Jersey City skyline punctuate the harbor views from this landscaped riverside walkway in a stunning residential/office complex at the lower edge of Manhattan. People loll on the benches reading the *Times,* coffee mugs in hand; dog owners walk frisky pets on leashes; in-line skaters and cyclists weave patiently through the crowd; and children hang on the inward-curved railings watching yachts cruise past on their way to the boat basin at the north end. No panhandlers, no T-shirt vendors, no ice-cream carts—it's a wonderfully civil scene.

◑ Brooklyn Heights Promenade. All ages. West of Columbia Heights, between Montague and Cranberry sts., Brooklyn Heights, Brooklyn. Subway: 2/3 to Clark St.; then follow Clark St. west to reach the Promenade.

The calm here is so palpable, you'd never know that the Brooklyn–Queens Expressway is rumbling underneath this cantilevered promenade. On one side are the back gardens of lovely Brooklyn Heights town houses; on the other, the East River and a drop-dead view of Lower Manhattan and the harbor. It faces west, which means that the view is especially terrific near sunset. Best of all, if you're with little kids, there's a superb neighborhood playground at the south end, near Pierrepont Street. Combine this with a walk across the Brooklyn Bridge or a visit to the New York Transit Museum (later in this chapter), and you've got a great day trip.

◐ Empire State Building. Ages 4 & up. Fifth Ave. and 34th St. ☎ **212/736-3100.** www.esbnyc.com. Admission $9 adults, $7 seniors, $4 children 11 and under. Daily 9:30am–midnight (ticket booth on concourse level, open until 11:20pm). Subway: B/D/F/N/R to 34th St.

To my mind, the Empire State Building is the classic skyscraper observation deck—after all, this is where Cary Grant and Deborah Kerr missed their rendezvous in *An Affair to Remember* and Tom Hanks and Meg Ryan made theirs in *Sleepless in Seattle.* And, of course, this is where Fay Wray and King Kong had their own kind of rendezvous. Shabby as much of the building has become, its art deco lobby is still impressive and the location puts you squarely in the middle of Manhattan, with close-up views to all sides. The small enclosed observation deck on the 86th floor (change elevators at the 80th floor) has narrow outdoor promenades on all sides, though the parapets are too high in many places for youngsters to see over; there's porthole-type window viewing from the 102nd floor (1,250 feet up). Gift shops in the main lobby and on the 86th floor sell all kinds of New York City, Empire State Building, and (of course) King Kong knickknacks.

For information on the **New York SkyRide** attraction inside the Empire State, see "Best Rides," later in this chapter.

Downtown Attractions

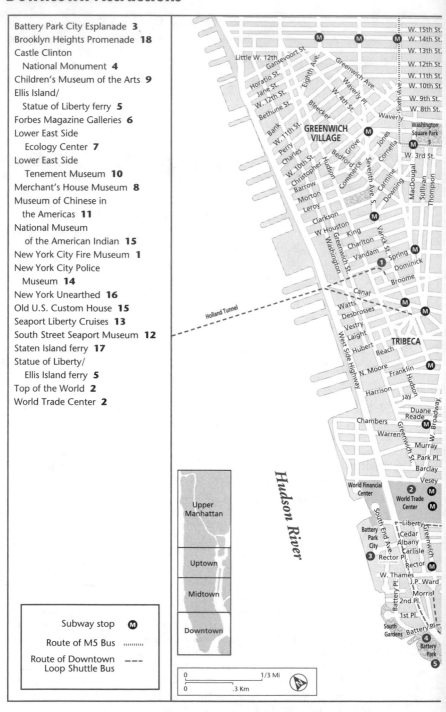

Subway stop ⓜ
Route of M5 Bus ....
Route of Downtown ‒ ‒ ‒
    Loop Shuttle Bus

Upper
Manhattan

Uptown

Midtown

Downtown

Hudson River

0   1/3 Mi
0   .3 Km

Riverside Church Bell Tower. Ages 4 & up. 120th St. and Riverside Dr. ☎ **212/ 870-6700.** Admission $2 adults, $1 students and children, free for children under 5. Tues–Sat 11am–4pm, Sun 12:30–4pm. Subway: 1/9 to 116th St. Bus: M5 to 120th St.

Though not nearly as high as its skyscraper competitors—only 355 feet in the air—this elegant church's bell tower has a glorious 360-degree view across and down Manhattan, not to mention jaw-dropping Hudson River vistas. It's rarely crowded—another decided plus—and the small observation deck puts you cheek to jowl with Gothic stone buttresses (sorry, no resident hunchback, but the mood is definitely dramatic). Only one thing to beware: An immense 74-bell carillon will be right beneath you, and it rings forth every 60 minutes on the hour, which can unnerve some youngsters. Others will be, like, whoa, dude!

Top of the World/World Trade Center Observation Deck. Ages 4 & up. 2 World Trade Center (bounded by West, Vesey, Liberty, & Church sts.). ☎ **212/323-2340.** www. wtc-top.com. Admission $13 adults, $9.50 seniors, $6.50 children 6–12, free for children 5 and under. June–Aug daily 9:30am–11:30pm, Sept–May daily 9:30am–9:30pm. Subway: A/C to Chambers St.; E to World Trade Center; N/R/1/9 to Cortlandt St.; 4/5 to Fulton St.

It may not be the world's tallest building anymore, but it's still New York's tallest and plenty high enough (1,377 feet) to produce a thrill. Because the World Trade Center is at the tip of Manhattan island, the views here include a sweeping vista of the harbor and the ocean beyond; the nighttime perspective is a tapestry of twinkling street lights to the north. Whiz upward in a superspeed elevator to the spacious 107th-floor observation deck, with windows on all four sides, powerful binoculars for zooming in on details, and computer consoles for identifying the sights you're seeing. In good weather, the 110th-floor open-air rooftop deck is opened, for those who are really into heights. As compared to the Empire State Building (see above), it's worth the extra money—higher, cleaner, more high-tech—though only if you're downtown anyway. Be prepared to endure long lines to get in. Admission also includes a simulated helicopter ride over New York City and a nightly laser show that'll beam visitors' messages out into space. Awesome!

3 More Manhattan Museums

Children's Museum of Manhattan. Ages 10 & under. 212 W. 83rd St. (between Broadway and Amsterdam Ave.). ☎ **212/721-1234.** www.cmom.org. Admission $6 adults and children, $3 seniors, free for children under 1. Sept–late June Wed–Sun 10am–5pm; late June–Aug Tues–Sun 10am–5pm; open school holidays. Subway: 1/9 to 79th or 86th St.; B/C to 81st St.

My children are always happy to come here, though its limited installations can wear thin if we go too often. Best for the under-8 crew, it's full of things they can touch, space for them to run and jump, make-believe environments, and opportunities to experiment. The main floor features an interactive exploration of the human body; the mezzanine's Word Play exhibit has seven activity areas cleverly designed to stimulate language development in kids 4 and under. The museum's four floors also include a playroom especially for 4-and-unders, a carpeted reading room with a puppet theater where kids can do their own impromptu shows, a few computers for older kids to mess around on, and an activity-packed basement area that's periodically remodeled, most recently with a delightful Dr. Seuss theme. The outdoor WaterWhirl and the recycling-oriented Urban Treehouse are fun, too, I'm told, though they seem to be closed whenever we're visiting. Young readers may appreciate the fun upstairs corridor that pays homage to Maira Kalman's nutty Max the Dog books.

There are always daily activities (check the posted schedules when you enter) like face painting, storytelling, and shows in the auditorium. Special weekend events focus on holidays. On rainy days and during school vacations, the joint gets pretty crowded, and the badly lit high-ceilinged spaces reverberate with noise; staff members posted in the galleries seem listless and uninvolved. It's a pity this place isn't better, but it's still worth checking out.

Children's Museum of the Arts. Ages 12 & under. 182 Lafayette St. (between Broome and Grand sts.). ☎ **212/274-0986.** Admission $5, free for children under 1; pay as you wish Wed 5–7pm. Wed noon–7pm, Thurs–Sun noon–5pm; open school holidays. Subway: 6 to Spring St.; N/R to Prince St.

Smaller than the Children's Museum of Manhattan (above), this is a good alternative if you're downtown, with lots of hands-on stuff for kids. Various art projects are set up; youngsters are encouraged to explore rhythm instruments; a couple of computers loaded with graphics programs are available; there's a small play area where infants and toddlers can work off their extra energy. This is less a museum than an indoor playground with an arts emphasis, with various weekend and after-school workshops; the afternoon we went, it was full of neighborhood preschoolers who acted like they owned the place and whose baby-sitters were too busy gossiping in a corner to supervise them. I think my son would've had a blast if he'd come with a playmate, though—next time, we'll know. On rainy or cold weekends, it's crowded to the rafters, so be warned.

✪ **The Cloisters. All ages.** In Fort Tryon Park at 193rd St. and Fort Washington Ave. ☎ **212/923-3700.** www.metmuseum.org. Suggested donation (includes same-day admission to the Metropolitan Museum of Art, earlier in this chapter) $10 adults, $5 students and seniors, free for children 11 and under. Mar–Oct Tues–Sun 9:30am–5:15pm; Nov–Feb Tues–Sun 9:30am–4:45pm. Closed Jan 1, Thanksgiving, and Dec 25. Free parking. Subway: A to 190th St. Bus: M4 to the end of line.

Of course your kids aren't into medieval art—that's not the point. For families, the point of the Cloisters, the Metropolitan's beautiful medieval art annex, is the sheer weirdness of it—a conglomeration of chapels and courtyards and refectories lifted from European convents and monasteries, brought in packing crates to America, and reconstructed here on a blufftop site in Fort Tryon Park. Wander from room to room, soaking up the time-stands-still atmosphere; go out on the terrace for splendid views of the Hudson River and the New Jersey Palisades, and poke around the monks' herb garden. Talk with your kids about unicorns before you go—there's one fascinating gallery devoted to a series of tapestries depicting a unicorn hunt (a medieval version of an adventure comic strip?).

It's a long trek up here, considering that children may not want to spend more than an hour in the museum, but they might actually enjoy the bus ride, which won't take forever if you're coming from the Upper West Side (combine the Cloisters with visits to St. John the Divine and Riverside Church for a full day of Gothic-ness). If you're doing this in the same day as the Metropolitan (which makes sense, since your admission covers both sites), compare what you see up here to the Met's first-floor medieval galleries, right next to the arms and armor department that many kids love.

Cooper-Hewitt National Design Museum. Ages 3 & up. 2 E. 91st St. (at Fifth Ave.). ☎ **212/849-8300** or 212/849-8400. Admission $8 adults, $5 students and seniors, free for children 12 and under; free Tues 5–9pm. Tues 10am–9pm, Wed–Sat 10am–5pm, Sun noon–5pm. Closed major holidays. Subway: 4/5/6 to 86th St.

Check to see what exhibit is currently running at this Smithsonian branch devoted to design and decorative arts: A surprising number of them appeal to kids (clothing, furniture, advertising posters), and the accompanying material is usually so lucid that even a young kid can grasp what's interesting about the displays. What's more, it gives you a chance to get inside industrial tycoon Andrew Carnegie's surprisingly homey neo-Georgian mansion—don't forget to check out the beautiful plaster ceilings, and point out to kids how low some of the doorways are (Carnegie, a short man, wanted the house built to *his* scale). My older son fell in love with the elegant leaded-glass conservatory; there's a nice garden out back and a super gift shop with a number of clever toys and kids' books (it's set in Carnegie's library—look at the inlaid designs in the wood paneling).

Forbes **Magazine Galleries. All ages.** 62 Fifth Ave. (at 12th St.). ☎ **212/206-5548.** Free admission. Tues–Wed and Fri–Sat 10am–4pm. Closed major holidays. Subway: 4/5/6 or N/R to 14th St./Union Square.

An obsessive collector, publishing magnate Malcolm Forbes had enough money to turn his obsessions into a strange and wonderful little museum. Basically, he collected six things: toy boats, toy soldiers, Monopoly games, medals and trophies, presidential papers, and lavishly bejeweled Fabergé eggs. Okay, younger kids may not care about the presidential papers, but that leaves plenty kids do love. This labyrinth of small galleries won't tax youngsters' attention spans, though they should be warned ahead that this is a sedate don't-touch kind of place. (No strollers permitted inside, either.) The display windows aren't always low enough for small children, so expect to do a lot of lifting. Don't expect your kids to linger as long as you may wish over the minutiae of the collection—remember, Forbes was a successful and influential grown-up when he collected this stuff, with a mere adult's eye to what made something valuable. But there's still enough here to make kids press their noses against the glass for a good half hour or so, more if they're older.

Guggenheim Museum. Ages 5 & up. 1071 Fifth Ave. (at 89th St.). ☎ **212/423-3500.** www.guggenheim.org. Admission $12 adults, $7 students and seniors, free for children 11 and under. Sun–Wed 9am–6pm, Fri–Sat 9am–8pm. Subway: 4/5/6 to 86th St.

The Guggenheim's rotating exhibits of 20th-century art may or may not appeal to your kids—Edward Hopper maybe yes, Mark Rothko maybe no. No matter. The main reason for including this museum in your NYC itinerary is the museum building itself: Frank Lloyd Wright's glorious, streamlined, totally wacky inverted spiral, which displays the art along one long ramp coiling down around a huge central atrium. I mean, can you imagine doing the Guggenheim on a *skateboard?* Since kids get in for free, it may be worthwhile to pay the adult admission just so you can enjoy this visionary interior for half an hour. In any case, the side galleries display some artworks kids might enjoy, by such masters as Degas, Cézanne, and Picasso.

✪ **Lower East Side Tenement Museum. Ages 5 & up.** 90 Orchard St. (at Broome St.). ☎ **212/431-0233.** www.tenement.org. Admission: Gallery, free; tenement tour and walking tour $9 adults, $7 seniors, students, and children; Confino Family tour $8 adults, $6 students, seniors, and children; any two tours $14 adults, $10 seniors, students, and children; all three tours $20 adults, $14 students, seniors, and children. Gallery daily 11am–5pm (opens Mon at noon). Tenement tours (every 30 min) Tues–Fri 1–4pm, Thurs at 6 and 7pm, Sat–Sun 11am–4:30pm. Walking tours Sat–Sun at 1 and 2:30pm (Apr–Dec only). Confino Family tour Sat–Sun at noon, 1, 2, and 3pm. Advance tickets for tours available through Ticket Web (☎ **800/965-4827;** www.ticketweb.com). Subway: B/D/Q to Grand St., J/M/2 to Essex St.

A narrow 1863 tenement building has been converted into this thoughtful small museum that picks up the immigrant story where Ellis Island leaves off—in the poor neighborhoods where the new arrivals landed. Once you've seen these bare, cramped living quarters, all too authentically furnished, your kids may never fight again over sharing a bedroom. (It's the perfect antidote to all those ornate period rooms at the Metropolitan Museum.) The gallery is basically a ticket desk and gift shop; the tours are the heart of the experience, so schedule your visit to include one. Various apartments in the tenement have been refurnished to tell the stories of immigrants from different homelands and eras of immigration; though more are in the works, the best one for kids would be the living-history tour of the Confino apartment, Sephardic Jews who emigrated from Turkey around 1916, which features costumed interpreters. It's held only on weekends at noon, 1, 2, and 3pm. Tours are limited to 15 people, so reserve slots in advance to avoid disappointment, especially for Sunday tours. Weekend walking tours widen the scope to include the whole neighborhood—they're wonderful if your kids are old enough to keep up with the pace.

Madame Tussaud's New York. Ages 5 & up. 234 W. 42nd St. (between Seventh and Eighth aves.). ☎ **800/246-8872**. Admission $19.95 adults, $17.95 seniors, $15.95 children 4–12. Sun–Thurs 10am–6pm, Fri–Sat 10am–8pm. Subway: A/C/E to 42nd St./Port Authority or 1/2/3/7/9/N/R to Times Square.

Transplanted from London, this wax museum to the stars has adapted its slightly creepy signature attraction to the Big Apple by featuring wax replicas of quintessential New Yorkers such as Mayor Rudolph Giuliani, Woody Allen, Joe DiMaggio, Yoko Ono, Jacqueline Kennedy Onassis, Donald Trump, and Andy Warhol. (Never fear, they'll still have Tussaud's favorites like Princess Di and the Beatles.) An extra attraction called "It Happened in New York" (included in the prices above) offers a virtual hansom cab ride through NYC history. Tussaud's opened in October 2000, just after we went to press, so I didn't have a chance to review it in time for this edition. Still, I figured you'd want to know it was around—another glitzy stop on the New 42nd Street.

Museum of American Folk Art. All ages. 2 Lincoln Square (between 65th and 66th sts.). ☎ **212/595-9533**. www.folkartmuseum.org. Suggested donation $3; $1 materials fee for children's workshops. Tues–Sun 11:30am–7:30pm; call for workshop schedule. Closed legal holidays. Subway: 1/9 to 66th St.

For whatever reason, even young kids get the point of folk art—in fact, young kids sometimes enjoy this stuff more than older kids who think they know what "good" art is. The shows here change continually, but every time we've ventured inside, my children have been charmed by the paintings and sculptures and collages, all by untutored artists, past and present—quilts, weathervanes, bottle-cap sculptures, an immense canvas covered with obsessively tiny handwriting, whatever. It's not an overwhelming museum; you can just walk in, browse around for 20 minutes, and walk out. The excellent gift shop (nearly as large as the museum itself) sells many handmade items, including a fairly interesting selection of toys you don't see everywhere else. A much larger space is slated to open at 45–47 W. 53rd St. in spring 2001.

Museum of Chinese in the Americas. Ages 5 & up. 70 Mulberry St. (at Bayard St.). ☎ **212/619-4785**. www.moca-nyc.org. Suggested admission $3 adults, $1 students and seniors, free for children 11 and under. Tues–Sat noon–5pm. Subway: N/R/6 to Canal St.

Nestled in the atmospheric heart of Chinatown, this museum mounts fascinating rotating exhibits, mostly drawn from its huge collection of photographs and artifacts—tiny shoes for a Chinese woman's bound feet, tin tea canisters, brocaded Chinese opera costumes, the heavy irons used in a laundry. Located on the second floor of a shabby old school building, the gallery is a stunning surprise, with 15 angled translucent walls creating the illusion of being inside a giant-sized Chinese lantern. Even if it holds your kids' attention for only 20 minutes, it'll give them a perspective on a very different side of New York.

What's in the Dollhouses?

Kids aren't the only ones fascinated by dollhouses, where every detail of life is obsessively re-created in miniature. The **Museum of the City of New York** has a wonderful collection of historic dollhouses upstairs in its Toy Gallery. Peer intently within and check off these tiny items as you find them:

- ❏ a mousetrap
- ❏ a leopard-skin rug
- ❏ a pincushion
- ❏ a snow globe
- ❏ a pack of playing cards
- ❏ a chess set
- ❏ a white bear rug
- ❏ two birdcages
- ❏ an old-fashioned handset telephone
- ❏ a basket of yarn and knitting needles
- ❏ a tiger-skin rug
- ❏ a lion-skin rug

✪ Museum of the City of New York. Ages 3 & up. 1220 Fifth Ave. (at 103rd St.). ☎ **212/534-1672.** www.mcny.org. Suggested admission $7 adults, $4 children, students, and seniors, $12 families. Wed–Sat 10am–5pm, Sun noon–5pm. Subway: 6 to 103rd St. Bus: M1/M2/M3/M4.

Don't drag your kids uptown just to see this museum, but if you're on Museum Mile already, it's worth stopping in for an hour or so (and skip across the street to Central Park's lovely Conservatory Garden afterward—see "Gardens," later in this chapter). The biggest draw for kids is the spectacular dollhouse exhibit in the Toys Gallery, though some kids I know like to come here just to parade up and down the gorgeous staircase in the entrance hall. My younger son also likes the Marine Gallery, tricked out to look like a little wharf, with ship models all around, a few weathered figureheads from old sailing ships, and a gigantic statue of Robert Fulton. Theater lovers will want to swing through the Broadway exhibit, displaying posters and mementos from the Great White Way (including a costume Barbra Streisand wore in *Funny Girl*). My daughter Grace was blown away upon seeing the black net "shadow" that Wendy sewed back onto Peter Pan's toes in the old Mary Martin musical—that's the kind of cool stuff this museum has hidden away.

✪ Museum of Modern Art (MoMA). All ages. 11 W. 53rd St. (between Fifth and Sixth aves.). ☎ **212/708-9400.** www.moma.org. Admission (includes movie admission) $10 adults, $6.50 students and seniors, free for children 15 and under; pay as you wish Fri 4:30–8:15pm. Thurs–Tues 10:30am–5:45pm (Fri until 8:15pm). Closed Thanksgiving and Dec 25. Subway: E/F to Fifth Ave.

If young kids don't get the point of modern art, it's not the fault of this world-class museum in Midtown: Saturday activities here include special tours for 4-year-olds, gallery talks for ages 5 to 10, interactive activity workshops for the entire family, and programs of classic short films chosen for a family audience. The "modern" in the museum's name no longer means cutting edge, but its large bright galleries do provide a retrospective of the best in 20th-century art, from Picasso to Pollock, from Rodin to Rothko.

The very young may be blissfully happy here because they don't care whether a painting looks like anything; preschoolers who've just learned how to make a tree look like a tree may be baffled by a canvas covered with mere stripes or squares or spatters of paint—steer them instead toward the bright pop art image of Andy Warhol's Marilyn Monroe portrait, the moody intensity of van Gogh's *Starry Night*, or the surreal images by Magritte or Dalí. My older son fell seriously in love with Picasso after a Sunday afternoon here, while my younger son preferred the meticulous architectural models upstairs; my daughter's favorite spot is the splendid sculpture garden, where she can run dizzying circles around three-dimensional masterpieces while the rest of us recline on a bench and muse on the art we've just enjoyed.

Museum of Television and Radio. Ages 5 & up. 25 W. 52nd St. (between Fifth & Sixth aves.). ☎ **212/621-6600.** www.mtr.org. Admission $6 adults, $4 students, $3 children 12 and under. Tues–Sun noon–6pm (Thurs until 8pm and Fri until 9pm for theaters). Closed major holidays. Subway: E/F to Fifth Ave. (53rd St.).

In this sleek Midtown museum (with a sister branch in L.A.), junior couch potatoes can gorge on all kinds of broadcast media, from vintage commercials to 1960s sitcoms to TV coverage of the first Moon walk. The catch: You've got to get here early in the day to make a reservation to use the library, where you can search the database on a Mac, then call up a program on an individual console with headphones. Failing that, you can stop by the fifth-floor radio listening room to sample sound bites from timely preselected programs or attend any of several screenings running frequently in a number of cushy small theaters. Weekends are the best time for kids, when there are hands-on workshops in the morning and uncrowded screenings of top international children's TV shows in the afternoon; the staff is genuinely friendly to youngsters. If your child's hooked on Nick at Nite, plan for several hours of browsing around.

National Museum of the American Indian. Ages 5 & up. 1 Bowling Green, beside Battery Park. ☎ **212/668-6624.** web1.si.edu/nmai. Free admission. Daily 10am–5pm (Thurs until 8pm). Closed Dec 25. Subway: 4/5 to Bowling Green; N/R to Whitehall St.; 1/9 to South Ferry.

A branch of the Smithsonian, this museum enjoys a fabulous setting in the ornate 1907 U.S. Customs House, a beaux arts gem that was a principal site in the movie *Ghostbusters II*. To enter the exhibition galleries, you pass through the awesome Great Rotunda—don't miss looking up at the painted dome. The museum has vast holdings, only a small portion of which are on display (another branch is set to open on the Mall in Washington, D.C., in 2002); it isn't big on interactivity, but you should be able to find several displays of interest, particularly if your kids have studied Native Americans in school. Wend your way through the labyrinth of small rooms looking for stuff that isn't over your children's head—a hanging bison hide they can stroke or the round glass case filled with hundreds of moccasins large and small. My kindergartener, who wouldn't know a Choctaw from a Cherokee, lingered in the two adjacent replica rooms from a contemporary reservation—one a family's living room, the other a schoolroom—and marveled over the fact that Indian kids play with Gumbys and watch TV just like he does. That cultural insight in itself was reason enough to come here.

❂ New York City Fire Museum. Ages 3 & up. 278 Spring St. (between Varick & Hudson sts.). ☎ **212/691-1303.** Suggested admission $4 adults, $2 students and seniors, $1 children 11 and under. Tues–Sun 10am–4pm. Subway: 1/9 to Houston St.; C/E to Spring St.

Though small, this two-story museum in a converted firehouse is worth the money if your kids are as much into fire trucks as my son was at a certain age (he has since graduated to warships, hence our frequent trips to the *Intrepid;* see listing earlier in this chapter). This place is full of antique fire engines, including several horse-drawn ones. The horses aren't on display, unfortunately, but there's a stuffed fire dog named Nig who used to be the mascot of one Brooklyn firehouse. A lot of the museum is most interesting to adults patient enough to pore over the mementos of 19th-century firefighting, but there are enough bells, alarms, pickaxes, and nozzles to hold young interest for 45 minutes or so. Our favorite room is a little back gallery on the first floor displaying loads of color snapshots from firehouses all over the five boroughs and embroidered badges from fire companies all over the world (we like the one from Maui, with a volcano on it, and the one from Houston, with the motto "You Light 'Em, We Fight 'Em").

New York City Police Museum. Ages 6 & up. 25 Broadway (between Morris St. and Battery Place). ☎ 212/301-4440. www.nycpolicemuseum.org. Free admission. Mon–Fri 10am–6pm, Sat–Sun 10am–4pm. Subway: 1/9/N/R to Rector St.; J/M/Z to Broad St.; 4/5 to Bowling Green.

With everything from vintage uniforms to a mock-up of a crime scene and a computer simulation of what it would be like to be confronted with a gun-wielding criminal, this collection of police memorabilia should mesmerize any child who's into cops and robbers. Confiscated weapons, counterfeit money, an old patrol car, badges and radios and alarms and nightsticks . . . the mind boggles. Expanded from a smaller gallery attached to the Police Academy, this privately run museum is staffed by NYPD officers and has a clear bias toward supporting law enforcement points of view. Keeping that in mind, this excursion into the world of *NYPD Blue* can be a trip.

New-York Historical Society. Ages 4 & up. 2 W. 77th St. at Central Park West. ☎ 212/873-3400. www.nyhistory.org. Suggested donation $5 adults, $3 students and seniors, free for children 11 and under. Tues–Sun 11am–5pm. Subway: B/C to 81st St.

While the general collection here is bigger on history than on fun, the interactive exhibit called Kid City downstairs should pique children's interests. Re-created from old photographs in the society's exhaustive collection, Kid City presents a New York neighborhood from 100 years ago, full of household objects and toys and the sorts of things kids notice about their world. A good three-dimensional hands-on history lesson. Older children may be ready to browse through the new fourth-floor exhibit space, which finally allows the society to display a larger portion of its vast holdings—Audubon's bird paintings, George Washington's camp bed from Valley Forge, the desk where Clement Clarke Moore wrote "A Visit from St. Nicholas," and a portrait of an early governor of New York dressed as a woman (makes Mayor Giuliani's penchant for wearing drag look like more of a New York tradition than we thought).

New York Public Library. Ages 6 & up. Fifth Ave. at 41st St. ☎ 212/930-0800. www.nypl.org. Free admission. Mon and Thurs–Sat 10am–6pm, Tues–Wed 11am–7:30pm. Subway: B/D/F/4/5/6 to 42nd St.; 7 to Fifth Ave.

Though most little kids fall in love with the regal pair of lions—Patience and Fortitude—poised beside the front steps, the exhibits mounted inside the New York Public Library are usually of interest to older kids only. (But you never know—there was an exhibit on garbage in 1995 that my boys thought was totally cool.) The library does have an extraordinary collection of first editions, manuscripts, letters, prints, maps, and other treasures on paper and often puts together fascinating shows, but whether or not your youngster will be intrigued all depends on the theme. Otherwise, pop in for a few minutes just to gape at the beaux arts architecture, from the dignified marble to the extraordinary Main Reading Room, where anyone can join the scholars and writers at endless ranks of tables poring over research materials from the NYPL's famous stacks. Note that behind the library is **Bryant Park.**

The NYPL's **Donnell Branch,** 20 W. 53rd St., between Fifth and Sixth avenues (☎ 212/621-0636), may be worth a stop, too, to see the original Winnie-the-Pooh animals displayed in the Central Children's room (generally open noon to 6pm, with some minor variations, and closed Sunday).

New York Unearthed. Ages 8 & up. 17 State St. at Battery Park (entrance on Pearl St. between Whitehall and State sts.). ☎ **212/748-8628.** Free admission. Mon–Fri noon–6pm. Closed holidays. Subway: 4/5 to Bowling Green; N/R to Whitehall St.; 1/9 to South Ferry.

A branch of the South Street Seaport Museum (earlier in this chapter), this gallery shows off all sorts of stuff that got dug up when construction crews excavated Manhattan sites in preparation for building skyscrapers. It's a tangible history of all the layers of civilization that have occupied this island, from early Native American flint tools to Dutch trade goods to 20th-century junk—which means that only school kids will get the point. (Exhibits are placed too high for younger kids anyway.) But gazing at all this random detritus of human lives can have its own weird fascination, and the glass-enclosed pit where you can watch real archeologists at work gives the place a proper field-trip aura. It makes a logical combination with the nearby National Museum of the American Indian (above); while you're here, young Indiana Joneses may want to go 2 blocks up Pearl Street to investigate the archeological excavations of an old Dutch city hall under a transparent panel in the sidewalk, beside the office building at 85 Broad St.

Pierpont Morgan Library. Ages 8 & up. 29 E. 36th St. (between Madison & Park aves.). ☎ **212/685-0008.** www.morganlibrary.org. Admission $8 adults, $6 students and seniors, free for children 12 and under. Tues–Thurs 10:30am–5pm, Fri 10:30am–8pm, Sat 10:30am–6pm, Sun noon–6pm. Closed holidays. Subway: 6 to 33rd St.

The Morgan Library's refined gallery space exhibits prints and drawings, which may or may not be of interest to kids—a recent show about St. Exupery's *The Little Prince* was just the ticket, but that isn't always the case. What kids will appreciate is the wing J. P. Morgan actually used as a library, especially his elegant wood-paneled study.

4 Museums in the Outer Boroughs

IN BROOKLYN

✪ **Brooklyn Children's Museum. All ages.** 145 Brooklyn Ave. (at St. Mark's Ave.) in Brower Park, Crown Heights. ☎ **718/735-4400.** www.bchildmus.org. Suggested admission $4 per person. Wed–Fri 2–5pm, Sat–Sun 10am–5pm; Jul[y–Aug Mon and Wed–Thurs noon–5pm, Fri noon–6:30pm, Sat–Sun 10am–5pm. Transportation: See below.

This futuristic museum building—erected in 1976 to replace an earlier pair of Victorian town houses—is technically the oldest children's museum in the country, founded in 1899. It's also one of the best in the country, with an array of hands-on exhibits that will interest kids up to age 14. The emphasis on technology, TV, and video will appeal to older children (witness the pair of hip New York boys aged 10 and 12 who wandered into a *Sesame Street* exhibit, saw themselves on a monitor, and wound up happily clowning around alongside various *Sesame Street* characters they thought they'd outgrown). There's also an emphasis on nature, with exhibits exploring animals' eating habits and plants' growing habits (in a greenhouse environment that's a collaboration with the Brooklyn Botanic Garden). During special animal programs, staff members bring out the museum's permanent animal inhabitants, including a beautiful and enormous amber-colored python named Fantasia, to demonstrate their traits. In the MusicMix studio, kids can experiment with how various instruments produce sounds; a "pizza parlor" lets children make pizzas out of felt and charge their parents play money from an antique cash register; a game room features hands-on exhibits about games and actual chess tournaments on weekends. Free Friday Family Fun nights in July and August add music, theater, or dance performances for families at 6:30.

Kids—and parents—will also be intrigued by the museum's subterranean architecture. You enter through a neon-lit tunnel and burrow into various large open spaces snuggled within a cluster of earth mounds. A terraced outdoor plaza is fun to romp around in fair weather. The museum has plenty of space, and crowds are not as overwhelming as at some of the Manhattan museums.

Getting There: By **subway,** take the no. 3 to the Kingston Avenue station, walk 6 blocks (with traffic flow) on Kingston Avenue to St. Mark's Avenue, and turn left for 1 block. Or take the no. 2 to the President Street station, walk 8 blocks on Nostrand Avenue (against traffic) to St. Mark's Avenue, turn right, and go 2 blocks. Or take the A to the Kingston Avenue station, walk 6 blocks on Kingston Avenue (against traffic) to St. Mark's Avenue, turn right, and go to Brooklyn Avenue. By **car,** take Atlantic Avenue east to Brooklyn Avenue, turn right, and drive 4 blocks south; or follow Eastern Parkway east from Grand Army Plaza to New York Avenue, turn left, and go 6 blocks north to St. Mark's Avenue, where you turn right and go 1 block east. Unmetered on-street parking is nearby. An alternative that's fun for kids is the museum's free **Trolley Express,** which runs Saturday and Sunday between 10am and 5pm, making three stops every hour—at Grand Army Plaza (at quarter past the hour), the Brooklyn Museum of Art (at 25 past the hour), and the Brooklyn Children's Museum (at a quarter to the hour). Call the museum for details.

✪ **Brooklyn Museum. Ages 4 & up.** 200 Eastern Pkwy., at Prospect Park, Brooklyn. ☎ **718/638-5000.** Admission $4 adults, $2 students, $2 seniors, free for children 11 and under. Wed–Fri 10am–5pm, Sat 11am–9pm (first Sat of the month 11am–11pm), Sun 11am–6pm. Parking $3 for 1st hr, $2 per hr after that. Subway: 2/3 to Eastern Pkwy.

The superb Egyptian collection, full of over-the-top mummy cases, is the best reason to visit this big underappreciated museum in Brooklyn, near neighbor to the Brooklyn Botanic Garden and Prospect Park; even if you're going to spend only an hour or so in the museum, there are enough other things to do nearby to justify the excursion. If your kids like history, they can wander past 27 detailed American period rooms from 1675 to 1928, including an eye-popping Moorish-style smoking room from John D. Rockefeller's town house. If they're old enough to appreciate great art, the American and European galleries are strong, with lots of impressionists and a load of Rodin bronzes. There's a special gift shop just for kids and lots of weekend drop-in programs for children.

Lefferts Homestead. All ages. Flatbush Ave., Prospect Park, Brooklyn. ☎ **718/965-6505.** Free admission. Apr–Oct Thurs–Fri 1–4pm, Sat–Sun 1–5pm; Nov Thurs–Sun 1–4pm. Subway: D/Q to Prospect Park.

This Dutch colonial farmhouse has been filled with exhibits for kids—old-fashioned toys, puppets, storybook corners, art activities—and absolutely everything in it is touchable. It's a little shabby, but who cares, when your kids are allowed to run up and down the stairs and jump off the porch and just enjoy themselves. On summer Sundays, come for the afternoon story hours under the big tree outside and go on to visit the nearby Prospect Park Wildlife Center (below) and take a spin on the stunning carved animals of the vintage Prospect Park Carousel.

✪ New York Transit Museum. Ages 3 & up. At the corner of Boerum Place and Scher-merhorn St., Brooklyn. ☎ **718/243-8601.** Admission $3 adults, $1.50 seniors and children 16 and under. Tues–Fri 10am–4pm, Sat–Sun noon–5pm. Closed Jan 1, Dec 24–25 and 31. Subway: 2/3/4/5 to Borough Hall; A/C/G to Hoyt/Schermerhorn sts.; F to Jay St./Borough Hall.

Another of my sons' favorite places (naturally, since it has to do with vehicles), this downtown Brooklyn museum is a snap to get to from Manhattan. The first great thing about this museum is that it's built in a disused subway station, with exhibits sprawling down the tunnels. The second great thing is the pair of bus cabs kids can climb into and pretend to drive. The third is the set of vintage subway cars kids can lope through, hanging on straps and swinging around poles. (Meanwhile, I got a kick out of reading the vintage subway ads on a couple of cars.)

Beyond that, the joint is full of things most kids will look at only for a minute or two—antique turnstiles and fare boxes and route maps and scale-model trolley cars and subway station mosaics and switching apparatuses. And there's only so long you can spend down in a subway tunnel without eventually starting to feel like a mole person. But the sheer amount of stuff makes this place good for an hour, more if you're transportation-obsessed (like my younger son). On weekdays, you may be battling school groups for that bus cab; on weekends, there are some wonderful workshops for kids—call ahead for a schedule.

IN THE BRONX

Yankee Stadium Tour. All ages. River Ave. and E. 161st St., the Bronx. ☎ **718/579-4531.** www.yankees.com. 1 hour tour $8 adults, $4 seniors and children 14 and under. Tour plus a short film on Yankee history $15 adults, $10 children and seniors. Reservations for groups of 12 or more. Group tours Mon–Fri 10am–4pm, Sat 10–11am; individual tours Mon–Sat at noon except for game days. Subway: 4 or C/D to 161st St.

The home of the Bronx Bombers, a.k.a. the House That Ruth Built, isn't exactly a museum—a shrine is more like it, at least to confirmed Yankees fans like my sons. These 1-hour tours give you a great behind-the-scenes glimpse of this historic sports stadium, seeing the view from the press box, learning how the scoreboard operates, gazing upon the plaques to Ruth, Mantle, DiMaggio, and other great Yankees in Monument Park—and, best of all, walking through the clubhouse where the players themselves actually suit up. My older son stared at Bernie Williams's guitar, propped up next to his locker, as if it were the Shroud of Turin. Individual tours do not need reservations; just show up several minutes before noon at the event ticket window near Gate 4. You can tour the stadium year-round, which is good to know if your Little Leaguer suffers from baseball deprivation during the off-season.

IN QUEENS

✪ American Museum of the Moving Image. Ages 10 & up. 35th Ave. and 36th St., Astoria, Queens. ☎ **718/784-0077.** www.ammi.org. Admission (includes film and video programs) $8.50 adults, $5.50 students and seniors, $4.50 children 5–18, free for children 4 and under. Tues–Fri noon–5pm, Sat–Sun noon–6pm. Subway: N to Broadway; R/G to Steinway St.

This superb resource for cinephiles is housed in the Kaufman Astoria Studio, where talkies were made long ago and *Sesame Street* is filmed today. At nine interactive work stations you can fiddle with sound effects, dub in new dialogue, call up different soundtracks, and even add your face (à la Woody Allen's *Zelig*) to classic movie scenes. You can record yourself making a series of funny faces into a video camera, which is then printed out in a flip book (thumb through it rapidly to re-create your moving facial expressions). At the digital animation stands, you can move cardboard cutouts around to create your own animated short. At other stations where the equipment is especially high-tech, museum staffers helpfully demonstrate the behind-the-scenes wizardry.

Many of the historic artifacts on display—a 1910 wooden Path camera, a 1959 Philco TV set—may inspire nothing but yawns from youngsters, but the extensive costume gallery should interest kids, with recognizable items like Robin Williams's dowdy padded housedress from *Mrs. Doubtfire*. The Monk's Coffee Shop set from *Seinfeld* is re-created here, along with a set of costumes worn by Jerry, Elaine, George, and Kramer on the sitcom. To illustrate the history of TV and movie merchandising, there's a fun display of tie-in toys and lunchboxes promoting TV shows from *Howdy Doody* to *The Simpsons*. The makeup exhibition has enough ghoulish masks to satisfy young Goosebumps readers. There's a cafe here too, which is convenient.

If your kid liked the interactivity of the Sony Wonder Technology Lab (above), this place should be a hit; less slick and commercial than a Universal Studios Tour, it's a great way to open kids' minds to the art and science of motion pictures.

✪ New York Hall of Science. Ages 3 & up. 47–01 111th St., Flushing Meadows–Corona Park, Corona, Queens. ☎ **718/699-0005.** www.nyhallsci.org. Admission $7.50 adults, $5 children 4–17 and seniors, free for children 3 and under; Science Playground $2 (6 and older only). Free admission Thurs–Fri 2–5pm except summer. Mon–Wed 9:30am–2pm, Thurs–Sun 9:30am–5pm (Tues and Wed until 5pm in summer); Science Playground open Apr–Nov, weather permitting. Closed major holidays. Parking $6. Subway: 7 to 111th St.

This is one of the great discoveries I made while researching this book. Like the wonderful Imaginarium in San Francisco, this is a completely hands-on type of museum that makes learning really fun—you can pedal furiously on a bicycle to turn a huge propeller; you can watch a bank of rotating electric fans create wind; you can hunt for microbes and fungi with microscopes; you can use colored Plexiglas tiles to make your own rainbow; you can watch your brother get really huge and then really tiny as he walks across an optically distorted room. Put your ear to glass pipes and you can hear different pitches; stand in front of a special light scope and you can cast three different-colored shadows at once.

The exhibits weren't over our 4-year-old's head, and yet they were plenty fascinating enough for my husband, who's no slouch when it comes to physics. Best of all, no activity takes more than a minute to execute, which means that kids sprint from one to another instead of hogging a demo station—we never had to wait our turn to try anything. Museum staffers were performing all kinds of cool demonstrations down on the main floor, but my boys were too busy to watch them. And the Science Playground is an awesome 30,000 square feet of outdoor fun with 27 interactive activities, including a gigantic teeter-totter, a light-activated kinetic sculpture, windmills, and a water-play area.

There's a limited cafe here, but you'd be better off packing a lunch—there aren't many options in the neighborhood. Definitely combine the science museum with a stop at the nearby Queens Wildlife Center (below), which won't add more than an hour to your expedition.

Queens County Farm Museum. All ages. 73–50 Little Neck Pkwy., Floral Park, Queens. ☎ **718/347-3276.** Free admission. Mon–Fri 9am–5pm (grounds only), Sat–Sun 10am–5pm (house and grounds). Subway: E/F to Kew Gardens/Union Turnpike; then Q46 bus to Little Neck Pkwy.

Still a working farm, this 18th-century homestead is a bucolic spot of fields and orchards and barns full of animals, with ongoing demonstrations of agricultural arts—plowing, planting, apple picking, reaping, milking cows, birthing foals, incubating chicks, and so on. Plan your trip to come on a weekend, when you can go inside the simple three-room frame farmhouse, built in 1772, and go on a hayride ($2).

Queens Museum of Art. Ages 8 & up. NYC Building (next to the Unisphere), Flushing Meadows–Corona Park, Queens. ☎ **718/592-5555.** www.queensmuse.org. Admission $5 adults, $2.50 students and seniors, free for children under 5. Wed–Fri 10am–5pm, Sat–Sun noon–5pm. Subway: 7 to Willett's Point/Shea Stadium—walk south over ramp into park and head for the Unisphere.

Besides the fact that it's parked next to the Unisphere, that famous stainless-steel globe from the 1964 World's Fair, the chief reason for children to visit this museum of 20th-century art is the Panorama, an awesomely huge three-dimensional re-creation of the New York skyline that's kept faithfully up-to-date. Kids will love picking out familiar landmarks; anyone who enjoys dollhouses, Polly Pockets, and MicroMachines can marvel over the incredibly detailed small-scale rendering of a city that's often all too large-scale.

ON STATEN ISLAND

✪ **Historic Richmond Town. Ages 5 & up.** 441 Clarke Ave., Staten Island. ☎ **718/351-1611.** Admission $5 adults, $2.50 children 6–18, free for kids 5 and under. Sept–June Wed–Sun 1–5pm; July–Aug Wed–Fri 10am–5pm, Sat–Sun 1–5pm. From the Staten Island Ferry, take bus no. S74 to Richmond Rd./Court Place.

Somewhat off the beaten track, this 100-acre re-creation includes 27 buildings spanning the 17th to the early 20th centuries—which may create a disjointed effect for historical purists, but kids generally don't care. Three little streets are set up like a small village, and kids can run in and out of the houses and basically just have a ball. Many buildings were moved here from other sites on Staten Island; they range from a neoclassical courthouse serving as a visitor center to a little schoolhouse dating from 1695, the oldest elementary school building in the country. Costumed interpreters are in action July and August, demonstrating crafts like basket weaving, spinning, weaving, tinsmithing, and printing. A good full day's expedition.

Staten Island Children's Museum. Ages 10 & under. 1000 Richmond Terrace, Staten Island. ☎ **718/273-2060.** Admission $4 adults and children, free for children under 2. Tues–Sun and most school holidays noon–5pm; July–Aug opens at 11am Tues–Sun. From the Staten Island Ferry, take the S40 bus (Richmond Terrace) to the Snug Harbor center, with its black wrought-iron gate. The museum is in Building M.

Another interactive children's museum with a raft of workshops to keep kids busy, the Staten Island contender has one advantage—a lovely setting on the lawns and gardens of the Snug Harbor Cultural Center, formerly a home for retired seamen—and one main disadvantage, which is that it's out on Staten Island, albeit only a short bus ride from the ferry terminus. Seven hands-on interactive exhibits help children explore the wonders of water, insects, computers, and animals, among other subjects, with an emphasis on fun.

5 Best Rides

For classic theme-park thrills, you can venture out to the honky-tonk amusement parks of **Coney Island** (take the D or F train to West 8th Street in Brooklyn), where in summer months the vintage **Cyclone** roller coaster, built in 1927, offers thrills to riders over 54 inches tall, and the landmark **Wonder Wheel,** a double Ferris wheel built in 1920, circles high over the boardwalk. To tell the truth, I've never ventured onto the boardwalk attractions there because they terrify my children, but if yours are more adventurous, give it a whirl. The attractions below are thrilling enough for us.

The Beast. Ages 7 & up. Board at Pier 83, W. 42nd St. at the Hudson River (Circle Line Cruises pier) or at Pier 16, South St. Seaport. ☎ **212/563-3200.** www.circleline.com. Fare $15 adults, $10 children 5–12, no children under 5. May–Sept daily 11am–dusk (no Wed am from Pier 83); Apr Sat–Sun from Pier 16 only, Oct Sat–Sun from both piers. Subway to Pier 16: 2/3/4/5 to Fulton St. or A/C to Broadway/Nassau St. Bus to Pier 83: Westbound M42 to Hudson River.

The hulls of these high-speed boats have been painted with huge chomping shark teeth to look like they're eating the waves before them. Cruising at speeds up to 45 mph, the Beast buzzes past the New York skyline, pausing briefly at the Statue of Liberty for a quick close-up, then zips back to port, all within an adrenaline-pumping 30 minutes. As a sightseeing cruise, it hardly covers all bases, but who said kids were into sightseeing?

Central Park Carousel. All ages. In Central Park, midpark near 64th St. ☎ **212/ 879-0244.** Ride $1. Apr–Nov daily (weather permitting) 10am–6pm; rest of year closes at 4:30pm. Subway: 1/9 to 66th St.; N/R to Fifth Ave.

The elaborate carving that graces this 1908 merry-go-round's wooden horses may be lost on your kids. No matter—it's a big, fast, classic carousel with a vintage calliope (playing tunes of a decidedly different vintage, like "Rainy Days and Mondays"). The 4-minute ride is a pleasant way to top off a Central Park expedition, considering you're not far from either the zoo or the Wollman Rink. (For more on Central Park, see chapter 6.) Younger, skittish kids may want to find one of the horses that doesn't go up and down or opt for one of the gilded swan cars.

Chelsea Screamer. Ages 7 & up. Board at Pier 62, Chelsea Piers, West 23rd St. at the Husdon River. ☎ **212/924-6262.** www.chelseascreamer.com. Fare $15 adults, $10 children 3–12, free for children under 2. Mid-May to Oct Mon–Fri noon–7pm or dusk, Sat–Sun 11am–7:30pm or dusk. Subway: 1/9, C/E, or F/N/R to 23rd St. Bus: M23 across 23rd St.

A trifle more sedate than the Beast (see above), the Chelsea Screamer narrated speedboat cruise lasts a full hour, tootling past the Statue of Liberty around the tip of Manhattan to the Brooklyn Bridge and back. You'll still be on an open deck and churning up a fair bit of wake. Buy tickets on the dock 30 minutes before departure; groups of eight or more can make reservations.

New York SkyRide. Ages 4 & up. In the Empire State Building (2nd floor), Fifth Ave. at 34th St. ☎ **888/SKYRIDE** or 212/279-9777. www.skyride.com. Admission $11.50 adults, $10 children 13–17, $8.50 seniors and children 4–12, $35 family (2 adults and up to 4 kids). Daily 10am–10pm. Subway: B/D/F/N/R/1/2/3/9 to 34th St.

For roller-coaster daredevils, this 8-minute simulation may seem tame, but my 7-year-old was a bit shaken by it. "Passengers" are seated on a large platform that begins to tilt and jolt and careen wildly while a big screen shows you "crashing" your way around New York landmarks, with lots of ear-splitting recorded sound effects. For some reason, James Doohan—"Scotty" on the original *Star Trek* crew—narrates the show. There's zero sightseeing information imparted—it's just a crazed simulation of speeding through the cityscape. Count on a long line, up to 30 minutes at times. For goofy, kitschy fun, it's worth considering if the prices don't put you off.

Prospect Park Carousel. All ages. Flatbush Ave. entrance, Prospect Park, Brooklyn. ☎ **718/ 965-8961.** Ride 50¢. Thurs–Fri 11am–3pm, Sat–Sun and holidays noon–6pm. Subway: D to Prospect Park.

This vintage merry-go-round, close cousin to Central Park's, has a greater variety of animals—not just horses but also giraffes and zebras and other exotics, painted in fanciful pastels. A carousel ride here makes a perfect add-on to a visit to the nearby

Prospect Park Wildlife Center (later in this chapter), the **Lefferts Homestead** (earlier in this chapter), or the **Brooklyn Botanic Garden** right across Flatbush Avenue (later in this chapter).

Riverbank Carousel. All ages. Riverbank State Park, 145th St. and Riverside Dr. ☎ **212/ 694-3600.** Ride 50¢. Fri–Sun 2–8pm. Bus: M11 or Bx19.

On a grassy terrace set high on the shores of the Hudson, this uptown park's restored carousel draws young visitors on their way to and from a swim or a skate. In contrast to the restored vintage carousels in other New York City parks, Riverbank's Totally Kids Carousel may be extra appealing to families because it was designed by kids in the late 1990s. The lucky schoolchildren whose drawings were chosen to be reproduced—fanciful creatures like winged frogs replacing the traditional horses—were awarded free rides for life. A good reason to visit this uptown park overlooking the Hudson.

Roosevelt Island Tram. All ages. Manhattan terminus: Second Ave. and 60th St. Fare $1.50. Subway: 4/5/6 to 59th St.

A pair of big red cable cars swing over the East River alongside the 59th Street/ Queensboro Bridge to Roosevelt Island. Though most of the trip is actually over an unglamorous wedge of East Side real estate, it does go over the river, and you're high up enough to get good views of Manhattan up and down. There are few seats—only a narrow hard bench at either end of a car that holds 30 or so—so get there early to grab a seat by the front windows.

Once you're on Roosevelt Island, site of a former smallpox hospital, you can turn right around and ride back—or you can take a ride on the red shuttle bus (fare 25¢) to loop around this island housing development. It's all forgettable modern apartment blocks, but there's lots of riverside green space and little playgrounds are tucked away everywhere. The village's main street looks like something out of the 1960s British TV series *The Prisoner*—a curved main street cutting between characterless shopfronts (one of everything: post office, library, church, deli, Chinese restaurant, bank, school). It has a middle-class, racially mixed population, and the whole place is wheelchair accessible—it would be a little utopia if only the architecture weren't so grim. Nevertheless, it's a quick, cheap trip to a place where kids can run around outside and play—and getting there on the cable car is more than half the fun.

✪ Staten Island Ferry. All ages. Departing from South Ferry in Battery Park. ☎ **718/ 727-2508.** Passengers free, cars $3. Subway: 1/9 to South Ferry.

Walk right on at the South Ferry Terminal and you can chug across New York Harbor, past the Statue of Liberty, to Staten Island, where you walk around the barriers and get on again for the return ride. The whole round-trip should take about an hour. Most of the ferry decks are now glassed in, alas, but the views are still great. A friend of mine tells me that his mother used to corral the kids onto the ferry on hot summer nights to sleep when their un-air-conditioned apartment got too stifling hot; that's the kind of wonderfully populist institution the Staten Island Ferry is in the hearts of New Yorkers.

6 Historic Houses

Manhattan doesn't have many full-fledged historic houses, maybe because real-estate values are too high for old homes to sit around waiting for a preservation society to snap them up. You can see the mayor's yellow frame home, **Gracie Mansion,** in Carl Schurz Park on the East River at 89th Street, but the public rooms on the main floor can be toured only on Wednesday (March to November, 10am, 11am, 1pm, or 2pm—call ☎ 212/570-4751 for reservations; admission $4). Older kids who really want the experience of another era do have a few choices (beyond the extensive period rooms at the **Metropolitan Museum of Art**), but most are well off the beaten track and may have limited visiting hours.

○ **Alice Austen House, Museum and Park. Ages 6 & up.** 2 Hylan Blvd., Staten Island. ☎ 718/816-4506. www.aliceausten.8m.com. Admission $2 adults, free for children 12 and under. Thurs–Sun noon–5pm. From the Staten Island Ferry terminal, take the S51 bus 2 miles to Bay St./Hylan Blvd. Walk 1 block toward water. Museum on right.

Many things about pioneer photographer Austen's house make it a great bet for kids. First, it's really just a cozy cottage, a low-slung gingerbread-trimmed bungalow with rolling lawns that offer dynamite views of New York harbor. Second, Austen herself is such an appealing character, a spunky turn-of-the-20th-century woman who started taking pictures when she was 10 and just never stopped. Lots of her work is on display, and the garden has been replanted according to her photos of the original grounds. Third, you get to ride the Staten Island Ferry over. What more could you ask?

Merchant's House Museum. Ages 8 & up. 29 E. 4th St. (between the Bowery and Lafayette St.). ☎ 212/777-1089. Admission $5 adults, $3 students and seniors, free for children 11 and under. Thurs–Mon 1–5pm. Subway: 6 to Astor Place or Bleecker St.

The most interesting thing about the Tredwell family—who lived in this house continuously from 1835 to 1933—is that they weren't famous or unusual at all, just a stable, prosperous, upper-middle-class family whose house and furniture happened to survive intact, wallpaper and all, until it became a house museum in the mid-20th century. The house itself is a fairly notable example of Greek Revival, but your kids will probably be more struck by the old-fashioned furnishings. A nice trip back in time on a quiet side street not far from NYU and the East Village's funky St. Mark's Place.

Morris–Jumel Mansion. Ages 10 & up. 65 Jumel Terrace (at 160th St.). ☎ 212/923-8008. Admission $3 adults, $2 students, free for children 11 and under. Wed–Sun 10am–4pm. Subway: B/C to 163rd St.

Dating back to 1765, this imposing mansion with its Georgian front columns had a major brush with history when Gen. George Washington used it as his headquarters in 1776. As they tour the house, however, your kids may become more interested in Eliza Jumel, the wealthy, brazen 19th-century woman who lived here for many years, during her marriage to, and after her divorce from, Aaron Burr. It's too bad this big, elegant mansion is off the beaten path for tourists . . . or then again, maybe that's its saving grace. As a bit of colonial history, Manhattan's oldest house is a gem.

Mount Vernon Hotel Museum and Garden. Ages 6 & up. 421 E. 61st St. (between First and York aves.). ☎ 212/838-6878. Admission $4 adults, $3 students and seniors, free for children 11 and under. Tues–Sun 11am–4pm (Tues until 9pm June–July). Closed major holidays and Aug. Subway: N/R or 4/5/6 to Lexington Ave./59th St.

Back in the 1820s and 1830s, when this part of the Upper East Side was considered a country retreat, the Mount Vernon Hotel stood here. What's surprising is how much this site still feels like a retreat, surrounded by city as it is: The surrounding gardens, planted in 18th-century style, offer a welcome whiff of horticulture, and nine period rooms inside this former carriage house—restored by the Colonial Dames of America as a museum of decorative arts and furniture—re-create what life in the old inn might've been like. Considering its convenient location, it's curious that this museum isn't better known, though the curators do all they can to draw in the public with workshops, candlelit tours, and other special events.

7 Zoos & Aquariums

Aside from the following, check out the **Bronx Zoo/Wildlife Conservation Park** and the **Central Park Wildlife Conservation Center** (see "Kids' Top 10 Attractions," earlier in this chapter).

New York Aquarium. All ages. Surf Ave. and W. 8th St., Coney Island, Brooklyn. ☎ **718/265-3400** or 718/265-FISH. www.nyaquarium.com or www.wcs.org. Admission $9.75 adults, $6 seniors and children 2–12. Daily 10am–5pm. Parking $6. Subway: D/F to W. 8th St. (Brooklyn).

After an hour-long subway ride from Manhattan—an adventure in itself—you hit the ocean at Coney Island beach, skirting the tawdry rides of Coney Island's amusement park, and walk to the left on the open part of the boardwalk (away from the cheesy stuff) to the aquarium. I'm a veteran aquarium lover and have to admit that this place disappointed me, perhaps because we went in spring—many of the exhibits are outdoors and it was still too chilly to linger while watching the seals and walruses. But having heard how crowded this place gets in summer (and how distracting the tinselly lights of Wonderland are, once the amusement park opens for summer), I'm glad we did it out of season, with the beach deserted and the ocean misty, cold, and gray. The kids still had a ball in the **Discovery Cove,** where they could get their hands on real sea creatures. Time your schedule so you can catch the dolphin and sea lion shows too. Pack a lunch if you're going in the cooler months, when the outdoor snack bar may be closed and nearby boardwalk joints are boarded up (it's several blocks to the nearest McDonald's).

☻ Prospect Park Wildlife Center. All ages. 450 Flatbush Ave., Prospect Park, Brooklyn. ☎ **718/399-7339.** www.wcs.org. Admission $2.50 adults, 50¢ children 3–12, free for children 2 and under. Apr–Oct Mon–Fri 10am–5pm, Sat–Sun and holidays 10am–5:30pm; Nov–Mar daily 10am–4:30pm. Subway: D to Prospect Park.

This is my kids' favorite of all New York City's zoos, probably because it's right at the level of preschoolers and young grade-schoolers. The fanciful abstract sculptures arching over the walkway from the side entrance tell you right away you're in kid territory, and on it goes, to the **Animals in Our Lives** petting zoo and the outdoor **Discovery Trail,** where kids can hop like a wallaby, squat on their own lily pads, or huddle inside a giant turtle shell. There's a miniamphitheater built in front of the glass-enclosed environment where a troop of hamadryas baboons scamper around—somebody knows which animals kids most like to watch. It's small, clean, safe, and tons of fun. Once you're out here, make it a full day by visiting nearby **Lefferts Homestead** (earlier in this chapter), New York's only historic house set up just for kids, and taking a ride on the gorgeous antique **Prospect Park Carousel** (earlier in this chapter), only steps from the zoo entrance. The subway ride from Manhattan isn't all that long, leaving you off only a block or so from the zoo.

Queens Wildlife Center. All ages. 53–51 111th St. (at 54th Ave.), in Flushing Meadows Park, Queens. ☎ **718/271-1500.** www.wcs.org. Admission $2.50 adults, $1.25 seniors, 50¢ children 3–12, free for children 2 and under. Mon–Fri 10am–5pm, Sat–Sun 10am–5:30pm (Nov–Mar daily until 4:30pm). Subway: 7 to 111th St. (Queens).

Though it may not rate a trip out to Queens from Manhattan on its own account, this smart little zoo is a natural add-on to a **New York Hall of Science** excursion (earlier in this chapter)—a good excuse for a tramp through the old World's Fair grounds. The zoo's focus is on North American species (don't expect exotics here, though my sons considered the American bison plenty exciting) arranged along a handsomely landscaped walking trail. You feel surrounded by wilderness, yet the pathway is actually pretty short—it won't tax young legs—and the loop shouldn't take more than 15 or 20 minutes. Across the park road is a minifarm with domestic animals that'll satisfy the yen for feeding and stroking warm furry creatures.

Staten Island Zoo. All ages. 614 Broadway, Barrett Park, Staten Island. ☎ **718/442-3101.** www.statenislandzoo.org. Admission $3 adults, $2 children 3–11, free for children 2 and under. Daily 10am–4:45pm. From the Staten Island Ferry, catch the S48 bus, get off at Broadway and Forest Ave., turn left, and go 2½ blocks up Broadway. Free parking.

The little Staten Island zoo isn't under the umbrella of the Wildlife Conservation Society, as are the other zoos around here, and it's definitely a poor cousin. But you may want to combine this with a visit to the **Staten Island Children's Museum** (earlier in this chapter), especially if you're into snakes—the reptile collection is a standout. The 8 acres are also home to a small aquarium and a fair number of birds. Feeding times are frequent attractions, and there's also a small children's zoo, for younger kids who like their nature hands-on.

8 Gardens

۞ Brooklyn Botanic Garden. All ages. 900 Washington Ave. (at Eastern Pkwy.), Brooklyn. ☎ **718/623-7200.** www.bbg.org. Admission $3 adults, $1.50 students and seniors, free for children 15 and under; free all day Tues and Sat am. Tues–Fri 8am–6pm, Sat–Sun and holidays 10am–6pm. Subway: 2/3 to Eastern Pkwy; D/Q to Prospect Park; 4/5 to Franklin Ave.

Every month something new is blooming at this 52-acre garden beside the Brooklyn Museum and across from Prospect Park. Starting in spring, **Daffodil Hill** dazzles the eye with a field of stunning yellow, then delicate pink cherry blossoms fringe the **Japanese Pond** (local Japanese families flock in for their annual blossom-viewing picnics). A riot of roses fills the **Cranford Rose Garden** as summer sets in, and thickets of rhododendron blossom near the Eastern Parkway entrance. There's also a **Fragrance Garden** for the blind and a sweet little **Shakespeare Garden** featuring all sorts of plants mentioned in Shakespeare's plays. Year-round, you can stroll through the **Steinhardt Conservatory,** with its outstanding bonsai collection, orchids, water lilies, and **Trail of Evolution,** a pathway lined with increasingly sophisticated plant forms. You'll also find a cafe, a lovely gardening gift shop, and frequent weekend programs for children and families. Kids may get a kick out of the **Celebrity Path,** inlaid with the names of famous Brooklynites from Mae West to Woody Allen.

Conservatory Garden. All ages. Central Park at 105th St. ☎ **212/860-1382.** www. centralparknyc.org. Free admission. Daily 8am–dusk. Free tours Apr–Oct Sat 11am. Subway: 6 to 96th St., then walk up Fifth Ave.

Central Park's only patch of formal garden is a delightful find in Manhattan and rarely crowded because it's so far uptown. Walk through glorious wrought-iron gates (which once fronted the Fifth Avenue mansion of Cornelius Vanderbilt II) and turn left to find the **Children's Garden,** with beds of flowers blooming around a wishing well with a statue of the children from Frances Hodgson Burnett's *The Secret Garden.* The central section of the garden is a long lush lawn flanked by a pair of walkways lined with flowering trees; the northern end has a circular design, with a fountain of the Three Graces surrounded by flower beds—a spectacular blaze of tulips in spring and chrysanthemums in fall. On spring and summer weekends, there's nearly always a wedding party here getting photographed; with rest rooms and a fair-weather outdoor cafe, it's a welcome refuge, a perfect place to let your kids stretch their legs after a Museum Mile trek.

New York Botanical Garden. All ages. 200th St. and Kazimiroff (Southern) Blvd., the Bronx. ☎ **718/817-8705.** www.nybg.org. Admission to grounds $3 adults, $2 students and seniors, $1 children 2–12, free for children under 2; combination ticket to all sections $10 adults, $7.50 students and seniors, $4.50 children 2–12; free on Wed. Tues–Sun and Mon holidays 10am–6pm (Nov–Mar until 4pm). Parking $5. Transportation: See below.

This lushly planted 250-acre park—five times bigger than the Brooklyn Botanic Garden (above)—is a real magnet for families. The stunning 8-acre **Everett Children's Adventure Garden** (separate admission $3 adults, $2 seniors and students, $1 children 2 to 12) tempts youngsters with cunning minitrails and mazes and topiaries and fanciful sculptures, not to mention hands-on stations where they can learn about pollination, chlorophyll, root systems, and all that good stuff. My kids simply adore it. Other highlights are the **Wild Wetland Trail,** which engagingly leads kids through a natural ecosystem; the **Ruth Rea Howell Family Garden,** where young city-dwellers can plant, weed, water, and compost tidy little garden plots; the 19th-century **Snuff Mill,** perched on its riverside terrace; a **rock garden** (admission $1 adults, 50¢ students, seniors, and children 2 to 12); a huge formal rose garden; a steep rhododendron valley; and the huge Victorian-era greenhouse complex of the **Enid Haupt Conservatory** (admission $3.50 adults, $2 students, seniors, and children 2 to 12), which alone makes the garden a delightful destination year-round.

A narrated **tram** ($1) swings around the grounds to help you cover the territory. Spring is intoxicating here, what with the huge stands of azaleas, magnolias, dogwood, and lilacs, but it's a blast even in winter, when the Holiday Garden Railway exhibit is set up—a large-scale model train wending its way through fanciful landscapes and cityscapes. Although the botanical garden is right next to the Bronx Zoo (see "Kids' Top 10 Attractions," earlier in this chapter), you'd have to be very ambitious (and very good walkers) to do both justice in 1 day, since their sites are so spread out—but if you're game, it can be done.

Getting There: Metro North trains from Grand Central Terminal make the 20-minute trip to the Botanical Garden Station; cross Southern Boulevard and you're at the entrance. One-way fare is $3.50 off-peak or $4.75 peak. By **car,** take the Henry Hudson Parkway to the Mosholu Parkway; at the end of the Mosholu, turn right onto Kazimiroff Boulevard and follow the garden perimeter to the entrance. By **subway,** take the D or no. 4 to Bedford Park Boulevard. Walk east 8 blocks or take Bx26 bus to Garden.

Wave Hill. All ages. 675 W. 252nd St., Riverdale, the Bronx (entrance at 249th St. and Independence Ave.). ☎ **718/549-3200.** www.wavehill.org. Admission $4 adults, $2 students and seniors, free for children 5 and under; free admission Sat 9am–noon, all day Tues, and daily mid-Nov to mid-Mar. Tues–Sun 9am–4:30pm (mid-May to mid-Oct until 5:30pm, Wed in June–Aug until dusk). Transportation: See below.

A very suburban enclave in the Bronx, Riverdale has some fine housing stock on its Hudson River shore, notably this 28-acre estate with two mansions and extensive gardens. Over the years many famous people lived here, as tenants or as guests—writers Mark Twain and William Makepeace Thackeray, conductor Arturo Toscanini, and Theodore Roosevelt; at one time the Tudor-style house was also the official residence of Great Britain's ambassador to the U.N. But there's not much to see inside the houses—just let your kids play on the grounds, which offer one of the few unobstructed views across the Hudson to the magnificent New Jersey Palisades.

Nobody minds if youngsters run on the grass, and the formal gardens are world-famous, well worth prowling around. My kids' favorites are the **Aquatic Garden,** with a pair of pergolas enclosing a formal pool; the nook-filled **Wild Garden;** and a terraced series of small walled gardens showing off cactuses and alpine flowers. Below the mansions' smooth lawns sprawls a 10-acre **woodland** with walking trails that give kids a nice bit of a hike. Excellent children's workshops are held on weekends in the learning center; make a phone call or check the Web site for a current schedule.

Getting There: Liberty Lines (☎ 718/652-8400) bus no. BxM1 (from the East Side) or BxM2 (from the West Side) goes to 252nd Street; then walk west across the parkway bridge and follow the signs to the main gate. The fare is $3 one-way; a child under 45 inches may sit on a parent's lap for free. Or take the **Metro North train** (☎ 212/532-4900) to the Riverdale stop, walk up 254th Street, turn right on Independence Avenue, and go to the main gate at 249th Street. The one-way fare is $4.75 peak and $3.50 off-peak. By **car,** take the Henry Hudson Parkway to the 246th Street exit and drive straight north to 252nd Street; turn left to cross the parkway overpass, turn left at the light, and drive south to 249th Street, where you turn right and follow it to the Wave Hill gate.

9 Nature Centers

Note that Central Park is covered in depth in chapter 6 under "Green New York: The Top Parks."

The Dairy. All ages. In Central Park, midpark at 65th St. ☎ 212/794-6564. Free admission. Tues–Sun 10am–5pm. Subway: 6 to 68th St.; 1/9 or A/B/C/D to Columbus Circle.

This charming 19th-century structure, with patterned roof tiles and gaily painted gingerbread trim, actually started life as a dairy, back in the days when people grazed cows on Central Park's meadows (children could stop in here and buy a cool cup of milk fresh from the udder). There aren't too many Guernseys left in Manhattan, so nowadays the Dairy is the park's chief visitor information center, with a roomful of displays about the park's landscape. There are always a few hands-on activities for youngsters, and it's a pleasant short stroll from either the carousel or the zoo, not to mention the Wollman Rink.

✪ **Dana Discovery Center. All ages.** In Central Park at 110th St., near Fifth Ave. ☎ 212/860-1370. Free admission. Tues–Sun 10am–5pm (until 4pm in winter). Subway: 2/3 to 110th St. Bus: M2, M3, or M4 to 110th St./Fifth Ave.

After Harlem Meer was dredged out in the early 1990s and its banks beautifully relandscaped, this pretty structure on its north shore opened as a nature study center, bringing visitors uptown for the first time in years. Weekend family workshops run year-round (usually at 1pm, but call for schedules), and a room overlooking the Meer's serene waters is set up with hands-on nature exhibits. Stroll around the Meer to the neighboring **Conservatory Garden** (see "Gardens," earlier in this chapter).

✪ **Henry Luce Nature Observatory at Belvedere Castle. All ages.** In Central Park, midpark at 79th St. ☎ 212/772-0210. Free admission. Apr–Oct Tues–Sun 10am–5pm; Nov–May Tues–Sun 10am–4pm. Subway: B/C to 79th St.

Besides studying the kid-friendly interactive exhibits on Central Park's natural habitats, young visitors to Belvedere Castle get a kick out of standing on the rocky terrace hanging high over **Turtle Pond** and the outdoor **Delacorte Theater** or walking onto the castle's upper-level terraces for some super views of the Upper West Side, including the American Museum of Natural History. The mere fact that it's a castle is intriguing enough, though it's an awfully tiny castle, built in 1872 as an optical illusion to make the lake to the south look bigger (the woods of the Ramble have since grown so high they nearly obscure the lake view). But this castle has a U.S. Weather Service station on top—note the twirling weathervanes on the tower. Stroll down the hillside west of the castle, a neatly planted **Shakespeare Garden** (appropriate, since the neighboring Delacorte is home to the Public Theater's free Shakespeare in the Park series), or scamper down the long slope to the east, where turtles and ducks populate the adjacent pond.

Inwood Hill Urban Ecology Center. All ages. Inwood Hill Park, 218th St. and Indian Rd. ☎ 212/304-2365. Free admission. Wed–Fri 11am–4pm, Sat–Sun 11am–5pm. Subway: 1 to 215th St., then walk several blocks to Indian Rd.

This art deco canoe house, tiled in aqua and white, holds weekend walking tours of the surrounding park, with its marsh, meadow, and steep rock cliffs. A telescope inside the center lets kids zoom in on details of the neighboring marsh and meadow; other exhibits include hands-on geology displays, an aquarium, and a flip-book of pictures of the native plants and animals. Few Manhattanites venture up to this northern tip of the island, but it's a stunning site.

Lower East Side Ecology Center. Ages 3 & up. E. 7th St. between Aves. B and C. ☎ 212/ 420-0621. Free admission. Wed 4–7pm, Fri–Sun 8am–5pm. Subway: 6 to Astor Place.

Though it looks at first like another abandoned Alphabet City lot, look closer and you realize that every structure has been built from discarded materials—coffee cans, plastic laundry detergent jugs, old tires—with some inventive sculptures amid garden works in progress. The neighborhood can be funky, but the walk across East 7th Street from Tompkins Square is fairly innocuous. Green guerrillas and other plucky souls may get a charge out of such a determinedly urban spin to nature studies.

10 Kid-Friendly Tours

BUS TOURS

Gray Line Tours Double-Decker Bus Tours. All ages. Main stop at Port Authority Bus Terminal (42nd St. and Eighth Ave.). ☎ 800/669-0051 or 212/397-2600. www.graylinenewyork.com. Full city tour: $59 adults, $39 children under 12. Upper or Lower Manhattan loop: $25 adults, $16 children under 12. Statue of Liberty/Ellis Island grand tour: $68 adults, $48 children under 12. Free for children under 5 if sitting in adult lap. Daily starting at 9am.

Though lengthy narrated bus tours can make some younger children squirm like crazy, they're convenient for helping you see a lot of sights without having to run your kids ragged. Hop-on/hop-off tours provide a happy medium—you get driven around and spoon-fed information, and when your kids get restless you just jump off at the next stop, expecting to get back on again later.

Operating both red double-decker buses and bright red trolley buses, Gray Line offers so many options it could make your head spin. Gray Line's tour guides are reliable too. Besides the 2-day **Grand Tour,** which would take 5 hours if you didn't indulge in hopping on and off, there's a **Lower Manhattan loop** and an **Upper Manhattan loop,** the **Grand Tour plus Statue of Liberty 2-day option,** and the **Lower Manhattan plus Statue of Liberty 1-day option.** More traditional escorted sightseeing tours—the kind where you have to stick with the same groups of bus pals throughout—include both half-day and full-day Manhattan routes that involve a buffet lunch, as well as escorted Harlem tours (the Sunday version includes a gospel church service), helicopter tours, and a harbor cruise add-on to the Grand Tour loop.

✪ **Magic Bus (M5 city bus). All ages.** Recommended starting point: 125th St. and Riverside Dr. Fare $1.50, exact change, MetroCard, or token.

It's an ordinary city bus route, but it happens to rumble past a host of sights you'd like to see in its 90-minute loop, and you may even get some narration over the PA.

You can board anywhere along the route, which is marked with a dotted line on the three city maps in this chapter. I recommend catching the bus at 125th and Riverside, where you'll first wheel past **Grant's Tomb** (122nd Street) and gleaming neo-Gothic **Riverside Church** with its carillon bell tower (120th Street). You'll proceed down handsome residential **Riverside Drive** (Riverside Park and the Hudson lie out the right-side window) to 72nd Street, where the route jogs east to Broadway, then south past **Lincoln Center.** At Columbus Circle, it turns east and goes across 59th Street—also called Central Park South, since the park lies on your left—to the Plaza, where the **Plaza Hotel** faces **FAO Schwarz** at 58th Street. Down Fifth Avenue you'll go, past **Tiffany & Company** (on your left on the south side of 57th Street), **St. Patrick's Cathedral** (on your left at 51st Street), **Rockefeller Center** (on your right from 51st to 48th streets), the main research library of the **New York Public Library** with its famous stone lions, Patience and Fortitude (on the right from 42nd to 40th streets), the **Empire State Building** (on the right at 34th Street), the narrow wedge-shaped **Flatiron Building** (on the left at 23rd Street), to the white triumphal arch of **Washington Square** (facing the foot of Fifth Avenue where 6th Street should cut through). After circling the square, you'll go back north up Sixth Avenue, which from 16th to 23rd streets takes you past **Ladies' Mile,** the late 19th-century department store district (many of the old stores have been recently restored for new megastore tenants like Barnes & Noble and Bed, Bath & Beyond); the Herald Square shopping intersection where **Macy's** department store presides at 34th Street; **Bryant Park** (on your right from 40th to 42nd streets), the New York Public Library's backyard, which was the site of a World's Fair in 1853; more of Rockefeller Center, including **Radio City Music Hall** (on your right at 50th Street); and back to 59th Street to retrace the route back north, as far as 178th Street.

BOAT TOURS

For the **Beast** and the **Chelsea Screamer** high-speed harbor rides, see "Best Rides," earlier in this chapter.

✪ **Circle Line Sightseeing Cruises. Ages 3 & up.** Departing from Pier 83, at the foot of W. 42nd St. at the Hudson River. ☎ **212/563-3200.** www.circleline.com. 3-hour tour $24 adults, $12 children 2–11; 2-hour tour $20 adults, $10 children 2–11. Parking $12–$15. Bus: Westbound M42 to the Hudson River.

Delivering a classic New York City experience, these low-slung little steamers chug right around Manhattan on a 3-hour tour (shades of *Gilligan's Island?*) with narration that can be very entertaining. Sit on the left-hand side of the boat for the best views. On the first leg you deconstruct the Midtown skyline, get a good look at the Chelsea Piers, pass Battery Park City and the World Trade Center, and swoop past Ellis Island and the Statue of Liberty. Then the boats cut across New York Harbor and go up the east side of the island, past Wall Street and South Street Seaport, and under the East River bridges, getting a view of the other end of Midtown, with the United Nations presiding over the river at 42nd Street. This is where the shortened Express Tour stops and turns around, but if you continue, you'll pass the Upper East Side, seeing Gracie Mansion, where the mayor lives, and you get to go through Hell Gate, where the East River merges with the Harlem River, and Spuyten Duyvil (Spite the Devil), where the Harlem River empties into the Hudson. Granted, there's not so much to see on the northern end of the island, but the guides gamely fill in with lots of trivia. And when you pass under the George Washington Bridge, you can spot the little red lighthouse featured in Hildegarde H. Swift's classic children's book *The Little Red Lighthouse and the Great Grey Bridge.*

The experience of being out on the water with the wind in your hair is marvelous by itself, but getting a minicourse in New York history and architecture is a definite bonus. Go early in your trip to get a firm sense of Manhattan as a whole. It really is the guide that makes the trip—the first time I went, the narrator was full of wonderful obscure trivia, but a more recent cruise with a lazier guide started to drag for me. And you're a captive audience—if your kid freaks out in the middle of the trip, or, like my 9-year-old and his friend, starts to complain that you didn't bring the Game Boys, you have no option but to endure the rest of the voyage. There are rest rooms and a snack bar on board, at least, and even without Game Boys the 9-year-olds decided at the end of the trip that "it really rocked," which I gather means they enjoyed it. They were adamant about doing the 3-hour circuit rather than the shorter route, because it's cool to go *all the way around.* That's the *point,* Mom. Gotcha.

The *Pioneer.* All ages. Departing from Pier 16 at South St. Seaport. ☎ **212/748-8590.** www.southstseaport.org. Admission $20 adults, $15 students and seniors, $12 children 12 and under.

Two-hour harbor cruises aboard a historic schooner depart a couple of times a day (schedules vary) from South Street Seaport. The time-warp experience of setting sail from this old seaport is somewhat diluted by the views of very modern downtown skyscrapers and the chug of barges, tugboats, and tour boats on the water around you, but it could still be a memorable throwback to an earlier era. New York viewed from the water is quite a sight.

Seaport Liberty Cruises. All ages. Departing from Pier 16 at South St. Seaport. ☎ **212/ 630-8888.** www.southstseaport.org. Admission $12 adults, $11 students, $6 children 12 and under.

These narrated harbor cruises last only an hour, which makes them a better alternative for younger kids than the Circle Line tours (above). You'll go from the Seaport down around Wall Street to Battery Park, swing around to pass by Ellis Island and the Statue of Liberty, then cruise past Brooklyn Heights and the Brooklyn shipyards, under the Brooklyn Bridge, and back to the Seaport. If just being out on the water is more important to you than getting a comprehensive view of Manhattan, bag Circle Line and do this one instead.

PRIVATE GROUP TOURS

Small Journeys, Inc. All ages. 114 W. 86th St., New York, NY 10024. ☎ **212/874-7300.** $230 per group for 4-hour tour.

These custom-designed group tours are too expensive for individual families, but if you can hook up with another two or three broods, go for it, because Steven Kavee and his guides really gear their tours to kids' interests. The company also designs behind-the-scenes field trips for school groups, going on-site to meet professionals in fashion, art, theater, music, interior design, whatever. Transportation costs—whether by van, by limo, by bus, or on foot—are additional, depending on the sights involved. Arrange well in advance.

WALKING TOURS

For detailed strolls around the city and even Brooklyn, you may want to check out *Frommer's Memorable Walks in New York.* Take into account, however, that some of the walks (such as the Greenwich Village literary tours) may not be of much interest to kids.

Several organizations run a number of tours; check the schedules in the *Big Apple Parent*, the *New York Family*, or the *New York ParentGuide*, available free at children's bookstores and clothing stores all over town.

ARTime (☎ 718/797-1573), as its name implies, runs walking tours oriented toward the fine arts, usually focusing on museums and galleries. Because they don't cover as much physical ground as some of the neighborhood and architectural tours (no more than 2 or 3 blocks between art galleries), they're quite suitable for younger kids—so long as the kids are into art. Tour guides gear their talks to children 5 to 10. Tours last about 1½ hours and cost $20 for one adult plus a child and $5 for each additional child (an extra adult tagging along is free). You can usually book a tour up to a day in advance—they run from September to June on Saturday 11am to 12:30pm.

Big Onion Walking Tours (☎ 212/439-1090; www.bigonion.com) are designed primarily for adults, but kids 8 and up will respond to many of their lively topics, which often touch on the multiethnic dimensions of New York's mosaic. Tours can last as long as 2 hours; they cost $12 for adults, $10 for students and children.

The **Grand Central Partnership** (☎ 212/883-2420), a coalition of business interests in the area around Grand Central Terminal, sponsors a free 1½-hour walking tour along East 42nd Street—an area that includes such Midtown classics as the Chrysler Building, the Daily News Building, the art deco Chanin Building, and the old Bowery Savings Bank. With its historical/architectural emphasis, this may be a bit scholarly for kids under 10, but the length (and the price) make it worth trying out. Tours depart Friday at 12:30pm from the Whitney Museum at Phillip Morris, 120 Park Ave. at 42nd Street.

The **Municipal Arts Society** (☎ 212/935-3960 for reservations and details, 212/439-1049 to get a schedule by mail; www.mas.org) runs fascinating tours that explore the city's architecture and neighborhoods from an urban-design perspective. The guides are top-notch—occasionally they'll talk over a kid's head, but they're so enthusiastic it's infectious, and their depth of knowledge means they can handle just about any question thrown at them. Tours run from 2 hours up to 6- or 7-hour excursions; weekday tours cost $10 for adults, $8 for students and seniors, and weekend tours cost $15. One very popular option is the hour-long lunchtime tour of fascinating Grand Central Terminal (suggested donation $5), which meets every Wednesday at 12:30pm (call the society to find out where to meet). Advance reservations aren't required for weekday tours, but for some of the popular weekend tours you may need to reserve a couple of weeks in advance; call for times.

Neighborhood Strolls 5

Manhattan is one of the great walking cities in the world. On this densely packed island, it seems there's something new to see every half a block—an intriguing shop, a museum, a beautiful piece of architecture, or an eccentric fellow pedestrian. Even children who normally drag their feet when forced to walk from the far end of a parking lot may cover several blocks without noticing, enticed on and on by the continual stream of sights. Almost every place you want to go can be reached on foot, often more quickly, and for sure more cheaply, than via taxi, subway, or bus. And along the way, you'll get a great window on the way New Yorkers live.

If you're already planning to go to one of the neighborhoods described in this chapter to visit an attraction, restaurant, or store, allow a little more time to explore the immediate area. Most of them are worth a visit simply so you can drink in the kaleidoscope of street life that is New York.

1 Midtown

LOBBY HOPPING ON FIFTH AVENUE

Start at the biggie: the **Empire State Building,** 34th Street and Fifth Avenue (see "Best Views" in chapter 4), whose streamlined 1931 interior includes murals of the Seven Wonders of the World. Then head up Fifth Avenue to the **New York Public Library** at 41st Street, where you can walk up the steps between the famous lions (Patience and Fortitude) and peek into the ornate lobby, eternally cool in white marble. The **Fred E. French Building,** Fifth Avenue at 45th Street, has a wonderfully Byzantine lobby with loads of mosaics. Up Fifth Avenue in Rockefeller Center, between 49th and 50th streets, **30 Rockefeller Plaza**—formerly the RCA Building, now the General Electric Building, still home to the NBC TV network—has another awesome deco lobby, sheathed in dark marble. Check out the ceiling mural inside the Rockefeller Plaza entrance, a very pro-labor statement that must have galled the Rockefellers when they first saw it. Continue up Fifth to glitzy modern **Trump Tower,** between 56th and 57th streets, full of rosy marble, shiny brass, greenery, and a waterfall.

LOBBY HOPPING ACROSS 42ND STREET

Start in the **Lincoln Building,** 60 E. 42nd St., between Madison and Park avenues, whose imposing Depression-era lobby holds a replica of the Daniel Chester French statue of Lincoln that occupies the Lincoln Memorial in Washington, D.C. Then pop into **Grand Central Terminal** on the north side of 42nd Street at Park Avenue, which, though technically not a lobby, has a gloriously restored main room that'll knock your socks off. Gaze up at the constellations painted or electrically twinkling on the soaring azure ceiling, check out the elegant waiting room, then descend into the marbled catacombs to find a shopping concourse and a food court, populated with commuters scurrying for their trains. Try out the whispering gallery in the large tiled vault outside the Oyster Bar—if two people face the walls in diagonal corners, they can hear each other's softest speaking voices. Exit from Grand Central Terminal through the 1930s deco lobby of the **Graybar Building,** Lexington Avenue at 43rd Street; as you step out onto Lexington Avenue, look at the awning built over the entrance and you'll see curious iron struts fashioned like a ship's mooring ropes, with round brackets to prevent cast-iron wharf rats from scrambling aboard. Go south on Lexington to the northeast corner of 42nd and Lex, where you can duck into the **Chrysler Building,** whose steel-tipped deco spire is so notable on the skyline. The small lobby is surprisingly warm and rich looking (think luxury car glove compartment), with black marble and inlaid wood. Continue east on 42nd Street—on the south side, step into the art deco **Daily News Building,** 220 E. 42nd St., with its spinning 12-foot globe and a floor inlaid with an immense bronze compass; on the north side of 42nd between Second and First avenues, the modern **Ford Foundation Building** is a complete contrast, with its tranquil atrium garden—a good place to sit for a few minutes and rest your weary feet. Feet not weary? Then head to the United Nations (see below).

UNITED NATIONS AREA

If you're staying in Midtown, sightseeing in Midtown, and dining in Midtown, you may crave a quick shot of residential calm—and you'll find it in **Tudor City,** a protected mock-Tudor enclave built in the 1920s on the East River end of 42nd Street. From Second Avenue and 41st Street, walk east up a steep hill to Tudor City Place, where you can turn left. Stand at the railings across the street, look east to the East River, and then down to see the traffic of 42nd Street thunder through the underpass, while all up where you are on the terrace remains calm. Linger in the neatly planted gardens on the west side of Tudor City Place, visit the playground (go down the steps on the south side of 42nd Street), or proceed north on Tudor City Place to 43rd Street, where you can look straight across First Avenue to see the **United Nations** complex. A flight of stairs takes you down into tiny paved **Ralph Bunche Park,** from which you can cross the street to the United Nations (technically, you're no longer on U.S. soil here—like the Vatican, the U.N. is its own nation). Even if you're not doing a tour (see chapter 4), walk around the U.N.'s beautiful **Rose Garden,** with broad paved walkways overlooking the East River.

ROCKEFELLER CENTER AREA

The heart of Midtown is Rockefeller Center, a huge streamlined office/retail complex of pale limestone built in the 1930s by the famously wealthy Rockefeller family. Start on Fifth Avenue between 49th and 50th streets at the **Channel Gardens,** which lie between the British building on the north and the French building on the south (like the English Channel lies between Britain and France—get it?). The Channel Gardens slope down to **Rockefeller Plaza,** the center's heart. Beneath the colossal gilded statue of the Greek god Prometheus, in winter there's a jewel of an ice-skating rink, in summer an open-air restaurant (the Rock Center Café—see

Manhattan Neighborhoods

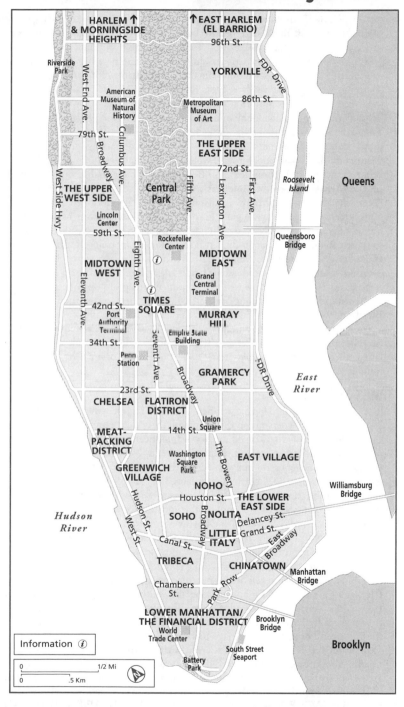

HARLEM ↑
& MORNINGSIDE
HEIGHTS

↑EAST HARLEM
(EL BARRIO)

96th St.

Riverside
Park

YORKVILLE

FDR Drive

West End Ave.

American
Museum of
Natural
History

Metropolitan
Museum
of Art

86th St.

79th St.

Columbus Ave.

THE UPPER
EAST SIDE

West Side Hwy.

Broadway

72nd St.

Roosevelt
Island

Queens

THE UPPER
WEST SIDE

Central
Park

Fifth Ave.

Lexington Ave.

First Ave.

Lincoln
Center

59th St.

Rockefeller
Center

Queensboro
Bridge

Eighth Ave.

ⓘ

MIDTOWN
EAST

MIDTOWN
WEST

Grand
Central
Terminal

East
River

ⓘ

Eleventh Ave.

42nd St.
Port
Authority
Terminal

TIMES
SQUARE

Seventh Ave.

MURRAY
HILL

34th St.

Empire State
Building

Penn
Station

Broadway

GRAMERCY
PARK

FDR Drive

23rd St.

CHELSEA

FLATIRON
DISTRICT

MEAT-
PACKING
DISTRICT

14th St.

Union
Square

Washington
Square
Park

EAST VILLAGE

GREENWICH
VILLAGE

The Bowery

Williamsburg
Bridge

NOHO

Houston St.

THE LOWER
EAST SIDE

Hudson
River

Hudson St.

SOHO

Broadway

NOLITA

Delancey St.

West St.

LITTLE
ITALY

Grand St.

East Broadway

Canal St.

TRIBECA

CHINATOWN

Manhattan
Bridge

Chambers
St.

Park Row

LOWER MANHATTAN/
THE FINANCIAL DISTRICT

World
Trade Center

Brooklyn
Bridge

South Street
Seaport

Brooklyn

Battery
Park

Information ⓘ

0   1/2 Mi
0   .5 Km

chapter 9). Behind Prometheus, where the giant Christmas tree stands every December, rises **30 Rockefeller Plaza,** home of the NBC TV network; step inside to see about taking the NBC Studio Tour and to buy souvenirs of your favorite NBC shows at the NBC Experience shop. Or if you're here between 7 and 9am, stop outside the big glass windows on the south side of 49th Street to watch the *Today Show* being broadcast live; hosts Katie Couric and Matt Lauer often take to the streets outside as well to film various segments.

Study the monumental lobby murals inside 30 Rock's Rockefeller Plaza entrance. You may then want to take the escalators down from the lobby in 30 Rock and prowl around the maze of concourses and tunnels connecting all the Rockefeller Center buildings in an underground world of shops and restaurants (good to know about on rainy days). If you leave 30 Rock through the entrance on Sixth Avenue (excuse me, Avenue of the Americas), turn around to see the glittering mosaics decorating the portico. My own kids' favorite 30 Rock doorway, however, is on 50th Street; they never fail to get a kick out of the massive stone bas-relief figures framing the doors, jauntily dressed in nothing but attitude and a little city soot. My sons are convinced the one on the left is intentionally mooning **Radio City Music Hall** across 50th street. Go west to Sixth Avenue for the best views of Radio City's neon-jazzed streamlined facade. This landmark art deco theater still has some live stage shows (see chapter 8) as well as a continual lineup of pop concerts.

Return to Fifth Avenue along 50th Street and turn left to pass the **International Building,** with its famous bronze statue of Atlas carrying the world. Across the street is Rockefeller Center's famous neighbor, **St. Patrick's Cathedral,** seat of the Archdiocese of New York. You may want to step inside for a look at this graceful late 19th-century Gothic-style church—if you're lucky, there'll be a wedding to watch.

TIMES SQUARE

There was a time, not so long ago, when New York families strenuously avoided the Times Square area when out on the town with their kids. Those days are gone, with the development of what's called the new 42nd Street, a family-friendly theme park of cinemas and restaurants and shops. This being New York, of course, there are plenty of curmudgeons around who bewail the death of the old sleazy Forty Deuce with its porn shops, XXX cinemas, and ragged street people. I cannot concur.

Start at the intersection of 42nd Street and Seventh Avenue, where there's a theme restaurant (the **ESPN Zone**) on the northeast corner and a theme store (the **Warner Bros. Studio Store**) on the northwest. As you head west on 42nd Street, you'll pass two gloriously restored theaters—Disney's ornate **New Amsterdam Theater** on the south side of the street and the **New Victory Theater** on the north—both of which specialize in family entertainment. On the north side of the drag you'll pass the **Museum Store,** a themed-to-the-max games arcade (**Broadway City**), and a **Yankees Clubhouse** store; the south side boasts a spiffed-up food court and a New York branch of **Madame Tussaud's.** Toward the end of the block, two megamultiplex cinemas face off across 42nd Street closer to Eighth Avenue— the 13-screen **Loews** (with a homage-to-Broadway lobby and a great retro neon sign flashing on the facade) and the 25-screen **AMC Empire,** which boasts the gilded moldings and frescoed dome of an old Broadway theater as its lobby. Flanking them are two new chain hotels: a Hilton on the south side and a Westin across the street.

If you head north up Broadway from 42nd Street, you'll pass a number of theme restaurants—**WWF New York** at 44th Street, the **Official All Star Café** at 45th,

Mars 2112 at 51st (see chapter 9). The **MTV studio** on the mezzanine level of 1515 Broadway (between 44th and 45th streets, on the west side) has floor-to-ceiling windows and cameras trained on the passing crowd below, while the *Good Morning America* gang holds court catercorner to MTV, on the southeast corner of 44th and Broadway. *Late Night with David Letterman* frequently films segments on the street outside the **Ed Sullivan Theater,** up at 53rd and Broadway. Tourists flock into the bright and busy **Times Square Visitors Center** on Seventh Avenue between 46th and 47th streets, which even has a 24-hour McDonalds (this is, after all, the City That Never Sleeps).

Kids may not even need to enter any particular attractions to enjoy the unabashed razzle-dazzle of Times Square, where immense advertising signs are designed to be as bright and as gimmicky as possible. Just plant yourselves on one of the mid-Broadway islands and crane your neck. My kids especially love the **Eight O'Clock Bean Coffee sign,** with steam rising from a giant cup of coffee. The **huge video screen** that faces uptown from a skyscraper at 43rd between Broadway and Seventh is distracting to drivers but fascinating to kids. Don't be ashamed to gawk; we all do.

2 Downtown

LOBBY HOPPING AROUND WALL STREET

In New York's financial center, you can almost *hear* the money being made. Even if the notion of rubbing shoulders with titans of commerce doesn't enthrall your children, they should be amazed by the urban canyons of this narrow-street, skyscraper crammed neighborhood, the prototype of many a futuristic movie or video game landscape.

Begin at the corner of Broad and Pearl streets, where the modern **85 Broad St.** building pays tribute to the archeological past: The curved lobby shows where old Stone Street used to run, and the Pearl Street sidewalks outside contain glassed-over pits revealing foundations of the old **Stadt Huys,** the town hall of 17th-century Nieuw Amsterdam. Follow Pearl Street down to State Street and turn left. Even if you're not visiting the National Museum of the American Indian (see chapter 4), go inside the **Alexander Hamilton Customs House** on Bowling Green, Broadway, and State streets, across from Battery Park. Just past the museum's front desk (admission is free) is the glorious Grand Rotunda, with a huge circular ceiling mural celebrating New York.

Heading up Broadway, stop in the **U.S. Post Office at 25 Broadway** to check out the painted vaulted ceilings, a glorious celebration of transatlantic travel dating from 1921, when this room was the booking office for the Cunard Lines's New York office. Continue on Broadway past the venerable Gothic-style **Trinity Church,** tucked among the skyscrapers at the head of Wall Street. Between Dey and Fulton streets is **195 Broadway**—built from 1915 to 1922 as AT&T headquarters—looking like a wedding cake stacked with several levels of classical columns. This facade has more columns than that of any other building in the world. Go in the lobby to see even more columns. Then proceed up to the **Woolworth Building** at Park Place and Broadway, which was the world's tallest building from 1913 to 1930. In its pre-deco heyday, the Woolworth Building was a prime exemplar of Gothic skyscraper design, and the lobby's sculptured ceiling is worth several minutes' study. Ask your kids to look for the self-portrait of the architect hugging his building in his arms and a Scrooge-like caricature of Mr. Woolworth hoarding his wealth.

GREENWICH VILLAGE

Start in the heart of the Village, **Washington Square,** with its white triumphal arch at the foot of Fifth Avenue. The red-brick houses facing the north side of the square look totally 19th century, dating from a time when Greenwich Village really was a separate country village. Much of the rest of Washington Square is now surrounded by the modern buildings of **New York University,** but the park's crowd is a democratic mélange of all sorts of New Yorkers, not just college students. Weekends usually attract street performers, and on many afternoons there are informal speed-chess competitions going on beneath the shade trees at the southwest corner of the park.

For a taste of the bohemian Village, go south from the park (down Thompson, Sullivan, or MacDougal) to **Bleecker Street,** lined with cheap ethnic restaurants and long-established music clubs. Go west on Bleecker Street across Sixth Avenue, where Bleecker takes an unpredictable angle north, like many of the West Village streets. This is an Italian part of the village, with some great food shops selling coffee, bread, pastries, cheese, and pork and sausage. If you've got older kids who are hardy walkers, follow Bleecker all the way across Seventh Avenue, turn left on Grove Street, and go west until Grove dead-ends at the charming church of **St. Luke's–in–the–Fields.** The well-preserved 19th-century look of this quiet neighborhood makes it popular for TV and movie shots; the apartment where TV's *Friends* supposedly live is on the corner of Grove Street and Bedford. Go north on Hudson to West 10th Street, turn right, and return east to Sixth Avenue.

At Sixth Avenue and West 9th Street, the castlelike red-brick building on your left is **Jefferson Market,** originally a courthouse and now a branch of the public library. Turn right (east) onto West 11th Street. The brick wall on your right surrounds a tiny cemetery, one of several belonging to **Shearith Israel,** the oldest Jewish congregation in the country. Continue down the block, lined with classic brick town houses, until you see one that's startlingly modern—**18 W. 11th St.** Inside the large picture window, the owner's stuffed Paddington bear is usually dressed in a timely fashion, with a yellow slicker on if it's raining, a Yankees or Mets cap in baseball season, depending on which team is winning. Soon after, you'll be back at Fifth Avenue—turn right to get back to Washington Square or left to make a stop at the Forbes Magazine Galleries (see "More Manhattan Museums" in chapter 4) with its collections of toy soldiers, toy boats, and Fabergé eggs.

THE EAST VILLAGE

Gentrified but still urban cool, the funky East Village is a magnet for preteens and teenagers determined to prove their hipness quotient. Start on **Astor Place,** the busy intersection of Fourth Avenue, Lafayette Street, and East 8th Street, where sidewalk peddlers usually hawk everything from hammered silver jewelry to vinyl LPs to well-thumbed paperbacks to secondhand lamps and furniture. The hulking brownstone building to the south is **Cooper Union,** a progressive school of architecture, art, and engineering founded in 1859. Head east on what should be 8th Street, here called **St. Mark's Place;** busy day and night, the block of St. Mark's between Third and Second avenues is lined with vintage-clothing stores, bookstores, coffeehouses, and cafes. Beatniks hung out here in the 1950s, hippies in the 1960s, punks in the 1970s. (Somewhat incongruously, this neighborhood also has long-established enclaves of Ukrainian immigrants, centered on 7th Street, and Russian immigrants, on 9th and 10th streets, as you can see if you stroll around farther.)

At Second Avenue, you may want to turn left and go 2 blocks north to the **Second Avenue Deli** (southeast corner of Second Avenue and 10th Street). Stars set in the sidewalk in front celebrate long-ago stars of the golden age of Yiddish theater, which was centered along this stretch of Second Avenue. On the northwest corner of this intersection, the fieldstone **St. Mark's–in–the–Bowery Church** is the city's oldest continually used church building—Peter Stuyvesant, the famous governor of the Dutch colony of Nieuw Amsterdam, used to worship here. In fact, this area used to be his farm, and **Stuyvesant Street,** which angles south back to Astor Place, is named for him. Stroll past the early 19th-century town houses on Stuyvesant Street and try to imagine what the Village looked like back then—before the beatniks, hippies, and punks took over.

If you're looking for club-kid coolness, follow St. Mark's Place until it ends at Avenue A. (Manhattan widens here, requiring a set of lettered avenues to be added east of the numbered ones—hence the neighborhood's nickname, Alphabet City.) You'll be at **Tompkins Square** (bounded by Avenue A, East 7th Street, Avenue B, and East 10th Street), the site of bloody confrontations in the late 1980s between the police and a resident camp of homeless people. Today it has been thoroughly spruced up—a controversial move in this politically conscious neighborhood, long the low-rent-or-no-rent domain of squatters, struggling artists, and drug dealers. Avenue A is lined with funky shops and cafes, well worth scoping out.

CHINATOWN

Begin on **Canal Street,** the major thoroughfare cutting across Manhattan at this point; Canal Street used to be the northern boundary of Chinatown before its population spilled over into Little Italy and the Lower East Side. Walk east from Centre Street to the Bowery on the south side of Canal Street, where a string of produce and fish stores offer wares on the sidewalks. Point out to your kids the Chinese lettering on every sign and the pagoda-shaped pay-phone stations. Turn right (south) at the Bowery. On the Bowery's east side, a gargantuan statue of the Chinese philosopher Confucius dominates the little plaza in front of **Confucius Plaza,** a modern red-brick residential development.

Continue south on the Bowery 2 blocks to the frantic intersection called **Chatham Square,** with its big Chinese arch in the middle. Then backtrack on the Bowery a few steps to narrow sloping Pell Street, where you turn left. A Hong Kong–like jumble of restaurants and neon signs, Pell leads you west 1 block to busy Mott Street, a crowded and decidedly unglitzy shopping street. Barbecued ducks hang in glass shopfronts, candy shops sell pastel-colored imported sweets, and twanging recorded music leaks out into the street. Turn right on Mott and go 1 block to Bayard Street, where you turn left and go 1 block to Mulberry. The **Museum of Chinese in the Americas** (see "More Manhattan Museums" in chapter 4) is on your right and Columbus Park on your left, where Chinatown residents old and young congregate. If your kids are young enough to enjoy a swing and slide, stop in **Columbus Park**'s playground for some closer contact with the locals.

LITTLE ITALY

There's not much left to this classic tenement neighborhood, what with Chinatown encroaching on the south and SoHo on the west; you and your kids can easily do the whole bit in half an hour, even if you stop along the way to check out the authentic little shops. From Canal Street, walk up **Mulberry Street** to Houston Street, past several Italian restaurants that thrive on the tourist trade; don't miss

Umberto's Clam House at 129 Mulberry St., site of a famous 1973 Mafia hit, when a wiseguy named Joey Gallo was rubbed out.

On Mulberry and the streets branching off it, look for stores selling religious medals and figures and others selling glorious foodstuffs—fresh pastas, imported olive oil and vinegars, Baci chocolates, tangy gelati (Italian ices). At the intersection of Mulberry and Broome streets, **Caffé Roma,** 385 Broome St., is a great old-fashioned tile-floored pastry shop where you can stop for cannoli and espresso. Look above the shop signs to see the tracery of iron fire escapes hanging out over the street, a distinguishing feature of these turn-of-the-20th-century tenement buildings, which slumlords designed to cram in as many small rooms as possible onto the narrow lots.

Things get quieter above Spring Street. At the leafy little paved **De Salvio Square** park, on the southeast corner of Spring and Mulberry, locals gather on summer weekend nights to watch **Italian classic movies,** projected on the wall by a filmmaker from Rome. Another block up Mulberry is **Old St. Patrick's Cathedral,** the 19th-century precursor to Midtown's big Catholic cathedral, now a parish church. Behind the red-brick walls lies a tiny cemetery where some of the city's early Roman Catholic bishops are buried; scenes from Martin Scorsese's seminal Little Italy film *Mean Streets* were shot here.

LOWER EAST SIDE

Once a teeming slum for waves of new immigrants, the Lower East Side has been "discovered" by artistic types, ever on the lookout for cheap apartments. The main shopping drag, **Orchard Street,** though still dominated by discount clothing and dry goods stores (mostly Jewish-owned—the district shuts up tight on Saturday), now has renovated storefronts and a sprinkling of trendy boutiques. The surrounding architecture, however, is still classic tenement buildings everywhere, and the district's immigrant past is preserved at the fascinating **Lower East Side Tenement Museum** (see chapter 4). While you're down here, wander around a little and enjoy a good nosh. Start out at the unassuming **Kossar's** (367 Grand St., between Orchard and Allen streets), a glorious time warp of a bagel factory where customers can watch the bakers slide trays full of ring-shaped dough into a vintage oven. The bialys are incredibly dense and flavorful, especially when you get them warm. Pickle lovers (you know who you are) should head east on Grand and turn up Essex to make a beeline for **Hollander Pickles** (35 Essex St., between Grand and Hester streets), which is where Peter Reigert worked in the film *Crossing Delancey.* Go back to Seward Park, which lies south of Grand and east of Essex, to work up a little appetite. Then go west on Grand to Orchard Street, turn right (north), and work your way past the many stores on Orchard Street until you reach East Houston Street. Turn left and go to Forsyth Street, where **Yonah Schimmel's Knishes** (137 E. Houston St.) is worth a stop for an amazing selection of those Yiddish delicacies—pockets of thin dough stuffed with everything from kasha to blueberries to sweet potatoes. Backtrack toward Orchard Street for **Russ and Daughters** (179 E. Houston St.), a long-established family deli specializing in cheese, whitefish, and herring. Most businesses depend on a son taking over, but the original Mr. Russ, a crusty Eastern European, found the key to his success by stationing his three pretty daughters behind the counter, and business has thrived for at least eight decades. If you still have any appetite left, put it to rest at **Katz's Delicatessen** (East Houston Street at Ludlow Street), where you can sit down and order blintzes, corned beef, and wonderful salami sandwiches.

3 Uptown

MORNINGSIDE HEIGHTS

The upper end of the Upper West Side, this neighborhood is Manhattan's college town, with Columbia University, Barnard College, the Union Theological Seminary, and the Jewish Theological Seminary all clustered along Broadway from 116th to 122nd streets. The place to start, however, is at 112th Street and Amsterdam Avenue, on the front steps of the Episcopal **Cathedral Church of St. John the Divine.** This will be the largest cathedral in the world if they ever finish building it; they've been at it for over a century, since 1892, but if your kids have studied medieval history at all, they'll know that most of the great European cathedrals took a couple of centuries to complete too. Notice how only two of the arches over the front doors have statues in them; empty niches in the other arches await future stone carvers' work. Go inside and stroll around, stopping on the north aisle at Poet's Corner, where paving stones honor selected American poets. St. John the Divine is so huge that the Statue of Liberty could fit under the central dome, and the tiny-looking figure of Christ you see in the rose window over the front doors is actually life-size. Stop in the wonderful gift shop, which has some books and toys for kids, to a see a model of what the cathedral should look like when completed. Then go out to the garden just south of the cathedral to see the Children's Fountain, a fanciful huge sculpture surrounded by peewee sculptures created by local schoolchildren. On the lawns of the surrounding cathedral close, you can sometimes spot a pair of peacocks strutting and preening.

Go north on Amsterdam Avenue. (If your kids are good walkers, you may want to detour at 113th Street, turn right to head over to Morningside Drive, and walk north to 116th Street for a great vista across the steep slope of Morningside Park and Harlem to the east.) At 117th Street and Amsterdam, pass through the wrought-iron gates into **Columbia University,** New York's entry in the Ivy League. As you cross the campus, notice the broad steps of Low Memorial Library on your right; parents may remember it as the site of the famous student protests in 1968, but kids will recognize it as the place where Dan Aykroyd, Bill Murray, and Harold Ramis decided to leave academic research and become full-time Ghostbusters.

Exit the campus through the matching set of gates onto Broadway and cross the street to enter the gates of **Barnard College,** Columbia's all-women sister college. Or head north on Broadway to 120th Street: Columbia's **Teachers College** is the big, dark, red-brick building on the northeast corner, and the **Union Theological Seminary** is the medieval-looking gray stone complex on the northwest corner. (**Jewish Theological Seminary** is a red-brick fortress on the northeast corner of Broadway and 122nd Street.) Turn left on 120th Street and go west to Riverside Drive, where **Riverside Church** stands on the right. If its pale limestone reminds you of a Gothic version of Rockefeller Center, it's no coincidence, since John J. Rockefeller was one of its founders in 1930. Step inside to take the elevator to the top of the 356-foot-tall bell tower. Across Riverside Drive and several yards north sits the columned neoclassical **Grant National Memorial Monument,** where President Ulysses S. Grant and his wife, Julia, are buried. (Ask your kids the corny old joke: "Who's buried in Grant's Tomb?") Admission is free—step inside and peer down into the sunken chamber where their dark marble tombs are laid. It can be deliciously creepy if you think about it, though the high-ceilinged memorial has a few other distractions, including a National Parks Service information stand and some interesting exhibits about Grant's life and the Civil War he won for the Union.

My kids' favorite part is outside, in the plaza around the tomb, with its nutty mosaic benches designed by New York's public school students. We usually repair afterward to the **Claremont Playground,** in the park just north of the memorial, then meander south down the broad sidewalk on the west side of Riverside Drive, overlooking shady **Riverside Park.**

4 Brooklyn

CROSSING THE BROOKLYN BRIDGE

As thrilling a sight as this beautiful brown-hued East River bridge is from afar, with its Gothic-style towers and lacy mesh of cables, the view from the bridge is even more thrilling. A **boardwalk-like pedestrian walkway** goes all the way across, raised slightly above the car traffic. One mile long, it should take about half an hour to traverse—except you'll be tempted to stop more than once to ooh and ahh at the vision of Manhattan's skyscrapers thrusting upward, with the great harbor and Verrazano Bridge beyond.

Why has the Brooklyn Bridge captured the popular imagination so much more than its neighbors to the north, the Manhattan and Williamsburg bridges? Well, for one thing, it scored one historic first—it was the first steel-wire suspension bridge in the world when it opened in 1883. Until then, the only way to get from Manhattan to Brooklyn, at that time separate cities, had been via ferry (crossing from Manhattan's Fulton Street to Brooklyn's Fulton Street, both named after steamship inventor Robert Fulton, who operated the ferry company). You can imagine what a difference the bridge made in consolidating the New York metropolis.

As you walk over, wow your kids with some of the bridge's history. It took 16 years to build, from 1867 to 1883, and you could say it seemed to have a bit of a curse on it—the original designer, John A. Roebling, died from tetanus contracted when his foot was crushed while surveying the site, and his son, Washington, who took over the job, fell ill with the bends after diving into the river to supervise the workmen laying the pilings. A virtual invalid afterward, Washington Roebling watched the bridge going up through a telescope from his house in nearby Brooklyn Heights, while his wife actually supervised much of the completion of the project.

Since then, however, the Brooklyn Bridge has become a byword in New York lore. The standard old joke defines a con artist as a guy trying to sell rubes the deed to the Brooklyn Bridge ("Brother, have I got a bridge to sell you. . . ."). Cocky teenage hoodlums have proved their bravado by shinnying up its cables, and suicides with a flair for the dramatic have plummeted to their deaths from those same cables into the tidal currents below. The bridge has appeared in countless movies and TV shows, its outline practically synonymous with New York City.

The entrance ramps to the bridge begin by the plaza in front of the city's **Municipal Building,** along Centre Street just south of Chambers Street. Be aware, though, that things get awfully windy once you're over the water, and the sensation of being suspended in midair gives some people vertigo. The bridge's pedestrian ramps empty out into Brooklyn's downtown, which is a bit of a wasteland on weekends. It isn't a far walk from here to **Brooklyn Heights,** one of the loveliest brownstone neighborhoods you'll ever see—but you'd better be armed with a map and look like you know where you're going. If your kids aren't hardy urban trekkers, consider walking just halfway to get the view and then doubling back to Manhattan. If you're on bicycles (and yes, the walkway is a perfectly fine place to bike, though it's a very long ascent) going all the way to Brooklyn is a better bet.

5 New York Movie Sites

Sometimes it seems that if New York hadn't existed, Hollywood would've had to invent it to get the perfect movie set. From its instantly recognizable skyline to such iconic sites as Rockefeller Plaza, the Plaza Hotel, Central Park, and the World Trade Center, much of Manhattan has appeared on film so often that most Americans feel they know it before they ever visit. The city government welcomes movie companies shooting on location, and my kids learned from an early age what it means when a phalanx of trailers, lighting equipment, and headset-wearing production assistants descends suddenly upon a neighborhood. And you know what? We still get excited when we see our hometown in the movies.

Fans of the 1988 hit **Big** will no doubt want to check out **FAO Schwarz,** the mega–toy store at 58th Street and Fifth Avenue where Tom Hanks tap-danced on a giant keyboard in the movie's signature scene. **Home Alone 2,** the sequel to Macaulay Culkin's first big hit, takes place in New York; Kevin stays at the **Plaza Hotel,** Fifth Avenue and 59th Street, conveniently across from Central Park—the robbers (played by Joe Pesci and Daniel Stern) spot him ice-skating at the park's **Wollman Rink.** Kevin also hangs out at **Rockefeller Plaza** to gape at the giant Christmas tree and has a heart-to-heart with the Pigeon Lady who lives in the attic of **Carnegie Hall,** Seventh Avenue at 57th Street. The climax is set in a fictitious Upper West Side brownstone on West 95th Street between Central Park West and Columbus Avenue.

The 1984 comedy **Splash,** starring Tom Hanks and Darryl Hannah, features the **Statue of Liberty,** in New York Harbor, where Hannah's mermaid first comes ashore; after Hanks takes her to his bachelor apartment in the **Tudor City complex** (east of Second Avenue between 41st and 43rd streets), she makes her way to **Bloomingdale's,** 59th Street and Lexington Avenue, where a session in front of a bank of TVs quickly teaches her to speak the language of dry land. Later, Hanks and his brother, played by John Candy, smuggle the mermaid away from scientists at the **American Museum of Natural History,** on Central Park West at 79th Street.

The 1978 **Superman,** starring Christopher Reeve and Margot Kidder, features the **Daily News Building,** 220 E. 42nd St., as the headquarters of the *Daily Planet.* Superman skims down the long sleek facade of the skyscraper at **9 W. 57th St.** to catch a falling child. Lex Luthor has his subterranean lair underneath **Grand Central Terminal,** 42nd Street and Park Avenue, and Lois Lane lives in the penthouse of **240 Central Park South,** just east of Columbus Circle—the outside terrace being handy for those fly-in dates with Superman.

The classic 1947 Christmas movie **Miracle on 34th Street** kicks off with the Macy's Thanksgiving Day Parade, as Maureen O'Hara fires a drunken parade Santa and hires Kris Kringle on **West 81st Street,** just off Central Park West. O'Hara's daughter, played by young Natalie Wood, watches the parade from their apartment window in an unspecified building along Central Park West. At the **Macy's** department store in Midtown, 34th Street and Broadway, Kringle revolutionized retailing by sending families across the street to the now-defunct Gimbel's store at 33rd and Broadway (where the Manhattan Mall is today) if Macy's didn't have the right toys. The main **U.S. Post Office** at Eighth Avenue between 31st and 33rd streets is where sacks of mail addressed to Santa Claus were collected and delivered to Kringle downtown at the **New York County Courthouse,** 60 Centre St., happily putting an end to his insanity trial.

Older kids may have seen that quintessential Manhattan movie **Breakfast at Tiffany's,** the 1961 charmer starring Audrey Hepburn and George Peppard.

Prominently featured is **Tiffany & Co.,** the elegant jewelry store at Fifth Avenue and 57th Street; the Upper East Side town house where Hepburn's Holly Golightly lives is at **171 E. 71st St.** (look for the distinctive green-striped awning). Hepburn and Peppard make an excursion to the **New York Public Library,** Fifth Avenue at 42nd Street, to find a copy of his recently published book; Peppard and Buddy Ebsen (as Holly's husband) have a poignant scene later at the **Bandshell in Central Park,** midpark just south of the Bethesda Fountain, at 72nd Street, now a popular weekend area for in-line skating.

One of the great Manhattan movies of all time, the 1984 film *Ghostbusters* really used the city well. It starts out in Midtown at the **New York Public Library,** Fifth Avenue at 42nd Street, where a little old lady librarian flips her card catalog at an onslaught of spirits. The team of paranormal researchers played by Dan Aykroyd, Harold Ramis, and Bill Murray teach uptown at **Columbia University,** Broadway and 117th Street, until they set up shop as Ghostbusters in an old fire station at **14 Moore St.,** at Hudson Street in TriBeCa. An urgent call from an attractive cellist, played by Sigourney Weaver, brings them to **55 Central Park West,** at 65th Street, where a spirit named Gozer has taken up residence in her refrigerator; looking up at this varicolored art deco building, however, you'll note that the top looks significantly different from the way it did in the movie—an elaborate rooftop was matted in. The nerdy accountant down the hall, played by Rick Moranis, becomes possessed and roams glassy-eyed outside **Tavern on the Green,** the festively lit restaurant across the street in Central Park at West 65th Street. And when the evil spirit turns into a giant Stay-Puft Marshmallow man, it wades up Central Park West from Columbus Circle, 59th Street and Central Park West, looking for all the world like a Macy's Parade balloon (the parade passes through Columbus Circle every Thanksgiving Day).

For the Active Family 6

It's a fallacy to assume that New Yorkers are soft, flabby city people who never get any exercise. On the contrary, we end up walking much more than car-dependent suburbanites do, and the city's complement of huge parks makes it supereasy to ride bikes, play tennis, jog or stroll, toss a Frisbee, fly a kite, skate, or skateboard, not to mention feed ducks or squirrels and watch boats drift lazily past.

But New York parents as a breed tend to be too compulsive to just laze around in the parks—at the drop of a hat they'll enlist their children in classes for anything from chess and computers to horseback riding and fencing. Staying active in New York is a 12-months-a-year proposition, and neither the dog days of summer nor the ice days of winter are allowed to slow down kids' activities. Though many classes and workshops are only available for full-series enrollment, I've listed below a number of drop-in classes, both weekday and weekend, for visiting families and for local kids who want to do something on the spur of the moment.

1 Green New York: The Top Parks

Though New York is studded with squares where you can find a patch of grass and some benches, it has only a handful of parks large enough for a real exploration. Some of these are somewhat off the beaten track: **Flushing Meadows–Corona Park** in Queens (take the no. 7 train to 111th Street or Willets Point/Shea Stadium) and **Van Cortlandt Park** in the Bronx (take the no. 1 or 9 train to 242nd Street) are both loaded with recreational facilities, but they're so big and spread out you can't just ramble around aimlessly. **Fort Tryon Park** at the northern end of Manhattan (take the A train to 190th Street), a wooded strip of park on high ground overlooking the Hudson River, is lovely if somewhat overgrown, but it's far enough off the beaten path that it's not worth a special trip unless you're already coming to visit the Cloisters branch of the Metropolitan Museum of Art (which you definitely should do—see chapter 4). Then there's compact **Riverbank State Park,** perched over the Hudson River at the western end of 145th Street, which offers a slew of topnotch recreational facilities (see "Sports & Games" below) but hardly any untrammeled grass. For other green pleasures in the city, see "Gardens" and "Nature Centers" in chapter 4.

New Yorkers, however, more than make do with the five great parks below. The larger three—Central Park, Riverside Park, and Prospect Park—were laid out in the 19th century by the team of Frederick Law Olmsted and Calvert Vaux, a pair of inspired amateurs who virtually invented the art of urban landscape design. These guys really knew how to maximize space, with twisting paths and artful hills and dales that make you feel as though you've left the city as soon as you're 10 paces inside the park. Later park commissioners slapped on recreational amenities like tennis courts and playgrounds that may not strictly have been what Olmsted and Vaux envisioned, but nothing has seriously marred the beauty of these detailed landscapes.

✪ **Central Park.** From 59th to 110th sts., between Central Park West (Eighth Ave.) and Fifth Ave. ☎ **212/360-3444.** Event hotline: 888/NY-PARKS or 212/360-3456. www.centralparknyc. org. Subway: 1/9 to Columbus Circle; B/Q to 57th St.; N/R to Fifth Ave.; B/C to any stop from Columbus Circle to 110th St.; 4/5/6 to any stop from 59th St. to 103rd St.

At 840 acres, this park—one of the world's greatest—is a vital resource for the city. Set right in the middle of things, with frequent entrances cut into its low brownstone wall, it separates the Upper West Side from the Upper East Side, lying between Midtown at the south end and Harlem at the north end. It's big enough to give you a real sense of escape, and when you're walking around the park the only roads you have to deal with are the circular park drive and one cross-cut at 72nd Street; both are closed to car traffic weekdays 10am to 3pm and 7 to 10pm, as well as 7pm Friday to 6am Monday (holidays are traffic-free too). Four other east–west streets cross the park—66th, 79th, 86th, and 96th—but they're cunningly hidden beneath overpasses so you'll never notice them.

The section of the park below 72nd Street is somewhat formal. Starting at 59th Street and Fifth Avenue—where **horse-drawn carriages** line up to give tourists a ridiculously overpriced ($34 for 20 minutes) ride through the park—you'll find the **Pond,** a picturesque small body of water reflecting Midtown skyscrapers. Just northwest of this lie the **Wollman Rink,** where you can ice-skate in winter and roller-skate in summer (see "Sports & Games," later in this chapter), and the **Dairy** visitor center (see chapter 4); from the Dairy, follow a path west under an arch to the **Carousel** (see chapter 4). The **ball fields** west and south of here are fun even for spectators on summer weekday evenings, when some very competitive after-work leagues slug it out. As you walk up the West Drive past **Tavern on the Green** restaurant (see chapter 9), your kids may be interested to know that it was originally built as a sheepfold in 1870 when the **Sheep Meadow,** the broad fenced-in green lawn on your right, still was used for grazing sheep; the sloping drive here is a prime spot for skateboarders and in-line skaters showing off their tricks. Midpark, east of the Sheep Meadow, is a paved road that swarms with volleyball games and in-line skaters on weekends. The **Mineral Springs Pavilion** just north of the Sheep Meadow has a **snack bar** and **rest rooms.**

Go north across 72nd Street to **Strawberry Fields,** a gem of a bit of landscape laid out in memory of Beatle John Lennon, who lived across Central Park West from here in the Dakota apartment building (he was shot out front). My sons, both of them next-generation Beatlemaniacs, love to hang out here. It seems there are always flowers laid in tribute to Lennon on the black-and-white mosaic medallion that reads IMAGINE. Across the drive to the northeast lies the **Lake,** a body of water larger than the Pond—large enough, in fact, for boating. To rent rowboats, cross the park along the 72nd Street Transverse. Along the way, though, stop off at two postcard views that even your kids may recognize from scores of movies and TV

Central Park Attractions

Information ⓘ

Subway stop Ⓜ

Path of Animal Statue Walk - - - - -

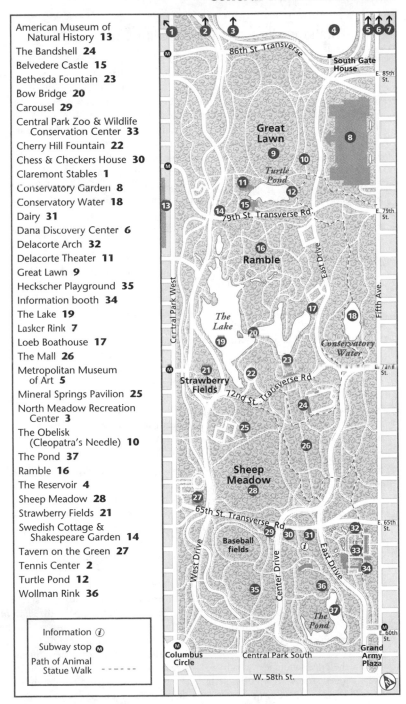

86th St. Transverse

South Gate House

E. 85th St.

Great Lawn

Turtle Pond

79th St. Transverse Rd.

E. 79th St.

Ramble

East Drive

Central Park West

The Lake

Conservatory Water

Fifth Ave.

E. 71st St.

Strawberry Fields

72nd St. Transverse Rd.

Sheep Meadow

65th St. Transverse Rd.

E. 65th St.

West Drive

Baseball fields

Center Drive

East Drive

The Pond

E. 60th St.

Grand Army Plaza

Columbus Circle

Central Park South

W. 58th St.

Stalking the Animal Statues in Central Park

In the course of half an hour's walk, you and your kids can bag a couple dozen animals in the wilds of Central Park—statue animals, that is.

Start on the northwest corner of East 79th Street and Fifth Avenue. A few steps into the park, on your right are **(1–3) three bronze bears,** a copy of a Paul Manship statue that's in the Metropolitan Museum directly north. Continue on the path into the park, going through a vaulted tunnel under the East Drive and veering to your left (south) to reach the east end of Turtle Pond. There you'll find King Jagiello of Poland astride a **(4) magnificent horse.** Stroll uphill to your left to the drive and walk downtown (south) on the road, keeping to the right-hand jogging path if there's car traffic in the park. About halfway down the hill, atop a massive rock outcropping on your right, crouches a **(5) bronze panther,** peering out of the foliage ready to pounce on unsuspecting joggers.

Cross the East Drive at the pedestrian crossing near the Loeb Boathouse and walk a few yards south to a dirt path cutting east over the grass; a short, steep slope brings you to a path leading south to the Conservatory Water. The Alice in Wonderland statue at the pond's north end has not only the **(6) White Rabbit** but also the **(7) Cheshire Cat,** Alice's **(8) kitten Dinah,** and **(9) assorted mice,** along with the usual number of children climbing all over the giant mushrooms. Swing around to the west side of the pond to find the **(10) Ugly Duckling** waddling past the statue of Danish storyteller Hans Christian Andersen.

Take either path leading south from the Conservatory Water up the hill to the 72nd Street Transverse; cross 72nd Street and go to the west side of the circular drive. On your right, the ground rises to the Rumsey Playground (less a playground these days than a plaza for special events). Set amid the steps rising to Rumsey's entrance gate is a big **(11) stone goose,** with who else but Mother Goose riding on its back. (Walk around to identify carved scenes from various nursery rhymes.) Go east past Rumsey and bear right, crossing the plaza in front

shows: Turn left at **Cherry Hill Fountain** and walk over lovely **Bow Bridge,** or take either the lakeside path or 72nd Street to **Bethesda Terrace,** a grand lakeshore plaza featuring the **Bethesda Fountain.** The lakeside path continues, winding north to the **Loeb Boathouse** (☎ 212/517-2233), where you can rent boats and also get something to eat at the **Boathouse snack bar** (the Park View restaurant here is an upscale affair and not particularly child-friendly, alas). The boathouse is open daily April to October, 10am to 6:30pm, depending on the weather; rowboat rental is $10 per hour (cash only, $30 deposit required), and there's also an honest-to-goodness gondola you can rent, April to October, for $30 per half hour.

Across East Drive and just above 72nd Street, the **Conservatory Water** is a fun area even for the littlest ones, with its large serene formal pool—the *Alice in Wonderland* statue at the north end features a giant mushroom that just begs to be clambered on. April to September, you can rent 41-inch-long radio-controlled model sailboats ($10 per hour) from a stand beside the boathouse here. There's a cafe on the pond's east side, which also has **rest rooms.** Stroll back south through a shady green strip with winding paths, passing a couple of good playgrounds (see "The Playground Lowdown," later in this chapter). As you head downhill toward a rugged stone arch, expect to see a gaggle of sidewalk performers on weekends, some of the Bandshell (watch for roller-skaters on weekends!). At the western edge of the plaza you'll find a **(12–13) pair of eagles** devouring a hapless **(14) mountain goat.** Continue west on 72nd Street. On your left, just before 72nd Street meets the West Drive, look up on another big outcropping to find the **(15) falcon** lighting on the glove of the Falconer.

Retrace your steps east on 72nd Street until you reach the Dead Road, that broad asphalt lane bordering the Sheep Meadow, where skaters and volleyball games proliferate on warm-weather weekends. Follow the Dead Road south to find the Indian hunter with his faithful **(16) dog.** Turn left, following the circular drive past the foot of the Mall; go under the drive via a brick-vaulted tunnel (try out the echoes). The path swings uphill on the east side of the drive to reach one of the most famous animal statues in the park, **(17) Balto the sled dog,** hero of a 1995 animated film.

From here the path leads south through another underpass past the gates of the Children's Zoo; look for a **(18–19) pair of goats** prancing atop the zoo's wrought-iron entrance arch. On through a second underpass, you'll come up to the red-brick Delacorte Arch. In a niche to the right of the arch is a bronze **(20) dancing bear,** and the glockenspiel on top of the arch features **(21–26) a hippo, a goat, a penguin, a kangaroo, an elephant, and a bear**—plus a **(27–28) pair of monkeys** squatting on top, hammering the bells. The musical clock performs on the hour and half hour; stick around to watch if possible. Then proceed south on the walkway past the Central Park Zoo; at the southern end of the zoo's red-brick structures, turn to your right to see another niche with a **(29) dancing goat** inside.

After stalking all this sculpted prey, your kids may well feel as mine did: "Mom, can we see some live animals now?" And here you are, right near the gates of the zoo, ready to grant their wish.

of whom are delightful to watch—allow for a little dawdling time. Passing through the arch brings you to the **Tisch Children's Zoo,** then south to the **Delacorte Arch,** with its delightful glockenspiel chiming every hour, and finally to the **Central Park Wildlife Center** (see chapter 4).

North of the Lake, the **Ramble** is a compact wilderness that's easier than you'd think to get lost in; navigate with care and stick to daylight hours when there are plenty of other folks around (unsavory types know it's the best place in the park for a mugging). Situated on a major North American flyway, this is, against all odds, a birdwatcher's paradise right in the middle of the big city, resonant with warbles, chirps, and hoots; the nature center at the nearby **Belvedere Castle** (see "Nature Centers" in chapter 4) can provide you with equipment to find and identify several species. Look overhead for nests and along the lake's marshy northern shore for frogs.

Above 79th Street, a pair of museums dominate the park: the **Metropolitan Museum of Art,** inside the park at East 82nd Street, and the **American Museum of Natural History,** facing the park at West 79th Street and Central Park West (see chapter 4). Midpark, between them, lies the **Great Lawn,** a huge stretch of grass and ball fields where crowds happily congregate in summer for events ranging from

Metropolitan Opera concerts to the special events such as the 1995 premiere of Disney's *Pocahontas* or the Sting concert in September 2000. At the south end of the Great Lawn, **Turtle Pond** protects a habitat for turtles, ducks, and dragonflies. To the west of it lie the **Delacorte Theater,** home of summer's free Shakespeare in the Park (and another essential set of **rest rooms**); the picturesque wooden **Swedish Cottage,** where daily marionette shows are held (see chapter 8); and, up on the hill, the **Shakespeare Garden** (see chapter 4) and **Belvedere Castle** with its nature center.

Between 86th and 96th streets, the major feature of the park is the **Jacqueline Kennedy Onassis Reservoir,** named in 1995 in honor of the presidential widow who lived for years nearby at 1040 Fifth Ave. (at 85th Street). A gravel path makes a 1.6-mile loop around the reservoir, much of it lined with cherry trees that are breathtaking in spring; there's also a bridle path circling the reservoir, where experienced riders can bring their mounts from the **Claremont Stables** on West 89th Street (see "Horseback Riding" under "Sports & Games," later in this chapter). Take a walk here, and you've got a very good chance of sighting horses, which is a treat for lots of kids. My boys like following the bridle path on the south end of the reservoir because it runs through the parking lot of Central Park's police precinct station, housed in an old set of red-brick stables along the 86th Street Transverse. North of the reservoir is the tan stucco **Tennis House** (see "Tennis" under "Sports & Games," later in this chapter), which also has **rest rooms.**

Above 96th Street, the east side of the park has two big attractions: the **Conservatory Garden,** at 105th Street and Fifth Avenue (see chapter 4), which has **rest rooms,** and **Harlem Meer,** the graceful pond at the northeast corner of the park, where the **Dana Discovery Center** (see chapter 4) runs nature workshops and hands out fishing poles so even youngsters can try their hand at angling in the meer. Midpark, right off of the 97th Street Transverse, the **North Meadow Recreation Center,** undiscovered by many Manhattanites, has lots of sports facilities, including well-groomed ball fields, handball courts, and climbing walls. See "Sports & Games," later in this chapter, for more details; the staff here will even lend you equipment for free (call ☎ **212/348-4867** to reserve equipment, and be sure to bring a valid photo I.D.). On the west side of the park, a stroll above 96th Street will take you to a picturesque and little-known area at West 100th Street: the **Pool,** a willow-fringed pond with a lively waterfall at the east end; my kids love to hang over the railing on the bridge and watch the cascading waters beneath. North of here, the **Great Hill** has a high, broad lawn perfectly suited to picnics. At the top of the park, at 110th Street, is the **Lasker Rink,** which converts in summer into the **Lasker Pool.** Be wary about going too deep into the park this far north, however, since it's less populated and the surrounding neighborhoods include some risky elements. I readily take my kids to the Pool and Harlem Meer on weekend days, and lots of families we know skate at Lasker Rink, but the social scene is rougher in summer when the rink turns into a pool. Be cautioned, too, that there are fewer people around on weekdays, and the possibility of a mugging rises proportionally.

Riverside Park. Between the Hudson River and Riverside Dr., from 72nd to 153rd sts. ☎ **212/408-0265** or 212/870-3070. Subway: 2/3 to 72nd St. or 96th St.; 1/9 to any stop from 72nd St. to 125th St.

Long, narrow Riverside Park really shows off designer Frederick Law Olmsted's ingenuity: Beneath it lie miles of underground railroad tracks, while the Henry Hudson Parkway, a major thoroughfare out of the city, bisects it lengthwise. You can't always get to the river shore as a result; the section of the park between the highway and the Hudson is overgrown and deserted in some spots and totally given over to playing fields in others. But between West 83rd and West 96th streets, Riverside Park features a broad paved **promenade** with stone railings where you can lean over and gaze west over the Hudson; the pavement here makes it super for leisurely biking and skating, though you'll have to weave through strolling crowds on summer Sundays. The **dog run** near 86th Street always manages to entertain children even if they don't have a pooch to exercise, and the **community garden** along the median strip at 91st Street is simply glorious.

At 72nd Street, 79th Street, and 86th Street, you can find paths going under the highway to the riverside promenade, a wide path leading past the **79th Street Boat Basin**—a marina full of bobbing houseboats, not all necessarily seaworthy. Most of the docks are private, but Pier A, the northernmost (just above 79th Street), is open to the public on weekends; stroll to the end and you'll get wonderful wide-open Hudson views, as well as close-up glimpses of the houseboats. The grassy shade behind the esplanade makes a good place for a picnic, or you can stop for a casual meal at the **West 79th Street Boat Basin Café** (see chapter 9).

The southern end of Riverside Park, from 72nd to 83rd streets, is flatter and more open than the rest of the park, and it is unbelievably beautiful in spring, when all the flowering trees unfurl. If you want to fly a kite, this can be a good place for it, with breezes blowing in from the river. The **playground** at 76th Street includes basketball courts where you can often watch some fierce hoop action. Above 96th Street the park gets more rustic and uncrowded, with some very steep paths plummeting down the slope from Riverside Drive. Up at 116th Street and in the lower section of the park at 96th Street, there are **tennis courts** (see "Tennis" under "Sports & Games," later in this chapter). Go all the way to 125th Street and you can visit the **Grant National Memorial Monument,** familiarly known as Grant's Tomb (see chapter 4). Nearby, at about 123rd Street, hunt for a much smaller and very touching memorial—a stone urn surrounded by iron palings, erected in memory of St. Clair Pollock, who died in 1797 at the age of 5.

Prospect Park. In Park Slope, Brooklyn. Bounded by Prospect Park West (Ninth Ave.), Eastern Pkwy., Flatbush Ave., Parkside Ave., and Prospect Park South. ☎ **718/965-8999.** www.prospectpark.org. Subway: 2/3 to Grand Army Plaza or Eastern Parkway; D to Prospect Park or Parkside Ave.; F to 15th St./Prospect Park.

Designers Frederick Law Olmsted and Calvert Vaux considered this park their crowning achievement, though it hasn't been kept up as well as Central Park. The main draws for kids are the super trio of attractions on the park's east side, along Flatbush Avenue: the **Prospect Park Wildlife Center,** the **Lefferts Homestead** house museum for children, and the **Prospect Park Carousel** (see chapter 4). Across Flatbush you'll find the **Brooklyn Museum** and the **Brooklyn Botanic Garden** (see chapter 4), which aren't part of the park proper but were always considered part of the overall scheme. On weekends and holidays, noon to 5pm, a free hourly trolley runs continually among all these attractions (call ☎ **718/965-8999** for schedule).

If outdoor activities are on your agenda, you may well want to head for the **Long Meadow,** 90 acres of rolling greensward just inside the park's ornate entrance on Grand Army Plaza. Warm-weather weekends always see plenty of picnic action on the meadow, with lots of families tossing Frisbees and working on little sluggers' pitching arms; it's not so great for kite-flying, since the meadow is set down in one huge gentle hollow. Brooklyn's sizable Middle Eastern and Caribbean populations give cookout hours here a special spicy aroma. In winter, the slopes along the edges of the meadow are just the ticket for trying out that new sled or pair of cross-country skis. The park's circular drive follows a 3.45-mile loop that's great for biking or in-line skating; follow it to the park's southern end, skirting the tangled woods and ravines in the middle of the park, and you'll find a 60-acre lake where you can rent four-person pedalboats (☎ **718/282-7789;** Thursday to Friday 11am to 4pm, Saturday, Sunday, and holidays noon to 6pm, $10 per hour); Prospect Park's own **Wollman Rink** sits on its northern shore.

Carl Schurz Park. Along the East River from East 84th to East 90th sts. Subway: 4/5/6 to 86th St.

Though not as extensive as its West Side counterpart, Riverside Park, Carl Schurz Park—named after a prominent 19th-century German immigrant who was a newspaper editor, senator, and cabinet member—offers some very good East River views, and, behind them, a few delicious green landscaped dells to wander through. Along the river, **John Finley Walk** (which actually continues south for several blocks past the park) is a paved promenade with wide-open views of the Triborough Bridge to the northeast, the railroad bridge spanning the rough waters of Hell Gate (a name that never fails to titillate my boys), and, across the river, the small lighthouse on the northern tip of Roosevelt Island; otherwise it's just warehouses and boxy modern apartment complexes across the water. No bikes or skating are allowed, but there's a dynamite enclosed **dog run** just inside the park about halfway up; come right before dinnertime and watch the dogs romp. Walk to the north end of the promenade, where it loops around **Gracie Mansion,** the mayor's yellow clapboard residence (built as a country house in 1799, when this still was country); stand by the railing and face south to see how this tranquil park actually is built over four lanes of car traffic, on the busy FDR Drive—another good example of New York City maximizing its real estate.

✪ **Hudson River Park/Battery Park City/Battery Park.** West of West St., from Chambers St. to the end of Manhattan. Subway: 1/2/3/9 to Chambers St.; C/E to World Trade Center; 4/5 to Bowling Green; 1/9 to South Ferry.

Although these three parks are operated by different authorities, in effect they create a nearly continuous strip of park along the Hudson shore from Manhattan's southern tip on north to Chambers Street and beyond, as plans progress for a bike path/promenade that may someday run all the way to 59th Street. Don't expect to find big green fields and woods; this is a narrow strip of landfill, much of it devoted to a paved riverside esplanade with inward-curving iron railings. But bicyclists and in-line skaters and joggers make good use of that esplanade, which connects to a bike path running along West Street up to the Village. Droves of other people simply lounge on the benches and stroll along gazing at the river and the harbor.

The oldest section, city-run **Battery Park,** is southernmost, occupying the tip of Manhattan Island. An expanse of grass with some fine old trees, it's crisscrossed by paved paths and dotted with statues; round brownstone **Castle Clinton** stands here, selling ferry tickets to the **Statue of Liberty** and **Ellis Island** (see chapter 4); the ferries embark from Battery Park's waterfront pilings. At the jutting prow of Manhattan Island, a delightful series of 37 cast-iron and bronze panels by Wopo Holup counterpoints scenes from city history with examples of its wildlife. Battery Park is generally thronged with tourists; hot-dog carts, T-shirt vendors, and street musicians are allowed in Battery Park but not in the other two parks, which are privately operated.

Battery Park City is a large mixed-use development, built in the early 1980s, with tony office/retail towers and some pleasant residential buildings. Its **Esplanade**

connects the whole. At the southern end, the **Museum of Jewish Heritage** presides over a terraced plaza with great harbor views. My kids are especially fond of the garden area around **South Cove,** where they can scamper over a small bridge and up into a postmodern gazebo echoing the Statue of Liberty's crown. At the heart of the **North Cove,** at the other end of the Esplanade, lies a grand yacht basin, surrounded by a pink granite plaza accented with fountains; opening onto this fine public space is the **Winter Garden Atrium** of the World Financial Center, an upscale retail development with stores and restaurants and lots of free cultural events.

North of the World Financial Center, the Esplanade runs on into **Hudson River Park,** which has a really excellent **playground** (see "The Playground Lowdown," below). There's a stunning **waterfall pool,** a large green lawn at the north end, and an outstanding **sculpture garden** so deliriously full of fancy that kids are bound to love it. Bronze figures run riot, perched atop lampposts and walls and even overtaking the drinking fountain: oversized pennies, human feet, frogs, cats, immense earthworms, and weird little round-headed people, all of which invite kids to climb on them. In the middle of this small paved wonderland is a railed-off centerpiece sculpture with a ring of rushing water for youngsters to wade in—sheer delight.

2 The Playground Lowdown

CENTRAL PARK

Central Park's "adventure playgrounds," most built in the 1980s, feature imaginative designs incorporating lots of places to climb, jump, slide, and hide out, as well as lots of sand to dig in or land safely on. In the 1990s, a new generation of playground began appearing, with rubber mat ground surfaces (as opposed to asphalt) and large, complex structures of metal bars coated with tough plastic, usually in primary colors. The playgrounds are surrounded by iron palings so kids don't wander away unsupervised; they all have drinking fountains, operational from Memorial Day to Labor Day, though none has rest rooms, and many have sprinklers to make summertime play a whole lot cooler (which makes up somewhat for the appalling lack of decent public pools).

The playgrounds listed below have bucket swings for toddlers and babies and either tire swings or flat swings for older kids. The Parks Department keeps playground equipment decently well maintained, often with the help of neighborhood parents who join in for monthly cleanup days.

THE WEST SIDE   The large **Heckscher Playground,** midpark at 62nd Street, could stand to be renovated; surrounded by chain-link fence, it's a relic of an era when gray-brick pyramids, metal slides, concrete ledges and tunnels, and a few brown timber climbing contraptions were the be-all and end-all of playground design. One area is set in a shallow expanse of rather dirty sand, but most of the rest of the playground is asphalt paved, and very little is shaded by trees. There are a few straightforward swings and seesaws at one end, which seem to be used mostly by sullen teenagers hanging out. There are working rest rooms here, but they're often locked up.

Just north of Tavern on the Green, the **West 67th Street Playground** has two sections: a 1960s-era playground atop a small hill and a smaller fenced area across the path with some newer primary-colored climbing structures and a set of bucket swings. The hilltop area is deliciously shady and better than most of this vintage, with undulating concrete forms, a nice bilevel brown timber tree house, and sprinklers set in a little concrete amphitheater that spills running water into a long raised basin. The sight lines aren't too bad, but the sand could be cleaner.

Manhattan Playgrounds

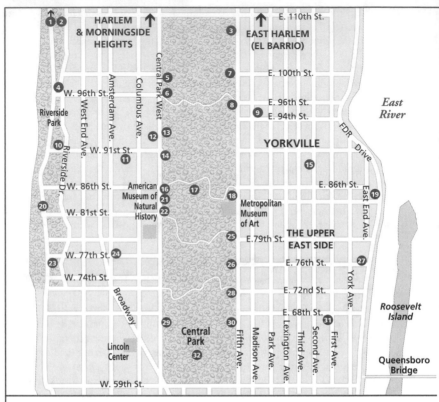

CENTRAL PARK PLAYGROUNDS

West Side
Diana Ross Playground **22**
Heckscher Playground **32**
Pinetum **17**
Rudin Playground **6**
Safari Playground **14**
Spector Playground **16**
West 67th Street Playground **29**
West 84th Street Playground **21**
West 99th Street Playground **5**
Wild West Playground **13**

East Side
Ancient Playground **18**
Bernard Family Playground **3**
East 72nd Street Playground **28**
East 96th Street Playground **8**
East 100th Street Playground **7**
James Michael Levin
  Playground **26**
Pat Hoffman Friedman
  Playground **25**
Rustic Playground **30**

RIVERSIDE PARK PLAYGROUNDS
Claremont Playground **1**
Dinosaur Park **4**
Elephant Park **23**
Hippo Park **10**
River Run Playground **20**
West 110th Street Playground **2**

OTHER MANHATTAN PLAYGROUNDS
The Upper West Side
St. Gregory the Great
  Playground **11**
Sol Bloom Playground **12**
Tecumseh Playground **24**
The Upper East Side
Carl Schurz Playground **19**
Hunter School Playground **9**
John Jay Park **27**
Ruppert Park **15**
St. Catherine's Playground **31**
Midtown
DeWitt Clinton Park **33**
Sutton Place Park **34**

Tudor City Playground **35**
Chelsea & the Flatiron District
Augustus Saint-Gaudens Park **37**
Clement Clarke Moore Park **36**
Union Square Playgrounds **38**
Greenwich Village & the East Village
32 Carmine Street Playground **42**
Bleecker Street Playground **39**
Mercer Playground **43**
Tompkins Square Park **41**
Washington Square Park Playground **40**
SoHo, Little Italy & Chinatown
Columbus Park **46**
De Salvio Playground **45**
Thompson Street Playground **44**
TriBeCa & Lower Manhattan
Battery Park City **49**
Hudson River Park Playground **48**
Pearl Street Playground **50**
Washington Market Park **47**

A BROOKLYN HEIGHTS PLAYGROUND
Pierrepont Street Playground **51**

The well-shaded **Diana Ross Playground** at West 81st Street—so named because the singer donated money to the park after violent incidents marred her Central Park concert in the early 1980s—was one of the first adventure playgrounds and now it could use some refurbishment. The weathered wood structures, set in sandpits, are complex enough to inspire some really fun games, with webs of chains to climb on, suspension bridges to bounce on, and fireman's poles to slide down. But the design isn't geared to younger kids, who may have some trouble climbing where they want to go (which means you'll have to climb up after them to give them a boost). There are two hulking climbing structures set right in the middle; the sight lines can be a problem. Two giant pluses: There are public rest rooms nearby (next to the Delacorte Theater—usually dirty but infinitely preferable to soiled undies), and you're only a block north of the American Museum of Natural History.

A nautical theme prevails at the **West 84th Street Playground,** which has boat-shaped climbing structures, rowboats to rock in, fish designs around the sprinklers, and lots of shade. A stone's throw away, the **Spector Playground** at West 85th Street sits on a rise of land with lots of picnickable grass around it. Its two best features are the nice fenced-off toddler area (baby swings, sandbox, sprinklers) and an irresistible rambling wooden tree house with a giant rope to swing on, Tarzan style. Many of the playground's structures are set in sand, however, and a long wooden bridge arches over the middle of the immense sandpit, which makes sight lines problematic if you're in the toddler area and trying to keep an eye on older kids down by the tree house. The paved sprinkler area gets very active in summer. Across the drive are some bucket swings midpark in the shady cool of the **Pinetum.**

The delightful **Safari Playground** at West 91st Street is an imaginative playscape where children scramble over a herd of hippo sculptures and hop in and out of a green rowboat embedded in the pavement. It has no swings or slides and only two rudimentary climbing structures, but kids hardly notice—they're so busy with jump ropes and hopscotch and sidewalk chalk and running in and out of the sprinklers. With picnic tables and lots of shade, it attracts swarms of preschoolers. At West 93rd Street, the **Wild West Playground** is extremely popular with uptown families, especially in summer, when sprinklers send water rushing down the long central gully into a circular wading pool at the far end. Four square fortlike wood towers at the center make this a great spot for playing all sorts of war games; three of the towers anchor big sandpits surrounded by low wooden palisades, with tire swings, slides, a bouncy suspension bridge, and weathered wood climbing structures (the fourth has a rubber mat surface that's good for playing ball). The towers in the center make the sight lines a bit of a problem, and the combination of water gully and sandpit means lots of wet gravelly muck in your kids' shoes when you get home.

At West 96th Street, the newer **Rudin Playground** is set on an island between two busy transverse roads, meaning a bit more noise and exhaust than at other playgrounds; the gate leads straight out to Central Park West, which can also be a problem. But in other respects it's a pleasant place, with a central paved sprinkler area, a vine-hung pergola shading a set of benches, and a trio of brightly colored climbing gyms that modulate from low toddler-friendly structures to a fairly demanding set of parallel bars and swinging rings. There's only one small concrete-edged sandbox, but there are lots of well-shaded bucket swings for babies.

The **West 99th Street Playground** is past its prime and looks it, but athletic kids can have a blast on its weathered wood structures, especially the concrete mountain with interior tunnels for reaching the top of a big metal slide. Essentially one large sandpit surrounded by asphalt, it's rarely crowded, but the sight lines can be a problem since the benches are on the perimeter. The gang here is fairly mixed, mostly neighborhood folks, but for whatever reasons it seems to be kept less tidy than playgrounds farther south, and the park here is a bit wilder and more overgrown. There are good lawns nearby for picnicking, and right across the drive are the North Meadow playing fields.

THE EAST SIDE   At East 67th Street, the **Rustic Playground** is one of the park's most imaginative play spaces. You enter through a leafy wooden arbor; straight ahead is an arched stone bridge that looks very much like the famous Bow Bridge over the Lake to the north, connecting a pair of lushly planted islands. On your left is a midsized sandpit with a slide, on your right a terrace with picnic tables. Best of all, behind the stone bridge, steps lead up a steep rock outcropping to the top of a long curved metal slide actually set into the face of the rock; daredevil kids in the know bring a square of corrugated cardboard to sit on to make the slide superfast, sort of like a waterless log flume ride. The big problem with the Rustic Playground is you can't see past the bridges and islands in the center; if one of your children is doing repeat trips down that slide—it can be addictive—you can't monitor the rest of the playground if your other children are elsewhere. Still, it's a wonderful place for a pre- or postzoo frolic.

The **East 72nd Street Playground** is another dinosaur from the era of brown timber, brick pyramids, metal slides, and concrete. These hulking shapes make the sight lines pretty bad, and the ground surface, mostly sand, looks a bit dirty. It's quite shady, though, and the entrance is set safely inside the park. Kids in this neighborhood prefer to go to the **James Michael Levin Playground,** set well inside the park near East 76th Street, with a small iron entrance gate everyone conscientiously keeps latched. The centerpiece of this graceful wide-open playground is a fountain featuring scenes from classic fairy tales; kids swarm between the climbing structure near the gate and a decent-sized concrete sandbox at the other end, with plenty of open pavement in between for skating, hopscotch, and the like. Sight lines are super, and the people here are pretty well behaved, but the place gets crowded after school. On the north side of East 79th Street, the **Pat Hoffman Friedman Playground** is a well-sheltered small area behind a replica of the Metropolitan Museum's American Wing's statue *Three Bears* by Paul Manship; there's not much here except bucket swings, a tiny concrete sandbox, a metal slide, and a few climbing bars. It's a handy place for a quick stop right after a visit to the Metropolitan, though only the 4-and-under set will be satisfied.

With its series of glazed-brick pyramids, the **Ancient Playground** at East 84th Street pays homage to the neighboring Metropolitan Museum's Egyptian Temple of Dendur, visible through the glass wall right across the road. Hulking concrete banks around the edges give this playground a bunkerlike quality, and, wedged between two busy transverse roads, it is about as bucolic as an interstate gas station. Most of the benches are set up at one end, grouped around concrete chessboard tables, which means baby-sitters congregating there have a hard time supervising their charges. But it's an extremely popular after-school spot for elementary school kids, who have a ball leaping all over the pyramids, thundering up and down the metal slides, and taking furious spins on the rope swings. A segregated area at the far end makes a safe toddler haven with a sandbox and bucket swings.

The popular **East 96th Street Playground** sits at the top of a short, steep rise from Fifth Avenue. A good-sized toddler area is set off by iron palings in the center; other separately defined areas include a rubber-matted zone with tire swings and wooden pilings to climb on; a large modern metal-bar structure with all sorts of bridges, ladders, towers, and plastic slides; a cool little tree house platform in a shady back corner; and a paved expanse surrounding a big water sprinkler. The sight lines are very good, and the Carnegie Hill crowd is pleasant to play with. The well-shaded **East 100th Street Playground** has a coil of red steel that becomes a run-through tunnel of spraying water in summer; the climbing structure is particularly imaginative, with lots of inspiring nooks for all sorts of make-believe. Best of all, this playground is wheelchair accessible. It's adjacent to an extensive lawn that sees lots of ball playing and picnic action on weekends. On the east shore of Harlem Meer, at 108th Street, the **Bernard Family Playground** is a very civilized area featuring a large steel-bar climbing apparatus, painted maroon and forest green, mounted on black rubber matting. It also has a small, clean sandbox, a paved sprinkler section, and a few bucket swings. The crowd is racially diverse and very harmonious; only a few yards away, there's a marvelous tiny sand beach where small children can happily dig, sift, and mold sand beside the lapping meer water.

RIVERSIDE PARK

The **Henry Neufield Playground** at West 76th Street is commonly known as the **Elephant Park** after a set of five plump little stone pachyderms set around an open expanse of asphalt. This pleasant playground also has two modern climbing structures, a fenced swing area, a small fenced sandbox with very clean sand, and rest rooms (hallelujah!) actually kept decently clean. There's an active set of basketball courts next to it. The only drawback is that traffic roars on the West Side Highway right past the bushes on the other side of the back fence. At the **River Run Playground** at West 83rd Street, a sprinkler feeds into a sculpted replica of the Hudson River; this, in turn, flows into a whimsical 35-foot sandbox, with sculptural forms of castles, classical gods, and woodland animals frolicking around it. Parents appreciate another form of running water here—the working rest rooms.

The **Hippo Park** (down a steep hill from Riverside Drive, at West 91st Street) derives its nickname from the wonderful hippopotamus sculptures in the middle, which children can climb on. It has swings for both tots and big kids, smallish sandboxes, and sprinklers in summer. An energetic group of neighborhood parents that banded together to raise money to renovate the park now organizes drop-in arts and crafts classes in summer, as well as regular attendants to keep the rest rooms clean and safe. A few blocks north at 97th Street and Riverside Drive, the **Dinosaur Park** also has sculptures (dinosaurs, naturally) and a huge sprinkler area, great for cooling off in summer, but the secret is out and the playground gets supercrowded after school. There are rest rooms here as well. Set alongside the Riverside Drive promenade on the park's upper level, the **West 110th Street Playground** has small climbing structures, bucket swings, and small sandboxes that make it especially good for toddlers. The farthest north, the shady **Claremont Playground,** at West 124th Street (right behind Grant's Tomb), has spouting porpoise sprinklers, a sandbox shaped like a huge rowboat, and—ta-dah!—more rest rooms.

THE UPPER WEST SIDE

Sandwiched between Central Park and Riverside Park, the Upper West Side needs fewer playgrounds of its own than the wider Upper East Side does—yet it seems to have more. Along Amsterdam Avenue at 77th Street (northeast corner), helpfully near the American Museum of Natural History, the **Tecumseh Playground** features a rootin' tootin' western theme, with climbing structures shaped like Conestoga wagons and longhorn cattle. On West 90th Street, between Columbus and

Amsterdam avenues, you'll find the **St. Gregory the Great Playground,** a small rubber-floored playground with a sprightly set of climbing structures built in 1995; walk through the **community garden** just east of it (taking time to smell the flowers, please) to reach another newly renovated playground with lots of shade on West 89th Street. On West 92nd Street between Central Park West and Columbus Avenue, the **Sol Bloom Playground** not only has two great climbing structures (one toddler-scaled) on a soft red-and-black checkerboard surface but also is the focus of lots of neighborhood athletics, with basketball hoops, a paved softball diamond, and a handball court.

THE UPPER EAST SIDE

St. Catherine's Playground, on the west side of First Avenue between 67th and 68th streets, is undeniably urban—iron palings, asphalt paving, traffic churning past on three sides—but it's definitely a welcome spot in this near-Midtown neighborhood, roomy and fairly shady with a couple of terraced levels. There's a set of happening basketball and handball courts on the other side of a chain-link fence. **John Jay Park,** on 76th Street east of York Avenue, has some nice up-to-date climbing structures for toddlers in the shady outer area and some for older kids inside the chain-link fence. There are also wide-open asphalt surfaces to run (and fall) on, a small East River lookout, and an outdoor pool open in summer (see "Swimming" under "Sports & Games," later in this chapter).

The **Carl Schurz Park Playground,** at 84th Street and East End Avenue, is my top choice on the East Side: This large, well-shaded playground has several multi-level climbing structures of red-and-green plastic-coated steel and weathered wood—ladders, slides, bridges, steering wheels, climbing chains, and sliding poles provide plenty of playtime interest. It also has a separate sprinkler area and lots of open pavement in the middle that just cries out for a rousing game of Red Rover or Prisoners All. You'll see lots of little girls in uniforms in the afternoons, after nearby Chapin and Brearley schools let out. Adjacent Carl Schurz Park has a superb riverside promenade (see "Green New York: The Top Parks," earlier in this chapter). Not far away is **Ruppert Park** (89th to 90th streets along Second Avenue); despite its limited playground equipment, smaller children have fun frolicking on the landscaped series of terraces, with lots of curved paths, flowerbeds, and benches for play-date tête-à-têtes. Another Upper East Side playground with some interest is the **Hunter School Playground** on Madison Avenue between 94th and 95th streets; its Madison Avenue entrance incorporates a red-brick castlelike facade preserved from a demolished turn-of-the-20th-century National Guard armory. (A similar armory, still intact, is down Park Avenue between 66th and 67th streets.) Though this playground is open to the public only after school hours, it may be worth a special detour to let your kids scamper up and down the steps between the stout brick towers, through a wide arch that just cries out for a moat and drawbridge.

MIDTOWN

At the east end of 42nd Street, the **Tudor City** residential complex is set on a terrace above First Avenue; halfway up the stairs that rise on the south side of 42nd Street just past Second Avenue is a small fenced playground with a rubberized surface and primary-colored climbing structures. Overlooking the river, **Sutton Place Park** is set in a quiet cul-de-sac where East 57th Street dead-ends just past Sutton Place. This tiny brick-paved play area is a few steps down from street level, on a terrace above the FDR Drive, with lots of shade and some great views of the 59th Street Bridge arching over the East River. It's best for infants and toddlers, though, since there's no playground equipment to speak of—nothing but wooden benches, one absurdly small iron-fenced sandbox, and a large bronze wart hog (Pumbaa!) on a pedestal. Over on the far West Side, in a grimy neighborhood once called Hell's Kitchen (nowadays more gentrified and politely relabeled Clinton), the **DeWitt Clinton Park** playground (between 52nd and 53rd streets on Eleventh Avenue) is set behind a balding set of ball fields, with the West Side Highway rumbling beyond a fence. Still, the playground equipment is excellent, set in pleasant shade, with a nicely executed Erie Canal theme (DeWitt Clinton was the politician who got the Erie Canal built a couple centuries ago—but you already knew that, right?). It's worth a stop if you're nearby, doing the Circle Line cruises or visiting the *Intrepid* (see chapter 4).

CHELSEA, THE FLATIRON DISTRICT & GRAMERCY PARK

Named for the clergyman who wrote *A Visit from St. Nicholas* (better known as *The Night Before Christmas*), **Clement Clarke Moore Park,** in western Chelsea (southeast corner of Tenth Avenue and 22nd Street), isn't much—a paved corner lot with a few benches and concrete sculptures, with one rubberized-steel climbing structure at the far end—but it's decently shady and quiet enough.

In the Flatiron District, the most centrally located are the two small but heavily populated playgrounds in **Union Square,** side-by-side near Broadway and 16th Street. The fenced-in one has a smart rubber-coated steel climbing gym in happy primary colors, with hordes of toddlers swarming all over it; outside the fence, many kids still insist on clambering over an older playground's outmoded metal structures, which look like geodesic dome skeletons. The Union Square Greenmarket, operating Monday, Wednesday, Friday, and Saturday, is only a few steps away, which makes playground picnics very handy. Somewhat off the beaten track in the Gramercy Park area is **Augustus Saint-Gaudens Park** (19th Street and Second Avenue), which has shade, good climbing structures, and lots of open pavement, some with basketball hoops.

GREENWICH VILLAGE & THE EAST VILLAGE

The focal point of the Village, **Washington Square Park,** at the foot of Fifth Avenue (between 4th and 6th streets, though the names are changed here for a couple of blocks), has on the north side a bustling playground with lots of up-to-date climbing structures, set off by a fence from the rest of the park. A pair of greenish tortoises spout water from their beaks in summer. Farther west, at Sixth Avenue and Bleecker Street, the **32 Carmine Street Playground** is buffered by a red-brick wall from the surrounding traffic; go through the iron gate and you'll find swings and wooden climbing structures in an asphalt-paved yard. Or follow Bleecker Street west to the point where it dead-ends at Hudson Street to find the always-hopping **Bleecker Street Playground,** fenced off with iron palings. It's got swings, a sandbox, picnic tables, and a stretch of asphalt just big enough for hopscotch or a round of double-dutch jump-roping. Older kids may be attracted more to the **Mercer Playground,** a long narrow strip on the west side of Mercer Street between Bleecker and West 3rd streets; instead of climbing equipment, it features a long skating path, a spray shower, plantings, and benches for socializing. The under-8 crowd is served with a small playground a short way down Mercer Street, in front of NYU's sports center.

Once-derelict **Tompkins Square Park** has become a leafy haven in the increasingly gentrified East Village, and it has no fewer than three good-sized fenced-off playgrounds with black rubberized ground surfaces and rubber-coated metal play structures in bold primary colors (my kids are downright envious of such an abundance). The biggest and busiest is along Avenue A at East 9th Street; the other two are along East 7th Street. After a vigorous play session, head down the avenue for pizza at Two Boots (see chapter 9).

SOHO, LITTLE ITALY & CHINATOWN

The **Thompson Street Playground,** on the east side of Thompson Street between Prince and Spring streets, is a welcome romping spot in oh-so-urban SoHo; it has large red timber climbing structures on an asphalt surface. Good for stretching limbs in fair weather, it's about halfway between the New York Fire Museum and the Children's Museum for the Arts, both on Spring Street. At the corner of Mulberry and Spring streets in Little Italy, the **De Salvio Playground** has a couple of bright modern climbers set in a pleasant fenced-in corner lot, neatly paved with a few benches under the trees. In tree-shaded **Columbus Park,** at Worth Street between Baxter and Mulberry streets in Chinatown, hordes of Asian and Asian-American children scramble over the climbing structures and dangle on the swings, while elderly men play chess nearby.

TRIBECA & LOWER MANHATTAN

One of Lower Manhattan's few really inviting green spaces is **Washington Market Park,** on Greenwich Street between Chambers and Duane streets, a 2½-acre lawn sprouting up where the city's rough-and-tumble wholesale food markets used to be. The gentle rises of the grassy area, punctuated with a delightful gazebo, are perfect for picnics and Frisbee games, and there's a fanciful maritime-themed wrought-iron fence at the south end, where P.S. 234 sits. The tidy playground is a small enclosed strip along the park's eastern wall.

The **Hudson River Park Playground,** at the west end of Chambers Street, is a thriving enclosed area across the esplanade from the river. The super climbing structures, made of weathered wood and royal-blue steel, provide bridges and platforms where kids can scamper above ground; on ground level are three good-sized sand areas, one wheelchair accessible. The northern section is set aside for toddlers, with a delicious bronze dodo set in a tiny splashing area; there's another sprinkler area for older kids, with a stone elephant and hippo. At the southern end is one of the coolest pieces of playground equipment in the city: a red steel whirligig seating eight, powered by pedals mounted beneath every other seat. Though most of the playground is unshaded, several wooden arbors along the sides allow parents and sleeping babies to duck out of the sun. While it isn't technically a playground, the same park's esplanade also features a fanciful sculpture park with a wade-in fountain that's irresistible to children (not to mention adults, who grin goofily as they inspect the whimsical bronze figures swarming over every available surface). Adjacent **Battery Park City** has a handful of other tiny fenced play areas tucked in around its residential buildings, many of them with no more than a yard-square sandbox and a couple of weathered-wood blocks for climbing on; the largest is a shady, spacious playground just west of West Street and south of Thames Street.

Across the street from South Street Seaport, iron fences surround a triangular lot at Fulton and Pearl streets, where the **Pearl Street Playground** has a delightfully complicated climbing structure where kids can let off steam.

BROOKLYN

At the south end of the Promenade in Brooklyn Heights, the excellent **Pierrepont Street Playground** has rest rooms (not always clean, however), a separate yard for the very young, lots of shade trees, and loads of slides. Add to that plenty of neighborhood buzz and a peerless view across the East River to Manhattan. The **Imagination Playground** in Prospect Park (east side of the park, near the Lincoln Road entrance) is as fanciful as its name promises: a bronze dragon spouts water, a black-and-white-striped bridge twists like a helix, child-sized masks are mounted for children to peek through, and a central sculpture features the little boy Peter and his dog Willie from Ezra Jack Keats's beloved children's books.

3 Sports & Games

BASEBALL

Organized Little League games around the city in spring snap up most of the groomed baseball fields on spring weekends; after work, grown-up leagues fill the parks on weekday evenings. Central Park has some very nice fields: at the **Great Lawn** (midpark between 81st and 86th streets), **Heckscher Ballfields** (midpark between 63rd and 66th streets), or the **North Meadow** (midpark between 97th and 100th streets). Anyone can reserve a ball field for use; call the parks department at ☎ **212/408-0209** or go online at **www.nyc.gov/parks** and find out what's available for the time you want. The cost is $8 per 2-hour session (after 5:30pm, $8 gets you a 1½-hour session). If you don't want to get that formal, try the North Meadow facilities, which are sometimes free on a walk-in basis, provided no one has reserved them; a handful of other Manhattan parks, including **DeWitt Clinton Park** (between 52nd and 53rd streets on Eleventh Avenue) and **Riverside Park** (west of Riverside Drive, in the section north of 103rd Street—take stairs down from the promenade level), have baseball diamonds with chain-link backstops that are usually free for pick-up games.

If your slugger just wants to work on batting form, check out the **batting cages** at the **Field House at Chelsea Piers,** 23rd Street and the West Side Highway, Pier 62 (☎ **212/336-6500;** $1 per 10 balls); at **Frozen Ropes NYC Baseball Center,** 202 W. 74th St., between Broadway and Amsterdam Avenue (☎ **212/362-0344;** $40 per half hour, $75 per hour, for one to five players); or at **Randall's Island Family Golf Center,** across the Triborough Bridge on Randall's Island (☎ **212/ 427-5689;** $2 for 15 pitches; for transportation details, see "Golf" later in this chapter).

BASKETBALL

Several city-run playgrounds have asphalt half courts where some pretty aggressive games of one-on-one take place. The famous courts at **Sixth Avenue and West 4th Street**—known as "The Cage"—are a breeding ground for serious hoop-dreamers; the action is so fast and furious, kids may be better off spectating than playing. Intrepid kids may, however, be able to get a pick-up game at **St. Catherine's Playground** (First Avenue between 67th and 68th streets), in **Central Park's** courts just northeast of the Great Lawn (midpark at 85th Street), **Riverside Park** at West 76th Street, the **Sol Bloom Playground** (West 92nd Street between Central Park West and Columbus Avenue), or **Goat Park** (Amsterdam Avenue and 99th Street)—named after Earl "the Goat" Manigault, a high-jumping, high-scoring street player who watched his peers win NBA offers while his own life unraveled in disappointment and drug addiction. Manigault redeemed himself by running athletic programs for kids in this very park, for which he will be forever remembered. If you didn't bring your own ball, head to the paved outdoor courts at Central Park's **North Meadow Recreation Center** (midpark, just north of the 97th Street transverse road); at the recreation center's offices right next to the courts, you can borrow a basketball along with a whole bag full of other sports equipment.

BICYCLING

The circular drive in **Central Park** is probably the city's most popular biking road, a 6-mile-long circuit that includes a couple of fairly grueling hills; younger kids should probably stick to the relatively flat lower loop, which shortcuts across at 72nd Street, or even the footpath looping around the Great Lawn, midpark from 81st to 86th streets; it's officially off-limits to bikes, but trikes are usually tolerated.

Or try this **suggested route:** Starting at East 79th Street and Fifth Avenue, pedal up Cedar Hill to the East Drive, turn right, and follow a flat stretch of the drive past the reservoir; at the crosswalk just south of 96th Street, turn left again (west) and follow the footpath that cuts west across the park, bearing left at the fork to go past the Tennis House and exit the park at 93rd Street; turn left and ride south on the Central Park West sidewalk to West 81st Street, where you can turn back into the park and follow paths across the foot of the Great Lawn back to your starting point. Park drives are closed to traffic weekdays 10am to 3pm and all weekend long; bike traffic circles the park clockwise. The wide sidewalk bordering the park walls is also good for young riders, with few cross streets to negotiate; follow it up either Fifth Avenue or Central Park West.

The circular road in Brooklyn's **Prospect Park** is another great traffic-free place to ride on weekends; it's only 3½ miles long and has only one really tough hill.

Riverside Park offers a flat, wide promenade from 83rd to 96th streets, as well as paths skimming down under the West Side Highway to let you ride for a few blocks right along the Hudson. (The downward path at 86th Street has the gentlest incline of the three; the 79th Street path entails negotiating around a busy West Side Highway off-ramp, while the 72nd Street path to the boat basin has a very steep hill just west of the highway. See "Green New York: The Top Parks," earlier in this chapter.) Like Central Park, Riverside is bordered by wide sidewalks, either of asphalt or of distinctive hexagonal paving stones, so you can cruise along the west side of Riverside Drive from 79th Street up to 125th Street with very few cross streets to worry about. A bike path now runs the length of Riverside Park on up to the George Washington Bridge, although those deserted upper reaches are not wise to pedal with kids. A sensible path would be to enter Riverside at 72nd Street, going under the archway and down the hill to the lower section of the park, and then follow the bike lane alongside the river north to 96th Street or even to 125th Street, where Grant's Tomb sits high above the park.

The **Battery Park Promenade** also runs along the Hudson, with some great harbor views, though it isn't all that long; you can extend your ride by following the bike path 2 more miles through **Hudson River Park,** running up to Christopher Street and West Street. On weekends, there's little traffic in Lower Manhattan, so you may have fun going across Liberty Street or Rector Street to the Wall Street area, where you can circle around the deserted skyscrapers. Swing north on Nassau Street and go up to City Hall, where broad entrance ramps lead onto the Brooklyn Bridge, with broad bike/pedestrian lanes leading you over the river (see "Crossing the Brooklyn Bridge" in chapter 5).

Now here's the catch: Very few of Manhattan's many bicycle rental shops stock bikes for kids; apparently the insurance costs are too prohibitive. The ones that do are **Larry & Jeff's Bicycles Plus,** 1690 Second Ave., between 87th and 88th streets (☎ **212/722-2201**), charging $7.50 per hour, $25 for a full day; and **Pedal**

Pusher, 1306 Second Ave., at 69th Street (☎ 212/288-5592; closed Tuesday), charging $3.95 per hour, $9.95 per day.

BOWLING

Bowlmor Lanes. 110 University Place (between 12th and 13th sts.). ☎ 212/255-8188. www.bowlmor.com. $6.45 per person per game ($5.45 Mon–Fri before 5pm); $17 (including shoe rental) for Night Strike, Mon 10pm–4am. Shoe rental $3. Tues–Thurs and Sun 10am–1am, Mon and Fri–Sat 10am–4am. Subway: 4/5/6/L/N/R to Union Square.

Down in the Village, 42-lane Bowlmor survives as a sort of hip throwback, with a long sleek bar, a restaurant, a VIP lounge, and lots of postmodern date bowling (deejays, glow-in-the-dark pins, nude bowling parties, and so on), alongside some ferocious league action at night. Daytimes, though, are relatively uncrowded. There's automatic scoring, and gutter bumpers are available to keep kids' balls in the alley. Trivia fans take note: The first *Bowling for Dollars* TV game show was shot here, and Nixon bowled here regularly in the 1950s.

✪ Chelsea Piers AMF Bowling. Pier 60 at Chelsea Piers, 23rd St. and the West Side Hwy. at the Hudson River. ☎ 212/835-2695. www.chelseapiers.com. $7 per person per game. Shoe rental $4. Sun–Thurs 9am–1am, Fri–Sat 9am–4am. Subway: 1/9, C/E, or F/N/R to 23rd St. stations. Bus: M23 across 23rd St.

This sparkling 40-lane facility, one of the newer additions at Chelsea Piers (it's in the building just south of the Field House), sees lots of family action on weekends. There's also a games arcade, and waiters from the on-site restaurant will bring food right to your lane. Gutter bumpers are much in demand here.

Leisure Time Bowling. 625 Eighth Ave., in the Port Authority Bus Terminal, 2nd level (enter at 40th St. and Eighth Ave.). ☎ 212/268-6909. $5.25 per person per game ($4.25 before 5pm). Shoe rental $3.50. Sun–Thurs 10am–11pm, Fri–Sat 10am–3am (arrive by 1am). Subway: A/C/E to 42nd St.

Budding bowlers should foray into the unattractive bus terminal because this surprisingly clean and modern 30-lane complex offers kids bumper bowling and a relatively low-key scene.

CHESS

It's possible to play at the outdoor chessboards beside the **Central Park Chess and Checkers House,** midpark at 67th Street, just west of the Dairy; the boards are built into the stone tables and you can pick up chess pieces at the Dairy. The real scene for kids, however, is in Greenwich Village, where two chess stores sit a few doors away from each other on Thompson Street between 3rd and Bleecker streets: **Chess Forum,** 219 Thompson St. (☎ 212/475-2369), and the **Chess Shop,** 230 Thompson St. (☎ 212/475-9580). Loads of kids stream in to play, especially on Saturday, and the chargés are minimal—officially $1 an hour per person, though the folks on staff rarely charge even that much. Either store can also arrange lessons for $25 an hour.

Kids can play for free at **New York Chess and Backgammon,** 120 W. 41st St., between Broadway and Sixth Avenue (☎ 212/869-6057). This club organizes tournaments for kids outdoors in Bryant Park (Sixth Avenue between 40th and 42nd streets) late June to September, every Saturday 11am to 2pm; there's a $7 entry fee, a lesson and lecture are thrown in, and many levels of players show up. School-age kids can also take chess lessons on Saturday 11am to 2pm and Sunday noon to 3pm at the **Manhattan Chess Club,** 481 Eighth Ave. at 34th Street (☎ 212/333-5888 for tournament information); the cost is $5 per class.

CLIMBING

Two venues in Manhattan cater to young climbers with walls scaled to their size: the **Chelsea Piers Field House,** Pier 62, 23rd Street and the West Side Highway (☎ **212/336-6500;** $17 admission for Open Gym & Climb sessions—call for schedule), and the **North Meadow Recreation Center,** Central Park, midpark at 97th Street (☎ **212/348-4867**), which offers 1-day climbing courses as well as occasional open climb sessions for experienced climbers.

FENCING

Fencers Club. 119 W. 25th St. (between Sixth and Seventh aves.), 5th floor. ☎ **212/807-6947.** www.fencersclub.com. Subway: 1/9 or E/F/N/R to 23rd St. stations.

Led by Peter Westbrook, one of the few Olympic-level American fencers, this fencing studio's youth program is outstanding.

Metropolis Fencing Club. 45 W. 21st St. (between Fifth and Sixth aves.), 2nd floor. ☎ **212/463-8044.** Subway: 1/9 or E/Γ/N/R to 23rd St. stations.

Starting at age 7, kids—even rank beginners—can book fencing lessons by the hour at this high-ceilinged, friendly studio. Equipment is provided.

FISHING

Dana Discovery Center. In Central Park at E. 110th St. ☎ **212/860-1370.** Free admission. Apr–Oct Tues–Sun 10am–4pm. Subway: 2/3 to 110th St. Bus: M2, M3, or M4 to 110th St./Fifth Ave.

Believe it or not, you actually can fish in Manhattan, at the north end of Central Park in the Harlem Meer. From April to October, take your kids to the red-brick boathouse on the meer's north shore and the staff will give them simple fishing poles; they'll even throw in some bait. (Don't worry, it's not live worms.) No one I know has ever successfully caught a fish up here, but fish did nibble at their lines and everyone reports having had a whale of a time.

FOLK DANCING

Central Park International Folk Dancing. In Central Park, on the east end of Turtle Pond, midpark at 81st St. ☎ **718/584-4578.** Free admission. Sun 2–6pm (weather permitting).

It's free, it's outdoors, and it's so uncool it's cool. A mismatched bunch of enthusiasts shows up every week to hop, skip, cross-step, and clap in time to various kinds of folk music, blared from Alex Quartner's tape deck; show up at 1:30pm or so and Alex will give you a little lesson. People come and go, joining in for a few dances or sitting on the base of the King Jagiello statue just to watch. Nothing is too difficult that you can't pick up the steps just by shuffling along behind the regulars, and nobody cares if you do it right—they're just happy you're participating. Though it's mostly adults, there are always a few kids hanging on the fringes until they figure out the steps (of course, the kids catch on faster than we bumbling adults do). Donations to help cover the organizer's costs are appreciated. Anyone who thinks New York is a cold, rude, overstimulated city should show up here on Sunday to see a very different face of the Big Apple.

GOLF

Golf Club at the Chelsea Piers. Pier 59 at Chelsea Piers, 23rd St. and the West Side Hwy., at the Hudson River. ☎ **212/336-6400.** www.chelseapiers.com. Minimum charge $15, which gets you 65 balls at peak times, 94 other times. Apr–Sept daily 5am–midnight; Oct–Mar daily 6am–midnight. Subway: 1/9, C/E, or F/N/R to 23rd St. stations. Bus: M23 across 23rd St.

This is truly an amazing facility: a four-level driving range, where 52 golfers at a time can slam balls out into a huge open space bounded by high-tech mesh. All the time, you're looking out at incredible Hudson River views. Modeled after multi-tiered ranges in Japan, where golf's popularity far outweighs the availability of land for golf courses, this is the first such facility in the United States. The stalls are heated for year-round play, and you don't have to lug around buckets of balls—a computerized system in the floor slides a new ball up on your tee as soon as you've hit the previous one. You pay for as many balls as you wish and get a magnetized card to swipe in a slot at the tee; the computer subtracts how many you hit and you can come back whenever you want to hit the rest. There's also a 1,000-square-foot practice putting green, and pros are available for lessons at the attached Jim McLean Golf Academy.

Pier 25 Mini-Golf. N. Moore St. at the West Side Hwy. ☎ **212/732-7467** or 212/941-6922. Admission $3 adults, $2 children. Daily 1–9pm in warm weather.

Community-based Manhattan Youth Recreation and Resources has developed this downtown pier, just north of Hudson River Park, as a children's play area, with a sand yard, a sprinkler plaza, a snack bar, and an 18-hole miniature golf course. The layout is ungimmicky, just green outdoor turf fairways with a few mock boulders, mini–sand traps, and blue-painted water to simulate the type of hazards you'd get on an actual course. Everybody we saw there was playing with young kids, which meant that everybody was forgiving if play wasn't exactly regulation. A great place to stop off, especially if you're riding or skating on the Hudson bike path.

Randall's Island Family Golf Center. On Randall's Island. ☎ **212/427-5689.** Driving range: $10 for bucket of 102 balls, $6 for 51 balls. Minigolf: $5 adults, $3 children under 16. Batting cages: $2 for 15 pitches. May–Oct Mon 1–11pm, Tues–Fri 8am–11pm, Sat 7am–11pm, Sun 7am–10pm (Nov–Apr closes daily at 10pm). Free parking; shuttle available (see below).

Randall's Island is one of the city's best-kept sports secrets; with an athletic stadium and lots of ball fields, it's a haven for amateur athletes and a quick drive across the Triborough Bridge from Manhattan. Along with a driving range, batting cages, a golf shop, and a snack bar, there's a nifty minigolf course at this golf complex on the island. If you don't have a car, you can take a shuttle bus, leaving from Modell's sporting goods store at 86th Street and Third Avenue; it costs $9 and leaves every hour on the hour 3 to 7pm weekdays and 10am to 6pm weekends.

HORSEBACK RIDING
Chelsea Equestrian Center. 63 North River (at 23rd St. and the Hudson River). ☎ **212/ 367-9090.** $50 per half-hour private lesson, $100 per 1-hour private lesson. Mon–Fri 7am–10pm, Sat–Sun 8am–5pm. Subway: 1/9, C/E, or F/N/R to 23rd St. stations. Bus: M23 across 23rd St.

Adding to the cluster of sports facilities adjoining Chelsea Piers, this horseback riding center is much more expensive than the others, but it may be a good place for an interested child to give riding a first try. Children as young as 5 years old can mount up here, even the rankest beginner (they'll lend boots and helmets to riders who don't have their own). Horses are available for lessons only (no trails nearby for riding, sorry) on either the outdoor ring or an indoor one with big windows overlooking the Hudson; riders can use either English or Western saddle. Book at least 3 days in advance, and be prepared to suit your time to the scheduled class for your designated riding ability.

✪ **Claremont Riding Academy.** 175 W. 89th St. (between Columbus and Amsterdam aves.). ☎ **212/724-5100.** $37.50 per 1-hour group lesson, $40 per half-hour private lesson. Mon–Fri 6:30am–10pm, Sat–Sun 8am–5pm. Subway: 1/9/B/C to 86th St.

The only riding stables close to Central Park, Claremont occupies a charming 1892 building that was freshly restored in 1998. There are lots of classes for kids 6 and up, riding in an indoor ring—English saddle only. Call a day or two in advance to schedule. Experienced riders can take their mounts into nearby Central Park for $40 per hour; the bridle trail runs nearly the length of the park, looping around the reservoir. Thundering along the shady trails, clattering under landmark arched bridges, is a wonderful experience. You must wear shoes with enough of a heel to catch hold in a stirrup; helmets are required, but the stable provides them free of charge.

Kensington Stables. 51 Caton Place, Brooklyn. ☎ **718/972-4588.** $40 per 1-hour private lesson, $25 per half-hour private lesson; $35 per hour semiprivate lesson; $30 per hour group lesson for 3 or more. Daily 10am–9pm for lessons, 10am–sundown for trail rides. Subway: F to Fort Hamilton Pkwy.

To me, this is one of the best horseback deals in New York City, provided the schlep to Brooklyn doesn't daunt you. For $20 per hour, you can join a guided trail ride through leafy Prospect Park, riding either English or Western saddle; because there's a guide along, even inexperienced riders can join in. Lessons at the stable can be English or Western saddle. Call ahead if you want to book a lesson; drop-ins are welcome for the trail rides.

Riverdale Equestrian Center. In Van Cortlandt Park at W. 254th St. and Broadway, Riverdale, the Bronx. ☎ **718/548-4848.** $67 per hour private lesson, $36 per half-hour private lesson; $49 per hour semiprivate lesson (for advanced riders only); $31 per half-hour semiprivate lesson; $27 and $40 per hour group lesson (depending on skill level). Tues–Fri 8am–9pm, Sat–Sun 9am–5pm. Subway: 1/9 to 242nd St. Bus: Liberty Lines BxM3.

All saddles are English. Call a few days in advance to book lesson time.

ICE-SKATING

Lasker Rink. In Central Park at 110th St. and Lenox Ave. ☎ **212/534-7639.** Admission $3 adults, $1.50 children. Skate rental $3.50. Nov–Apr Mon–Thurs 10am–3pm, Fri 10am–2pm and 5–9pm, Sat 11am–10pm, Sun 11am–6pm. Subway: 2/3 to 110th St.

Cheaper and less crowded than its Central Park cousin, the Wollman Rink, uptown's Lasker is well populated by families on weekends. The ice here doesn't get as chewed up as Wollman's, but the rental skates are not great quality.

Riverbank State Park. 145th St. and Riverside Dr. ☎ **212/694-3642.** Admission $4 adults, $2 children 12 and under. Skate rental $3. Late Oct–Mar Fri 6–9pm, Sat–Sun noon–3pm and 4–7pm. Subway: 1/9 to 145th St. Bus: M11, Bx19.

This roomy, open-air rink on Riverbank's topmost level is very much in demand with school hockey teams, but public skating sessions are leisurely and pleasant—a boon for tentative young skaters. It's rarely crowded, though some fast and furious teenage skaters here don't always watch out for little ones. In summer, it converts to a roller rink.

Rockefeller Plaza Rink. Lower Plaza, Rockefeller Plaza (off Fifth Ave. between 49th and 50th sts.). ☎ **212/332-7654.** Admission Mon–Thurs $8.50 adults, $7 children 11 and under; Fri–Sun $11 adults, $7.50 children 11 and under. Nov–Dec Mon–Fri $13 adults, $9 children 11 and under; Sat–Sun, holidays, and Dec 24–Jan 1 $15 adults, $10 children 11 and under. Skate rental $6 (Nov–Dec $7). Oct–Apr 45-minute sessions daily; call for schedule. Subway: B/D/F/Q to 47th–50th sts./Rockefeller Center.

No doubt the most famous rink in town—and the easiest to find if you're a first-time visitor staying in a Midtown hotel—the Rockefeller Plaza Rink does have undeniable charm, especially in December, when you get to skate under the gargantuan Christmas tree. The golden statue of Prometheus reclines at rinkside, and tourists crowd around the railings above, staring down as you pirouette around (though the ice is sunken far enough below street level you're hardly aware of your audience). It's expensive (particularly around the holidays), you have to pay again if you want to skate for more than 45 minutes, and the rink is so small you can't get up much speed; there's usually a crowd, which means a wait in line to get in as well as a bit of jostling once you're on the ice. But do it once for the glamour of it.

✪ **Sky Rink.** Pier 61 at Chelsea Piers, 23rd St. at the Hudson River. ☎ **212/336-6100.** www.chelseapiers.com. Admission $11 adults, $8 children 12 and under. Skate rental $5, helmet rental $3, coin-operated lockers 75¢ (bring 3 quarters). Call for schedule of public skating sessions. Subway: 1/9, C/E, or F/N/R to 23rd St. stations. Bus: M23 across 23rd St.

Open 7 days a week year-round, this facility offers not one but two permanent ice rinks—the benefit of permanent ice being that the skating surface has more give than ice rinks laid down on top of other surfaces. (This is how Sky Rink justifies its relatively high prices.) The East Rink is booked up pretty solid with figure-skating classes and hockey programs, but the West Rink is open for general skating sessions every afternoon, more or less noon to 5pm, and some evenings to 9pm (call for the current schedule). If you're a good enough skater to look around, you can gaze out the windows to a wide-open Hudson view. It's a special treat to skate here in summer, wearing a T-shirt and shorts.

Wollman Rink. In Central Park—enter at E. 62nd St. ☎ **212/396-1010.** Admission $7 adults, $3.50 children 11 and under. Skate rental $3.50. Oct–Mar Mon–Tues 10am–3pm, Wed–Thurs and Sun 10am–9:30pm, Fri–Sat 10am–9pm.

Central Park's chief skating rink, at the southern end of the park nearest to Midtown, makes a super place to spin around the ice outdoors, with rock-music soundtrack piped in and a skyscraper skyline rising right beyond the trees. After school and on weekends, the ice can be thronged, but since skaters aren't limited to set session times, you can still get your money's worth if you hang out at the rink for a while, maybe refortifying yourself with food and hot chocolate from the snack bar while the Zamboni re-slicks the ice surface.

IN-LINE SKATING & ROLLER-SKATING

In **Central Park,** the top places for skating on weekends are the plaza by the Bandshell (just south of 72nd Street, at the end of the Mall), the Dead Road just east of the Sheep Meadow, and the West Drive near Tavern on the Green. The entire 6-mile loop of the circular drive is generally thronged with skaters on weekends, though it includes some challenging hills that may be too much for young skaters; the so-called Inner Loop, from 72nd Street down to 60th Street, is mostly level, however. At the **Wollman Rink,** midpark at 62nd Street (☎ **212/396-1010**), you can rent skates for use in the park, costing $15 for a whole day ($100 deposit, in cash or with a credit card).

Other favorite skating pavements around the city are the promenade in Riverside Park, West 83rd to 96th streets; the ramped areas for aggressive skating in **Riverside Park** at about 108th Street (below the promenade level—open May to October, admission $3); the Upper East Side's walkway on the bank of the East River from 60th Street on north; Union Square; the riverside Promenade in Battery Park City; and the pavements of Washington Square Park (bounded by Waverly Place and West 4th Street, at the foot of Fifth Avenue).

Skate-rental outlets have proliferated in Manhattan along with the in-line skating craze, but not all rent skates in children's sizes. Try **Blades Board & Skate** at one of its seven Manhattan locations: 120 W. 72nd St., between Columbus Avenue and Broadway (☎ **212/787-3911**); 1414 Second Ave., between 73rd and 74th streets (☎ **212/249-3178**); 160 E. 86th St., between Lexington and Third avenues (☎ **212/996-1644** or 212/336-6199); 901 Sixth Ave., between 32nd and 33rd streets, in the Manhattan Mall, 4th floor (☎ **212/563-2448**); at Chelsea Piers, 23rd Street and the West Side Highway (☎ **212/336-6299**); 659 Broadway, between Bond and Bleecker streets (☎ **212/477-7350**); and 128 Chambers St., at West Broadway (☎ **212/964-1944**). If you don't have your own wheels, you'll have to go to the following rinks, where skates are available for use at the rink only.

Riverbank State Park. 145th St. and Riverside Dr. ☎ **212/694-3642.** Admission $1. Skate rental $4. May–Sept daily 3–6pm (Fri also 7–10pm, Sat–Sun also 11am–2pm and 7pm–2am). Subway: 1/9 to 145th St. Bus: M11.

Perched above the banks of the Hudson, this sizable roofed rink catches lots of cooling breezes in summer, though it's an uptown trek.

Roller Rink. Pier 62 at Chelsea Piers, 23rd St. and the West Side Hwy., at the Hudson River. ☎ **212/336-6200.** www.chelseapiers.com. Admission $6 adults, $5 children 12 and under. Skate rental (including protective gear) $15 adults, $10 children. Credit-card deposit required. Subway: 1/9/C/E/F/N/R to 23rd St. Bus: M23 across 23rd St.

A pair of open-air roller-skating rinks are set out on the northernmost of Chelsea's recreational piers. Though roller hockey leagues keep the rinks busy, at least one or the other is open for general skating Saturday and Sunday noon to 5pm; there's also a grooving skate disco on Saturday 8 to 11pm. In-line skating instruction is offered as well. Between the rinks is an "aggressive skate park" for those who want to do stunt skating or skateboarding; it's open Monday to Friday 3 to 7pm, Saturday 10am to 7pm, and Sunday 10am to 6pm at $8 per session ($14 per day on weekends).

Wollman Rink. In Central Park—enter at E. 62nd St. ☎ **212/396-1010.** Admission $4 adults, $3 children 12 and under. Skate rental $6.50 (includes safety gear), $3 for safety gear only. Lessons available. Late May–Labor Day Thurs–Fri 11am–5pm, Sat–Sun 11am–8pm.

Considerably less crowded in the roller-skating season than it is in ice-skating season—probably because all the park's sidewalks and roads are also available for skating that covers more territory—in summer the Wollman hosts a hardy crew of in-liners who prefer circling around a rink with rock music blaring over the PA system. The fact that it's not crowded may make it an excellent place for beginning skaters to try out their wheels; it sure helps to have those wooden rink walls to crash into when you still haven't learned how to brake.

SKATEBOARDING

Two primo sites in Manhattan for trick skateboarders are **Central Park's West Drive,** between 66th and 70th streets (near Tavern on the Green), where hot-doggers set up jumps and obstacles to show off their moves; and the swerving concrete ramps around the **entrance to the Brooklyn Bridge,** near City Hall and the Municipal Building, Centre Street just south of Chambers Street. If you don't mind paying an admission fee, try the ramps set up for aggressive skateboarding in **Riverside Park,** at about 108th Street, west of the promenade (☎ **212/408-0239;** May to October, admission $3), and at **Chelsea Piers,** Pier 62, 23rd Street and the West Side Highway (☎ **212/336-6200;** admission $6 adults, $5 children 12 and under). Two other sidewalk options are in and around **Union Square** (14th to 17th streets, Broadway to Park Avenue South) and the island around the cube sculpture at **Astor Place** (East 8th and Lafayette streets, in the East Village). The primo sources for boards, either sale or rental, is **Blades Board & Skate;** of its several locations all over town, the two handiest for these skateboarding sites are at 120 W. 72nd St., between Broadway and Columbus Avenue (☎ 212/787-3911), and 128 Chambers St. at West Broadway (☎ **212/964-1944**).

SWIMMING

This is one severe shortage in New York's recreation facilities: There are very few clean, well-run pools open to the public. If you're visiting and a place to swim is important to you, zone in one of the hotels that has its own pool (see chapter 10). If you live here and you're dying to take a swim, enroll your child in swim classes or join a health club. Another option worth knowing about is that you can pay for a 1-day drop-in swim at the Upper East Side's **Asphalt Green,** York Avenue between 90th and 92nd streets (☎ **212/369-8890**). A 1-day pass is $15 for adults and $7 for kids 16 and under; public swimming sessions are Monday to Friday 5:30am to 3pm and 8 to 10pm and Saturday and Sunday 8am to 8pm. Asphalt Green has two marvelous, clean pools: one 25 yards long and the other an Olympic-sized 50-meter pool; the big pool is used for public swimming only on Sunday. The city's only other Olympic-sized pool is at **Riverbank State Park,** 145th Street and Riverside Drive (☎ **212/694-3665**), which also offers a smaller outdoor pool in summer; use of the Riverbank pools is far cheaper than Asphalt Green, at $2 for adults and $1 for kids 5 to 15. Call for public swimming schedules. A pricier option is a day-use pass for the atrium rooftop pool and health club at **Le Parker Meridien** hotel, 118 W. 57th St., between Sixth and Seventh avenues; passes cost $50 per person, child or adult, and you must call the health club at ☎ **212/245-1144** to check on availability.

To be frank, I wouldn't advise taking your kids to swim in the city parks' pools, which often are overrun; conditions can be less than sanitary, and there have been some alleged incidents of sexual harassment. I wish the situation were better, but it hasn't improved yet. For the record, here are the three main city-run indoor pools: **East 54th Street,** 348 E. 54th St., between First and Second avenues (☎ 212/397-3154); **Carmine Street,** Clarkson Street and Seventh Avenue South (☎ 212/242-5228); and **West 59th Street,** 533 W. 59th St., between Tenth and Eleventh avenues (☎ 212/397-3159). Carmine Street also has an outdoor pool open in summer. The best of the city's outdoor pools, which are open July and August only, are at Carmine Street, at **John Jay Park,** East 77th Street and Cherokee Place, just east of York Avenue (☎ **212/794-6566**), and at Central Park's **Lasker Pool,** midpark at East 106th Street (☎ **212/534-7639**).

TENNIS

Very few public tennis courts are available in Manhattan, where most serious tennis players belong to private clubs. You'll find two fairly decent sets in **Riverside Park,** Riverside Drive at either 96th or 116th Street; play is first-come, first-served, but there's not usually much of a wait. At the city's premier public facility, the **Central Park Tennis Center,** midpark at West 93rd Street, matters are somewhat more complicated. Players who have bought an annual tennis permit ($50 adults, $20 seniors, $10 juniors) can make advance reservations by phone for $5 on weekdays between noon and 2pm (call ☎ **212/280-0201** for information and reservations). Anyone else can get a single-play ticket for $5 at the Tennis Center on the day of play, entitling you to an hour of court time. You can sign up for a specific court time—in person only—or put your name on the no-show list to take the next available court; players who don't show up 15 minutes before their booked court time get bumped, so plenty of folks from that stand-by list do get to play. When the hourly bell rings, there's a mass exodus from the courts—26 Har-Tru and 4 hard courts (doubles players, however, can reserve 2 hours at a time). If you don't have your own racquet, you can rent one at the pro shop ($5 for 2 hours), and they do have kid-sized racquets. April to November, the Tennis Center is open daily 6:30am to dusk.

It may be worth an excursion into Queens just to play on the site of the U.S. Open, the **U.S.T.A. National Tennis Center** in Flushing Meadows–Corona Park (take the no. 7 subway to the Shea Stadium stop). Call the center at ☎ **718/760-6200** to reserve a court, no more than 2 days in advance. Fees are $11 to $23 per hour for outdoor courts; for indoor courts, which are open year-round, per-hour rates are $30 to $44. The center is open daily 8am to midnight.

4 Indoor Playgrounds

The winter play scene in Manhattan is relieved by these huge rooms with innovative, brightly colored structures encouraging all sorts of active and fantasy play. While these can be lifesavers on a cold or rainy day when the kids are climbing the walls, when you arrive you may find that everybody else in town has had the same bright idea. They're popular party locales too, which makes for sardinelike crowds on weekends.

Chelsea Piers Field House. Pier 62 at Chelsea Piers, 23rd St. and the West Side Hwy., at the Hudson River. ☎ **212/336-6500.** Admission $10 to Toddler Gym, $17 to Open Gym & Climb, $7 for soccer field or basketball courts, $1 per 10 balls in batting cages. Call for schedule. Subway: 1/9, C/E, or F/N/R to 23rd St. stations. Bus: M23 across 23rd St.

Calling this recreation facility an indoor playground is kind of like calling the Superdome a football field. What a fabulous resource this is: batting cages, basketball courts, artificial turf fields that can be adapted for soccer or volleyball or lacrosse, an indoor climbing wall scaled perfectly for young climbers, and a gymnastics area you have to see to believe—spring floors, in-ground trampolines, deep foam pits for practicing dismounts, and loads of bars, beams, rings, horses, and vaults. Most of the facility is booked up with ongoing classes and league play, but kids 4 and older can check out the Field House at an Open Gym session, while children 1 to 4 can occupy themselves happily in the Toddler Gym, a separate playroom with soft climbing structures.

Early Childhood Resources & Information Center. 66 Leroy St. (between Hudson St. and Seventh Ave. South). ☎ **212/929-0815.** Free admission. Mon–Sat 1–4:30pm. Subway: 1/9 to Houston St.

This public library branch in the West Village has a little-known bonus: a large indoor area set aside for infants and toddlers (under age 6 only), with small slides and other equipment for stretching those muscles. Best of all, it's free.

✪ **PlaySpace.** 2473 Broadway (at 92nd St.). ☎ **212/769-2300.** www.playspaceny.com. Admission $7.50 per person. Daily 9:30am–6pm. Subway: 1/2/3/9 to 96th St.

This large, colorful playroom is custom-designed for the 6-and-under crowd, with a special carpeted area set aside for infants and their grown-ups. Large windows let in plenty of light, making it feel less claustrophobic than some of the other indoor playgrounds. There's a huge sand area with lots of digging toys and incredibly white sand (you could never keep sand this clean outdoors in the parks); a wide-open area of blond hardwood floor allows toddlers to trundle around on sturdy little bikes and minicars, and there are a couple of waist-high troughs for water play. Best of all is the imaginative bilevel structure running along the north wall, incorporating little nooks and crannies for block-building and dress-up and puppet play with a series of ladders and tunnels and towers and bridges. There's also a small cafe where kids can refuel and parents can prop themselves up with coffee and a newspaper. Everything is spick-and-span and well supervised, and nothing seems too hokey or contrived—no ball mazes for small children to get lost and frightened in, either. When this place first opened, I thought it was overpriced, but now that I've seen all the competition I realize how superior PlaySpace is.

Rain or Shine. 202 E. 29th St. (at Third Ave.). ☎ **212/532-4420.** Admission $6.95 per child, free for adults. Daily 10am–5pm. Subway: 6 or N/R to 28th St.

Best for children 6 and under, this rain forest–themed play space is a godsend in this between-neighborhoods part of town. Dramatic play is encouraged in the main area with a curtained stage, dress-up costumes, puppets, and a good-sized playhouse (complete with a picket fence), as well as a few slides and tunnels to work off energy. My children were drawn like magnets to the mini–roller coaster—a riding toy on a track with very gentle hills—which is extremely popular (giving rise to lots of impromptu lessons on sharing). It also has a super sandbox, a big walk-in pit with a slide, lots of big plastic dump trucks, and sparkling white sand. The enclosed infant area is small but cozy, and an open art room provides an outlet for kids at the older end of the spectrum. This long, narrow space is easily flooded by arriving birthday parties, but once they vanish to the downstairs gym and party room, things calm down. There's a limited selection of snacks for sale, with a cafe counter running the length of the main space so noshing parents can keep an eye on their kids.

5 Classes & Workshops

ART & SCIENCE WORKSHOPS

ArtsConnection. 120 W. 46th St. (between Sixth Ave. and Broadway). ☎ **212/302-7433.** www.artsconnection.org. Workshops $2, performances $6. Subway: B/D/F/Q to 47th–50th sts./Rockefeller Center; N/R to 49th St.; 1/2/3/9 to 42nd St./Times Square; C/E to 50th St.

Call in advance for a schedule of this useful organization's Saturday workshops for kids, from October to May. The range of interests is huge: dance, puppetry, storytelling, hands-on art, art history, music appreciation, and more.

Dana Discovery Center. In Central Park at the Harlem Meer, 110th St. at Lenox Ave. ☎ **212/860-1370.** Subway: 2/3 to 110th St. Bus: M2, M3, M4 to 110th St./Fifth Ave.

Summer weekends usually see free entertainment out on the plaza here, and arts-and-crafts workshops, science displays, puppet shows, and the like are regularly held inside this beautiful pondside facility, a short walk north of the Conservatory Garden. Call for schedules.

92nd Street Y. 1395 Lexington Ave. (at 92nd St.). ☎ **212/996-1100.** Subway: 4/5/6 to 86th St.

Affiliated with the YMHA (Young Men's Hebrew Association), this is one of the city's greatest cultural resources, with loads of evening programs in music and the arts and a vast roster of sign-up classes for adults and children. Call to ask what is currently available on a drop-in basis.

Sony Wonder Technology Lab. 550 Madison Ave. (entrance on 56th St.). ☎ **212/ 833-8100.** www.sonywondertechlab.com. Subway: E/F to Fifth Ave.

Many Saturdays and Sundays, this super Midtown attraction runs Fundays@The Lab: 3-hour workshops and activity sessions exploring different themes in communications technology—3-D effects, mirrors, animation, robotics, and so on. Most are designed for ages 5 to 8 and charge a $5 materials fee (Sony Wonder admission itself is free); call ahead for a schedule of upcoming classes.

DROP-IN CRAFTS

Craft Studio. 1657 Third Ave. (between 92nd and 93rd sts.). ☎ **212/831-6626.** Subway: 4/5/6 to 86th St.; 6 to 96th St.

Plasterwork painting is a big draw here—superheroes, harlequin masks, rainbows, cars, picture frames, puppies, kittens, dinosaurs, you name it, you can paint it (with a little help from the friendly staff). You pay according to the price of the piece you choose. Terra-cotta pots are available for painting (think Mother's Day presents), as are assorted other ceramic items. The space is roomy and well lit, with a rain-forest decor, and the shop carries a good number of excellent crafts and toys.

Little Shop of Plaster & Pottery. 431 E. 73rd St. (between First and York aves.). ☎ **212/717-6636.** Subway: 6 to 68th or 77th St.

Pick a piece of precast plaster from the racks lining the walls, and you can paint it whatever colors you choose, daub on designs in finger wax, sprinkle glitter all over, and just generally make it your own masterpiece. There's no charge except the price of the plaster pieces, which are $9.95 and up. The staff helps out as much as you need; teenagers labor intently for hours over incredibly detailed curlicues, while little kids are allowed to happily slap on paint as they please. (Our assistant just grinned and winked when my 4-year-old solemnly painted his entire car yellow, then covered it all up with red, then covered it completely again with purple.) They also carry a full line of functional pottery pieces to decorate. You can't take these home for about a week, but shipping is available for out-of-towners. Sand bottle art (a good bet for younger brothers and sisters) and custom hand-painted "tattoos" are also on the menu. It's a friendly, relaxed place, and the painting is more fun than I expected; come on weekday afternoons, and you might have the place practically to yourself.

Our Name Is Mud. (1) 1566 Second Ave. (between 81st and 82nd sts.). ☎ **212/ 570-6868.** www.ournameismud.com. Subway: 4/5/6 to 86th St. (2) 506 Amsterdam Ave. (between 84th and 85th sts.). ☎ **212/579-5575.** Subway: 1/2/3/9 to 86th St. (3) 59 Greenwich Ave. (at Seventh Ave.). ☎ **212/647-7899.** Subway: 1/2/3/9 to 14th St.

The ceramic items that customers paint here must be glazed and fired in a kiln, which means you pick them up a week after you've painted them—not as good on the instant gratification score as the plaster-painting shops above. On the other hand, you'll end up with a real piece of pottery, from a mug to a piggybank to a pitcher to a platter, a real keepsake that's also functional, and my kids are always delighted to see me using the mugs they made for me for Mother's Day. Pieces range from $5 to $60.

MUSEUM WEEKEND WORKSHOPS

On weekends, a number of major Manhattan museums seek to attract families by offering children's workshops, usually free with museum admission. Times vary, so plan on calling ahead.

The **Children's Museum of Manhattan,** 212 W. 83rd St., between Amsterdam Avenue and Broadway (☎ 212/721-1223; admission $6, free for children under 1), always has a lineup of fun workshops, often themed to holidays. The **Children's Museum of the Arts,** 182 Lafayette St., between Broome and Grand streets (☎ 212/274-0986; admission $5, free for children under 1), sets up hands-on art projects every weekend, providing materials for kids to create anything from papier-mâché masks to found-art collages to giant mobiles. **Midtown's Museum of Television and Radio,** 25 W. 52nd St. (☎ 212/621-6600; admission $5), has fun Saturday workshops, including a series in which kids can re-create old radio scripts. Up in Riverdale, **Wave Hill,** 675 W. 252nd St., the Bronx (☎ 718/549-3200; admission $4 adults, $2 students, free for children under 6), organizes superb hands-on children's workshops combining arts and crafts with nature study, helping children to appreciate the estate's magnificent gardens and Hudson River landscape.

The **Jewish Museum,** 1109 Fifth Ave., at 92nd Street (☎ 212/423-3200; admission $8 adults, $5.50 students, free for children under 12), is closed on Friday and Saturday for the Jewish Sabbath, but on Sunday it often offers some lively workshops based on Judaic history or holidays. Down in Battery Park City, the **Museum of Jewish Heritage—A Living Memorial to the Holocaust,** 18 First Place, at Battery Place (☎ 212/509-6130; admission $7 adults, $5 students, free for children under 5), also closes early on Friday and all day Saturday, but it has frequent engaging Sunday workshops for children.

The **Asia Society,** 725 Park Ave., at 70th Street (☎ 212/288-6400; admission $4 adults, $2 students, free for children 12 and under), comes up with really super workshops exploring various facets of different Asian cultures—Chinese story-tellers, Indonesian puppets. And, less frequently, the **China Institute,** 125 E. 65th St., between Park and Lexington avenues (☎ 212/744-8181; suggested donation $5 to $10), offers similar workshops usually around the Chinese New Year or connected with current rotating shows in its galleries.

Among the city's art museums, the best programs for kids are probably those offered by the **Museum of Modern Art,** 11 W. 53rd St., between Fifth and Sixth avenues (☎ 212/708-9400; admission $10 adults, $6.50 students, free for children under 16), which organizes Saturday tours for 4-year-olds, gallery talks for ages 5 to 10, hands-on classes for the entire family, and family-oriented programs of classic short films. The **Whitney Museum of American Art,** 945 Madison Ave., at 75th Street (☎ 212/570-3600; admission $10 adults, $8 students, free for children 11 and under); the **Museum of American Folk Art,** 2 Lincoln Square, between 65th and 66th streets (☎ 212/595-9533; free admission, $1 materials fee for children's workshops); and the **Studio Museum in Harlem,** 144 W. 125th St., between Lenox Avenue and Adam Clayton Powell Boulevard (☎ 212/864-4500; admission $5 adults, $3 students, $1 children 11 and under), present frequent art workshops highlighting aspects of their collections or current exhibitions.

Shopping with Your Kids

7

New York City kids are trained to be conspicuous consumers, with a wide range of options for spending money—deluxe children's clothing boutiques, toy stores crammed with imported marvels, wondrous hobby shops, and comic-book and trading card dealers stocked with rarities. Some of these can be downright overwhelming, not to mention astronomically priced (come on, what kid really needs that $450 party frock from Bonpoint or that $600 stuffed King Kong from FAO Schwarz?). And while adults can safely indulge in mere window-shopping, it's a rare kid who's content to look without trying to coerce you to buy.

One happy thing about Manhattan toy stores is that most of them (not FAO, of course) have a wall of under-$5 toys to pacify your child if you decide against that $150 Playmobil castle. Otherwise, it's best to know what you're shopping for and head straight for the store most likely to have it.

1 The Shopping Scene

SHOPPING HOURS & SALES TAX

Neighborhood stores are generally open daily 10am to 6pm, though some of the upscale East Side boutiques are closed on Sunday. Stores that are open on Sunday may not open until noon, however. Some small Midtown boutiques are closed on weekends, but not the tourist-dependent Fifth Avenue showcases. Street fairs and flea markets are generally weekends-only operations.

An 8.25% **sales tax** is levied on clothing and shoe purchases over $110. Take-out food, groceries, and services are exempt from sales tax.

SHOPPING DISTRICTS

THE UPPER WEST SIDE   Lots of families live in this neighborhood, and its toy and clothing shops tend to be down-to-earth, if occasionally too earnestly wholesome. You'll probably be here at some point anyway, visiting the American Museum of Natural History or the Children's Museum of Manhattan or PlaySpace, so check out the outstanding toy stores between 76th and 87th streets—**Unique Science, Penny Whistle Toys,** and **West Side Kids**—where toys are chosen with an eye toward durability, educational value, and reasonable price. The West Side is good for one-of-a-kinders, like **Shoofly,** a marvelous children's hat store (it sells shoes too), and **Plain Jane,** selling adorable nursery antiques.

THE UPPER EAST SIDE   This is the best area of town, hands-down, for pricey, gorgeous kids' clothes and precious toy boutiques. If you're shopping without kids in tow, a serious Madison Avenue expedition could take all day—all the designer kids' boutiques are here, between 62nd and 96th streets (**Jacadi** and **Bonpoint** even have two Madison Avenue locations). Shops along Lexington and Third avenues are a little more reasonable, but there are still some darling finds, especially in the toy realm: **Mary Arnold Toys,** the **New York Doll Hospital,** and **Big City Kites,** not to mention the **Store of Knowledge,** a gleaming PBS-affiliated emporium with loads of nifty puzzles and gadgets and science-tinkering stuff. On East 86th Street, **Barnes & Noble** has one of the city's biggest and best children's book departments, and if you need to get your child's locks chopped, three of the kids' hair salons I list in this chapter are here, between 78th and 92nd streets.

MIDTOWN   Primarily a business area, Midtown doesn't have many children's stores, and what it does have seems designed for indulgent grandparents and foreign tourists intent on stocking up on licensed-character items. There's **FAO Schwarz,** of course, the toy store to end all toy stores; joining it along formerly chichi Fifth Avenue are the **Warner Bros. Studio Store** and the **Disney Store,** which between them pretty much have the lock on cartoon character–driven merchandise (you'll also find **Warner Bros.** at Times Square and the **Disney Store** near Lincoln Center).

At the other end of Midtown, Herald Square (34th Street and Broadway) has a cluster of less glitzy stores to attract kids: **Macy's** department store, a grubby multilevel **Toys 'Я' Us** in a dismal vertical mall once owned by Imelda Marcos, and a handful of chain stores in **Manhattan Mall,** Sixth Avenue at 32nd Street (☎ 212/465-0500), a surprisingly bright and busy vertical mall with glass elevators shooting up and down the central atrium—a very un-Manhattan refuge. A number of small specialty shops, mostly for collectors, are tucked into spaces around high-rent Midtown.

CHELSEA   There's one reason for shopping in Chelsea if you have kids: **Books of Wonder,** the dean of children's bookstores in Manhattan.

GREENWICH VILLAGE   Between **Forbidden Planet** and **Village Comics,** Greenwich Village is the place to interest older kids who are into comics, trading cards, vintage records, and sci-fi/fantasy stuff. It's also Chess Central on Thompson Street just south of Washington Square, where the **Chess Shop** and the **Chess Forum** sell some beautiful chess sets and let kids play for hours. Funky-but-chic clothes rule down here, in stores like **Ibiza Kidz, Village Kidz, Bombalulu's,** and **Peanut Butter & Jane.** Older kids whose idea of fashion lies more at the grunge end of the spectrum may want to troll Broadway below Astor Place, where warehouselike stores sell vintage clothes and army surplus and Doc Martens.

THE EAST VILLAGE   The shops here are just plain way out, especially when it comes to toys and accessories; work your way across East 9th Street and you'll see what I mean—starting with the relatively staid **Dinosaur Hill** and getting stranger as you go east to **It's a Mod, Mod World** or down Avenue A to **Alphabets.** Preteens and teens will find this edgy neighborhood eye-opening, though younger ones may not be clued in.

SOHO & TRIBECA   Parents down here tend to be loft-living urban pioneers with a highly developed visual sense, and the kids' stores reflect this with a very cool, sophisticated, miniature-adult sensibility (the **Enchanted Forest** toy store is a prime example).

WALL STREET This area is hardly a target zone for shopping for kids. The occasional children's shop is geared to guilt-ridden working parents picking up a last-minute gift/bribe. There are a couple of mall-type destinations: **South Street Seaport** features a characterless mix of midrange chain stores and odd theme boutiques (a whole store for butterflies, for instance, or for soft sculptures), many of them under a roof in the Pier 17 pavilion. The **World Trade Center** has a concourse of shops where commuters can buy essentials before whizzing home on the PATH trains. For upscale recreational shopping, try the **World Financial Center,** across the street in Battery Park City; though few stores cater to kids, the complex's Winter Garden Atrium is a stunning space with a long cascade of marble steps that toddlers seem to find irresistible, and outside is a yacht basin and long Hudson River esplanade.

STREET MARKETS

The long-running Sunday flea market on the Upper West Side at **P.S. 44,** Columbus Avenue at 76th Street, has loads of junk to sort through in the schoolyard, with loads of friendly West Siders jostling one another. On Saturday and Sunday the **Annex Flea Market,** Sixth Avenue at 26th Street ($1 parking/admission), has some finds if you're into nostalgia and kitsch.

The **Union Square Greenmarket,** 16th Street between Broadway and Park Avenue South, runs Monday, Wednesday, Friday, and Saturday and has some truly glorious produce from rural New York State, New Jersey, and Pennsylvania. There's a bustling playground directly south of the greenmarket, so pick up lunch (crisp Macoun apples, fresh cheddar cheese, hearty seven-grain bread) and eat on a bench while the kids clamber away.

May to October, various stretches of Manhattan streets are closed to traffic for **street fairs** featuring booths selling everything from T-shirts to audiotapes to potted palms and hand-knit Peruvian sweaters. The food booths are even more fun—sizzling-hot stir-fries or heaping tacos or foot-long hot dogs. Sometimes there'll be a petting zoo or one of those inflated castles kids can bounce around in. You tend to see the same vendors weekend after weekend, and little that's for sale is really special. But the main thing is the crowd, the sunshine, and the car-free strolling. Look for posters in store windows.

2 Shopping A to Z

My listings are mainly for kid-specific stores and merchandise. If you want to check out what New York offers adult shoppers, see *Frommer's New York City.*

BABY & PRESCHOOLER CLOTHES

Au Chat Botte. 1192 Madison Ave. (at 87th St.). ☎ **212/722-6474.** Subway: 4/5/6 to 86th St.

In sizes 0 to 2, you'll find beautiful and dressy European imports at stiff prices— $350 for an exquisite fawn-colored velvet frock with an ivory lace collar. The nursery furnishings shop next door offers some lovely crib beddings. Closed Sunday.

Baby Gap. (1) 1037 Lexington Ave. (at 74th St.). ☎ **212/327-2614.** www.gap.com. Subway: 6 to 77th St. (2) 341 Columbus Ave. (at 76th St.). ☎ **212/875-9196.** Subway: B/C to 79th St.

Although there are Baby Gap departments inside several of the Gap Kids stores (see "Everyday Clothing," later in this chapter), these two branches are exclusively for baby sizes up to 4XL. Sturdy, simple knits with a casual sense of style, like all Gap clothes.

Bloomers. 1042 Lexington Ave. (between 74th and 75th sts.). ☎ **212/570-9529.** Subway: 6 to 77th St.

The refreshing mix here is women's lingerie and children's clothes up to 6X, all in cozy, casual cotton knits. Labels include Green Babies, New Potatoes, Big Fish, and Marimekko. Closed Sunday.

✪ **Bombalulu's.** 101 W. 10th St. (between Sixth and Greenwich aves.). ☎ **212/463-0897.** Subway: B/D/F/A/C/E to West 4th St.

Funky, casual, colorful clothing in sizes up to age 5—a nice counterpoint to all the Upper Madison Avenue frills. Lots of toys too.

Calypso Enfants. 284 Mulberry St. (between Prince and Houston sts.). ☎ **212/965-8910.** Subway: B/D/F/Q to Broadway/Lafayette St.

Imported French designer ensembles for newborns to size 12 draw fashion-conscious downtown parents to this SoHo shop.

Farmer's Daughter and Son. 1001 First Ave. (at 55th St.). ☎ **212/421-0731.** Subway: E/F to Lexington Ave. and 53rd St.

Amid the drapey, casual women's clothes at this Midtown shop, you'll find a limited but tasteful selection of little children's clothes, plus a few wholesome toys. Well worth a stop if you're nearby.

✪ **Jacadi.** (1) 1281 Madison Ave. (between 91st and 92nd sts.). ☎ **212/369-1616.** www.jacadiusa.com. Subway: 4/5/6 to 86th St. (2) 787 Madison Ave. (between 66th and 67th sts.). ☎ **212/535-3200.** Subway: 6 to 68th St.

Imported from France, this lovely upscale line of baby clothes (and stuff for older kids) features stylish simplicity in rich colors and pastels, with cottons and knits that last.

Julian & Sara. 103 Mercer St. (between Prince and Spring sts.). ☎ **212/226-1989.** Subway: N/R to Prince St.

This tiny SoHo shop sells frilly, pretty upscale things in sizes for newborns to 12 years for girls and boys.

Koh's Kids. 311 Greenwich St. (between Chambers and Reade sts.). ☎ **212/791-6915.** Subway: 1/2/3/9 to Chambers St.

This is the TriBeCa source for funky, contemporary, casual clothes for the newborn to size 10 set, including American labels like Cozy Toes.

La Layette. 170 E. 61st St. (between Lexington and Third aves.). ☎ **212/688-7072.** Subway: 4/5/6 to 59th St.

Lace, smocking, and embroidery turn these infant clothes (to size 2) into frilly fashion statements; if you don't mind seeing a newborn spit up Similac over that $150 moiré silk dress, indulge yourself. Other new-baby gifts are engraved silver picture frames, hand-painted nursery furniture, personalized pillows, and lovely ruffly crib bedding.

La Petite Etoile. 746 Madison Ave. (between 64th and 65th sts.). ☎ **212/744-0975.** www.lapetiteetoile.com. Subway: 6 to 68th St.

Christening gowns and flower-girl dresses head the lineup of pretty clothes—casual as well as dressy—at this trim shop along the Mad Ave boutique strip.

Lester's. 1522 Second Ave. (at 79th St.). ☎ **212/734-9292.** Subway: 6 to 77th St.

The layette department at this roomy East Side clothing shop features imported and designer styles, at fairly reasonable prices.

Magic Windows. 1186 Madison Ave. (at 87th St.). ☎ **212/289-0028.** Subway: 4/5/6 to 86th St.

Here you'll find East Side–conservative, traditional baby clothes (sizes up to 6X), all in pastel blues and pinks, as well as a selection of snowy linens for bassinet and crib. The tiny white cotton sweaters are adorable.

○ **Nursery Lines.** 1034 Lexington Ave. (at 74th St.). ☎ **212/396-4445.** www.nurserylines. com. Subway: 6 to 77th St.

Lots of hand-embroidered baby clothing, much of it imported from Italy, and precious hand-knit sweaters fill this tasteful corner shop. You can also order stunning custom-designed nursery furniture, and there's even a baby-gift registry. Sizes up to 4 years.

Plain Jane. 525 Amsterdam Ave. (between 85th and 86th sts.). ☎ **212/595-6916.** Subway: 1/9 to 86th St.

There are only a few baby clothes here, and they're all darling, from the lacy antique christening gowns to a nutty one-piece knit that'll make your infant look like a Campbell's Soup can. Somebody here is having fun. Closed Sunday.

Tartine Et Chocolat. 1047 Madison Ave. (at 80th St.). ☎ **212/717-2112.** Subway: 6 to 77th St.

Luxe children's clothing, imported from France, is carried here in sizes up to 10 years, for boys and girls. The smock dresses and delicate little jackets are *fantastique;* so are the prices.

Wicker Garden's Children. 1327 Madison Ave. (at 93rd St.). ☎ **212/410-7001.** Subway: 6 to 96th St.

The downstairs section has loads of frilly stuff, predominantly in eye-blinding white. (I had nervous visions of splattered juice and mushed peas all over those starched pique pinafores.) They carry up to size 4, for boys as well as girls, though the boys' duds are definitely only for dress-up. The shop is on the pricey end of the spectrum. Closed Sunday.

Wynken, Blynken and Nod. 306 E. 55th St. (between First and Second aves.). ☎ **212/ 308-9299.** Subway: E/F to Lexington/Third aves.

A convenient shop for the Sutton Place crowd, this boutique with a nostalgic 1950s look carries a range of quality children's wear, from casual to dressy. It's mostly designer stuff but not too outrageously priced, for sizes newborn to 6. The shop has a significant toy section as well, including many wooden toys and puzzles. Closed Sunday and Monday.

○ **Z'Baby Company.** (1) 100 W. 72nd St. (at Columbus Ave.). ☎ **212/579-BABY.** Subway: 1/2/3/B/C to 72nd St. (2) 996 Lexington Ave. (at 72nd St.). ☎ **212/472-2229.** Subway: 6 to 68th St.

Both the slick West Side shop and its new East Side partner feature casual clothes (boys' sizes newborn to 7, girls up to 14) with upscale labels like Erin's Babies, Petit Bateau, Alphabet, and Lily Pulitzer. My son saw a $200 black leather baby biker jacket here that he badgered me to buy for about 15 minutes.

BOOKS

☉ Bank Street College Book Store. 610 W. 112th St. (at Broadway). ☎ **212/678-1654.** www.bankstreetbooks.com. Subway: 1/9 to 110th St.

This narrow, bright uptown store has a wonderful selection of over 40,000 titles and an extremely knowledgeable staff. It's connected to an outstanding education college, so there's also a great section for parents and teachers.

Barnes & Noble. (1) 240 E. 86th St. (between Second and Third aves.). ☎ **212/794-1962.** www.bn.com. Subway: 4/5/6 to 86th St. (2) 2289 Broadway (at 82nd St.). ☎ **212/362-8835.** Subway: 1/9 to 79th St. (3) 1972 Broadway (at 66th St.). ☎ **212/595-6859.** Subway: 1/9 to Lincoln Center. (3) Citicorp Building (at Third Ave. and 54th St.). ☎ **212/750-8033.** Subway: E/F to Lexington Ave. (4) Rockefeller Center, 600 Fifth Ave. (at 48th St.). ☎ **212/765-0590.** Subway: B/D/F/Q to Rockefeller Center. (5) 675 Sixth Ave. (at 21st St.). ☎ **212/727-1227.** Subway: F to 23rd St. (5) 105 Fifth Ave. (at 18th St.). ☎ **212/807-0099.** Subway: 1/9 to 18th St. (6) 4 Astor Place (between Broadway and Lafayette St.). ☎ **212/420-1322.** Subway: 6 to Astor Place. (7) Union Square, 33 E. 17th St. (between Broadway and Park Ave.). ☎ **212/253-0810.** Subway: 4/5/6/L/N/R to Union Square.

A lot of people grouse about how this big chain bookstore drove small specialty stores out of business. Yes, I miss Eeyore's and Storyland, too. But get over it, folks—these megastores have great children's sections (the 86th Street one has the largest), with some informed salespeople, plenty of room for kids to frolic, frequent story hours and author appearances, and just about any book you could ever want for your kids. Story hours (half hours, really) at various branches of this big bookstore chain often feature the authors themselves. On the Upper West Side, the branch near Lincoln Center (66th Street) runs its story times Saturday at 10:30am and Wednesday at 4:30pm, while the Broadway and 82nd Street branch has a Tuesday story hour at 10:30am. In Midtown, the Citicorp branch has Wednesday story hour at 10am. The Union Square story hour is at 2pm Saturday. Story hours at the 86th Street branch vary, so you're advised to call ahead. The store has even added kids' meals to the upstairs cafe menu, so you know they're serious about attracting family business. The Fifth Avenue and Rockefeller Center locations have good children's sections, but don't have story hours or entertainment.

Bookberries. 983 Lexington Ave. (at 71st St.). ☎ **212/794-9400.** Subway: 6 to 68th St.

A cozy little carpeted nook has been partitioned off for kids in this small East Side store. The selection is fairly good, though the picture books may be haphazardly alphabetized—probably because so many little hands have pulled them out. A good sign.

☉ Books of Wonder. 16 W. 18th St. (between Fifth and Sixth aves.). ☎ **212/989-3270.** Subway: 1/9 to 18th St.

One of the few specialty children's bookstores left in town, this great Chelsea shop has a lot of hard-to-find titles, as well as collectors' items (the Oz books, original Nancy Drews). Friendly, helpful, knowledgeable staff. Story hour is Sunday at 11:45am.

Borders Books & Music. (1) 5 World Trade Center (corner of Church and Vesey sts.). ☎ **212/839-8049.** www.borders.com. Subway: E to World Trade Center. (2) 461 Park Ave. (at 57th St.). ☎ **212/980-6785.** Subway: 4/5/6 to 59th St. (3) 576 Second Ave. (at 32nd St.) in Kips Bay Plaza. ☎ **212/685-3938.** Subway: 6 to 33rd St.

This chain megastore was much needed in the bookstore void known as Wall Street; the fact that it has a strong and welcoming children's section is the icing on the cake. In the Wall Street branch, regular story time is Tuesday at 10am; story hours for the

Park Avenue store are Tuesday and Thursday at 10am; and there are three regular story times at the Kips Bay Plaza branch—Tuesday and Saturday at 10am and Sunday at 2pm.

Gryphon Bookshop. 2246 Broadway (between 80th and 81st sts.). ☎ **212/362-0706.** Subway: 1/9 to 79th St.

This excellent little used bookstore—narrow, dusky, with books to the ceiling—has a strong children's section, with some real finds.

Logos Bookstore. 1575 York Ave. (between 83rd and 84th sts.). ☎ **212/517-7292.** Subway: 4/5/6 to 86th St.

Near Carl Schurz Park, this pleasant shop has a good children's corner at the back, near the small but leafy outdoor garden, a delightful place for reading in fair weather. While the store's specialty is religious books, this isn't heavily emphasized in the kids' selection, which does include some interesting titles from smaller publishers.

Shakespeare and Company. 939 Lexington Ave. (between 68th and 69th sts.). ☎ **212/570-5148.** Subway: 6 to 68th St.

This surviving East Side branch of the old Upper West Side literary hangout offers a decent children's section, with pint-sized chairs and a carpet for in-store reading. Definitely worth a visit if you want to park the youngsters while you browse. The selection is intelligent, if skewed toward "worthy" picture books and classics.

CANDY, CHOCOLATE & SWEETS

☉ **Elk Candy Co.** 1628 Second Ave. (between 84th and 85th sts.). ☎ **212/650-1177.** Subway: 4/5/6 to 86th St.

Wonderful marzipan creations and molded chocolate entice sweet tooths here; it has a very European flavor, a holdover from the days when Yorkville was the German part of town.

Li-Lac Chocolates. (1) 120 Christopher St. (between Hudson and Bleecker sts.). ☎ **212/242-7374.** Subway: 1/9 to Christopher St. (2) Park Ave. and 42nd St., The Food Market at Grand Central Terminal. ☎ **212/370-4866.** Subway: 4/5/6/7/S to Grand Central Terminal.

These charming shops sell handmade chocolates molded into a delightful variety of shapes.

Mondel Chocolates. 2913 Broadway (near 114th St.). ☎ **212/864-2111.** Subway: 1/9 to 116th St.

This old-fashioned little shop in the Columbia University area has beautiful hand-made chocolates and other gift items for the sweet tooth.

Sweets from Heaven. (1) 2052 Broadway (between 70th and 71st sts.). ☎ **212/712-2216.** Subway: 1/2/3/9 to 72nd St. (2) 148 E. 86th St. (between Third and Lexington aves.). ☎ **212/860-8773.** Subway: 4/5/6 to 86th St.

A bright, modern equivalent of the old penny candy store, Sweets from Heaven is full of clear acrylic bins full of loose candies (wrapped and unwrapped) that customers scoop into bags and buy by weight. There are also shelves of imported candy bars (homesick British and Irish nannies make quick stops here to stock up on Cadbury Flake and Yorkie bars) and a wall of M&Ms in designer colors.

COMIC BOOKS & SPORTS CARDS

It depends on what your young collector is looking for: All these stores have a wide stock of cards and/or comics, but whether they've got that rare item you're looking for is always a question. If you're really on a quest for something special, call the whole lot until you strike gold. Otherwise, drop in for a browse at whichever shop you're nearest.

Alex's MVP Cards. 256 E. 89th St. (at Second Ave.). ☎ **212/831-2273.** Subway: 4/5/6 to 86th St.

This friendly neighborhood store specializes in comics and sports cards and wax packs, as well as a decent supply of nonsports toys and supplies.

Chameleon Comics. (1) 3 Maiden Lane (between Nassau St. and Broadway). ☎ **212/ 587-3411.** Subway: A/C to Broadway/Nassau St.; 2/3/4/5 to Fulton St. (2) 36–59 Main St., Flushing, Queens. ☎ **718/461-4675.** Subway: 7 to Main St., Flushing.

Here you'll find Marvel comics and sports cards. Closed Sunday.

Collector's Universe. 124 E. 40th St. (between Park and Lexington aves.). ☎ **212/922-1110.** Subway: 4/5/6/7/S to Grand Central.

This large, sensible Midtown shop covers all ends on sports and superheroes. Closed Sunday. A store for true aficionados, this place stocks comic books—millions of comic books.

Cosmic Comics. 36 E. 23rd St. (near Madison Ave.). ☎ **212/460-5322.** Subway: 6 to 23rd St.

This is a good source for comics, in addition to action figures, nonsports trading cards, T-shirts, models, paperback books, and videos.

Forbidden Planet. 840 Broadway (at 13th St.). ☎ **212/473-1576.** Subway: 4/5/6/L/N/R to Union Square.

This overwhelming store is a valuable source for comics and assorted sci-fi and fantasy paraphernalia.

Gotham City Comics. 800 Lexington Ave. (at 62nd St.). ☎ **212/980-0009.** Subway: 4/5/6 to 59th St.

A wide-ranging stock of comics, sports cards, action figures, T-shirts, with some rarities—it's one of those places where collectors can browse happily for a long time.

It's "A" Nother Hit. 131 W. 33rd St. (between Sixth and Seventh aves.). ☎ **212/ 564-4111.** www.itsanotherhit.com. Subway: 1/2/3/9/B/D/F/N/Q/R to 34th St.

Close to Madison Square Garden, this store sells sports cards and autographed memorabilia, as well as some superhero comics and Pokemon cards.

Jim Hanley's Universe. 4 W. 33rd St. (between Fifth Ave. and Broadway). ☎ **212/ 268-7088.** www.jhuniverse.com. Subway: B/D/F/N/Q/R to 34th St.

Comic books old and new, plus fantasy role-playing games, can be found here.

Manhattan Comics and Cards. 228 W. 23rd St. (between Seventh and Eighth aves.). ☎ **212/243-9349.** Subway: 1/9/C/E to 23rd St.

A reliable source for collectibles, this store specializes in magazines, sports cards, gaming cards, *X-Files* collectibles, paperback books, and action figures.

St. Mark's Comics. (1) 11 St. Mark's Place (between Second and Third aves.). ☎ **212/ 598-9439.** Subway: 6 to Astor Place (2) 138 Montague St., Brooklyn. ☎ **718/935-0911.** Subway: 2/3/4/5/M/N/R to Court St./Borough Hall, Brooklyn.

Anything comic-related can be bought here, including books, magazines, action figures, and toys; the shop has its own subculture buzz.

Village Comics. 214 Sullivan St. (between W. 3rd and Bleecker sts.). ☎ **212/777-2770.** Subway: A/B/C/D/E/F/Q to W. 4th St.

This store is renowned in the comic collector community as a superb source for Marvel cards, action figures, toys, and other collectors' supplies, as well as comics.

World Collectible Center. 18 Vesey St. (between Church St. and Broadway). ☎ **212/267-7100.** Subway: E to World Trade Center; N/R to City Hall; 4/5/6 to Fulton St.

This is a great source for old action figures, such as *Star Wars* and GI Joe. The abundant stock also contains old magazines, comic books, and trading cards. Closed Saturday and Sunday.

DEPARTMENT STORES

Bloomingdale's. 1000 Third Ave. (at 59th St.). ☎ **212/355-5900.** Subway: 4/5/6 to 59th St.

Bloomie's prides itself on glitz, which doesn't translate well into family-oriented merchandise. The layette department is extravagant, geared toward pregnant shopaholics going on a final binge before the demands of motherhood put their shopping days to an end. The kids' clothing departments are claustrophobic and overpriced, and there's no toy department to speak of.

Lord & Taylor. 424 Fifth Ave. (at 39th St.). ☎ **212/391-3344.** Subway: B/D/F/Q to 42nd St.

This slightly dowdy Midtown matron stocks traditional layette stuff and children's clothes. Its meticulous window displays at Christmas are the best in town—collectors of American Girl dolls will want to linger over the detailed historic scenes with their tiny costumed moving figures.

Macy's. At the northwest corner of Herald Square (Broadway and 34th St.). ☎ **212/695 4400.** Subway: B/D/F/N/Q/R to 34th St.

Macy's flagship in Midtown is one of the world's biggest department stores, with a solidly middle-class orientation. The children's departments are huge and carry a broad range of merchandise, including lots of sturdy playwear for boys and girls. This is the only Manhattan department store with a significant toy department, though the selection is fairly run-of-the-mill; my kids actually get more of a kick out of the electronic games department or the sample room setups on the vast furniture floor. At Christmastime, Macy's still mounts a Santaland, a state-of-the-art extravaganza with long lines and Santa himself taking requests.

Saks Fifth Avenue. 611 Fifth Ave. (at 50th St.). ☎ **212/753-4000.** Subway: B/D to Rockefeller Center.

Sleek and chic, Saks does best for the very young, with a fairly good infant-wear department; for older kids, Saks's fashion sense—usually right on target when it comes to adults—is decidedly off kilter.

DOLLS & DOLLHOUSES

✪ **Doll House Antics.** 1343 Madison Ave. (at 94th St.). ☎ **212/876-2288.** www.dollhouseantics.com. Subway: 6 to 96th St.

This big, sunny, well-stocked store boasts loads of marvelous tiny things. They take care to carry sturdy, affordable items for kids as well as incredible miniatures and handcrafted pieces for adult collectors. My daughter's first serious dollhouse came from a kit we bought here (still, ahem, a work in progress).

Iris Brown Antique Dolls. 253 E. 57th St. (between Second and Third aves.). ☎ **212/593-2882.** Subway: 4/5/6 to 59th St.

This is a long-established source for Victorian dolls and miniatures—not necessarily dolls for playtime. Closed Sunday.

Prowling the Pet Stores

When your child decides he or she can no longer tolerate another museum or toy store, try this boredom-buster: Visit one of Manhattan's many pet stores. Whether or not you're actually in the market to buy a pet, it never hurts to drop by and take a look. Many specialize in one kind of animal, whether it be cats, birds, or fish; your family might see some exotic animals you may have previously seen only in zoos.

For instance, there's **33rd and Bird,** 40 E. 33rd St., between Park and Madison avenues (☎ 212/447-0021), which carries not only your standard parakeets and canaries but also exotic parrots and cockatoos. If someone in your family just can't go home without one of these rare birds, the store offers worldwide shipping. The Upper West Side's **Amsterdam Aquarium and Pet Shop,** 652 Amsterdam Ave., between West 91st and 92nd streets (☎ 212/724-0536), carries reptiles, rabbits, birds, and exotic small animals like snakes and frogs.

New World Aquarium, 5 W. 8th St., between Fifth and Sixth avenues (☎ 212/460-9390), is the place to go if your child is fascinated by fish. This Greenwich Village store specializes in marine fish, African chichlids, and rare and exotic freshwater fish, and it's open daily as late as 9pm.

If your kids are demanding to see puppies and kittens, stop at the **International Kennel Club,** 1032 Second Ave., between East 54th and 55th streets (☎ 212/755-0100); **American Kennels,** 798 Lexington Ave., between East 61st and 62nd streets (☎ 212/838-8460); or **Pets-on-Lex,** 1271 Lexington Ave., between East 85th and 86th streets (☎ 212/426-0766). Upscale **Just Cats,** 244 E. 60th St., between Second and Third avenues (☎ 212/888-2287), is a self-described East Side "feline boutique" selling pedigreed kittens and cats as well as toys, accessories, and food for your feline friends (as well as a growing selection of cat-themed merchandise for their humans).

And then there's the Upper East Side's **Le Chien Pet Salon,** 1044 Third Ave., at East 61st Street (☎ 212/861-8100), unique not because of the animals it carries but because of the clientele it serves: The cats and dogs that come for grooming arrive via limousine, and the puppies and kittens for sale, needless to say, are all pedigreed.

✪ **Manhattan Doll House Shop.** 236 Third Ave. (between E. 19th and 20th sts.). ☎ **212/253-9549.** www.manhattandollhouse.com. Subway: 6 to 23rd St.

Besides a truly awesome selection of kits and finished dollhouses, this Gramercy store has all the furnishings, right down to electrical fixtures. Full-size dolls are also repaired and sold, with a specialty in Madame Alexander.

✪ **Mary Arnold Toys.** 1010 Lexington Ave. (between 72nd and 73rd sts.). ☎ **212/744-8510.** Subway: 6 to 77th St.

This top-notch East Side toy shop includes a wonderful doll section—Madame Alexander, Corolle, Götz, and the like.

New York Doll Hospital. 787 Lexington Ave. (between 61st and 62nd sts.), 2nd floor. ☎ **212/838-7527.** Subway: 4/5/6 to 59th St.

Since 1900, young New Yorkers have climbed the stairs to this musty space bearing their precious dolls and stuffed animals in need of repairs. You can also buy antique and discontinued dolls and kitschy collectibles like a Charlie McCarthy doll, a

Howdy Doody, a Daddy Warbucks tie-in from the movie *Annie,* or a Pee-Wee Herman doll (from back before scandal shut down *Pee-Wee's Playhouse*). A wonderful jumble of dolls' heads, arms, and legs on the floor gives the place a slightly *Twilight Zone*-ish atmosphere.

Tiny Doll House. 1146 Lexington Ave. (between 79th and 80th sts.). ☎ **212/744-3719.** Subway: 6 to 77th St.

In this small, well-organized shop, rows of perfectly put-together miniature rooms flank the side walls, while a few empty doll mansions preside regally over the center of the room. Wallpaper, carpeting, lamps, cutlery—a tasteful selection of all the tiny furnishings you'll ever need. Before you go inside, warn little would-be customers not to touch, as the staff is somewhat gun-shy about kids breaking the delicate miniatures.

EVERYDAY CLOTHING

Baby Depot at Burlington Coat Factory. At the corner of W. 23rd St. and Sixth Ave. ☎ **212/229-2247.** Subway: F to 23rd St.

Clothing up to size 12, boys' and girls', can be found on the third floor of this big discount store in the megastore shopping district wedged between Chelsea and the Flatiron District. The brands are quite respectable—Carter's, Buster Brown, Guess—but not very appealingly displayed, jammed onto racks under fluorescent lighting.

Children's Emporium. 293 Court St., in Cobble Hill, Brooklyn. ☎ **718/875-8508.** Subway: F to Bergen St.

It may be worth a trip across the river to take advantage of the savings at this off-price children's boutique, where prices are 35% to 75% off on quality labels like Flapdoodle, Deux Par Deux, and Mulberibush, not to mention Elefanten shoes and Sara's Prints pajamas.

Children's Place. (1) In Manhattan Mall, 901 Sixth Ave. (at 33rd St.), 2nd level. ☎ **212/268-7696.** Subway: B/D/F/N/Q/R/1/9 to 34th St. (2) 173 E. 86th St. (between Third and Lexington aves.). ☎ **212/831-5100.** Subway: 4/5/6 to 86th St. (3) 2039 Broadway (at 70th St.). ☎ **917/441-2374.** Subway: 1/9 to 66th St. (4) 2187 Broadway (at 77th St.). ☎ **917/441-9807.** Subway: 1/9 to 79th St. (5) 1460 Broadway (at 41st St.). ☎ **212/398-4416.** Subway: 1/2/3/7/9/N/R to Times Square. (6) 22 W. 34th St. (at Broadway). ☎ **212/904-1190.** Subway: 1/2/3/9 to 34th St. (7) 36 E.16th St. (at Union Square). ☎ **212/529-2201.** Subway: L/N/R/4/5/6 to 14th St./Union Square. (8) 400 World Trade Concourse, World Trade Center. ☎ **212/432-6100.** Subway: E to World Trade Center, 1/9 to Cortlandt St.

This chain store sells its own label of bright, simply cut casual wear in sizes newborn to 12. It's like a slightly cheaper version of The Gap, in all respects, but to fill out a wardrobe, a $10 polo shirt or plain $14 sundress isn't such a bad idea.

Conway's. (1) 201 E. 42nd St. (at Third Ave.). ☎ **212/992-5030.** Subway: 4/5/6/7/S to Grand Central. (2) 11 W. 34th St. (between Fifth and Sixth aves.). ☎ **212/967-1370.** Subway: 1/2/3/9/B/D/F/N/Q/R to 34th St. (3) 49 W. 34th St. (between Fifth and Sixth aves.). ☎ **212/967-6454.** Subway: 1/2/3/9/B/D/F/N/Q/R to 34th St. (4) 1333 Broadway (at 35th St.). ☎ **212/967-3460.** Subway: 1/2/3/9/B/D/F/N/Q/R to 34th St. (5) 450 Seventh Ave. (between 34th and 35th sts.). ☎ **212/967-1371.** Subway: 1/2/3/9/B/D/F/N/Q/R to 34th St. (6) 225 W. 34th St. (between Seventh and Eighth aves.). ☎ **212/967-7390.** Subway: 1/2/3/9/B/D/F/N/Q/R to 34th St. (7) 45 Broad St. (between Broadway and Beaver sts.). ☎ **212/943-8900.** Subway: 4/5 to Bowling Green. (8) 151 William St. (between Fulton and Nassau sts.). ☎ **212/374-1072.** Subway: A/C to Broadway/Nassau St.

Budget-conscious parents can be spotted all over town carrying Conway's pink plastic bags, bulging with basic clothing bought at low prices. Conway's has heavily colonized the 34th Street shopping district, and it has locations downtown among the discount stores as well.

Daffy's. (1) 111 Fifth Ave. (at 18th St.). ☎ **212/529-4477.** Subway: 4/5/6/L/N/R to Union Square. (2) 335 Madison Ave. (at 44th St.). ☎ **212/557-4422.** Subway: B/D/F/Q to 42nd St. (3) 1311 Broadway (at 34th St.). ☎ **212/736-4477.** Subway: B/D/F/N/Q/R to 34th St. (4) 125 E. 57th St. (between Park and Lexington aves.). ☎ **212/376-4477.** Subway: 4/5/6 to 59th St. (5) 462 Broadway (at Grand St.). ☎ **212/334-7444.** Subway: B/D/Q to Grand St.

The price is definitely right at this smart discount clothing chain that has been rapidly expanding its children's departments thanks to popular demand. For straightforward play and school clothes, most items are under $20, and I'm talking perfectly acceptable quality and styles.

Gap Kids. (1) 57th St. and Broadway. ☎ **212/956-3140.** www.gap.com. Subway: 1/9/A/B/C/D to Columbus Circle. (2) 2 World Financial Center. ☎ **212/945-4090.** Subway: E to World Trade Center. (3) Sixth Ave. between Washington Square and West 4th St. ☎ **212/777-2420.** Subway: A/B/C/D/E/F/Q to W. 4th St. (4) 17th St. and Fifth Ave. ☎ **212/989-0195.** Subway: 4/5/6/L/N/R to Union Square. (5) 60 W. 34th St. (at Broadway). ☎ **212/643-8995.** Subway: B/D/F/N/Q/R to 34th St. (6) 657 Third Ave. (at 42nd St.). ☎ **212/697-9007.** Subway: 4/5/6/7/8 to Grand Central. (7) 42nd St. and Broadway. ☎ **212/302-1266.** Subway: 1/2/3/7/9/N/R/S to Times Square. (8) 1066 Lexington Ave. (between 75th and 76th sts.). ☎ **212/988-4460.** Subway: 6 to 77th St. (9) 86th St. and Madison Ave. ☎ **212/517-5202.** Subway: 4/5/6 to 86th St. (10) 87th St. and Third Ave. ☎ **212/423-0033.** Subway: 4/5/6 to 86th St. (11) 2300 Broadway (at 83rd St.). ☎ **212/873-2044.** Subway: 1/9 to 86th St.

You know the look—jeans, khakis, sweatshirts, T-shirts, denim jackets. You've gotta hand it to them: The Gap provides a mix-and-match backbone for kids' wardrobes, giving the casual look a spin of adultlike cool. Wait for sales and you can clean up.

Gymboree Store. (1) 1332 Third Ave. (at 76th St.). ☎ **212/517-5548.** www.gymboree. com. Subway: 6 to 77th St. (2) 1132 Madison Ave. (between 83rd and 84th sts.). ☎ **212/717-6702.** Subway: 4/5/6 to 86th St. (3) 1049 Third Ave. (at 62nd St.). ☎ **212/688-4044.** Subway: 4/5/6 to 59th St. (4) 2015 Broadway (at 69th St.). ☎ **212/595-7662.** Subway: 1/9 to Lincoln Center. (5) 2271 Broadway (between 81st and 82nd sts.). ☎ **212/595-9071.** Subway: 1/9 to 79th St.

This clothing chain has some fun looks for younger kids: durable knits in bold colors and kindergartenish prints. Cut roomy for easy moving, they're a sensible, reasonably stylish bet for everyday wear.

Kids Are Magic. 2293 Broadway (between 82nd and 83rd sts.). ☎ **212/875-9240.** Subway: 1/9 to 79th St.

Here you'll find substantial discounts on name-brand clothing, plus a few toys and accessories. This store has minimal class, but often you can find super deals. West Side moms zoom in on end-of-season sale days, especially in midsummer, when you can pick up $3 knit tops and $6 swimsuits.

Morris Brothers. 2322 Broadway (at 84th St.). ☎ **212/724-9000.** Subway: 1/9 to 86th St.

Having cut back on its children's departments, Morris Brothers has lost its former West Side monopoly on kids' basics, but it's still a decent source for winter hats, umbrellas, socks, underwear, pajamas, jeans—all the untrendy stuff you need to fill out a wardrobe (that's not to say you can't find some trendy outfits as well). Very solid, not particularly low priced.

New York City Kids. 495 Seventh Ave. (between 36th and 37th sts.). ☎ **212/868-6925.** Subway: 1/2/3/9 to 34th St.

Almost everything is under $100 at this discount store in the Garment District, and with labels like Calvin Klein and Guess, that's netting you some substantial savings. There is a tendency toward children's clothes that look like Mini-Me versions of what parents wear; lots of little boys' three-piece suits and girls' glam-o-rama party dresses.

Old Navy. (1) 610 Sixth Ave. (at 18th St.). ☎ **212/645-0663.** www.oldnavy.com. Subway: F to 14th St.; 1/9 to 18th St. (2) 503–511 Spring St. (entrance on Broadway between Spring and Broome sts.). ☎ **212/226-0838.** Subway: B/D/F/Q to Broadway/Lafayette St., 6 to Spring St. (3) 150 W. 34th St. (at Broadway). ☎ **212/594-0049.** Subway: 1/2/3/9/A/C/E/B/D/F/Q/N/R to 34th St. (4) 125th St. and Frederick Douglas Blvd. (in Harlem USA Mall). ☎ **212/531-1544.** Subway: 2/3 or A/B/C/D to 125th St.

Featuring sturdy, classic casual wear in The Gap mold, this clothing superstore along the old Ladies' Mile in Chelsea has a big second-floor section for kids. Prices are as down-to-earth as the superwearable styles.

OshKosh B'Gosh. 586 Fifth Ave. (between 47th and 48th sts.). ☎ **212/827-0098.** www.oshkoshbgosh.com. Subway: B/D to Rockefeller Center.

The Rockefeller Center showcase for this sturdy kids' play clothes line has all the cutest stuff for toddlers and preschoolers. A mecca for Europeans.

FASHIONS

Bambini. 1367 Third Ave. (at 78th St.). ☎ **212/717-6742.** Subway: 6 to 77th St.

This beautiful, humorless, blond-wood store stocks European children's clothes (brand names like Simonetta and Cacharel) and shoes. The clothes are indeed handsome, but at princess prices—$49 for a dead-plain polo shirt or $375 for a stunning smocked party frock.

Bebe Thompson. 1216 Lexington Ave. (between 82nd and 83rd sts.). ☎ **212/249-4740.** Subway: 4/5/6 to 86th St.

A whiff of sophisticated style sets apart the clothes at this smart little shop. Much (but not all) is imported; I get a kick out of the tiny Geisswein boiled-wool jackets from Austria, which would make your toddler look perfectly ripe for the Junior League.

Bonne Nuit. 30 Lincoln Plaza (at 63rd St.). ☎ **212/489-9730.** Subway: 1/9 to Lincoln Center.

This shop carries adult lingerie and a choice selection of designer duds for kids (mostly for girls) in sizes up to 12 years.

Bonpoint. (1) 1269 Madison Ave. (at 91st St.). ☎ **212/722-7720.** Subway: 4/5/6 to 86th St. (2) 811 Madison Ave. (at 68th St.). ☎ **212/879-0900.** Subway: 6 to 68th St.

This stunning boutique takes the cake—it has the most expensive and probably the most beautiful children's clothes in town (up to size 16 girls and 12 boys). Everything sold is the store's private label, and the fabrics are gorgeous, no question about it; the styles are classic, chic, and perfectly cut. Closed Sunday.

Catamimi. 1284 Madison Ave. (between 91st and 92nd sts.). ☎ **212/987-0688.** Subway: 6 to 96th St.

These French kids' clothes (up to size 12) show an ineffable sense of style, with sassy prints and deep-colored solids cut into simple, roomy clothes with real flair. The store has a bold, clean look and friendly, hip staff. The clothes aren't cheap, but they're casual and sturdy enough that you may get a fair bit of wear out of them.

✪ **Cooo & Z.** 222 Columbus Ave. (at 70th St.). ☎ **212/721-0415.** Subway: 1/2/3/9/B/C to 72nd St.

This friendly, adorable boutique for sizes newborn to 10 carries some very wearable duds from makers like Flooby, Metropolitan Prairie, and Baby Lulu, at prices in the $25-to-$75 range. Maybe they just have a knack for displaying things well, but I had a hard time getting out of this shop without buying anything. Its sibling store, **Co2,** 284 Columbus Ave., between 73rd and 74th streets (☎ **212/721-4966**), carries the whole aesthetic into the preteen arena, sizes 7 to 16.

G. C. William. 1137 Madison Ave. (between 84th and 85th sts.). ☎ **212/396-3400.** Subway: 4/5/6 to 86th St.

Very Upper East Side boutique for Armani-bound youth. You'll find resort wear, club wear, and party wear but not school wear, since most shoppers here go to private schools that have uniforms.

Greenstones & Cie. (1) 442 Columbus Ave. (at 81st St.). ☎ **212/580-4322.** Subway: B/C to 79th St. (2) 1184 Madison Ave. (between 86th and 87th sts.). ☎ **212/427-1665.** Subway: 4/5/6 to 86th St.

Upper-scale imported kids' clothes, with a kind of yacht-club look (every sweater has a design, it seems), are sold in sizes from 3 months to 12 years (the East Side shop carries up to size 8 only, however). Lots of items that are well-nigh irresistible.

Ibiza Kidz. 42 University Place (at 9th St.). ☎ **212/505-9907.** Subway: N/R to 8th St.

Annexed to a gorgeous women's clothing boutique, this Village shop sells some dreamy children's clothes with a bohemian sensibility. Shoes, books, and toys can be found next door.

✪ **Infinity.** 1116 Madison Ave. (at 83rd St.). ☎ **212/517-4232.** Subway: 4/5/6 to 86th St.

As a friend of mine says, "At a certain age all girls want to look like either a construction worker or a tramp": This is the store for both looks. T-shirts and jeans and skimpy knit dresses rule, along with lots of the huge dumpy backpacks every school kid has to have. Infinity doesn't necessarily try to be hip; it just stocks what kids like to wear, damn the parents. Bring your preteen here to prove you do indeed get it. Closed Sunday.

Jacadi. (1) 1281 Madison Ave. (between 91st and 92nd sts.). ☎ **212/369-1616.** www.jacadiusa.com. Subway: 4/5/6 to 86th St. (2) 787 Madison Ave. (between 66th and 67th sts.). ☎ **212/535-3200.** Subway: 6 to 68th St.

A French chain, Jacadi sells expensive, stylish, sturdy clothes, cut for comfort, for boys and girls up to age 12. Each season's line is color coordinated, handy for mixing and matching, and the store looks tidy and very put-together as a result.

Julian & Sara. 103 Mercer St. (between Prince and Spring sts.). ☎ **212/226-1989.** Subway: N/R to Prince St.

The upscale, style-conscious clothes at this SoHo store attract downtown kids up to size 12.

Koh's Kids. 311 Greenwich St. (between Chambers and Reade sts.). ☎ **212/791-6915.** Subway: 1/2/3/9 to Chambers St.

Located in TriBeCa, this shop lines up funky, contemporary, casual clothes in sizes up to 10 years.

La Petite Etoile. 746 Madison Ave. (between 64th and 65th sts.). ☎ **212/744-0975.** www.lapetiteetoile.com. Subway: 6 to 68th St.

A top luxury children's chain from France, La Petite Etoile carries sizes up to 12 at its only U.S. store. These are classic good-looking clothes, with embroidered designs on dress collars and little crests on the boys' jackets, and the concept is that everything a child wears—shirt, sweater, pants, dress, socks, hair bows, shoes, underwear—should match, which sounds fine when you see the shelves lined with color-coordinated accessories. (They even carry parfum for the young.) The total wardrobe idea is pretty staggering, though, when you look at the prices—I saw a $193 price tag on a simple striped cotton frock.

Lester's. 1522 Second Ave. (at 79th St.). ☎ **212/734-9292.** www.lestersclothing.com. Subway: 6 to 77th St.

This is an East Side staple for clothing and shoes, ages newborn to 12—most of the stock is imported and designer styles, but the prices aren't too wild. Many of the clothes show a daring sense of style compared to nearby Talbots Kids or the Madison Avenue boutiques.

M. W. Teen. 1188 Madison Ave. (at 87th St.). ☎ **212/289-0181.** Subway: 4/5/6 to 86th St.

When you graduate from Magic Windows (see "Baby & Preschooler Clothes," above), you get to buy precociously chic party dresses from M. W. Teen next door. The clothes really are pretty, if a trifle too adult for my tastes—but then, my daughter's not a teenager yet.

✪ Marsha D. D. 1324 Lexington Ave. (between 88th and 89th sts.). ☎ **212/534-8700.** Subway: 4/5/6 to 86th St.

Two small neighboring storefronts—one for girls, one for boys—are stuffed with stylish casual clothes, strong on urban hipness and streetwise sophistication. These are clothes your kids will feel very cool wearing. Closed Sunday.

Oilily. 870 Madison Ave. (between 70th and 71st sts.). ☎ **212/628-0100.** Subway: 6 to 68th St.

Cherry red, tangerine orange, banana yellow—as you enter this spotless store, Oilily's trademark Trix-hued fabrics hit you like an LSD flashback. As a friend of mine says, Oilily is the only line of clothing that believes boys can wear flowered pants. They last absolutely forever, which may or may not be a good thing.

PaPoose. 311 E. 81st St. (between First and Second aves.). ☎ **212/639-9577.** Subway: 4/5/6 to 86th St., 6 to 77th St.

Imported from Europe, the clothing in this winning little shop on a quiet East Side side street is very tempting, from smocked dresses to sunsuits to fine-spun sweaters.

✪ Peanut Butter & Jane. 617 Hudson St. (at Jane St.). ☎ **212/620-7952.** Subway: A/C/E/L/1/2/3/9 to 14th St.

Packed to the rafters, this utterly wonderful small store carries real-life clothes at real-life prices—print leggings, tie-dyed T-shirts, denim jackets, cotton dresses in dusky floral prints. Both the sporty and the dressy items have a funky sense of style; sizes go up to 10 for boys, 16 for girls. There are lots of dress-up costumes as well, to feed the imagination, and the clutter of toys in the back is irresistible. My friends in the West Village look on this shop as a life-support system.

Robin's Nest. 1168 Lexington Ave. (at 80th St.). ☎ **212/737-2004.** Subway: 6 to 77th St.

This small undistinguished store carries a lot of the same upscale imported clothes you'll see at the Madison Avenue boutiques—cute, casual outfits mostly. Closed Sunday.

San Francisco Clothing. 975 Lexington Ave. (between 70th and 71st sts.). ☎ **212/ 472-8740.** Subway: 6 to 68th St.

This long-established East Side women's clothing store has a surprisingly darling line of little girls' and boys' clothing, in well-cut mini-preppie styles and top-quality fabrics. Don't let the wood-paneled decor and snooty staff put you off—with play clothes under $50 and dresses under $75, this is an upscale shop worth checking out.

Small Change. 964 Lexington Ave. (at 70th St.). ☎ **212/772-6455.** Subway: 6 to 68th St.

Still more expensive children's clothing ($280 for a boy's navy blazer!). The store buyers clearly have a sense of style, though. Closed Sunday.

Space Kiddets. 46 E. 21st St. (between Broadway and Park Ave. South). ☎ **212/ 420-9878.** Subway: 6/N/R to 23rd St.

Come here for some very cute downtown-trendy stuff for wee ones—it can be pricey, but the sales are good. Closed Sunday.

Spring Flowers Children's Boutique. (1) 1050 Third Ave. (at 62nd St.). ☎ **212/758-2669.** Subway: 4/5/6 to 59th St. (2) 905 Madison Ave. (at 72nd St.). ☎ **212/717-8182.** Subway: 6 to 68th St.

In the realm of upscale children's clothing, Spring Flowers strikes a healthy balance: The big-skirt party gowns run only $75 to $175. You can find some casual wear and shoes, but it's the dress-up stuff that catches the eye, round racks bulging with petticoats and pinafores. Imported brand names include Cacharel, Le Petit Bateau, Sophie Dess—all the usual suspects.

Talbots Kids. 1523 Second Ave. (at 79th St.). ☎ **212/570-1630.** www.talbots.com. Subway: 6 to 77th St.

For all the country-club matron image of the adult Talbots store, this junior version (for newborns to teens) is surprisingly bright and casual and cool, like a Gap without the grunge: loads of khaki pants and polos and tank tops in solid colors and traditional stripes, at prices that seem just right for simple well-made clothes. When my older son finally agreed to wear a navy blazer and rep tie, this is where we bought the blazer—it fit, it looked great, and I didn't pay through the nose for something he'll wear only three times.

Tigers, Tutus, and Toes. 128 Second Ave. (between 7th and 8th sts. at St. Mark's Place). ☎ **212/228-7990.** Subway: 6 to Astor Place.

This sister store to the groovy Ibiza Kidz (see above) supplies bohemian kids with clothes, shoes, and accessories in the East Village. The look is stylish, not grungy, with a sense of whimsy.

Tutti Bambini. 1490 First Ave. (between 77th and 78th sts.). ☎ **212/472-4238.** Subway: 6 to 77th St.

Carrying a wide range of labels—imported, made in the U.S.A., whatever—this busy little East Side shop knows its look: funky and fun. It carries sizes up to 10, with brand names like Spaghetti & Confetti and Cozy Toes, and tends toward designs adults wouldn't mind wearing. Most of the other shoppers I saw had kids in tow, which means they were picking out clothes the kids themselves like to wear—always a good sign.

Village Kidz. 3 Charles St. (at Greenwich Ave.). ☎ **212/807-8542.** Subway: 1/9 to Christopher St.; F to 14th St.

Village Kidz has perfectly adorable clothing for newborns to size 12, with high-end labels like Jean Bourget, Miniman, and Skivvydoodles. Some styles are over the top, like the zipper-infested black leather biker jacket in size 4T and the sweet cross-stitched pinafores in cotton so thin it looks like it'd rip in a minute, but there's plenty here to tempt you. Good for shoes too. Closed Sunday.

Zitomer Department Store. 969 Madison Ave. (between 75th and 76th sts.). ☎ **212/ 737-2037.** Subway: 6 to 77th St.

Bursting at the seams, this drugstore's upstairs children's clothing department has some very upscale imported clothes (dresses in the $50 to $500 range) that manage to look cheesy in the fluorescent light, jammed together on chrome racks as they are. It's worth a stop if you're on a quest for something special, though the setting is hardly conducive to leisurely browsing.

GAMES

Chess Forum. 219 Thompson St. (between 3rd and Bleecker sts.). ☎ **212/475-2369.** www.chessforum.com. Subway: A/B/C/D/E/F/Q to W. 4th St.

Competing head-to-head with the Chess Shop right up the street, the Chess Forum is big on chess lessons for kids, along with selling a large variety of exquisite sets for chess, backgammon, cribbage, and dominoes. Celebrity customers include David Lee Roth, Sean Lennon, Yoko Ono, and Harvey Keitel.

Chess Shop. 230 Thompson St. (between 3rd and Bleecker sts.). ☎ **212/475-9580.** Subway: A/B/C/D/E/F/Q to W. 4th St.

Come here for exotic chess sets, esoteric chess manuals, and a slew of related computer software, as well as clocks for speed chess.

Compleat Strategist. 11 E. 33rd St. (between Fifth and Madison aves.). ☎ **212/685-3880.** Subway: 6 to 33rd St.

This specialist shop stocks a fairly mind-boggling array of games, from chess and backgammon to military simulations and role-playing games, but doesn't neglect board games for the younger set, including some noncompetitive games for non-readers. Fun for browsing. Closed Sunday.

Dart Shoppe. 30 E. 20th St. (between Broadway and Park Ave. South). ☎ **800/552-9830** or 212/533-8684. Subway: 6/N/R to 23rd St.

This quirky little store in a Gramercy Park brownstone stocks everything relating to darts, period. Not a dart player? Not to worry—they can give you lessons.

✪ **Game Show.** (1) 1240 Lexington Ave. (between 83rd and 84th sts.). ☎ **212/472-8011.** Subway: 4/5/6 to 86th St. (2) 474 Sixth Ave. (between 11th and 12th sts.). ☎ **212/633-6328.** Subway: F to 14th St.

A little less specialty-oriented than the Compleat Strategist (above), this well-stocked bright store has lots of board, card, and puzzle games to choose from, including a good range for kids of all ages.

Neutral Ground. 122 W. 26th St., 4th floor (between Sixth and Seventh aves.). ☎ **212/ 633-1288.** www.neutralground.com. Subway: 1/9 to 28th St.

Along with selling an eclectic array of games, especially role-playing games, this store sponsors Magic the Gathering tournaments, role-playing campaigns, and miniature battles. To get a monthly calendar of events, check their Web site.

GIFTS & GADGETS

E.A.T. Gifts. 1062 Madison Ave. (between 80th and 81st sts.). ☎ **212/861-2544.** Subway: 6 to 77th St.

Next door to the absurdly overpriced E.A.T. cafe, this gift store isn't really designed for kids—it's crowded and there's an annoying "don't touch" factor—but somehow every time we wander in there's something one of my children can't live without. Little gift books, bath toys, tiny shaped soaps and crayons, chocolate novelties—it's like quicksand for the reluctant shopper.

Hammacher Schlemmer. 147 E. 57th St. (between Lexington and Third aves.). ☎ **212/421-9000.** www.hammacher.com. Subway: 4/5/6 to 59th St.

You want gadgets? They've got gadgets—high-quality gadgets to do everything under the sun, including some things you've never thought of doing before. Older kids and adults get a kick out of the unique and ingenious products, and don't worry if most items are way out of your price range—the ratio of browsers to buyers is usually pretty high. Closed Sunday.

It's a Mod, Mod World. 85 First Ave. (between 5th and 6th sts.). ☎ **212/460-8004.** Subway: 6 to Astor Place.

For lovers of Day-Glo vinyl, this East Village shop's collection feels utterly 1960s, though a lot of the surreal items are recent artist-created *objets*—lamps, clocks, decoupaged ashtrays, altered Barbie dolls, and other groovadelic stuff. The impulse-buy toys near the door are less nostalgia-oriented than simply kitschy: wind-up robots that send off sparks, boxing nun hand puppets, and the like. Cute and a hoot.

New York Firefighter's Friend. 263 Lafayette St. (between Prince and Spring sts.). ☎ **212/226-3142.** Subway: N/R to Prince St.

A sore disappointment to my son the fire truck lover, this is really a store for firefighters (there's a station two doors down), where they can buy adult-sized turnout gear and badges and FDNY T-shirts. There are a few items in stock for junior firefighters, like plastic red helmets and axes, but not many toy fire engines, and a whole case of what they do have is special-edition collectors' stuff at $25 to $80 (too high for something that's gonna get lost in the sandbox).

P.S. I Love You. 1242 Madison Ave. (between 89th and 90th sts.). ☎ **212/722-6272.** Subway: 4/5/6 to 86th St.

Preteen girls love this neighborhood boutique, crammed with stickers, candles, T-shirts, jewelry, pogs, stampers, and other neat little gifts. Sheer impulse buys, nothing horribly expensive.

Sharper Image. (1) 4 W. 57th St. (between Fifth and Sixth aves.). ☎ **212/265-2550.** www.sharperimage.com. Subway: N/R to Fifth Ave. (2) 900 Madison Ave. (at 73rd St.). ☎ **212/794-4974.** Subway: 6 to 77th St. (3) Pier 17 at South Street Seaport. ☎ **212/693-0477.** Subway: 2/3/4/5 to Fulton St.; A/C to Broadway/Nassau St.

Now that it has spread to malls all across the country, this high-end gadgetorium chain isn't so much of a draw—it can't beat Hammacher Schlemmer (above) for one-of-a-kind-ism. Still, it can be a fun stop for kids, since so many of the hands-on items on display move and do stuff.

HAIRCUTS

✪ **Cozy's Cuts for Kids.** (1) 1125 Madison Ave. (at 84th St.). ☎ **212/744-1716.** www.cozyscutsforkids.com. Subway: 4/5/6 to 86th St. (2) 448 Amsterdam Ave. (between 81st and 82nd sts.). ☎ **212/579-2600.** Subway: 1/9 to 79th St.

Spanking clean and bright, Cozy's plays videos to keep kids happy in the chair—which may be a regular barber chair or a yellow Jeep. *Après*-cut, the little shavers get lollipops, balloons, favors, all the usual bribes. Cozy's has enough quality toys to double as a toy store, which unfortunately means you've got to ward off toy requests when you come in only for a haircut; but what the hey, at least you have no trouble getting the kids in the door. Closed Sunday.

Fun Cuts. 1567 York Ave. (between 83rd and 84th sts.). ☎ **212/288-0602.** Subway: 4/5/6 to 86th St.

Two things make Fun Cuts a restful alternative for parents: the soft hues with which it's painted and the fact that there are few toys for sale to raise the "gimme" quotient. There are, however, videos to distract young haircuttees, and quick-working, low-key hairdressers. My squirmy toddler daughter got a superb short cut here after she hacked off her own hair with kindergarten scissors, and we've returned time and again and never been disappointed.

Kids Cuts. 201 E. 31st St. (at Third Ave.). ☎ **212/684-5252.** Subway: 6 to 33rd St.

If you're in Midtown, this small salon may be more convenient; its slightly lower prices also reflect the fact that it's not part of the Upper East Side yup-scale hub. They cut adult hair as well, which is a real bargain. Closed Monday.

Michael's. 1263 Madison Ave. (between 90th and 91st sts.). ☎ **212/289-9612.** Subway: 4/5/6 to 86th St.

The most expensive East Side haircut joint is also the oldest and dirtiest, and I've been told of occasional unpleasant incidents with Michael himself, though the other barbers are real sweeties. But my husband prefers Michael's because, even though it specializes in children, it looks like a regular barbershop (except they've got hobbyhorse-shaped booster seats for the chairs and a couple of battered autos that rise on a pole for kids to sit in). The gray-haired barbers have cut so many little mops that no tantrum can faze them—and can they work fast. Very liberal with lollipops after the cut. No reservations; closed Sunday.

Paul Mole. 1031 Lexington Ave. (at 74th St.). ☎ **212/535-8461.** Subway: 6 to 77th St.

Well known for stylish men's cuts, the Paul Mole salon also has a thriving business in cutting the hair of those stylish men's children (mostly sons), at 10¢ less per cut than adult prices.

Tortoise and the Hare. 1470 York Ave. (at 78th St.). ☎ **212/472-3399.** Subway: 6 to 77th St.

My boys love getting their hair cut here, mostly because I cave in and buy them toys from the considerable selection taking over the front of the store—the last couple of times it was electronic miniguitars like the ones they were handed as distractions during the cut. Kids can choose to watch a video or play Nintendo and Sony PlayStation games. Closed Sunday and Monday.

HOBBY SHOPS

Ace Hobbies. 35 W. 31st St. (between Fifth Ave. and Broadway), 4th floor. ☎ **212/268-4151.** Subway: B/D/F/N/Q/R to 34th St.

This store is big on model kits, especially planes and naval craft. Closed Sunday.

Jan's Hobby Shop. 1557 York Ave. (between 82nd and 83rd sts.). ☎ **212/861-5075.** Subway: 4/5/6 to 86th St.

This stocked-to-the-rafters shop is a wondrous source for all kinds of wooden models—in everything from balsa wood to mahogany—as well as plastic model kits (loads of Revell planes and race cars) and die-cast metal items for collectors. The display cases of military models are awesome. This is currently my 8-year-old's favorite store in the world.

Mach 1 Hobbies. 249-A W. 29th St. (between Seventh and Eighth aves.). ☎ **212/947-0157.** Subway: 1/9 to 28th St.

This is a serious source for model makers, juvenile and adult, with discounted prices to boot. Closed Sunday.

Red Caboose. 23 W. 45th St. (between Fifth and Sixth aves.); enter the lobby and go down stairs at the back. ☎ **212/575-0155.** Subway: B/D to Rockefeller Center.

New York's most intense model railroad shop, the Red Caboose has been selling all gauges and scales of trains since 1942, as well as equipment and supplies desired by modelers. The stock of train and automobile kits is growing all the time, too. Closed Sunday.

Train World. 751 McDonald Ave., Brooklyn. ☎ **718/436-7072.** Subway: F to Ditmas Ave., Brooklyn.

True electric train fanatics may want to venture out to this huge store for train sets.

MAGIC & GAGS

✪ **Abracadabra.** 19 W. 21st St. (between Fifth and Sixth aves.). ☎ **212/627-5194.** Subway: F to 23rd St.

Harry Potter fans can indulge some serious fantasies at this ever-growing magic superstore, so large it even has a stage and a cafe on site. Its several thousand feet of space are stocked with every magic trick, costume, and gag under the sun. Warning to parents of skittish youngsters: Some of the masks on display are extremely lifelike and gruesome as all-get-out.

Flosso Hornmann Magic Co. 45 W. 34th St. (between Fifth and Sixth aves.), 6th floor. ☎ **212/279-6079.** Subway: B/D/F/N/Q/R to 34th St.

Houdini himself once owned this outfit, which claims to be the oldest magic shop in the country. There's something subtle in the air here, like a *Twilight Zone* set just waiting for creepy things to start happening. Closed Sunday.

Tannen's Magic. 24 W. 25th St. (between Broadway and Sixth aves.). ☎ **212/929-4500.** www.tannenmagic.com. Subway: F/N/R to 23rd St.

Amateur or professional, magicians shop here, in a slightly raffish commercial neighborhood of storefronts and warehouse lofts. In the interests of developing future magicians, Tannen's also runs magic camps (for ages 12 to 20) and hosts a fall magic conference in the Catskills; magic is serious business here. Closed Sunday.

MUSIC

Bleecker Bob's Golden Oldies. 118 W. 3rd St. (between Sixth Ave. and MacDougal St.). ☎ **212/475-9677.** www.bleeckerbobs.com. Subway: A/B/C/D/E/F/Q to W. 4th St.

Like a scene out of the movie *High Fidelity,* this famous Village hangout still has bins full of vinyl, with some very obscure albums, and staff who really know their arcane music trivia. Older kids who are into esoterica and nostalgia may dig it.

HMV. (1) 1280 Lexington Ave. (at 86th St.). ☎ **212/348-0800.** Subway: 4/5/6 to 86th St. (2) 57 W. 34th St. (enter on Sixth Ave.). ☎ **212/629-0900.** Subway: B/D/F/N/Q/R to 34th St. (3) 565 Fifth Ave. (between 46th and 47th sts.). ☎ **212/681-6700.** Subway: B/D/F/Q to Rockefeller Center. (4) 308 W. 125th St. (between Frederick Douglas Blvd. and St. Nicholas Place). ☎ **212/932-9619.** Subway: A/B/C/D/2/3 to 125th St.

Big, big, big store for tapes and CDs, good for browsing for the latest mainstream sounds in rock, jazz, and classical; decent sections also on world music, show tunes, and country, though nothing too obscure. Sizable video and DVD section as well.

House of Oldies. 35 Carmine St. (between Bleecker and Bedford sts.). ☎ **212/243-0500.** www.houseofoldies.com. Subway: A/B/C/D/E/F/Q to W. 4th St.

Like Bleecker Bob's (above), the House of Oldies prides itself on hard-to-find vintage recordings, especially 45s and LPs. If your kids don't know what a "record" is, bring them here for a history lesson.

Manny's Music. 156 W. 48th St. (between Sixth and Seventh aves.). ☎ **212/819-0576.** Subway: B/D to Rockefeller Center.

On Midtown's Music Row, Manny's is one store that welcomes kids to fiddle around on the instruments for sale.

Tower Records. (1) 1961 Broadway (at 66th St.). ☎ **212/799-2500.** Subway: 1/9 to Lincoln Center. (2) 725 Fifth Ave. (at 57th St.). ☎ **212/838-8110.** Subway: N/R to Fifth Ave. (3) 692 Broadway (at 4th St.). ☎ **212/505-1500.** Subway: 6 to Bleecker St.

The name's a bit of a misnomer, since there's precious little vinyl for sale anymore. But Tower remains a massive source for recorded music. Despite its terminal hipness, the Upper West Side branch near Lincoln Center has an especially strong classical music department. The newest branch on Broadway in Midtown feeds on its proximity to the 57th Street theme restaurants and licensed merchandise stores; the original store in Greenwich Village is perhaps a bit past its 15 minutes of utter downtown coolness.

Virgin Megastore. (1) 1540 Broadway (at 45th St.). ☎ **212/921-1020.** Subway: 1/2/3/7/9/N/R/S to Times Square. (2) 52 E. 14th St. (at Park Ave.). ☎ **212/598-4666.** Subway: 4/5/6/L/N/R to 14th St./Union Square.

Everybody's favorite hip Brit tycoon Richard Branson moved into Times Square in a big way with this three-story megamart for recorded music—along with a bookstore, cafe, and movieplex. The music selection is good and deep, and there are lots of listening posts around so you can sample the sounds before you buy. Dig the smoke-blowing weird bronze facade of the Union Square megastore, equally immense, which opened in 1999.

SCIENCE STUFF

Maxilla and Mandible. 451 Columbus Ave. (between 81st and 82nd sts.). ☎ **212/724-6173.** www.maxillaandmandible.com. Subway: B/C to 79th St.

Being a block away from the American Museum of Natural History makes sense for this odd and wonderful little shop selling collectible bones and fossils (yep, that's right). Less gruesome items include butterflies pinned under glass, rock samples, and crystals. Fun for junior naturalists. Closed Tuesday, January through June; closed Sunday, July through Labor Day.

Star Magic. (1) 745 Broadway (at Astor Place). ☎ **212/228-7770.** Subway: 6 to Astor Place; N/R to 8th St. (2) 1256 Lexington Ave. (at 85th St.). ☎ **212/988-0300.** Subway: 4/5/6 to 86th St.

New Agers, Trekkies, and kids alike love this space-themed gift store, which takes its mission pretty loosely—stuff like wind chimes and lava lamps and crystals and tarot cards and Rubik's cubes go along with the astronomy books and telescopes and star charts. Both parents and kids can browse happily for a long time.

✪ **Store of Knowledge WNET.** (1) 1091 Third Ave. (at 64th St.). ☎ **212/223-0018.** www.storeofknowledge.com. Subway: 6 to 68th St. (2) 1 World Trade Center, in The Mall at World Trade Center. ☎ **212/321-2855.** Subway: E to World Trade Center; 1/9 to Cortlandt St.

My family has long loved Boston's WGBH Store of Knowledge in Harvard Square, so we were thrilled when the local PBS station, WNET, opened its own branches. Lots of magnets, building toys, flying toys, dinosaur stuff, planetary models, and nature study kits, along with a small computer section, make this a great source for budding scientists (which means any kid with a healthy curiosity about how the world works). Prices are quite decent, many products here won't be seen in other stores, and there are plenty of clear plastic bins around the store with clever under-$5 toys so you can satisfy your child's lust to buy.

✪ **Unique Science.** 410 Columbus Ave. (between 80th and 81st sts.). ☎ **212/712-1899.** Subway: B/C to 79th St.

Slightly more upscale than Star Magic (above), Unique Science has a quality selection of intriguing toys, books, and gift items with a scientific bent—globes, crystals, gyroscopes, experiment kits. Great location right by the Natural History museum, so you can stop in while your kids are still buzzing with interest.

SHOES

East Side Kids. 1298 Madison Ave. (between 92nd and 93rd sts.). ☎ **212/360-5000.** Subway: 6 to 96th St.

Free popcorn is dispensed to shoe-shopping kids, which means the place looks like a pigsty by the end of the day. But the range of shoes is wide, some chic and some totally playground-friendly.

Great Feet. 1241 Lexington Ave. (at 84th St.). ☎ **212/249-0551.** Subway: 4/5/6 to 86th St.

Carrying the Stride Rite standard on the Upper East Side, Great Feet looks like a super tree house, with separate areas (each decked out with boredom-fighting activities) for different age groups. An essential stop for durable midpriced shoes and for wider feet.

Harry's Shoes. 2299 Broadway (at 83rd St.). ☎ **212/874-2035.** www.harrys-shoes.com. Subway: 1/9 to 86th St.

A West Side institution. The kids' department is strong on Stride Rites; moms and dads buy boots and sandals and casual shoes here too. It's always a zoo and hardly a bargain, but the weary staff is pretty professional. Fashion is less the point here than solid quality.

Ibiza Kidz. 42 University Place (at 9th St.). ☎ **212/505-9907.** Subway: N/R to 8th St.

Next door to its sibling clothing store, this Village kids boutique sells shoes, books, and animals, and the stock shows some real flair.

Lester's. 1522 Second Ave. (at 79th St.). ☎ **212/734-9292.** Subway: 6 to 77th St.

This all-purpose children's clothing store (see "Fashions," above) provides one-stop shopping with a full-service shoe department in the back.

Little Eric. (1) 1331 Third Ave. (at 76th St.). ☎ **212/288-8987.** Subway: 6 to 77th St. (2) 1118 Madison Ave. (at 83rd St.). ☎ **212/717-1513.** Subway: 4/5/6 to 86th St.

Style is the watchword—get your 4-year-old shod here if you want to wow the admissions officer at your Brearley or Buckley interview. Yes, they've got plain patent-leather Mary Janes and classic penny loafers in peewee sizes, but also cowboy boots and other trendy styles.

✪ **Shoofly.** (1) 465 Amsterdam Ave. (between 82nd and 83rd sts.). ☎ **212/580-4390.** www.shooflynyc.com. Subway: 1/9 to 79th St. (2) 42 Hudson St. (between Duane and Thomas sts.). ☎ **212/406-3270.** Subway: 1/2/3/9 to Chambers St.

A whimsical collection of designer hats for kids hangs from tree branches poking out of one wall; low shelves and bins and steamer trunks overflow with a wild assortment of shoes, sandals, socks, mittens, hair bows, belts, and ties, running the gamut from goofy to glam. The downtown store carries infant gifts and toys, too. It's always fun shopping here, even if you don't buy. The prices aren't outlandish, but the sense of style is—just what little New Yorkers need to look really cool.

Tip Top Kids. 149 W. 72nd St. (between Broadway and Columbus Ave.). ☎ **212/874-1004.** Subway: 1/2/3/9 to 72nd St.

Bright, cheerful, and relaxed, this children's annex to Tip Top Shoes is the antidote to crazed Harry's Shoes (see above): You can almost always get waited on immediately, the staff handles children with good humor, and the selection offers quality shoes at fair prices. Brands like Elefanten, Aster, Timberland, Sperry, and Bass, as well as Stride Rite and Skechers and Adidas.

Village Kidz. 3 Charles St. (at Greenwich Ave.). ☎ **212/807-8542.** Subway: A/B/C/D/E/F/Q to W. 4th St.

Come here for downtown shoe styles that are very with it, like little brown leather lace-up boots and patent-leather hightops. No bargains. Closed Sunday.

SHOWER & BABY GIFTS

Art & Tapisserie. 1242 Madison Ave. (between 89th and 90th sts.). ☎ **212/722-3222.** Subway: 4/5/6 to 86th St.

Make sure you bring the correct spelling of the new baby's name: The cheery jumble here is geared to items that can be personalized—picture frames, footstools, clocks, bookends, and other nursery accents. There are some other toys, but nothing to die for.

✪ **Little Extras.** 674 Amsterdam Ave. (at 93rd St.). ☎ **212/721-6161.** Subway: 1/9 to 86th St.

Though there are a few toys here for older kids (pacifying gifts for displaced older siblings, perhaps), baby gifts reign: music boxes, picture frames, picture albums, nursery lamps, soft wall hangings, baby towel sets, silver cups and spoons and rattles, personalized footstools, and toy chests. This place never lets me down when I'm en route to a shower, christening, or bris and need a present in a hurry.

Tiffany's. 727 Fifth Ave. (at 56th St.). ☎ **212/755-8000.** www.tiffany.com. Subway: N/R to Fifth Ave.

Wanna score points? A silver spoon, rattle, teething ring, or baby cup from Tiffany's is still the classy way to celebrate a new arrival, and no new parent minds duplicates of these classics. Get the spoon or cup engraved for an extra touch; you can do it all by phone or online, though visiting this fabled store is usually a pleasure. All except the cup are under $100, so why not go for it? A child is born only once.

SOFTWARE & ELECTRONIC GAMES

Cybergames. 2662 Broadway (between 101st and 102nd sts.). ☎ **212/666-2662.** Subway: 1/9 to 103rd St.

Nintendo and Sony Playstation games are for sale, along with trading cards, and there are a couple of in-store sets where you can try out games you're interested in.

Sometimes, this place has the atmosphere of a grungy arcade, but it's a good source to know about.

Electronic Boutique. (1) 901 Sixth Ave. (at 33rd St.). ☎ **212/564-4156.** Subway: B/D/F/N/R to 33rd St. (2) 1217 Third Ave. (between 70th & 71st sts.). ☎ **212/879-9544.** Subway: 6 to 68th St.

Racks full of computer software and accessories, as well as those GameBoy, Playstation, and Nintendo games kids think they can't live without.

✪ **Game Quest.** 1596 Third Ave. (between 89th and 90th sts.). ☎ **212/423-0697.** Subway: 4/5/6 to 86th St.

The people who run this jam-packed little shop have proven their parents wrong: It *will* help you to find a job if you play Nintendo day and night, at least to get a job in this store. Staff members know their stuff so well, they talk about it in some kind of incomprehensible code, dude. They seem to have everything, and to get it first.

Software Etc. (1) 1120 Sixth Ave. (at 44th St.). ☎ **212/921-7855.** Subway: B/D/F/Q to 42nd St. (2) 128 E. 86th St. (between Park and Lexington aves.). ☎ **212/423-1844.** Subway: 4/5/6 to 86th St. (3) 1282 Broadway (at 33rd St.). ☎ **212/967-9070.** Subway: B/D/F/N/Q/R to 33rd St. (4) 2330 Broadway (between 84th and 85th sts.). ☎ **917/441-4160.** Subway: 1/2/3/9 to 86th St. (5) 2764 Broadway (at 106th St.). ☎ **212/864-4292.** Subway: 1/9 to 103rd St. (6) 743 Broadway (between 7th & 8th sts.). ☎ **212/979-7678.** Subway: 6 to Astor Place, N/R to 8th St.

These stores carry a reliable, if somewhat middle-of-the-road, selection of software and electronic games, along with magazines, computer accessories, videos, and some game- and cartoon-related collectible toys. Our family makes a supply stop here at least once a month.

Stop 'n' Save Software. (1) 1470 Third Ave. (at 83rd St.). ☎ **212/288-5370.** Subway: 4/5/6 to 86th St. (2) 687 Broadway (between W. 3rd and W. 4th sts.). ☎ **212/473-6571.** Subway: 6 to Astor Place, N/R to 8th St., B/D/F/Q to Broadway/Lafayette St.

Prices here aren't stupendously lower than at other software stores, but on some items you may save a buck or two, and the staff make it their business to know about the latest hot games, even if it means steering you away from a rip-off. Lots of Pokemon accessories make this an essential stop for my boys.

SPORTS STUFF

Blades Board & Skate. (1) 120 W. 72nd St. (between Broadway and Columbus Ave.). ☎ **212/787-3911.** Subway: 1/2/3/9/B/C to 72nd St. (2) 659 Broadway (between Bond and Bleecker sts.). ☎ **212/477-7350.** Subway: B/D/F/Q to Broadway/Lafayette St. (3) 128 Chambers St. (at West Broadway). ☎ **212/964-1944.** Subway: 1/2/3/9 to Chambers St. (4) Chelsea Piers (West 23rd St. and the West Side Highway). ☎ **212/336-6299.** Subway: C/E to 23rd St. (5) 901 Sixth Ave. (between 32nd and 33rd sts., in the Manhattan Mall). ☎ **212/563-2448.** Subway: B/D/F/N/Q/R to 34th St. (6) 160 E. 86th St. (between Lexington and Third aves.). ☎ **212/996-1644.** Subway: 4/5/6 to 86th St. (7) 1414 Second Ave. (between 73rd and 74th sts.). ☎ **212/249-3178.** Subway: 6 to 77th St.

In-line skaters and skateboarders gear up at this chain of specialty stores, where you can have your own board custom-built for $500 or so. Get your helmets and kneepads here as well. Rentals are available. See chapter 6 for skateboarding info.

Eastern Mountain Sports. (1) 20 W. 61st St. (between Broadway and Columbus Ave.). ☎ **212/397-4860.** Subway: 1/9/A/B/C/D to Columbus Circle. (2) 611 Broadway (at Houston St.). ☎ **212/505-9860.** Subway: B/D/F to Broadway/Lafayette St.

This place is big on camping gear and outdoor wear, along with equipment for climbing walls. The ideal place to buy a sleeping bag that doesn't have Mickey Mouse or Batman all over the lining.

Mets Clubhouse Shop. 143 E. 54th St. (at Lexington Ave.). ☎ **212/888-7508.** Subway: E/F/6 to 53rd St.

Mets fans stock up on blue-and-orange team paraphernalia and memorabilia here. You can buy game tickets here, too. Let's go, Mets!

Modell's. (1) 1535 Third Ave. (between 86th and 87th sts.). ☎ **212/996-3800.** Subway: 4/5/6 to 86th St. (2) 200 Broadway (between Fulton and John sts.). ☎ **212/964-4007.** Subway: 2/3/4/5 to Fulton St. (3) Manhattan Mall, 901 Sixth Ave. (at 33rd St.). ☎ **212/594-1830.** Subway: B/D/F/N/Q/R to 34th St. (4) 498 Seventh Ave. (between 36th and 37th sts.). ☎ **212/822-1000.** Subway: 1/2/3/9 to 34th St. (5) 51 E. 42nd St. (between Vanderbilt and Madison aves.). ☎ **212/661-4242.** Subway: 4/5/6/7/S to Grand Central. (6) Harlem USA Mall, 300 W. 125th St. (between St. Nicholas Place and Eighth Ave.). ☎ **212/280-9100.** Subway: 2/3/A/B/C/D to 125th St. (7) 606 W. 181st St. (at St. Nicholas Place). ☎ **212/568-3000.** Subway: 1/9 to 181st St.

When you gotta go to Mo's, you gotta go. Though not totally kid-oriented, Mo's is an important destination for any family harboring a young athlete, because of its sheer size and its attention to some of the less mainstream sports as well. Equipment, clothing, and some sports fan gear as well—it's hard to get out of here without buying more than you expected to.

NikeTown. 6 E. 57th St. (between Fifth and Madison aves.). ☎ **212/891-6453.** Subway: N/R to Fifth Ave.

This glitzy temple to sports and sneakers is more of a museum/attraction than a place to buy shoes, with several interactive stations where kids can measure their feet, test their reach and reflexes, and generally try to be like Mike (or Tiger, perhaps, these days).

Paragon Sports. 867 Broadway (at 18th St.). ☎ **212/255-8036.** Subway: 4/5/6/L/N/R to Union Square.

Paragon is good for rugged sports clothing and total gear, including lots of camping equipment, ski stuff, and a golf department with a tiny putting green.

Sports Authority. (1) 401 Seventh Ave. (at 33rd St.). ☎ **212/563-7195.** Subway: 1/2/3/9 to 34th St. (2) 51st St. and Third Ave. ☎ **212/355-9725.** Subway: 6 to 51st St. (3) 57th St. and Sixth Ave. ☎ **212/355-6430.** Subway: B/Q to 57th St.

Though not quite as comprehensive as Mo's, this is another good clean Midtown source for sports equipment and apparel, as well as tickets and fan gear to support a pro sports spectating habit.

Yankees Clubhouse Shop. (1) 393 Fifth Ave. (between 36th and 37th sts.). ☎ **212/685-4693.** Subway: 6 to 33rd St. (2) 110 E. 59th St. (between Park and Lexington aves.). ☎ **212/758-7844.** Subway: 4/5/6 to 59th St.

Bronx Bomber fans can indulge their merchandise-buying addictions here. Also a good source for tickets.

STROLLERS, CRIBS & FURNITURE

Albee Baby Carriage Co. 715 Amsterdam Ave. (at 95th St.). ☎ **212/662-5740.** Subway: 1/2/3/9 to 96th St.

This store may be crowded and a little grimy and disorganized, but what these folks don't know about nursery equipment ain't worth knowing. There's always an unwieldy mother-to-be collapsed in a glider rocker, looking glassy-eyed as she (and her mother and/or husband) order a couple thousand dollars' worth of baby stuff—I wonder how many labors have started here over the years.

Baby Depot at Burlington Coat Factory. 116 W. 23rd St. (entrance on Sixth Ave.). ☎ **212/229-2247.** Subway: F to 23rd St.

Toil up to the third floor of this discount emporium to find a Toys 'Я' Us–ish collection of layettes, cribs, strollers, car seats, and clothing. The prices are fairly low—just don't expect top-of-the-line furnishings for your nursery.

Baby Palace. 1410–16 Lexington Ave. (between 92nd and 93rd sts.). ☎ **212/426-4544.** Subway: 6 to 96th St.

This friendly store is a well-stocked solid option for everything from cribs to strollers to toys and baby wear. Closed Saturday.

Bellini. 1305 Second Ave. (between 68th and 69th sts.). ☎ **212/517-9233.** Subway: 6 to 68th St.

At this expensive baby furniture boutique, the service can be offhand (unless, of course, you're dropping a bundle). The look is pretty with an edge of fun, nothing too unusual. If you want to start your infant off with upscale tastes, this is where to do it.

Ben's for Kids. 1380 Third Ave. (between 78th and 79th Sts.). ☎ **212/794-2330.** Subway: 6 to 77th St.

Ben's is to the East Side what Albee's (above) is to the West, the main difference being that Ben's is actually pretty clean and has a substantial toy department. Closed Sunday.

Boston & Winthrop. No address. ☎ **212/410-6388.**

This firm designs some really wonderful custom-painted children's furniture; call for an appointment. They come to you, not you to them.

Bunnies. 100 Delancey St. (between Ludlow and Essex sts.). ☎ **212/529-7567.** Subway: F to Delancey St.

The downmarket Lower East Side location reflects this store's mission to sell baby equipment (makers like Century and Evenflo) and clothing up to size 16 (labels like OshKosh and Guess) at very reasonable prices.

Chelsea Kids Quarters. 33 W. 17th St. (between Fifth and Sixth aves.). ☎ **212/627-5524.** Subway: 1/9 to 18th St.

Smart-looking custom-made furniture for kids' bedrooms—bunks, trundles, and loft beds, bookcases, dressers, and student desks, with many configurations scaled just right for apartment dwellers.

Children's Room. 140 Varick St. (at Spring St.). ☎ **212/627-2006.** Subway: 1/9 to Canal St.

Here you'll find bunk beds galore, as well as kid-sized desks, dressers, toy chests, and the like. Nothing tremendously flashy, but everything is well designed and high quality, with prices to match.

Cradle & All. 110 W. 86th St. (between Columbus and Amsterdam aves.). ☎ **212/580-3801.** Subway: 1/9/B/C to 86th St.

Nursery furniture and furnishings, along with some adorable layette items and infant toys, grace this cheery Upper West Side shop, the upscale alternative to Albee's (see above).

Kids Supply Co. 1325 Madison Ave. (between 93rd and 94th sts.), 2nd floor. ☎ **212/426-1200.** Subway: 6 to 96th St.

This boutique sells some intriguing children's furniture, featuring warm woods and bold colors and a sophisticated sense of style. Quality stuff, built to withstand children.

Little Folks Shop. 123 E. 23rd St. (between Park and Lexington aves.). ☎ **212/982-9669.** Subway: 6 to 23rd St.

Little Folks sells a solid range of nursery outfittings and strollers, plus layettes and clothes up to size 14. Closed Saturday.

Plain Jane. 525 Amsterdam Ave. (between 85th and 86th sts.). ☎ **212/595-6916.** Subway: 1/9 to 86th St.

This kicky little West Side boutique specializes in antique nursery furniture, country-look bedding, quilts, and some newer stuff with a retro sensibility—truly one-of-a-kind items like a $500 decoupaged toy chest accented with kids' faces straight from some *Dick and Jane* primer. Closed Sunday.

Schneider's. 20 Avenue A (at 2nd St.). ☎ **212/228-3540.** Subway: F to Second Ave.

This downtown source for baby equipment, on a rundown East Village block, is a lot cleaner than the surrounding neighborhood. A staple for below-14th-Street new moms. Closed Sunday.

Wicker Garden's Children. 1327 Madison Ave. (at 93rd St.). ☎ **212/410-7001.** Subway: 6 to 96th St.

While the baby clothes downstairs are lovely, the upstairs section is the real heart of this shop—nursery furniture that puts the cheap white laminated stuff utterly to shame. Decorate your baby's nest with these country-house reproductions (it's not all wicker) and even Mark Hampton would approve. Closed Sunday.

THEME STORES

Disney Store. (1) 711 Fifth Ave. (at 55th St.). ☎ **212/702-0702.** Subway: E/F to Fifth Ave. (2) 39 W. 34th St. (between Fifth and Sixth aves.). ☎ **212/279-9890.** Subway B/D/E/F/N/Q/R to 34th St. (3) 141 Columbus Ave. (at 66th St.). ☎ **212/362 2386.** Subway: 1/9 to Lincoln Center. (4) 300 W. 125th St. and Seventh Ave. ☎ **212/749-8390.** Subway: 2/3/A/B/C/D to 125th St.

This three-story studio store brings to Manhattan the world's largest selection of Disney merchandise under one roof: images of Mickey, Donald, and the gang painted, embroidered, and embossed on every imaginable item, from baseball hats to bedside lamps—and, of course, wristwatches. If you think this is cheap stuff, the top floor's collectibles department will set you straight, a veritable gallery of animation art, glass art, and exquisite ceramics. The first floor is dedicated to clothing, for children and adults; make a beeline for the second floor, where all the toys and games are in stock. There's always a captivating video clip playing on a huge screen somewhere, to mesmerize your children while you shop.

NBA Store. 666 Fifth Ave. (between 52nd and 53rd sts.). ☎ **212/515-6221.** Subway: E/F to Fifth Ave.

This three-story player in the Fifth Avenue Parade of Theme Stores celebrates hoop dreams in a big way.

NikeTown. 6 E. 57th St. (between Fifth and Madison aves.). ☎ **212/891-6453.** Subway: N/R to Fifth Ave.

Eye-popping design and lots of sports videos build the buzz at this sneaker palace.

Warner Bros. Studio Store. (1) 1 E. 57th St. (at Fifth Ave.). ☎ **212/754-0300.** Subway: N/R to Fifth Ave. (2) 1 Times Square (at 42nd St., Seventh Ave., and Broadway). ☎ **212/840-4040.** Subway: 1/2/3/7/9/N/R/S to Times Square.

The intersection of Fifth Avenue and 57th Street has become known as the Four Carats since carrot-chompin' Bugs Bunny joined the high-end jewelry stores here;

in 1997, Warner Bros. also cornered a very prime piece of Times Square real estate, right below where the ball drops on New Year's Eve. Both megastores occupy three floors and are usually crowded to the gills. There's absolutely nothing New Yorkish about them, but they're indubitably loads of fun for little cartoon hounds, with endless cartoon videos on the huge monitors and pictures of the Looney Tunes crowd painted, embroidered, and embossed on every kind of clothing and gift item.

TOYS

Alphabets. (1) 115 Ave. A (at 7th St.). ☎ **212/475-7250.** Subway: 6 to Astor Place (2) 2284 Broadway (between 82nd and 83rd sts.). ☎ **212/579-5702.** Subway: 1/9 to 79th St. (3) 47 Greenwich Ave. (between Sixth and Seventh aves.). ☎ **212/229-2966.** Subway: 1/2/3/9 to 14th St.

The East Village sensibility of this wacky gift-a-torium translates well to more mainstream neighborhoods; central to the concept is lots of campy kids' stuff— Etch-a-Sketch and Mr. Potato Head, yes, but also some truly goofball stuff like a chess set with the Simpson family (Homer and Bart, that is)—which is probably bought by as many adults as children. Loads of one-of-a-kind T-shirts and a very big line of Hello Kitty stuff from Japan (hot with downtown club kids).

A Bear's Place. 789 Lexington Ave. (between 61st and 62nd sts.). ☎ **212/826-6465.** Subway: 4/5/6 to 59th St.

For some reason, this strikes me as a girl's toy store, maybe because it has the biggest stock I've seen of equipment for mothering baby dolls, along with wooden toys, games, puppets, big teddy bears, dolls, and the entire line of imported Battat toys for babies and toddlers. You can order some hand-painted nursery furnishings here.

Ben's for Kids. 1380 Third Ave. (between 78th and 79th sts.). ☎ **212/794-2330.** Subway: 6 to 77th St.

Though principally for nursery equipment, Ben's has enough toys in the front to qualify as a toy store. The emphasis is on playthings for babies and toddlers, with lots of Fisher-Price and such standard brands. Closed Sunday.

Big City Kites. 1210 Lexington Ave. (at 81st St.). ☎ **212/472-2623.** www.bigcitykites.com. Subway: 4/5/6 to 86th St.

Beyond all the great wind-worthy kites promised in the name, this handy little shop stocks loads of other flying toys, from Frisbees to balsa-wood gliders; a serious collection of yo-yos and juggling equipment rounds out the inventory. A good stop if you're on the way to Central Park on a windy spring afternoon. Closed Sunday September to March.

✪ **Children's General Store.** (1) Grand Central Terminal, Lexington Passage. ☎ **212/ 682-0004.** Subway: 4/5/6/7/S to Grand Central. (2) 2473 Broadway (at 92nd St.). ☎ **212/580-2723.** Subway: 1/2/3/9 to 96th St.

This charming toy boutique is a welcome addition to the shopping at Grand Central Terminal; the West Side original, handily downstairs from Playspace (see chapter 6), first won customer loyalty for offering some unusual handmade and imported toys you don't see in most other stores. The emphasis is on well-made toys with a certain imagination-sparking value. The West Sider crams an awful lot into its small space; thank goodness the Grand Central space will give them room to show what they can really do.

Classic Toys. 218 Sullivan St. (between Bleecker and W. 3rd sts.). ☎ **212/674-4434.** Subway: A/B/C/D/E/F/Q to W. 4th St.

The "classic" in the name works both ways: both vintage toys (wind-ups, trains) and the kinds of solid, quality new toys that'll endure.

Cozy's Cuts for Kids. (1) 1125 Madison Ave. (at 84th St.). ☎ **212/744-1716.** Subway: 4/5/6 to 86th St. (2) 448 Amsterdam Ave. (between 81st and 82nd sts.). ☎ **212/579-2600.** Subway: 1/9 to 79th St.

Besides haircuts (above), Cozy's deals in a small stock of well-chosen toys, including lots of arts and crafts.

Craft Studio. 1657 Third Ave. (between 92nd and 93rd sts.). ☎ **212/831-6626.** Subway: 6 to 96th St.

The rain forest–themed site for plaster-painting parties has an excellent front section with lots of crafts kits, art materials, puzzles, and other toys.

Dinosaur Hill. 306 E. 9th St. (near Second Ave.). ☎ **212/473-5850.** www.dinosaurhill.com. Subway: 6 to Astor Place.

Selling imported toys, mobiles, wooden blocks, art supplies, and puppets—notably an extensive line of handmade marionettes—this airy East Village shop also has a battery of under-$2 stuff so no child will have to leave empty-handed.

Enchanted Forest. 85 Mercer St. (between Spring and Broome sts.). ☎ **212/925-6677.** Subway: N/R to Prince St.; 6 to Spring St.

Befitting its SoHo location, this is a boutique for the Toy as Art—handmade wooden song flutes from the rain forest, exquisite hand-sewn stuffed animals and hand puppets, phantasmagorical pop-up books, amazing kaleidoscopes. The fanciful decor makes it more or less a gallery, highly browseable, and about as far away from Toys 'Я' Us as a toy store can get.

✪ **FAO Schwarz.** 767 Fifth Ave. (at 58th St.). ☎ **212/644-9400.** Subway: N/R to Fifth Ave.

What can I say? Vacationing families are duty-bound to visit this mecca, though locals rarely venture inside. This huge place isn't just a toy store, it's a destination—the immense mechanical music box/clock on the ground floor is worth at least 10 minutes of staring and marveling in itself. Larger-than-life stuffed animals, the FAO trademark, dominate the ground floor; upstairs (via escalator or glass-walled elevator) are incredible toy cars, a Barbie boutique, an overwhelming Lego department, an immense Brio train setup, and more electronic robots and toys and games than you've ever seen. Not everything is imported, by any means—Fisher Price and Playskool take their place alongside the somewhat precious toys made exclusively for FAO. (Remember, this place is now a chain, with all the mass-market mentality that implies.) Grandmas with big bucks are the prime audience for all this conspicuous consumption, but persevere and you'll no doubt find some toys you could justify buying.

Geppetto's Toybox. 10 Christopher St. (between Greenwich Ave. and Gay St.). ☎ **212/620-7511.** Subway: 1/9 to Christopher St.

Kids and collectors alike shop at this light-filled Greenwich Village boutique, its varnished blond wood surfaces echoed by the number of quality wooden toys. The selection tends toward high-end dolls, collectible bears, and artist-designed toys, as well as some very sturdy playthings for infants and toddlers.

✪ **Hombons.** 1500 First Ave. (between 78th and 79th sts.). ☎ **212/717-5300.** Subway: 6 to 77th St.

Crowded into this storefront is a deep selection of stuff to play with, best for its art-and-crafts materials, puzzles, board games, Playmobils, and other small-motor activities. It's definitely a place that rewards a long, slow browse.

Kay-Bee Toys. (1) In Manhattan Mall, 901 Sixth Ave. (at 33rd St.). ☎ **212/629-5386.** Subway: B/D/F/N/Q/R to 34th St. (2) 2411 Broadway (at 89th St.). ☎ **212/595-4398.** Subway: 1/9 to 86th St.

Sometimes you need a chain toy store to get that Malibu Barbie or G.I. Joe your kid is pining for. Utterly mass market, very dependable.

Kidding Around. (1) 60 W. 15th St. (between Fifth and Sixth aves.). ☎ **212/645-6337.** Subway: 4/5/6/L/N/R/F to 14th St./Union Square. (2) 68 Bleecker St. (between Broadway and Lafayette St.). ☎ **212/598-0228.** Subway: 6 to Bleecker St.

This pair of shops brings the uptown toy-buying aesthetic to downtown—imports and educational toys in a clean well-lighted space. Lots of rugged plastic wildlife in baskets on the floor.

Little Extras. 674 Amsterdam Ave. (at 93rd St.). ☎ **212/721-6161.** Subway: 1/9 to 86th St.

Alongside some lovely baby gifts, this West Sider has a pleasant stock of painted wooden toys, hand puppets, backpacks, puzzles, and art kits, not to mention personalized little-boy yarmulkes and nifty junior jewelry. A fun place to browse.

✪ **Mary Arnold Toys.** 1010 Lexington Ave. (between 72nd and 73rd sts.). ☎ **212/744-8510.** Subway: 6 to 77th St.

One of the best toy stores in town, Mary Arnold's is intelligently laid out with nooks where children can fiddle and browse without clogging the aisles. Quality toys—Legos, Brios, Playmobils—many shelves of board games, lots of dress-up costumes, and a very impressive doll department make this a never-fail destination to satisfy kids of any age or interest.

✪ **Penny Whistle Toys.** (1) 448 Columbus Ave. (at 81st St.). ☎ **212/873-9090.** www. pwt-toys.com. Subway: B/C to 79th St. (2) 1283 Madison Ave. (at 91st St.). ☎ **212/369-3868.** Subway: 4/5/6 to 86th St.

This outstanding shop has more or less defined what upscale New York parents want in a toy store: imported, quality, educational toys, well made but with a sense of fun. Nothing too precious, nothing too commercial. Mechanical bears outside both stores blow soap bubbles in fair weather, which makes it very hard to get your kids past without stopping.

Promises Fulfilled. 1592 Second Ave. (between 82nd and 83rd sts.). ☎ **212/472-1600.** Subway: 4/5/6 to 86th St.

This narrow, crowded, little shop specializes in kids-room accessories with hand-painted designs and personalization. A few toys as well; handy if you're in the neighborhood.

Stationery & Toy World. 125 W. 72nd St. (between Columbus Ave. and Broadway). ☎ **212/580-3922.** Subway: 1/2/3/9 to 72nd St.

There's a delightfully unpretentious clutter of mass-market toys amid the spiral notebooks and ballpoint pens at this friendly West Side storefront (which, my kids never fail to remember, is just down the street from the Krispy Kreme Doughnuts shop). A good place for reward and bribe toys and fun little surprises. Closed July and August.

Store of Knowledge WNET. (1) 1091 Third Ave. (at 64th St.). ☎ **212/223-0018.** Subway: 6 to 68th St. (2) 1 World Trade Center, in The Mall at World Trade Center. ☎ **212/321-2855.** Subway: E to World Trade Center; 1/9 to Cortlandt St.

Along with awesome stuff for junior physicists, astronomers, entomologists, and paleontologists (see "Science Stuff," above), this large PBS-sponsored store has lots of good baby toys, books, and tie-in toys to all those great PBS kids' shows.

(Now you can assemble a complete family of stuffed Arthur, D.W., and Baby Kate, or construct the entire Island of Sodor Railway in Brio track.) Kids of all ages will find a section to gravitate to.

Toys 'Я' Us. (1) 1293 Broadway (at 34th St.). ☎ **212/594-8697.** Subway: B/D/F/N/Q/R to 34th St. (2) 24–32 Union Square East (at 15th St.). ☎ **212/674-8697.** Subway: 4/5/6/L/N/R to Union Square.

I'm not a snob, and there certainly have been times when I've trekked here to get that Fisher Price trike or Hot Wheels set that the high-end Manhattan toy stores don't stock. But frankly, in the context of New York toy shopping, these immense toy-o-ramas are a pretty lackluster alternative; the stock looks battered, customers wander around in a shell-shocked daze, there's hardly any sales help, the toys don't even have price tags (you have to lug them over to a scanner to have the bar code read electronically), and, for all the miles of shelves, sometimes you still can't find that mass-market toy your son saw advertised on the Cartoon Network and is bugging you for. The prices aren't even significantly lower. A new giant branch is supposed to open in Times Square in 2001 or so—maybe that flagship location will be clean, bright, and cheerfully efficient. I'll keep my fingers crossed.

◑ West Side Kids. 498 Amsterdam Ave. (at 84th St.). ☎ **212/496-7282.** Subway: 1/9 to 86th St.

This superb West Side store has room enough to stock every toy a parent could want—lotsa Legos, T.C. Timber, Playmobils, every crafts kit known to youth, an impressive board game selection, and a whole wall of great imported infant and toddler items, as well as one of those great bin corners where the toy equivalent of penny candy is handily laid out (there have been days when I'd never have gotten my kids safely out of the store if I hadn't been able to buy each of them a $1 toy from the bins). The staff is knowledgeable, the selection intelligent and responsible. When I've got a birthday or Christmas coming up and have no time to troll the stores, I can count on one-stop shopping here.

Zany Brainy. (1) 112 E. 86th St. (between Park and Lexington aves.). ☎ **212/427-6611.** Subway: 4/5/6 to 86th St. (2) 2407 Broadway (at 88th St.). ☎ **917/441-2066.** Subway: 1/9 to 86th St.

Face it: Who has time to browse delightedly for toys these days? Your kid's heart is set on a certain Brio component, or you've got two cooped up with chicken pox who are climbing the walls. Where do you go to get relief fast? Try Zany Brainy, a reliable place for efficient toy shopping. Though it may lack the kind of personality and charm a small independently owned shop might have, this large chain store has a broad-ranging stock of quality toys, without any snobbery against commercial stuff like Barbies and Nerf guns. The prices are decent (at least by Manhattan standards), and the space is clean and bright. The selection of children's audiotapes and CDs is particularly extensive, and there's a generous section of arts-and-crafts kits, as well as good board games and puzzles. Beanie Baby collectors note: This is one of the city's best sources for current Beanies, where the prices remain fair.

Zittles. 969 Madison Ave. (between 75th and 76th sts.). ☎ **212/737-2040.** Subway: 6 to 68th St.

This East Side drugstore's toy department just kept expanding and crowded out the second floor; now it's got its own name and a floor to itself. Finally, this overflowing selection of toys has room to be properly displayed, even with a little flair. For a good mix of quality items and unsnobby mainstream toys, it's a source worth knowing about.

8 Entertainment for the Whole Family

Being the theater capital of the United States doesn't necessarily make New York City the children's theater capital—most of those struggling actors and playwrights and directors are too intent on breaking into the Big Time to pay much mind to kid stuff. On the other hand, the major classical music venues—Lincoln Center and Carnegie Hall—have in the past few years seen the wisdom of introducing children to music *early,* perhaps because impresarios realize (with panic) that their core audience is rapidly aging and needs to be replaced. In any case, there's a lot of talent hanging around this city, and when enterprising organizers decide to put on a show for young audiences, the production values are generally high.

Two important players entered the scene in the 1990s. The Disney organization has waded into New York theater in a big way, topping its live stage version of the animated hit *Beauty and the Beast* with an even more successful *Lion King* production in the stunningly renovated New Amsterdam Theater on West 42nd Street (see "The Big Venues"). The New Victory Theater, another 42nd Street rehab, opened well before Disney, paving the way with a vigorous series of family-oriented productions that has already improved the cultural life of the under-14 set (see "The Big Venues").

New York parents tend to be culture hounds, so plays and concerts for children are usually well attended—which means that, as for adult productions, you've got to reserve in advance. Compared to the $75 you can pay for orchestra seats in the big Broadway theaters, ticket prices for kids' events aren't usually outrageous, though a few major annual events—like the Big Apple Circus and *The Nutcracker*—get away with higher prices.

FINDING OUT WHAT'S ON   The three local parents' monthlies—*Big Apple Parent,* 9 E. 38th St., 4th floor, New York, NY 10016 (☎ 212/889-6400; www.parentsknow.com); *New York Family,* 141 Halstead Ave., Suite 3D, Mamaroneck, NY 10543 (☎ 914/381-7474; www.parenthoodweb.com); and *Parent Guide,* Parent Guide Media, 419 Park Ave. South, New York, NY 10016 (☎ 212/213-8840; www.parentguidenews.com)—carry invaluable calendars of upcoming cultural events kids would enjoy. You can usually pick up free copies at public libraries, toy stores, and kids' clothing stores.

Call to get recorded listings of events for **Lincoln Center** at ☎ **212/875-5400** or **Central Park** at ☎ **888/NY-PARKS.**

Every Friday, the *New York Times* runs a "Family Fare" column in its Weekend entertainment section, detailing special events in the upcoming week. Three weeklies—*New York* magazine, *Time Out New York,* and the *Village Voice*—include sections on children's events in their comprehensive listings.

GETTING TICKETS   In marked contrast to the adult entertainment scene, children's events in New York City don't tend to sell out far in advance. The Radio City Christmas show and seasonal runs like *The Nutcracker,* the Big Apple Circus, and the Ringling Brothers and Barnum & Bailey Circus should be reserved a few weeks in advance, but for most other events you'll be fine calling a week ahead or even walking in the day of the show. For pro sports events, ticket availability is a matter of how well the team's been doing lately (Knicks tickets are impossible, but you can just about always walk into a MetroStars game). You can usually find flocks of scalpers hovering around Madison Square Garden, if seeing a Knicks game is the most important thing on your youngster's agenda. You'll pay through the nose and might be sold bogus tickets, but it may be worth the gamble for you.

Madison Square Garden events and major theater productions offer their tickets through **Ticketmaster** (☎ **800/755-4000,** 212/307-4100, or 212/307-7171; www.ticketmaster.com) or through **Tele-Charge** (☎ **800/432-7250** or 212/239-6200; www.telecharge.com). **Madison Square Garden** events also have their own box office (☎ **212/465-MSG1;** www.thegarden.com). For smaller children's theater companies and puppet shows, contact the box office numbers in separate listings below (some are simply answering machines where you leave your number so the organizer can call you back)

Same-day tickets for many Broadway and Off-Broadway events can be bought in person at the **TKTS booths** (☎ **212/768-1818**): in Midtown on the pedestrian island called Duffy Square at 47th Street and Broadway (open daily 3 to 8pm for evening performances, Wednesday and Saturday 10am to 2pm for matinees, Sunday 11am to closing for evening and matinee shows) or Downtown on the mezzanine of 2 World Trade Center (open Monday to Friday 11am to 5pm, Saturday 11am to 3:30pm; tickets for Wednesday, Saturday, and Sunday matinees on sale the day before only 11am to closing). Most tickets are sold at half price, though some are discounted only 25%, but you'll have to have cash or traveler's checks—no plastic. A $2.50 TKTS service charge is added. The Times Square booth often has long lines, which move fairly fast, but not fast enough for restless small kids. The surrounding assemblage of wild lit-up signs can provide some distraction while you're waiting, and sometimes mimes and jugglers and street musicians work the crowd. But if you can swing it, one parent should take the youngsters for a walk while the other hangs out in line.

1 The Big Venues

Brooklyn Academy of Music (BAM). 30 Lafayette Ave., Brooklyn. ☎ **718/636-4100.** www.bam.org. Tickets $8–$12. Subway: 2/3/4/5/D/Q to Atlantic Ave., Brooklyn; G to Fulton St., Brooklyn; B/M/N/R to Pacific St., Brooklyn.

Theater, dance, music, puppetry—an impressively international selection of productions rolls through BAM in the course of a year, with a decided tendency toward the avant-garde. In the lineup you can count on a handful of reasonably priced performances suited to youngsters, always worth a trek out to Brooklyn. Also look out for the 2-day BAMKids Film Festival in the spring. Age levels are specified for each performance.

Madison Square Garden. Seventh Ave. between 31st and 33rd sts. ☎ **212/465-MSG1.** www.thegarden.com. Subway: A/C/E to Penn Station; 1/2/3/9 to 34th St.

B-ball, hockey, WWF wrestling, ice shows, the big-top circus, and megarock concerts occupy this large arena in a grubby part of Midtown. It can be an intimidating space for a small child, but older kids will recognize it for what it is: a big-league venue with lots of urban electricity. Tickets for most events here are also handled through Ticketmaster. The **Theater at Madison Square Garden,** part of the Garden complex, hosts concerts and live touring stage shows like *Sesame Street Live.*

New Amsterdam Theater. 214 W. 42nd St. (between Seventh and Eighth aves.). ☎ **212/ 282-2900** or 212/307-4747 (Ticketmaster) for tickets. Subway: 1/2/3/7/9/N/R/S to Times Square; A/C/E to 42nd St.

Ornate and gilded to the max, this classic Broadway theater reopened in spring 1997 with the brilliantly inventive stage version of *The Lion King,* which won a slew of Tony awards. This Disney production is sold out absurdly far in advance, but same-day tickets are often released; line up outside the box office around noon to try your luck.

New Victory Theater. 209 W. 42nd St. (between Seventh and Eighth aves.). ☎ **212/ 382-4000** or 212/239-6200 (TeleCharge). www.newvictory.com. Tickets $10–$35. Subway: 1/2/3/7/9/N/R/S to Times Square; A/C/E to 42nd St.

This lovely renovated theater on 42nd Street—originally built by impresario Oscar Hammerstein in 1900—has an impressive lineup of entertainment totally for kids: international circus troupes, operas, dance, mimes, storytellers, movies, and many acts that defy categories. There's a lot of high-profile talent, like London's Young Vic Theatre Company, Circus Oz, Mabou Mines, Australia's zany Flying Fruit Fly Circus, the British "junk opera" *Shockheaded Peter,* and the Flying Karamazov Brothers. But New York parents have learned to book tickets far in advance even if they've never heard of the artists, because chances are you'll open the *New York Times* the morning after a new New Victory show opens and read rave reviews and then discover the entire 3-week run is already sold out. Target age groups vary, but there's a good deal of stuff for kids 8 to 12—too old to get a thrill out of puppet shows but still too young to really enjoy most Broadway shows. The lineup of shows keeps the place hopping most of the year, except July and August.

Radio City Music Hall. 1260 Sixth Ave. (at 50th St.). ☎ **212/247-4777** or 212/307-1000 (Ticketmaster). Subway: B/D to Rockefeller Center.

The art deco interior of this Rockefeller Center showcase is a marvel in itself, but kids probably won't notice—they'll be too busy gaping at the vast proscenium of the stage. Besides mounting its own live stage shows twice a year (see "Seasonal Events," below), Radio City hosts concerts, including the occasional family show. (We went to the Barney stage show a couple of years ago, packed with jabbering toddlers and vendors hawking licensed merchandise. Never again.)

Symphony Space. 2537 Broadway (at 95th St.). ☎ **212/864-5400.** www.symphonyspace. org. Subway: 1/2/3/9 to 96th St.

Besides the Just Kidding series (see "Weekend Shows," later in this chapter), this Upper West Side theater hosts an eclectic variety of events: international dance troupes, Gilbert & Sullivan operettas, and, in spring, a really great series of short-story readings by famous actors and writers. Although a new apartment tower was built above it in 2000, Symphony Stage remains snuggled into the base, decidedly shabby and very PC—a vintage piece of the Upper West Side.

2 Seasonal Events

Madison Square Garden, Seventh Avenue between 31st and 33rd streets (☎ 212/ 465-6741), hosts various ice shows when they skate through town—**Disney on Ice, Sesame Street on Ice,** and others of that ilk. Tickets are usually available through Ticketmaster.

✪ Big Apple Circus. All ages. In Damrosch Park at Lincoln Center, Broadway and 64th St. ☎ **212/268-2500.** (Mailing address: 35 W. 35th St., New York, NY 10001.) Tickets $12–$55; free for children under 2. Subway: 1/9 to Lincoln Center.

Kids too young for clamorous Ringling Bros. and Barnum & Bailey delight in this wonderful one-ring circus that performs in a tent (heated, of course) at Lincoln Center from October to January. In 2¼ hours the Big Apple Circus manages to pack in clowns, elephants, trapeze artists, bareback riders, and something for everyone. Skilled circus artists and a sophisticated sense of humor make this a good show for adults who'd rather be charmed than stunned. A splendid time is guaranteed for all.

A Christmas Carol. **Ages 6 & up.** The Theater at Madison Square Garden, Seventh Ave. between 31st and 33rd sts. ☎ **212/465-MSG1** or 212/307-4747 (Ticketmaster). Tickets $29–$69. Subway: A/C/E to Penn Station; 1/2/3/9 to 34th St.

With songs by perennial Oscar winner Alan Menken (*Aladdin, Beauty and the Beast*), this glossy holiday musical based on the Dickens chestnut arrives for an annual run, late November to December. A trifle slick and you know how it's gonna end, but hey, this story didn't become a classic for nothing—it still pulls in the crowds.

The Nutcracker. **Ages 10 & up.** At the New York State Theater in Lincoln Center, Broadway and 64th St. ☎ **212/870-5570.** Tickets $25–$80. Subway: 1/9 to Lincoln Center.

This is where the city's best *Nutcracker* is staged every December by the New York City Ballet, with several stunning effects (like a Christmas tree that grows up out of the stage to gi-normous proportions).

The Nutcracker. **Ages 5 & up.** Florence Gould Hall, 55 E. 59th St. (between Park and Madison aves.). ☎ **212/355-6160.** Tickets $20 adults, $10 children 12 and under. Subway: 4/5/6 to 59th St.; N/R to Lexington Ave.

The New York Theater Ballet's abbreviated version of Tchaikovsky's holiday classic ballet lasts about 1 hour, cutting out a lot of the first act to focus on the magical elements of the story. Alongside the classical ballet elements, bits of juggling have been thrown in, and Herr Drosselmeyer has some speaking parts to set up the story. Children are allowed—even expected—to make noises and jump out of their seats. A nice introduction to the ballet for younger audiences.

Radio City Music Hall Christmas Show. Ages 3 & up. 1260 Sixth Ave. (at 50th St.). ☎ **212/247-4777** or 212/307-1000 (Ticketmaster). Tickets $32–$80. Subway: B/D to Rockefeller Center.

The Rockettes gotta perform somewhere, and this is it. Radio City's elegant art deco interior, with its immense stage, cries out for a stage extravaganza like this—lots of music, lavish stage effects, corny holiday motifs, and that classic precision kick line. The Christmas Spectacular runs early November to the first week in January, usually one show a day until the holidays loom close, when up to five shows a day

Street Performers

The cream of New York's street performers may be the Crowtations puppet ensemble (see "Puppet Shows," later in this chapter), which has been playing Central Park on weekends for years. Top spots for catching jugglers are at South Street Seaport, by the Statue of Liberty ferry line in Battery Park, by the TKTS line in Duffy Square, by the steps of the Metropolitan Museum of Art, by the fountain in Washington Square Park, and near the Tisch Children's Zoo in Central Park (near 65th Street).

The subways see their fair share of freelancers—there's actually a great space set up for them in the Times Square station, near the Times Square shuttle platform, where jazz combos gravitate for the great acoustics. The 34th Street station for the B, F, N, and R trains often attracts good musicians as well, including an Andean pipe band that's really primo.

There's no guarantee these people will be any good, of course. Standouts in my mind include the guy who plays electric harmonica on the IND platforms in Midtown; a juggler my husband and I nicknamed Bope, who used to work the crowds at movie houses around 57th Street on weekend nights; and a totally whacked-out saxophonist who used to play the *Twilight Zone* theme over and over on the West Side IRT (memorable more for his crazy patter than for his musical technique—people used to pay him to *stop* playing). Remember, you're under no obligation to give these people money, but if you think they're good, you should. Unlike panhandlers, these people are at least doing something for their money.

are performed. It's an annual tradition, and the magic still works, dazzling the Nickelodeon generation.

Ringling Bros. and Barnum & Bailey Circus. Ages 6 & up. At Madison Square Garden, Seventh Ave. between 31st and 33rd sts. ☎ **800/755-4000,** 212/465-MSG1, or 212/307-4100 (Ticketmaster). www.ringling.com. Tickets $10–$22.50 (VIP boxes $42.50). Subway: A/C/E to Penn Station; 1/2/3/9 to 34th St.

This glitzy, humongous circus takes up residence at the Garden for 6 weeks every spring, beginning in late March, starring death-defying aerialists, wild animal acts, lumbering elephants, snarling bears, hordes of clowns, the whole shebang. Smaller kids may be overwhelmed by the sheer size of the Garden, not to mention the flashing lights and eardrum-blasting music. Adults may be overwhelmed by the barrage of vendors selling junk food and junky souvenirs at wildly inflated prices. Still, it's the Greatest Show on Earth and pretty darn impressive.

3 Weekend Shows

Henry Street Settlement Abrons Arts Center. Ages 4 to 12. 466 Grand St. (at Pitt St.). ☎ **212/598-0400.** Tickets $6 adults, $4 children 4–12. Subway: F to Delancey St.; B/D/Q to Grand St.

On weekends, this Lower East Side cultural center—a longtime mainstay of the neighborhood—runs a series for kids and their parents at 2pm, with performances twice a month. The company does a wide variety of shows, including dance performances, plays based on updated fairy tales, improv sessions, and puppet shows, all nicely multicultural and very professional. I recommend you call for reservations a week in advance.

Museum of Television and Radio. Ages 3 & up. 25 W. 52nd St. (between Fifth and Sixth aves.). ☎ **212/621-6600.** www.mtr.org. Tickets $6 adults, $4 students, $3 children 12 and under. Subway: E/F to Fifth Ave.

What's called the International Children's Television Festival runs November to May, offering screenings on Saturday and Sunday afternoons. Each month has a different theme; the museum selects outstanding live and animated kids' TV shows from around the world and shows them in screening rooms in the museum. If your kids are older, definitely check out the museum's fascinating Saturday morning "Re-creating Radio" workshops (ages 9 to 14, $5 per child), which let kids re-create the golden age of radio by recording a show themselves.

Symphony Space. Ages 5 & up. 2537 Broadway (at 95th St.). ☎ **212/864-5400.** www.symphonyspace.org. Tickets $8. Subway: 1/2/3/9 to 96th St.

One Saturday a month, November to April, the Just Kidding series here presents 11am performances by and for kids—anything from live theater to children's movie screenings. Eclectic, multicultural, and fun.

4 Theater

LONG-RUNNING SHOWS

It's always hard to predict which Broadway and Off-Broadway shows will still be running by the time you read this (much less by the time you get to New York), but these five are a pretty safe bet—they've been running for a long time with no sign of letting up. Most of them (except *The Lion King*) are usually available for half price at the TKTS booth at 47th Street and Broadway and the World Trade Center.

Beauty and the Beast. **Ages 5 & up.** At the Lunt–Fontanne Theater, 205 W. 46th St. ☎ **212/575-9200.** Tickets $25–$80. Subway: 1/9 to 50th St.

The beloved Disney film has been turned into a hit Broadway musical (2½ hours long) that keeps regular Broadway hours—8pm shows Wednesday to Saturday, 2pm matinees Wednesday and Saturday, a 1pm Sunday matinee, and an early-bird 6:30pm Sunday night show (June through September there's only a 3pm matinee on Sunday). Tickets should be reserved in advance, but it may be possible to get them at the TKTS booth or at the box office an hour before the start of the show.

Blue Man Group: Tubes. **Ages 10 & up.** At the Astor Place Theater, 434 Lafayette St. (between E. 4th and E. 8th sts.). ☎ **212/254-4370.** www.blueman.com. Tickets $45 and $55. Subway: 6 to Astor Place.

Faces painted blue, this trio has been committing weird mayhem on stage since 1992, with lots of flashing strobes and percussion effects. The hip performance art elements are directed to adults, but preteens dig the show too—there are often birthday parties in the audience. The show runs slightly under 2 hours.

The Fantasticks. **Ages 5 & up.** At the Sullivan Street Playhouse, 181 Sullivan St. (between Bleecker and Houston sts.). ☎ **212/674-3838** or 212/307-4100 (Ticketmaster). Tickets $37.50–$40. Subway: A/B/C/D/E/F/Q to W. 4th St.

Why has this show been running since 1960? Well, it's a sweet fable about young lovers, with very hummable tunes (the showstopper is "Try to Remember"), and in this intimate Village playhouse it's a good way to introduce kids to live grown-up theater. Call well in advance, since the theater's small and fills up quickly.

✪ *The Lion King.* **All ages.** At the New Amsterdam Theater, 214 W. 42nd St. (between Seventh and Eighth aves.). ☎ **212/282-2900** or 212/307-4747 (Ticketmaster). Tickets $25–$90. Subway: 1/2/3/7/9/N/R/S to Times Square.

One of the hottest tickets in town, improbably enough, is for this adaptation of a Disney animated movie. Why all the fuss? Because Tony-winning director Julie Taymor discarded glitzy special effects and made stage magic instead with puppets, dancers, masks, billowing cloths, and imagination. Drawing strongly on African folk traditions, this production is genuinely moving, even—dare I say it?— better than the movie. Call for tickets many months in advance, line up outside for same-day returns, or splurge on a ticket agent, but somehow get your children to see this play.

Stomp. **Ages 8 & up.** At the Orpheum Theater, 126 Second Ave. (between 7th and 8th sts.). ☎ **212/477-2477** or 212/307-4100 (Ticketmaster). Tickets $29.50–$49.50. Subway: 6 to Astor Place.

What kid hasn't made music by tapping a broom handle on the floor or crashing two pot lids together? This troupe of eight athletic-looking dancers does the same sort of rhythmic stuff with everyday objects for an hour and a half, and it's undeniably captivating. Kids with a short attention span may weary, but others will be fascinated by the endless variations. Early evening performances Saturday and Sunday make it possible to see this without being out too late.

CHILDREN'S THEATER COMPANIES
Grove Street Playhouse. Ages 2 to 12. 39 Grove St. (between Bedford and Bleecker sts.). ☎ **212/741-6436.** Tickets $8.50. Subway: 1/9 to Christopher St.

Miss Majesty's Lollipop Playhouse presents adaptations of classic tales like *The Gingerbread Man, The Three Little Pigs, Pocohontas,* and *The Little Mermaid* on weekends at 1:30 and 3:30pm September to June. All performances are audience-participation comedies, and a rollicking time is usually had by all.

Here. Ages 4 & up. 145 Sixth Ave. (near Spring St.). ☎ **212/647-0202.** www.here.org. Tickets $5–$10. Subway: C/E to Spring St.

This multiarts collaborative in SoHo runs programs for kids on Saturday throughout the year—works like a spirited retelling of *Beowulf* and a popular *Pied Piper.*

✪ **Paper Bag Players. Ages 4 to 9.** At the Sylvia and Danny Kaye Playhouse, Hunter College, 68th St. between Park and Lexington aves. ☎ **212/772-4448** or 212/362-0431. Tickets $15–$20. Subway: 6 to 68th St.

January to March, this veteran troupe presents original plays with a pleasant edge of nuttiness, on Saturday at 2pm and Sunday at 1 and 3pm. The company's trademark is using everyday materials like paper bags and corrugated cardboard for all the costumes, sets, and props, giving the productions a homegrown look that somehow makes them very appealing to kids.

Shadow Box Theater. Ages 4 & up. 30 Third Ave. (at Atlantic Ave.), Brooklyn. ☎ **212/724-0677** or 212/877-7356. (Mailing address: 325 West End Ave., New York, NY 10023.) Tickets $8. Subway: 2/3 to Nevins St., Brooklyn.

The children's theater-in-residence at the Brooklyn YWCA specializes in original musicals with multicultural themes, featuring singing, dancing, and puppetry. November to May, they present four to five productions, each running about a month, with weekday and weekend performances. Call ahead for a schedule.

Theater for a New Audience. Ages 8 & up. At The American Palace Theatre, 111 W. 46th St. (between Broadway and Sixth Ave.). ☎ **212/229-2819.** www.tfana.org. (Mailing address: 154 Christopher St., New York, NY 10014.) Tickets $10–$45. Subway: B/D/F/Q to Rockefeller Center, 1/2/3/7/9 to Times Square, N/R to 49th St.

This top-notch Off-Broadway company devotes itself to the classics, mostly Shakespeare. By no means for children only, its vigorous productions do attract lots of school groups, because they're a great way to introduce youngsters to the Bard. January to April, there are two or three productions, playing Tuesday to Saturday nights, with a Saturday matinee.

۞ Theatreworks USA. Ages 5 & up. At the Auditorium at Equitable Tower, 787 Seventh Ave. (at 51st St.). ☎ **212/627-7373** or 212/239-6200 (TeleCharge). www.theatreworksusa. org. Tickets $19. Subway: 1/9 to 50th St.; N/R to 49th St.; B/D/E to Seventh Ave.

One of the city's top choices for kids, this long-running troupe presents witty, vivid musical versions of classic books—real books like *The Lion, the Witch, and the Wardrobe, Charlotte's Web, The Boxcar Children,* and *Ramona Quimby,* not just fairy tales. They put on a dozen or so plays each year, with several performances of each, so you can count on something every weekend at 12:30pm September to March. Babes in arms aren't allowed.

Thirteenth Street Repertory Theater. Ages 4 & up. 50 W. 13th St. (between Fifth and Sixth aves.). ☎ **212/675-6677.** Tickets $7. Subway: 1/2/3/9/F to 14th St; 4/5/6/L/N/R to Union Square.

This company puts on two original shows on Saturday and Sunday at 1 and 3pm year round. With recorded music and special effects, shows like *Danger Dinosaurs* are perfectly calibrated for a young audience, with healthy doses of humor. Reservations are recommended a couple of days in advance of the performance.

Tribeca Performing Arts. Ages 5 & up. 199 Chambers St. (between Greenwich St. and the West Side Hwy.). ☎ **212/346-8510.** Tickets $13 adults, $8 children 12 and under. Subway: 1/2/3/9/A/C to Chambers St.

Offering a mixed bag of events—some starring kids, others with adult performers, others with puppets or dancers or actors performing in sign language—this downtown arts center brings to town a full season of children's entertainment with its Family, Folk, and Fairy Tale series (October to June, Saturday or Sunday at 1:30pm). Past productions have included musical versions of classics like *Hans Brinker* and *The Reluctant Dragon* as well as retellings of award-winning children's books.

KIDS ON STAGE

City Lights. Ages 4 & up. 130 W. 56th St. (between Sixth and Seventh aves.). ☎ **212/262-0200.** Tickets $7 adults, $5 children. Subway: 1/9 to 28th St.

Twice a year, students 7 to 18 who've taken classes at the City Lights school perform—one production is an original play, the other a musical. There are also three stage readings for family audiences throughout the year. Call ahead for schedules.

New Media Repertory Company. Ages 3 to 7. 512 E. 80th St. (between York and East End aves.). ☎ **212/734-5195.** Tickets $8 adults, $6 children. Subway: 6 to 77th St.

These performances are by and for kids, with lots of participation for the kids in the audience. Each season (late December to May) there's a new original nonmusical adventure story written by New Media's director, Miranda McDermott. Performances are on Saturday at 3pm. Between the young performers (students at the program's acting workshops) and the interaction with a young audience, the shows stay fresh throughout the 5-month run. Make reservations.

✪ **TADA!. Ages 3 & up.** 120 W. 28th St. (between Sixth and Seventh aves.), 2nd floor. ☎ **212/627-1732.** www.tadatheater.com. Tickets $12 adults, $6 children. Subway: 1/9 to 28th St.

The most energetic and successful of NYC's theater schools for kids, TADA! has even performed at the White House. A diverse group of professional kid performers, ages 8 to 17, star in TADA!'s sprightly original musicals. They play weekends in January, March, and December (including one Friday night show, unusual for children's companies; two Saturday matinees; and two Sunday matinees). In July—when most other children's entertainment dries up—TADA! comes to the rescue with weekday shows as well. Even adults without children have been known to see TADA!'s shows, which tells you something about how lively they are.

5 Concerts

Brooklyn Center for the Performing Arts. Ages 4 & up. At Brooklyn College, 1 block west of Flatbush and Nostrand aves., Brooklyn. ☎ **718/951-4500.** Tickets $10. Subway: 2 to Flatbush Ave., Brooklyn.

The center's FamilyFun Series presents six productions a year, plus an annual November *Nutcracker* ($20 adults, $10 children) Sunday at 2pm. The programs are a grab bag of cultural events appealing to kids—circuses, puppet shows, jugglers, classical music concerts, and ballet, with many events of a multicultural flavor.

Carnegie Hall Family Concerts. Ages 7 & up. At Carnegie Hall, at the corner of 57th St. and Seventh Ave. ☎ **212/247-7800.** www.carnegiehall.org. Tickets $5. Subway: N/R to 57th St.

Three Saturdays a year, Carnegie Hall presents hour-long concerts at 2pm, preceded by 1pm activities like demonstrations, craft workshops, and storytelling. There are also concerts by such classical music stars as cellist Yo-Yo Ma and clarinetist Richard Stoltzman. Advance reservations are recommended.

Carnegie*Kids*. Ages 3 to 6. Kaplan Space at Carnegie Hall, corner of 57th St. & Seventh Ave. ☎ **212/903-9670.** www.carnegiehall.org. Tickets $3. Subway: N/R to 57th St.

These 45-minute weekday morning concerts are designed especially for preschoolers and kindergarteners, using storytellers and musicians who interact with the children in the audience, letting them sing and move around to the music.

Growing Up with Opera. Ages 4 & up. At the Metropolitan Opera Guild in Lincoln Center, Broadway and 64th St. ☎ **212/769-7008.** www.operaed.org/guwo.htm. Tickets $10–$15. Subway: 1/9 to Lincoln Center.

The Metropolitan Opera Guild sponsors this series as a way to get young people hooked on opera; they start out with First Stop Opera, a sampler program presenting a mix of scenes from operas, then work up to an entire opera—usually a crowd-pleasing choice like *The Barber of Seville*, with easy-to-follow action and tunes any cartoon fan will recognize. Three or four productions are staged annually, with four public performances of each, on Saturday and Sunday afternoons November to March. Performances are in various venues around town rather than in the overwhelming Metropolitan Opera House.

Jazz for Young People. Ages 5 & up. 33 W. 60th St., New York, NY 10023. ☎ **212/721-6500** or 212/258-9800. www.jazzatlincolncenter.org. Tickets $15 adults, $10 children. Subway: 1/9 to 66th St./Lincoln Center.

Under the aegis of superstar trumpeter Wynton Marsalis, this series is run by Jazz at Linclon Center, Lincoln Center's embrace of jazz as a serious art form. There are three Saturday performances a year, sometime from September to June.

Performances will eventually take place in Jazz at Lincoln Center's sparkling new space on Columbus Circle; until then, look for shows at Alice Tully Hall in Lincoln Center, Broadway at 65th Street, or at the Apollo Theater, 253 W. 125th St.

☼ Little Orchestra Society. Ages 3 to 12. At Avery Fisher Hall in Lincoln Center, Broadway at 64th St., or Florence Gould Hall, 55 E. 59th St. **☎ 212/971-9500.** (Mailing address: Box 2624, Times Square Post Office, New York, NY 10108.) Tickets $15–$32. Subway: 1/9 to Lincoln Center.

Two series—Happy Concerts for Young People (ages 6 to 12) and Lolli-Pop Concerts (ages 3 to 5)—are designed to introduce kids to classical music, using first-class professional artists (moonlighting Philharmonic members, New York City Ballet stars, and the like). This organization has been around since the 1950s, and the quality is top-notch. There are three Happy Concerts a year, held on Saturday (two performances each) at Lincoln Center's **Avery Fisher Hall.** The Lolli-Pop series, which uses cutesy costumed figures to help teach wee ones about music, is more extensive, with three 3-concert series (fall, winter, spring) and four performance times for each; these are held at **Florence Gould Hall.** You pretty much have to buy a whole series (at $96 a head) for the Lolli-Pops, but there are some non-subscription events every year, like *Peter and the Wolf* and the annual Menotti's *Amahl and the Night Visitors,* a fully staged opera with live animals, the works.

Meet the Music. Ages 6 to 12. At Alice Tully Hall in Lincoln Center, Broadway and 64th St. **☎ 212/875-5788.** www.chambermusicsociety.org. Tickets $12; $40 for 4-concert subscription. Subway: 1/9 to Lincoln Center.

The Chamber Music Society of Lincoln Center puts in its bid for young audiences with this four-concert Sunday afternoon series. Not all the chamber music performed dates back to the baroque era—modern pieces by Aaron Copland or even Andrew Lloyd Webber might qualify, so long as they're played by a small group of musicians, one player to a part. With narrators, props, and audience participation, the concerts engage fidgety youngsters admirably.

Young People's Concerts. Ages 6 to 12. At Lincoln Center, Broadway and 64th St. **☎ 212/721-6500** or 212/875-5656. Tickets $6–$21. Subway: 1/9 to Lincoln Center.

Want to turn your kid into a hardcore classical music fan? Four Saturdays a year, the New York Philharmonic trots out musicians like violin prodigy Sarah Chang and conductors Kurt Mazur and Leonard Slatkin to introduce kids to major selections from the classical repertory—not just the chestnuts like *Eine kleine Nachtmusik,* but pieces by moderns like George Gershwin and Charles Ives. Topping it off, free 12:45pm Children's Promenades precede the 2pm concerts, with hands-on demonstrations and workshops with orchestra members. Older kids (12 to 17) can graduate to Philharmonic Teens, which gives them discount seats to the orchestra's weekday Rush Hour Concerts (at 6:45pm), along with free pre- and postconcert meet-the-artist events.

6 Films

If it's standard feature-film fare you want, Manhattan is packed with cinema screens, including the busy 12-screen **Sony Lincoln Square complex** at 68th and Broadway, where each theater entrance evokes a different classic New York movie palace; the multiplex **Loews** and **AMC Empire** cinemas, both located on West 42nd Street between Broadway and Eighth Avenue; and the 16-screen **Battery Park City** theater inside the Embassy Suites at Vesey and West streets downtown. For more unusual films, geared for a young audience, here are your choices:

BAMKids Film Festival. Ages 3 to 13. At the Brooklyn Academy of Music (BAM) Rose Cinemas, 30 Lafayette Ave., Brooklyn. ☎ **718/623-2770.** www.bam.org. Tickets $5. Subway: 2/3/4/5/D/Q to Atlantic Ave., Brooklyn; G to Fulton St., Brooklyn; B/M/N/R to Pacific St., Brooklyn.

For 2 days each spring, BAMKids treats its young audience to an array of international feature-length films and shorts. Selections have ranged from animated favorites like *Babar: King of Elephants* to quality classics like *The Red Balloon*. Guest appearances by featured animators and directors make the experience for youngsters even more meaningful. Call for a schedule.

Family Films. Ages 6 to 12. At the Metropolitan Museum of Art, Fifth Ave. at 82nd St. ☎ **212/570-3932.** Tickets free with museum admission ($10 adults, $5 students and seniors, free for children 12 and under). Subway: 4/5/6 to 86th St.

On Saturday and Sunday at 12:30pm in the spring, and Tuesday to Friday at noon in the summer, the museum shows short films from around the world in the Uris Auditorium. If you're going to be visiting the museum anyway, this provides a good break from gallery strolling.

IMAX Theater. Ages 3 & up. At the American Museum of Natural History, Central Park West at 79th St. ☎ **212/769-5100.** www.amnh.org. Tickets $15 adults, $11 seniors and students (includes museum admission), $9 students 2–12. Subway: B/C to 81st St.

The screen here isn't quite as huge as the one at the Sony IMAX (below), but unless you get out your measuring tape you'd never know. The main thing is that your whole field of vision is occupied, which somehow doubles the sensory impact of a movie—something to consider before you take young, skittish children inside. You have a choice of IMAX movies every day, some more intense than others, though all have an educational bent. Whether you're in outer space, underwater, or deep in the rain forest, the sights and sounds tend to include a speeding camera taking you on a visual thrill ride that swoops over rising and falling terrain, the hallmark of the IMAX experience.

Buy the combination ticket when you enter—if you didn't or if you entered free as a member, stop by the ticket counter near the museum's 77th Street entrance to buy tickets. There's a movie every 45 minutes or so, though school groups get first dibs on seats weekday mornings (the public is then admitted on a first-come, first-served basis). The museum is open daily year-round, except on Thanksgiving and Christmas.

Movies for Kids. Ages 4 & up. At the Walter Reade Theatre in Lincoln Center, 165 W. 65th St., plaza level. ☎ **212/875-5370.** www.filmlinc.com. Tickets $3. Subway: 1/9 to Lincoln Center.

This special series run by Lincoln Center Inc. and the Lincoln Center Film Society (the same folks who run the top-drawer New York Film Festival) shows movies on Saturday or Sunday at 2pm, October through June. The selection each month is organized along a specific theme—one on cars, for instance, included *Chitty Chitty Bang Bang* and *The Phantom Tollbooth*. Most are full-length features, with some shorts or cartoons thrown in; generally these are American films, but occasional series focus on international movies from anywhere from Africa or Iran to Scandinavia.

New York Public Library. Ages 3 to 8. Various branches around Manhattan.

Along with story hours, children's rooms at several Manhattan branch libraries may run once a month an hour-long program of short films, many of them made from children's books—*Madeline, Curious George, Doctor deSoto,* and so on. For a monthly schedule ahead of time, contact the NYPL at 8 W. 40th St., New York, NY 10018 (☎ **212/221-7676;** www.nypl.org), or stop by any branch when you get to town.

Sony IMAX Theater. Ages 3 & up. At Broadway and 68th St. ☎ **212/336-5000.** Tickets $9.50 adults, $6 children 12 and under. Subway: 1/9 to Lincoln Center.

Not just IMAX but 3-D IMAX—awesome. The screen is 8 stories high, and you get this cool headset that puts you in the extraspatial dimension. Needless to say, there isn't a lot of film material for this format and some of the offerings aren't 3-D. But Sony has managed to get movies that go beyond documentaries into actual story-telling features—like *Across the Sea of Time,* which tells of a young Russian immigrant boy searching for relatives in Manhattan (think of it as a live-action *An American Tale*). And features like *Michael Jordan: To the Max* will definitely excite sports fans, young and old. Most shows run about 45 minutes to an hour. Target ages for the scheduled films vary, so check ahead—and, as always with IMAX, consider whether your youngster is suited to the medium's heightened sensory impact.

7 Dance

American Ballet Theatre. Ages 8 & up. At the Metropolitan Opera House in Lincoln Center, Broadway and 64th St. ☎ **212/362-6000.** www.abt.org. Tickets $17–$125. Subway: 1/9 to Lincoln Center.

On this enormous stage, the spring season (May to June) features both modern works and some classic story ballets like *Swan Lake* and *Coppelia*—just the thing for budding ballerinas.

Dance Theater Workshop. Ages 4 & up. 219 W. 19th St. (between Seventh and Eighth aves.). ☎ **212/924-0077.** Tickets $8–$20. Subway: C/E to 23rd St.; 1/9 to 18th St.

One of the city's leading promoters of modern dance, the workshop presents among other things a Family Matters series, Sunday matinee events appropriate for parents and kids of all ages (not necessarily purely dance). The season usually runs September to June; due to construction beginning in 2001, performances will be held at other venues around town until renovation is complete at the 19th Street theater. I recommend you call the box office for ticket availability.

Ice Theatre of New York. Ages 5 & up. At Rockefeller Plaza skating rink, Riverbank State Park (145th St. and Riverside Dr.), or Sky Rink at the Chelsea Piers, 23rd St. at the Hudson River. Tickets around $20. ☎ **212/929-5811** or 212/307-7171 (Ticketmaster).

Unlike typical ice-show companies, Ice Theatre leads figure-skating strongly in the direction of dance, even commissioning noted nonskating choreographers to create new pieces for their lyrical, intriguing performances. With guest artists like Nancy Kerrigan and Paul Wylie, the skaters take to the ice in free lunchtime shows January to March at **Rockefeller Center** (last Wednesday of the month) and **Riverbank State Park** (last Thursday of the month); other performances (not free) are at the **Sky Rink** at Chelsea Piers in October.

☉ Joyce Theater. Ages 6 & up. 175 Eighth Ave. (at 19th St.). ☎ **212/242-0800.** www.joyce.org. Tickets $26–$38. Subway: C/E to 23rd St.; 1/9 to 18th St.

This Chelsea theater devoted to modern dance does an admirable job of bringing in young audiences. The 40-member Kids Dance company, made up of young dancers in the Feld Ballet school, performs weekend matinees throughout the Feld's 6-week season, a mainstay in the Joyce's annual schedule. On 10 other Saturdays throughout the year, touring dance companies booked into the Joyce are asked to design special family matinees as well. After these matinees, dancers in the cast—still in costume—show up in the lower lobby to meet audience members and give autographs.

New York City Ballet. Ages 10 & up. At the New York State Theater in Lincoln Center, Broadway and 64th St. ☎ **212/870-5570.** Tickets $25–$72. Subway: 1/9 to Lincoln Center.

For technique, many critics feel this troupe surpasses its Lincoln Center cousin, the ABT (above), but young balletomanes may not get the point of the more abstract pieces the NYCB presents, following the tastes of founder George Balanchine. However, this is where the city's best *Nutcracker* is staged every December. The ballet offers two seasons—April through June and Thanksgiving through February—with nightly performances (except Monday) and weekend matinees.

8 Puppet Shows

✪ **Crowtations. All ages.** At Bethesda Fountain in Central Park (midpark at 72nd St.). Free admission (pass the hat). Subway: B/C to 72nd St.

Since 1977, this sassy quartet of puppeteers has been charming crowds in Central Park on many fair-weather Saturday and Sunday afternoons with their Muppet-sized crow puppets performing to vintage Motown tunes. The four crows (Otis, John Jay, Junior, and Fast Eddie) have delightfully different personalities, and the byplay among them is truly funny, for adults as well as kids. Best of all, you can just stroll by, watch for a few minutes, then leave when your young ones' attention span has run out (but don't forget to drop some money in the hat). They aren't always there—these guys are, after all, street performers—but their shows are so magical, it's worth checking to see if they show up.

Leni Suib Puppet Playhouse. Ages 2 to 5. At Asphalt Green, 555 E. 90th St. (between York and East End aves.). ☎ **212/369-8890.** Tickets $6. Subway 4/5/6 to 86th St.

The Leni Suib Puppet Playhouse has been running for years and years; Leni Suib is a major player in the puppet world, up there with Bill Baird and Burr Tillstrom. Every weekend September to May, kids can take in a different show, with different puppets and a different theme (nonpuppet antics, like juggling and mime, are often thrown in, just to keep things hopping). Show times are Saturday and Sunday at 10:30am and 12:30pm. Reservations aren't accepted (except for groups of 10 or more), so get there 20 minutes before show time to be sure of a seat.

Puppetworks—Park Slope. Ages 3 to 7. At the Children's Aid Society, 219 Sullivan St., Manhattan; 338 Sixth Ave., Brooklyn. (Mailing address: 338 Sixth Ave., Brooklyn.) ☎ **718/965-6058** or 718/965-3391. www.puppetworks.org. Tickets $7–$8 adults, $5 children. Subway: B/D/F to Broadway/Lafayette St.; F to Seventh Ave. in Brooklyn.

Using both hand puppets and marionettes, these puppeteers retell classic children's stories. The season runs year-round, with performances on weekends at 1:30 and 3:30pm in Manhattan, 12:30 and 2:30pm in Brooklyn. Reservations required.

Swedish Cottage Marionette Theatre. Ages 3 to 10. In Central Park (West Dr. at 81st St.). ☎ **212/988-9093.** Tickets $5 adults, $4 children; reservations required. Closed mid-Aug through Sept. Subway: B/C to 79th St.

This alpine-looking cottage holds a small stage where near-life-sized marionettes prance and caper in hour-long productions of classic fairy tales—recorded soundtrack, spot lighting, full scenery, the works. Because these are such elaborate shows, one production is designed per year, performed throughout the season. A puppeteer prefaces performances with a helpful miniseminar on the kinds of puppets (the *Cinderella* we saw included a shadow puppet interlude as well as a couple of stick puppets). The pace is a little slow, the sense of humor gentle. Call 3 or 4 weeks in advance for a reservation—there are usually two shows a day, Tuesday to Saturday (Monday to Friday in summer), but they fill up fast with school groups.

9 Spectator Sports

New Jersey Devils. Ages 8 & up. Continental Airlines Arena, East Rutherford, NJ. ☎ **201/935-6050** (or 201/935-3900, for single-game tickets). www.newjerseydevils.com. Tickets $75–$110. Parking $8. For game-time bus service from Manhattan's Port Authority Bus Terminal, call New Jersey Transit ☎ 800/772-2222.

Winners of the 1995 and 2000 Stanley Cups, the Devils have lately been stealing the thunder from the New York area's older hockey teams, the Rangers and the Islanders. The season runs from October to mid-April, and though much of the arena gets sold out with season tickets, individual tickets for cheaper seats may be available. It's always worth checking the day of a game to see if some seats have been released.

New Jersey Nets. Ages 8 & up. Continental Airlines Arena, East Rutherford, NJ. ☎ **800/7NJ-NETS,** 201/935-3900 (for single-game tickets), or 201/507-8900 (Ticketmaster). www.nba.com/nets. Tickets $25–$500. Parking $8.

The past few seasons have been frustrating ones for New York's "other" basketball team; despite the presence of such promising players as Stephon Marbury and Keith Van Horn, injury and bad luck seemed to have dogged the team—all of which is another way of saying they could be contenders any time now—watch your backs, Knicks. The season runs November to mid-April—longer if they get into the play-off action.

New York Giants. Ages 8 & up. At Giants Stadium in the Meadowlands, East Rutherford, NJ. ☎ **201/935-8222** (or 201/935-3900, for single game tickets). www.giants.com. Tickets $45 and $50. Parking $10.

With a seeming revolving door of coaches, the Giants dance in and out of contention. Because football teams play only once a week, there are fewer home games in the course of their September-to-December season, and just about the whole stadium goes with season ticket holders—to get tickets you have to know somebody or be *somebody* or spring for a scalper. On game days, there's a New Jersey Transit bus from Port Authority Terminal, Eighth Avenue between 40th and 42nd streets—call ☎ 212/564-1114 for information.

Warning: It's an open-air stadium, so it gets bitterly cold by the end of the season.

New York Islanders. Ages 8 & up. At Nassau Coliseum, Hempstead Turnpike, Uniondale, NY. ☎ **516/794-4100** or 631/888-9000 (Ticketmaster). www.newyorkislanders.com. Tickets $15–$115.

A lively force in recent NHL seasons, the Islanders skate on their home ice out on Long Island (hence the name) from October to mid-April. Take the Long Island Rail Road from Penn Station, Seventh Avenue between 31st and 33rd streets.

New York Jets. Ages 8 & up. At Giants Stadium in the Meadowlands, East Rutherford, NJ. ☎ **516/560-8200** (or 201/935-3900, for single-game tickets). www.newyorkjets.com. Tickets $50 and $60. Parking $10.

Playing in the same stadium as the Giants, the Jets—who have had some loser seasons in the recent past—were reenergized under Bill Parcells (formerly the Giants' coach), but with Parcells's departure at the end of the 1999 season, it's now up to Al Groh to keep up the momentum. Jets fans are die-hards, and both individual and season tickets are pretty well sold out. On game days there's a New Jersey Transit bus from Port Authority Terminal, Eighth Avenue between 40th and 42nd streets—call ☎ 212/564-1114 for information. The regular season runs September through December.

Milestones in New York Sports History

In all the major pro sports, the lucrative New York area market is able to sustain at least two teams, and at some period (baseball in the 1950s, hockey today), three teams. New Yorkers, spoiled by years of sport success, aren't big on rooting for underdogs (with the exception of the 1969 Mets). Then again, we aren't used to having underdogs. Cynics point out that it's because all the money in the New York area allows team owners to buy the best sports talent available. Actually, that's a pretty fair assessment—from Babe Ruth to Wayne Gretzky to Stephon Marbury, top athletes get lured by high salaries away from their former teams to maintain New York's winning profile. But New York fans, hooked on those championship titles, still can't get enough. Here's the sort of thing we're talking about:

- 1921–23: Two New York baseball teams—the Giants and the Yankees—meet in the World Series for 3 consecutive years. The Giants win the first 2 years; the Yankees finally take the title in 1923, establishing a taste for victory they'll never shake.
- 1927–28: Two consecutive World Series victories for the Yankees, both of them four-game sweeps. Babe Ruth sets his home run record at Yankee Stadium in 1927.
- 1928: New York Rangers win hockey's Stanley Cup.
- 1932: Another Yankee World Series sweep.
- 1933: The Rangers take the Stanley Cup again; the Giants win the World Series.
- 1936–37: Two more Yankees–Giants World Series match-ups—the Yankees win both times.
- 1938–39: The Yankees continue their streak, sweeping the Cubs and then the Reds to make four World Series titles in a row.
- 1940: Yet another Rangers victory in the Stanley Cup championship.
- 1941: The Yankees play the Brooklyn Dodgers in the World Series; the Yankees win.
- 1943: Another Yankees Series win.
- 1947: It's the Dodgers versus the Yankees in the Series; the Yankees win again.

New York Knicks. Ages 8 & up. At Madison Square Garden, Seventh Ave. between 31st and 33rd Sts. ☎ **212/465-MSG1** or 212/465-JUMP. www.nyknicks.com. Tickets $10–$220 and up. Subway: A/C/E to Penn Station; 1/2/3/9 to 34th St.

The Knicks play 41 regular-season home games a year, November to mid-April. An aging team that has suffered from injuries the past few seasons, under coach Jeff Van Gundy the Knickerbockers have still proven their mettle in the NBA playoffs, and getting tickets is next to impossible, unless you're Spike Lee. Seats usually sell out for the season within an hour of the time they go on sale. There's still hope: On the day of the game, the box office sometimes releases a small number of tickets (call ☎ 212/465-6040), and there are always scalpers who'll be happy to let you pay top dollar for tickets.

- 1949–56: New York dominates baseball, with one of its teams winning the World Series every year—the Yankees for 5 years straight, then the Giants in 1954, the Dodgers in 1955 (finally beating the Yankees!), only to have the Yankees vanquish the Dodgers again in 1956. Six World Series in this 8-year period are "Subway Series"—the Yankees face the Dodgers five times and the Giants once.
- 1958: Having gotten into the habit of winning World Series, the Yankees take another one.
- 1961–62: Two more Yankee World Series championships. Yankee Roger Maris breaks Babe Ruth's home run record in 1961.
- 1969: The New York Jets win the Super Bowl; the "Miracle" Mets win the World Series.
- 1970: The New York Knicks take the NBA championship.
- 1973: The Knicks are NBA champions again.
- 1977–78: The Yankees beat the Dodgers—who are now the Los Angeles Dodgers—in the World Series 2 years in a row.
- 1980–83: The New York Islanders dominate hockey, winning the Stanley Cup 4 years in a row.
- 1986: The Mets win another World Series.
- 1987: The Giants win the Super Bowl.
- 1991: The Giants win another Super Bowl.
- 1994: The Rangers win another Stanley Cup.
- 1995: This year it's the New Jersey Devils' turn to win the Stanley Cup.
- 1996: After a long dry spell, the resurgent Yankees win another World Series.
- 1998: The Yankees take the World Series in a four-game sweep.
- 1999: The Yankees win their 25th World Series, another four-game sweep.
- 2000: The New Jersey Devils win the Stanley Cup once more; at long last, another Subway Series, with the Yankees meeting the Mets for the first time in post-season play. The Yanks win the World Series for the third straight year.

New York Liberty. Ages 6 & up. At Madison Square Garden, Seventh Ave. between 31st and 33rd sts. ☎ **212/465-MSG1** or 212/307-7171 (Ticketmaster), 212/564-WNBA for info. www.nyliberty.com. Tickets $8–$210. Subway: A/C/E to Penn Station; 1/2/3/9 to 34th St.

The success of professional women's basketball surprised all the pundits, who never expected the public to respond so immediately to its brand of clean, fast, non-trash-talking basketball. Kids, especially girls, have been an important part of the Liberty's audience all along (it helps that its June-to-August season coincides with school vacation); plenty of on-court activities during the breaks, along with a lively dog mascot who patrols the stands looking for kids to shake paws with, boosts the entertainment quotient for younger ones. The team has been riding strong at the top of its division in the past couple of seasons.

New York MetroStars. Ages 6 & up. At Giants Stadium in the Meadowlands, East Ruther-ford, NJ. ☎ **888/4-METROTIX,** 201/583-7000, 201/935-3900; or 212/307-7171 and 201/507-8900 (Ticketmaster). www.metrostars.com. Tickets $15–$30. Parking $10.

Playing March to October, the MetroStars have built an audience from all those kids and parents who've been bit by the soccer bug through youth leagues, and their strong 2000 season put them in contention for the U.S. Cup. Games are usually Wednesday night or weekend days or evenings. Major league soccer offers plenty of action on the field, though not a lot of scoring, but it's reasonably easy for a kid to follow even if he or she hasn't played. And sitting outdoors in the Meadowlands is a lot nicer in summer than in November. For game-time bus service from Manhattan's Port Authority Bus Terminal, call New Jersey Transit (☎ **800/772-2222**).

New York Mets. All ages. At Shea Stadium in Flushing, Queens. ☎ **718/507-METS.** www.mets.com. Tickets $12–$37. Subway: 7 to Shea Stadium.

Baseball can be awfully slow-moving for a young kid, but Shea does what it can to jazz things up, what with the loud taped music and the big DiamondVision screen broadcasting pictures of the audience (no back-flipping mascot yet, thank goodness). It's an open-air stadium, which somehow makes matters less overwhelming for younger kids and makes a fine summer afternoon a real treat. Seats cost considerably less than they do for the other sports, and unlike the theater, you don't have to worry about keeping your child quiet. Even night games are a distinct possibility—if your kids get bored or sleepy, you can always leave early. The regular season for New York's National League team runs mid-April to early October; throughout this stretch, 81 home games are played at Shea. Tickets can be purchased in advance, but even given the Mets' recent success, you may still be able to get tickets at the stadium on game day. The food is typical arena fare: nachos, hot dogs, and soda. **NY Waterway** runs a Mets Express ferry to the ballpark ($14 adults, $10 children 11 and under, or $50 for game ticket plus transportation); call ☎ **800/ 533-3779** or order from www.nywaterway.com. Ferries depart from Weehawken, New Jersey, South Street Seaport, 34th Street at the East River, and 90th Street at the East River.

New York Rangers. Ages 8 & up. At Madison Square Garden, Seventh Ave. between 31st and 33rd sts. ☎ **212/465-MSG1** or 212/307-7171 (Ticketmaster), 212/308-NYRS for info. www.newyorkrangers.com. Tickets $25–$150. Subway: A/C/E to Penn Station; 1/2/3/9 to 34th St.

The Rangers play 41 hockey games, mostly at night, at Madison Square Garden during their season October to mid-April. Celebrities and CEOs pay as much as $500 for prized behind-the-bench seats, but in "Blue Heaven"—the cheap seats high above the ice—true hockey fans make Rangers games an audience participation sport. Rangers tickets usually sell out a couple of months before the season starts, so buy in advance.

New York Yankees. All ages. At Yankee Stadium in the Bronx. ☎ **718/293-6000** or 212/307-1212 (Ticketmaster). www.yankees.com. Tickets $8–$43. Subway: D to 161st St. Subway: 4/C/D to 161st St.

Yankees fans have never minded watching their team roll effortlessly over all the competition, and after a lean decade or so, the Bronx Bombers are once again keeping them very happy indeed; the team's handy four-game sweeps of the 1998 and 1999 World Series were no less than what their legions of supporters expected. Our family was lucky enough to attend pitcher David Wells's perfect game in May 1998, and it's an experience none of us will ever forget. There's a long-running soap opera over whether owner George Steinbrenner will let them continue to play at this grand old ballpark in the Bronx—as the fanfares play on an electric organ, you almost expect to see the scoreboard changed by hand. New York's American League team plays 81 home games at Yankee Stadium mid-April to early October; order tickets in advance or buy them at the stadium ticket office on game day (when they're playing well, ticket availability gets tight toward fall). The refreshments here run in the traditional peanuts and popcorn and Cracker Jack vein, along with hot dogs and jumbo sodas. Show up a couple of hours early and you may be able to watch batting practice. To make it a really special outing, take the **NY Waterway** Yankee Clipper ferry to the stadium ($14 adults, $10 children 11 and under, or $56 for game ticket plus transportation); call ☎ **800/533-3779** or order from www.nywaterway.com. Ferries depart from Weehawken, New Jersey, South Street Seaport, 34th Street at the East River, and 90th Street at the East River.

10 Story Hours

Bank Street College Bookstore. Ages 2 to 6. 2871 Broadway (at 112th St.). ☎ **212/ 678-1654.** Free admission. Subway: 1/9 to 110th St.

This intelligent Upper West Side bookstore runs story hours for preschoolers at 10:30am on Wednesday.

Barnes & Noble. Ages 2 to 7. (1) 240 E. 86th St. (between Second and Third aves.). ☎ **212/794-1962.** Free admission. Subway: 4/5/6 to 86th St. (2) 2289 Broadway (at 82nd St.). ☎ **212/362-8835.** Subway: 1/9 to 79th St. (3) 1972 Broadway (at 66th St.). ☎ **212/ 595-6859.** Subway: 1/9 to Lincoln Center. (4) Citicorp Building (at Third Ave. and 54th St.). ☎ **212/750-8033.** Subway: E/F to Lexington Ave. (5) Rockefeller Center, 600 Fifth Ave. (at 48th St.). ☎ **212/765-0590.** Subway: B/D/F/Q to Rockefeller Center. (6) 675 Sixth Ave. (at 21st St.) ☎ **212/727-1227.** Subway: F to 23rd St. (7) 105 Fifth Ave. (at 18th St.). ☎ **212/807-0099.** Subway: 1/9 to 18th St. (8) 4 Astor Place (between Broadway and Lafayette St.). ☎ **212/420-1322.** Subway: 6 to Astor Place. (9) Union Square, 33 E. 17th St. (between Broadway and Park Ave.). ☎ **212/253-0810.** Subway: 4/5/6/L/N/R to Union Square.

Story hours at various branches of this big bookstore chain often feature the authors themselves. On the Upper West Side, the branch near Lincoln Center (66th Street) runs its story times Saturday at 10:30am and Wednesday at 4:30pm, while the Broadway and 82nd Street branch has a Tuesday story hour at 10:30am. In Midtown, the Citicorp branch has Wednesday story hours at 10am. The Union Square ones are at 2pm Saturday.

✪ **Books of Wonder. Ages 3 to 7.** 16 W. 18th St. (between Fifth and Sixth aves.). ☎ **212/989-3270.** Free admission. Subway: 1/9 to 18th St.

This great Chelsea shop runs friendly story hours on Sunday at 11:45am.

Borders Books, Music & Cafe. Ages 2 to 8. (1) 461 Park Ave. (at 57th St.). ☎ **212/ 980-6785.** Free admission. Subway: 4/5/6 to 59th St. (2) 5 World Trade Center (at Church and Vesey sts.). ☎ **212/839-8049.** Subway: C/E to World Trade Center. (3) Second Ave. and 32nd St. ☎ **212/685-3938.** Subway: 6 to 33rd St.

The Midtown branch of this superstore book chain has two weekly story hours, Tuesday and Thursday at 10am. The World Trade Center branch has a 10am Tuesday story time, and the Second Avenue store has story hours on Tuesday and Saturday at 10am and Sunday at 2pm.

Central Park. Ages 2 to 8. At the Hans Christian Andersen Statue, on the west side of Conservatory Water (at 74th St.). Free admission. Subway: 6 to 77th St.

On summer Saturdays, there are story hours here at 11am, rain or shine; New York Public Library librarians also run story hours in July, on Wednesday at 11am. The park organizes a Sandbox Stories program that rotates around various playgrounds in July; look for schedules posted on bulletin boards at the larger playgrounds.

Lefferts Homestead Children's Museum. Ages 3 to 8. In Prospect Park, Brooklyn. ☎ **718/965-6505.** Free admission. Subway: D to Prospect Park, Brooklyn.

July and August, this restored farmhouse next to the zoo and carousel in Prospect Park holds cozy storytelling hours, outside under a tree, at 2 and 3:30pm on Sunday (call to see if some Saturday dates have been added as well).

Line Reading for Children. Ages 4 to 8. At the Drawing Center, 35 Wooster St. (between Broome and Grand sts.). ☎ **212/219-2166.** Free admission. Subway: A/C/E to Canal St.

Once a month, this SoHo arts center presents Sunday illustrated storytelling performances, usually at 3pm. It's hip, it's downtown.

New York Public Library. Ages 2 to 8. Various branches around Manhattan. Free admission.

Nearly every weekday, some Manhattan branch library holds a story hour or shows short films about children's books or holds some kind of cool workshop—and it's all free. You can contact the NYPL at 8 W. 40th St., New York, NY 10018 (☎ 212/221-7676), for a monthly brochure of events for children. Better yet, stop by the **Donnell Library,** 20 W. 53rd St. (☎ 212/621-0636), the main children's branch for the system, and pick up a brochure—while you're there, don't miss the original Pooh animals and Mary Poppins's umbrella on display.

11 Arcades

✪ **Broadway City. Ages 7 & up.** 241 W. 42nd St. (between Broadway and Eighth Ave.). ☎ **212/997-9797.** www.broadwaycity.com. Subway: 1/2/3/7/9/N/R/S to Times Square; A/C/E to 42nd St.

If you have to go to arcades—and with boys my sons' ages, it seems you have to go to arcades—this would be my choice: clean, with a reasonable mix of games (not all of which involve shooting at a menacing enemy), and relatively secure. The trilevel arcade is separated into various theme areas, with actual decor—one section is decorated to look like Yankee Stadium, another like Coney Island, another like a public school playground, another like Wall Street—and games of a similar nature are grouped in each section, so you can steer children away from the more violent ones. There's a roller-coaster simulator and a snack bar as well. You buy a magnetically encoded card for however much money you want to spend; when it's used up, you refill it or leave. Many games reward players with tickets that can be redeemed for unbelievably skimpy prizes. A few games are coin-operated as well. Most games cost between 25¢ and $1 to play.

Chelsea Piers AMF Bowling. Ages 7 & up. Pier 60 at Chelsea Piers, 23rd St. and the West Side Hwy. at the Hudson River. ☎ **212/835-2695.** Subway: 1/9, C/E, or F/N/R to 23rd St. stations. Bus: M23 across 23rd St.

A well-lighted, clean space at the back of this bowling alley has a dozen or so relatively wholesome games involving car-driving or shooting or ball-throwing skills. A good amusement stop if you're at the Piers anyway.

Cybergames. Ages 9 & up. 2662 Broadway (between 101st and 102nd sts.). ☎ **212/ 666-2662.** Subway: 1/9 to 103rd St.

Way uptown, on the way to Columbia University, this neighborhood storefront selling Nintendo and Playstation games (as well as trading cards) has several consoles for in-store play as well as a few big arcade-type games near the front door.

Generally a nonthreatening place to hang out, but it all depends on the crowd that's there at the moment.

ESPN Zone. Ages 7 & up. 1472 Broadway (at 42nd St.). ☎ **212/921-3776.** Subway: 1/2/3/9 to 42nd St.

Games here, on an upper floor of this clean and glossy theme restaurant (thus less walk-in street trade, which is a plus), tend to be sports-oriented—baseball, hockey, soccer, driving simulators, that sort of thing, rather than sci-fi–based shoot-'em-ups. Children under 18 are not admitted without an accompanying adult, which lessens the teen hangout factor.

Lazer Park. Ages 7 & up. 163 W. 46th St. (between Sixth and Seventh aves.). ☎ **212/398-3060.** www.lazerpark.com. Subway: 1/2/3/7/9/N/R/S to Times Square.

Somewhat more state-of-the-art than your typical arcade, Lazer Park offers laser tag and a virtual reality ride simulator as well as a battery of arcade games. The destination of choice for third- and fourth-grade boys' birthday parties.

XS New York. Ages 8 & up. 1457 Broadway (between 41st and 42nd sts.). ☎ **212/398-5467.** Subway: 1/2/3/7/9/N/R/S to Times Square.

Like Lazer Park (above), this is a high-tech version of the old arcades; various activities (priced $1 to $6) include laser tag and virtual reality, as well as video games. Most of the crowd here seem to be adults (don't these people have jobs?) and there are several games that are rated mildly violent. With two street-level entrances, one on Broadway and one on Seventh Avenue, security is none too strict. All told, this isn't an atmosphere for younger children, but older kids may find it way cool.

9 Family-Friendly Restaurants

In the gastronomic universe, New York has a fair number of star-quality restaurants, but are they worth it if you're eating out with your kids? Fuhgeddaboudit. Le Bernardin and Alain Ducasse be damned—what I look for these days is a restaurant that's noisy and casual, where the service is relatively speedy, and where the menu includes at least one or two items from my kids' major food groups: chicken fingers, burgers, pasta, pancakes, and pizza, any or all of which could come with a side of fries. You can find plenty of such restaurants in New York, and they won't cost you an arm and a leg.

DINING OUT WITH YOUR KIDS You know a restaurant welcomes kids when they've printed up a placemat for young customers to color and when you get to keep the crayons you're given to color it with. If they've gone to the trouble of developing a specific children's menu, you've hit gold. A number of tourist-dependent restaurants around Times Square have gone this route, and we're grateful for them in a pinch. For us adults, however, the food is generally mediocre and the only thing that's relaxing about the ambience is that we don't have to do the dishes afterward.

Because we don't want to be limited to these family restaurants, we try to venture beyond the round of Pizzeria Uno and Houlihan's. Stressful as it can be to eat out with children, we do it at least once a week, and as a result our kids have become relatively restaurant savvy. Ethnic restaurants are one good option—our kids will always eat pasta and rice—and New York, this great immigrant city, is rich in these. Coffee shops are another option, and I don't mean just the corner Greek joints with the revolving showcase of whipped cream–topped desserts. A number of trendy retro coffee shops have opened in recent years, adding upscale parent-pleasing food to the traditional menu of burgers and omelets and grilled cheese sandwiches.

I'm not a big fan of eating at sidewalk tables—I'd rather get *away* from traffic and exhaust—but as soon as the weather warms up, many families brunch alfresco at restaurants that have room to expand their seating out onto the pavement. The open-air arrangement minimizes your child's noise, provides endless distraction, and makes messes less important (there's always a pigeon or two around to peck up dropped french fries after you've cleared off).

Most Manhattan restaurants serve continuously—you can generally order dinner as early as 5pm if that's what you're used to, though most New Yorkers eat around 7 or 8pm. If you're dining anywhere in the Theater District (the West 40s) or near Lincoln Center (the West 60s), you'll be competing with lots of other people trying to finish dinner before an 8pm curtain time; unless you're trying to make that curtain too, delay your arrival until 7:30 or so, when most of these restaurants seem just about ready to draw a sigh of relief and relax. Similarly, lunch hours at Midtown and Lower Manhattan restaurants can be very busy about 11:30am to 2:30pm.

I've noted in this chapter if a given restaurant doesn't take reservations or if reservations are generally necessary to ensure a table. If there's no notation about reservations, assume you have a fair chance of being seated even if you haven't called ahead, though making a reservation is always smart. Although some posh Manhattan restaurants still cling to formal dress codes, requiring men to wear a jacket and tie, none of the restaurants I list here do.

I should make it clear that my kids are all still under age 10, so, knowing how many Manhattan restaurants are not for wee ones, I've tried to address the more pressing needs of families with smaller children. That's not to say all the restaurants I've included in the following list are for preschoolers only—I've also suggested some restaurants that would appeal only to older kids. If your youngsters are well-behaved, adventurous eaters, your choice of eating places is obviously much broader.

Because we do keep eating out regularly, I have high hopes for the future. Our kindergartener no longer needs me to bring toys to keep her occupied at the table (especially not if the restaurant has a jukebox or big streetside picture window to view the passing show), and our 9-year-old is getting a little more adventurous in his tastes—he'll at least try something new to see if he likes it. As soon as our daughter gets to that stage, we may be ready to try Tavern on the Green.

A NOTE ABOUT PRICES   The following reviews include a range of specific menu prices as often as possible; I've also categorized the restaurants as Expensive, Moderate, or Inexpensive, based on rough estimates of what it would cost to feed a family of four—two parents and two children, assuming that one of the kids is young enough to be satisfied with either a kids' meal or a half portion or just an appetizer-sized portion. If this mythical family would have to spend $75 or more for dinner (excluding any bar tab), I've classed that restaurant as **Expensive;** between $50 and $75, **Moderate;** under $50, **Inexpensive.** I haven't included in these price categories those places I recommend for afternoon tea, ice-cream sundaes, or pastries, since you won't be eating a full meal there; I also haven't given a price category to the various fast-food spots and food courts I've suggested, since prices there are uniformly low.

THE CHAIN GANG   Besides the restaurants covered in detail below, there are a number of kid-friendly chains—some local, some national—with several properties in New York City that can be very handy if you're in the neighborhood anyway; I've given them abbreviated listings at the end of each neighborhood section.

Among the local burger restaurant chains, **Jackson Hole** stands out, with burgers so thick and juicy they'll make your buns soggy (whatever that means), as well as grilled chicken sandwiches, some salads, and less successful Mexican dishes. Another decent choice for burgers and fries is **Burger Heaven,** a coffee shop–ish chain with long counters dishing out flavorful hamburgers a notch above fast food. Geared toward the office crowd, they close at 8pm and all day Sunday.

The local Mexican food chain **Mary Ann's** serves homemade-on-premises dishes that go way beyond burritos and tamales and chimichangas, embracing grilled meats and seafood, as cooked in Acapulco or the Yucatán or Puerta Vallarta (warning: there's no gringo menu). No reservations are necessary, and they don't take American Express. Another local ethnic chain worth seeking out is **Lemongrass Grill,** for Thai food. **Blockhead's Burritos** is a fun addition to the city's dining scene, with a menu of tortilla-wrapped meals that go well beyond the Mexican standards (like the West Indian vegetable casserole tortilla or the Bar-B-Cuban Chicken); teenagers in particular like its hipster decor and healthy emphasis on fresh vegetables, lean meats, and lard-free cooking. Bargain-hunters like the casual **Dallas BBQ** restaurants, where you can get big portions for under $10. The menu holds no surprises: barbecued chicken, barbecued baby-back ribs, barbecued sliced beef, half-pound burgers (turkey or beef). Just beware if you see a tour bus parked out front.

Pizzeria Uno is a known commodity: swift, cheery service, child-friendly amenities (kids' menu, crayons, flimsy activity booklet, drinks served in lidded plastic cups), and a saloonish decor with wooden booths, black-and-white tiled floors, and exposed brick walls. Both the deep-dish and the thin-crust pizzas are decent; it's when they go beyond pizzas that you can't always be sure of what you'll get. **Houlihan's** and **T.G.I. Friday's,** both owned by the same organization, are dimly lit bar-and-burger joints with several superconvenient locations, mostly in Midtown and Downtown. The service is fast, the regular menu spans everything from stir-fries to pastas to burritos, and the $6.95 kids' menu rivals a Happy Meal any day—a choice of hamburger, chicken fingers, spaghetti, or grilled cheese, served with not only fries and a drink but also veggies and dip, ice cream for dessert, and a toy. Prices run a bit higher than at the other chains I've mentioned—expect entrees to cost $11 to $27.

A NOTE ABOUT FAST FOOD   The reality of eating out with small children is that fast-food joints are sometimes a blessing. Most of those in high-traffic areas of Manhattan are spanking clean and recently renovated; somehow, there's always a McDonald's or a Burger King or a Sbarro's just where you need one. There's also a McDonald's delivery service operating in Manhattan (how New Yorkers do love to phone out for their food): Call ☎ **212/337-3278** to get your Happy Meals and Big Macs brought to your door.

1 Restaurants by Cuisine

AMERICAN

America (p. 219)
Anglers and Writers (p. 228)
Bar Odeon (p. 238)
Barking Dog Luncheonette (p. 197)
Bubby's (p. 239)
Chat 'n' Chew (p. 220)
Elephant and Castle (p. 227)
ESPN Zone (p. 209)
Fanelli's (p. 234)
Flight 151 (p. 218)
Flight 1668 (p. 202)
Friend of a Farmer (p. 220)
Good Enough to Eat (p. 190)
Hard Rock Café (p. 210)

Internet Café (p. 230)
Jackson Hole (pp. 202, 204, 217)
Jekyll & Hyde Club (p. 210)
Kitchenette (p. 239)
Luke's Bar & Grill (p. 199)
Manhattan Chili Company (p. 215)
Mickey Mantle's (p. 205)
Miss Elle's Homesick
    Bar & Grille (p. 195)
NoHo Star (p. 225)
Odeon (p. 238)
O'Neal's (p. 190)
Peanut Butter & Co. (p. 228)
Popover Café (p. 191)
Route 66 (p. 216)

79th Street Boat Basin Café (p. 195)
Tavern on the Green (p. 185)
Telephone Bar & Grill (p. 230)
Tennessee Mountain (pp. 211, 233)
Texas Texas Restaurant and Saloon
(p. 212)
Treehouse (p. 225)
Virgil's Real Barbecue (p. 213)
WWF New York (p. 213)

AMERICAN DINER

Bendix Diner (pp. 218, 230)
Black Sheep Luncheonette (p. 200)
Comfort Diner (pp. 201, 214)
EJ's Luncheonette (pp. 188, 198,
224)
Ellen's Café & Bake Shop (p. 239)
Ellen's Stardust Diner (p. 209)
Empire Diner (p. 218)
Googie's Luncheonette (p. 198)
Kiev (p. 231)
Lexington Candy Shop (p. 202)
Miss Rita's (p. 219)
Moondance (p. 234)
Official All Star Café (p. 205)
Serendipity 3 (p. 199)

AMERICAN SOUTHERN

Emily's (p. 198)
Brother Jimmy's (pp. 193, 200, 201)
Duke's (p. 220)
Hog Pit (p. 225)
Old Devil Moon (p. 229)

BAKERY

Caffé Roma (p. 236)
Cupcake Café (p. 214)
Ferrara (p. 236)
DeRobertis Pasticceria (p. 233)
Veniero's (p. 233)

BARBECUE

Brother Jimmy's (pp. 193, 200, 201)
Brothers Barbeque (p. 226)
Dallas BBQ (pp. 197, 204, 229, 233)
Duke's (p. 220)
Hog Pit (p. 225)
Rodeo Grill (p. 221)
Tennessee Mountain (pp. 211, 233)
Texas Texas Restaurant and Saloon
(p. 212)
Virgil's Real Barbecue (p. 213)

BRITISH

Telephone Bar & Grill (p. 230)

BURGERS

Big Nick's Burger &
Pizza Joint (p. 192)
Burger Heaven (p. 217)
Corner Bistro (p. 226)
Hamburger Harry's (p. 215)
Hard Rock Café (p. 210)
Jackson Hole (pp. 202, 204, 217)
Johnny Rockets (p. 227)
Luke's Bar & Grill (p. 199)
Sassy's Sliders (p. 203)

CAJUN

Two Boots (p. 231)

CALIFORNIAN

California Pizza Kitchen (p. 201)
Planet Hollywood (p. 205)

CHINESE

China Fun (pp. 193, 201, 214)
China Shalom (p. 232)
HSF (p. 237)
Hunan Balcony (p. 194)
LiLi's Noodle Shop and Grill (p. 203)
Lin's Dumpling House (p. 237)
New York Noodletown (p. 237)
NoHo Star (p. 225)
Ollie's Noodle Shop (pp. 195, 216)
Pig Heaven (p. 199)
Ruby Foo's (pp. 185, 208)
Tai Hong Lau (p. 236)
Wong Kee (p. 235)

CONTINENTAL

Cloister Café (p. 229)
Palm Court (p. 217)
Tavern on the Green (p. 185)
Treehouse (p. 225)

CUBAN-CHINESE

La Caridad Luncheonette (p. 194)

DELI

Artie's Delicatessen (p. 192)
Barney Greengrass (p. 192)
Carnegie Deli (p. 209)
Second Avenue Deli (p. 229)
Stage Deli (p. 216)

Famous Ray's Pizza (p. 227)
Il Fornaio (p. 235)
John's Pizza (pp. 194, 202, 215, 227)
Lombardi's Pizza (p. 235)
Patsy's Pizzeria (pp. 195, 203, 216, 228)
Pizza Box (p. 228)
Pizzeria Uno (pp. 197, 204, 229, 233, 240)
T & R Pizzeria (p. 196)
Two Boots (p. 231)
V & T Pizzeria-Restaurant (p. 196)
Vinnie's Pizzeria (p. 196)

SEAFOOD

Go Fish (p. 198)

TEX-MEX/SOUTHWESTERN

Cowgirl Hall of Fame (p. 224)
Manhattan Chili Company (p. 215)
Rodeo Grill (p. 221)

THAI

Bendix Diner (pp. 218, 230)
Kelley & Ping (p. 233)
Lemongrass Grill (pp. 190, 229)
Rain (p. 191)

UKRAINIAN

Kiev (p. 231)

VIETNAMESE

Monsoon (p. 190)
Nha Hang (p. 238)

2 The Upper West Side

EXPENSIVE

Ruby Foo's. 2182 Broadway (at 77th St.). ☎ **212/724-6700.** High chairs, boosters. Reservations recommended. Lunch $20–$25; dinner $30–$35 (average per person, including drinks). AE, DISC, MC, V. Sun 11:30am midnight, Mon–Thurs 11:30am–12:30am, Fri–Sat 11:30am–1am. Subway: 1/9 to 79th St. CHINESE/JAPANESE/PAN-ASIAN.

The Suzy Wong–style decor of this bilevel rice palace is eye-popping, and the menu hits all the high notes of Asian cuisine, from dim sum to sushi to maki rolls to Thai curries. Compared to more authentic Chinese, Japanese, or Thai restaurants, the food is only competent, but the stunning setting makes up for it—you'll feel like you're inside a jewel-toned lacquered box, with Chinese lanterns glowing overhead, your linen napkin crisply folded into a fan, chopsticks set before you in a gleaming metal stand. Don't expect to get in without a reservation, and don't expect the service to be speedy.

Tavern on the Green. In Central Park at W. 67th St. ☎ **212/873-3200.** Reservations recommended. Kids' menu, sassy seats. Lunch $13.75–$27.50; dinner $21.50–$33.75; kids' menu $8.50–$10. AE, CB, DC, DISC, MC, V. Mon–Thurs 11:30am–3pm and 5–10:45pm, Fri 11:30am–3pm and 5–11:30pm, Sat 10am–3pm and 5–11:30pm, Sun 10am–3pm and 5–10:45pm. Subway: 1/9 to 66th St.; B/C to 72nd St. AMERICAN/CONTINENTAL/ECLECTIC.

Local wisdom has it that only tourists go to Tavern on the Green, drawn by scores of movies featuring this huge Central Park site with its Tiffany glass lamps, crystal chandeliers, surrounding gardens, and twinkling outdoor lights. To celebrate a special event, however, even New Yorkers find themselves considering this undeniably enchanting place. The menu features such American dishes as grilled salmon, roasted rack of lamb, and aged sirloin, along with a handful of Italian dishes (risotto, gnocchi, frittata) and all sorts of variations on the mashed potato; presentation is dramatic, and accompaniments like braised fennel and vegetable ragout show gourmet flair. The children's menu is surprisingly ordinary—fish-and-chips, grilled cheese, chicken fingers, pasta   but it does indicate a commitment to family business. I'd save this place for a special celebration, and only with kids old enough to appreciate the glitz and glamour, because the service can be deadly slow and sloppy—and you know how fatal that is when you've got restless children.

Uptown Dining

Artie's Delicatessen **17**
Bagelry **50 58 65**
Barking Dog Luncheonette **53 78**
Barney's Greengrass **12**
Barron's Pizza **52**
Bella Luna **11**
Big Nick's Burger & Pizza Joint **30 40**
Black Sheep Luncheonette **59**
Blockhead's Burritos **69**
Brother Jimmy's Bait Shack **56**
Brother Jimmy's BBQ **77**
Brother Jimmy's BBQ & Booze **20**
California Pizza Kitchen **88**
Carmine's **10**
China Fun **39 85**
China Shalom **8**
Chirping Chicken **4 31 63**
Ciao Bella Café **51**
Comfort Diner **61**
Dallas BBQ **42 81**
Dougie's BBQ and Grill **36**
EJ's Luncheonette **18 80**
Emack & Bolio's Ice Cream **27**
Emily's **49**
Ernie's **32**
Flight 1668 **54**
Gabriela's **7 33**
Go Fish **55**
Good Enough to Eat **16**
Googie's Luncheonette **75**
Gray's Papaya **38**
H&H Bagels **24**
H&H Bagels East **70**
Houlihan's **48**
Hunan Balcony **4**
Jackson Hole **14 57 67 86**
John's Pizza **47 87**
Joseph's Café **41**
La Caridad Luncheonette **28**
Lemongrass Grill **6**
Lexington Candy Shop **66**
LiLi's Noodle Shop and Grill **64**
Luke's Bar & Grill **72**
Mary Ann's **9 73**
Miss Elle's Homesick Bar & Grille **26**
Monsoon **21**
O'Neal's **46**
Ollie's Noodle Shop **2 15 44**
Patsy's Pizzeria **35 83**
Payard Patisserie **79**
Peppermint Park **84**
Petaluma **82**
Pick a Bagel **74 76**
Pig Heaven **71**
Pizzeria Uno **22 62**
Popover Café **13**
Presto's **1**
Rain **19**
Ruby Foo's **29**
Sassy's Sliders **60**
Serendipity 3 **89**
79th Street Boat Basin Café **23**
Soma Soup **37**
T & R Pizzeria **25**
Tavern on the Green **45**
Tony Di Napoli **68**
Trattoria Sambucca **43**
V & T Pizzeria-Restaurant **3**
Vinnie's Pizzeria **34**

E. 106th St.
E. 105th St.
E. 104th St.
E. 103rd St. Ⓜ
E. 102nd St.
E. 101st St.
E. 100th St.
E. 99th St.
E. 98th St.
E. 97th St.
E. 96th St.
E. 95th St.
L. 94th St.
E. 93rd St.
E. 92nd St.
E. 91st St.
E. 90th St.
E. 89th St.
E. 88th St.
E. 87th St.
E. 86th St.
E. 85th St.
E. 84th St.
E. 83rd St.
E. 82nd St
E. 81st St.
E. 80th St.
E. 79th St.
E. 78th St.
E. 77th St.
E. 76th St.
E. 75th St.
E. 74th St.
E. 73rd St.
E. 72nd St.
E. 71st St.
E. 70th St.
E. 69th St.
E. 68th St.
E. 67th St.
E. 66th St.
E. 65th St.
E. 64th St.
E. 63rd St.
E. 62nd St.
E. 61st St.
E. 60th St.
E. 59th St.

Ward's Island Footbridge

Ward's Island
Park
Ward's Island

Upper
Manhattan

Uptown

Midtown

Downtown

Carl Schurz
Park

Gracie
Mansion

**UPPER EAST
SIDE**

Fifth Ave.
Madison Ave.
Park Ave.
Lexington Ave.
Third Ave.
Second Ave.
First Ave.
York Ave.
East End Ave.

*The
Reservoir*

The Great
Lawn

Metropolitan
Museum of Art

Sheep
Meadow

Central
Park
Zoo

Wollman
Rink

Central Park South

FDR Dr.

East River

Roosevelt Island

Roosevelt Island
Tram

Queensboro Bridge

Sutton Pl.

From Lower
Level

To
Upper Level

0   1/3 Mi
0   .3 Km

MODERATE

⊙ **Bella Luna.** 584 Columbus Ave. (between 88th and 89th sts.). ☎ **212/877-2267.** High chairs, boosters. Reservations recommended. Main courses $8.95–$16.95; kids' portion of pasta $5.95. AE, MC, V. Daily noon–midnight. Subway: 1/9/B/C to 86th St. ITALIAN.

This cool and sophisticated restaurant with art-hung white walls and dreamy blue lights rimming the plate-glass windows looks like it'd be strictly for grown-ups—and in fact it's the choicest dining spot above 86th Street on Columbus. But the owners have young children, and from Day One the place has been extremely easygoing about young diners, always happy to bring them a small portion of plain pasta. The Tuscan-style pasta dishes are truly superior, as are the salads, the bruschetta, and the glorious mixed antipasto starter (practically a meal in itself); my kids often fill up on the crusty, dense bread. We eat here just as often without the kids as we do with them, even bringing clients—the food's that good.

Carmine's. 2450 Broadway (between 90th and 91st sts.). ☎ **212/362-2200.** High chairs, boosters. Reservations accepted Mon–Fri 5–7pm; other times for parties of 6 or more only. Family-style main courses (serve 2–3 people) $14–$46. AE, MC, V. Mon–Thurs 11:30am–3pm and 5–11pm, Fri 11:30am–3pm and 5pm–midnight, Sat 11:30am–midnight, Sun 2–10pm. Subway: 1/9 to 86th St. ITALIAN.

The original location of this popular northern Italianer still is tough to get into, but reservations are accepted for parties of six or more. My advice is to get here early if you don't want to make your children wait. That said, this lively, hearty restaurant is fun, with a decor that's a 1960s throwback (dark wood trim, chrome bar stools) and a menu of superbly executed standards like shrimp scampi, rigatoni with sausage, chicken marsala, veal scaloppine, and big thick steaks. The portions are served family-style and legendarily huge, so order accordingly—insist on your children splitting orders, even if they're extremely big eaters.

EJ's Luncheonette. 447 Amsterdam Ave. (between 81st and 82nd sts.). ☎ **212/ 873-3444.** Kids' menu, high chairs, boosters. Reservations not accepted. Breakfast $4.50–$8.50; lunch $6.50–$9; dinner $9.95–$14.75. No credit cards. Sun–Thurs 8:30am–10:30pm, Fri–Sat 8:30am–11pm. Subway: 1/9 to 79th St. AMERICAN DINER.

With its blue leatherette banquettes, pressed-tin ceiling, and chrome-trimmed Formica-topped tables, this is a museum-perfect replica of a classic American diner, and the menu strives to match—burgers, omelets, salads, sandwiches—though it gives away its yup-scale 1990s character with a number of vegetarian specials. The kids' menu tries to add some class by putting the peanut butter and jelly on challah bread, which utterly violates my sons' eating codes, but they're totally content to go instead for the fluffy stack of flapjacks. A feel-good sorta place, EJ's couldn't be nicer to kids, at least at lunchtime. Halfway between the Children's Museum of Manhattan and the American Museum of Natural History, it's a natural for the family trade.

Ernie's. 2150 Broadway (between 75th and 76th sts.). ☎ **212/496-1588.** Kids' menu, high chairs, boosters. Reservations recommended. Lunch $7.95–$14.95; dinner $7.95–$18.95; kids' menu $6.50. AE, DC, DISC, MC, V. Sun–Thurs noon–11pm, Fri–Sat noon–midnight. Subway: 1/2/3/9 to 72nd St. ITALIAN.

Back when I was single, I avoided Ernie's because this cool, high-ceilinged setting opening onto the Broadway sidewalk was so noisy I couldn't hear my date talk. Now I have kids and think the noise is great—that way no one can blame my children for disturbing the peace. Having lost some of its hip-joint cachet in recent years, Ernie's depends more than ever on the family business, which is good news for you. This is currently my second-grader's favorite Sunday brunch place; we never have

The Best of the Bagels

Why is it that bagels in other cities just don't taste as good as New York bagels? There can't be such a mystery, after all, to baking what's essentially a chewy bread doughnut. Yet we know many transplanted New Yorkers who beg us to bring real bagels with us when we come to visit. (Even New Jersey suburbanites make special treks into the city to get their bagels.) And bagels are such a great kid-pleasing food—New Yorkers even use them to pacify teething infants—that we'd hardly know what to do without them.

In my opinion, the premier outlet is **H&H Bagels,** 2239 Broadway, at 80th Street (☎ 212/595-8003), and 639 W. 46th St., between Eleventh Avenue and the West Side Highway (☎ 212/595-8000; call ☎ 800/NY-BAGEL for shipping anywhere). Besides selling bagels hot out of the oven to the public, H&H supplies bagels to delis and grocery stores all around the city, so look for signs boasting WE HAVE H&H BAGELS. The only problem with H&H is that it has no seating and doesn't serve bagels with any spread (in local parlance, a "schmear"), though you can separately buy little tubs of cream cheese, chopped liver, egg salad, herring in cream sauce, whatever. At least the store has finally installed a coffee machine so you can get a cup of coffee to go. **H&H Bagels East,** 1551 Second Ave., near 80th Street (☎ 212/734-7441), is a former branch that had to litigate for the right to keep using the name; it too has wonderfully chewy bagels, with the added convenience of a deli counter where countermen can cut and dress your bagels. I know many people who'd award the crown to **Ess-a-Bagel,** 359 First Ave., at 21st Street (☎ 212/260-2252), and 831 Third Ave., at 51st Street (☎ 212/980-1010), which is a full-service bagel deli where you can sit down and eat. Then, if you really want to get authentic, you might journey down to the Lower East Side to try **Kossar's Bagels & Bialys,** 39 Essex St. (☎ 212/387-9940).

Among the chains, **Pick a Bagel** is a favorite on the Upper East Side and elsewhere: 1101 Lexington Ave., at 77th Street (☎ 212/517-6590); 1473 Second Ave., between 76th and 77th streets (☎ 212/717-4662); 200 W. 57th St., between Seventh and Eighth avenues (☎ 212/957-5151); 601 Sixth Ave., between 17th and 18th Streets (☎ 212/924-4999); and 297 Third Ave., between 22nd and 23rd Streets (☎ 212/686-1414). The **Bagelry** is another perfectly good place to buy chewy, freshly baked bagels with a limited number of accompaniments: 1380 Madison Ave., at 96th Street (☎ 212/423-9590); 1324 Lexington Ave., at 88th Street (☎ 212/996-0567); 1228 Lexington Ave., at 83rd Street (☎ 212/717-2080); 425 Third Ave. at 30th St. (☎ 212/679-9845); 200 W. 14th St., at Seventh Avenue (☎ 212/352-2604); and 502 Hudson St. at Christopher St. (☎ 212/367-8809).

trouble walking in and getting a table, and they're always superfriendly to kids. Not only is there a kids' menu (pizzas, pastas, burgers, chicken-and-chips) and crayons to color on the paper tablecloths, but also you can order any main course to be served family-style. Some of the many pasta dishes are overspiced and drenched in tomato sauce, and the French toast and waffles are rather heavy, but the burgers, sandwiches, and salads are just fine. The garden room in back is a nice place to sit, though it's not always open at brunch. Do call before 5pm to reserve for a weekend night.

Good Enough to Eat. 483 Amsterdam Ave. (between 83rd and 84th sts.). ☎ **212/496-0163.** Kids' menu 4–7pm. Reservations not accepted. Main courses $9–$22. AE, MC, V. Mon–Fri 8am–10:30pm, Sat 9am–10:30pm, Sun 9am–10pm. Subway: 1/9 to 86th St. AMERICAN.

The kids' menu here is hand-drawn by a kid, which is a good sign. *Homey* is a very good word to describe this charming little restaurant, which grew out of a bakery, so you can bet the pies and cakes are excellent. Tables are small, with weathered wood pickets around to strike a rustic note; cut flowers add another farmhouse touch. Though the menu focuses on old-fashioned American dishes like macaroni-and-cheese, meat loaf, and a classic turkey dinner, chef/owner Carrie Levin trained at the Russian Tea Room and the Four Seasons, and is perfectly capable of turning out stunning daily fish specials and lemon parmesan chicken breast and a vegetable napoleon that's memorable indeed. Pasta and chicken fingers are still available on the kids' menu, never fear, so you can keep finicky eaters happy while indulging grown-up palates as well.

Lemongrass Grill. 2534 Broadway, at 95th St. ☎ **212/666-0896.** High chairs. Reservations accepted for parties of 6 or more only. Main courses $6.95–$14.95. AE, DC, MC, V. Sun–Thurs noon–11:30pm, Fri–Sat noon–12:30am. Subway: 1/9 to 86th St. THAI.

Succulent spring rolls and grilled skewers of chicken start you off right at this dependable Thai restaurant with its restful tropical-colonial decor (ceiling fans, bamboo, wooden rafters). Our youngsters feast on those appetizers and plain white rice, while we indulge in stir-fried beef and green-curry chicken and spicy pork chops. The tables are set close together and things can get pretty busy, but the upside is that no one minds kids' mess and noise—the staff actually seems to like children, and the service is attentive if not chatty.

Monsoon. 435 Amsterdam Ave. (at 81st St.). ☎ **212/580-8686.** Reservations recommended. Main courses $12–$20. AE, DC, MC, V. Sun–Thurs 11:30am–11:30pm, Fri–Sat 11:30am–midnight. Subway: 1/9 to 79th St. VIETNAMESE.

If your kids can handle the spicier types of Asian cooking, Monsoon is a good place to learn about Vietnamese food. This attractive, softly lit restaurant has lots of wood trim and plants (the colonial look, don't you know) and the staff is very tolerant of children. Grilled meat on skewers or the fine grilled pork chops are favorites with my kids, as well as the tender, savory spring rolls; my husband and I venture farther afield with the curries, stir-fries, elaborately shredded vegetable salads, and deeply flavored seafood casseroles. Your kids will feel grown-up and you will all feel well fed.

O'Neal's. 49 W. 64th St. (between Broadway and Central Park West). ☎ **212/787-4663.** Kids' menu, high chairs, boosters. Reservations recommended, especially for dinner or brunch. Main courses $7.95–$23.95. AE, CB, DC, MC, V. Mon–Fri 11am–4am, Sat–Sun 10am–4am. Subway: 1/9 to 66th St. AMERICAN.

Opened in 1964 as the Ginger Man, this perennial Lincoln Center-area favorite is a great place, so long as you can steer around the pre-performance rush. The staff is adept at getting diners out in time for the 8pm curtain, but if you want a relaxed meal, come for dinner after 8pm, or do weekday lunch or an early weekend brunch. The rambling dining rooms have the authentic look of a turn-of-the-20th-century saloon—brass fittings, wood trim, tile floors—and the unpretentious menu runs the gamut from burgers to seafood with more than a bit of panache. The chicken paillard and broiled shrimp curry are two unfailing winners, but the daily specials are always worth considering, and the burgers are some of the best in town. Look for the huge mural of a group of people in 1970s garb, many of them famous dancers (Lynn Seymour, Peter Martins, Edward Villella, Cynthia Gregory, Anthony

Dowell, Helgi Tomasson) who hung out at the O'Neal brothers' other restaurant, the now-defunct O'Neals' Baloon.

Popover Café. 551 Amsterdam Ave. (at 87th St.). ☎ **212/595-8555.** Kids' menu (except weekend afternoons), high chairs, boosters. Reservations not accepted. Lunch $8.95–$15.50; dinner $11.95–$21; kids' menu $3.95–$5.75. AE, MC, V. Mon–Thurs 8am–10pm, Fri 8am–11pm, Sat 9am–11pm, Sun 9am–10pm. Subway: 1/9/B/C to 86th St. AMERICAN.

This pleasantly upscale cafe's signature teddy bears lined up in the front windows have always deluded folks into thinking it's a restaurant for kids—but it's not particularly so, and the staff has been burned enough by unsupervised brats that they've added a note on children's manners to their menu. With an unpretentiously handsome decor (red plaid banquettes, cadet blue walls, granite-speckled Formica tabletops), it serves the West Side equivalent of the East Side ladies-who-lunch crowd, wholesome chic types who appreciate sprout-bedecked salads and soul-warming soups accompanied by a light-as-air baked popover. Still, the owner seems somewhat to have accepted the family fate, serving milk in a lidded paper cup and adding a kids' menu of sorts—yet a grilled cheese cooked on hearty home-baked peasant bread isn't necessarily as good as one made with Wonder bread, if you're 4 years old. The staff's patient tolerance for youngsters helps too. I find our lunches here more memorable than my kids do, but they're perfectly happy to accompany me, so long as it's not for weekend brunch, when the lines are ridiculous.

✪ Presto's. 2770 Broadway (between 106th and 107th sts.). ☎ **212/222-1760.** Boosters. Reservations recommended for parties of 6 or more. Main courses $8–$14.95. DISC, MC, V. Mon–Thurs noon–11pm, Fri noon–midnight, Sat 4pm–midnight, Sun 4–11pm. Subway: 1/9 to 103rd St. or 110th St. ITALIAN.

One of my family's all-time favorites is this comfy neighborhood pasta place with big front windows opening onto upper Broadway. First off, the fresh-baked bread is so delicious my kids can go through two baskets of it before their pasta's served. Second, the pasta dishes are some of the best I've eaten anywhere: rigatoni with eggplant and artichoke, a four-cheese pasta, linguine with grilled shrimp and veggies in a sauce of basil and goat cheese. Individual thin-crust pizzas are another hit, topped with a truly tasty pizza sauce. And seafood is routinely done well, though with few fancy flourishes. The decor is simple—white walls, a couple of ficus trees, darkwood chairs, white tablecloths—with tables spaced out decently; and the crowd is an easygoing mix of old-time West Siders, Columbia professors and grad students, and a few undergrads dining out with their parents. We don't generally see other children here, but I don't know why, since the waiters have always treated our kids with unfailing kindness and calm. It's a real winner.

Rain. 100 W. 82nd St. (at Columbus Ave.). ☎ **212/501-0776.** High chairs, boosters. Reservations recommended. Lunch $6.50–$15; dinner $12–$23. AE, DC, DISC, MC, V. Mon–Thurs noon–3pm and 6–11pm, Fri noon–3pm and 6pm–midnight, Sat noon–4pm and 5pm–midnight, Sun noon–4pm and 5–10pm. Subway: 1/9/B/C to 79th St. PAN-ASIAN/THAI.

The dreamy Maugham-esque decor of this upscale West Sider perfectly matches its exotic cuisine, principally Thai but borrowing accents from Malaysia and Vietnam—peanut sauces, coconut-milk soups, grilled meats, stir-fries, and lemongrass, chile, and lime flavorings. Though there's no kids' menu, many young diners are happy with the chicken skewers, noodle dishes, and rice. The place certainly is family-friendly, especially at lunch, despite the romantic calm of its softly lit dining room, with lots of drapes and rattan chairs and potted plants and fringed lamp shades. An added plus: It's very handy to the Natural History Museum—repair here after a morning in the Asian animals gallery and you'll feel you've really been to the Far East.

Trattoria Sambucca. 20 W. 72nd St. (between Columbus Ave. and Central Park West). ☎ **212/787-5656.** Kids' menu, high chairs, boosters. Reservations recommended. Main courses $20 (family-sized portions); kids' menu $5. AE, DC, DISC, MC, V. Mon–Thurs 5–10pm, Fri–Sat 5–11pm, Sun 3–10pm. Subway: B/C to 72nd St. ITALIAN.

We like to come here for family birthday celebrations: The waiters are very friendly to kids, you can color on the paper tablecloths, and the food is straightforward Italian classics, served in robust portions. (We have to remind our kids not to fill up on the delicious bread beforehand.) Dishes are served family-style, so don't overorder—our family of five chose two entrees and left a lot of food on the platters. The chicken piccata was a real winner, as was the penne with eggplant and mozzarella. The dining room is pleasantly soft-hued and contemporary, with sponged orange walls, iron sconces, and Tuscan painted pottery on wall brackets. Very casual, but you still get that special dining-out feeling.

INEXPENSIVE

Artie's Delicatessen. 2290 Broadway (at 83rd St.). ☎ **212/579-5959.** Kids' menu, high chairs, boosters. Reservations not accepted. Sandwiches $5.95–$12.95; main courses $7.95–$16.95; kids' menu $4.95–$6.95. AE, DC, MC, V. Daily 9am–midnight. Subway: 1/9 to 86th St. DELI.

The glossy, retro decor of this deli/coffee shop knockoff appeals to many Upper West Siders; it's been busy since it opened. Pastrami is a cornerstone of the huge menu, and I must say I was disappointed by it—too fatty and salty for my tastes. I did love the pickles set in a bowl on the table and the crisp, tangy coleslaw; next time I'll maybe go for an omelet, burger, roast chicken, or hot open turkey breast, which other people with me had and liked. Hot dogs, potato pancakes, and grilled cheese sandwiches are other kid-friendly choices. Service is quick and friendly, and the white-tiled setting is always noisy enough that no one minds if kids add to the din.

Barney Greengrass. 541 Amsterdam Ave. (at 86th St.). ☎ **212/724-4707.** Reservations not accepted. Egg dishes $4–$16.50; sandwiches $1.50–$11.75; smoked fish platters $18.50–$69.75. MC, V (no credit cards on weekends and holidays). Tues–Fri 8:30am–4pm, Sat–Sun 8:30am–5pm. Subway: 1/9 to 86th St. DELI.

A West Side institution since 1908, Barney Greengrass looks like it hasn't been redecorated in half a century—the chipped Formica tabletops, beige linoleum floor, stained brownish wallpaper, and fluorescent lighting are an aggressive statement of the fact that the food's so good, you come here anyway. I'm not a smoked salmon expert, but the fish here is so silky, so meltingly tender, it converted me for life (problem is, nobody else's lox is ever gonna live up to this standard). The service is famously laconic, even gruff, but food arrives quickly. Sodas come in cans, the plates are plain white institutional china—who cares? Your kids may not get the time-warp charm of this place, but if they're at all inclined to try classic deli food—lox, chopped liver, cold borscht, chopped herring, whitefish salad, with omelets and bagels as safe alternatives—they'll love it. Good for breakfast, too.

Big Nick's Burger & Pizza Joint. (1) 70 W. 71st St. (at Columbus Ave.). ☎ **212/ 799-4444.** Main courses $4.45–$15.50; weekday lunch specials $4.95. MC, V. Daily 10am–5am. Subway: 1/2/3/9/B/C to 72nd St. (2) 2175 Broadway at 77th St. ☎ **212/ 362-9238.** Open 24 hours. Subway: 1/9 to 79th Street. BURGERS/PIZZA.

Cacophonous, crowded, and utterly unpretentious, this burger joint is great for kids. You squeeze in past a long counter with chrome stools, hoping one of the cramped leatherette booths in the back is free. Head shots of customers, famous or not, fill the brick-faced walls alongside hand-scrawled signs advertising dozens of specials (all this on top of a menu that's almost bewilderingly extensive). Even the regular burgers are obscenely huge—my carnivore son, Tom, could barely get his hands around one—and the pizzas are gooey with crisp crusts (whole pies only, no slices). There are also steaks, pot pies, sandwiches, and lots of Greek dishes such as souvlaki, spanokopita, and gyros, all in huge portions, but keep one thing in mind: Big Nick's sees greasy food as a good thing. If you agree, you will be tremendously happy here.

Brother Jimmy's BBQ & Booze. 428 Amsterdam Ave. (between 80th and 81st sts.). ☎ 212/501-7515. Kids' menu, high chairs, boosters. Reservations accepted for parties of 8 or more only. Main courses $9.95–$15.95; salads and sandwiches $3.95–$9.95. AE, CB, DC, DISC, MC, V. Mon–Thurs 5pm–midnight, Fri 5pm–1am, Sat noon–1am, Sun noon–midnight. Subway: 1/9/B/C to 79th St. BARBECUE/AMERICAN SOUTHERN.

The word *booze* in the name shouldn't be taken lightly; as the evening wears on, this low lit, cluttered joint does become a noisy, beery Southern frat party, especially on nights when UNC and Duke square off in basketball. But the three Brother Jimmy's restaurants very definitely like kids and prove it by letting the under-12 set eat free (two kids eat free with each paid adult meal). And the barbecue is some of the city's best, with meaty, spicy ribs, pulled pork, and chicken cooked slowly over hickory wood and slathered with a tangy sauce. Add a little cornbread, candied yams, fried okra, and black-eyed peas, and it's a welcome break from pizza and burgers. (Kids may want to play it safe with corn on the cob or french fries.) Your kids' noise level won't be a problem, that's for sure.

China Fun. 246 Columbus Ave. (between 71st and 72nd sts.). ☎ 212/580-1516. High chairs, boosters. Reservations accepted for parties of 6 or more only. Main courses $6.95–$13.95; noodles and rice $4.95–$7.95; dim sum 95¢–$4.95. MC, V. Sun–Thurs 11am–midnight, Fri–Sat 11am–1am. Subway: B/C/1/9 to 72nd St. CHINESE.

The grand-niece of Gen. Chiang Kai-shek, Dorothea Wu, is now a restaurateur in New York, and she runs this smart bilevel Mandarin-style place on the Columbus Avenue restaurant row. The look is clean and modern, with a bright abstract mural splashed on the high back wall; the food is classic and delicate, with lots of barbecued meats hanging in the glass-walled kitchen and dim sum carts trundling about. This is a good place to introduce your children to wonton soups and dumplings without hauling them all the way to exotic Chinatown, though there are some more inventive dishes on the menu as well, including pineapple curry fried rice and chicken in peach sauce garnished with sesame seeds. The kids' menu, for take-out and delivery only, goes the safe route of chicken nuggets, plain lo mein noodles, Jell-O, and a toy; at $3.25, it's a bargain—why they don't offer it in the restaurant is a puzzlement indeed.

✪ **Gabriela's.** (1) 685 Amsterdam Ave. (at 93rd St.). ☎ 212/961-0574. Kids' menu, high chairs, boosters. Reservations accepted for parties of 6 or more only. Main courses $6.95–$12.75; tacos and tortas $2.25–$4.75; kids' menu $4.95–$7.95. AE, MC, V. Mon–Thurs 11:30am–11pm, Fri–Sat 11:30am–midnight, Sun 11:30am–10pm. Subway: 1/2/3/9 to 96th St. (2) 311 Amsterdam Ave. (at 75th St.). ☎ 212/875-8532. Mon–Thurs noon–11pm, Fri–Sat noon–midnight, Sun noon–10pm. Subway: 1/2/3/9 to 72nd Street. MEXICAN.

Gabriela's serves up astonishingly good regional dishes that go well beyond rote Mexican combo platters. On the menu is exotic stuff even adults may not want to try—roast cactus, for example—but you can't go wrong with any of the marvelous spicy stews and casseroles and pozole soups. The roast chicken is a marvel, succulent and delicately spiced; quesadillas are light, crisp, and flavorful; and there's a corn soup to die for. As for kids, there are plenty of simpler tacos and sandwiches, served up with great rice and beans, as well as a number of fruit drinks and fruit shakes, not to mention chocolate milk, which you don't find on many restaurant menus. Gabriela's is fantastically popular, so there's usually a line for dinner; go early or go for lunch. The staff is cordial and accommodating; the clean, modern-looking coffee-shop decor (enlivened with colorful lacy doilies hanging from the ceiling) includes nice blue banquettes, which kids may prefer to chairs.

Hunan Balcony. 2596 Broadway (at 98th St.). ☎ **212/865-0400.** High chairs, boosters. Reservations recommended. Lunch specials $4.75–$5.95; dinner $4.75–$13.50. AE, DC, MC, V. Daily noon–1am. Subway: 1/2/3/9 to 96th St. CHINESE.

The Upper West Side has long been well served by Chinese restaurants, and Hunan Balcony is the granddaddy of them all. It's a big operation, smartly run, with a menu that tries hard to meet everybody's tastes—noodles, seafood, steamed items, spicy Hunan dishes, even sushi, plus the classic chow meins and egg rolls that characterized another American generation's idea of Chinese food. Purists will realize that the cooking isn't as authentic as you'll find in Chinatown, but it's usually delicious (I've eaten here so often over the past 20 years that I've occasionally hit an off night, but that's rare). Everyone's happy to serve the dishes family-style; children can drop all the rice they want and no one seems to mind.

John's Pizza. 48 W. 65th St. (between Broadway and Central Park West). ☎ **212/721-7001.** Reservations not accepted. Pizzas $11.90–$50. AE, MC, V. Daily 11:30am–11:30pm. Subway: 1/9 to 66th St. PIZZA.

Considering how few cheap places to eat there are around Lincoln Center, this branch of the famous Village pizzeria (see below for other locations) is a welcome addition to the neighborhood. Thin-crust pizzas, baked in a brick oven—*delicioso.*

La Caridad Luncheonette. 2199 Broadway (at 78th St.). ☎ **212/874-2780.** Reservations not accepted. Main courses $5.95–$8.95. No credit cards. Mon–Sat 11:30am–1am, Sun 11:30am–10:30pm. Subway: 1/9 to 79th St. CUBAN-CHINESE.

There's often a line at this cheap, authentic corner storefront spot, but customers move in and out fast—a hearty meal materializes on your Formica-topped table minutes after you order. The clientele seems split pretty evenly between those ordering white-rice dishes (savory Chinese stir-fries, chop sueys, and soups) and those going for the yellow-rice side of the menu (pork chops, fried chicken crackling, and a divine Cuban pot roast my daughter attacked with gusto). This isn't a place for picky eaters—the mere sight of yucca and fried plantain side dishes send my boys into total appetite arrest—but anyone who's willing to try the food comes away happy. Though the place is cramped, crowded, and crazily busy, the taciturn Asian waiters never blink at a stroller blocking the aisle or a bread crust flung on the floor. What you see is what you get, and what you get is delicious.

Mary Ann's. 2452 Broadway (at 91st St.). ☎ **212/877-0132.** Kids' menu, high chairs, boosters. Reservations accepted Mon–Thurs only. Main courses $6.95–$11.95; kids' menu $3.95–$4.75. MC, V. Sun–Thurs 11:30am–10:30pm, Fri–Sat 11:30am–11:30pm. Subway: 1/9 to 86th St.; 1/2/3/9 to 96th St. MEXICAN.

The West Side branch of this Mexican chain is its most kid-friendly, with a junior menu that includes quesadillas, tacos, chicken fajitas, and a red-cheese enchilada; there's spaghetti for kids who won't try Mexican. The earth-toned decor is movie-set Mexican, with tiled-topped tables and a sombrero or two on the walls; the food is uniformly good, delicately spiced rather than fiery, with fresh tomatilla salsa and handmade tortillas. A decent choice for families who want to sample good-as-homemade Mexican.

Miss Elle's Homesick Bar & Grille. 226 W. 79th St. (between Amsterdam Ave. and Broadway). ☎ **212/595-4350.** Reservations accepted. Main courses $10.50–$19.50; lunch special $5.95; early-bird special (4:30–6:30pm) $13.50; brunch $11.95. AE, CB, DC, DISC, MC, V. Daily 11:30am–midnight. Subway: 1/9 to 79th St. AMERICAN.

Comfort food like macaroni-and-cheese and pot roast dominate the menu at this homey restaurant; the garden room, reached through a long front bar area, is light and cool beneath a skylight roof, with ceiling fans, trailing plants, lacy tablecloths, and a crystal chandelier, giving it just the right air of faded gentility. Service is genial, and while there's no specific kids' meal, most children opt for the section of the menu entitled "Make Believe Food," which has fun stuff like English muffin pizzas, beans 'n' franks, fried ravioli, and "Tastes Just Like Chicken" (which is, in fact, very tasty chicken tenders). The whole place is a little out of the ordinary, and though it's not as naive as it pretends to be, a mixed neighborhood crowd ambles in and enjoys the funky ambience. Children are just as welcome as everybody else.

Ollie's Noodle Shop. (1) 2315 Broadway (at 84th St.). ☎ **212/362-3111.** Reservations not accepted. Main courses $6.95–$14.95; lunch specials $4.95–$5.25. AE, MC, V. Sun–Thurs 11:30am–midnight, Fri–Sat 11:30am–1am. Subway: 1/9 to 86th St. (2) 1991 Broadway (near 68th St.). ☎ **212/595-8181.** Sun–Thurs 11:30am–midnight, Fri–Sat 11:30am–1am. Subway: 1/9 to 66th St./Lincoln Center. (3) 2957 Broadway (at 116th St.). ☎ **212/932-3300.** Mon–Sat 7am–2am, Sun 7am–midnight. Subway: 1/9 to 116th St. CHINESE.

The roast poultry hanging in the front window is a promising sign, and the cheery bustle inside carries out the promise of simple, filling Chinese food—nothing exotic to challenge the taste buds. Besides the usual spring rolls, dumplings, and steamed buns for appetizers, the menu features lots of fish, grilled or steamed or braised or sautéed, and a fairly classic range of Chinese dishes (lemon chicken, double-sautéed pork, eggplant sautéed in garlic sauce). Nothing's too heavy, too greasy, or too spicy. My kids usually opt for lo mein noodles or the broader chow fun noodles, topped with chunks of chicken and a few shredded vegetables. The service is brisk and tolerant; it can get pretty crowded on a weekend night, but tables empty quickly. The Ollie's uptown near the Columbia campus may be the best choice if your kids aren't Chinese-savvy; it offers diner standards like burgers, chef's salads, and omelets. The Midtown location is covered later in this chapter.

Patsy's Pizzeria. 64 W. 74th St. (at Columbus Ave.). ☎ **212/579-3000.** High chairs, boosters. Reservations not accepted. Pizzas $11.50–$13.50; pasta $7.95–$12.95. No credit cards. Sun–Thurs noon–11pm, Fri–Sat noon–midnight. Subway: 1/2/3/9/B/C to 72nd St. PIZZA.

Given their decades-long rivalry for pizza supremacy in New York, it was perhaps inevitable that as soon as John's Pizza (above) began to expand beyond Bleecker Street, Patsy's would want to move beyond its East Harlem original location, which it has done speedily (other locations are on the Upper East Side, in Midtown, and in the Village, below). The good news is that the pizzas are still superlative, as are mouth-watering pastas, all at very reasonable prices and with a casual, family-friendly atmosphere. The Upper West Side branch is only a few blocks from the Natural History Museum, an added benefit.

✪ 79th Street Boat Basin Café. W. 79th St. at the Hudson River, in Riverside Park. ☎ **212/496-5542.** Kids' menu. Reservations not accepted. Main courses $3–$18; kids' menu $2.50–$3.50. AE, DC, MC, V. Early May–late Sept, weather permitting, daily noon–11pm. Subway: 1/9 to 79th St. AMERICAN.

A stroke of genius, to put a restaurant here overlooking the houseboat marina in lower Riverside Park. Not only are there great views west over the Hudson (time it right and you'll get a sunset show to die for), the arched stone vaults of this open-air structure have a kind of Venetian charm all their own. And the food is head-and-shoulders above what you'd expect at an outdoor cafe: superb burgers, zestfully seasoned salads and sandwiches, and excellent grilled seafood. The trappings are supercasual—checked vinyl tablecloths, sturdy plastic chairs, folding tables, fries heaped in a plastic basket on wax paper—and the service can dawdle, but our kids didn't seem to mind, they were so busy counting boats on the river. They're smart enough to serve the kids' menu sandwiches on white bread and not to blacken the hot dogs on the grill; the lemonade was too sour for our kids, but once they realized they could pour packets of sugar into their glasses, they were delighted. This cafe is run by the management of the excellent **O'Neal's** restaurant (see above), which also operates two other seasonal restaurants: the **Hudson Beach Café** in Riverside Park at about 105th St and the **Ballfields Café** in Central Park, midpark at 65th St. by the Heckscher ballfields.

Soma Soup. 2067 Broadway (between 71st and 72nd sts.). ☎ 212/721-7662. High chairs, boosters. Main courses $4.95–$11.95. AE, MC, V. Daily 11am–11pm. Subway: 1/2/3/9 to 72nd St. ECLECTIC.

All there is to eat here are soups and their cold equivalent, fruit smoothies, but if your kids like those, you're in business. The decor is groovy and contemporary, with light neutral colors, slick surfaces, and lots of curves; the upholstered settees at the tables make you almost forget that this is basically a fast-food place. Menu boards tell you what soups are on today, and you can choose which size to have, along with breadsticks, drinks, and brownies. Think globally—soup recipes come from Asia, Africa, the Mediterranean, Europe, and the New World (that's us). Fun for a lunchtime change of pace.

T & R Pizzeria. 411 Amsterdam Avenue (at 79th St.). ☎ 212/787-4093. Reservations not accepted. Medium pie $10.75. No credit cards. Daily 11am to midnight. Subway: 1/9 to 79th St. PIZZA.

Need a pizza near the Natural History Museum? Here's the place for a quick slice or a pie to go—a very dependable neighborhood storefront pizzeria. No fancy airs or graces, just good pizza.

V & T Pizzeria-Restaurant. 1024 Amsterdam Ave. (between 110th and 111th sts.). ☎ 212/663-1708. Boosters. Main courses $6–$13. AE, DISC, MC, V. Daily 11am–midnight. Subway: 1/9 to 110th St. PIZZA/ITALIAN.

With its brick walls, low lighting, and red-checkered tablecloths, V & T looks just like the campus pizza joint it is, the campuses in question being nearby Columbia and Barnard. The pizzas are fabulous, with thin crusts, runny cheese, and robust tomato sauce; other southern Italian dishes, like lasagna and baked ziti, are heartwarmingly good too, and the prices can't be beat. Not much on ambience, but then you don't get a lot of attitude, either.

Vinnie's Pizzeria. 285 Amsterdam Ave. (between 73rd and 74th sts.). ☎ 212/874-4382. Reservations not accepted. Pizza $1.60 (slice)–$21 (pie); pasta $5–$9. No credit cards. Mon–Wed 11am–1am, Thurs–Sun 11am–2am. Subway: 1/2/3/9 to 72nd St. PIZZA/ITALIAN.

One of the best by-the-slice walk-in pizzerias in the city, Vinnie's also provides table service if you want to go beyond the wonderful pies and order pasta, antipasti, or salads. At $1.60 a slice, the pizza is a good deal, flavorful and nicely goopy. The location is handy too.

ICE CREAM & SWEETS

Emack & Bolio's Ice Cream. 389 Amsterdam Ave. (between 78th and 79th sts.). ☎ 212/362-2747. No credit cards. Sun–Thurs 2–11pm, Fri–Sat 2pm–midnight. Subway: 1/9 to 79th St. ICE CREAM.

Creamy, delicious full-fat ice cream, cups or cones, with toppings or not, as well as fruit smoothies, shakes, and other yummy potables. Trademark flavors include grasshopper pie, cosmic crunch, and vanilla bean speck.

THE CHAIN GANG

The **Houlihan's** at 1900 Broadway, at 63rd Street (☎ **212/339-8862**), is a good option when the Lincoln Center restaurants are crammed before an 8pm curtain. Handy to the American Museum of Natural History is the **Pizzeria Uno** at 432 Columbus Ave., at 81st Street (☎ **212/595-4700**). There's a **Dallas BBQ** at 27 W. 72nd St., between Central Park West and Columbus Avenue (☎ **212/873-2004**). The **Jackson Hole** at 517 Columbus Ave., at 85th Street (☎ **212/362-5177**), has sidewalk seating and lots of parked strollers on weekends.

FAST FOOD

Kids may not go for the milky, sweet, refreshing papaya juice at **Gray's Papaya,** 2090 Broadway, at 72nd Street (☎ **212/799-0243**), but there's also fruit punch and soda; as far as food goes, your best bet is a plump, succulent hot dog, costing about a buck. Prices are low, low, low and you're handed your food in a jiffy, but don't expect to sit down—a few high stools at a counter is about the extent of it. My favorite of the city's many grilled-chicken take-outs is **Chirping Chicken,** 350 Amsterdam Ave. at 77th Street (☎ **212/787-6631**), and 2680 Broadway at 103rd St. (☎ **212/280-3500**), where they throw a pita bread on the grill atop the chicken to absorb some juices (okay, to absorb the flavorful grease). Corn on the cob and fries are among the sides you can order.

3 The Upper East Side

EXPENSIVE

Petaluma. 1356 First Ave. (at 73rd St.). ☎ **212/772-8800.** www.petalumanyc.com. High chairs, boosters. Reservations accepted. Main courses $13–$28. AE, DC, DISC, MC, V. Mon–Fri 11am–3:30pm and 5–11:30pm, Sat–Sun noon–3:30pm and 5–11:30pm. Subway: 6 to 68th St. ITALIAN.

A good place to take a well-behaved child for a special meal out, though you'll see plenty of neighborhood types bringing toddlers here. The atmosphere is indeed friendly to kids, and the thin-crust pizzas from the brick oven go down well with youngsters. But with such upscale food—grilled focaccia, gnocchi, swordfish with tomatoes, capers, and olives—it'd be nice to have a child appreciate it. The dining room is mellow and contemporary, with saffron-colored walls and plenty of room between tables; service is attentive but low-key.

MODERATE

✪ **Barking Dog Luncheonette.** (1) 1678 Third Ave. (at 94th St.). ☎ **212/831-1800.** Boosters, sassy seats. Reservations not accepted. Main courses $10.50–$14.50; sandwiches and salads $4.50–$8.95. No credit cards. Daily 8am–11pm. Subway: 6 to 96th St. (2) 1453 York Ave. (at 77th St.). ☎ **212/861-3600.** Daily 8am–11pm. Subway: 6 to 77th St. AMERICAN.

The Barking Dog isn't automatically a family restaurant, but that's what I like about it. Convenient to the 92nd Street Y and Carl Schurz Park, this sleek retro diner is suffused with a mellow glow from golden walls, wood-trimmed booths, and parchment-shaded lamps at every table. The dog motif amuses my daughter: Posters, cookie jars, and even bulldog hood ornaments from Mack trucks put dogs all around the room, and there's a dog bar outside, a blue-tiled corner trough with a polished spigot. But what really makes this place work for families is that it serves breakfast until 4pm—kids can feast on waffles or blueberry pancakes while parents get a chance to eat something suitably grown-up, like a salad of field greens with goat-cheese croutons or a grilled fillet of salmon sandwich. For dinner, there's a good fried chicken with real mashed potatoes, baked ham, pot roast, and a homey meat loaf, as well as more sophisticated stuff like the pan-roasted breast of chicken with piquant Mediterranean-flavored ragout. Bribe your children with old-fashioned ice-cream sodas and sundaes, served from a shiny vintage soda fountain.

EJ's Luncheonette. 1271 Third Ave. (at 73rd St.). ☎ **212/472-0600.** Kids' menu, high chairs, boosters. Reservations not accepted. Breakfast $4.50–$8.50; lunch $6.50–$9; dinner $9.95–$14.75. No credit cards. Mon–Sat 8am–11pm, Sun 8am–10:30pm. Subway: 6 to 77th St. AMERICAN DINER.

Breakfast is an especially good time to check out this re-creation of an old-style lunch-counter diner (see also Upper West Side and Greenwich Village), but the classic repertoire of burgers, salads, and sandwiches—plus daily specials like skinless fried chicken and turkey meat loaf—makes it a good bet for lunch or dinner too, so long as you can get in. The tile floor and high ceiling usually ring with noise.

Emily's. 1325 Fifth Ave. (between 111th and 112th sts.). ☎ **212/996-1212.** High chairs, boosters. Reservations accepted. Main courses $6.95–$16.95. AE, DC, DISC, MC, V. Daily 11am–midnight. Subway: 2/4 to 110th St. AMERICAN SOUTHERN/JAMAICAN.

The crowd is lively and racially mixed, everyone crowding in for good ol' Southern home cooking—stuff like baby-back ribs, Louisiana catfish strips, crab cakes, and pork chops. There's a significant Jamaican influence on the menu, too, with jerk chicken and a fine red snapper in West Indian sauce. Things get even better at dessert, with peach cobbler and sweet potato pie stoking the sugar cravings. Kids who like to stick to the tried-and-true can still get chicken fingers or a cheeseburger or fried chicken. Breakfast here is something to know about, too, including biscuits and grits and corned beef hash as well as omelets and French toast and waffles. Nothing glamorous about the way uptown setting, or about the food, and that's the point.

Go Fish. 1675 Third Ave. (between 93rd and 94th sts.). ☎ **212/410-4900.** Kids' menu, high chairs, boosters. Reservations recommended. Main courses $9.95–$19.95. AE, DC, MC, V. Sun–Thurs 5–11pm, Fri–Sat 5pm–midnight. Subway: 6 to 96th St. SEAFOOD.

With its tropically bright yellow walls, the weathered spar hung from ropes in the middle of the dining room, and sea gull mobiles and big plastic fish overhead, Go Fish trumpets its seafood specialty pretty clearly. But we all know what Go Fish is–a kids' card game, right?—and that's a signal of how family-friendly this place can be. Children enjoy the live fish flitting around in a big tank, as well as the fish-festooned bathrooms; try to snag a table at the back so you can sit by windows looking onto a pleasant garden terrace. The so-called Squid's Menu features chicken fingers and the like as well as light and crispy fish-and-chips. For bigger appetites, there's a nice mix-and-match option: Choose one of four featured fishes, then select your method of preparation, and then decide which of the 11 zappy sauces should go on it. The possibilities are endless (well, not endless, but 132 different combinations ain't bad). Or go for the steamed mussels, the raw bar's clams and oysters, pan-seared trout, lump crab cakes—or, if you must, roasted chicken or filet mignon. The upbeat, jovial atmosphere here puts everyone at ease. If that's what it takes to get your kids to eat fish, go for it.

Googie's Luncheonette. 1491 Second Ave. (at 78th St.). ☎ **212/717-1122.** Boosters, sassy seats. Reservations not accepted. Sandwiches $5.95–$8.95; main courses $7.95–$16.95.

AE, DC, DISC, MC, V. Sun–Wed 9am–midnight, Thurs 9am–1am, Fri 9am–1:30am, Sat 9am–2am. Subway: 6 to 77th St. AMERICAN DINER.

This upscale coffee shop's bright, clean, pastel-toned decor lacks the sassy retro atmosphere of EJ's or the Barking Dog (above), but the food is perfectly fine, especially if your kids, like mine, are pasta omnivores. It's usually bustling, and though the service can be slipshod, no one will hurry you out the door. The menu features a fair number of Italian dishes along with typical diner fare—burgers, club sandwiches, omelets, or even a fairly decent sirloin steak, to be accompanied if at all possible with the excellent shoestring fries. The pasta sauces are a little less spicy than I like, but my kids seem to prefer 'em that way. Googie's is a useful option for a late breakfast, with Italian frittatas in addition to standard waffles, pancakes, and French toast.

✪ Luke's Bar & Grill. 1394 Third Ave. (between 79th and 80th sts.). ☎ **212/249-7070.** Boosters, sassy seats. Reservations accepted for parties of 6 or more only. Main courses $5.95–$15.95. No credit cards. Mon–Thurs 11am–2am, Fri 11am–3am, Sat–Sun 10am–2am. Subway: 6 to 77th St. AMERICAN/BURGERS.

It's hard for me to analyze why I like Luke's—it just seems to me like a very civilized place where children are included as a matter of course. Lots of brick and wood give it a warm, clubby look that's also somehow young and casual; there's definitely an active bar scene here, but it never overwhelms the pleasant, relaxing restaurant. Things never get too loud or rowdy, but it's not reverently hushed either. Luke's burgers are really wonderful, firm and yet juicy, with an ever-so-slightly charred outside, and the salads are big, fresh, and well conceived. My younger ones don't like burgers, so they go for the grilled cheese sandwich, roast chicken, or one of the pasta dishes. There's no attitude on the part of the waiters: They seem genuinely happy to serve youngsters, even babies. If only more restaurants were like this.

Pig Heaven. 1540 Second Ave. (between 80th and 81st sts.). ☎ **212/744-4333.** Reservations recommended. Main courses $8.50–$17.95. AE, DC, DISC, MC, V. Sun–Thurs 11:30am–11:15pm, Fri–Sat 11:30am–12:15am. Subway: 6 to 77th St. CHINESE.

A makeover of this East Side designer Chinese spot has done away with the old pig-themed decor, putting something very sleek and contemporary in its place, though a back room still has the farmhouse look. More important, somebody gave the kitchen a much-needed shot in the arm, and the food is wonderful again, after several lackluster years. The barbecue and pork specials are the way to go; we also liked the spring rolls and dry-cooked string beans (something about Chinese sauces gets my kids to eat vegetables they'd never touch otherwise). The staff treats children well, if not effusively, and even my pickiest eater filled up on boiled white rice to her heart's content.

Serendipity 3. 225 E. 60th St. (between Second and Third aves.). ☎ **212/838-3531.** Boosters. Reservations accepted for full meals only. Main courses $6.95–$18. AE, CB, DC, DISC, MC, V. Sun–Thurs 11:30am–midnight, Fri 11:30am–1am, Sat 11:30am–2am. Subway: 4/5/6 to 59th St. AMERICAN DINER/ICE CREAM.

This cheery, bright restaurant with its snugly deep booths and Tiffany-style lamps has a classic coffee-shop menu, with especially good burgers. But it's best known in the under-12 population as a source for huge, wickedly rich desserts, fountain sodas, and ice-cream sundaes. The Outrageous Banana Split is priced at $12 and worth every penny.

Tony di Napoli. 1606 Second Ave. (between 83rd and 84th sts.). ☎ **212/861-8686.** High chairs, boosters. Reservations recommended. Main courses (serve 2–3 people) $11–$36; kids' pasta portions $5. AE, CB, DC, DISC, MC, V. Mon–Fri 5pm–midnight, Sat 2pm–midnight, Sun 2–11pm. Subway: 4/5/6 to 86th St. ITALIAN.

Hearty southern Italian food is served family-style at this genial Upper East Side neighborhood spot, which opens a big sidewalk cafe in fair weather. Polaroids of satisfied customers in the front window and black-and-white head shots of race-car drivers on the yellowed plaster walls give it the look of a vintage family-owned red-sauce joint, though in fact it's part of the Dallas BBQ restaurant empire. Sunday lunch is the most popular time for families (Tony's doesn't serve lunch on weekdays), but you'll find kids sprinkled around the boisterous dining room on weeknights too. The family-style menu is strong on pasta dishes, with several chicken and veal offerings as well, plus a two-person steak for dedicated carnivores. If your family can't agree on dishes, half portions can be ordered for individuals, as well as kid-sized portions of pasta (there's no separate kids' menu). Though I prefer the similar food at Carmine's (on the Upper West Side, above, and in Midtown, below), the scene here is less trendy and the prices are certainly reasonable, considering you can get away at $20 a head, including wine for adults. Note that there isn't room to park strollers beside tables.

INEXPENSIVE

Barron's Pizza. 1426 Lexington Ave. (at 93rd St.). ☎ 212/410-6600. Slice $1.50; plain pie $10. Daily 7am–11pm. No credit cards. Subway: 6 to 96th St. PIZZA.

We stumbled into this pizzeria one Sunday noontime and had some of the best pie of our lives—tangy sauce, fresh mozzarella, crisp chewy crust—along with friendly counter service. The decor is a little different from your standard storefront pizza shop, with some mosaic tile designs and wrought-iron cafe chairs. This is the sort of place you might not seek out without a recommendation, so take it from me— it's well above average. We go back whenever we're in the neighborhood.

Black Sheep Luncheonette. 1725 Second Ave. (at 89th St.). ☎ 212/348-1144. Kids' menu, high chairs, boosters. Reservations not accepted. Breakfast $3.25–$6.25; lunch/dinner $4.50–$9.50. No credit cards. Daily 8am–10:30pm. Subway: 4/5/6 to 86th St. AMERICAN DINER.

Another retro coffee shop, but the look here is cleaner and more light-filled, with lots of white tile accented with pale grays and greens. A pressed-tin ceiling and ceiling fans add that vintage look. The chef used to work at EJ's Luncheonettes (see above and below) and has every intention of pulling off the same sort of feat here: classic American food with a little flair, served in casual dinerlike surroundings. Breakfast is served all day, which is a plus for my pancake-loving children, but there's also a L'il Lambs menu with chicken nuggets and buttered noodles and P-B-and-J sandwiches and the like. Adult-friendly options include lots of salads and grilled sandwiches and wraps; try the buffalo-meat burgers if you want something low-fat and very tasty.

Brother Jimmy's Bait Shack. 1644 Third Ave. (at 92nd St.). ☎ 212/426-2020. Kids' menu, high chairs, boosters. Reservations accepted for parties of 8 or more only. Main courses $9.95–$15.95; salads and sandwiches $3.95–$9.95. AE, CB, DC, DISC, MC, V. Mon–Fri 5pm–midnight, Sat noon–1am, Sun noon–11pm. Subway: 6 to 96th St. BARBECUE/ AMERICAN SOUTHERN.

The rowdy roadhouse charm of this Brother Jimmy's is scarcely dimmed by its emphasis on seafood, which means simply that an oyster bar, blackened catfish, and peel-and-eat shrimp are featured on a menu otherwise heavy on barbecued chicken, ribs, and pork. The kitchen doesn't stint on the spices, and beer flows plentifully. But kids are welcomed warmly, with a kids-eat-free policy that can't be beat anywhere else in town. (Two kids per parent, and they have to be under 12, but it's still a great deal.) A variety of nightly "events" like All-U-Can-Eat Sundays and White Trash Wednesdays make every evening a party here.

☻ Brother Jimmy's BBQ. 1461 First Ave. (at 76th St.). ☎ **212/288-0999.** Kids' menu, high chairs, boosters. Reservations accepted for parties of 8 or more only. Main courses $9.95–$15.95; salads and sandwiches $3.95–$9.95. AE, CB, DC, DISC, MC, V. Sun–Thurs 5–11pm, Fri–Sat 5pm–1am. Subway: 6 to 77th St. BARBECUE/AMERICAN SOUTHERN.

If God were a man he'd be a Tarheel. With a jumble of frat-party paraphernalia littering the walls, low-lit Brother Jimmy's brings hickory-smoked Carolina barbe-cue to New York City. No baby-back ribs here, only thick 'n' meaty St. Louis–style ribs, served in hefty dinners that also include cornbread and a choice of country sides—if your kids aren't into collard greens (yeah, right), you can satisfy them with creamed corn or french fries or macaroni-and-cheese. Two kids 11 and under eat free for each adult meal, which is a bargain you can't refuse: Kids' meals include burgers, hot dogs, grilled cheese, or chicken fingers. My oldest son has taken friends here for dinner his past two birthdays and it's been memorable, in a good way. The southern roadhouse atmosphere is laid-back, as is the service, for better or worse. It may be best to get here early, before the frat party gets in high gear.

California Pizza Kitchen. 201 E. 60th St. (at Third Ave.). ☎ **212/755-7773.** Kids' menu, high chairs, boosters. Reservations not accepted. Main courses $6.25–$11; kids' menu $4.95. AE, DC, MC, V. Sun–Mon 11:30am–10pm, Tues–Sat 11:30am–11pm. Subway: 4/5/6 to 59th St.; E, F to Lexington Ave. PIZZA/CALIFORNIAN.

Frankly, I think the idea of a pizza topped with barbecued chicken or shrimp is an abomination, but this cheery chain restaurant surmounts that objection for me because it's so darned kid-friendly. The menu does include other items, like salads and soups and pasta dishes, and you can order more traditional pizzas, which come out of a brick oven on the ground floor. My younger son pronounced the pepper-oni pizza the best he'd ever had (but remember, he was under the influence of being given crayons and an activity sheet and a take-home plastic cup). Service is decently prompt, and the kids' menu is smartly focused on pizza and pasta, including perfectly plain (no sauce) spaghetti and penne. I found the food tasted rather bland, light on salt and fat but heavy on scallions and vinegar. (Like in California, dude.) The black-and-yellow decor is clean and modern, neither beachy nor barlike, and the noise level is just right—we could hear one another talk but didn't feel self-conscious when the kids became exuberant. It's a middle-of-the-road option that comes in real handy.

China Fun. 250 E. 65th St. (at Second Ave.). ☎ **212/752-0810.** High chairs, boosters. Reservations accepted for parties of 6 or more only. Main courses $6.95–$13.95; noodles and rice $4.95–$7.95; dim sum 95¢–$4.95. AE, MC, V. Sun–Thurs 11am–midnight, Fri–Sat 11am–1am. Subway: 6 to 68th St. CHINESE.

Named after the Mandarin word for "noodle," China Fun lives up to the English sense of the word as well, being a bright and lively informal spot with an immense menu of Chinese standards. Crispy duck, noodle soups, and grilled sea bass are some of the standouts in the kitchen; service is efficient and pleasant, and there's enough clatter and bustle to absorb child ruckus. Like its West Side sibling (above), it's run by Shanghai-born, Taiwan-raised Dorothea Wu, a grand-niece of Chiang Kai-shek, and it's even kosher—go figure.

Comfort Diner. 142 E. 86th St. (at Lexington Ave.). ☎ **212/426-8600.** Kids' menu, high chairs, boosters. Reservations not accepted. Main courses $5.95–$13.95; kids' menu $4.95. DC, MC, V. Sun–Wed 8am–11pm, Thurs 8am–midnight, Fri–Sat 8am–2am. Subway: 4/5/6 to 86th St. AMERICAN DINER.

This branch of the kid-friendly Midtown diner (below) is in a prime Upper East Side family location. Diner standards like meat loaf and honey-dipped fried chicken are mixed with a few more 1990s dishes, like wild mushroom potato pancakes, a spinach portobello wrap, or a chicken pot pie with Southwestern accents such as black beans and jalapeños thrown in. Kid-friendly features include crayons for coloring at the booth and free ice cream for those who've cleaned their plates (and the waiters aren't too strict on the policy—if you didn't eat your crusts you may still qualify).

Flight 1668. 1668 Third Ave. (between 93rd and 94th sts.). ☎ **212/426-1416.** Boosters. Reservations not accepted. Main courses $5.95–$12.95. AE, MC, V. Mon–Wed 4pm–2am, Thurs–Fri 4pm–4am, Sat 11am–4am, Sun 11am–2am. Subway: 6 to 96th St. AMERICAN.

The aviation-themed decor is the chief draw for my second son, who couldn't take his eyes off the model biplane suspended from the high ceiling. Though the place has that dimly lit bar look, neighborhood families do come here in the early evening for the straightforward comfort food—pastas and burgers and curly fries topped with cheese, a house specialty. Hot dogs and chicken fingers are standard kid choices on the menu. Though it can get noisy as the evening wears on, it certainly feels like a grown-up place, a plus for older kids. There's a sister spot in Chelsea, Flight 151 (below), also named after the numbers in its address.

Jackson Hole. 1270 Madison Ave. (at 91st St.). ☎ **212/427-2820.** Booster seats. Reservations not accepted. Burgers and sandwiches $4.30–$10.90. AE, MC, V. Mon–Fri 7am–11pm, Sat 8am–11pm, Sun 8am–10pm. Subway: 4/5/6 to 86th St.; 6 to 96th St. AMERICAN/ BURGER.

The largest and sleekest of this chain's handful of Manhattan restaurants, the wood-trimmed Carnegie Hill branch of Jackson Hole deserves special mention because it's perpetually mobbed after 3pm with kids from the clutch of private schools nearby—Spence, Nightingale, Sacred Heart, St. David's, St. Bernard's, Lycée Française, and so on. The main thing here is the burgers, which are fat and luscious (prepare to wipe your child's chin), or is it the substantial french fries? The long list of grilled chicken sandwiches are pretty good, topped with whatever cheese or bacon or chili or salad items you want. No one rushes you and kids feel totally welcome.

John's Pizza. 408 E. 64th St. (between First and York aves.). ☎ **212/935-2895.** Reservations accepted for parties of 5 or more only. Pizzas $10–$13.50; pastas $6.50–$7.95. AE, MC, V. Daily 11:30am–11:30pm. Subway: 4/5/6 to 59th St. PIZZA.

The great Village pizzeria (below) has also opened this East Side branch for thin-crust, brick-oven pies, substantial green salads, and a few well-executed pasta dishes. The menu's limited enough so that every dish on it is delectable.

✪ Lexington Candy Shop. 1226 Lexington Ave. (at 83rd St.). ☎ **212/288-0057.** Boosters, sassy seats. Reservations not accepted. Main courses $3.95–$10.50. AE, DC, DISC, MC, V. Mon–Sat 7am–7pm, Sun 9am–6pm. Subway: 4/5/6 to 86th St. AMERICAN DINER.

Walking through the door of the Lexington Candy Shop is like passing through a time warp: Inside is a perfectly preserved old luncheonette that makes EJ's (above) look like Planet Hollywood. It's been around since 1925 and looks it. There's a counter with chrome-rimmed stools and a handful of wooden booths, where you can down creamy milk shakes and malteds, fresh lemonade, buttery grilled cheese sandwiches, super BLTs, outstanding cheeseburgers, and crinkle fries. And best of all, the staff seems to positively perk up when they see kids coming. The candy shop component doesn't consist of much more than a rack of Milky Ways and Hershey Bars just inside the door; the front window is also crammed full of stuffed animals for sale, which guarantees that my children never pass by without stopping. And I don't mind, because it's the sort of place that warms the cockles of my heart.

✪ LiLi's Noodle Shop and Grill. 1500 Third Ave. (between 84th and 85th sts.). **☎ 212/639-1313.** High chairs, boosters. Reservations accepted. Main courses $8–$15. AE, DC, MC, V. Sun–Thurs 11:30am–11:30pm, Fri–Sat 11:30am–12:30pm. Subway: 4/5/6 to 86th St. CHINESE.

My kids are big fans of this kind of noodle-shop/rotisserie food, and LiLi's is their favorite place for it. The food is delicately spiced and not too greasy, which is a feat considering how barbecue-roasted pork and chicken can be. We also like the noodle dishes, even plain lo mein; the soups come in enormous bowls and can be a challenge to finish, but the broth is light and flavorful, filled with fresh noodles and vegetables. Light varnished woods and streamlined shapes give the decor a smart, modern feel, and the service is efficient, casual, and friendly.

Mary Ann's. 1503 Second Ave. (between 78th and 79th sts.). **☎ 212/249-6165.** Kids' menu, high chairs, boosters. Reservations accepted weeknights for parties of 8 or more only. Main courses $5.25–$18.95. MC, V. Mon–Thurs noon–3pm and 5pm–midnight, Fri–Sat noon–4pm and 5pm–midnight, Sun noon–4pm and 5–10:30pm. Subway: 6 to 77th St. MEXICAN.

Mary Ann's on the East Side is fairly family-oriented, though I've heard complaints of occasional rudeness. The food is fresh and authentic and the atmosphere casual and down-to-earth.

Patsy's Pizzeria. 1312 Second Ave. (at 69th St.). **☎ 212/639-1000.** High chairs, boosters. Reservations not accepted. Pizzas $11.50–$13.50; pasta $7.95–$12.95. No credit cards. Sun–Thurs noon–11pm, Fri–Sat noon–midnight. Subway: 6 to 68th St. PIZZA.

Superb thin-crust pizza and wonderful filling pastas make this casual pizzeria a worthwhile destination for families. Though there's no kids' menu per se, smaller-sized pizzas and small portions of pasta make good kid options, so everybody can be satisfied with different choices from the menu.

Sassy's Sliders. 1530 Third Ave. (at 86th St.). **☎ 212/828-6900.** Reservations not accepted. Burgers 89¢–99¢. No credit cards. Mon–Thurs 11am–11pm, Fri–Sat 11am–1am, Sun noon–10pm. Subway: 4/5/6 to 86th St. BURGERS.

The decor is very 1950s—wall tiles, Formica tables, and linoleum, all in Fiestaware colors—and so is the fast-food concept: 2-inch hamburgers steamed with onions, so small and moist they slide whole down your throat, hence the name "sliders." I've personally been addicted to them ever since I was a kid going to White Castle, and I've turned my older son into a fan as well. But Sassy's Sliders are much better than White Castle's, and with other choices like grilled chicken, ground turkey, or veggie burgers as well, this nifty little spot should satisfy everyone in the family. The slider is a perfect-sized burger for a kid anyway, and at these incredibly low prices, you may be able to feed the whole gang for less than $20. Most of its business is takeout and delivery, but there are a few tables inside.

AFTERNOON TEA

Payard Patisserie. 1032 Lexington Ave. (between 73rd and 74th sts.). **☎ 212/717-5252.** Reservations recommended. Tea $16–$21; lunch $10–$24; dinner $23–$29. AE, CB, DC, DISC, MC, V. Tea served Mon–Sat 3:30–5pm. Subway: 6 to 77th St. FRENCH.

I'm always wary of dining establishments that post signs in the front windows advising patrons that strollers are not allowed. Considering the already high prices, that should rule out eating with kids at this elegant wood-paneled East Side pastry shop–cum–bistro. However, I'm willing to make an exception when it comes to afternoon tea, which is generally only for children who know how to dress up and behave. The prix-fixe teas entitle you to an array of mini-sandwiches, scones with jam, and other delicate little pastries, along with a pot of tea or coffee or hot chocolate. If that's too stuffy and formal, you can always buy pastries from the glass cases in front and eat them at the tiny cafe tables. Just don't bring your stroller.

ICE CREAM & SWEETS

Ciao Bella Café. 27 E. 92nd St. (at Madison Ave.). ☎ **212/831-5555.** No credit cards. Mon–Thurs 11:30am–9pm, Fri–Sun 11:30am–8pm. Subway: 6 to 96th St. ICE CREAM.

A favorite hangout for various private schools in the neighborhood, this simple pink-walled little spot has served hand-mixed cones to nearly every member of each school's student body. Gelato is the star, straight from Ciao Bella's SoHo factory. Fruit smoothies and a few food items are also available.

Peppermint Park. 1225 First Ave. (at 66th St.). ☎ **212/288-5054.** No credit cards. Mon–Thurs 11am–11pm, Fri 11am–1am, Sat 10am–1:30am, Sun 10am–11pm. Subway: 6 to 68th St. ICE CREAM.

The tiled floor and wrought-iron cafe tables give this place a sweetly old-fashioned air; the glass case full of luscious pastries is well-nigh irresistible to anyone with a sweet tooth. There is also a dinerlike selection of hot food, but the ice cream's the thing that draws birthday parties in the grade-school set.

THE CHAIN GANG

Besides the famous Carnegie Hill branch (above), there are two other **Jackson Hole** locations: 234 E. 64th St., between Second and Third avenues (☎ 212/371-7187), and 1611 Second Ave., at 84th Street (☎ **212/737-8788**). There's also a good-sized **Pizzeria Uno** at 220 E. 86th St., between Second and Third avenues (☎ **212/ 472-5656**), a **Dallas BBQ** at 1265 Third Ave., at 73rd Street (☎ 212/772-9393), and a **Chirping Chicken** at 1260 Lexington Ave., at 85th Street (☎ **212/ 517-9888**). You'll find one of the new-age wacky-tacky **Blockhead's Burritos** restaurants at 1563 Second Ave., between 81st and 82nd streets. (☎ **212/ 879-1999**).

4 Midtown

EXPENSIVE

Benihana. (1) 120 E. 56th St. (between Park and Lexington aves.). ☎ **212/593-1627.** Booster seats. Reservations recommended. Lunch $7.50–$14; dinner $15–$42. AE, CB, DC, DISC, MC, V. Sun–Thurs noon–11pm, Fri–Sat noon–midnight. Subway: 4/5/6 to 59th St.; E/F to Lexington Ave./Third Ave. (2) Benihana West. 47 W. 56th St. (between Fifth and Sixth aves.). ☎ **212/581-0930.** Sun–Thurs noon–11pm, Fri–Sat noon–midnight. Subway: B/Q to 57th St.; E/F to Fifth Ave. JAPANESE.

Watching the Benihana chefs at work with their flying knives, slicing and dicing the meat, seafood, and vegetables they'll grill on the teppanyaki right at your table, is always quite a show. As far as Japanese food goes, this doesn't require as adventurous a palate as, say, sushi does, so it's a good choice for kids—not to mention the awesome thrill of watching these kitchen samurai at work. For adults, the grilled food is a decent nongreasy option; the portions looked a little small to me, but I felt perfectly full afterward. What with the minimalist decor and the low tables, kids may feel they're getting an exotic Eastern experience, though this operation is slickly tourist-oriented, and, truth to tell, the chefs look pretty bored with their work. You wouldn't want to come here every night, but it's an interesting one-night stand.

Mickey Mantle's. 42 Central Park South (between Fifth and Sixth aves.). ☎ **212/ 688-7777.** Kids' menu, high chairs, boosters. Reservations recommended. Main courses $11.95–$25; kids' menu $8.95. AE, CB, DC, DISC, MC, V. Mon–Fri 11:30pm–1am, Sat 9am–1am, Sun 10am–midnight. Subway: N/R to Fifth Ave. AMERICAN.

Young fanatics hungering for a brush with athletic celebrity may not get the point of this sleek blond-wood sports shrine owned by the late great baseball star Mickey Mantle: Among the many autographed jerseys displayed on the walls are those of Ted Williams, Hank Aaron, Stan Musial, Yogi Berra, and Joe DiMaggio, guys I recognize from my brother's baseball cards back in the days when they gave you bubble gum with your cards. Oh, yeah, there's a Shaquille O'Neal autographed basketball, but who's this Johnny Unitas whose name is scrawled on the football next to it?

If all your junior leaguer is interested in is big-name memorabilia, go to the Official All Star Café (see below); if, however, your family is looking for a smart, friendly, casual restaurant that takes pride in its food, come here. A couple of upscale dishes like grilled swordfish, herb-roasted chicken, and wild mushroom ravioli grace the menu, but most of it is studiedly down-home; Mick's own picks include chicken fried steak, Texas barbecued ribs, and grilled sirloin chili with blue-corn tortillas. The Little League menu has the usual range of chicken fingers, grilled cheese, spaghetti, and burgers. Dig the Scooter Pie sundae. TV monitors everywhere are usually tuned to some sports event, and oil paintings of baseball players festoon the walls of the quieter, carpeted back room.

Official All Star Café. 1540 Broadway (at 45th St.), 2nd floor. ☎ **212/840-8326.** Reservations accepted for parties of 20 or more only. Main courses $10.95–$19.95. Daily 11am–midnight. AE, DC, DISC, MC, V. Subway: 1/2/3/7/9/N/Q/R/S to Times Square. AMERICAN DINER.

It's owned by Joe Montana, Ken Griffey Jr., Wayne Gretzky, Andre Agassi, Monica Seles, Tiger Woods, and Shaquille O'Neal, and if you have to ask who these people are, then this isn't the place for you. Projection screens play videos of these athletes' days of glory, while big TVs play current sports events; diners sit in booths that resemble giant baseball mitts; à la Planet Hollywood (same designer, same part-owner), the stars' personal memorabilia are on display, including Agassi's chopped-off ponytail and the first backboard Shaq ever shattered. Each owner has chosen a favorite dish for the menu—Gretzky's is steak and Agassi's is red-sauce spaghetti—and there are 51 kinds of burgers and 5 kinds of hot dogs (each from a different ballpark). Big portions and lotsa distractions make this an overwhelming place to treat a young sports fan.

Planet Hollywood. 140 W. 57th St. (between Sixth and Seventh aves.). ☎ **212/333-7827.** Reservations not accepted. Main courses $8–$21. AE, CB, DC, DISC, MC, V. Daily 11am–midnight. Subway: B/N/R/Q to 57th St. CALIFORNIAN.

As a tribute to movies—make that late 20th-century movies—this blockbuster theme restaurant scores more on noise and razzle-dazzle than it does on substance. The walls are covered with props and costume items donated by movie-star pals of the owners (Stallone and Willis are the marquee names attached), though the vaguely whacked-out decor looks more like outer space than it does like Tinseltown. *Beware:* Skittish youngsters may find it hard to eat with a stuffed Chewbacca from *Star Wars*, Freddy Krueger's sweater and claw, and the Terminator's ripped-open bionic head looming nearby.

There's a movie trivia quiz on the placemats to entertain you while you wait for service, after you've waited on the sidewalk and then in the bar area to get in. The

Midtown Dining

America **71**
Angelo's Coal Oven Pizza **35**
Bagelry **63**
Bendix Diner **29**
Benihana **39**
Benihana West **38**
Blockhead's Burritos **12 45 62**
Burger Heaven **41 43 48 54**
Café SFA **47**
Carmine's **18**
Carnegie Deli **5**
Chat 'n' Chew **73**
Chelsea Market food court **31**
China Fun **9**
Chirping Chicken **66**
Citicorp Building food court **42**
Comfort Diner **52**
Cupcake Café **24**
Duke's **69**
Ellen's Stardust Diner **11**
Empire Diner **27**
ESPN Zone **22**
Ess-a-Bagel **44 67**
Flight 151 **30**
42nd Street food court **23**
Friend of a Farmer **72**
Great American Health
   Bar **37**
H&H Bagels **15**
Hamburger Harry's **49**
Hard Rock Café **2**

Jackson Hole **60**
Jekyll & Hyde Club **36**
John's Pizza **17**
Kosher Delight **51 56**
La Bonne Soupe **40**
Le Gamin **28**
Mangia e Bevi **8**
Manhattan Chili Company **7 21**
Manhattan Mall food court **57**
Mars 2112 **10**
Mary Ann's **32**
Mickey Mantle's **33**
Miss Rita's **26**
Official All Star Café **16**
Ollie's Noodle Shop **19**
Palm Court **34**
Patsy's Pizzeria **61**
Pick a Bagel **1 65 70**
Planet Hollywood **3**
Rock Center Café **46**
Rodeo Grill **64**
Route 66 **4**
Ruby Foo's **13**
Stage Deli **6**
The T Salon **68**
Tennessee Mountain at
 Times Square **50**
Texas Texas Restaurant and
 Saloon **14**
Virgil's Real Barbecue **53**
Won Jo **59**
WWF New York **20**

Subway stop Ⓜ

menu has a California bias, but this being a theme restaurant, it's big on burgers; other popular choices are Cajun chicken breast, Cobb salad, grilled Tuscan chicken sandwich, Caesar salad, and barbecued pork sandwich. There's a long list of no-alcohol cocktails with cutesy names like Total Recall, Home Alone, and Ace Ventura. You can't deny that this place has a buzz about it.

😊 **Rock Center Café.** 20 W. 50th St. (at Rockefeller Center). ☎ **212/332-7620.** Kids' menu, high chairs. Reservations recommended, especially for lunch. Lunch $14–$28; dinner $15–$28; kids' menu $8.95. AE, CB, DC, MC, V. Mon–Fri 7:30am–10pm, Sat 10am–10pm, Sun 10am–9pm. Subway: B/D/F/Q to 47th–50th sts./Rockefeller Center. ITALIAN.

If it weren't at Ground Zero in Midtown, this restaurant might have cause to be snooty about children, with its sleek mahogany-trimmed contemporary decor and upscale Italian food (stylish pastas, roasted chicken, frittatas, fish, and steak). But as they say in the real estate biz, location is everything, and this location couldn't be more of a tourist magnet: set right on the lower plaza of Rockefeller Plaza, where you can watch the ice-skaters in winter and sit out under Prometheus in summer. (And if that isn't enough of a thrill, you can ride a tiny glass-enclosed elevator down from sidewalk level to the restaurant.) Where tourists flock, there are bound to be children, and the Rock Center Café has shrewdly decided to make the most of them with a decent children's menu—chicken tenders, handmade penne pasta, and a grilled cheese made with fontina cheese on Italian bread. Everything about this place spells Special Event.

Ruby Foo's. 1626 Broadway (at 49th St.). ☎ **212/489-5600.** High chairs, boosters. Reservations recommended. Lunch $20–$25; dinner $30–$35 (average per person, including drinks). AE, DISC, MC, V. Sun–Thurs 11:30am–midnight, Fri–Sat 11:30am–1am. Subway: 1/9 to 50th St. CHINESE/JAPANESE/PAN-ASIAN.

This Theater District location of the Asian-themed restaurant is good for special events—the decor is as stunning as a movie set, the food precisely presented, the whole atmosphere trendily abuzz. The menu ranges all over Asia, with dim sum, sushi, hand rolls, and Thai curries. Best for older kids who can appreciate the setting and are willing to sample exotic dishes.

MODERATE

Café SFA. In Saks Fifth Avenue, 611 Fifth Ave. (between 49th and 50th sts.), 8th floor. ☎ 212/940-4080. Kids' menu, high chairs, boosters. Reservations accepted for parties of 5 or more only. Main courses $8–$15; afternoon tea $18.50; kids' menu $5.25–$8. AE, DC, DISC, MC, V. Tues–Sat 11am–5pm (Thurs until 7pm), Sun noon–5pm. Subway: E/F to Fifth Ave.; B/D to Rockefeller Center. ECLECTIC.

Many things recommend this department store cafe for lunch or afternoon tea: its high-floor views over Rockefeller Center and St. Patrick's (insist on a window table), the harpist playing weekdays 3 to 5pm, and the smart kids' menu—soup and sandwich, miniburgers, a hot dog, or a peanut-butter-and-jelly sandwich, with a choice of drinks that includes chocolate milk. Grown-ups will feel very ladies-who-lunch-ish with selections like grilled salmon, turkey club, Cobb salad, a portobello focaccia sandwich, and an asparagus-and-mushroom risotto. The decor is thick-carpeted and pleasant, with golden hues and mahogany-stained wood trim. Just one bit of advice: If you've got older boys, steer to the right when you step off the elevator, because you'll be walking through the ladies' lingerie department—better for them to see the negligees than the bras and garter belts.

Carmine's. 200 W. 44th St. (between Seventh and Eighth aves.). ☎ 212/221-3800. High chairs, boosters. Reservations after 6pm accepted for parties of 6 or more only. Family-style main courses (serve 2–3 people) $14–$46. AE, MC, V. Sun–Mon 11:30am–11pm, Tues–Sat 11:30am–midnight. Subway: 1/2/3/9/N/R/S to Times Square. ITALIAN.

Northern Italian, and lots of it. Family-style dinners make this a natural if you're eating out with kids, especially if yours are the kind that suck up spaghetti with gusto. The noisy, casual atmosphere absorbs a lot of tantrums, and service is prompt (if you can't move customers in and out quickly in the Theater District, you're done for). The original branch is on the Upper West Side (above).

Carnegie Deli. 854 Seventh Ave. (between 54th and 55th sts.). ☎ **212/757-2245.** High chairs, boosters. Reservations recommended. Breakfast $2.95–11.95; sandwiches and main courses $6.45–$19.95. No credit cards. Daily 6:30am–3:30am. Subway: B/D/E to Seventh Ave. DELI.

A classic delicatessen restaurant, straight out of Woody Allen's *Broadway Danny Rose*, the Carnegie Deli may borrow its name from nearby Carnegie Hall, but the atmosphere is anything but refined and stuffy. Every table has a little bowl of crisp dill pickles on it, and the sandwiches are piled so high you can hardly get your mouth around them—corned beef, pastrami, brisket, chopped liver, the works, with Russian dressing the condiment of choice. You can also get kosher dairy dishes like blintzes and pirogue and matzoh brei, or Eastern European home-cooking like chicken paprikash, Hungarian goulash, and stuffed cabbage. The menu is as huge as the servings. Ya wanna know what New York was like in the 1940s and 1950s? Come here, order an egg cream, borscht, or gefilte fish, and schmooze away.

✪ Ellen's Stardust Diner. 1650 Broadway (at 51st St.). ☎ **212/956-5151.** High chairs, boosters. Breakfast $3.95–$6.95; sandwiches and tapas $8.25; main courses $6.95–$13.95. AE, DC, DISC, MC, V. Sun–Thurs 7:30am–midnight, Fri–Sat 7:30am–1am. Subway: 1/9 to 50th St. AMERICAN DINER/ECLECTIC.

This *Happy Days*-style diner is a block from my husband's office and it's our kids' hands-down favorite place to eat when we visit Dad at work. Enter through what looks like a vintage red subway car and you're in a nostalgic time warp—streamlined chrome trim, turquoise vinyl and Formica, vintage movie posters and ads, and a wall full of subway posters introducing a bevy of Miss Subways (owner Ellen Hart was herself voted Miss Subways in 1959). But what my kids like best are the model train zipping around on an elevated track above our heads and the TV monitors showing *Ed Sullivan* segments. The food—your basic grab bag of burgers and fries/salads/omelets/tacos/sandwiches—tastes decent and comes in good-sized portions; Nick at Niters may get a kick out of the cutesy names for menu items, like Fred Mertz-arella Sticks or the Cesar Romero Salad. The wait staff is super-congenial, and Wednesday through Saturday nights they even sing, as part of a slightly goofy dinner-hour floor show my sons haven't stopped talking about since they witnessed it.

ESPN Zone. 1472 Broadway (at 42nd St.). ☎ **212/921-3776.** Kids' menu, high chairs, boosters. Reservations not accepted. Sandwiches $5.25–$10.95; main courses $10.95–$21.95; kids' menu $5.25. AE, DISC, MC, V. Mon–Fri 11:30am–11pm, Sat–Sun 11am–1am. Subway: 1/2/3/9 to 42nd St. AMERICAN.

It's definitely a theme-restaurant scene, with a line out front, a gift shop, multiple floors, an arcade upstairs, and big-screen TVs putting sports in your face everywhere you turn. But the streamlined blond-wood decor is not too cluttered, the noise level is tolerable, smokers are segregated to their own floor, and the menu offers a decent range of standard dishes, with some salads and lighter food amid all the fried stuff that kids and jock types are expected to love. Meat is, however, a linchpin of the menu: steaks, ribs, chops, pot roast, cheese steak, burgers, barbecued chicken, along with tailgate-party-worthy appetizers like chicken wings, queso chips, and cheese fries. Though the kids' menu is pretty standard, there are two unusual items—corn dogs and sliders (mini-hamburgers)—and maybe the best thing about the place is that the children's menu comes in a Viewmaster that you can hold up to the light and read at your table. That alone made it worth the visit for my kids.

Hard Rock Café. 221 W. 57th St. (between Broadway and Seventh Ave.). ☎ **212/489-6565.** Reservations accepted for parties of 20 or more only. Main courses $7.95–$13.50. AE, DC, DISC, MC, V. Daily 11:30am–midnight (open Wed & Sat at 11am; open Fri–Sat until 2am). Subway: N/R to 57th St.; B/D/E to Seventh Ave. AMERICAN/BURGERS.

Looking like it was rear-ended by a Cadillac, this brassy burger joint promotes its rock-and-roll theme with such memorabilia as a pair of John Lennon's wire-rims with a cracked lens, a broken guitar used in Nirvana's *Smells Like Teen Spirit* video, and a rhinestone-studded jumpsuit actually worn by Elvis. Various trippy 1960s slogans pepper the place, scripted in neon or proclaimed on posters, but the target audience isn't baby boomers nostalgic for Woodstock: It's teenagers, who regard the place as a museum of their parents' goofy past. Despite its lowbrow Disneyland-ish cachet, the Hard Rock is really not an awful restaurant; the burgers and milk shakes are perfectly fine, the prices aren't out of sight, and there's something infectious about the blaring rock soundtrack. And if you've got teenagers in tow, the fact that the place is packed with callow teenagers might even be a plus. (Unless, of course, your teenager is too sophisticated for the place already.)

Jekyll & Hyde Club. 1409 Sixth Ave. (near 57th St.). ☎ **212/541-9505.** Reservations accepted for parties of 15 or more only. Main courses $7.95–$17.95. AE, DC, DISC, MC, V. Daily 11:30am–midnight (open Wed at 11am, Fri–Sat at 10:30am). Subway: B/Q to 57th St. AMERICAN.

My young kids are terrified of this place—I can barely get them to walk past the entrance, where ghoulish skull heads dangle and there are always throngs of older kids lined up, dying to get in. Other theme restaurants have staid display cases full of memorabilia; Jekyll & Hyde delivers a thrill-ride experience, from the crashing ceiling in the vestibule to the creepy artwork that stares back at you from the walls. The waiters all look decked out for Halloween, and there's a continual floor show of ghastly figures telling even ghastlier jokes. The food is somewhat beside the point, but for the record I'll tell you that they serve popcorn shrimp, pizzas, veggie burgers, baby-back ribs, and more; you can choose between the smaller Batty Burger or the Monster Burger, which comes topped with the works. The kitchen's general strategy seems to be to smother things with cheese if at all possible and to grill anything that's grillable.

✪ La Bonne Soupe. 48 W. 55th St. (between Fifth and Sixth aves.). ☎ **212/586-7650.** Kids' menu, seat cushions. Reservations recommended in winter. Main courses $8.95–$19.25; kids' menu $9.25. AE, CB, DC, MC, V. Mon–Sat 11:30am–midnight, Sun 11:30am–11pm. Subway: B/Q to 57th St. FRENCH.

One rainy Sunday we left the Museum of Modern Art, all five of us starving, not knowing where to go for lunch. (Yes, it happens to us, too.) We wandered into La Bonne Soupe simply because there wasn't much else open nearby on a Sunday, and it was one of the pleasantest discoveries we ever made. This is a cozy, charming bistro, French but not snooty, which truly welcomes *les enfants*. The quiches are splendid, as is the onion soup gratinee, and there are a few fine fondue dishes (talk about throwbacks). Omelets, salads, and filet mignon fill out the menu. My kids ordered from the kids' menu *steak haché*—a.k.a. chopped steak, a.k.a. hamburger—and were astonished when it arrived with no bun and no ketchup. But the accommodating waitress quickly sliced up French bread and discovered some ketchup in the kitchen, and, *voilà!* we were all set. There are two floors, the lower one softly lit and paneled, the upper floor with a cheery look more like an Alpine chalet, checkered tablecloths and all. Service isn't speedy, but it's pleasant, and no one minded when my daughter vanished under the table for while. A very delightful change of pace.

Mangia e Bevi. 800 Ninth Ave. (at 53rd St.). ☎ **212/956-3976.** Booster seats, high chairs. Reservations for 4 or more only. Main courses $8.95–$16.95. AE, DC, DISC, MC, V. Mon–Sat noon–midnight, Sun noon–11pm. Subway: C/E to 50th St. ITALIAN.

Graffiti-ish murals outside do their best to stop traffic on Ninth Avenue, drawing customers to this hearty Italian restaurant on the western edge of Midtown. *Boisterous* is the word to describe what goes on inside, with the small tables crammed together and speakers pouring out standard Italian music (we actually heard *O Sole Mio*). The decor is pointedly rustic, with rough white plaster, wood trim, and red-checkered tablecloths, though no true Adriatic taverna would cover the tablecloth with paper and give diners Crayolas to color with. But the southern Italian food is up to the most sophisticated Manhattan standards—truly marvelous gourmet pastas, grilled seafood, and some of the best bruschetta I've ever tasted. Many pasta dishes are available in half orders to suit small appetites, but my three kids shared a pizza with a divinely thin, crispy crust and big splatters of fresh mozzarella, plenty big enough for three. Our waiter was a tad sullen but totally efficient, and everybody in the restaurant seemed delighted to have the kids there, even our 20- and 30-something fellow diners, who thought our dimply baby daughter was cute (if they only knew . . .).

○ Mars 2112. 1633 Broadway (at 51st St.). ☎ **212/582-2112.** www.mars2112.com. Kids' menu, high chairs, boosters. Reservations not accepted. Main courses $9.95–$24.95; kids' menu $8.95. AE, DC, DISC, MC, V. Mon–Thurs 11:30am–10pm, Fri 11:30–midnight, Sat 11am–midnight, Sun 11am–10pm. Subway: 1/9 to 50th St. ECLECTIC.

A visit here is truly a treat for kids. The sci-fi theme is carried out with real imagination: You enter through a simulator that gives guests an "interplanetary ride" to the lower-level restaurant (never fear, skittish kids and pregnant women can enter through a back door instead), and the restaurant itself looks like a cavernous subterranean mining colony, weirdly lit with futuristic trappings. You can watch intraspace broadcasts on a giant screen, and a staff member dressed as a Martian circulates among the tables, greeting guests in a very nonthreatening manner. The kids' menu offers standard pizza, pasta, chicken fingers, and burgers, but the adult menu has a nice Californian/Asian spin, stuff like pepper-crusted tuna steak and pork roast confit and a thin-crust pizza with roasted chicken and pesto (what's more, these fussy fusion dishes actually come out tasting pretty good). I'd call this a total entertainment experience rather than a theme restaurant; my kids just call it a blast and beg to go back.

Tennessee Mountain at Times Square. 121 W. 45th St. (between Sixth and Seventh aves.). ☎ **212/869-4545.** Kids' menu, boosters, sassy seats. Reservations recommended. Main courses $6.50–$16.95; kids' menu $4.25–$5.95. AE, CB, MC, V. Mon–Sat 11:30am–11:30pm, Sun 11:30am–10pm. Subway: 1/2/3/9/N/R to Times Square; B/D/F/Q to 42nd St. AMERICAN/BARBECUE.

Going head-to-head with Virgil's (below) a block away, Tennessee Mountain brings its Southern-style cooking all the way up north from SoHo to the newly family-friendly precincts of Times Square. The barbecued ribs and chicken don't match Virgil's for authentic flavor, but Tennessee Mountain has the edge in catering to

Pizza Etiquette

Pizza by the slice is a ubiquitous New York food that's a real life-saver when you're out and about with kids. Most kids, even picky eaters, like pizza, and between the tomato sauce and the cheese, it actually makes a fairly well-balanced meal. Sometimes it seems there's a narrow little neighborhood pizzeria on every corner here, though of course when you really need one you may not find one for blocks.

Several pizza dynasties have contended for superiority for nearly a century now; the oldest, **Lombardi's** (see Little Italy), declared its coal-oven pizzas the best, but the brick-oven pies at **John's Pizza** in Greenwich Village and **Patsy's Pizzeria** up in East Harlem drew an equal number of supporters. The mid-1990s saw a sudden expansion of both John's and Patsy's, with branches being opened all over town (see Greenwich Village, the Upper West Side, the Upper East Side, and Midtown); surprisingly enough, they've maintained a high level of quality and are well worth a visit. But these are real pizza restaurants, where you sit down and order a whole pie; the sort of storefront spot that sells pizza by the slice is another thing altogether.

The overwhelming majority of pizza places in New York have the name *Ray* somewhere in the title: Famous Ray's, World Famous Ray's, Famous Original Ray's, Original Ray's, Ray's Famous, Ray's House of Pizza, Ray's Real Pizza. Most of these are trying to cash in on the enormous success of **Famous Ray's Pizza of Greenwich Village** (see Greenwich Village), where you'll often have to stand in line just to buy a slice to go. In most neighborhood pizzerias, a single slice of plain cheese pizza will cost between $1.50 and $2.50, with higher prices for additional toppings.

Most New Yorkers eat pizza without utensils, which can be pretty hard if the crust is nice and thin and the tomato sauce suitably runny. The New York solution: Fold the triangular slice in half lengthwise, hold it by the thick end, and eat it like a sandwich from the narrow end up. Younger kids may need to have their pizza cut up, which is tricky when you're sawing away on a thin paper plate with a plastic knife. Try slicing it into long triangular strips.

families, with a sizable kids' menu offering lots of non-barbecue items like chicken fingers and grilled cheese; the adult menu ranges as far afield as quiche and salads. The laid-back informality of the SoHo original may be compromised somewhat in the pretheater rush, but it's still an easygoing place where families comfortably chow down in Midtown.

Texas Texas Restaurant and Saloon. 1600 Broadway (at 48th St.). ☎ **212/956-7427.** Kids' menu, high chairs, boosters. Reservations recommended. Main courses $10–$25. AE, CB, DC, MC, V. Mon–Thurs 11:30am–midnight, Fri–Sat 11:30am–1am, Sun noon–11:30pm. Subway: 1/9 to 50th St. AMERICAN/BARBECUE.

The fare at this handy Times Square spot—predominantly ribs and chicken, with some burgers and salads and sandwiches thrown in for good measure—is better than you'd expect, with good fresh bread and crisp coleslaw (never mind the unnaturally yellow corn on the cob). The barbecue sauce may not be authentic, but it's neither sugary nor too thick, and there are plenty of nonbarbecued choices as well. The choices on the kids' menu are predictable (burgers, chicken fingers) but taste more than decent, with very good ungreasy french fries. Big, well-lit, and clean, the place has friendly, helpful waiters and a Western-themed decor that's not too hokey, plus large picture windows to take in the Broadway razzle-dazzle.

◐ Virgil's Real Barbecue. 152 W. 44th St. (between Broadway and Sixth Ave.). ☎ **212/921-9494.** Kids' menu, high chairs, boosters. Reservations recommended. Main courses $11.95–$17.95; kids' menu $5.95. AE, DC, MC, V. Mon 11:30am–11pm, Tues–Sat 11:30am–midnight, Sun 11:30am–10pm. Subway: 1/2/3/7/9/N/R/S to Times Square. AMERICAN/BARBECUE.

Your cutlery is wrapped in a maroon hand towel atop the plastic tablecloth, which tells you all you need to know about Virgil's—this is barbecue, and you're expected to get messy eating it. Along with the wood-smoked barbecued specialties, you get sides of down-home stuff like turnip greens, a slaw made with mustard greens, and buttery cornbread, as well as more mainstream choices like french fries and coleslaw for folks whose home isn't below the Mason-Dixon line. Kids who can't handle ribs are offered some safer choices like grilled cheese and hot dogs. The decor is roadhouse chic, with polished wood paneling, ceiling fans, and a clutter of vintage livestock photos. Casual and friendly as it is, Virgil's has a postmodern self-consciousness—come on, that wood pile inside the front door is not there just to stoke the barbecue. But you might as well play along with the game when the food is this good, this hearty, this authentic.

Won Jo. 23 W. 32nd St. (between Broadway and Fifth Ave.). ☎ **212/695-5815.** High chairs. Reservations recommended. Main courses $9.95–$18.95. AE, MC, V. Daily 24 hours. Subway. B/D/F/N/Q/R to 34th St. KOREAN.

Skip the Japanese sushi bar downstairs and head straight upstairs for do-it-yourself barbecue, Korean style. Each of the wooden tables has a small built-in grill and you choose what you want to grill on it—beef, pork, chicken, or mushrooms. The result is food that can be as simple as you want it and an experience that's fun for kids (the same kids who'd be bored to death watching you cook at home). Just make sure they're old enough to refrain from burning themselves on the grill. Other Korean specialties are kimchee (pickled vegetables), a variety of buckwheat noodle dishes, and broiled fish. There are a lot of authentic Korean restaurants in the immediate vicinity, but this one's a standout.

WWF New York. 1501 Broadway (at 43rd St.). ☎ **212/398-0893.** Kids' menu, high chairs, boosters. Reservations accepted for parties of 20 or more only. Main courses $14.95–$31.95; kids' menu $5.25–$7.25. AE, DC, DISC, MC, V. Sun–Fri 11:30am–midnight, Sat 11am–1am. Subway: 1/2/3/9 to 42nd St. AMERICAN.

The restaurant of choice for fourth- and fifth-grade boys these days, simply because it celebrates the goofy world of pro wrestling and its dubious celebrities. Like it or not, you may want to come here just to score big points with the kids. It doesn't pretend to be anything other than what it is: The smell of fried food hits you as you thread your way through the gift shop to the restaurant downstairs. The cafe itself has a forbidding prisonlike aura, with rock music pounding, tables harshly spotlit, and chain-link fences separating dining areas; you can't get away from the big-screen TVs endlessly showing wrestling matches. The menu is oriented toward the high-cholesterol end of things, with steaks and veal chops and burgers (an appetizer of hot crab slammers, corn fritters, and fried okra would help anybody bulk up to heavyweight class), though there are pizzas, pastas, and salads as well (including a crispy fried chicken salad with bacon and cheddar cheese—they just can't resist adding the artery-clogging stuff, can they?). To quote one of my son's most cool-dude friends, "Never, never, never, never buy anything in the gift shop there because it's really, really, really, *really* expensive." So I guess this joint qualifies as an educational experience after all.

INEXPENSIVE

Angelo's Coal Oven Pizza. 117 W. 57th St. (between Sixth and Seventh aves.). ☎ 212/333-4333. Pizzas $11.50–$17; main courses $8.95–$36.95 (family-style). AE, MC, V. Mon–Thurs 11am–11pm, Fri–Sat 11am–midnight, Sun 11:30pm–11pm. Subway: B/N/Q/R to 57th St.; B/D/E to Seventh Ave. ITALIAN/PIZZA.

Yet another claimant to the title of New York's most authentic pizza, with ties to the much-disputed Patsy's dynasty, Angelo's (which is actually run by Angelo's nephew, John) is an upscale two-level pizzeria dishing up crisp thin-crust pies as well as calzones, salads, and pastas, which can be ordered in family-sized servings to share. The look of the place is old-world, with wood trim, green marble-topped tables, and parchment yellow walls; you can't get a single slice of pizza here, but you can get a superb cannoli. I still wouldn't rate it as high as John's (see below), but it's certainly fine traditional pizza, not a bad choice for a Midtown meal.

China Fun. 1653 Broadway (at 51st St.). ☎ 212/333-2622. High chairs, boosters. Reservations accepted for parties of 6 or more only. Main courses $6.95–$14.95; noodles and rice $4.25–$8.25; dim sum 95¢–$4.95. AE, MC, V. Sun–Thurs 11am–midnight, Fri–Sat 11am–1am. Subway: 1/9 to 50th St. CHINESE.

Our kids like this place because it's clean, fast, and friendly, and the chunky grilled chicken sticks are so yummy (not to mention the steamed broccoli, the roast pork, and the rice). We parents like it because, well, it's clean, fast, friendly, and not too expensive, and our kids will actually eat the food here with no fuss. The Midtown spot's less stylish than the uptown branch; with plain light-wood tables and chairs, room-length mirrors, and a lobster tank in the back, it looks only a notch better than a fast-food outlet. But the food's a lot healthier than fast food, and the table service is prompt and reliable. While Ollie's and LiLi's (earlier in this chapter) have slightly better roasted meats, China Fun is still tasty, and it's an especially welcome option for the Theater District. We often come here before a movie or a show, and always manage to get in and out in well under an hour.

Comfort Diner. 214 E. 45th St. (between Second and Third aves.). ☎ 212/867-4555. Kids' menu, high chairs, boosters. Reservations not accepted. Main courses $5.95–$13.95; kids' menu $4.95. AE, DC, MC, V. Mon–Fri 7:30am–11pm, Sat–Sun 9am–11pm. Subway: 4/5/6/7/S to Grand Central. AMERICAN DINER.

This is a great place to know about if you're visiting the U.N. or if you're suburbanites on your way into or out of Grand Central. The Comfort Diner certainly lives up to its name, with generous portions of satisfying diner classics—macaroni-and-cheese, open-faced hot turkey sandwich, chili, tuna melt, BLT, and burgers, as well as a substantial breakfast menu served all day. The clean, cheery look is classic too, with booths and banquettes and a long chrome-trimmed counter with stools; you almost expect the waitress to call you "honey." Service is quick and kids are welcomed, with a joke-laden menu they can color and good-bye prizes "for good eaters." The kids' menu is wonderfully sensible, with PB&J, a pancake, buttered noodles ("with no green stuff"), and a tuna fish sandwich along with the usual burger/grilled cheese/macaroni-and-cheese stuff. Somebody running this place must have young children. Brunch, served weekends 9am to 4pm, is popular with families.

Cupcake Café. 522 Ninth Ave. (at 39th St.). ☎ 212/465-1530. Reservations not accepted. Breakfast and lunch under $5.75. No credit cards. Mon–Fri 7am–7pm, Sat 8am–7pm, Sun 9am–5pm. Subway: A/C/E to 42nd St. BAKERY.

The menu here is extremely limited: a couple of soups, slices of quiche, and waffles on weekends, plus a selection of bakery items like muffins, bagels, doughnuts, and tray after tray of beautiful, mouth-watering cupcakes. The setting is so grungy it's hip, with worn wood floors, a pressed-tin ceiling, and about half a dozen small bare tables for customers to sit at; signs on the glass pastry cases are handwritten on paper plates. The clientele is very cutting edge ("Daddy, why is that man's hair green? And why does he have an earring in his tongue?") and yet perfectly friendly and laid-back. When my stubborn toddler planted herself right in front of the front door, not one person in the steady stream of customers coming in or out failed to smile as they stepped around her. A good offbeat choice for a quick, cheap breakfast or lunch, especially if you've got older kids who're dying to be cool.

Hamburger Harry's. 145 W. 45th St. (between Broadway and Sixth Ave.). ☎ **212/ 840-0566.** Booster seats. Reservations accepted for parties of 6 or more only. Main courses $7.50–$15.95. AE, MC, V. Mon–Thurs 11:30am–11pm, Fri–Sat 11:30am–11:30pm. Subway: 1/2/3/7/9/N/R/S to Times Square. BURGERS.

This handy Midtown restaurant is more upscale than your typical burger joint, with dark blue walls and light-wood floors, tables, and chairs. Its hearty 7-ounce hamburgers are mesquite-grilled, which is no longer the newest foodie craze but still tastes awfully good; the menu veers into other territory as well, with burritos, barbecued ribs, and even Cajun catfish, and non–meat eaters may find some refreshing options, like the Mexican sandwich (tortilla stuffed with cheese, guacamole, sour cream, and salsa) or the veggie burger with melted cheddar and sprouts. The burgers come with curly fries, which somehow taste very exotic to young palates. Coloring the placemat helps keep youngsters occupied, and the bustling, casual atmosphere feels very comfortable.

۞ John's Pizza. 260 W. 44th St. (between Broadway and Eighth Ave.). ☎ **212/391-7560.** High chairs, boosters. Reservations not accepted. Pizzas $11–$14.50; pastas $7–$10.50. AE, DISC, MC, V. Daily 11:30am–11:30pm. Subway: 1/2/3/9/N/R to Times Square; A/C/E to 42nd St. PIZZA.

As good as all the John's branches are, this one deserves special mention because it fills such a need in the Theater District for a quick, unpretentious, fabulous meal. The simple white-walled space is stunning too, a two-story dining room converted from a church, with a stained-glass dome in its upper reaches. Pizzas slide out of the brick ovens with incredibly thin, crisp crusts; the satisfying green salads are huge enough for two to split, and the stuffed homemade rolls are a special treat. Okay, so they don't take reservations, but even in the height of the pretheater crush, you might wait 20 minutes at most for a table, and service is prompt enough to get you out again before your curtain. It's too good to be true.

۞ Manhattan Chili Company. (1) 500 Broadway (at 43rd St.). ☎ **212/730-8666.** Kids' menu, high chairs, boosters. Reservations recommended. Main courses $9.95–$14.95; salads and sandwiches $4.95–$10.95; kids' menu $5.50. AE, DISC, MC, V. Sun–Mon 11:30am–11pm, Tues–Sat 11:30am–midnight. Subway: 1/2/3/7/9/N/R/S to Times Square. (2) 1697 Broadway (between 53rd and 54th sts.). ☎ **212/246-6555.** Sun–Mon 11:30am–11pm, Tues–Sat 11:30am–midnight. Subway: 1/9 to 50th St.; B/D/E to Seventh Ave. AMERICAN/MEXICAN/TEX-MEX.

This bright and busy little Times Square restaurant welcomes kids with open arms, which is smart as can be considering it's right around the corner from the New Victory Theater and the Warner Bros. Studio Store. (The Broadway location is downstairs from the Ed Sullivan Theater, where the *Late Show with David Letterman* is taped Monday through Friday.) The day we went, it was crowded with lunching office workers, yet my 5-year-old still felt totally at home, thanks to the friendly, attentive staff. There are two colorful cartoon murals of the city on the side walls, one of which is reproduced in the paper placemat they give kids to color—my son thought that was really cool. Kids who aren't chili eaters still have plenty of choices; I like the kids' menu because it includes grilled veggies as well as the standards. My chili was spicy and slightly bitter (heavy on the cumin), which I liked a lot as soon as my palate got accustomed to it, but besides the 11 chili varieties there are lots of fajitas, quesadillas, nachos, and even a few burgers for those who don't like Mexican. Noisy, festive, and clean as a whistle, this is definitely one of your better choices around Times Square.

Ollie's Noodle Shop. 200B W. 44th St. (between Seventh and Eighth aves.). ☎ 212/921-5988. High chairs, boosters. Reservations accepted for parties of 6 or more only. Main courses $6.95–$16.95. AE, MC, V. Mon–Thurs 11:30am–midnight, Fri–Sat 11:30am–1am, Sun 11:30am–11:30pm. Subway: A/C/E to 42nd St. CHINESE.

The Midtown branch of this popular Upper West Side noodle shop does a brisk business in the Chinese standards Americans are most comfortable with—egg rolls, barbecued spare ribs, wonton soup, sweet-and-sour pork—with a nod to newer favorites like Mandarin noodle soups, a sizzling tofu platter, and a grilled tuna kebab with teriyaki sauce. At these prices, who could complain? Fast, noisy, casual, and dependably edible, it may work better for families if you can avoid the pretheater madhouse. See also the Upper West Side branches above.

Patsy's Pizzeria. 509 Third Ave. (between 34th and 35th sts.). ☎ 212/689-7500. High chairs, boosters. Reservations not accepted. Pizzas $11.50–$13.50; pasta $7.95–$12.95. No credit cards. Sun–Thurs noon–11pm, Fri–Sat noon–midnight. Subway: 6 to 68th St. PIZZA.

Not far from the Empire State Building and the Morgan Library (see chapter 4), this branch of the great pizzeria makes a good choice for families, especially in this less-touristed section of Murray Hill. The kids can feast on a small pizza while parents go for memorable, if not too fancy, pastas and salads.

Route 66. 858 Ninth Ave. (between 55th and 56th sts.). ☎ 212/977-7600. High chairs, boosters. Reservations accepted except for weekend brunch. Main courses $10–$18. AE, DC, DISC, MC, V. Daily 8am–midnight. Subway: 1/9 to 59th St. AMERICAN.

The open-road murals and the clutter of artifacts decorating this place give it a nice, breezy, Southwestern feel; the food is contemporary casual stuff, some of it with a Southwestern accent (a little jalapeño thrown in here and there), but nothing too contrived or exotic. Grilled tuna, spinach ravioli, and steamed mussels all sound good, but somehow we always end up with burgers and the Popeye salad (spinach, naturally), or one of the omelets. We like it for Sunday brunch, after soccer games or before plays at Theatreworks USA (see chapter 8), though my husband confesses he often comes here for weekday lunch with people from his office. Tables are set close together, and the noise level is, well, lively, but everybody seems happy and relaxed, and that's not a bad thing.

Stage Deli. 834 Seventh Ave. (between 53rd and 54th sts.). ☎ 212/245-7850. Kids' menu, high chairs. Reservations not accepted. Sandwiches $7.95–$14.95. AE, DISC, MC, V. Daily 6am–1:30am. Subway: B/D to Seventh Ave. DELI.

Doggedly trying to compete with the Carnegie Deli up the street (above), the Stage Deli promotes more of a theatrical connection; besides the requisite black-and-white glossies of stars plastered all over the place, near the door there's a large display case of Polaroids taken of more recent stars (I use the term loosely for folks like Pauly Shore and David Faustino, along with reliables like Dom DeLuise—who, judging from the numbers of pictures posted in restaurants around town, must've eaten everywhere). On many factors—the overstuffed sandwiches, dill pickles on every table—the Stage Deli competes head-to-head with its rival, and there are some who even claim its corned beef is better; the cheesecake here is smooth as satin and of heroic proportions. The menu is more limited, sticking mostly to sandwiches. On the whole, the Stage Deli is a little less chummy and a whole lot less authentic-feeling than the Carnegie, if ambience is what you're after. Lunch and pretheater hours are crazed, which may mean impatient service, something you don't need when you're with kids.

AFTERNOON TEA

Palm Court. In the Plaza Hotel, 768 Fifth Ave. (between 58th and 59th sts.). ☎ **212/546-5350.** High chairs. Reservations recommended for brunch. High tea $29; breakfast $30; main courses $19–$30. Daily 6:30am–2:45pm and 3:45pm–midnight (high tea Mon–Thurs 3:45–7pm, Fri–Sat 3:45–8pm, Sun 4–7pm). AE, CB, DC, DISC, MC, V. Subway: N/R to Fifth Ave. CONTINENTAL.

The classic choice for a special-occasion outing with grandparents or godparents, the Plaza Hotel's elegant lobby cafe is at its best in the afternoon, with the discreet clink of china teacups and the rustle of shopping bags mingling with soft classical music. The desserts are as ornate as the 19th-century decor, all curlicued gilt and creamy marble. Kids should be on their best behavior; I even saw, honestly, a 5-year-old boy dressed in a sailor suit (let's hope he was European), which tells you what you need to know about the target clientele. The dress code is business casual or dressier—don't try to show up in skimpy shorts.

THE CHAIN GANG

Among **Houlihan's** many branches, the three best locations for families are 122 E. 42nd St near Grand Central (☎ **212/922-5660**); 2 Pennsylvania Plaza by Penn Station (☎ **212/630-0349**); and 350 Fifth Ave., at 34th Street (☎ **212/630-0339**), on the ground floor of the Empire State Building. There's a **Jackson Hole** at 521 Third Ave., at 35th Street (☎ **212/679-3264**). **Burger Heavens** are sprinkled all around Midtown, though they're usually open only until 8pm: 20 E. 49th St., between Fifth and Madison avenues (☎ **212/755-2166**); 536 Madison Ave. at 54th Street (☎ **212/753-4214**); 9 E. 53rd St. at Fifth Avenue (☎ **212/752-0340**); and 291 Madison Ave. at 41st Street (☎ **212/685-6250**). A hipper and healthier alternative may be **Blockhead's Burritos,** which has three Midtown locations: 499 Third Ave., between 33rd and 34th streets (☎ **212/213-3332**); 954 Second Ave., between 50th and 51st streets (☎ **212/750-2020**); and 322 W. 50th St., between Eighth and Ninth avenues (☎ **212/307-7070**).

FOOD COURTS

A handy place to know about if you're doing movies or theater on 42nd Street is the industrial-chic-looking **42nd Street Food Court** at 234 W. 42nd St. (between Seventh and Eighth avenues), which has a nice mix of counters including Ranch 1 Chicken, Jody Maroni's, California Pizza Kitchen, Cinnabon, and Manchu Wok, as well as full-service restaurants Ruby's Dinette and Chili's (there's an Applebee's one level down as well). On the top floor of the **Manhattan Mall,** an oddly suburban vertical shopping center at Sixth Avenue and 33rd Street, nearly a dozen food vendors offer a pretty varied smorgasbord of food choices: at last visit, Japanese, Chinese, Indian, Cajun, vegetarian, fish-and-chips, and good old American hamburgers and cheese steaks and hot dogs. The marble-clad mall is a bit noisy and the food court's tables are tiny; there are big bathrooms handy, though my husband

and sons reported that the men's room was messy and populated by rummies (the women's room was fine—draw your own conclusions). At any rate, you'll ride up in glass-enclosed elevators, which should thrill your little daredevils. The angle-topped **Citicorp Building,** a stunning white skyscraper between Lexington and Third avenues and 53rd and 54th streets, has a food court in its sunken atrium plaza, with a range of take-out choices: pizza, bagels, frozen yogurt, and so on. There are also several restaurants around the atrium to choose from.

5 Chelsea

MODERATE

Empire Diner. 210 Tenth Ave. (at 22nd St.). ☎ **212/243-2736.** Booster. Reservations not accepted. Main courses $9.95–$17.95; salads and sandwiches $4.95–$11.95. AE, DC, DISC, MC, V. Daily 24 hours (except closed Tues 4–8am). Subway: C/E to 23rd St. AMERICAN DINER.

The enduring popularity of this deco-ish chrome diner, stretching like a waiting limo along Chelsea's far west Tenth Avenue, is no doubt because it stays open to all hours of the morning—the club-happy crew that tramps through here at 5am is a sight to behold. There's only one booster seat in the whole joint, which tells you how little they value family business. But if your kids are older and have developed some restaurant manners, this is a dependable choice in a neighborhood that doesn't offer many places to eat. The whimsically footnoted menu's big on omelets, burgers, meat loaf, and the like, which won't threaten a youngster's palate, but you can still find chic dishes like grilled portobello and goat cheese salad or linguine with smoked salmon. One thing you can be sure of—you'll feel like you're in Manhattan.

Flight 151. 151 Eighth Ave. (between 17th and 18th sts.). ☎ **212/229-1868.** Kids' menu, boosters. Reservations not necessary. Lunch $3.95–$7.95; dinner $5.95–$13.95; brunch buffet $6.95; kids' menu $2.95. AE, MC, V. Daily 11am–2am. Subway: A/C/E to 14th St. AMERICAN.

Like its sibling Flight 1668 on the Upper East Side (above), this relaxed neighborhood hangout is a welcome spot for families at lunch and dinner, before the drinking crowd settles in for the night. Vintage plane memorabilia decorates the space, an added plus for aircraft-loving kids. The food is middle-of-the-road standards—burgers, pastas, crab cake sandwich, steak, chicken marsala—with chicken fingers, hot dogs, grilled cheese, and penne on the kids' bill of fare. Service is friendly and blessedly tolerant.

INEXPENSIVE

Bendix Diner. 219 Eighth Ave. (at 21st St.). ☎ **212/366-0560.** High chairs, boosters. Reservations not accepted. Main courses $3.25–$7.95. AE, MC, V. Tues–Sat 8am–2am, Sun–Mon 8am–11pm. Subway: C/E to 23rd St. AMERICAN DINER/THAI.

Garish cartoony murals on the walls give a hip jolt to this friendly Chelsea diner, which proclaims as its happy motto "Get Fat!" The menu mixes American diner specialties—your typical burgers, Greek salads, BLTs, and tuna melts—with some pretty passable Thai food. If you've never tried Thai, at least order the chicken satay appetizers: skewered grilled chicken with peanut sauce that even toddlers may find delectable. The more adventurous should undertake pad thai noodles, soft noodles that come stir-fried with chicken, shrimp, bean sprouts, turnips, and tofu; the garlicky fried tofu with broccoli is another good choice. The meeting of East and West works well, and any place that lets me eat pad see eew while my kids share a stack of silver-dollar pancakes is A-okay.

Le Gamin. 183 Ninth Ave. (at 21st St.). ☎ **212/243-8864.** Reservations not accepted. Main courses $5–$10. No credit cards. Daily 8am–midnight. Subway: C/E to 23rd St. FRENCH.

The vintage Parisian look of this corner café—faded yellow walls, dark wood trim, a chalkboard menu, wicker cafe–style chairs—perfectly suits a place whose specialties are crêpes, croque monsieurs, and quiches. Tell your kids that a croque monsieur is an open-faced grilled cheese with ham and they should go for it, though they may be more interested in the delicate crêpes, which are really only stuffed pancakes, right? Tables are tiny and set fairly close together, but hey, it's atmospheric. (Never mind that the atmosphere isn't New York at all.) So long as you don't expect to make this a long, leisurely meal, you should do very well.

Miss Rita's. Pier 60, Chelsea Piers. ☎ **212/604-0441.** Kids' menu. Main courses $3.50–$8.50. AE. Mon–Sat 11am–10pm, Sun11am–7pm. Subway: C/E to 23rd St. Bus: M23 to Chelsea Piers. AMERICAN DINER.

The best family choice at Chelsea Piers is this pink-hued and western-themed corner diner at Pier 60, which dishes up beef burgers and barbecued and fried chicken and salads, with an upbeat rock soundtrack. Items like veggie burgers, homemade potato salad, peppered catfish sandwich, and chilled gazpacho vary from diner standards; the vinegar coleslaw is a specialty. Good-natured service puts children at their ease, though the food doesn't always arrive in a hurry—even burgers may take up to 15 minutes as they are slow-grilled for maximum juiciness (if you're in a hurry, order the miniburger instead, which is actually better suited to a kid's appetite). Quality ingredients and a little extra care raise this food above your normal coffee-shop fare; besides, any place that serves a jumbo chili dog is A-okay.

FOOD COURT

Definitely the coolest place to eat in Chelsea is at the **Chelsea Market,** 75 Ninth Ave., between 15th and 16th streets (entrance also on Tenth Avenue), a rambling series of food shops set in a rehabbed Nabisco factory. Older kids with a sense of style will appreciate the industrial chic look, with scrubbed brick walls, exposed pipes, and utilitarian light fixtures; the focal point is a ripped-open water main gushing into a crumbling brick cavity in the floor. Among fish stores and produce stalls you'll find hip little take-out eateries like Amy's Bread, Sarabeth's Bakery, Bimmy's Sandwiches, the Juice Factory, and Hale and Hearty Soups, all with tiny cafe tables nearby where you can enjoy the food.

THE CHAIN GANG

The original location of **Mary Ann's,** at 116 Eighth Ave., at 16th Street (☎ 212/ 633-0877), is less kid-oriented than its Uptown counterparts, but the Mexican food is dandy.

6 The Flatiron District & Gramercy Park

MODERATE

✪ **America.** 9 E. 18th St. (between Fifth Ave. and Broadway). ☎ **212/505-2110.** High chairs, boosters. Reservations recommended. Main courses $7.95–$19.95; salads and sandwiches $3.95–$14.95. AE, DC, DISC, MC, V. Sun–Thurs 11:30am–midnight, Fri–Sat 11:30am–1am. Subway: 4/5/6/L/N/R to Union Square. AMERICAN/ECLECTIC.

A giant American flag hangs over the entrance and a Statue of Liberty presides over one end of the raised bar area, while figures of Washington and Lincoln hold a confab at the other end. From Albuquerque nachos to Yazoo City fried okra, this

USA-themed restaurant assigns every item on the menu a hometown, some of which seem far-fetched—why should alphabet noodle soup belong to Kalamazoo, Michigan, a tuna melt to Minnesota, or the Reuben sandwich to Nebraska? But why quibble with such a big, fun menu, especially when so many selections are kid-pleasers, even for kids too young to get the geography gimmick. Even picky eaters should find something they like, whether it's a Georgia peach pancake, a Fluffernutter sandwich, macaroni-and-cheese, or a trio of tiny Velveeta-topped slider hamburgers; meanwhile, parents can sample exotic items like Puget Sound wild-mushroom ragout, Creole jambalaya, or air-dried duck salad. And surprisingly, the kitchen does a pretty good job with nearly everything. The big dining room's cool minimalist decor will flatter older kids into thinking this is a grown-up restaurant, but never fear—America attracts lots of younger diners and is well used to dealing with them.

Friend of a Farmer. 77 Irving Place (between 18th and 19th sts.). ☎ 212/477-2188. Kids' menu, high chairs, boosters. Lunch $7–$9; dinner $8–$17; kids' menu $6. AE, DC, DISC, MC, V. Mon–Thurs 8am–10pm, Fri 8am–11pm, Sat 9:30am–11pm, Sun 9:30am–10pm. Subway: 4/5/6/L/N/R to Union Square. AMERICAN.

Like a little piece of upstate New York plunked down just south of Gramercy Park, rustic low-ceilinged Friend of a Farmer does the country cafe thing right—fresh-baked breads and muffins, hearty soups, filling casseroles, and pot pies on a menu that also offers steaks, roast chicken, pastas, and salads. Young farmhands can choose from macaroni-and-cheese, chicken with pasta, grilled cheese, or PB&J. Casual and low-key it may be, but the wooden tables are small and set close, service can dawdle a bit, and the lunching neighborhood folks may look askance if rowdy juveniles shatter the usual calm. All the same, I keep coming here to get the kind of home cooking I never have time to do at home; so long as I have only one kid in tow at a time, it can be a wonderfully relaxing experience.

INEXPENSIVE

Chat 'n' Chew. 10 E. 16th St. (between Fifth Ave. and Union Square West). ☎ 212/243-1616. Kids' menu, high chairs, boosters. Reservations recommended for parties of 5 or more. Main courses $7.25–$12.75; salads and sandwiches $6–$9.95; kids' menu $2.95 at brunch, $3.95 at lunch/dinner. AE, MC, V. Mon–Thurs 11:30am–11pm, Fri 11:30am–11:30pm, Sat 10am–11:30pm, Sun 10am–11pm. Subway: 4/5/6/L/N/R to Union Square. AMERICAN.

Are they serious about that name? Of course not, and neither should you be. Something about this cozy Flatiron place just makes me smile as soon as I walk in the door. Maybe it's the (nudge, nudge) "down-home" decor—red-painted floors, dark-stained wood, farm implements and road signs on the walls—or maybe it's the casual, friendly way they treat you. The menu's fun to read, with names like the Cesar Romero Salad, Uncle Red's Addiction (honey-dipped fried chicken), 110% Veggie Chili, and the Holy Cow (a 9-oz. hamburger); the fried catfish po' boy is especially moist and delicious, and the meat loaf comes with "skin-on" smashed potatoes. Kids get offered a fairly standard menu of favorites, but the names alone will intrigue them: Monster Burger, Flying Saucer Pancakes, Mars Fried Chicken (two pieces of mutant chicken with alien fries). Tongue-in-cheek it may be, but it's not too hip to welcome families, unlike the Coffee Shop and the Union Square Café and all those other trendies down the street.

Duke's. 99 E. 19th St. (between Park Ave. South and Irving Place). ☎ 212/260-2922. Kids' menu, high chairs, boosters. Reservations required for parties of 6 or more. Main courses $6.95–$13.95; kids' menu $6.95. AE, MC, V. Sun–Wed noon–11pm, Thurs noon–midnight, Fri–Sat noon–1am (in summer, opens at 4pm weekends). Subway: 4/5/6/N/R to Union Square. AMERICAN SOUTHERN/BARBECUE.

Yet another haven for transplanted Southerners, this roadhouse-style hangout believes in huge portions, a steady noise level, and being friendly to kids. Expect a rock-and-roll soundtrack, vintage clutter on the weathered-looking walls, and Tennessee-style barbecue (ribs, chicken, fish) that's not terribly authentic. The kids' menu is your usual burger, chicken fingers, and the like, but it includes a drink and a hot fudge sundae, which makes it a decent deal. It doesn't have quite the kitschy sense of fun as Chat 'n' Chew (above), but we thought the food was a half notch above Rodeo Grill (below), with a similar down-home atmosphere.

Rodeo Grill. 375 Third Ave. (at 27th St.). ☎ **212/683-6500.** Kids' menu, high chairs, boosters. Reservations accepted for parties of 6 or more only. Main courses $5.95–$14.95; kids' menu $3.50. AE, CB, DC, DISC, MC, V. Daily 11:30am–2am. Subway: 6 to 28th St. BARBECUE/TEX-MEX.

Someone had a lot of fun decorating this bilevel space, with the feed-grain silo on the upper landing and the huge stuffed bison on a ledge above the bar. The weathered-wood walls are hung with old highway signs and lots of animal horns; Western music twangs and a basket of taco chips arrives on your table in a flash. Children are a welcome part of the mix—on Monday night they even eat free. The menu is heavy on burgers, steaks, barbecue, fajitas, and burritos, but there are a fair number of vegetarian items and a short list of salads as well. Children are offered (once again) burgers, chicken fingers, and grilled cheese, with mounds of fries. I found the salsa and hot sauce pretty acrid, but our family enjoyed our meal nevertheless, which just goes to prove that dining out with kids isn't about eating good food.

AFTERNOON TEA

T Salon. 11 E. 20th St. (between Fifth Ave. and Broadway). ☎ **212/358-0506.** Boosters. Main courses $6–$28. AE, MC, V. Daily 10:30am–8pm. Subway: N/R to 23rd St. ECLECTIC.

This cozy spot is full of artistic types brooding over cups of fragrant brew (herbal as well as caff and no-caff) chosen from a list as long as the wine list at most restaurants. Low ceilings, soft lighting, and settees and armchairs covered in William Morris-y dark brocades complete the look of boho British gentility. Besides tea, the bill of fare has a refreshingly low pastry component, leaning more toward soups, salads, sandwiches, and delicate crêpes. Twelve-year-old girls who love Jane Austen movies should eat this place up.

THE CHAIN GANG

There's a handy **Chirping Chicken** at 377 First Ave., between 22nd and 23rd streets (☎ **212/529-4211**).

7 Greenwich Village

MODERATE

Arturo's Restaurant-Pizzeria. 106 W. Houston St. (at Thompson St.). ☎ **212/677-3820.** Boosters. Reservations not accepted on weekends. Pizzas $10 and up; main courses $8–$22. AE, DC, MC, V. Mon–Thurs 4pm–1am, Fri–Sat 4pm–2am, Sun 3pm–midnight. Subway: 1/9 to Houston St. ITALIAN/PIZZA.

Crowded, dimly lit, and busy, this vintage hangout right on the border between the Village and SoHo—near the Italian part of the West Village, around Father Demo Square—serves some very good thin-crust pizzas; they're slung on your table fresh from a coal-fired oven, so hot the mozzarella could burn the roof of your mouth. You can get various pasta dishes too (go for the baked stuff like ziti and lasagna) or

Downtown Dining

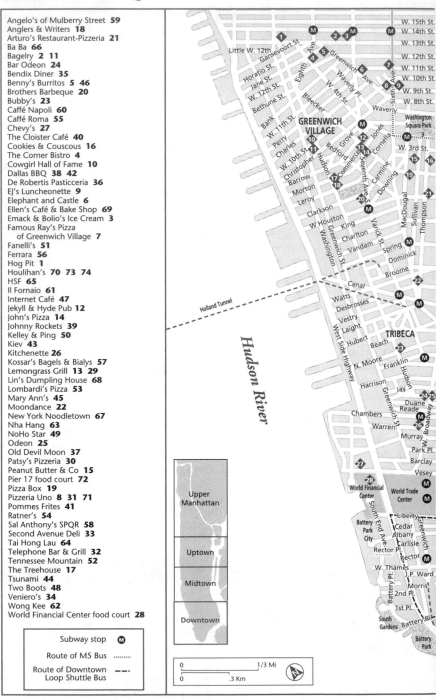

Subway stop   Ⓜ

Route of M5 Bus   ·········

Route of Downtown   — ·· —
Loop Shuttle Bus

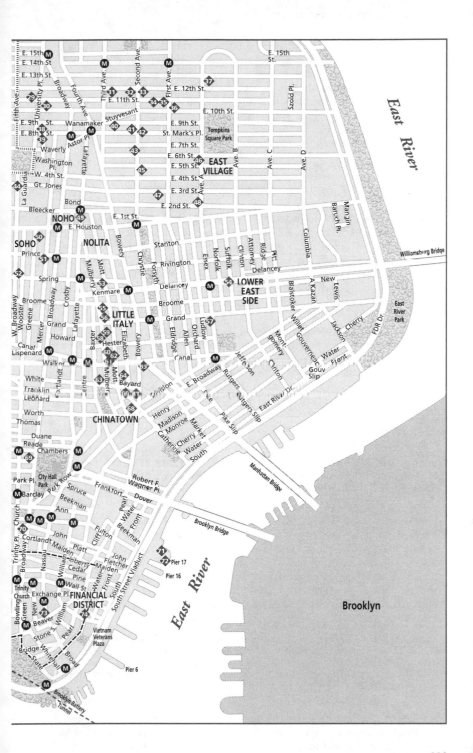

even surf-and-turf, though that seems a bit beside the point here: Pizzas are the thing to order. Several notches above storefront by-the-slice pizzerias, it's still a casual sort of place where drinks come in plastic tumblers and side salads come in plastic fake-wood bowls, which bodes well if you've got kids in tow. You may have to wait in line, though, and at particularly frantic meal times it can be hard to get your waiter's attention. There's live jazz every night, which may make waiting easier. Arturo's is certainly as authentic as any place officially in Little Italy—and a good deal less touristy.

Cookies & Couscous. 230 Thompson St. (between Bleecker St. and W. 3rd St.). ☎ 212/ 477-6562. Reservations recommended. Main courses $9–$19. No credit cards. Daily noon–11pm (Sun until 10pm). Subway: A/B/C/D/E/F/Q to West 4th St. ECLECTIC/ NORTH AFRICAN.

Moroccan-born chef/owner Moha Orchid is so enthusiastic about feeding his guests, it's hard not to be pleased. My kids happen to love couscous, that delicate small-grained pasta that's such a staple in North Africa; here it's mixed maybe with vegetables, maybe with meat, whatever is fresh and seasonal. Other dishes they enjoy are grilled marinated lamb on brochette, the grilled half chicken, and the superb Kefta burger, which is really a high-quality hamburger livened up with Moroccan spices. For those with more adventurous palates, the soups, salads, and stews are all exotic and wonderful. But wait! There's more! The chef also has a flair for Viennese pastries, especially cookies and tarts with buttery, sweet crusts, and his homemade sorbets are a marvel, coming in intense flavors like mango/lavender and red plum/anise and watermelon/absinthe (okay, that one may not be for kids). Although the menu doesn't seem like a natural for families, lots of regulars have started bringing their youngsters and the chef welcomes them, even to the point of tailoring his spices to suit a child's taste buds. The sweet and homelike dining room, with its butter-yellow walls, lace curtains, and cushioned seats, will be decorated with Moroccan antiques as soon as Moha has time to visit home. The way this place is hopping, that may not be for a while.

Cowgirl Hall of Fame. 519 Hudson St. (at 10th St.). ☎ 212/633-1133. Kids' menu, high chairs, boosters. Reservations recommended. Main courses $7.95–$16.95; kids' menu $2.95–$5.95. AE, MC, V. Daily 11:30am–11pm. Subway: 1/9 to Christopher St. TEX-MEX.

Think the Old West motif of this West Village theme spot is corny? You're darn tootin' it's corny, and that's why kids get into it. Cowboy hats, boots, and lassos adorn the walls; steer horns poke from the mirrors and antlers from the chandeliers; younger customers are handed crayons to color a paper Indian headdress. Passable barbecue, hearty chili, and a mess of fried catfish are included in the menu round-up; kids' options feature some offbeat items such as corn dogs and cheese quesadillas along with the obligatory chicken fingers. The operation's a little too perky and slick for my tastes (this is part of a small national chain), but kids are easily taken in by all the kitsch.

EJ's Luncheonette. 432 Sixth Ave. (between 9th and 10th sts.). ☎ 212/473-5555. Kids' menu, high chairs, boosters. Reservations not accepted. Breakfast specials $4.50–$8.50; lunch specials $6.50–$9; dinner specials $9.95–$14.75. AE. Mon–Thurs 8:30am–11pm, Fri–Sat 8:30am–11:30pm, Sun 8:30am–10pm. Subway: A/B/C/D/E/F/Q to West 4th St. AMERICAN DINER.

Yet another in this trio of popularissimo retro-1950s diners (see Upper West Side and Upper East Side, above), the Village EJ's follows the same drill: From French toast and flapjacks to meat loaf and mashed potatoes, it's the kind of comfort food your mom used to make (or the kind you wished she had).

Hog Pit. 22 Ninth Ave. (at 13th St.). ☎ **212/604-0092.** Reservations recommended for parties of 6 or more. Lunch $8.95–$13.95 lunch; dinner $11.95–$15.95. AE, MC, V. Sun–Thurs noon–11pm, Fri–Sat noon–1am. Subway: A/C/E/L to 14th St. AMERICAN SOUTHERN/ BARBECUE.

Three things you should know before venturing into the Hog Pit: It's got stuffed boar's heads snarling down from all the walls, the air is permeated with cigarette smoke, and the jukebox plays only raucous Southern rock. What else would you expect from a barbecue joint in the meat-packing district that has pressed-tin walls, a back room with pool table and foosball, and Johnny Cash posters mounted over the tables? Yep, this is a dive all right, but a dive that serves fine down-home food, and older kids will appreciate the adventure of coming here (though I wouldn't bring kids here too late into the evening, after the bar scene gets going). Go for the baby-back ribs (which are actually cooked in an oven, not a pit, but the taste is still spicy and savory); fried chicken and chicken fried steak are other specialties. Collard greens, black-eyed peas, mashed potatoes—sugar, you got yourself a fine meal, and you should wind it up with pecan pie and hope you can find a cab home. (Don't worry—cab drivers know this is a burgeoning restaurant neighborhood, and you can usually find a taxi at Ninth Avenue and 14th Street outside the Old Homestead Steak House.)

Jekyll & Hyde Pub. 91 Seventh Ave. South (between Barrow and W. 4th sts.). ☎ **212/ 989-7701.** Boosters. Reservations not accepted. Sandwiches $7.95–$10.95; main courses $8.95–$16.95. AE, DC, DISC, V. Sun–Thurs noon–2am, Fri–Sat noon–4am. Subway: 1/9 to Christopher St. ECLECTIC.

The original outpost of this horror-themed restaurant, the Village's Jekyll & Hyde is slightly more casual than the Midtown spot (above), in a dining room that opens right onto Seventh Avenue South, and waiting in line is less of a factor here. The menu is slightly different but still features a fairly standard range of burgers, salads, pizza, pasta, and steaks, gussied up with hokey names. And there's a whole new repertoire of spooky special effects, with an ongoing floor show that definitely goes for corny punch lines. Boasting an extensive range of international beers, plus exotic drinking vessels to quaff your brew from, Jekyll & Hyde shoots for an adult crowd, which is all the more reason why teenagers and adolescents think it's cool. This place falls somewhere between Disney World and Madame Tussaud's on the entertainment spectrum; if that's up your kid's alley, you could all have a ball—so long as you don't expect the food to be much good.

NoHo Star. 330 Lafayette St. (at Bleecker St.). ☎ **212/925-0070.** Boosters. Reservations not accepted. Main courses $7–$24.50. AE, DC, DISC, MC, V. Mon–Fri 8am–midnight, Sat–Sun 10:30am–midnight. Subway: 6 to Bleecker St. AMERICAN/CHINESE.

Just a block above Houston Street, this airy loftlike space has a very SoHo-ish feel, with brightly painted columns and an arty tile mural of a newspaper (the fictional NoHo Star). Burgers, pastas, and very good omelets are winners for lunch and brunch; the dinner menu goes upscale with items like seared sea scallops, steak frites, a top-drawer Caesar salad, and a range of superb, zestfully spiced Chinese dishes. The best time to come, though, is at breakfast, when it's quiet and never crowded—kids can dive into a stack of pancakes while parents nurse a cup of good coffee. The atmosphere is always relaxed and relaxing, and the waiters are totally friendly to kids.

Treehouse. 436 Hudson St. (between St. Luke's Place and Morton St.). ☎ **212/989-1471.** High chairs, boosters. Reservations recommended. Lunch $8–$16.95; dinner $9–$22; brunch $9.50. AE, MC, V. Mon–Thurs noon–3pm and 5:30–11pm, Fri noon–3pm and 5:30–11:30pm, Sat 11am–4pm and 5:30–11:30pm, Sun 10am–4pm and 5:30–10pm. Subway: 1/9 to Christopher St. or Houston St. AMERICAN/CONTINENTAL/ECLECTIC.

With tree branches growing in through the windows, this country-charming restaurant in the far West Village seems miles away from Manhattan, and its kid-friendly attitude is decidedly un-urban too. Though there's no specific kids' menu, the kitchen is happy to improvise to suit a child's tastes—buttered pasta, perhaps, or a small portion of fish; the thick homemade fries could be a meal in themselves. At weekend brunches, children join in a cookie baking session and happily run around while their parents enjoy the prix-fixe menu. The menu ranges widely, with several French dishes among the American favorites: burgers, steaks, seafood, soups, and salads.

Tsunami. 70 W. 3rd St. (between La Guardia and Thompson sts.). ☎ **212/475-7770.** Boosters. Reservations accepted. Sushi $1.50 per piece; main courses $15. AE, DC, MC, V. Mon–Thurs 11:30am–11pm, Fri 11:30am–midnight, Sat noon–midnight, Sun 2–11pm. Subway: A/B/C/D/E/F to W. 4th St. JAPANESE.

The name means "tidal wave," the reference presumably being to the fact that this serene sushi restaurant has an actual water canal encircling the central sushi bar. The sushi chefs set little dishes of sushi on the small boats, which drift around the oval; if you see something you like, just lift the plate off the boat. On leaving, your bill is totaled according to the colors of the various plates you've taken. It's a charming gimmick that always fascinates my kids, even though they'd rather watch than dare to eat sushi. Luckily, the menu also offers other Japanese standards like steak teriyaki, grilled chicken, soba noodles, a hearty ramen soup, and a particularly fluffy and golden shrimp tempura, and you can order these even if you're sitting canalside at the sushi counter. The staff tends to be very sweet with youngsters, though the Zen-like mood doesn't really suit a rambunctious toddler.

INEXPENSIVE

Benny's Burritos. 113 Greenwich Ave. (at Jane St.). ☎ **212/727-0584.** Boosters. Reservations not accepted. Main courses $7–$12. AE, MC, V. Sun–Fri 11:30am–11pm, Sat 11:30am–midnight. Subway: 1/2/3/9 to 14th St. MEXICAN.

Casual, cheap, and often crowded, Benny's is the kind of little Village joint everyone drifts into sooner or later. (If you can't get a table, hit the take-out shop across the street at 112 Greenwich.) Though there's no kids' menu per se, you can order several items on the regular menu in smaller portions—which is a relief, when you see how gargantuan the burritos here can be.

Brothers Barbeque. 225 Varick St. (at Clarkson St.). ☎ **212/727-2775.** Kids' menu, high chairs, boosters. Reservations accepted. Main courses $11–$15; kids' menu $6–$7. AE, MC, V. Sun–Thurs 11am–11pm, Fri–Sat 11am–1am. Subway: 1/9 to Houston St. BARBECUE.

Set on a corner where Greenwich Village begins to fade into TriBeCa, this is a top downtown spot for falling-off-the-bone tender barbecue. For the record, Brothers subscribes to the North Carolina school of barbecue, with its peppery vinegar sauce; the pulled pork sandwich is a standout, which is great since that happens to be my older son's favorite barbecue dish. The decor is your usual faux-roadhouse clutter, and the music gets cranked up as the evening wears on, but if your kids are barbecue lovers, this is a fun option.

Corner Bistro. 331 W. 4th St. (at Jane St. and Eighth Ave.). ☎ **212/242-9502.** Reservations not accepted. Main courses $4.50–$5.75. No credit cards. Daily 11:30am–4am. Subway: 1/2/3/9/A/C/E to 14th St. BURGERS.

Here are your choices: hamburger, cheeseburger, bacon cheeseburger, or chicken sandwich. No doubt about it, this place is a bar, and a dark and smoky one at that, the kind where people huddle in wooden booths and initials have been carved into the tabletops. Which is precisely why some kids will think it's totally cool to come here; others will simply dig into the thick, juicy burgers and piles of fine fries. And if that's not enough, there's a pretty darn good jukebox. Though the Corner Bistro can get full of drinkers later in the night, at midday or in the early evening it's wonderfully mellow and kids aren't out of place.

Elephant and Castle. 68 Greenwich Ave. (at 11th St.). ☎ **212/243-1400.** Boosters. Reservations not accepted. Main courses $6–$12.50. AE, CB, DC, MC, V. Mon–Fri 8:30am–midnight, Sat–Sun 10am–midnight. Subway: 1/2/3/9 to 14th St. AMERICAN.

Like a holdover from the 1970s, this mellow-eats parlor continues to churn out good burgers and crêpes and fluffy omelets and other stuff kids will generally accept. A cheery, well-lit space, it's best for leisurely brunches; bring a few toys for your offspring and a copy of the Sunday *Times* for you to browse through. Though it isn't inherently child-oriented, E&C is informal and friendly enough that families blend right in.

Famous Ray's Pizza of Greenwich Village. 465 Sixth Ave. (at 11th St.). ☎ **212/243-2253.** Reservations not accepted. Pizza $1.90 (slice)–$13.50 (pie). AE, DC, DISC, MC, V. Sun–Thurs 11am–2am, Fri–Sat 11am–3am. Subway: F to 14th St.; A/B/C/D/E/F/Q to W. 4th St. PIZZA.

Definitely the most renowned corner pizzeria in town is Famous Ray's—the Ray's that all those other ersatz Ray's Pizzas around town are hoping you'll confuse them with. Set right in the midst of the Village's prettiest town-house streets, Ray's is easy to spot by the lines snaking out onto the sidewalk, with all sorts of people hungry for a slice to go. A wait is nearly inevitable, but the line moves quickly. Many pizza lovers rave about the extra-cheese pizza here; I find it a bit excessive, but I do like the plain pizza's chewy crust and tangy sauce. All sorts of designer toppings are also available—pesto, eggplant, lettuce, even pineapple and ham (say it ain't so, Ray!)— but why mess around with a classic?

Johnny Rockets. 42 E. 8th St. (at Greene St.). ☎ **212/253-8175.** Kids' menu, high chairs, boosters. Burgers $4.45–$6.35. AE, DISC, MC, V. Daily 11am–midnight. Subway: N/R to 8th St.; 6 to Astor Place. BURGERS.

As chains go, this is one that doesn't offend me at all: The 1950s soda shoppe look is executed smartly, with lots of gleaming white tile and chrome, and the menu really works for kids. You get perfectly fine burgers, creamy milk shakes, good fries that aren't too greasy—and, get this, a jukebox at every table (though our waiter confessed to me that they don't always work and it's a pain to find mechanics who can fix them). With $4.25 kids' meals and menus to color, this is a good bet to please most kids. The staff seems cheerful enough, at least at lunchtime, and the NYU crowd hasn't taken over (not grungy enough for students, I suppose, and the music on the jukes is too old-fashioned).

✪ John's Pizza. 278 Bleecker St. (near Jones St.). ☎ **212/243-1680.** Reservations not accepted. Pizzas $9.50–$19.50; pasta $6–$8.75. No credit cards. Sun–Thurs 11:30am–11:30pm, Fri–Sat noon–12:30am. Subway: 1/9 to Christopher St. PIZZA.

This is the kind of place that's often described as having no ambience, when in fact it has plenty—classic no-frills pizzeria ambience, with harsh lighting and bare-topped tables and an open view of the brick ovens where the pizzas are baked. Folks in the Village are always lamenting that John's doesn't sell pizza by the slice, but families should have no problem polishing off a whole pie. The crust is crunchy thin, with savory tomato sauce, bubbly melted mozzarella, and a host of fresh toppings to pick from (nothing too trendy, though). After eating at John's, you can say you've truly sampled New York pizza at its best.

Patsy's Pizzeria. 67 University Place (between 10th and 11th sts.). ☎ **212/533-3500.** High chairs, boosters. Reservations not accepted. Pizzas $11.50–$13.50; pasta $7.95–$12.95. No credit cards. Sun–Thurs noon–11pm, Fri–Sat noon–midnight. Subway: N/R to 8th St.; 4/5/6/L/N/R to Union Square. PIZZA.

On this restaurant strip just north of the New York University campus, this branch of the Patsy's chain finally gives Village pizza lovers a good alternative if their legs are too tired to walk west to the original John's Pizza on Bleecker Street (above). Classic pizzeria look and an informal atmosphere that works great with kids.

Peanut Butter & Co. 240 Sullivan St. (between Bleecker St. and W. 3rd St.). ☎ **212/ 677-3995.** www.peanutbutterco.com. High chairs, boosters. Sandwiches $4–$7. AE, DC, DISC, MC, V. Sun–Wed noon–9pm, Thurs noon–10pm, Fri–Sat noon–midnight. Subway: A/B/C/D/E/F/Q to West 4th St. AMERICAN.

Born of owner Lee Zalben's obsession, this is a quirky little store/restaurant that serves mostly, you guessed it, peanut butter. Peanut butter memorabilia decorates the golden-hued little cafe, and jars of the house brand are for sale, along with jam and marshmallow Fluff and other suitable accompaniments. The menu's a hoot, with items like Ants on a Log (a celery stalk coated with peanut butter and raisins), your traditional Fluffernutters, and the Elvis (grilled peanut butter sandwich with bananas and honey). If you really must, you can also get a grilled cheese, a tuna-fish sandwich, or a baloney sandwich, you spoilsport you. But the peanut butter is superb, freshly ground from high-quality peanuts with only enough oil to make it spreadable, just like Mom used to make (honest, my mom used to make it just like this, in her Waring blender). Every sandwich is served with potato chips and carrot sticks and they'll even cut off the crusts for you. You should be drinking milk with your PB&J, but Welch's grape juice is also available, as are fountain treats such as egg creams, black cows, and a cherry lime rickey. And for dessert, what else but peanut butter cookies or chocolate peanut butter pie?

Pizza Box. 176 Bleecker St. (between MacDougal and Sullivan sts.). ☎ **212/979-0823.** Reservations not accepted. Pizza $1.50 (slice)–$11 (pie). No credit cards. Daily 11am–midnight. Subway: A/B/C/D/E/F/Q to W. 4th St. PIZZA.

The hippielike scruffiness of this stretch of Bleecker Street reminds you that you're close to a major university campus (NYU), but among the cheap ethnic hole-in-the-walls lies this pleasant and unpretentious pizza spot, worth noting for its restful back garden, open in fair weather. The pizza is perfectly fine, though connoisseurs may want to head west to John's (above). Pizza Box's advantage is that you don't have to buy a whole pie, as you do at John's, and it has waiter service at tables, unlike Famous Ray's (above). If you've ODed on pizza but your child is clamoring for it, you can indulge him while you have pasta or a hero and enjoy the garden.

AFTERNOON TEA

Anglers and Writers. 420 Hudson St. (at St. Luke's Place). ☎ **212/675-0810.** Reservations recommended for parties of 5 or more. Main courses $7–$13.50. No credit cards. Mon–Sat 9am–10:30pm, Sun 10am–10:30pm. Subway: 1/9 to Houston St. AMERICAN.

In a large, airy corner storefront, this relaxed and civilized restaurant seems like a Merchant-Ivory cast-off, with shelves of worn books for browsing, fishing gear hung on the walls, and mismatched china—just like my Aunt Hazel's Adirondack cottage. The problem is, all that West Village serenity is geared to literary adult tastes and the long lines for brunches virtually rule it out for families. Weekdays at teatime is when to go, perhaps as a treat for a 7-year-old daughter; the pastries, while pricey, are wonderfully flaky.

ICE CREAM & SWEETS

Emack & Bolio's Ice Cream. 56 Seventh Ave. (at 14th St.). ☎ **212/727-1198.** No credit cards. Sun–Thurs 2–11pm, Fri–Sat 2pm–midnight. Subway: 1/2/3/9 to 14th St. ICE CREAM.

West Village branch of New England's top ice-cream vendor, starring flavors like grasshopper pie, cosmic crunch, and vanilla bean speck. A fine lick for a summer's night.

THE CHAIN GANG

There are two **Lemongrass Grill**s in the Village, one at 37 Barrow St., at Seventh Avenue South (☎ 212/242-0606), and another at 80 University Place, at 11th Street (☎ 212/604-9870). The **Dallas BBQ** down the street, at 21 University Place, at 8th Street (☎ 212/674-4450), caters largely to a budget-conscious NYU student crowd. The first **Pizzeria Uno** branch in the city was the bustling one at 391 Sixth Ave., at 8th Street (☎ 212/242-5230).

8 The East Village

MODERATE

Cloister Café. 238 E. 9th St. (between Second and Third aves.). ☎ **212/777-9128.** Reservations not accepted. Main courses $4.95–$22.95. No credit cards. Daily 11am–midnight. Subway: 6 to Astor Place. CONTINENTAL.

The main reason to come here is for the courtyard garden, with umbrella-shaded tables set out on crooked paving stones and a tiny fountain trying its best to gurgle. The menu's rather predictable fare runs a tired range from salads (the avocado salad isn't bad) to pastas (cheese ravioli, linguine with clam sauce) to veal, chicken, and seafood dishes (grilled red snapper, shrimp scampi). The lemonade is refreshingly sour; kids may want to add their own sugar. Service can be slapdash at times, but the garden is a treat, day or night, and things are plenty casual enough to come here with kids.

Old Devil Moon. 511 E. 12th St. (between Ave. A and Ave. B). ☎ **212/475-4357.** Reservations recommended. High chairs, boosters. Main courses $7.50–$21. AE, MC, V. Daily 5–11pm. Subway: L to 1st Ave. AMERICAN SOUTHERN/ECLECTIC.

The junk-shop decor of this urban Love Shack is a little out of hand, though it's often too dark inside to see all the stuff on the walls. Younger kids may be overwhelmed, but for preteen would-be hipsters and for anyone who appreciates Southern home cooking, it's a worthy stop. Not that this is traditional Southern cooking—no Mississippi mama would dream of putting andouille sausage in with the macaroni-and-cheese, let alone whipping up a batch of chicken fried tofu (c'mon, where did that idea come from?). But hey, you're in the East Village, so get over it. The catfish, jerk chicken, and po' boy sandwiches are plenty satisfying, and the jambalaya and greens 'n' beans taste like they've been simmering on the stove for hours, swapping their juices deliciously around. Best of all are the pies for dessert (the chocolate pecan pie will require several days of penance afterward). Come here on weekends, too, for breakfasts of country ham, grits, and fresh-baked biscuits. Whoo-*eee!*

Second Avenue Deli. 156 Second Ave. (at 10th St.). ☎ **212/677-0606.** Main courses $10.95–$17.50. AE, DC, DISC, MC, V. Sun–Thurs 7am–midnight, Fri–Sat 7am–3am. Subway: 6 to Astor Place. DELI/KOSHER.

Once upon a time, Second Avenue was the Yiddish equivalent of Broadway (look for the brass stars embedded in the sidewalk outside the restaurant, commemorating great stars of the Yiddish theater). Though the old theaters down the street have been taken over by hip Off-Off-Broadway productions, this great kosher deli survives. It may look like just an ordinary coffee shop, but the food is flavorful and authentic, served in generous portions—you haven't tasted chopped liver till you've tried it here, and the chicken soup with matzoh balls can cure more than the common cold. There's plenty on the menu to satisfy plain-eatin' kids, including bagels and omelets and sandwiches stuffed fat with cold cuts. The waiters are famously grumpy; don't worry that your kids are annoying them—they treat everybody that way. Go figure.

Telephone Bar & Grill. 142 Second Ave. (between 11th and 12th sts.). ☎ **212/529-5000.** Kids' menu, high chairs. Reservations accepted. Lunch $7.95–$12.95; dinner $7.95–$18.95. AE, CB, DC, DISC, MC, V. Subway: 6 to Astor Place; 4/5/6/L/N/R to Union Square. AMERICAN/BRITISH.

Instead of East Village grunge, what you get here is an ersatz British pub, as signaled by the red phone box out front. This place has been around for years, serving Stuyvesant Square squares more than Tompkins Square hipsters; its very middle-of-the-roadness is the key to its survival. There are several sidewalk tables, or you can go inside for brick-walled coziness. The shepherd's pie and fish-and-chips are quite decent, and you'll get them on the $5 kids' menu as well, along with hamburgers and grilled cheese sandwiches. The rest of the adult menu covers all the American bases, from salads to burgers to steaks and seafood. Weekend brunch is popular here; the restaurant also serves a proper Irish breakfast every morning, with oatmeal and Irish bacon. The bar scene is not too intrusive, though the large indoor dining room has no divider to block out the inevitable smoke factor—that may be why they leave the sidewalk tables up for so much of the year. Service is attentive and the whole atmosphere of the place is casual and relaxed.

INEXPENSIVE

Bendix Diner. 167 First Ave. (between 10th and 11th sts.). ☎ **212/260-4220.** High chairs, boosters. Main courses $6.95–$12.95. AE, MC, V. Daily 8am–11pm. Subway: 6 to Astor Place; L to First Ave. AMERICAN DINER/THAI.

An East Village branch of the popular Chelsea hangout (earlier in this chapter), Bendix combines diner classics like burgers and tuna melts with some delicious Thai dishes and yet never seems schizophrenic. Breakfast is served all day, which suits my kids just fine. Weekends can be busy; service is fast but sometimes sloppy.

Benny's Burritos. 93 Ave. A (at E. 6th St.). ☎ **212/254-2054.** Booster seats. Reservations not accepted. Main courses $7–$11.50. AE, MC, V. Sun–Thurs 11am–midnight, Fri–Sat 11am–1am. Subway: 6 to Astor Place. MEXICAN.

Monster-sized burritos and other hearty, healthy Mexican fare are dished up at this East Village branch of the West Village Benny's (earlier in this chapter).

Internet Café. 82 E. 3rd St. (between First and Second aves.). ☎ **212/614-0747.** Reservations not accepted. Sandwiches, salads, and pastries $3–$7. MC, V. Mon–Sat 11am–2am, Sun 11am–midnight. Subway: 6 to Bleecker St.; F to Second Ave. AMERICAN.

This long, narrow, Zen-like space decorated in deep, bold colors invites computer users to linger over the PCs, sustaining themselves with casual low-priced food, designer coffees, and microbrews. The front of the restaurant doubles as an art gallery, with changing shows. Though the software on hand isn't heavy on kids' titles, they do have a few games available, and the place is surprisingly child-friendly, welcoming everyone from infants snoozing in Perego strollers to teenage

Net surfers. (When I asked if they had booster seats, the laughing reply was, "No, but we've got the world's largest collection of phone books."). And a big plus: There's a back courtyard open in good weather.

Kiev. 117 Second Ave. (at 7th St.). ☎ **212/674-4040.** High chairs. Sandwiches $2.25–$6.50; main courses $3.95–$11.50. AE, DC, DISC, MC, V. Daily 24 hours. Subway: 6 to Astor Place. AMERICAN DINER/UKRAINIAN.

Prowl around the East Village and you'll find, beneath the hipster surface, a neighborhood that's still the heart of New York's Ukrainian immigrant community (particularly along 7th Street between Second and Third avenues). Of the handful of restaurants hereabouts catering to that clientele, Kiev is the most accessible and family-friendly. It carries off a balancing act between the old and new East Villages, serving omelets as well as pirogues (dumplings filled with potatoes or cheese), burgers as well as feather-light blintzes and robust borscht, in a modern coffee-shop-like setting. Kiev's Eastern European specialties certainly taste wonderful, and it's an added pleasure to be able to sample them at a place where my kids can have omelets and fries too.

Pommes Frites. 123 Second Ave. (at 9th St.). ☎ **212/674-1234.** French fries $3–$6. No credit cards. Sun–Thurs 11:30am–1am, Fri–Sat 11:30am–2am. Subway: 6 to Astor Place. FRENCH.

Not really a restaurant but a narrow storefront takeout joint, with a bill of fare that's pretty straightforward: nothing but thin, crispy, Belgian-style french fries, with all manner of sauces to dip them into. Considering that my children often eat nothing but fries anyway at sit-down restaurants, this isn't such a bad option for a lunchtime pit stop.

☺ Two Boots. (1) 37 Ave. A (at 2nd St.). ☎ **212/505-2276.** Kids' menu, high chairs, boosters. Reservations accepted for parties of 6 or more only. Main courses $6.95–$9.95; pizzas $5.50–$20.95; kids' menu $3.95–$5.50. AE, DISC, MC, V. Mon–Fri 5pm–midnight, Sat–Sun noon–midnight. Subway: F to Second Ave. (2) 241 Grand Central Terminal (in the food concourse). ☎ **212/557-7992.** No reservations. Mon–Thurs 11am–10pm, Fri–Sat 11am–11pm, Sun 11am–9pm. Subway: 4/5/6/7/S to Grand Central. CAJUN/ITALIAN/PIZZA.

This dandy East Village restaurant couldn't be better for kids. To start, you've got this witty junk-shop decor (strings of Christmas lights shaped like red chiles, old movie posters, and a pair of cowboy boots hanging on a pink wall); then when you're seated, the kids get whole coloring books to scribble in, though you don't get to take them with you. You know these people are used to dealing with kids when you see that the milk is served in plastic cups; grown-ups get their drinks in glass mugs shaped like boots, which our boys find hilarious. The service can be pretty casual, but the waitresses relate to kids instantly, which always seems to make my children behave better. The kids' menu has a little originality: mini-raviolis, spaghetti, chicken fingers, fish sticks, or a Pizza Face, a kid-sized individual pizza with vegetables arranged to form eyes, nose, and grin. My boys, who normally refuse any toppings at all, adore Pizza Faces. Bigger pizzas are served on cake stands, which is also kind of a kick. I opt for a spicy Cajun sandwich on good chewy bread—the kind of food I can't normally get in the kinds of restaurants my kids like. We all walk out with smiles on our faces.

Take-out locations: 36 Ave. A, at 2nd Street (☎ 212/505-5450; Subway: F to Second Avenue); 74 Bleecker St., between Broadway and Crosby Street (☎ 212/777-1033; Subway: 6 to Bleecker Street); 75 Greenwich Ave., between Seventh Avenue and 11th Street (☎ 212/633-9096; Subway: 1/2/3/9 to 14th Street).

Kosher Restaurants

Even if you don't maintain a kosher diet, New York offers the best kosher family dining outside of Israel. The important thing to remember is that a kosher restaurant will either be meat, dairy, or parve (*parve* means the food doesn't contain either meat or dairy products)—you won't find a cheeseburger or chicken parmigiana on any menu unless either the meat or the cheese is really an imitated product. This may sound restricting, but restaurants have learned to make do and become extremely creative in the process.

Joseph's Café, 50 W. 72nd St., between Central Park West and Columbus Avenue (☎ 212/595-5004; dairy), for example, has created such delicacies as imitation pepperoni to top the pizzas and other fake meat products for the Mexican and Italian dishes. The menu is eclectic, ranging from salads to veggie burgers, pizzas, and pastas. If you don't need to go the parve route, **China Shalom,** 686 Columbus Ave., between 93rd and 94th streets (☎ 212/662-9676; meat), offers pretty usual Chinese fare at pretty steep prices, but the service staff is accommodating to families—there's even a kids' menu, with egg rolls, spare ribs, fried chicken nuggets, and french fries.

A trip to **Ratner's,** 138 Delancey St., between Norfolk and Suffolk streets (☎ 212/677-5588; dairy), is like visiting a Catskills resort in the 1950s: Plastic-covered booths and hideous wallpaper may be an eyesore to some, but many make the trip to the Lower East Side just for Ratner's ambience. The menu is pretty straightforward, but the potato pancakes and blintzes are specialties; in a pinch, kids can't go wrong with the spaghetti in tomato sauce.

In Midtown, **Kosher Delight,** 1365 Broadway, at 36th Street (☎ 212/563-3366; meat), and 1156 Sixth Ave., at 45th Street (☎ 212/869-6699; meat), is the kosher answer to McDonald's and Burger King. Grilled burgers and chicken sandwiches are standard, but you can also choose from a small Chinese menu and Middle Eastern specialties like falafel. Kosher Delight also has free delivery to any location in Manhattan (it's not guaranteed your food will arrive hot or within a reasonable amount of time). The **Great American Health Bar,** 35 W. 57th St., between Fifth and Sixth avenues (☎ 212/355-5177; dairy), proves that healthy food doesn't have to be boring and flavorless, offering a varied menu from salads to vegetarian chili to pastas. There are wonderful fresh fruit health shakes blended with milk and yogurt, and kids may get a kick out of the pita pizza—tomato sauce, melted cheese, and vegetables baked on top of pita bread. Unlike most of these restaurants, the Health Bar also serves breakfast, opening at 8am; it's also the only one of these restaurants that doesn't close Friday night and Saturday for the Sabbath.

Finally, the West Side's popular **Dougie's BBQ and Grill,** 222 W. 72nd St., between Broadway and West End Avenue (☎ 212/724-2222; meat), offers crayons on all tables to keep kids occupied while they're waiting for their food. The service is fast-paced and friendly. Burgers and hot dogs are popular items, but the ribs and pasta dishes shouldn't be passed up.

Note: Because of the Sabbath, most kosher restaurants vary their hours on Friday and Saturday, depending on when sundown is on Friday night and when the Sabbath ends on Saturday night. (Some simply close all day Friday.) Call ahead to be sure when they'll be open if you plan to dine on Friday or Saturday.

ICE CREAM & SWEETS

DeRobertis Pasticceria. 176 First Ave. (between 10th and 11th sts.). ☎ **212/674-7137.**
AE, MC, V. Tues–Thurs 9–11pm, Fri–Sun 9am–midnight. Subway: 6 to Astor Place;
4/5/6/L/N/R to Union Square. BAKERY.

Smaller and not as commercially successful as Veniero's (below), DeRobertis, run by
four generations of the DeRobertis family since 1904, still gives its around-the-
corner neighbor a run for its money in the realm of Italian pastries: creamy
cannolis, anise cookies, fruit tarts, cheesecake. A more relaxed local crowd drifts in
here to skip the line at Veniero's. The back room, with its pressed-tin ceiling and
small marble tables, feels as authentic as any place in Little Italy.

Veniero's. 342 E. 11th St. (between First and Second aves.). ☎ **212/674-7264.** AE, DISC,
MC, V. Daily 8am–midnight. Subway: 6 to Astor Place; 4/5/6/L/N/R to Union Square. BAKERY.

This spiffed-up dessert cafe often has a line waiting outside in the evenings, full
of people craving after-dinner delights from cakes to cookies to cannolis, plus
cappuccino and espresso that put Starbucks to shame. I know many New Yorkers
who judge this as the city's best Italian pastry shop, in or out of Little Italy. With
kids, though, your best bet is to come in the afternoon, when you'll have no
trouble getting a table.

THE CHAIN GANG

Beatniks must be turning in their graves to see St. Mark's Place, that bastion of
bohemian hipness, invaded by **Dallas BBQ** at 132 Second Ave. (☎ **212/777-5574**).
Next thing you know, **Pizzeria Uno** will be moving in around the corner . . . oops, it
already has, at 55 Third Ave., between 10th and 11th streets (☎ **212/995-9668**).
There's also a suitably laid-back **Mary Ann's**, 86 Second Ave., at 5th Street (☎ **212/
475-5939**), serving authentic Mexican food and many margaritas to latter-day
beatniks.

9 SoHo

MODERATE

Kelley & Ping. 127 Greene St. (between Houston and Prince sts.). ☎ **212/228-1212.** High
chairs, boosters. Reservations not accepted. Lunch $5.95–$7.50; dinner $5.50–$14. AE, MC, V.
Daily 11:30am–5pm and 6–11pm. Subway: N/R to Prince St. JAPANESE/PAN-ASIAN/THAI.

With its pressed-tin ceiling and wooden factory floor, Kelley & Ping looks very
SoHo, but its friendliness to kids is unusual in this hyper-urban-chic neighborhood.
It started out as an Asian grocery store but soon added an open kitchen in the center of the room; there are still stocks of bottled sauces and woks for sale along the
walls. The noodles, stir-fries, and grilled meats (Vietnamese pork chops, chicken
satay) go down well with children, though some dishes can be super-spicy—ask for
your waiter's guidance. Unlike many Asian restaurants, this one does have milk for
kids to drink; for dessert, try the fried bananas or the red-bean ice cream.

Tennessee Mountain. 143 Spring St. (at Wooster St.). ☎ **212/431-3993.** Kids' menu,
boosters, sassy seats. Reservations recommended. Main courses $7–$18.50; kids' menu $2.
AE, CB, DC, MC, V. Mon–Wed 11:30am–11pm, Thurs–Sat 11:30am–midnight, Sun
11:30am–10pm (later on holiday weekends). Subway: N/R to Prince St.; C to Spring St.
AMERICAN/BARBECUE.

The setting is a farmhouse dating from 1807 (back when this part of town was
country, long before all the cast-iron architecture went up), which from the outside

looks very historic and sedate. Inside, though, the exposed brick walls and simple wooden tables host casual crowds looking for Southern barbecue, served with sides of yams, fries, coleslaw, and whatever. Rib purists, who can be a very critical crowd, tell me this isn't the world's best barbecue, but it seemed plenty tasty to me—what do I know? If barbecue isn't your thing, there's also chili and plenty of blander choices like quiches, salads, and seafood. The kids' menu covers a good range with BLTs and tuna salad sandwiches as well as the usual burgers, chicken fingers, and ribs; they do give kids crayons and a white paper chef's hat, which helps buy parents time to chow down.

INEXPENSIVE

Fanelli's. 94 Prince St. (at Mercer St.). ☎ **212/226-9412.** Reservations not accepted. Main courses $6–$15. AE, MC, V. Mon–Thurs 10am–2am, Fri–Sat 10am–4am, Sun 11am–2am. Subway: N/R to Prince St. AMERICAN.

This 19th-century saloon claims to be the second-oldest drinking spot in the city, being descended from a grocery store that opened on this site in 1847 and soon had a good side business as a "porter shop" (saloon); it became a speakeasy after Michael Fanelli bought it in 1922. Atmospheric Fanelli's still has the requisite carved mahogany bar, pressed-tin ceilings, beery smell, and filtered light, but the fare is refreshingly simple pub grub—burgers, omelets, quiches, pastas, fried chicken, shepherd's pie. Families gravitate to the back room, which is a little sunnier and quieter, for casual lunches and early dinner; later on, it may be hard to compete with the drinking scene. The service is friendly and laissez-faire. If the trendy SoHo scene gets you down, retreat here.

Moondance. 80 Sixth Ave. (at Grand St.). ☎ **212/226-1191.** Booster seats. Reservations accepted. Salads and sandwiches $3–$10.95; main courses $6.95–$13.95. AE, DC, MC, V. Mon–Wed 8am–midnight, Thurs 8am–4am, Fri 8am–Sun midnight. Subway: C/E to Spring St. AMERICAN DINER.

Stranded on the western edge of SoHo, where Holland Tunnel traffic tends to back up, this nifty little diner—shiny with aluminum panels inside and out—is a hoot for kids who want to feel plugged into the downtown buzz. Like the SoHo art world, the menu's a tad schizophrenic, offering burgers and chili dogs as well as health-foody grilled vegetables and whole-wheat fusilli pasta and pesto scrambled eggs; comfort-food standbys like meat loaf and mashed potatoes are thrown in for good measure. The wide range of pancakes, waffles, and French toast served at all times makes my kids happy. Stick to the simpler stuff if you want to be safe. There's only a handful of tables, plus a few stools at the counter, but you'll rarely have to wait to be seated in daytime or early evening; the real scene happens late at night. Even at breakfast and lunch, you'll still spot plenty of rumpled arty types dressed in black.

10 Little Italy

EXPENSIVE

Sal Anthony's SPQR. 133 Mulberry St. (between Grand and Hester sts.). ☎ **212/ 925-3120.** High chairs, boosters. Reservations recommended. Two-course fixed-price lunch $7.95; dinner $15.50–$25. AE, CB, DC, MC, V. Mon–Fri noon–11pm, Sat–Sun noon–midnight. Subway: 6/N/R to Canal St. ITALIAN.

Lots of bustle and brightness define this big, high-ceilinged dining hall, where people on all sides are happily digging into Italian food: High-gloss as it is, you can tuck your napkin into your collar here with no fear. Despite the brick walls and potted plants, the look is modern, not vintage trattoria. But what it lacks in coziness and atmosphere it more than makes up in efficiency, big portions, and party spirits; it seems there are always a few large tables occupied by extended families, bonding over fusilli and linguine. Pastas are consistently good, as are the hearty meat dishes, especially the macho veal chop. A good place to celebrate a special family event.

MODERATE

Angelo's of Mulberry Street. 146 Mulberry St. (between Grand and Hester sts.). ☎ 212/966-1277. Sassy seats. Reservations recommended. Main courses $12–$17. AE, CB, DC, MC, V. Tues–Thurs and Sun noon–11:30pm, Fri noon–12:30am, Sat noon–1am (closed Mon). Subway: 6/N/R to Canal St. ITALIAN.

This crowded, crowd-pleasing Little Italy favorite, which has been around since 1902, turns out an incredibly long list of southern Italian pasta dishes with zestful flavor, all at around $12.50. Make a reservation so you won't get stuck in the line of tourists waiting to get in, but don't be dissuaded by the place's low-brow popularity—this is Little Italy, after all, where tourists flock to eat, and no restaurant here that's any good would be without a line. Order anything with garlic, anything with tomato sauce. If your kids like their pasta plain, as mine do, even they'll benefit from the fresh homemade quality of the food.

Caffé Napoli. 191 Hester St. (at Mulberry St.). ☎ 212/226-8705. High chairs. Reservations accepted for parties of 6 or more only. Main courses $11–$25. AE, MC, V. Daily 10:30am–2am. Subway: 6/N/R to Canal St. ITALIAN.

Though there's a string of more renowned "fine-dining" restaurants to the north on Mulberry Street, for a leisurely dinner out with family I'd rather go to a place like Caffé Napoli and its annex, **Trattoria Canta Napoli** (☎ 212/226-8705). The food is upscale enough to feel like a treat, with seafood alongside the pasta dishes (Naples is a seaport, remember); specialties include the stuffed veal chop and the pasta malefemmina. The softly lit dining room has been tastefully decorated—Neapolitan pictures and artifacts are strewn about, but there's no attempt to make it look like "the Old Country." Diners are encouraged to linger over their meals; waiters are attentive but not intrusive. And families are definitely welcome—they'll cheerfully do half portions of pasta for kids.

INEXPENSIVE

Il Fornaio. 132A Mulberry St. (between Canal and Hester sts.). ☎ 212/226-8306. Reservations not accepted on weekends. Main courses $5.95–$15.95. AE, CB, DC, DISC, MC, V. Daily 11am–11pm. Subway: 6/N/R to Canal St. PIZZA.

The sign outside is explicit: KIDS WELCOME. And, it goes without saying, no one will get too upset about spills or crying or food left on the plate in this unpretentious cafe. It's small enough that you can't miss the shouted exchanges between waiters and cooks, but the pizza here has a longstanding reputation for excellence, so don't be surprised if you have to wait a few minutes for a table on a weekend. (And once you get in, don't be surprised if you're hustled back out again fairly soon—not a bad thing if you're with kids.) Pizza, pasta, calzones, and muffalettas—the menu has many kid-friendly choices, so who needs a chicken-fingers-and-burgers kids' menu?

Lombardi's Pizza. 32 Spring St. (between Mott and Mulberry sts.). ☎ 212/941-7994. Boosters. Reservations accepted for parties of 6 or more only. Pizzas $10.50–$20 (feed 2 or more). No credit cards. Mon–Thurs 11:30am–11pm, Fri–Sat 11:30am–midnight, Sun 11:30am–10pm. Subway: 6 to Spring St. PIZZA.

Claiming to be a resurrection of New York's first pizza restaurant, which opened at 53 Spring St. in 1905—and where all the other pizza maestros learned their trade—the new Lombardi's is owned by a grandson of the original Gennaro Lombardi, and it does have an authentic coal oven, taken over from an old bakery. It's a bit far north from the main Little Italy strip along Mulberry Street, in an area that many think of as SoHo these days, but the look is nice and atmospheric, with the obligatory red-checkered tablecloths, brick walls, and white tiled floor. Its wonderful pizzas more than hold their own among the top contenders (John's, Patsy's, Angelo's), with lightly charred thin crusts and totally fresh ingredients. The clam pie is so good that it actually justifies the weird idea of putting seafood on a pizza. Don't expect to just pick up a slice: Sit your family down in a booth and apply yourselves to consuming a whole pie. Eat, already.

ICE CREAM & SWEETS

Caffé Roma. 385 Broome St. (at Mulberry St.). ☎ **212/226-8413.** No credit cards. Daily 8am–midnight. Subway: 6 to Spring St.; B/D/Q to Grand St. BAKERY.

This old-fashioned corner pastry shop with hexagonal-tile floors and tiny wrought-iron cafe tables is a great place to duck into for cannoli, those ricotta-filled roll-ups of sweet crisp pastry. Kids can drink frothy hot chocolate or chilled lemonade while parents indulge in cappuccino or espresso, made the classic way (no half-caffé mocha double latte here).

Ferrara. 195 Grand St. (between Mulberry and Mott sts.). ☎ **212/226-6150.** AE, DC, DISC, MC, V. Daily 8am–midnight. Subway: B/D/Q to Grand St. BAKERY.

Larger, cleaner, and brighter than Caffé Roma (above), Ferrara has display cases crowded with mouth-watering pastries to go or to stay. There's almost always a crowd, day or night. If your kids want to sample Italian gelato (ice cream), this is a good place for that too.

11 Chinatown

MODERATE

Ba Ba. 53 Bayard St. (at Elizabeth St.). ☎ **212/766-1318.** Reservations recommended. Main courses $3.95–$17.95. No credit cards. Daily 10:30am–2am. Subway: 6/N/R to Canal St. MALAYSIAN.

Not even a Chinese restaurant, and far more trendy-upscale than most of its neighbors—the brick walls, hammered metal accents, and Lucite table tops make it look positively SoHo—Ba Ba doesn't fit neatly into the Chinatown profile, but it has attracted a steady stream of customers nevertheless. Curry and coconut feature strongly in the spicy Malaysian style of cooking, but the menu here also borrows from other Asian cultures, chiefly Thai and Chinese. Children may like the crispy roti canai pancakes, the grilled chicken or beef on skewers (though they may not choose to dip them in the accompanying peanut sauce), or the Hainanese steamed chicken. Parents, of course, are welcome to try anything from crispy squid to fish heads to chicken feet (though the menu advises you to consult with your waiter before ordering these), though any of the fish or rice dishes or casseroles should show off the kitchen's skill.

Tai Hong Lau. 70 Mott St. (between Bayard and Canal sts.). ☎ **212/219-1431.** Reservations recommended. Main courses $8.95–$18.95, except for Peking Duck ($35). AE. Mon–Fri 10am–11:30pm, Sat–Sun 9am–11:30pm; dim sum daily 10am–4pm. Subway: 6/N/R to Canal St. CHINESE.

With its chandeliers, carpeting, and white tablecloths, Tai Hong Lau is much more dignified than the other places listed here, and therefore should be saved for special occasions with older children. If you don't want to splurge on the Peking Duck, you can still dine well on a number of Cantonese specialties such as boneless chicken with lemon sauce; the menu is strong on seafood and bean-curd dishes, so vegetarian teenagers may be pleased. The restaurant is open for dim sum until late afternoon, but be prepared: It's very hard to keep track of how many of those tempting-looking delicacies you've chosen from the little carts being wheeled about, and the price can mount up fast.

INEXPENSIVE

HSF. 46 Bowery (near Canal St.). ☎ **212/374-1319.** Boosters. Reservations recommended. Main courses $7.95–$16.95. AE, DC, DISC, MC, V. Daily 8am–midnight; dim sum daily 8am–5pm. Subway: 6/N/R to Canal St. CHINESE.

Unprepossessing from the outside, this slightly rundown spot with hand-lettered signs in Chinese taped on the walls is one of the best dim sum places in town. They start wheeling out the carts as early as 8am to satisfy regular customers; tiny dishes with all kinds of delectable dumplings and skewers and rolls are laid out on the carts, and diners choose whatever looks good to them. At the end of the meal, they count up your dishes and tell you how much you owe. You don't have to read a menu or communicate with the staff to choose yourself a meal full of wonderful surprises; in fact, you may never learn the name of certain mouth-watering dishes. Eating dim sum is a novel experience that can be loads of fun for older kids who are willing to blindly sample new foods, though no item is really that far from standard Chinese dishes. The only problem may be discovering how high a bill you've run up, taste-testing all those tempting morsels. Lovers of Chinese barbecue (that's my kids) may also want to check out the annex, **Yummy Noodles,** right across the alley at 48 Bowery (☎ 212/374-1327), a neater and more modern-looking spot that features roast meats and noodle dishes.

Lin's Dumpling House. 25 Pell St. (between Bowery and Mott sts.). ☎ **212/577-2777.** Reservations accepted. Main courses $7.50–$15.95; dumplings $4.25–$5.95. No credit cards. Sun–Thurs 11am–10:30pm, Fri–Sat 11am–11pm. Subway: 6/N/R to Canal St. CHINESE.

Though my kids aren't dumpling fans (foods aren't supposed to touch each other, you see), a lot of kids do like them, and this is the place to come for very succulent dumplings. The pork with leek dumpling is especially delicious. Other recommended dishes are the sesame shrimp, the romantically named Romeo and Juliet (prawns and flank steak with peppers and water chestnuts), and the Chicken Delight, which is chunks of chicken fried with vegetables. But face it, you won't get kids to try the pig's intestine with sour cabbage. This place is a good choice for families who are put off by the hole-in-the-wall look of most of the other restaurants in this price category: It's a soothing, respectable setting, with lots of dark wood, etched glass panels, and green tablecloths.

New York Noodletown. 28½ Bowery (at Bayard St.). ☎ **212/349-0923.** Reservations not accepted. Main courses $3.25–$14.95. No credit cards. Sun–Thurs 9am–4am, Fri–Sat 9am–5am. Subway: 6/N/R to Canal St. CHINESE.

Noodles are one Asian food that even picky-eater kids can often be persuaded to try, and the noodles in this bustling Chinatown spot are delectable, simmered in broth or coated with various savory sauces; a wide range of menu choices mix 'n' match the noodles with grilled or roasted meats and stir-fried veggies. Be prepared to elbow your way in and endure hurried service; smaller kids may have to sit in your lap, as there are no boosters or high chairs.

Nha Hang. 73 Mulberry St. (between Bayard and Canal sts.). ☎ **212/233-8988.** High chairs. Main courses $4–$14.50. AE, MC, V. Daily 10:30am–10:30pm. Subway: 6/N/R to Canal St. VIETNAMESE.

The first Vietnamese restaurant interloper in Chinatown, Nha Hang made it easier for the others to follow because its popularity spread the word. The space is bright, modern, and simply decorated, with lightly varnished wood furnishings—nothing too exotic, until you taste the food. Less sauce-driven than Chinese food, Vietnamese cooking is big on spices and grilling, so watch out for those red stars on the menu if you don't like hot foods (there are plenty of soothing noodle soups for those who prefer to play it safe, as well as more subtly spiced dishes). My kids like both spring rolls and barbecued beef, so the dish that combines the two of those on vermicelli noodles was a hit; there's also a fine green papaya salad with beef, and a curry shrimp with string beans and coconut milk over rice that'll really clear your sinuses.

Wong Kee. 113 Mott St. (between Canal and Hester sts.). ☎ **212/966-1160.** Boosters. Reservations accepted for parties of 5 or more only. Main courses $5.95–$15.75. No credit cards. Daily 11am–9:45pm. Subway: 6/N/R to Canal St. CHINESE.

A consistently reliable choice, Wong Kee is contemporary-looking (some might say sterile), but the Cantonese food is deeply authentic, the sauces sweet and pungent, and the seafood ultrafresh. The roast pork and noodle dishes are excellent, as are their steak specialties and Hong Shiu chicken, crisp-fried chicken slathered with Chinese vegetables. The waiters have a reputation for speed, which means they may rush you a bit, but at least you won't have to worry about your children getting restless because it's taking so long for their order to get to the table.

12 TriBeCa & Lower Manhattan

MODERATE

Odeon. 145 W. Broadway (at Thomas St.). ☎ **212/233-0507.** Kids' menu, high chairs. Reservations recommended. Brunch $10–$18.50; lunch $10–$19.75; dinner $10.50–$23.95. AE, DC, DISC, MC, V. Mon–Thurs 11:45am–2am, Fri 11:45am–3am, Sat 11:30am–3am, Sun 11:30am–2am. Subway: 1/2/3/9/A/C to Chambers St. AMERICAN.

The mellow art deco look of Odeon, with its wooden blinds and comfy banquettes, helped make it one of TriBeCa's first hot spots way back in the early 1980s, notable for its late-night scene. Standards have been kept up surprisingly well into the 21st century, but now it's not too hip to welcome families. The brasserie menu is inventive and constantly changing, but there's always simple classic food like burgers, roast chicken, steak frites, and pastas. I happen to like the seared tuna sandwich with arugula and wasabi mayonnaise, as well as the grilled stuffed chicken breast with melted Gruyère cheese. This is also a good place to make a meal of two appetizers, with some excellent salads and a fine country pâté available. There's very little attitude and a lot of smart cooking going on here—no wonder Odeon has survived.

INEXPENSIVE

Bar Odeon. 136 W. Broadway (between Thomas and Duane sts.). ☎ **212/285-1155.** Kids' menu, high chairs, boosters. Reservations recommended. Lunch $8–$14.50; dinner $8.50–$22; kids' menu $5. AE, DC, DISC, MC, V. Mon–Fri 11:30am–midnight, Sat–Sun 11am–midnight. Subway: 1/9 to Franklin St.; A/C/1/2/3/9 to Chambers St. AMERICAN.

The brasserie menu at this retro diner is reminiscent of that at its more famous neighbor, Odeon (see above): burgers, omelets, roast chicken, grilled tuna, steak frites. The kids' menu isn't much more adventurous, but it does throw in salad with the fish sticks and chicken nuggets and hot dogs, and there is a pizza offering. Informal and totally kid-friendly, Bar Odeon allows parents to feel TriBeCa hip while their children loll happily on the Naugahyde banquettes.

Bubby's. 120 Hudson St. (at N. Moore St.). ☎ **212/219-0666.** Kids' menu, high chairs, boosters. Reservations recommended; no reservations accepted for weekend brunch. Lunch $8–$10; dinner $10–$15; kids' menu $1.50–$3. AE, CB, DC, DISC, MC, V. Mon–Thurs 8am–11pm, Fri 8am–midnight, Sat 9am–midnight, Sun 9am–10pm. Subway: 1/9 to Franklin St.; A/C/E to Canal St. AMERICAN.

Homey is the word for this comforting TriBeCa restaurant, with its wooden chairs, soft recorded jazz, and kitschy clutter. The food is comforting as well, with sandwiches, burgers, and pastas, not to mention breakfast food (served until 4pm—good to know if you've got kids who like scrambled eggs and French toast for lunch), with a few more upscale salads and chicken and fish dishes to please adults. It's the sort of place that understands that kids may like their spaghetti with butter and parmesan instead of tomato sauce and that cooked carrots go down better if you drizzle maple syrup on top. Service may dawdle a bit, but the laid-back ambience somehow makes children willing to linger. The Saturday and Sunday brunch tends to be very popular, but weekdays are generally uncrowded; it's a good halfway stop between the Fire Museum in SoHo and the World Trade Center.

Chevy's. 102 North End Ave. (entrance on Vesey St. between West St. and North End Ave.), in Battery Park City. ☎ **212/786-1111.** Kids' menu, high chairs, boosters. Main courses $8.99–$19.99. AE, CB, DC, DISC, MC, V. Daily 11am–1am. Subway: A/C to World Trade Center. MEXICAN.

This Mexican chain restaurant, located in the base of the Embassy Suites hotel (right around the corner from the new Regal Cineplex) offers families a decent option in a neighborhood where restaurants are all too often geared to Wall Streeters. The menu is fairly standard: burritos, quesadillas, fajitas, chimichangas, occasionally with a little Texas-style barbecued chicken thrown in. Some safer alternatives show up on the kids' menu, to take care of little gringos who don't do spicy food—stuff like burgers and chicken fingers. Expect a rock soundtrack, roadhouse decor, and some rowdy spirits, especially at happy hour.

Ellen's Café & Bake Shop. 270 Broadway (at Chambers St.). ☎ **212/962-1257.** Boosters, sassy seats. Reservations recommended. Main courses $9–$12. AE, DC, DISC, MC, V. Mon–Fri 6am–7:30pm, Sat 7:30am–5pm. Subway: 4/5/6/N/R to City Hall; 2/3 to Park Place; A/C to Chambers St. AMERICAN DINER.

Catering to the Wall Street lunch crowd (note the limited hours), this downtown branch of Ellen Hart's diner empire is a handy alternative to the fast-food outlets around here. The look is more saloonish than Ellen's Stardust Diner (above), but the atmosphere is 100% kid-friendly. The wide-ranging menu includes omelets, salads, burgers, and sandwiches, not to mention a brimming display case of yummy baked goods by the front door.

✪ Kitchenette. 80 W. Broadway (at Warren St.). ☎ **212/267-6740.** Kids' menu (dinner only), high chair. Breakfast $3.75–$7.75; lunch $5–$8; dinner $9.50–$17. AE. Mon–Fri 7:30am–10pm, Sat–Sun 5–10pm. Subway: 1/2/3/9/A/C to Chambers St. AMERICAN.

This artfully weathered little cafe looks like it belongs on Cape Cod or in upstate New York, not in the shadow of the World Trade Center, but that's its charm. Farmhouse-style breakfasts, featuring things like blueberry pancakes and buttermilk biscuits, start out weekdays; the lunch menu starts to drift toward hipness with choices like goat-cheese sandwich, roast eggplant, or Tuscan tuna salad alongside your standard grilled cheese, B.L.T., and tuna melt. By dinnertime, the transformation is complete, with inventive dishes like cornmeal-crusted fish, crab cakes with pineapple salsa, and grilled pork loin with roasted garlic puree. But there's always the house special turkey meat loaf with mashed potatoes (this is really, really good), as well as burgers and club sandwiches. The dinnertime kids' menu offers grilled cheese, B.L.T., or a small burger, all for $6, and the signature meat loaf for $8. It's the best of both worlds: The kids eat happy, you can eat upscale, and everything's copasetic.

THE CHAIN GANG

Houlihan's crops up in three locations: 196 Broadway, at John Street (☎ 212/240-1280); 50 Broad St., near Beaver Street (☎ 212/483-8310); and 7 Hanover Square, at the intersection of Wooster and Pearl streets (☎ 212/483-8314). If you're at South Street Seaport and your kids hate fish, head for that old standby **Pizzeria Uno,** 89 South Street Seaport (☎ 212/791-7999).

FOOD COURTS

On the top floor of the **Pier 17** pavilion at South Street Seaport, a sparkling big food court enjoys the kind of picture-window river views normally reserved for the toniest restaurants. The various food vendors whose booths surround the public seating include several ethnic varieties; there's often live music as well. There are many fast-food places underground near the subway and PATH train stations in the World Trade Center, but for a more upscale experience take the walkway over West Street and head for the food court in the **World Financial Center.** Connected to the Winter Garden shopping atrium, the food court features a cluster of sit-down, table-service restaurants, but the ambience is casual enough for kids. Sushi, chicken-finger appetizers, and hoagies are available along with good seafood at Johnney's Fish Grill; across the way is Donald Sacks, which has lots of sandwiches, salads, burgers, and a few more upscale entrees; at the end is the sparkling-clean California Burrito Co., which dishes out a mess of burritos named after various California towns.

Family-Friendly 10
Accommodations

One big problem families have with New York hotels is that the overwhelming majority are in Midtown, between 30th and 59th streets—not the best part of town for parents to be in with their children. The traffic, the noise, the absence of greenery, and the lack of a resident population at night all make Midtown less than desirable. On top of that, Midtown's tourist attractions—the Theater District, Fifth Avenue and Madison Avenue shopping, gourmet restaurants—are less relevant when you've got kids in tow. Of course, Midtown does boast superb hotels whose facilities and service level more than compensate for the location; there are also decent moderately priced hotels that cater well to families. But the list of hotels I recommend also includes nearly every choice in other neighborhoods. If you can, why not stay near Central Park or the American Museum of Natural History or the Metropolitan Museum of Art? Even Lower Manhattan hotels at least are close to South Street Seaport, the Statue of Liberty/Ellis Island ferry, and Hudson River Park.

The other big problem is the cost. Manhattan hotels sit on some very expensive real estate, pay staff wages in a top urban job market, and (often serving as flagships of various lodging chains) definitely tilt toward the high end of the luxury spectrum. Consequently, the city has the highest average room rate in the country—$224.83 per night in the first half of 2000. Occupancy rates are high too, often topping 85%, which means hotels don't have to discount to fill their beds. And many hotels market themselves to business travelers and conventioneers, whose expense accounts presumably cover those hotel bills—so why court penny-pinching families? (That line of thinking, of course, ignores the fact that more and more business travelers and conventioneers are trying to bring their families with them, turning a business trip into a family vacation as well.)

If a swimming pool is important to you and your kids, I warn you now: Few Manhattan hotels have had the room to include them and some that do have had to maximize their investment by turning their pool/health club into a profit center, selling memberships to adult New Yorkers who may not care to have the pool taken over by a bunch of kids doing cannonballs in the deep end. I've listed nearly every hotel that does have a pool but tried to give you an idea of how welcoming those pools really are for families.

One thing my family has always made use of when traveling is a kitchenette—if you can throw together breakfasts and lunches in your room, you can easily save $100 a day, not to mention keep your children's stress levels lower by not requiring them to use their restaurant manners three times a day. Suite hotels in general get my vote whenever they include some kind of kitchen facilities; they're also great with younger kids, because you can put toddlers to bed at 8pm and repair to the other room for a room-service dinner, a movie on cable TV, whatever. Seems a shame to spend your evening this way when you're in Manhattan, but for one or two evenings of a 1-week stay it can be a restful relief.

On this built-up island, there just isn't the range of properties you'd find even in other expensive markets, like London and Paris. You've got flea bags, you've got palaces—and not a whole lot in between. But face it: In between is where most families need to be. I've concentrated on ferreting out midrange hotels that are at least decent if not always charming and atmospheric. When I do include some of the high-priced four-stars, it's because they offer something families especially value—not necessarily stunning decor, hushed privacy, and meticulous valet service (three things that don't mix well with small children anyway), but a pool, a kids' program, or a family-friendly location.

WHEN IS HIGH SEASON?   Funny thing about Manhattan hotels: There are two definite patterns of activity. Some report that their slow time is January to early March; others say that July and August are their slow times. I gave up trying to predict which would be which—it seems to have nothing to do with location, price range, or whether they depend more on business travelers or leisure travelers. Just about all hotels, however, are booked way in advance from Thanksgiving to mid-December. When a big convention hits town, it can be impossible to find a room for love or money, as I discovered when I started doing hotel visits during the big PC Expo in June. Moral of the story: Call for reservations as soon as you know you're coming to New York, to make sure you won't get shut out. But the other side of the coin is also true—call at the last minute and you may get lucky even at one of the most popular properties.

Because New York attracts lots of business visitors as well as tourists, it's also hard to predict whether a given hotel is more likely to have a room free on weekends or on weekdays. A few hotels offer weekend packages to bolster occupancy rates when corporate types have gone home at the end of a working week, so it's always wise to check.

RESERVATION SERVICES   Central Reservations (☎ 800/356-1123) will book you into any of 35 hotels, including all the Manhattan East suite hotels, the Plaza, the Empire Hotel, the Doubletree Guest Suites, the Crowne Plaza, Le Parker Meridien, and chains like the Dorals; there's no charge and they can often get you discounts of 25% to 40%. The nationwide **Central Reservation Service** (☎ 800/873-4683) also offers a discount, quoted as 10% to 40%, when they help you book rooms in New York; mostly they handle chain hotels. The **Hotel Reservations Network** (☎ 800/96-HOTEL; www.180096hotel.com.com) offers discount hotel booking, at savings of up to 65%, in several large cities across the country, including New York.

A NOTE ABOUT HOTEL SERVICES   Certain services are so standard in Manhattan hotels I haven't noted them in individual reviews. Because tall buildings here interfere badly with TV reception, every hotel that offers in-room TVs—and that's virtually all of them—offers **cable TV,** which means you'll have a range of channels to surf. Most hotels also have Spectravision or Pay Per View or some other

in-room movie service feeding into the TVs. In the more expensive hotels, **dry cleaning** and **laundry services** are usual. No hotels provide their own **baby-sitters,** but just about every concierge or front desk has a list of sitters they've used before, usually provided by one of the city's many child care agencies. Rates can be steep—around $12 per hour, with additional fees for more children, plus cab fare to get home afterward ($5 to $7). What you'll get will be professional baby-sitters, many of them from Europe, Asia, or South America as well as North America. They'll come to your hotel room and take care of your children there.

Parking at just about all these Manhattan hotels, whether the hotel has its own garage or merely gives you a discount at nearby garages (the latter being more usual), is based on a per-night rate that assumes you won't be taking your car in or out during the day. Once you start moving the car, you'll have to pay more. Just another reason for not using your car while you're visiting Manhattan.

A NOTE ABOUT PRICES   I've categorized hotels according to a fairly basic rate for a family of four. In some hotels, that'll be the price for a double room with two double beds. In others, it may require a connecting pair of double rooms (though hardly any hotels will guarantee you'll get two rooms that connect—they're covering themselves in case the folks next door don't check out as expected—but, in general, if you request connectors, you'll get them). In some hotels I've had to base things on the assumption that a small suite will be the best family deal. At any rate, I call a hotel **Inexpensive** if that fictional family of four can stay for less than $200 a night; **Moderate** if their bill will run $200 to $275; **Expensive,** $275 to $350; and **Very Expensive,** over $350. (Those terms are, of course, relative to the Manhattan lodging price structure in general.) Quoted rates don't include the 13.25% New York City hotel tax or the occupancy tax, which is $2 per room per night.

These are based on "rack rates," the hotel's standard rates for peak times: Corporate discounts and package deals can bring them in at as much as $100 lower a night, so I've also noted which hotels regularly offer good discounts. Some hotels regularly offer summer packages, while others are likely to activate package deals at the last minute, when occupancy rates appear to be falling short of projected levels. (Yield management is the name of the game, with hotels as well as with airlines.) Even if you've already secured a room at rack rates at a lower-priced hotel, just before you arrive you might call a couple of pricier places to see if any special deals have kicked in. You could get a premium room for less, if you're lucky.

1 The Upper West Side

EXPENSIVE

Empire Hotel. 44 W. 63rd St. (at Broadway), New York, NY 10023. ☎ **800/333-3333** or 212/265-7400. Fax 212/315-0349. www.empirehotel.com. 375 units. A/C MINIBAR TV TEL. $175–$350 double; $300–$780 suite. Children 18 and under stay free in parents' room. Roll-away or crib $20. Corporate packages available. AE, CB, DC, DISC, MC, V. Parking $25. Subway: 1/9 to 66th St.

For visitors focused on Lincoln Center, the Empire Hotel, across from the center's plaza, is the logical place to stay—petite dioramas of Metropolitan Opera stage sets

Best Hotel Bets

See chapter 1 for a list of my hotel favorites—the most family-friendly, the best views, and more.

Uptown Accommodations

244

E 106th St.
E 105th St.
E 104th St.
E 103rd St. Ⓜ
E 102nd St.
E 101st St.
E 100th St.
E 99th St.
E 98th St.
E 97th St. Ⓜ
E 96th St.
E 95th St.
E 94th St.
E 93rd St.
E 92nd St.
E 91st St.
E 90th St.
E 89th St.
E 88th St.
E 87th St.
E 86th St. Ⓜ
E 85th St.
E 84th St.
E 83rd St.
E 82nd St.
E 81st St.
E 80th St.
E 79th St.
E 78th St.
E 77th St. Ⓜ
E 76th St.
E 75th St.
E 74th St.
E 73rd St.
E 72nd St.
E 71st St.
E 70th St.
E 69th St.
E 68th St. Ⓜ
E 67th St.
E 66th St.
E 65th St.
E 64th St.
E 63rd St. Ⓜ
E 62nd St.
E 61st St.
E 60th St.
E 59th St.

Mount Sinai Hospital

The Reservoir

Fifth Ave.
Madison Ave.
Park Ave.
Lexington Ave.
Third Ave.
Second Ave.
First Ave.
York Ave.
East End Ave.
Sutton Pl.

The Great Lawn
Metropolitan Museum of Art

Sheep Meadow

Central Park Zoo

Wollman Rink

Central Park South

UPPER EAST SIDE

Wards Island Footbridge

Carl Schurz Park

Gracie Mansion

FDR Drive

East River

Roosevelt Island

Roosevelt Island Tram

Queensboro Bridge

From Lower Level
To Upper level

0   1/3 Mi
0   .3 Km

Upper Manhattan

Uptown

Midtown

Downtown

8
10
11
12
13
14
15
9

are displayed on the handsome lobby's paneled walls, along with a couple of full-length canvases of great opera stars of the past, and CD players in every room bespeak a clientele that includes many performers as well as classical music fans. For families, however, the rooms, with their bland, upscale traditional decor, can be a bit cramped. Don't try to economize by going for a standard room and bringing in an extra bed; upgrade to one of the front-facing rooms with two double beds—those will actually work better than the smaller suites, which have only one bed in the bedroom and a foldout couch in the sitting room.

More than a century old, the Empire was thoroughly renovated in 1990, in a glossy if somewhat superficial makeover: The baths are fitted with hair dryers and makeup mirrors and a profusion of little amenities, but the molding in the rooms still looks lumpy from years of painting and repainting, and new phone lines have been strung along the molding rather than buried in the walls. There are VCRs in every room and 24-hour video rental is available, but the closets are unbelievably tiny. The long halls are painted one of the most lurid shades of pink I've ever seen.

Bright, clean, and perfectly respectable, the Empire still doesn't have the boutique pizzazz of most other properties owned by Schrager Hotels, but at least it's outside of Midtown. The location isn't as restful as that of most other Upper West Side hotels, however, since this stretch of Broadway is lined with hulking modern buildings, and the Empire is at the bottom of a frantic intersection where Broadway cuts diagonally across lower Columbus Avenue. But Central Park is only a block away.

Dining: The excellent but fairly formal West 63rd Street Steakhouse is on the premises. Another, hipper restaurant, Iridium, is in the same building but not affiliated; kids might like to pop in here just to see the slightly surreal decor. The neighborhood is loaded with restaurants, and every one of them is full at dinnertime before Lincoln Center's 8pm curtains.

Amenities: Concierge, room service (6am to 11:30pm), laundry/valet, VCRs and video rentals, CD players and CD rentals, access to New York Sports Club health club ($10).

On the Ave. 2178 Broadway (entrance on 77th St.), New York, NY 10023. ☎ **800/ 509-7598** or 212/362-1100. Fax 212/787-9521. 253 units. A/C TV TEL. $240–$300 double; $320 suite; $300–$450 penthouse rooms and suites. Roll-away $20. AE, CB, DC, MC, V. Parking $20 in nearby garage. Subway: 1/9 to 79th St.

Definitely the hip choice on the Upper West Side. The trendy lobby looks like something out of South Beach, with cool, pale stone walls, a slick dark-wood floor, and a few scattered pieces of black leather furniture. It's been smartly renovated upstairs as well, with a Japanese-like simplicity—neutral carpet, gauze curtains, stainless-steel sinks, a sleek panel of varnished wood morphing from headboard into canopy over the bed. Rooms are smallish and contain only a king or queen bed, which means that a family will need to snag connecting rooms (of which there are about 30 in the hotel) or go for the penthouse suites, which have sitting areas and, often, balconies. Though this stylish newcomer launched itself into the market with some great bargains, prices are creeping upward as On the Ave gains popularity, especially with younger travelers. The location is very convenient, with the Natural History Museum only 2 blocks away and Lincoln Center a 10-block stroll down Broadway. While there's no restaurant, Big Nick's Burger and Pizza Joint (see chapter 9) provides room service, and morning coffee is set out in the lobby.

MODERATE
✪ **Beacon Hotel.** 2130 Broadway (at 75th St.), New York, NY 10023. ☎ **800/572-4969** or 212/787-1100. Fax 212/724-0839. www.beaconhotel.com. 230 units. A/C TV TEL. $195–$225

double; $250–$550 suite. Children 16 and under stay free in parents' room. Roll-away $15; crib free. AE, DC, DISC, MC, V. Parking garages nearby. Subway: 1/2/3/9 to 72nd St.

Converted from an apartment building in the early 1990s (some residents still live in the building), the Beacon offers just what we need more of in this city: clean, respectably furnished rooms with all the important amenities and none of the glitzy frills, in a neighborhood great for kids. Riverside Park is 2 blocks west and Central Park 3 blocks east; the American Museum of Natural History and the Children's Museum of Manhattan are just a few blocks up the street, and Lincoln Center isn't far down Broadway. You'll find a quiet marble-clad lobby; wide, well-lit corridors; and good-sized rooms freshly done up in a traditional decor (glossy dark Queen Anne–style furniture, muted rose and tan color schemes, framed botanical prints on the walls). There's a full kitchenette with microwave in every room; the baths aren't large but look sparkling clean and have proper drinking glasses and tidy little amenities baskets.

Even the doubles are big enough for a family, since they have two double beds and enough space for a crib or roll-away. Suites add on a sitting room with a foldout couch; if you've got more than four people staying in a suite, there's a $15 charge per extra adult. There's no room service, but a coffee shop is right on the corner. Though this is a busy stretch of Broadway, the rooms are pretty well soundproofed; since the 25-story hotel is one of the tallest buildings in the neighborhood, the upper-floor rooms facing west have nice views over Riverside Park and the Hudson. As you'd expect, the Beacon gets a steady stream of business, so reserve as far in advance as possible, especially in June and October; weekdays tend to be less busy than weekends, so plan accordingly.

⊙ **Mayflower.** 15 Central Park West (at 61st St.), New York, NY 10023. ☎ **800/223-4164** or 212/265-0060. Fax 212/265-5098. 365 units. A/C TV TEL. $210–$225 double; $210–$900 suite. Roll-away $20; crib free. AE, CB, DC, DISC, MC, V. Valet parking $28. Subway: 1/9/A/B/C/D to Columbus Circle.

The Mayflower seems like a perfect name for this old-line dowager overlooking Central Park. Renovations throughout the year 2000 have seen gleaming new bathroom fixtures installed, and rooms will have new fabrics and paint jobs, but this genteel hotel still has the aura of another era—and that's the beauty of it. These rooms are truly spacious (a crib or roll-away will fit easily into one of the doubles) and the large windows (which you can actually open) let in loads of light, especially if you've paid the extra $25 or so for a breathtaking park view. The traditional decor opts for sensible plain colors and dark woods; closets are huge and plentiful, and nearly every room has a simple, functional pantry alcove with a refrigerator and sink but no cooking facilities.

To get a family-friendly room configuration, ask about the several connecting doubles, though a suite is probably a better deal—with two double beds in the bedroom and a queen-sized sleeper sofa in the sitting room, they comfortably sleep six. There's a $20 charge for an extra person in a double, though they hardly ever charge it for kids under 14—except over Thanksgiving weekend, when the park-view rooms are one of the city's prime places to watch the Macy's parade pass by.

The small, pleasant Conservatory restaurant serves all meals, with room service until 11:30pm. A small second-floor exercise room caters to fitness addicts, but kids will more likely want to hit the park across the street. Lincoln Center is conveniently nearby; Midtown is only a couple of blocks away, close enough to walk to. The staff's easygoing, unpretentious manner adds to the sense that the Manhattan hustle just doesn't apply to the Mayflower.

INEXPENSIVE

✪ **Excelsior Hotel.** 45 W. 81st. St. (between Central Park West and Columbus Ave.), New York, NY 10024. ☎ **800/368-4575** or 212/362-9200. Fax 212/721-2994. www.excelsiorhotelny. com. 146 units. A/C TV TEL. $149–$189 double; $179–$389 suite. Children under 14 stay free in parents' room. Roll-away $10; crib free. AE, DC, DISC, MC, V. Parking garages nearby. Subway: B/C to 81st St.

Perhaps feeling the competition from the nearby Beacon (above), this longtime neighborhood bargain hotel—perfectly situated right across the street from the city's top family attraction, the American Museum of Natural History—underwent a top-to-toe renovation in 1997, exchanging its shabby shag carpeting and wicker headboards for a smart French provincial motif in soothing greens and soft rosy browns. The bathroom fixtures are sparkling new and up-to-date, with nice country-French tile accents. The rooms are good-sized—a family of four could fit comfortably into one of the double-doubles (double room with two double beds), though a one-bedroom suite, with its pullout couch in the smallish sitting room, would give even more privacy (some one-bedroom suites have two doubles in the bedroom, so request this if your family needs to sleep more than four). The small but handsome wood-paneled lobby has an ornate plasterwork ceiling, and there's a small fitness room on site. Unfortunately, the renovations did away with all the kitchenettes, and there's no room service, but complimentary continental breakfast is available on premises in a breakfast room.

You can't deny the location is superb—facing the wooded side yard of the American Museum of Natural History, on a clean and relatively quiet West Side block of luxury apartment buildings. You're half a block from Central Park, and there are loads of good restaurants and stores around the corner on Columbus Avenue. Now that's it's been brought up to snuff, the Excelsior is busier than ever, particularly with weekend business—reserve a couple of months ahead, if you can.

Milburn Hotel. 242 W. 76th St. (between Broadway and West End Ave.), New York, NY 10023. ☎ **800/833-9622** or 212/362-1006. Fax 212/721-5476. www.milburnhotel.com. 114 units. A/C TV TEL. $119–$165 double; $159–$195 suite. Roll-away or crib $10. AE, CB, DC, MC, V. Parking $20. Subway: 1/9 to 79th St.; 1/2/3/9 to 72nd St.

As a happy mother checking out reported to me the day I visited, "What's not to like? It's clean, cheap, and friendly to kids." The hallways are cramped-looking and the rooms are smaller than those at the Beacon and Excelsior (see above), but the simple, modern furnishings are attractive and everything is crisply maintained. (Okay, the wallpaper in the hallways has been dinged a few times, but it's a tight fit for big luggage going around some of those corners.) Adding a crib or roll-away would make one of the doubles seriously snug; a family should probably go for a suite, which adds a sitting room with foldout couch. Kitchenettes have been smartly crammed into room corners: an up-to-date microwave, unstocked minifridge, coffeemaker, two-burner range, and tiny sink. The hotel has a small fitness room (extra charge) and you can rent Playstations from the front desk.

The Milburn's entrance is just around the corner from Broadway, making it convenient for shopping and restaurants—a plus, since it has no restaurant or room service (they do offer some dining discounts at good local restaurants). Considering you'll have a kitchenette, it's good to know that food shopping is especially great in this neighborhood, with the Fairway market and Citarella's fish market a couple blocks south and H&H Bagels and Zabar's gourmet emporium a few blocks north. Riverside Park is only 2 blocks away too. All told, an excellent deal.

Cool Pools

The largest pool has to be the blue Olympic-sized one at the **Travel Inn,** which has a very pleasant patio area around it for lounging but is surrounded by wings of the hotel—no views. The small rooftop pool at the **Days Hotel Midtown** has decent views of surrounding skyscrapers, though it's only 15 stories up; the **Holiday Inn Midtown 57th Street** has a small outdoor rooftop pool, but again it's not on top of a very tall building and the surrounding buildings are undistinguished. Neither of these latter two pools permits diving, which might be a drag for rambunctious kids.

You'll get better views—and get them year-round—at the glass-enclosed atrium pool at **Le Parker Meridien,** which is up 42 stories with panoramas of Central Park and the Midtown skyline. The enclosed pool at the **Regal U.N. Plaza Hotel** may be only 27 stories up, but it's right on the East River, which means not only river views but also unobstructed skyline views south (you can even see the World Trade Center). What's more, the Regal U.N. Plaza's pool is especially lovely, with handsome tile work and an exotic spangled canopy overhead. Also in Midtown, the **Crowne Plaza Manhattan** has a 50-foot indoor lap pool with a nice view, if that matters to you. Farther west, the **Skyline Hotel** has a smallish enclosed rooftop pool with big windows grabbing a bit of a Hudson River view; hours are limited, however, because of swimming classes held throughout the day.

Downtown, the busy 50-foot pool at the **Marriott World Trade Center** is on the 22nd floor and has boffo harbor views. The **Millenium Hilton's** 40-foot fifth-floor pool looks right out on the spire of St. Paul's Church; the **New York Marriott Financial Center's** 50-foot pool has no views but is sparkling clean and quiet. Across the East River in Brooklyn, the **New York Brooklyn Marriott** has a 75-foot-long lap pool where kids can cavort after a day of sightseeing.

Quality Hotel on Broadway. 215 W. 94th St. (between Broadway and Amsterdam Ave.). ☎ **800/228-5151** or 212/866-6400. Fax 212/866-1357. www.bestnyhotels.com. 450 rooms. A/C TV TEL. $149–$219 double; $199–$350 suite. Roll-away or crib $15. AE, CB, DC, MC, V. Parking $18. Subway: 1/2/3/9 to 96th St.

Don't let the unglamorous upper Broadway environs put you off: You're half a block from an express subway stop, where trains can whisk you to the Theater District in minutes, and with several good casual restaurants nearby (not to mention top playgrounds and sports facilities in both Riverside and Central parks), this neighborhood works very well for families. The hotel itself is unexceptional, with tight corridors, a ho-hum traditional decor (subtly patterned wallpaper, mauve carpeting, rose-hued bedspreads, cherry-veneered reproduction furniture), and window air-conditioners (not that there's any view to block). Bathrooms, though neatly modernized, are on the small side. Still, a double room with two double beds can squeak into the Inexpensive rate category, and the suites aren't that much more (a junior suite, with a queen bed and a foldout couch, is a good option for families). Lots of tour operators know about this place, so book well ahead. Weeknights are considerably cheaper than weekends, if you can take advantage of that fact, and summer offers lower rates, though even then rooms book up fast. There's no room service, but there are plenty of nearby coffee shops; rooms have coffeemakers and you can rent an in-room fridge for $15 a night. It's a sensible option for families who plan to be out and about most of the time anyway.

2 The Upper East Side

VERY EXPENSIVE

✪ **The Carlyle.** 35 E. 76th St. (at Madison Ave.), New York, NY 10021. ☎ **800/227-5737** or 212/744-1600. Fax 212/717-4682. 192 units. A/C MINIBAR TV TEL. $450–$695 double; $650–$2,800 suite. AE, DC, MC, V. Parking $39. Subway: 6 to 77th St.

In my opinion, this is the best hotel in Manhattan—and lots of people seem to agree with me. The roster of celebrity guests includes everyone from Jack Nicholson to JFK, from Brooke Astor to David Bowie, from Jessica Lange and Sam Shepard to Goldie Hawn and Kurt Russell. Many of the staff, from the bellmen to the concierges, make working at the Carlyle a lifetime career, delivering white-glove service that's rare indeed. Surprisingly enough, all this makes the Carlyle a great family hotel, if the prices aren't beyond your budget. The neighborhood is wonderfully quiet and well behaved and the rooms are huge—even a double is big enough for a smaller family, with a crib or roll-away brought in.

All the rooms are done in beautiful traditional style, with gorgeous chintzes and drapes and thick carpets; from its first decorator in the 1930s, Dorothy Draper, to more recent refurbishments by Mark Hampton, the Carlyle has been furnished by Manhattan society's top residential designers. *Residential* is the key word—if a room has shelves, they'll be stocked with books; vases and china dishes and ormolu clocks are set out on the occasional tables; every sitting room and bedroom has its own entertainment center with a VCR and CD player. More than a dozen rooms have grand pianos, some of them Steinways, others Baldwins like the one Bobby Short plays downstairs in the Café Carlyle. The suites have sleek modern kitchens, while even the double rooms at least have an alcove with a sink and well-stocked minibar. The baths are big and gleaming, with Givenchy toiletries, thick towels, terrycloth robes, hair dryers, and makeup mirrors; most tubs have whirlpools in them.

The hotel is 35 stories tall, so if you're lucky enough to snag a room overlooking Central Park, you'll have a view you could gaze at for hours, day or night. Carlyle guests are near enough to the park to scamper right over and play, as well as being close to the Fifth Avenue museums and to the glorious children's shops of upper Madison Avenue.

Dining/Diversions: The dark, romantically ornate Carlyle Restaurant serves breakfast, lunch, and dinner, with a lavish luncheon buffet every day except Sunday. Bistro-style suppers and Sunday brunches are served in the Café Carlyle, best known as the cabaret ($50 cover charge) where pianist/singer Bobby Short has performed for three decades; in the months he's not there, Eartha Kitt, Dixie Carter, or Barbara Cook may fill in, and on Monday evening Woody Allen plays the clarinet with the Eddy Davis New Orleans Jazz Band. Bemelmans Bar is an atmospheric cocktail lounge even children will want to visit, to see the murals painted by Austrian artist Ludwig Bemelmans, creator of the Madeline books ("In an old house in Paris, covered in vines, lived twelve little girls in two straight lines. . . ."). Jazz vocalist Barbara Carroll performs at night in the bar ($10 cover). Breakfast coffee, afternoon tea, cocktails, and posttheater snacks are served in the Turkish-style red-velvet Gallery, a lobby area with a few small tables.

Amenities: Concierge, 24-hour room service, twice-daily maid service, secretarial services, VCRs and CD players; small health club with sauna, steam room, exercise machines.

Hotel Wales. 1295 Madison Ave. (at 92nd St.), New York, NY 10128. ☎ **212/876-6000.** Fax 212/876-7139. 87 units. A/C TV TEL. $305 double; $440–$895 suite. Rates include continental breakfast. Roll-away $20; crib free; extra person $20. AE, DC, DISC, MC, V. Valet parking $28. Subway: 6 to 96th St.

There's more than a touch of Edwardian Kensington to this charming century-old hotel in Carnegie Hill, a historic Upper East Side neighborhood full of top-notch private schools and well-off families. Only a block from Central Park and Museum Mile, the hotel is smack in the middle of upper Madison's strip of upscale children's shops. The lobby looks like the entry hall in a private mansion, with its marble stair-case, carved wood banisters, dark wainscoting, and striped wallpaper, and the room decor is tastefully traditional—beautiful restored woodwork, original cabinets, and cedar-lined closets. Absolutely the only drawback to staying in this hotel is that the rooms are so small you can barely fit in a crib—better to go for a suite, which consists of a fair-sized bedroom and an adjoining sitting area with a pullout sofa. (There are no connecting doubles.) The baths are tiny yet outfitted with top-quality fixtures. No rooms have kitchenettes, but you can have a mini-refrigerator on request. Every room has a VCR and CD player; the Wales's growing popularity with families has resulted in the addition of many more kids' movies to its VCR library. Kids might get a kick out of the hotel's Puss-in-Boots theme, discreetly carried out with framed prints on the walls and designs on the bath toiletries.

Dining/Diversions: The Pied Piper Room, where guests can help themselves to a granola-and-muffins breakfast, is a big comfy space with potted palms and Victorian settees where chamber music is played at teatime and on Sunday evening. Popular Sarabeth's Restaurant, though separately owned, is right downstairs and provides room service 7am to 11pm.

Amenities: Fitness studio, VCRs and rentals, CD players.

The Mark. 25 E. 77th St. (at Madison Ave.), New York, NY 10021. ☎ **800/843-6275** or 212/744-4300. Fax 212/744-2749. 180 units. A/C MINIBAR TV TEL. $480–$530 double; $675–$2,500 suite. Children under 17 stay free in parents' room. Roll-away $30; crib free. Corporate, weekend, and summer packages available. AE, CB, DC, DISC, MC, V. Parking $35. Subway: 6 to 77th St.

Compared to its near neighbor the Carlyle (above), the Mark looks hipper and more corporate, though it's still one of the city's finest hotels. (Don't worry—they've fixed up the room Johnny Depp so famously trashed.) Many of its guests are visiting New York on business, and 40% of the clientele is European—not surpris-ing, since the hotel is part-owned by a Monaco-based hotel company, the Rafael Group. But families still fit into the mix pretty well, especially since summers and weekends—prime times for family travel—are less busy here.

One thing the Mark offers that few other uptown hotels do: connecting doubles that can be closed off with their own private doorway and vestibule. Double rooms have either twin beds or a king-sized bed, and rooms are plenty large enough for a crib to be brought in. The so-called executive suite is another good option for families, with a queen-sized bed in one room and a foldout couch in the other. The decor is neoclassical English-Italian, with lots of warm browns, overstuffed chairs, and eye-catching draperies. The baths are bigger than average, with stunning black-and-white tiles and fixtures, including deep tubs, separate shower stalls, and heated towel bars (my kids always find these a kick for some reason—well, it is pretty nice to swathe yourself in a warm towel when you step out of a bath). The neighbor-hood is restful, with a sort of monied calm, and Central Park is only a block away. At 16 stories, the Mark offers views over many neighboring rooftops. The small but state-of-the-art second-floor health club is hardly ever used, so no one may mind if kids pop in to goof around on the treadmills, Exercycles, and Stairmasters.

Dining: Mark's, consistently rated one of the city's top restaurants, serves breakfast, lunch, dinner, Sunday brunch, afternoon tea, and posttheater drinks and desserts. It's a handsome clublike dining room with velvet banquettes, brass railings, mahogany armchairs, and tables spaced well apart. Mark's Bar is a snug, dark-walled lounge serving cocktails (with some light food) and late supper.

Amenities: Concierge, 24-hour room service, limousines, business services, laundry/valet, VCRs, in-room fax capability; twice-daily shuttle to Wall Street, weekend shuttle to the Theater District; small health club with sauna, steam room, exercise machines.

Stanhope. 995 Fifth Ave. (at 81st St.), New York, NY 10028. ☎ **800/233-1234** or 212/774-1234. Fax 212/894-5430. www.hyatt.com. 185 units. A/C MINIBAR TV TEL. $395–$450 double; $500–$2,000 suite. Roll-away or crib $35. Weekend packages (including continental breakfast). AE, CB, DC, DISC, MC, V. Parking $40. Subway: 4/5/6 to 86th St.; 6 to 77th St.

With its small gold-leaf-trimmed lobby and large plush rooms, the Stanhope, which is now part of the Park Hyatt collection, is definitely one of the Upper East Side's handful of true luxury hotels, and you can't beat that location right across from the Metropolitan Museum of Art. Few rooms have park views, since the museum is in the way, but museumgoers find it awfully handy to be just steps from the Metropolitan and right on Museum Mile, in one of Manhattan's calmest, safest, and most elegant neighborhoods (Jackie O used to live 4 blocks up the street).

The rooms, with floral fabrics, pastel wall coverings, and ornate furniture (the decorator clearly was into chinoiserie), are easily big enough for a crib or roll-away, but if you have more than one kid, go for a one-bedroom suite, which on weekends costs only a little more than a double does on weekdays. The suites have excellent pullout sleeper sofas, a second bath, and two TVs; request one with a kitchenette and you'll be set. Only guests have key access to the elevator, which means security isn't a worry here (and, hey, this neighborhood is hardly Times Square). Though it may seem a trifle too sedate for families, the Stanhope certainly welcomes kids, provided they don't pry the inlaid wood out of the armoires.

Dining: The hotel's restaurant, Melrose, serves contemporary American cuisine; it's super for ladies who lunch but perhaps a bit too refined if you've got vocal kids in tow. The Terrace, the popular small sidewalk cafe on Fifth Avenue, or the Tahitian-style Lobby Bar, may be your better bet for drinks or a light meal. If your kids are really into etiquette, dress them up in their cotillion clothes and treat them to afternoon tea served in the library, with scones and finger sandwiches and the works.

Amenities: Concierge, 24-hour room service, VCRs, CD players, in-room fax capability, business center, kitchenettes in deluxe doubles and suites, fitness center with sauna, complimentary limo to Midtown.

EXPENSIVE

The Barbizon. 140 E. 63rd St. (at Lexington Ave.), New York, NY 10021. ☎ **800/223-1020** or 212/838-5700. Fax 212/888-4271. 306 units. A/C MINIBAR TV TEL. $250–$325 superior; $275–$350 deluxe; $400–$500 1-bedroom suite; $600–$1,200 tower suite. Children under 13 stay free in parents' room. Roll-away $20; crib free. AE, DC, DISC, MC, V. Valet parking $29. Subway: N/Q/R to Lexington Ave.; 4/5/6 to 59th St.

In its days as a ladies' residence hotel, the Barbizon Hotel for Women—a tawny Spanish-Gothic brick tower close to Bloomingdale's—was home to such future luminaries as Grace Kelly, Ali McGraw, and Candice Bergen, as well as legions of other young women starting their careers in Manhattan. The tiny studios of those days were revamped in 1997 to create bigger rooms for the transient market, making it a very viable option for families, considering the clean East Side location. Superior and deluxe doubles hold either a king- or a queen-sized bed or a pair of double beds, and they are roomy enough for a crib or roll-away as well. One-bedroom suites have a queen-sized bed in the bedroom and a pullout sofa in the sitting room. The tower suites are even more special, with narrow wrap-around terraces that let you step outside and drink in the sky.

Now operated by the very savvy Schrager Hotels, the renovated Barbizon has a cool, restful, sophisticated decor of pale woods, soft garden colors, white louvered shutters, and wrought-iron bedsteads; the pristine white baths are smallish but well fitted. Though the breakfast room is open only 6:30 to 11am, there's room service (until 11pm), and the neighborhood is swimming in restaurants, several of which let you can charge your meals to your Barbizon room account. The on-site Equinox health club has an indoor pool, but there's a day-use fee for hotel guests, and no one under 18 is allowed to use it.

Amenities: Concierge, newspaper delivery, CD players and rentals, in-room fax capability, laptops to rent.

Lyden Gardens Suite Hotel. 215 E. 64th St. (between Second and Third aves.), New York, NY 10021. ☎ **800/ME-SUITE** or 212/320-8022. Fax 212/465-3697. 130 units. A/C TV TEL. $324–$649 suite. Roll-away $20; crib free. AE, DC, DISC, MC, V. Children under 13 stay free in parents' room. Parking $20 at nearby garage. Subway: 4/5/6 to 59th St.; 6 to 68th St.; B/Q to Lexington Ave.

Manhattan East Suites hotels offer great deals for extended-stay visitors or families: reasonably priced suites with fully equipped kitchens (the staff will even do your grocery shopping—for a modest fee), along with essential hotel services. (There's room service from 7:30am to 10:30pm, some nearby restaurants will deliver, and there are loads of family-friendly restaurants nearby.) The Lyden Gardens attracts a lot of business from the cluster of hospitals around 68th Street and York Avenue, but this relatively residential neighborhood also makes sense for families on a short stay. From the stylish small lobby on, the decor is clean, simple, and contemporary—good innocuous surroundings to crash in after a long day. Request a junior suite with a pullout couch as well as two double beds, or go for the one- or two-bedroom suites, which have separate bedrooms and sitting rooms, with sleeper sofas. There's also an on-premises Laundromat and a health club with weight-training equipment and a Stairmaster. In general, the staff seems helpful and friendly, accommodating whatever requests guests have.

☼ Surrey Hotel. 20 E. 76th St. (at Madison Ave.), New York, NY 10021. ☎ **800/ME-SUITE** or 212/288-3700. Fax 212/628-1549. 131 units. A/C TV TEL. $330–$350 studio suite; $395–$415 1-bedroom suite; $625–$725 2-bedroom suite. Roll-away $20; crib free. Weekly and monthly discount rates available. AE, CB, DC, DISC, MC, V. Valet parking $35. Subway: 6 to 77th St.

If you haven't got the dough to stay nearby at the Carlyle or the Mark (above), you can still enjoy this ace East Side neighborhood with a much more affordable suite at the Surrey. Its clean, well-maintained rooms are positively huge—you could easily fit a crib or roll-away into the so-called studio suites. The one-bedroom suites could sleep six, with two double beds in the bedroom and a foldout sofa in the sitting room. The decor is tasteful, if not fussy, with Chippendale-ish reproductions. The baths are sparkling clean, though the fixtures aren't necessarily luxurious. Every unit has a kitchen or kitchenette, with a mini-refrigerator, sink, stove, cutlery, and plates, and guests here really do seem to use their kitchens—the staff will even do your food shopping for only $5 (plus the cost of the groceries, of course). If cooking's not your idea of a vacation, there are scads of restaurants within a short walk and the room service is provided (7:30am to 10pm) by the kitchen of one of Manhattan's most stellar chefs, Daniel Boulud, whose Café Boulud is downstairs.

The ample reception area, with marble columns, a chandelier, and a genteelly faded Oriental rug, resembles many Upper East Side apartment building lobbies—indeed, staying here is one way to discover what it's like to live in New York as a family, as you troll the Madison Avenue children's shops and hang out at the East 76th Street Playground in Central Park. The Surrey's residential air is enhanced by the fact that many guests are on long stays—corporate relocations, local families holing up during apartment renovations (laundry facilities in the basement make life easier for those folks, as do VCRs and a small exercise room). Nevertheless, the Surrey welcomes short-stay guests, especially on weekdays and in the July/August slow period, so don't hesitate to check if there's a room, even on short notice.

MODERATE

Gracie Inn. 502 E. 81st St. (between York and East End aves.), New York, NY 10028. ☎ **212/628-1700.** Fax 212/628-6420. 12 units. A/C TV TEL. $169–$199 studio suite; $199–$249 1-bedroom suite; $299–$399 penthouse. Rates include continental breakfast. Roll-away $25; crib free. Discounts offered for weekly and monthly stays. AE, DC, DISC, MC, V. Parking garages nearby. Subway: 6 to 77th St.

If only New York had more places like the Gracie Inn! First off, there's the neighborhood—Upper East Side, on a side street near the East River, not far from Carl Schurz Park. This is the part of the East Side where middle-class families live and shop and go to school. Then there's the thoughtful service and quiet un-hotel-like atmosphere, which make this a welcome retreat from Manhattan bustle—the sort of bed-and-breakfast boutique hotel you can find all over Europe but rarely in the States.

Once you get past the unprepossessing exterior and minuscule lobby, the five-story town house (with elevator) has individually decorated suites. Antiques, stenciled wallpapers, rag rugs, hardwood floors, and lace curtains go for a country inn look that's never too frilly or precious; fresh flowers are set out in the rooms and plump snowy duvets are on the beds. Every suite has a tidy little kitchen with all utensils, and a continental breakfast is brought to your room each morning. Cribs or roll-aways could fit handily even in the studios, though a one- or two-bedroom suite would be better for a family, especially the penthouse duplex (kids will have a blast running up and down the snug wooden staircase). With skylights, a greenhouse wall, and weathered wood terraces, the penthouse suites get loads of sun, but even rooms on the lower floors are fairly light. Don't expect to walk to the subway—York Avenue is a long way east from the subway line—but buses and taxis are easy to find and the neighborhood has plenty of good, reasonably priced restaurants.

3 Midtown West

VERY EXPENSIVE

The Plaza. 768 Fifth Ave. (between 58th and 59th sts.), New York, NY 10019. ☎ **800/759-3000** or 212/759-3000. Fax 212/546-5234. 815 units. A/C MINIBAR TV TEL. $260–$550 double; $650–$15,000 suite. Roll-away $30; crib free; extra person $35 (after first 2 in room). AE, CB, DC, DISC, MC, V. Valet parking $40. Subway: N/R to Fifth Ave.

The only New York hotel designated a National Historic Landmark, the Plaza is truly lovely. Even if you're not staying here, you should stroll up the red-carpeted steps to have a walk through the turn-of-the-20th-century baroque lobby: From the neoclassical mosaic floors to the dazzling crystal chandeliers to the gilded cornices with inset heirloom tapestries, it's a sight to behold. (Don't miss a peek into the Edwardian Room and Oak Room to see their inimitable carved Gothic rafters and burnished wood paneling.) It's surprising, then, especially considering the steep rates, that the clientele looks so unsophisticated—an uncanny number of folks in shorts and polo shirts assiduously snapping photos of themselves "in the Plaza." The gracious concierge desk busily books guests into stodgy expensive restaurants, while the theater ticket window seems to do a brisk business in *Beauty and the Beast* tickets. The moral: Don't be intimidated by the Plaza—if you opt to stay here, you'll certainly feel you're someplace special but won't have to worry about being outclassed.

Lots of families stay here (Did everybody see *Home Alone 2*? Has every child dreamed of living here like Eloise?), and management has very intelligently responded by setting up the Young Plaza Ambassadors, a VIP program for kids 6 to 18. Free with a 2-night stay, two siblings ($50.75 for additional sibs) get turn-down cookies and milk; in-room movies; coupons and special perks at restaurants, shops, and museums around the city; and discounts on various kid-oriented events around the hotel. A lounge has been set up on the 17th floor, with videos, a bulletin board, games, and space for kids to meet other kids.

Families should steer away from the standard double rooms, which have only a double bed and not enough room for a crib or roll-away. For that, you'd have to get what they call a Classic room; better yet, get a Deluxe room that has two double beds. By that time, you're up to at least $450 a night. Of course, if you'd like to go all out, the Astor Suite costs a mere $4,000 a night! You'll get a huge living room, a formal dining room, a full kitchen, and three bedrooms, all fitted out in Versailles-style gilt and brocade—not to mention a master bath with Central Park views from the whirlpool. (The gold swan-shaped faucets are an Ivana Trump touch—she supervised the refurbishment of the hotel when she and the Donald ran the place.)

All the guest rooms betray a taste for the palatial—but, then, what else would go with 14-foot-high ceilings, ornamental plaster moldings, and original crystal chandeliers? Here's a tip: If you're paying the extra $200 or so a night for a room facing Central Park, insist on floors 5 to 8—you'll be up high enough to see, and, by virtue of the exterior's Parisian wedding-cake design, the windows are much larger there than on the higher floors. Or save dough by opting for a Fifth Avenue view, where you can look down on Grand Army Plaza's gilded statue and fountain, not to mention FAO Schwarz across the street.

Dining: Breakfast, lunch, and dinner are served in the Palm Court (see chapter 9). The Oak Room (for grilled American food; closed Saturday lunch and Sunday dinner) and the Oyster Bar (for seafood) serve lunch and dinner; both are very pricey and not what you'd call kid-friendly.

Amenities: Concierge desk (four Clefs d'Or on staff), 24-hour room service, VCRs, in-room fax capability; spa with fitness machines (no one under 18 allowed); business center; shopping arcade; courtesy car to the theater if you dine in the hotel.

EXPENSIVE

✪ **Le Parker Meridien.** 118 W. 57th St. (between Sixth and Seventh aves.), New York, NY 10019. ☎ **800/543-4300** or 212/245-5000. Fax 212/307-1776. 700 units. A/C MINIBAR TV TEL. $325–$365 double; $395–$2,500 suite. Roll-away or crib free. Weekend packages available. AE, CB, DC, DISC, MC, V. Valet parking $38. Subway: B/N/Q/R to 57th St.

Midtown Accommodations

With its splendid glass-enclosed atrium pool, sundeck, eighth-of-a-mile roof jogging track, and top-notch health club, this French-owned hotel is a super choice for any athletic family. The 57th Street location is in the middle of all the theme restaurants and not far from FAO Schwarz, the Warner Bros. Store, and the Disney Store; several rooms on the 42-story hotel's upper floors—say, from 20 on up— offer Central Park views. The property looks snooty enough, with a marble-columned lobby and a sleek guest-room decor that calls to mind both Japanese minimalism and hipster Italian fashion—but Le Parker Meridien does a good job of making families feel welcome.

On arrival, kids are given a packet containing stuff like crayons and coupons for kid-appealing activities. Items like high chairs, night lights, bottle warmers, and safety plugs are available on request. The suites have full kitchenettes (pots and plates and condiments can be requested), and all rooms have CD players and VCRs. The rooms are of good size by Manhattan standards—a double with two double beds could accommodate a family for a short stay—though the Tower Suites aren't a bad deal, with a king-sized bed in one room, a pullout couch in the other, a bath, a kitchenette, and an awesome skyline view on upper floors.

Dining: Norma's serves breakfast and brunch, and Seppi's offers French cuisine for lunch and dinner, as well as live jazz in the evening. Jack's Bar is also on premises.

Amenities: Concierge, 24-hour room service, business center, CD players, VCRs, kitchenettes, indoor pool, extensive health club with squash and racquetball courts, spa, sauna, sundeck, jogging track.

The Paramount. 235 W. 46th St. (between Broadway and Eighth Ave.), New York, NY 10036. ☎ **800/225-7474** or 212/764-5500. Fax 212/354-5237. 610 units. A/C MINIBAR TV TEL. $260–$350 double; $425 1-bedroom suite; $600 2-bedroom suite. Roll-away $20; crib free. AE, DC, DISC, MC, V. Parking $38. Subway: A/C/E to 42nd St.; C/E to 50th St.; 1/2/3/7/9/N/R/S to Times Square.

Not many families stay here, maybe because the parents feel intimidated by the aggressively hip decor by ultratrendy Philippe Starck: Stepping into the minimalist gray lobby with its asymmetrical rug, cartoonishly shaped armchairs, and free-standing stairway of brushed stainless steel can be unnerving. The rooms have severe-looking white linen bedcovers, black-and-white checkerboard carpets, and oversized gilt frames for headboards; the baths have an inverted cone of brushed steel for a sink.

Truth to tell, though, it's stunning, and kids might really get into its futuristic weirdness. If the guest-room decor's not a problem, the size may be—some double rooms do have two double beds, but that doesn't leave a whole lot of space. The west-of-Times-Square location is no longer a turnoff, with the increasing gentrification of neighborhoods to the west (a trickle-down effect from 42nd Street's remarkable transformation). The Paramount is close to Broadway theaters, so there are always lots of people around, and Eighth Avenue still boasts some cheap ethnic restaurants and coffee shops that may be fun for families. All in all, I think this is a super place for a few nights' stay, provided your kids are sophisticated enough to appreciate the hypercoolness.

Dining: The Mezzanine Restaurant—its tiny tables lit by jewel-toned lamps, set on a narrow mezzanine overlooking the lobby—serves breakfast, lunch, and dinner, as does the Library Lounge. Coco Pazzo Teatro is also available for lunch and dinner. A smart Dean & Deluca espresso bar is off the lobby, and the Whiskey Bar is a happening place for after-work singles.

Amenities: Concierge, 24-hour room service, VCRs and video rentals, fitness room with exercise machines, business center.

Renaissance New York. 714 Seventh Ave. (between 47th and 48th sts.), New York, NY 10036. ☎ **800/682-5222**, 800/HOTELS-1, or 212/765-7676. Fax 212/765-1962. 305 units. A/C MINIBAR TV TEL. $265–$495 double; $475–$600 suite. Children 15 and under stay free in parents' room. Roll-away or crib free. AE, DC, DISC, MC, V. Valet parking $35. Subway: N/R to 49th St.; B/D/F/Q to 47th–50th sts./Rockefeller Center; 1/9 to 50th St.

Sleek and corporate-looking as it is, the Renaissance isn't the kind of hotel families automatically gravitate to, but those who do wind up here might be very pleasantly surprised. First, you're right in the thick of the exciting Times Square action, but in a good way—the famous neon Coca-Cola sign hangs on the hotel's south wall, the TKTS half-price ticket booth is a few steps away, many rooms look out onto one or another of the fabled supersigns, and the hotel's Foley's Fish House restaurant offers the best panoramic view of the Times Square intersection. (You couldn't ask for a better ringside seat on New Year's Eve.) Yet the riffraff gets screened out by the ground-floor security lobby (the guest lobby is up on the third floor), and double-paned windows do an amazing job of keeping out traffic noise.

Inside, everything is mahogany and brass and marble and truly handsome. Families can fit nicely into the doubles, which are roomier than most Midtown doubles—go with a king-sized-bedded room with a roll-away or a room that has two queen-sized beds. Suites consist of a king-sized-bedded sleeping room and a sitting room with a pullout couch. Minibars are set under a marble countertop with a coffeemaker, which makes a handy place for fixing snacks or lunches, and 1 VCR (tucked into a cabinet with a video player) have 25-inch screens.

Dining: On the third floor off the guest lobby, Foley's Fish House—which has dark glass windows on three sides offering a thrilling view of the Great White Way—serves lunch and dinner. Breakfast is served in the Dining Room nearby. A cocktail lounge (closed Sunday and Monday), also on the third floor, has windows overlooking Broadway too, though facing away from Times Square. A pianist plays here about 5:30 to 8pm.

Amenities: Concierge, 24-hour room service, newspaper delivery, video players, small gym with fitness machines.

MODERATE

✪ **Crowne Plaza Manhattan.** 1605 Broadway (between 48th and 49th sts.), New York, NY 10019. ☎ **800/2-CROWNE** or 212/977-4000. Fax 212/333-7393. 770 units. A/C MINIBAR TV TEL. $200–$400 double; $450–$1,050 suite. Children 19 and under stay free in parents' room. Roll-away $20; crib free. AE, DC, DISC, MC, V. Valet parking $34. Subway: 1/9 to 50th St.; N/R to 49th St.

With the ongoing turnaround of Times Square, the Crowne Plaza is nicely positioned to grab a big chunk of the Midtown market. With a reception area one floor up from Broadway (security is thorough but not oppressive) and tight soundproofing, you can feel removed from the tumult but not bunkered in—many windows overlook the razzmatazz, including some around the pool and at the end of every corridor. The guest floors begin on the 16th story (several floors of offices are in between the lobby and the guest rooms), so many rooms have great skyline or river views. Yet this contemporary 46-story building sticks firmly to the middle of the road, in style as well as rates. Its lobby has some marble and brass and plush touches, but it's not overbearing; the room decor is traditional and corporate, with greens and browns and lots of table lamps.

Families have several layout options: a double room with two double beds; connecting doubles; a smallish sitting room with your choice of one or two bedrooms connecting; or a large sitting room (complete with a minibar/serving area and dining table) with your choice of one or two bedrooms connecting. Along with pullout sofas, the Crowne Plaza has some pull-down Murphy beds, which kids might enjoy. Some extra amenities (terry bathrobes, a jar of hard candies) are offered on Crowne Plaza Club floors, for which you'll pay $30 to $50 more, but it might be worth it if only because you can get continental breakfast free in the lounge, a huge windowed parlor with dynamite views; once the corporate travelers have cleared out at 9am or so, the room is virtually empty. The health club is an obvious attraction for families, though there are some caveats: The fitness center is run by the New York Sports Club, whose members get priority over hotel guests weekdays at lunchtime and after work. The 50-foot lap pool, however, is open to guests at all times; if you want to make sure there's room, call ahead to reserve a lane.

Dining: Samplings, a contemporary-looking continental restaurant off the lobby, serves dinner along with some stunning second-floor Times Square views. The Broadway Grill serves more casual fare—pizza, pasta, burgers—for lunch and dinner. The Balcony Café does breakfast and lunch, with a big buffet at both meals, as well as à la carte service. Another morning option is to pick up a light breakfast to go from the Lobby Bar—coffee, juice, muffins, bagels—just enough to satisfy kids before you dash off for sightseeing.

Amenities: Concierge, 24-hour room service (with kids' menu), theater desk, tour desk, newspaper delivery, 50-foot indoor pool, 29,000-square-foot health club (with exercise machines, aerobics classes, sauna, massage), business center, shopping arcade.

✪ Doubletree Guest Suites. 1568 Broadway (at 47th St. and Seventh Ave.), New York, NY 10036. ☎ **800/222-8733** or 212/719-1600. Fax 212/921-5112. 460 units. A/C MINIBAR TV TEL. $249–$399 suite. Children 17 and under stay free in parents' room. Crib free. AE, CB, DC, DISC, MC, V. Valet parking $30. Subway: 1/9 to 50th St.; N/R to 49th St.; B/D/F/Q to 47th–50th sts./Rockefeller Center.

Quite possibly the most family-oriented hotel in Manhattan, the Doubletree more than makes up for what might be an off-putting location, smack dab on Times Square. There are two entire floors fitted out for families with younger children—plastic drinking cups, childproofed power outlets, padded bump guards on furniture edges, spout covers in the tubs. Older children might prefer (or insist, if they're like my nieces) to stay on the two floors designated as Green Suites, which are cleaned with environmentally sound cleansers and offer recycling and optional fewer linen changes. The suite concept is a natural for families anyway, since you automatically get sleeping space for four or six, depending on whether you request a king-sized bed or two doubles in the bedroom (there's a foldout sofa in the sitting room). All suites have kitchenettes that include a microwave, a coffeemaker, a sink, a marble counter, and an empty mini-refrigerator, as well as a stocked minibar. The low-key contemporary decor features calm grays and subdued geometric designs that don't show spills. Both rooms have TVs, and you can request VCRs.

Now let's get to the really unusual ways the Doubletree provides for families: There's no charge for cribs, playpens, and strollers, and you can request that the cable movie service be shut off if you're worried your kids will go wild with the remote. Next to the restaurant and health club is a delightful large playroom with a stunning Statue of Liberty design on the carpet; it's equipped with well-chosen picture books, big stuffed animals, colorful large foam blocks, and a clever wall-mounted city maze around which kids can steer small taxis. Security is good, though not forbidding: There's a ground-floor foyer with monitored elevators leading up to the guest lobby, and a separate bank of elevators going up to guest-room floors. After 11pm guests have to show their key card to be admitted into the guest-room elevators. At 43 stories, the Doubletree does have some high-floor rooms with Midtown views, but what's more important about the height is that it means there are lots of rooms, so more families can take advantage of this great deal.

Dining: The Center Stage Café has whimsical wall murals carrying out its Broadway theater theme—face one way and you'll feel like an audience watching the stage; face the other and you'll feel like performers looking up at the audience in the painted balcony. The restaurant serves a breakfast buffet, lunch, and dinner and has a kids' menu.

Amenities: Room service (until 4am), newspaper delivery, kitchenettes, VCRs and video rentals, small fitness room with exercise machines, children's playroom.

INEXPENSIVE

Days Hotel Midtown. 790 Eighth Ave. (at 48th St.), New York, NY 10019. ☎ 800/572-6232, 800/325-2525, or 212/581-7000. Fax 212/974-0291. 367 units. A/C TV TEL. $119–$400 double. Third person $20; children 12 and under stay free in parents' room. Roll-away $20; crib free. AE, CB, DC, DISC, MC, V. Parking $11. Subway: C/E to 50th St.

The Days Hotel is the kind of place New Yorkers love to sneer at, because it's a mass-market chain popular with low-end tour groups (high school class trips, foreigners on package trips), but there's really nothing seriously wrong with the place. So long as you avoid the sleazy peep show strip south of the hotel along Eighth Avenue (between 42nd and 45th streets, mostly), this location actually isn't all that bad—just to the north on Eighth Avenue you'll find the Worldwide Plaza office complex (which has a great multiplex cinema) and several casual trendy restaurants.

The Days Hotel may be as bland as a suburban mall, but it's respectably clean, with a marble-and-brass lobby and neat, fresh, motel-like traditional furnishings in the rooms. Considering how small many Manhattan hotel rooms are, these are relatively large, with space for a crib or roll-away even if you opt for a room with two double beds. At these prices, though, larger families may be able to afford two connecting doubles, of which there are lots. The rooftop pool, one of the Days Hotel's bigger drawing points, is a bit of a disappointment—it's not big enough for lap swimming, and you aren't allowed to dive in. The small sundeck surrounding the pool is crammed with cheap lounge chairs; there's also a poolside snack bar. Just off the lobby, the bright but bare Metro Deli serves casual food 6am to midnight and provides room service (an unexpected perk in this price range) while it's open.

Holiday Inn Midtown 57th Street. 440 W. 57th St. (between Ninth and Tenth aves.), New York, NY 10019. ☎ 800/HOLIDAY or 212/581-8100. Fax 212/581-7739. 599 units. A/C TV TEL. $159–$289 double; $350–$700 suite. Roll-away $15; crib free. AE, DC, DISC, MC, V. Parking $13.50. Subway: 1/9/A/B/C/D to Columbus Circle.

This characterless motor inn suits its characterless surroundings on Midtown's far west fringe. If you're driving into Manhattan, the low parking rate from the attached garage may appeal to you, especially since this property is close to the West Side Highway. And if you think your kids can't survive a vacation without a pool handy, the outdoor rooftop pool (open in summer only) may be a draw. But otherwise this hotel has few virtues to overcome its out-of-the-way location (it's a long walk even to the Hard Rock Café) and its typical chain-motel layout, with large modern windows looking out at nothing particularly scenic.

The double rooms are of decent size by Manhattan standards—out-of-towners may think they're cramped, but they do fit two double beds comfortably, which means a whole family may be able to fit in. There are a number of connecting doubles, if your family wants more space to spread out. Rooms have neutral-toned contemporary-style furnishings; those who are interested in swimming might try to snag one in the south tower, where the pool is. The Gotham Café serves breakfast, the Via Strada restaurant serves Italian food for lunch and dinner, and Skylight Lounge (bar) serves food, as well; room service operates 6:30am to 10:30pm, and there's a fitness center.

Skyline Hotel. 725 Tenth Ave. (between 49th and 50th sts.). ☎ **800/433-1982** or 212/586-3400. Fax 212/582-4604. 230 units. A/C TV TEL. $129–$169 double. Roll-away $15; crib free. AE, DC, DISC, MC, V. Free parking (no in/out during stay). Subway: A/C/E to 50th St.

With the transformation of the gritty Hell's Kitchen neighborhood into respectable Clinton, the Tenth Avenue location of the Skyline is no longer a drawback. After their 1998 renovation, the rooms are tastefully decorated—green carpets, mottled rosy walls, flowered bedspreads—with up-to-date bathrooms (though small, most have bathtubs). Even better, most rooms are large enough to hold two double beds, which means that families may be able to get by with one room. We're talking bargain here, and many Europeans have already found it, so book well ahead. Okay, so outside corridors on guest-room floors are narrow, and even high floors don't have exciting views. The small rooftop indoor pool is freshly tiled with lots of surrounding windows, but there's a catch—a local swim teacher has several prime daytime hours reserved for his classes (excellent classes, by the way—Hi, Jim! Hi, Dwight!). For these prices, people are happy to work around such minor inconveniences.

Off the lobby, Restaurant 1050 is a casual spot serving American bistro-style food, three meals a day, room service runs from 6:30am to midnight, and there's a wealth of fun restaurants 1 block away on Ninth Avenue (not to mention those cheap-by-Manhattan-standards movie tickets at the Worldwide Plaza cinema). Yes, it's a trek from here to most sights (the *Intrepid* and the Circle Line are the only close attractions—see chapter 4), but it's generally easy to hail a cab outside the hotel door. Now that it's no longer scary to walk this far west on 49th or 50th streets, the Skyline makes a lot of sense if you're trying to save a buck or two.

Travel Inn. 515 W. 42nd St. (between Tenth and Eleventh aves.), New York, NY 10036. ☎ **800/869-4630** or 212/695-7171. Fax 212/967-5025. 160 units. A/C TV TEL. $150–$175 double. Roll-away $20; crib free. AE, DC, DISC, MC, V. Free parking. Subway: A/C/E to 42nd St./Port Authority. Bus: M42.

One of New York's very best deals is this bright, clean, sprucely decorated motor inn way at the end of 42nd Street—beyond the sleaze, beyond Theater Row, in an area of warehouses and parking lots and not much else. One reason to stay here is you get free parking; of course, what you save in parking you could easily spend in taxi fare, since the only attractions within walking distance are the Circle Line boat tours and the *Intrepid* Sea-Air-Space Museum (see chapter 4). Still, the Travel Inn remains very busy—there are many times when it's sold out months and months in advance—partly because it's so handy for conventioneers attending meetings at the nearby Javits Convention Center.

If you don't mind the grungy surroundings (the hotel certainly seems secure enough), you could save a whole lot by staying here: A family could fit comfortably in these rooms, which have two double beds, a desk, a dresser, and upholstered chairs. The decor is modern, and everything is well kept up; the baths are spotless.

And as befits a true motor inn, there's a big lap pool (open Memorial Day to Labor Day), set in a spacious tiled area with lots of lounge chairs and room to stroll around. A number of rooms overlook the pool area from balconied walkways—request one of these, as opposed to the ones overlooking the street. A fitness room with weights and exercise machines has recently been added. There's no room service (What do you expect at this price?), but the attached Riverwest Cafe and Deli will deliver up to your room 6am to 8pm.

4 Midtown East

VERY EXPENSIVE

Four Seasons. 57 E. 57th St. (between Madison and Park aves.), New York, NY 10022. ☎ **800/332-3442** or 212/758-5700. Fax 212/758-5711. www.fourseasons.com. 370 units. A/C MINIBAR TV TEL. $615–$990 double; $1,350–$10,000 suite. Extra person $50. Roll-away or crib free. AE, CB, DC, DISC, MC, V. Parking $42. Subway: 4/5/6 to 59th St.

Now owned by Ty Warner of Beanie Baby fame, this stunning 57th Street hotel designed by I. M. Pei has set new standards in New York for service, upscale chic, and high prices. The tortoise-shell onyx skylight and soaring octagonal limestone columns in the cathedral-like foyer instill a sense of awe, and everything from there on is hushed and decorous and knowingly subtle. Smartly dressed guests wander through the lobby toting the right designer shopping bags; the attentiveness of the staff is wonderful, without a trace of fawning or condescension. The guest rooms are furnished with sleek built-in cabinetry of blond English sycamore, beautifully streamlined stuff Frank Lloyd Wright would approve of. The marble baths are huge and superbly appointed, with roomy adjacent dressing areas.

The room layouts aren't particularly handy for families. A maximum of one extra bed is allowed per room (crib or roll-away) and there are only a few adjoining doubles that could be set off by shutting a common door to the corridor. Larger families will have to go for a suite, which knocks you up into the $1,000-plus range. All the suites are on the higher floors, 31 and above (the hotel is 52 stories tall), which gives many of them stunning Central Park views. But the Four Seasons does value its young guests enough to have welcoming cookies and milk, as well as a gift pack.

Dining: The Fifty Seven Fifty Seven restaurant serves contemporary American food, and the Lobby Lounge serves light American/continental fare for breakfast, lunch, tea, and dinner.

Amenities: Concierge, 24-hour room service; health club with exercise machines, whirlpool, sauna, spa services; business center.

Regal U.N. Plaza Hotel. 1 United Nations Plaza (44th St. and First Ave.), New York, NY 10017. ☎ **800/222-8888** or 212/758-1234. Fax 212/702-5051. 427 units. A/C MINIBAR TV TEL. $299–$399 double; $450–$1,500 suite. Roll-away $35; crib free. Weekend packages available. AE, CB, DC, DISC, MC, V. Valet parking $27. Subway: 4/5/6/7/S to Grand Central.

The Regal U.N. Plaza's neighborhood hardly qualifies as Midtown—across from the United Nations, it's deliciously quiet, safe, and residential. When you combine that with the peerless views (all rooms are on the 28th floor or above, overlooking the East River or the skyline, uptown or down), the premium prices start to make sense. The clientele is heavily international, with foreign businesspeople as well as some United Nations visitors, and one signature note of the hotel's decor is the many international textiles hanging framed in the halls, echoed in the rooms by interesting textures in the upholstery, drapes, and bedspreads. Although it's a sleek corporate-style hotel, families may well be attracted not only by the neighborhood but by the fact that it has a great pool—what may well be the prettiest pool in town, with a haremlike canopy hanging overhead and those dynamite views from windows on two sides.

There are two towers to choose from, connected by a disconcertingly slick lobby: the original East Tower, built in 1976, and the newer West Tower, built in 1980. While the East Tower is on the same elevator bank as the pool and has better river views, the West Tower makes up for it with floor-to-ceiling windows that really let you drink in the panorama. (Each room that ends in 31 is a lush two-bedroom suite, with a wedge-shaped living room that enjoys both river and skyline views, perfectly heavenly day or night.) The rooms feel slightly like ocean-liner cabins to me, with their richly hued wood trims, streamlined modern decor, and tidy built-in cabinets and desks and dressers. They're on the small side, which can be a problem for families. The double rooms have only a king-sized bed or two twins— there are no doubles with two double beds—and fire laws permit only one extra bed. Larger families will have to go for a suite (with kitchenette) or hope they can get connecting doubles (not guaranteed but almost always possible).

Dining: The Ambassador Grill serves American grill fare, with an open kitchen showing off the wood-fired rotisserie spits. Breakfast, lunch, and dinner are available, with brunch replacing the lunch menu on weekends.

Amenities: Concierge, 24-hour room service, newspaper delivery, in-room fax capability; health club with pool, exercise machines, weights, saunas; indoor tennis court on the 39th floor; business center; complimentary limo to Wall Street and Park Avenue weekdays, transportation to the Theater.

EXPENSIVE

✪ Beekman Tower. 3 Mitchell Place (First Ave. at 49th St.), New York, NY 10017. ☎ **800/ ME-SUITE** or 212/355-7300. Fax 212/753-9366. www.mesuite.com. 174 units. A/C TV TEL. $335 studio suite; $420 1-bedroom suite; $685 2-bedroom suite. Roll-away $20; crib free. AE, DISC, MC, V. Valet parking $23. Subway: E/F to Lexington/Third aves.

In many respects, the Beekman Tower offers the best of all worlds. You're convenient to Midtown but in the posh residential East 50s, where peace and safety reign. You have all the roominess of a small apartment but with lots of hotel services. You get some super views but don't have to pay through the nose for them.

This orange-brick deco tower rising on a slope just north of the United Nations is known to New Yorkers for the Top of the Tower, a pleasant and unpretentious restaurant and lounge with a wonderful view of the skyline and East River. What New Yorkers don't seem to know is what a great deal this all-suite hotel is. Its smallest suite, the studio, will work only for a small family—it has a queen- or full-sized bed and a small sofa (not all of them fold out), but there's plenty of room for a crib or roll-away, and it has a kitchenette. The one-bedroom suites are perfectly fine, with a foldout couch in the spacious living room and a separate bedroom with a king- or queen-sized bed.

And they have full kitchens—a four-burner stove, a full refrigerator, a big sink, a microwave, a coffeemaker, pots and pans, and, incredibly enough, a dishwasher. With clean, up-to-date appliances and a grocery-shopping service ($5 charge), these are kitchens people really can use. Ask for a "C-line suite" and you'll also get a dynamite East River view. The traditional room decor is easy to live with. Other hotel perks include a Laundromat, a small fitness room (free to guests), a concierge, and room service until 1am; deluxe suites also have VCRs, in-room fax machines, and, on top floors, balconies. The Top of the Tower serves lunch and dinner, and the Zephyr Grill serves upscale American food for breakfast, lunch, and dinner. On top of it all, the staff is very accommodating. July and August are particularly good times to snag a room; you may be able to negotiate on rates then.

The Beekman Tower is part of Manhattan East Suites hotels, as are the **Surrey** and **Lyden Gardens** (earlier in this chapter). Other Manhattan East Suites hotels in Midtown are the **Dumont Plaza,** 150 E. 34th St., between Third and Lexington avenues (☎ **212/481-7600**); **Eastgate Tower,** 222 E. 39th St., between Second and Third avenues (☎ **212/687-8000**); the **Lyden House Suite Hotel,** 320 E. 53rd St., between First and Second avenues (☎ **212/888-6070**); the **Plaza Fifty Suite Hotel,** 155 E. 50th St., at Third Avenue (☎ **212/751-5710**); the **Shelburne Murray Hill Suites,** 303 Lexington Ave. at 37th Street (☎ **212/689-5200**); and the **Southgate Tower,** 371 Seventh Ave. at 31st Street (☎ **212/563-1800**). All are in roughly the same price category, and reservations at any of them can be made by calling ☎ **800/ME-SUITE.**

Crowne Plaza at the United Nations. 304 E. 42nd St. (between First and Second aves.). ☎ **212/986-8800.** Fax 212/986-1758. www.crowneplaza un.com. 300 units. A/C MINIBAR TV TEL. $159–479 double; $189–$509 executive room; $489–$689 suite. Crib free. AE, CB, DC, DISC, MC, V. Parking $34 ($44 for extra-sized cars). Subway: 4/5/6 to Grand Central.

Down at the quiet end of 42nd Street lies this European-like boutique hotel, known for years as the Hotel Tudor (look high on the west-facing facade for the neon Hotel Tudor sign, protected as a city landmark). Now run by the Crowne Plaza folks, it's often booked solid September through December, when the diplomats flock into town for General Assembly sessions at the nearby United Nations. It's a great bet for families, though, convenient to Midtown sights yet in a peaceful area on the fringe of residential Tudor City (see chapter 5 for a walking tour). Note that weekend and summer rates are considerably lower than September to May weekly rates, often bumping you down into the Moderate price category.

Hallways are narrow but bright, and the rooms are comfortably sized, with a traditional decor in a bright rose-and-green color scheme. The recently renovated bathrooms have red marble vanities. I like the hushed lobby, narrow but very deep (linking the hotel's two towers) with old-fashioned touches like red plush armchairs, marble floors, columns, drapes, and potted palms. The staff, many of whom have worked here for years, are very friendly and accommodating. Go for superior rooms with two double beds, or even better, take the upgrade to executive rooms, which also have a sitting area and access to a lounge serving complimentary continental breakfast.

Dining: Cecil's Bistro, a cozy place with a small but well-tuned contemporary menu, serves all three meals.

Amenities: Concierge, room service 6:30am to 10pm, fitness rooms, in-room movies.

Drake Swissôtel. 440 Park Ave. (at 56th St.), New York, NY 10022. ☎ **800/73-SWISS** or 212/421-0900. Fax 212/371-4190. www.swissotel.com. 495 units. A/C MINIBAR TV TEL. $285–$425 double; $450–$1,000 suite. Roll-away $35; crib free. AE, CB, DC, DISC, MC, V. Valet parking $41. Subway: 4/5/6/N/R to 59th St.

The Drake is owned by Swiss Air, which may or may not have any connection to the fact that the wood-paneled lobby has an intricate big clock in a glass cube, its gears exposed and different faces showing the time in different time zones. This is a business-oriented property, with a top-notch business center and a corporate-looking room decor. Still, it has some definite virtues for families. The Drake has been around since the 1920s under one ownership or another, but it has the virtue of really good-sized rooms—a double with two double beds doesn't feel too cramped. The Park Avenue location is relatively safe and serene, handy to both

Midtown attractions and Upper East Side museums and shopping. For families tagging along with a parent on business in New York, the Drake works extremely well.

Dining: The Drake Café and Bar, at one end of the lobby, is a popular place, well set up for breakfast, lunch, and dinner, as well as drinks (it really hops at happy hour). The American menu has some Swiss specialties.

Amenities: Concierge, 24-hour room service, newspaper delivery, weekday morning limo to Wall Street, in-room fax capabilities; health club with sauna, spa facilities; excellent business center with private computer work stations to rent, secretarial support, color laser printers and color copiers, four private conference rooms, and cell phones, pagers, and laptops to rent.

Radisson Hotel New York East Side. 511 Lexington Ave. (at 48th St.), New York, NY 10017. ☎ **800/448-4471** or 212/755-4400. Fax 212/751-4091. 701 units. A/C TV TEL. $239–$379 double; $279–$419 business-class room; $500–$700 suite. Roll-away $20; crib free. AE, DC, DISC, MC, V. Parking nearby $25–$35. Subway: 6 to 51st St.; 4/5/6/7/S to Grand Central.

This handsome 1920s vintage property along Lexington's Midtown hotel strip looks like an upscale boutique hotel, but at 27 stories and 700-plus rooms it's much larger than it feels. Look and listen and you'll notice it has a sophisticated international clientele (not surprising in the U.N. vicinity). From the spiffy porte-cochère above the 48th Street entrance to the two-story mahogany-paneled lobby with textured fabrics and brushed-nickel fixtures, the Radisson East Side has been smartly renovated for a contemporary look without sacrificing the property's charm.

The guest-room decor shows quiet verve, with a palette of muted earth tones, nubbly carpeting, pleated gauze shades that let in loads of light, and framed black-and-white art photographs on the walls. Bathrooms have been tidily modernized with gray marble floors and modern white fixtures. Amenities like coffeemakers, full-length mirrors, large desks, and data ports with high-speed Internet access bespeak the Radisson's attention to traveling executives. What families may appreciate more, though, is room size: The one-bedroom suites are positively rambling, with a huge bedroom and sitting room (some even have little terraces where you can step outside and study the skyscrapers all around). Business-class rooms are large doubles with either two double beds or a king bed and foldout couches; the great thing about these is that they have two bathrooms. Deluxe rooms have either a king, queen, or two single beds, but there's plenty of room for a roll-away. The whole place seems well run, with thoughtful, friendly service; it's dignified enough to be restful, but not at all stuffy.

Dining: Breakfast, lunch, and dinner are served in Raffles, a cheery dinerlike corner coffee shop, and all three meals are also served in Vuli, an Italian bistro just off the lobby. The hotel's upscale restaurant is J. Sung Dynasty, a lovely gourmet Chinese restaurant that does a brisk lunch and dinner business with nonguests as well as guests. The Lobby Bar and a multilevel supper club, the House of Bordeaux, are scheduled to open by the end of 2000.

Amenities: Concierge, room service (7am to 9pm), small fitness room with exercise machines, minibars on request.

✪ **Roger Smith.** 501 Lexington Ave. (at 47th St.), New York, NY 10017. ☎ **800/445-0277** or 212/755-1400. Fax 212/758-4061. 133 units. A/C TV TEL. $265–$295 double; $330–$435 suite. Rates include continental breakfast. Extra person $20. Roll-away or crib free. Seasonal packages available. AE, CB, DC, DISC, MC, V. Valet parking $24. Subway: 4/5/6/7/S to Grand Central.

The Roger Smith is decidedly quirky, which may be why so many musicians and artists and Europeans choose to stay here. The small oval lobby is a mini-gallery in itself, with paintings and sculptures and polished wainscoting (there's more art next door in an actual art gallery run by Roger Smith). Upstairs, however, the look is more like a country inn, with individually decorated rooms featuring such items as canopy beds, stocked bookshelves, and chintz upholstery and bedspreads. Lots of hotels boast of a homey feeling, but the rooms here really do qualify. There's a variety of room layouts, including some connecting rooms and a junior suite that has a double bed and a foldout couch in the same room. For the price of a double at the Waldorf or the Plaza, here you can get a suite that includes not only a pullout couch in the sitting room and a double bed in the bedroom but also a second cozy bedroom with a twin bed.

Though none of the rooms has a full kitchen, all suites have pantries with a refrigerator and coffeemaker. And as if that weren't enough, continental breakfast is included (rare enough in New York hotels), served every morning in Lily's, a spunky little bistro with gaudy murals; Lily's also serves an interesting continental menu for lunch and dinner (closed weekends). For $10 a day, Roger Smith guests can get a day pass to the New York Sports Club, an excellent health club, only 4 blocks away. This lively, fun hotel does a pretty brisk business, but its slowest months are July and August—peak family travel time—so cross your fingers and call ahead if you're visiting New York in summer.

○ Waldorf-Astoria. 301 Park Ave. (between 49th and 50th sts.), New York, NY 10022. **☎ 800/WALDORF,** 800/HILTONS, or 212/355-3000. Fax 212/872-7272. 1,407 units. A/C MINIBAR TV TEL. $245–$695 double; $345–$950 suite. Children under 18 stay free in parents' room. Roll-away or crib free. Weekend packages available. AE, CB, DC, DISC, MC, V. Parking $37. Subway: 6 to 51st St.

This is my sentimental favorite among Manhattan's grand hotels, because I stayed here at age 13 when my dad came to New York for a convention. That was long before the Waldorf became a Hilton, but the chain has kept up this flagship property beautifully, devoting a lot of taste and money to maintaining its character. The wide stately corridors, the vintage deco door fixtures, the white-gloved bellmen, the luxe shopping arcade, and that knockout lobby all trumpet Grand Hotel, and there's a certain electric thrill about being here, even among the well-heeled guests. Enter from the Park Avenue side and you'll cross a stunning round mosaic under an immense crystal chandelier; in the main lobby, the four-sided freestanding Waldorf clock, covered with bronze relief figures, should fascinate your children as much as it did me all those years ago.

Upstairs, the silent plush-carpeted corridors seem to run on forever. The room decor is pleasant if unremarkable—a sort of traditional English country-house-style look. The standard double rooms are larger than those at the Plaza (above)—the Waldorf was, after all, built 24 years later; request a room with two double beds if you've got more than one kid. A minisuite, combining one king-sized-bedded room with a sitting room, might work better, though not all have foldout couches; some suites have kitchenettes, so ask for one if that's important. There's also a number of connecting doubles you can request. The staff seems unfailingly gracious, though in such a large hotel you won't get the personal service you might at a smaller place. There are 244 rooms in the Waldorf Towers, with a separate entrance; the duke and duchess of Windsor and John F. Kennedy are among the guests who've resided here. Staying in the pricier Towers, which have more distinctive antique-laden decor, snags you some extra amenities, like complimentary continental breakfast and hors d'oeuvres in a lounge on the 26th floor.

Dining: The Waldorf has four restaurants: The American brasserie, Oscar's, is the only one that serves all three meals; the ornate French restaurant, Peacock Alley, acclaimed for its smart cuisine, serves breakfast and dinner; you can also get lunch or dinner in the Japanese Inagiku or the clubby steak-and-seafood the Bull and Bear. Sir Harry's Bar, fitted out like an African safari, serves drinks.

Amenities: Concierge, 24-hour room service, health club with steam rooms and exercise machines ($14 charge to guests per day or $17 for entire stay), business center, shopping arcade.

MODERATE

✪ The Kimberly. 145 E. 50th St. (between Lexington and Third aves.), New York, NY 10022. ☎ **800/683-0400** or 212/755-0400. Fax 212/486-6915. 186 units. A/C MINIBAR TV TEL. $245–$325 double; $279–$435 1-bedroom suite; $409–$675 2-bedroom suite. Children under 18 stay free in parents' room. Roll-away or crib free. Weekend rates and summer packages available. AE, CB, DC, DISC, MC, V. Valet parking $23. Subway: 6 to 51st St.; E/F to Lexington/Third aves.

More people ought to know about this plush smaller hotel on a spruce Midtown East block heading toward the town houses of Turtle Bay. The glitzy small lobby, full of pale shiny marble and gilt rococo furnishings, has pizzazz but not a high snobbery quotient, thanks to a friendly, unpretentious veteran staff. Since the 30-story building was designed in the mid-1980s as an apartment building (though it was turned into a hotel immediately), the rooms are all big—even the standard doubles don't feel crowded when they have two double beds in them (a great setup for families on a short visit). The closets are sizable, as are the nicely appointed baths. The one-bedroom suites could sleep six, with two double beds in the bedroom and a pullout couch in the sitting room. The decor is traditional, with quality furniture in dark woods; vases and framed prints and other accents give each room a bit of a residential flair. All suites have kitchenettes, galley kitchens with cooking burners, pots and pans, and full-sized refrigerators. And now here's the kicker: Almost every room has a balcony where you can sit and have breakfast or cocktails while watching the Manhattan ad execs, lawyers, and publishing types scurry to or from their offices far below.

Dining: Breakfast, lunch, and dinner are served in L'actual, a modern French bistro. The hotel's nightclub, 151, serves lunch and dinner, as well as drinks.

Amenities: Concierge, room service (6am to 11pm), newspaper delivery; complimentary access to all branches of the New York Health & Racquet Club (same owner), with Saturday morning swim session for kids; limo service to nearby NYHRC branch; complimentary sailing on NYHRC party yacht from South Street Seaport; kitchenettes; and balconies.

Loews New York. 569 Lexington Ave. (at 51st St.), New York, NY 10022. ☎ **800/836-6471** or 212/752-7000. Fax 212/752-3817 for reservations, 212/758-6311 for guest use. 722 units. A/C TV TEL. $199–$265 double; $229–$399 junior suite; $450–$650 1-bedroom suite; $650–$950 deluxe suite. Extra person $20; children 12 and under stay free in parents' room. Roll-away $20; crib free. AE, DC, DISC, MC, V. Parking $30. Subway: 6 to 51st St.; E/F to Lexington/Third aves.

Surprisingly smart and sophisticated for its price range, the Loews has a spirited air that begins in the streamlined lobby with its mahogany-and-chrome neo-deco look. All the rooms sport a contemporary decor that carries on the vaguely Japanese/art deco/Frank Lloyd Wright feel. A double with two double beds is probably the way to go—the reasonably priced junior suite isn't really two rooms but a large room divided by a built-in cabinet into sleeping and sitting areas (the sitting area does have a pullout couch, but still . . .).

A refreshingly unstuffy sort of place, the Loews enjoys a decent location in the cleaner part of Midtown, handily above a subway station—and many of the guests who stay here look like people who aren't above using the subway. Both the restaurant and room service have kids' menus. The staff has put together a handout for families, recommending restaurants, stores, and museums (but since you already have this book, it'll contain nothing you don't already know).

Dining: The sleek but reasonably priced Lexington Avenue Grill serves American fare for breakfast, lunch, and dinner. The grill and its bar are open to the lobby, which makes for good people-watching.

Amenities: Concierge, room service (until midnight), health club (no one under 16 allowed), business center, shopping arcade. Business-class rooms have newspaper delivery, coffeemakers, in-room fax machines, and complimentary breakfast.

INEXPENSIVE

Vanderbilt YMCA. 224 E. 47th St. (between Second and Third aves.), New York, NY 10017. ☎ **212/756-9600.** Fax 212/752-0210. 415 units (5 with bathroom). A/C TV. $86 double without bathroom, $138 double with bathroom; $138 quad (2 bunk beds) without bathroom. AE, MC, V. Parking $20–$25 nearby. Subway: E/F to Lexington/Third aves.; 6 to 51st St.; 4/5/6/7 to Grand Central.

You can't reserve the quad rooms in advance at this clean, big, friendly Midtown East Y, but if your kids are old enough that you'd be willing to stay here even in two separate doubles, it's a great money-saving option. The rooms are pleasant if dormlike, but they do have curtains and mirrors and a TV on a stand in the corner, and the down-the-hall baths are quite clean; many rooms have washbasins, which means you don't have to trot down the hall every time you want to wash your face or brush your teeth. The five en-suite rooms have an adjoining bathroom (shower only) and private phones. There's even a Laundromat and a tour desk on premises. And the location can't be beat, on a clean, safe block not far from the United Nations. The on-premises International Café serves decent, cheap deli fare, but there are so many good restaurants nearby you probably won't use it much. Best of all, the Y has extensive up-to-date sports facilities, including an indoor jogging track, loads of classes for kids, and two stellar indoor pools, which guests can use for free during their stay.

5 Gramercy Park

INEXPENSIVE

Gramercy Park Hotel. 2 Lexington Ave. (between Gramercy Square and 22nd St.), New York, NY 10010. ☎ **800/221-4083** or 212/475-4320. Fax 212/505-0535. 509 units. A/C TV TEL. $190 double; $230–$250 suite. Roll-away $10; crib free. AE, CB, DC, DISC, MC, V. Parking garage nearby. Subway: 6 to 23rd St.

Not only does this hotel have views of leafy green Gramercy Park—a delightful London-style enclosed private square—but guests can even get a key to go inside the iron fence and stroll around on the gravel paths, a privilege many New Yorkers would envy. To me, this isn't enough incentive to stay here, but the Gramercy Park doesn't seem to be hurting for business. The clientele is an odd mix of bedraggled hipsters (rock musicians, alternative journalists, fashion world hangers-on) and bewildered Middle American tourists, whose travel agents must've picked the hotel out of some directory. The rooms are certainly large enough to spread out in, but the furniture is battered and mismatched; the closets are huge, but the baths have old fixtures and don't look all that clean. If you're staying here to save money, request one of the double rooms that have two double beds, as opposed to the ones with a king-sized bed. Suites have a king-sized bed in one room and a foldout couch in the other, so you won't be getting more bed for the money, only more awkward space.

The hotel is 18 stories high, but only floors 12 and above have real views, and only rooms in the 02, 03, 04, and 05 lines have park views (they hardly compete with the Central Park views at the Mayflower or Carlyle, earlier in this chapter). Some suites have kitchenettes; all other rooms have, instead of a minibar stocked with little liquor bottles and expensive snacks, an empty mini-refrigerator that can be handy for keeping children's essentials like milk, apple juice, and bologna. Right off the knotty pine–paneled lobby is a stodgy dining room, serving a continental menu straight out of the 1960s, and a dimly lit, shabby cocktail lounge. At the far end of a corridor is a tiny beauty salon that looks lost in a time warp. Room service (7:30am to 10:30pm) is reasonably priced compared to what some hotels charge, and there's a discount rate arranged with a nearby health club.

6 Greenwich Village

INEXPENSIVE

✪ **Washington Square Hotel.** 103 Waverly Place (between Sixth Ave. and MacDougal St.), New York, NY 10011. ☎ **800/222-0418** or 212/777-9515. Fax 212/979-8373. 170 units. A/C TV TEL. $142 double; $174 quad (two double beds). Rates include continental breakfast. Roll-away $20; crib free. AE, MC, V. Parking at nearby garages. Subway: A/B/C/D/E/F/Q to W. 4th St.

With its fantastic location at the corner of Washington Square Park, the focal point of Greenwich Village—Bob Dylan and Joan Baez lived here, when it was the Hotel Earle in the folkie 1960s—the Washington Square Hotel would probably do well even if it weren't so nice. The good news is that this small hotel is a winner on its own account: clean, cheery, and tastefully furnished—and very low priced. Absolutely book a room here as soon as you know you're coming to New York, because lots of people have found out about this gem and it's nearly always full.

The rooms are just big enough to comfortably accommodate a crib or roll-away, but at these prices a family might as well spring for a quad room, which has two double beds; request no. 902, the largest, which is in front with a super view of leafy Washington Square Park. (Any front room on the fifth through ninth floors has good park views.) If you want to spring for connecting doubles—and at these prices, why not?—request Rooms 219 and 220, which share a bath. All other rooms have their own small but spruce white tiled baths; the bedrooms are simply furnished in restful tones, with bleached wood and padded headboards creating a contemporary look that seems more Californian than New York. There are plenty of generous-sized mirrors and reading lamps, operating on the novel assumption that guests might actually like to read in bed.

After the Parisian-looking little lobby, with its wrought-iron gate and marble staircase, the Holiday Inn–ish decor of the rooms might disappoint some, but only those who haven't seen what else is available in this price range in Manhattan. There's even a small exercise room, with all the essential machines, right off the lobby. Guests get continental breakfast free in the CIII restaurant downstairs, which serves an eclectic menu that draws locals on its own merits. There's no room service, but this part of the Village is crawling with restaurants in all price ranges that stay open all hours, and walking around here is a pleasure at night. True, street musicians may be performing into the wee hours in the park across the street, but compared to the bustle of Midtown that's a minor annoyance.

Downtown Accommodations

Best Western Seaport Inn **6**
Embassy Suites **3**
Holiday Inn Downtown **2**
Marriott World Trade Center **4**
Millenium Hilton **5**

New York Brooklyn
  Marriott **7**
New York Marriott
  Financial Center **8**
Washington Square Hotel **1**

7 Lower Manhattan

EXPENSIVE

✪ **Embassy Suites.** 102 North End Ave. (between Murray and Vesey sts.). ☎ **800/EMBASSY** or 212/945-0100. Fax 212/945-3012. www.embassynewyork.com. 463 units. A/C MINIBAR TV TEL. Weekends $229–$279 double, weekdays $350–$500 double. Crib free. Children under 18 stay free in parents' room. AE, CB, DC, DISC, MC, V. Valet parking $45. Subway: C/E to World Trade Center; 1/9 to Cortlandt St.

This sparkling new property in Battery Park City, with views of the harbor on one side and of the World Trade Center on the other, can be a great deal for families on weekends, when the rates fall well down into the Moderate category. (On weekdays, you may slide up into Very Expensive.) Lots of corporate types book the place up during the week, but every unit is totally suitable for a family, with a king-bedded bedroom and a separate living room with foldout couch (bigger families may gravitate toward one of the rooms with two double beds in the bedroom). Bathrooms are big, with tubs, and there's always a table big enough for paperwork or art projects, not to mention room-service meals. The place has a with-it sort of buzz, from the curvy bright yellow wall behind the reception desk, to the soaring atrium dominated by an 11-story purple-and-blue Sol LeWitt abstract painting, to the sleek room decor, all neutral tones and textured fabrics and striking art prints commissioned expressly for the hotel. A complimentary breakfast buffet is served each morning in the Broker's Loft, one of two hotel restaurants operated by American cuisine's man-of-the-hour, Larry Forgione. And my son wants me to make sure to tell you that there are Sony Playstations provided in every suite, an amenity that he considers worthy of rating this place with a star. (I would have given it a star anyway.)

The Embassy Suites building also contains several other restaurants, as well as a 16-screen movie theater. The excellent playgrounds of Hudson River Park are only steps from the hotel, as is the gorgeous Hudson River promenade of Battery Park City. There's shopping and more dining next door in the World Financial Center's Winter Garden Atrium, and enough downtown attractions to keep a family happy for a complete weekend.

Dining: Manhattan Prime Steak House and the Broker's Loft seafood restaurant, both run by Larry Forgione, are in the hotel. The Broker's Loft serves all three meals, and Manhattan Prime serves lunch and dinner.

Amenities: Concierge, 24-hour room service, CD players, video players, Sony Playstations, Web TV, newspaper delivery, business center, free access to New York Sports Club fitness center, coin-op and valet laundry.

Millenium Hilton. 55 Church St. (between Fulton and Dey sts.), New York, NY 10007. ☎ **800/HILTONS** or 212/693-2001. Fax 212/571-2316. 561 units. A/C MINIBAR TV TEL. $300–$360 double; $450–$1,500 suite. Children 12 and under stay free in parents' room. AE, CB, DC, DISC, MC, V. Parking $35. Subway: 1/9 to Cortlandt St.; C/E to World Trade Center.

This slim black-glass high-rise plinth faces the World Trade Center across Church Street and soot-blackened historic St. Paul's church across Fulton Street. The place positively screams V.I.P., with a beautiful but spare lobby and sleek, subtle room decor. Streamlined golden maple cabinets and built-ins pack a lot into the guest rooms, while large windows let in floods of light; floors 31 to 55—the high-rise rooms, on a separate elevator bank—have astounding daytime views of neighboring skyscrapers, as well as snatches of the Hudson and the harbor and the East River. The baths are quite upscale, with black marble counters and all the chichi amenities.

Families will probably do best with the double-doubles (double rooms with a pair of double beds); the suites are tailored to high-level execs who need to do some entertaining, so they have only minimal kitchen facilities and don't necessarily have pullout couches. Why should a family stay here? One reason is that there's a lovely 40-foot pool that seems empty most of the time, overlooking the landmark church next door. The views can be great, and the location is handy, though Lower Manhattan does get deserted at night. Children are welcomed with a gift at check-in, and toys and games are available on loan during their stay.

Dining: American food is served for lunch and dinner in the upscale Taliesin restaurant (named after Frank Lloyd Wright's home, presumably because Wright influenced the hotel's sleek decor). The Connoisseur Grille is a more casual alternative serving breakfast, lunch, and dinner.

Amenities: Concierge, 24-hour room service, newspaper delivery, indoor pool, fitness center with exercise machines, in-room fax capability, business center.

MODERATE

Holiday Inn Downtown. 138 Lafayette St. (between Canal and Howard sts.), New York, NY 10013. ☎ **800/HOLIDAY** or 212/966-8898. Fax 212/966-3933. 227 units. A/C TV TEL. $179–$269 double; from $229 suite. Roll-away $15; crib free. AE, CB, DC, DISC, MC, V. Valet parking $25. Subway: 6/N/R to Canal St.

At the nexus of Chinatown, Little Italy, and SoHo, this modern midrange hotel occupies a converted factory/warehouse a block north of Canal Street. Take your basic contemporary Holiday Inn decor and add Asian accents—a stylized floral still life here, a subtle woven wallpaper there—and you've got an idea of what this place looks like: sparkling clean and only a bit impersonal-looking (the staff, many of whom are Asian, seem very helpful).

The lobby is one floor up from the busy, grubby commercial street; the rooms haven't been well soundproofed and the windows are a bit high, which makes things feel institutional. The rooms aren't large (high ceilings make them look smaller), so only a limited number of doubles contain two double beds; larger families may want to get connecting doubles, which might have a king-sized or a queen-sized bed, or two twin beds. The Pacifica restaurant serves all meals, including a big breakfast buffet, with a menu that straddles both Western and Chinese cuisine. Room service runs until 11pm. About 40% of the clientele is foreign, which may simply mean that travel agents in other countries can spot a good deal when they see one.

Marriott World Trade Center. 3 World Trade Center, New York, NY 10048. ☎ **800/228-9290** or 212/938-9100. Fax 212/444-3444. www.marriotthotels.com. 818 units. A/C MINIBAR TV TEL. $155–$339 double; $425–$1,750 suite. Roll-away or crib free. Weekend and summer packages available. AE, CB, DC, DISC, MC, V. Valet parking $30 (unlimited in/out). Subway: C/E to World Trade Center; 1/9 to Cortlandt St.

As the Vista Hotel, this gleaming 22-story property went through a multimillion-dollar renovation after "the incident," as people at the World Trade Center refer to the 1993 terrorist bombing. Marriott took over in late 1995 and hasn't had to do much since, except watch business climb back up. What's special about this hotel is its in-the-thick-of-it location—walk out the back doors and you're on the World Trade Center's sprawling plaza, with its huge fountain, pushcart cafes, and occasional free outdoor entertainment; you're right next door to the WTC observation deck, so you can beat the lines first thing in the morning. Just about all the rooms have excellent views, especially those overlooking Battery Park City and the Hudson to the west (it's worth having room-service dinner just to watch the sunsets).

There's also a super rooftop health club—open to nonguest members, however, which means it can get overly busy at peak lunch and after-work hours. The 50-foot indoor pool has panoramic windows on both sides, but exercise machines have been set up around it, which is quite disconcerting. Guest rooms are of a decent size, with upscale traditional decor. If you get a double with two double beds, there's still room for a crib or roll-away, but not much left over. Basically, this is a big, rather soulless hotel with a can't-be-beat location; it's full of corporate types on weekdays, but book on a weekend and you may save as much as a $100 off weekday rates.

Dining: The Greenhouse Café is a cheery, casual atrium restaurant serving American food for breakfast, lunch, and dinner, with a standard kids' menu (and placemats to color) at all meals. The Tall Ships Bar & Grill is a clubby spot for lunch or dinner.

Amenities: Concierge, 24-hour room service, indoor pool, full-service health club (jogging track, saunas, exercise machines, massages), business center.

✪ New York Marriott Financial Center. 85 West St. (at Albany St.), New York, NY 10006. ☎ **800/228-9290** or 212/385-4900. Fax 212/227-8136. www.marriotthotels.com. 504 units. A/C MINIBAR TV TEL. $145–$339 double; $450–$1,600 suite. Roll-away or crib free. Weekend packages available. AE, CB, DC, DISC, MC, V. Valet parking $30. Subway: C/E to World Trade Center; 1/9/N/R to Rector St.

Smaller than its sister hotel in the World Trade Center, less snooty than the nearby Millenium Hilton, the New York Marriott Financial Center is a good choice for families. It has the same wonderful skyline and harbor views as the Marriott World Trade Center and has its own 50-foot pool, bigger than the one at the Millenium Hilton and more private than the one at the Marriott WTC. So what if the pool has no views? When they're splashing in the water, kids don't care if there are glorious vistas at hand. The small lobby is less of a knockout than those other two, with a more traditional marble-and-mahogany look, but it's less intimidating too.

Though guest rooms here don't give you the same kind of space to stretch out in as the Embassy Suites, the double rooms with two double beds are roomy enough to take a crib or roll-away, and there are plenty of connecting doubles. The executive suite is a decent option for families, with a pullout couch in the sitting room. Some rooms have a traditional neoclassical decor, while others tend toward Japanese contemporary. The baths are good-sized, and the staff is very accommodating. If you're going to be in Manhattan for the weekend, ask if weekend packages are in effect—they could save you nearly $100 a night over the weekday rates, plus throwing in a complimentary breakfast. You'll be right across from Battery Park City, within walking distance of the Statue of Liberty/Ellis Island ferry, and not far from South Street Seaport—and have a very comfy hotel room to boot.

Dining: Roy's serves an American-style buffet breakfast and Euro-Asian cuisine at lunch and dinner. The Battery Park Tavern serves lunch and dinner.

Amenities: Concierge (limited hours), room service (until midnight), indoor pool, fitness room with exercise machines, business center.

INEXPENSIVE

Best Western Seaport Inn. 33 Peck Slip (between Front and Water sts.), New York, NY 10038. ☎ **800/HOTEL-NY** or 212/766-6600. Fax 212/766-6615. 72 units. A/C TV TEL. $159–$219 double. Rates include continental breakfast. Children 17 and under stay free in parents' room. Roll-away $25; crib free. AE, DC, DISC, MC, V. Parking $20 nearby. Subway: 4/5/6 to City Hall.

This spunky little hotel in a converted 19th-century red-brick building has an offbeat location—on a cobbled street just north of the Fulton Fish Market, a couple of blocks up from South Street Seaport, in the lee of the Brooklyn Bridge's Manhattan entrance ramps (a delightful trompe-l'oeil mural on a brick building just east of the hotel shows you what the view through the bridge's arches would look like if the building weren't in the way). Walk through the front door to find a spruce Federal-style decor, a cheerful staff, and goofy laser-disk flames blazing away in a mock fireplace; upstairs are quiet, bright corridors and quite decent guest rooms. Some have two double beds, while others have a queen-sized bed plus a fold-out couch. The baths are up-to-date and dazzlingly clean—so what if they have wrapped plastic drinking tumblers? (This *is* a Best Western.) While you don't get kitchenettes, there's an unstocked mini-refrigerator in every room, as well as a VCR (pick up a tape at the lobby's self-service rental machine). Some upper-floor rooms have Astroturfed terraces with lawn furniture and partial views of the East River and Seaport; some have whirlpools.

The immediate area's a bit deserted and some nearby buildings look derelict, but you'll be fine walking around here during the day (Pace University is a block away) and there's no trouble getting cabs at night if you walk the block to Pearl Street. Though the inn has no restaurant and no room service, local restaurants will deliver, and there are some fun, casual spots quite near, including the Bridge Cafe a block north; Chinatown is quite close, too. For what you save on frills, you can easily afford to spend a little money on cabs by staying here.

8 Brooklyn

MODERATE

New York Marriott Brooklyn. 333 Adams St., Brooklyn, NY 11201 ☎ **888/436-3759** or 718/246-7000. Fax 718/246-0563. www.marriotthotels.com. 376 units. A/C TV TEL. $209–$309 double; $349–$600 suite. Roll-away or crib free. AE, CB, DC, DISC, MC, V. Parking $20. Subway: A/C/F to Jay St./Borough Hall; 4/5 to Borough Hall; N/R to Court St.

Brooklyn Heights is said to be America's first suburb, and many Manhattanites still have the notion that Brooklyn is not quite "New York." But anyone who's spent time there knows better. In addition to having its own attractions (including a top-notch children's museum), Brooklyn is very much part of New York City, not to mention wonderfully convenient to downtown Manhattan—the Wall Street area, Battery Park, and the Statue of Liberty ferry are only one subway stop away. Located in downtown Brooklyn, near picturesque Brooklyn Heights, the Marriott is also a mere 7-minute subway ride from trendy SoHo, and, of particular interest to families, only a few blocks away from the famous Brooklyn Bridge (see chapter 5), with its pedestrian walkway where energetic kids can run off steam while their parents enjoy breathtaking views. Don't be put off by the location on Adams Street, a busy, nondescript thoroughfare feeding the Brooklyn Bridge; the hotel itself is spacious, comfortable, attractive, and well organized without being the least bit uptight or intimidating.

Kids will love the domed ceiling that soars above the entryway and mezzanine lobby, a stunning mural of the sky behind a white trellised gazebo. As you sweep up to the lobby on the escalator between huge potted plants, for a split second you feel as if you're flying. Otherwise, there's a businessy feel to the place, with its network of conference rooms off the main lobby. Guest rooms (and their views) are unremarkable, with standard hotel antique reproduction furniture, but higher ceilings make rooms feel even more spacious. There are some connecting rooms, and the doubles themselves have two double beds and just enough extra space to fit a crib or cot. Room decor is reasonably cheery, with red-gold-and-green patterned bedspreads and soft green carpeting. Each room is stocked with a coffeemaker, a refreshment center, a blow dryer, and an iron.

The hotel has a restaurant that serves breakfast, lunch, and dinner, and kids will enjoy some of the reasonably priced family restaurants on nearby Montague Street in Brooklyn Heights, a 5-minute walk from the hotel. Another plus for families is the 75-foot lap pool; several kids were swimming happily the day we visited.

Dining: The Archives Restaurant off the lobby lounge takes its name from the Brooklyn memorabilia it proudly exhibits (on loan from the Brooklyn Historical Society). There's an appealing kids' menu, crayons are at every table, and children's paper placemats offer $1 off admission to the Brooklyn Children's Museum.

Amenities: Concierge, 24-hour room service, baby-sitting, indoor pool, fitness room with exercise machines, business center, valet laundry.

Side Trips from New York City

by Mercer Warriner

Though New York City has enough attractions to keep even the most active child busy and interested, sometimes it's tempting (at least for parents) to get away from all the bustle, honking horns, and crowded streets—if only for a little while. When the weather's nice, a day trip from Manhattan can be just the ticket.

The following places are all within an hour of the city, and in some cases are close enough to each other to combine in a day—the Hudson Valley Children's Museum and Philipsburg Manor, for example, are just across the Tappan Zee Bridge from each other.

A car would be the most convenient way to reach these places. But if you have the time and want to make getting there part of the experience, a train or boat ride to Philipsburg Manor would be fun (though the boat excursion is an awfully long sightseeing trip for kids under 12).

If you're interested in exploring farther afield, you might want to check out *Frommer's Wonderful Weekends from New York City.*

1 Liberty Science Center

Approximately a 20-minute drive or a 40- to 45-minute train ride from Manhattan

GETTING THERE

BY CAR   Take the Lincoln Tunnel, the Holland Tunnel, or the George Washington Bridge to the New Jersey Turnpike heading south; go to exit 14B and follow the signs to the Science Center. Parking is $5.

BY TRAIN   Take the **PATH train** from its various Manhattan stations (along Sixth Avenue at 33rd Street, 23rd Street, 14th Street, or 9th Street; or Christopher Street; or the World Trade Center) to Exchange Place station in Jersey City, where the **Hudson–Bergen light rail** runs regular service to the Science Center for $1.50 adults and 75¢ kids.

CHECKING OUT THE MUSEUM

The enormous four-story ✪ **Liberty Science Center,** 251 Philip St., Jersey City, N.J. (☎ **201/200-1000;** www.lsc.org), seems to vibrate with energy the moment you enter. On the main floor you're instantly greeted by the sight of a 700-pound steel expandable **geodesic globe,** continually opening and closing. Just up the escalator are interactive exhibits on **health,** including the **Perception Alley,** which shows how our eyes see accurately and how they can play tricks. The array of crazy funhouse mirrors will entertain young and old alike. There's also a fully equipped ambulance to explore. But the second floor's highlight is indubitably the **Touch Tunnel,** a pitch-black 100-foot-long tunnel that takes about 5 minutes to crawl through, with only your sense of touch to guide you. Forget it if you're the least bit claustrophobic—kids 6 and under aren't even allowed.

The top floor's theme is the **environment,** and here you're treated to a number of fascinating displays of live insects, including some giant cockroaches from Central America that'll make your skin crawl. But kids of all ages love this floor, which includes a **rock wall** for climbing, exhibits of estuaries with live fish, and the **Bug Zoo** featuring insects from around the world (you can even hold some of them in the Greenhouse). And you can't miss the 20-foot "lighthouse," with a solar telescope inside. On the bottom floor, the focus is **invention.** Here, among other things, you can try out a flight simulator and a phonograph invented by Thomas Edison.

If you decide to visit during school hours, be advised that it's fairly crowded with school groups. In general, kids 5 and under might feel overwhelmed by the noise and activity. Since the exhibits are fairly sophisticated, school-age children and their parents would be most apt to enjoy this excursion.

Special exhibits at certain times are worth inquiring about. In addition to the exhibits, there's the **Kodak OMNI theater,** the nation's largest domed IMAX theater, with a six-story screen showing 3-D films like *Everest, Wolves,* and *Thrill Ride: The Science of Fun.* The **3-D laser light show** *Brain Storms: Creativity in Flight* is an especial draw.

Admission: Museum only, $9.50 adults, $7.50 seniors 62 and older and children 2 to 18; museum plus IMAX, $13.50 adults, $11.50 seniors and children 2 to 18. **Open:** Daily 9:30am to 5:30pm, except for Thanksgiving and Christmas.

WHERE TO EAT

The **Laser Lights Cafe** on the center's main floor has decent inexpensive food that'll appeal to a range of tastes. A cheese pizza is $1.50, while the most expensive item on the menu the day I was there was the special, a chicken burrito with salad for $4.95.

2 Hudson Valley Children's Museum

Approximately 45 minutes from Manhattan

GETTING THERE

BY CAR Take the Henry Hudson Parkway north to the George Washington Bridge; exit after the bridge onto the Palisades Parkway going north. Take exit 9 to get onto the New York State Thruway (I-87), heading east toward the Tappan Zee Bridge. At exit 11, take N.Y. 59 going east, which becomes Main Street. Turn right on Broadway to the first left on Burd Street and go 1½ blocks to 21 Burd St. There's free parking adjacent to the museum.

SEEING THE MUSEUM

Kids 1 to 12 will love the friendly **Hudson Valley Children's Museum,** 21 Burd St., Nyack, N.Y. (☎ **914/358-2191;** www.hvcm.org), where learning through hands-on exploration is actively encouraged. My sons were immediately drawn to the **Gadget Garage,** where they were greeted by a 1966 Deux Chevaux Citröen;

the hood of the car has been replaced by glass, so kids can see what happens inside the engine when they push the pedals. Also in the Gadget Garage is a workbench where children of all ages have fun experimenting with gears, pulleys, and tools. The **Hudson River Dive** is devoted to Hudson River ecology and art. In the back of the museum, the **Royal Bubble Factory** includes all sorts of bubble-making devices. Kids seem especially delighted by the bubble hoop—as they hoist this hoop, a giant bubble immediately grows up around them. There's also an enormous globe of the world with steps leading up to it, a workshop area built of imaginatively recycled materials, and the **Young People's Theater,** which features a piano, costumes, and family performances. A continual lineup of art workshops draw kids into various hands-on projects; **Tot Time** (Tuesday and Thursday at 2:45pm) offers an hour of arts-and-crafts projects for preschool kids, and **Tot Tunes** (Wednesday and Friday at 2:45pm) is a music time for preschoolers. The **Early Childhood Area** makes a safe haven for kids 5 and under, though these younger kids will definitely want to explore the rest of the museum, too. Parents will appreciate the gorgeous views of the Hudson River outside.

Admission: $5. **Open:** Tuesday to Saturday 10am to 5pm, Sunday noon to 5pm. Also open on most Monday school holidays.

WHERE TO EAT

Bring sandwiches and eat at tables in **Memorial Park,** a wonderfully scenic park on the banks of the Hudson River. As you leave the museum, head left out the door and then take your first left, onto Piermont Avenue. The park, which also includes a nice playground, is 2 blocks down Piermont on the left.

3 Philipsburg Manor

Approximately 45 to 50 minutes from Manhattan

GETTING THERE

BY CAR Take the Henry Hudson Parkway north to the Saw Mill River Parkway, which you follow to exit 20, turning west onto the New York State Thruway (I-87/287) toward the Tappan Zee Bridge and Albany. Get off I-87 at exit 9, Tarrytown, the last exit before the Tappan Zee Bridge. Go left on N.Y. 119, then take a quick right onto U.S. 9 north. Philipsburg Manor is 2 miles north on the left. The small parking lot next to the entrance can get crowded; for overflow parking, turn right out of the driveway, take another immediate right, and then turn right again into a gravel lot that says Kykuit (another manor owned by Historic Hudson Valley). Follow the path toward the visitor center.

BY TRAIN Metro North (☎ 800/METRO-INFO or 212/532-4900) offers local train service from Grand Central Terminal directly to Philips Manor (a 50-minute ride) or express train service to Tarrytown (a 40-minute ride). One-way adult fares are $5.50 to $7.50, depending on whether you travel at peak or off-peak times; children's fares are 50¢ (ages 5 to 11 with an adult). If you get off at the Philips Manor station, you can walk to your destination (one-third mile). From the Tarrytown station, you'll need to take a cab, which costs about $6. Call for details.

BY BOAT NY Waterway (☎ 800/53-FERRY for reservations) runs a Sleepy Hollow Cruise once a day, on weekends and holidays, from Pier 78 at West 38th Street and 12th Avenue. A shuttle bus meets the ferry in Sleepy Hollow. The fare (including boat, bus, and Philipsburg Manor admission) is $38 adults, $19 children

12 and under. The ferry departs at 10:30am and returns at 6pm. Estimated time on the ferry is 1½ hours, but the full-day round-trip takes 7½ hours and also includes sightseeing at **Sunnyside,** Washington Irving's manor in Sleepy Hollow, which would interest adults and teenagers but not necessarily younger kids.

TOURING THE MANOR

Philipsburg Manor, U.S. 9, Sleepy Hollow, N.Y. (☎ 914/631-8200; www. hudsonvalley.org), is an 18th-century colonial farm with a working gristmill, a yard full of animals, a farmhouse, and a tenant house. It's a great excursion for children 6 to 17. Alongside the mill pond is a narrow stream—kids may be awed to learn that 300 years ago it was wide enough to accommodate ships for loading and unloading cargo. A long wooden bridge crosses the mill pond, connecting the gift shop area with the farmhouse, mill, and barn; kids love running across it not only because it's long and close to the water but also because it gives the feeling of sweeping you straight into the 18th century once you reach the other side.

The guides, decked out in 18th-century dress, demonstrate various farm activities of that era: milling, sheep shearing, plowing, and dairying. Every half hour a guide gives a **tour of the farmhouse,** where the wealthy Philipse family once lived. (It was African slaves who actually worked the property for the Philipse family, however, laboriously threshing their wheat and grinding it into flour—there's a history lesson here that should stick with your kids.) The **stone manor house,** built between 1682 and 1720, includes interesting details of colonial life, including a night box to guard candles from rat attacks and a big white mound in the kitchen you later learn is sugar (the guide allows kids several guesses on that one).

Older children (8 and up) would most likely enjoy the tours and historic information, but there's less here to occupy younger children. While they'll certainly get a kick out of the sheep, chickens, cows, and cats wandering about the **barnyard,** they're not allowed to pat the animals and will quickly tire of the lectures on 18th-century life. But if you're trying to accommodate several ages and interests, don't despair: Your older child can learn about history while your younger child explores the spacious grounds outside. Just be aware that with the pond and the stream so close, parental supervision is necessary at all times.

Admission: $8 adults, $7 seniors, $4 children 6 to 17, free for children 5 and under. **Open:** April through December 10am to 5pm daily except Tuesday; November and December 10am to 4pm daily except Tuesdays, Thanksgiving, and Christmas; closed January and February; March Saturday and Sunday 10am to 4pm.

WHERE TO EAT

To the left of the gift shop is a small **cafe** where you can buy decent gourmet-type sandwiches or salads (under $6). There's not much here to entice children, though, so it might be easier to bring a picnic lunch and eat at the tables by the mill stream.

4 Playland

Approximately 50 minutes from Manhattan

GETTING THERE

BY CAR Take the Henry Hudson Parkway north to I-95, the Cross Bronx Expressway. Take I-95 to exit 19 in Rye (Playland Parkway) and then follow the signs to Playland. Parking costs $4 Tuesday to Friday, $5 Saturday and Sunday, and $7 holidays.

BY TRAIN   Metro North trains (☎ 800/METRO-INFO or 212/532-4900) take about 45 minutes from Grand Central Terminal to the Rye station. Adult one-way fares are $6.75 peak and $5 off-peak; children travel for 50¢. From the Rye station, take bus no. 75 to Playland. Metro North also organizes Playland packages, which include train and bus fare and a book of Playland tickets. These packages are likely to be cheaper than buying train tickets and Playland tickets separately. Call Metro North for details.

ENJOYING THE PARK

In 1923, the Westchester County Park Commission announced it would create an "unequaled seaside public park to provide clean, wholesome recreation for the people of Westchester County." So **Playland,** Playland Parkway, Rye, N.Y. (☎ 914/925-2701; www.westchestergov.com), opened in 1928 and since then has lived up to its lofty declaration—except it doesn't get too self-righteously hung up on the wholesome part, thank goodness. Situated right on Long Island Sound, Playland is the sort of place kids 2 and over overwhelmingly tend to love; it features so many rides, food stalls, game booths, and other amusements it would be impossible to list them all here. Plan on staying for several hours—your kids will insist on nothing less.

No mere rinky-dink midway, Playland is actually listed on the National Register of Historic Places. You'll be happy to know this is not only the cleanest amusement park I've ever seen but that it has also retained its fun retro look: striped awnings, painted wooden fences enclosing the rides, and festive-looking ticket booths. In fact, it's a lovely spot, with wide water views, meticulous landscaping, and art deco buildings (this was the first of several famous deco projects designed by the award-winning architectural firm Walker and Gillette).

Kids 5 and under should be steered straight to **Kiddyland,** which has rides tailored to their size: The **Kiddy Whip, Kiddyland Bumper Cars, Turtle Aviators,** and **swings** are especially popular. For older kids, the park is their oyster. Some of the most thrilling rides are the **Go-Carts** (for 12 and up only), the **Hurricane Coaster,** the **Whip,** the **Ferris Wheel,** and the **Dragon Coaster.**

In addition to the rides, Playland has a **beach,** a **pool,** and a **lake** for boating, which are open seasonally.

Admission: Free, but you must buy tickets for rides, which cost three to five tickets each: 75¢ per ticket, $8 for a book of 12, $15 for a book of 24, $19 for a book of 36. **Open:** May 30 through October Wednesday and Thursday 10am to 4pm, Friday 10am to midnight, Saturday noon to midnight, Sunday noon to 11pm. Closed Monday and Tuesday.

WHERE TO EAT

Playland offers many types of food in **concession stands**—and just the kind of junky food kids go crazy for. There are also attractive picnic areas.

5 Long Island Children's Museum

Approximately 50 minutes from Manhattan

GETTING THERE

BY CAR   Take the Midtown Tunnel to the Long Island Expressway, then exit heading east on the Grand Central Parkway, which becomes the Northern State Parkway. Turn south on the Meadowbrook Parkway, which you follow south to exit M3 west. At the first light, go right onto Stewart Avenue and continue 1½ miles to the free parking lot on your right, directly across from 550 Stewart Ave.

BY TRAIN   Take the **Long Island Rail Road** (☎ 718/217-5477) from Penn Station to the Garden City station. One-way adult fares are $4.25 to $6.25, depending on time of travel; children's fares (ages 5 to 11) are 50¢ to $3. A cab ride from the station to the museum costs about $6.

EXPLORING THE MUSEUM

The **Long Island Children's Museum,** 550 Stewart Ave., Garden City, N.Y. (☎ 516/222-0207; www.licm.org), occupies a block-shaped white building with a stark entryway, but the moment you step inside, you and your child will be richly rewarded by the staff's abundant creativity. Though the space is small (5,000 square feet), the hands-on exhibits go a long way toward stretching the imaginations of kids 2 to 12. The museum is planning to move to larger quarters by the fall of 2001.

In the **Communication Station** there are no limits—the entire world is there for a kid via the Internet (parents will be reassured to know there are checks and balances on this system to make sure whatever's accessed is appropriate). Also in this corner is a mock TV station that was a big hit during my visit—children see themselves projected on a giant TV screen as big-time news broadcasters (needless to say, they're instantly captivated). Nearby is a phone exhibit where kids can play with telephones from all different eras. Next to the Communication Station is **Working on the Railroad,** with everything a train-obsessed kid might want: a virtual train for children to drive, train crew clothes to dress up in, an explanation of signal lights, Long Island Rail Road maps, and a ticket punch game, among other things.

Hands On is a fun exhibit about . . . well, hands—kids have their fingerprints taken, study various animal hands, and look at all kinds of gloves. Children 6 and up enjoy an exhibit called **What If You Couldn't . . . ,** aiming to sensitize kids to certain disabilities. Though it may sound too PC, kids really get enthralled here: There are wheelchairs and crutches to experiment with, braille to touch, lenses showing what the world looks like to people with diminished sight, a phone that plays only muted conversation, and writing as it might appear to a dyslexic child. And then there's the **bubble room,** where you can make bubbles of all sizes to your heart's content, and a **giant kaleidoscope** guaranteed to captivate kids of all ages.

The museum also offers special events and workshops on Saturday and Sunday—call ahead for details.

Admission: $5; free for children under 2; tickets are sold on a first-come, first-served basis; time tickets are sold when crowded. In inclement weather, call ahead for time ticket schedule. **Open:** Tuesday to Friday 10am to 4pm, Saturday and Sunday 10am to 5pm (in summer, opens at noon on Sunday).

WHERE TO EAT

There's no on-site food service or any place to picnic within walking distance (the museum is on a busy road). However, there are a number of **fast-food restaurants** along Stewart Avenue between the museum and the entrance to the Meadowbrook Parkway. Nearby **Roosevelt Field Mall** has some good kid restaurants upstairs; to reach the mall, turn left from the museum parking lot onto Stewart Avenue, then take your first left at the light.

6 Maritime Aquarium at Norwalk

Approximately 1 hour from Manhattan

GETTING THERE

BY CAR   Take I-95 heading east/north to the South Norwalk exit (exit 14) off I-95 and follow the signs to the Maritime Center; it's about a 6-minute drive from the highway. Or take the Hutchinson River Parkway north, which becomes the Merritt Parkway in Connecticut. From the Merritt Parkway, take exit 39A and follow the signs on U.S. 7 to the Maritime Center. There's parking at the center, which costs up to $3.

BY TRAIN   Metro North trains (☎ **800/METRO-INFO** or 212/532-4900) run frequently to South Norwalk; the one-way fare is $8 to $10.75 adults, 50¢ children 5 to 11, free for children under 5. Travel time is about 60 minutes. Call for details. From the South Norwalk station, take a short taxi ride or walk—it's only about 3 blocks. When you get off the train, turn left and go down the stairs at the end of the platform; turn right at the bottom of the stairs, walk under the bridge, and go 1½ blocks to the first traffic light, at the intersection of Main and Monroe streets. Turn left onto Main Street and go to the next traffic light, then turn right onto Washington Street. Go under another bridge and continue past shops and restaurants to the next traffic light, at the corner of Washington and Water streets. You'll see the large red-brick Maritime Aquarium on your left.

SEEING THE AQUARIUM

The **Maritime Aquarium at Norwalk,** North Water Street, Norwalk, Conn. (☎ 203/852-0700, www.maritimeaquarium.org), gives families a fascinating hands-on look at the animals and ecology of Long Island Sound. Go up freestanding stairs in the lobby and across a midair bridge to the second-floor entrance, where carpeted walkways lead through a softly lit series of 20 marine habitats, progressing from salt marsh to the ocean depths. You'll see a thousand or so marine creatures of more than 125 species; my kids' favorites were the sleek speckled harbor seals that flop around an indoor/outdoor pool in the lobby (**seal feedings** at 11:45am and 1:45 and 3:45pm are extremely popular), but the bright-eyed otters in the woodland shoreline habitat run a close second. The sand tiger sharks circling and glaring at you through the glass in the enormous ocean tanks are also mesmerizing (12:45pm **sand tiger shark feeding** time), as is the **Jellyfish Encounter** at the ocean end of the long walkway. Kids who want to get really close to some less creepy sea creatures—sea stars, horseshoe crabs, whelks—can linger at the **Touch Tank,** or, if they're bold enough, pet a live ray at the **Ray Touch Pool.**

Beside the series of environments, the two-story **Maritime Hall** has loads of interactive educational displays on fish, but my friend's younger son and brother-in-law were just as interested in the displays on navigation and the boat shop for building wooden boats. The aquarium also boasts Connecticut's only **IMAX theater,** showing a rotation of several megascreen natural history films. An excellent gift shop lies in wait to cash in on all the parental goodwill created by the exhibits. It's just as pleasant a place to view marine life as the New York Aquarium in Coney Island (see chapter 4), and if you've got a car it's perhaps easier to get here; it's certainly easier to get here from Manhattan than it is to visit the Mystic Aquarium at the other end of Connecticut.

The aquarium is planning a huge expansion to be completed by early 2001, adding 33,000 square feet to the existing 100,000, making room for a much larger gift shop on the first floor and a new cafeteria on the second floor, and freeing up space in the present building for more animal exhibits.

Admission: Museum only, $8.25 adults, $7.50 seniors, $6.75 children 2 to 12; IMAX only (call for scheduled), $6.75 adults, $5.75 seniors, $5 children 2 to 12; museum plus IMAX, $12.50 adults, $11 seniors, $9.75 children 2 to 12. **Open:** Daily (except for Thanksgiving and Christmas) 10am to 5pm (July to Labor Day until 6pm); IMAX open for evening shows Friday to Sunday.

WHERE TO EAT

The **Oyster Bar,** at the end of Maritime Hall, offers some fairly good seafood, not all of it fried, at reasonable prices. It's open Saturday and Sunday 11:30am to 3pm, and operates daily July to Labor Day; until the new cafeteria opens, you can also grab a hot dog or other simple fare at the more pedestrian **snack bar** nearby. Table seating is provided.

Appendix:
For Foreign Visitors

New York is the largest city in the United States, and even other Americans can be intimidated by this fast-forward metropolis with its seemingly impenetrable (and largely unwritten) codes of conduct and rules of navigation. Especially with a family tagging along, you don't want to take chances. That's why we've prepared this information to help you navigate New York successfully.

Rule No. 1: Always ask for advice from a passerby, your hotel concierge, a restaurant waiter, a museum staffer, a bus driver—anyone who can clear up any confusion you may have about the best route to take or the proper way to accomplish something. Despite their bustling demeanor, New Yorkers are generally willing and eager to help visitors.

Rule No. 2: Take it easy—don't jump on that bus if you're not sure it's the right one, even though the locals may be dashing madly for the door. It won't be the last bus of the day.

1 Preparing for Your Trip

ENTRY REQUIREMENTS

Immigration laws are a hot political issue in the United States these days, and the following requirements may have changed somewhat by the time you plan your trip. Check at any U.S. embassy or consulate for current information and requirements, or plug into the U.S. State Department's Web site at **http://travel.state.gov**. Click on Visa Services for the latest entry requirements, or Links to Foreign embassies to find contact information for U.S. embassies and consulates worldwide.

VISAS

The U.S. State Department has a **Visa Waiver Pilot Program** allowing citizens of certain countries to enter the United States without a visa for stays of up to 90 days. At press time, this visa waiver program applied to citizens of these countries: Andorra, Argentina, Australia, Austria, Belgium, Brunei, Denmark, Finland, France, Germany, Iceland, Ireland, Italy, Japan, Liechtenstein, Luxembourg, Monaco, the Netherlands, New Zealand, Norway, Portugal, San Marino, Singapore, Slovenia, Spain, Sweden, Switzerland, the United Kingdom, and Uruguay. (Greece is in the preliminary stages of approval, but at press time visas were still required.) Citizens of these countries need only a valid passport and a round-trip air or cruise ticket in their possession upon arrival. If they first enter the United States, they may also visit Mexico, Canada, Bermuda, and the Caribbean islands and return to the United States without a visa. Further information is available from any U.S. embassy or consulate.

Canadian citizens may enter the United States without visas; they need only proof of residence.

Citizens of all other countries must have: (1) a **valid passport** that expires at least six months later than the scheduled end of their visit to the United States; and (2) a **tourist visa,** which may be obtained without charge from any U.S. consulate.

OBTAINING A VISA   To obtain a visa, you must submit a completed application form (either in person or by mail) with a 1½-inch-square photo, and you must demonstrate binding ties to a residence abroad. Usually you can obtain a visa at once or within 24 hours, but it may take longer during the summer rush, June through August. If you cannot visit your closest U.S. embassy or consulate in person, contact it for directions on applying by mail. A travel agent or an airline office may also be able to provide you with visa applications and instructions. The U.S. consulate or embassy that issues your visa will determine if you will be issued a multiple- or single-entry visa and any restrictions regarding the length of your stay. You can learn more about visas and the application process by calling the **U.S. State Department visa office** (☎ 202/663-1225).

MEDICAL REQUIREMENTS

Unless you're arriving from an area known to be suffering from an epidemic (particularly cholera or yellow fever), inoculations or vaccinations are not required for entry into the United States. If you have a disease that requires treatment with narcotics or syringe-administered medications, carry a valid signed prescription from your physician to allay any suspicions that you may be smuggling narcotics (a serious offense that carries severe penalties in the United States).

For HIV-positive visitors, requirements for entering the United States are somewhat vague and change frequently. If an HIV-positive non-citizen applying for a non-immigrant visa knows that HIV is a communicable disease of public health significance but checks "no" on the question about communicable diseases, INS may deny the visa on the grounds that the applicant committed fraud. If a non-immigrant visa applicant checks "yes," or if INS suspects the person is HIV-positive, it will deny the visa unless the applicant asks for a special waiver for visitors. This waiver is for people visiting the United States for a short time, to attend a conference, for instance, to visit close relatives, or to receive medical treatment.

For up-to-the-minute information concerning HIV-positive travelers, contact the **HIV/AIDS Treatment Information Service** (☎ 800/HIV-0440 or 301/519-0459; www.hivatis.org), the **Centers for Disease**

Immigration Questions

Automated information and live operator assistance regarding U.S. immigration policies and laws are available from the **U.S. Immigration and Naturalization Service (INS) Customer Information Center** (☎ 800/375-5283; www.ins.usdoj.gov), or the **New York Immigration Hotline** (☎ 718/899-4000).

Control and Prevention National AIDS Hotline (☎ 800/342-2437, or 800/344-7432 in Spanish; www.cdc.org), or **Gay Men's Health Crisis** (☎ **800/AIDS-NYC** or 212/807-6655; www.gmhc.org).

DRIVER'S LICENSES

Foreign driver's licenses are mostly recognized in the United States, although you may want to get an international driver's license if your home license is not written in English.

PASSPORT INFORMATION

Safeguard your passport in an inconspicuous, inaccessible place like a money belt. If you lose it, visit the nearest consulate of your native country as soon as possible for a replacement (a list of major consulates can be found in "Fast Facts: For the Foreign Traveler," at the end of this chapter). Passport applications are downloadable from the Internet sites listed below.

FOR RESIDENTS OF CANADA   You can pick up a passport application at one of 28 regional passport offices, most travel agencies, or the central **Canadian Passport Office,** Department of Foreign Affairs and International Trade, Ottawa, K1A 0G3 (☎ **800/567-6868;** www.dfait-maeci.gc.ca/passport). A passport is valid for five years. Children under 16 may be included on a parent's passport, but they need their own passport to travel if unaccompanied by the parent. An application must be accompanied by two identical passport-sized photographs and proof of Canadian citizenship. Processing takes 5 days if you apply in person, or about 10 days upon receipt if you apply by mail. Check the Web site or call for an updated list of fees.

FOR RESIDENTS OF THE UNITED KINGDOM   To pick up an application for a regular 10-year passport, visit a passport office, major post office, or travel agency, or contact the **UK Passport Agency** (☎ 0870/321-0410, www.ukpa.gov.uk).

FOR RESIDENTS OF IRELAND   Passport applications are available at all Garda stations, at post offices with Passport Express Service, and from the **Passport Office at Setanta Centre,** Molesworth Street, Dublin 2 (☎ 353-1/671-1633), or the **Passport Office at 1a South Mall,** Cork (☎ 353-21/272-525 or 353-21/276-964). For additional information, visit the **Department of Foreign Affairs** Web site at **www.irlgov.ie/iveagh** and click on Travelling Abroad.

FOR RESIDENTS OF AUSTRALIA   You can apply at a State Passports Office or at most local post offices. For further information, see the government's **Department of Foreign Affairs and Trade** Web site at **www.dfat.gov.au/passports.**

FOR RESIDENTS OF NEW ZEALAND   Complete information and downloadable applications can be found online at **www.passports.govt.nz;** or call the Passport Office at ☎ 0800/22-50-50.

CUSTOMS

WHAT YOU CAN BRING IN   Every visitor over 21 years of age may bring in, free of duty, the following: (1) 1 liter of wine or hard liquor; (2) 200 cigarettes, 100 cigars (but none from Cuba), or 3 pounds of smoking tobacco; and (3) $100 worth of gifts. These exemptions are offered to travelers who spend at least 72 hours in the United States and who have not claimed them within the preceding 6 months. It is altogether forbidden to bring into the country foodstuffs (particularly fruit, cooked meats, and canned goods) and plants (vegetables, seeds, tropical plants, and the like). Foreign tourists may bring in or take out up to $10,000 in U.S. or foreign currency with no formalities; larger sums must be declared to U.S. Customs upon entering or leaving, which includes filing form CM 4790. For more specific information regarding U.S. Customs, contact your nearest U.S. embassy or consulate, or the **U.S. Customs office** (☎ 202/927-1770; www.customs.ustreas.gov).

WHAT YOU CAN TAKE HOME   Check with your country's Customs or Foreign Affairs department for the latest guidelines—including information on items that are not allowed to be brought in to your home country—just before you leave home.

U.K. citizens should contact **HM Customs & Excise Passenger Enquiries** (☎ 0181/910-3744; www.open.gov.uk).

For a clear summary of Canadian rules, visit the comprehensive Web site of the **Canada Customs and Revenue Agency,** at **www.ccra-adrc.gc.ca.**

Citizens of Australia should request the helpful Australian Customs brochure *Know Before You Go* (☎ 1-300/363-263 within Australia or 61-2/6275-6666 from abroad). For additional information, go **www.dfat. gov.au** and click on Hints for Australian Travellers.

For New Zealand customs information, contact the **New Zealand Customs Service** (☎ 09/359-6655; www.customs.govt.nz).

INSURANCE

Although it's not required of travelers, health insurance is highly recommended. Unlike many European countries, the United States does not usually offer free or low-cost medical care to its citizens or visitors. Doctors and hospitals are expensive, and in most cases require advance payment or proof of coverage before they render their services. Travel insurance policies can cover everything from the loss or theft of your baggage and trip cancellation to the guarantee of bail in case you're arrested. Good policies will also cover the costs of an accident, repatriation, or death. Packages such as Europ Assistance in Europe are sold by automobile clubs and travel agencies at attractive rates. **Worldwide Assistance Services, Inc.** (☎ 800/777-8710, ext. 409, or 703/204-1897; www.worldwideassistance.com) is the agent for Europ Assistance in the United States.

Though lack of health insurance may prevent you from being admitted to a hospital in non-emergencies, don't worry about being left on a street corner to die: The American way is to fix you now and bill the living daylights out of you later.

FOR BRITISH TRAVELERS   Most big travel agents offer their own insurance, and will probably try to sell you their packages when you book a holiday. Think before you sign. Britain's Consumers' Association recommends that you insist on seeing the policy and reading the fine print before buying travel insurance. The **Association of British Insurers** (☎ 0171/600-3333) gives advice by phone and publishes the free *Holiday Insurance,* a guide to policy provisions and prices. You might also shop around for better deals: Try **Columbus Direct** (☎ 0171/375-0011; www.columbusdirect.net).

FOR CANADIAN TRAVELERS   Canadians should check with provincial health plan offices or call **HealthCanada** (☎ 613/957-2991) to determine the extent of their coverage and what documentation and receipts they must take home in case they are treated in the United States.

CURRENCY The U.S. monetary system is painfully simple: One U.S. **dollar** ($1) = 100 **cents** (100¢). The most common **bills** (all ugly, all green) are the $1 (colloquially, a "buck"), $5, $10, and $20 denominations. There are also $2 bills (seldom encountered), $50 bills, and $100 bills (the last two are usually not welcome as payment for small purchases). Note that redesigned $100, $50, $20, $10, and $5 bills have been introduced in the last few years, but the old-style bills are still legal tender.

There are six denominations of coins: 1¢ (1 cent, or a *penny*); 5¢ (5 cents, or a *nickel*); 10¢ (10 cents, or a *dime*); 25¢ (25 cents, or a *quarter*); 50¢ (50 cents, a *fifty-cent piece,* or a *half-dollar*); and the rare $1 piece (the older large *silver dollar,* the small silver-colored *Susan B. Anthony coin,* and a new gold-toned *$1 piece*). Note that a series of quarters minted beginning in 1999 feature different state emblems on the reverse instead of the long-standing American eagle icon; these are perfectly legal currency.

CURRENCY EXCHANGE The foreign-exchange bureaus so common in Europe are rare even at airports in the United States, and they're nonexistent outside major cities. You'll find them in New York's prime tourist areas like Times Square, but expect to get extorted on the exchange rate.

American Express (☎ 800/AXP-TRIP; www.americanexpress.com) has many offices throughout the city, including at the **New York Hilton,** 1335 Sixth Ave., at 53rd Street (☎ 212/664-7798); the **New York Marriott Marquis,** 1535 Broadway, in the 8th floor lobby (☎ 212/575-6580); on the mezzanine level at **Macy's Herald Square,** 34th Street and Broadway (☎ 212/695 8075); and **65 Broadway,** between Exchange Place and Rector Street (☎ 212/493-6500).

Thomas Cook Currency Services (☎ 800/223-9920; www.thomascook. com) has locations throughout the city, including JFK Airport and 41 E. 42nd St. Call for additional locations.

It's best not to expect to change foreign money (or traveler's checks denominated in a currency other than U.S. dollars) at a small-town bank, but many bank branches in Manhattan, such as Chase, are equipped to exchange a number of the most common foreign currencies. On the whole, it's better to leave any currency other than U.S. dollars at home—it may prove a greater nuisance to you than it's worth.

TRAVELER'S CHECKS Though traveler's checks are widely accepted, make sure they're denominated in U.S. dollars, as foreign-currency checks are often difficult to exchange. The three traveler's checks that are most widely recognized—and least likely to be denied—are **Visa, American Express,** and **Thomas Cook/MasterCard.** Be sure to record the numbers of the checks, and keep that information separately in case they get lost or stolen. Most businesses are pretty good about taking traveler's checks, but you're better off cashing them in at a bank (in small amounts, of course) and paying in cash. Remember that you'll need identification, such as a driver's license or passport, to change a traveler's check.

CREDIT CARDS & ATMs **Credit cards** are the most widely used form of payment in the United States: **Visa** (BarclayCard in Britain), **MasterCard** (Eurocard in Europe, Access in Britain, Chargex in Canada), **American Express,** and the somewhat less widely accepted **Diners Club, Discover,** and **Carte Blanche.** New York vendors may also accept international cards like **enRoute, Eurocard,** and **Japan Credit Bank,** but not as universally as American Express, MasterCard, or Visa. There are, however, a

Travel Tip

Be sure to keep a copy of all your travel papers separate from your wallet or purse, and leave a copy with someone at home should you need it faxed in an emergency.

handful of stores and restaurants that do not take credit cards, so be sure to ask in advance. Most businesses display a sticker near their entrance to let you know which cards they accept. Also, be aware that often businesses require a minimum purchase price, usually around $10 or $15, to use a credit card.

It is strongly recommended that you bring at least one major credit card. Hotels, car-rental companies, and airlines usually require a credit-card imprint as a deposit against expenses, and in an emergency a credit card can be priceless. Using a credit card to make store purchases may often save you money, since the credit card company will calculate your charges using the bank exchange rate—often better than the rate you'll be charged to convert your foreign denomination traveler's checks to cash

You'll find **automated-teller machines (ATMs)** on just about every block in Manhattan. Some ATMs will allow you to draw U.S. currency against your bank and credit cards. Check with your bank before leaving home, and remember that you will need your personal identification number (PIN) to use any ATM. Most accept Visa, MasterCard, and American Express, as well as ATM cards from other U.S. banks. Expect to be charged up to $3 per transaction, however, if you're not using your own bank's ATM.

SAFETY

Tourist areas in Manhattan are generally safe, and the city has experienced a dramatic drop in its crime rate in recent years. Still, crime is a national problem, and U.S. urban areas tend to be less safe than those in Europe or Japan. You should always stay alert, use common sense, and trust your instincts. If you feel you're in an unsafe area or situation, you probably are and should leave as quickly as possible.

GENERAL SAFETY SUGGESTIONS Leave your valuables at home if you can live without them. Don't display expensive cameras or flashy jewelry as you walk around the city. If you are using a map, consult it as discreetly as possible, with one eye on what's going on around you at all times. Always keep your children within sight, even if it means making a young boy go with his mother into the women's restroom (other women inside the restroom will generally be understanding). If you do send your child into a restroom alone, it's not a bad idea to stick your own head in first to scope out the other folks inside and to wait right outside the restroom door.

Remember that hotels are open to the public, and in a large hotel, security may not be able to screen everyone entering. Always lock the door to your room—don't assume that, once inside your hotel, you are automatically safe and no longer need to keep an eye on your valuables or be aware of your surroundings.

Avoid deserted areas, especially at night, and don't go into public parks at night unless there's a concert or similar occasion that will attract a crowd.

For more about personal security in Manhattan, see "Fast Facts: New York City" in chapter 3.

DRIVING   A rule of thumb for visitors to New York: Don't even think of driving within the city. Like many cities, New York has its own arcane rules of the road, confusing one-way streets, incomprehensible street-parking signs, and very expensive parking garages. Public transportation—whether buses, subways, or taxis—will get you anywhere you want to go quickly and easily, and that's where you'll be most comfortable.

If you do drive to New York in a rental car, return it as soon as you arrive and rent another when you're ready to leave the city. Always keep your car doors locked. Never leave any packages or valuables in sight, because thieves may break car windows. If someone attempts to rob you or steal your car, don't resist. Report the incident to the police department immediately.

2 Getting to the United States

In addition to the domestic airlines listed in chapter 2, many international carriers serve John F. Kennedy International and Newark airports. **British Airways** (☎ 0345/222-111 in the U.K., 800/AIRWAYS in the U.S.; www.british-airways.com) has daily service from London as well as direct flights from Manchester and Glasgow. **Virgin Atlantic** (☎ 01293/747-747 in the U.K., 800/862-8621 in the U.S.; www.virgin-atlantic.com) flies from London's Heathrow to New York.

Canadian readers might book flights on **Air Canada** (☎ 800/776-3000; www.aircanada.ca), which offers direct service from Toronto, Montréal, Ottawa, and other cities; and **Canadian Airlines** (☎ 800/426-7000; www.cdnair.ca).

Aer Lingus flies from Ireland to New York (☎ 01/886-8888 in Dublin, 800/IRISH-AIR in the U.S., www.aerlingus.ie).

The following U.S. airlines fly to New York from most major European cities. **Continental** (☎ 01293/776-464 in the U.K., 800/525-0280 in the U.S.; www.continental.com); **TWA** (☎ 0181/815-0707 in the U.K., 800/221-2000 in the U.S.; www.twa.com); **United** (☎ 0845/8-444-777 in the U.K., 800/538-2929 in the U.S.; www.ual.com); **American** (☎ 0181/572-5555 in the U.K., 800/433-7300 in the U.S.; www.americanair.com); and **Delta** (☎ 0800/414-767 in the U.K., 800/221-1212 in the U.S.; www.delta.com).

Qantas (☎ 13-13-13 in Australia, 800/227-4500 in the U.S.; www.qantas.com.au) and **Air New Zealand** (☎ 0800/737-000 in New Zealand, 800/262-1234 in the U.S.; www.airnewzealand.co.nz) fly to the West Coast and can book you straight through to New York City on a partner airline.

AIRLINE DISCOUNTS

The idea of traveling abroad on a budget is something of an oxymoron, especially when pricey New York is your destination, but you can reduce the price of a plane ticket by several hundred dollars if you take the time to shop around. For example, overseas visitors can take advantage of the **APEX (Advance Purchase Excursion)** reductions offered by all major U.S. and European carriers. For more money-saving airline advice, see "Getting There" in chapter 2. For the best rates, compare fares and be flexible with the dates and times of travel.

Operated by the **European Travel Network, www.discount-tickets. com** is a great online source for regular and discounted airfares to New York and other destinations around the world. You can also use this site to compare rates and book accommodations, car rentals, and tours. Click on Special Offers for the latest package deals. Students should also try **Usit Campus Travel** (☎ 0171/730-2101; www.usitcampus.co.uk).

Some major U.S. carriers—including Delta and Continental—offer travelers on their transatlantic or transpacific flights special low-price tickets on U.S. continental flights under the **Discover America program** (sometimes called **Visit USA,** depending on the airline). Offering one-way travel between U.S. destinations at significantly reduced prices, this coupon-based airfare program is the best and easiest way to tour the U.S. at low cost.

These discounted fare coupons aren't available in the United States and must be purchased abroad, in conjunction with your international ticket. You should ask a travel agent or an airline reservations agent about this program well in advance of your departure date—preferably when you buy your international ticket—since the regulations may govern your trip planning, and conditions can change without notice.

IMMIGRATION & CUSTOMS CLEARANCE

Visitors arriving by air, no matter what the port of entry, should expect to have their patience sorely tested as soon as they set foot on U.S. soil. Getting through immigration control may take as long as 2 hours on some days, especially on summer weekends, so forewarn your children and have on hand something to read or play with as you shuffle through the long lines. Add the time it takes to clear customs, and you'll see that you should make a 2- to 3-hour allowance for delays when you plan your connections between international and domestic flights.

In contrast, for the traveler arriving by car or rail from Canada, the border-crossing formalities have been streamlined to the vanishing point. People traveling by air from Canada, Bermuda, and some places in the Caribbean can sometimes clear customs and immigration at the point of departure, which speeds up the process considerably.

Fast Facts: For the Foreign Traveler

See "Fast Facts: New York City" in chapter 3 for more New York City–specific information.

Automobile Organizations   Auto clubs supply maps, suggested routes, guidebooks, accident and bail-bond insurance, and emergency road service. The **American Automobile Association (AAA)** is the major auto club in the United States. If you belong to an auto club in your home country, inquire about AAA reciprocity before you leave. You may be able to join AAA even if you're not a member of a reciprocal club; to inquire, call ☎ **800/222-4357,** or visit **www.aaa.com.** AAA is an organization of regional auto clubs, so you can also look under "AAA Automobile Club" in the White Pages of the telephone directory. AAA has a nationwide emergency road service telephone number (☎ **800/AAA-HELP**).

Automobile Rentals   To rent a car in the United States, you need a valid driver's license, a passport, and a major credit card. The minimum age is usually 25, but some companies will rent to younger people for an added surcharge. It's a good idea to buy maximum insurance coverage unless you're positive your own auto or credit-card insurance is sufficient. All major car-rental agencies have branches in Manhattan; try **Hertz** (☎ **800/654-3131;** www.hertz.com), **National** (☎ **800/227-7368;** www.nationalcar.com), or **Avis** (☎ **800/230-4898;** www.avis.com). Stick to the major companies, because what money you might save with smaller companies might not be worth the headache if you have mechanical or other troubles on the road. Rates vary, so it pays to call around. Child safety seats are required for children aged 5 and younger in many states—ask your car rental agency if it provides them (a fee may be charged).

Business Hours See "Fast Facts: New York City" in chapter 3.

Currency & Currency Exchange See "Money" under "Preparing for Your Trip," earlier in this chapter. For the latest market conversion rates, point your Internet browser to **www.cnn.com/travel/currency**.

Drinking Laws The legal age for purchase and consumption of alcoholic beverages is 21; proof of age is required and often requested at bars, nightclubs, and restaurants, so it's always a good idea to bring ID when you go out. Liquor stores, the only retail outlets for wine as well as hard liquor in New York, are closed on Sundays, holidays, and election days while the polls are open. Beer can be purchased in grocery stores and delis all day Monday to Saturday and Sunday after noon.

Do not carry open containers of alcohol in your car or any public area that isn't zoned for alcohol consumption. The police can, and probably will, fine you on the spot. And nothing will ruin your trip faster than getting a citation for DUI ("driving under the influence"), so don't even think about driving while intoxicated.

Electricity Like Canada, the United States uses **110 to 120 volts AC** (60 cycles), compared to 220 to 240 volts AC (50 cycles) in most of Europe, Australia, and New Zealand. If your small appliances use 220 to 240 volts, you'll need a 110-volt transformer and a plug adapter with two flat parallel pins to operate them here. Downward converters that change 220–240 volts to 110–120 volts are difficult to find in the United States, so bring one with you.

Embassies/Consulates All foreign embassies are in Washington, D.C. Some countries have consulates general in major U.S. cities, and most have a mission to the United Nations in New York City. If your country isn't listed below, call for directory information in Washington, D.C. (☎ 202/555-1212), or point your web browser to **www.embassy.org/embassies** for the location and phone number of your national embassy.

Australia: Embassy, 1601 Massachusetts Ave. NW, Washington, D.C. 20036 (☎ 202/797-3000; www.austemb.org); consulate general, 150 E. 42nd St., New York, NY 10117 (☎ 212/351-6500).

Canada: Embassy, 501 Pennsylvania Ave. NW, Washington, D.C. 20001 (☎ 202/682-1740; www.cdnemb-washdc.org); consulate general, 1251 Ave. of the Americas, New York, NY 10020 (☎ 212/596-1628; www.canada-ny.com).

Ireland: Embassy, 2234 Massachusetts Ave. NW, Washington, D.C. 20008 (☎ 202/462-3939; www.irelandemb.org); consulate general, 345 Park Ave., New York, NY 10154-0037 (☎ 212/319-2555).

Japan: Embassy, 2520 Massachusetts Ave. NW, Washington, DC 20008 (☎ 202/238-6700; www.embjapan.org).

New Zealand: Embassy, 37 Observatory Circle, Washington, D.C. 20008 (☎ 202/328-4800; www.emb.com/nzemb); consulate general, 780 Third Ave., New York, NY, 10017 (☎ 212/832-4038).

United Kingdom: Embassy, 3100 Massachusetts Ave. NW, Washington, D.C. 20008 (☎ 202/588-6500; www.britainusa.com/bis/embassy/embassy/htm); consulate general, 845 Third Ave., New York, NY 10022 (☎ 212/745-0200; www.britainusa.com/bis/consular/ny/ny.stm).

Emergencies   Call ☎ **911** to report a **fire, call the police,** or **get an ambulance** anywhere in the United States. This is a toll-free call (no coins are required at public telephones).

If you have a medical emergency that doesn't require an ambulance, you can walk into a hospital's 24-hour emergency room (usually a special emergency entrance). For a list of hospitals, see "Fast Facts: New York City" in chapter 3. Otherwise, call ☎ **212/737-2333,** a referral service available 8am to midnight, for doctors who make house calls. Don't be surprised if the first question you are asked is, "Do you have medical insurance?"

Gasoline (Petrol)   Petrol is known as *gasoline* (or simply *gas*) in the United States, and petrol stations are known as both *gas stations* and *service stations.* Gasoline costs less than it does in Europe (about $1.50 per gallon at press time), and taxes are already included in the advertised price. One U.S. gallon equals 3.8 liters, or 0.85 Imperial gallons.

Holidays   Banks, government offices, post offices, and many stores, restaurants, and museums are closed on the following legal national holidays: January 1 (New Year's Day), the third Monday in January (Martin Luther King, Jr. Day), the third Monday in February (Presidents' Day, Washington's Birthday), the last Monday in May (Memorial Day), July 4 (Independence Day), the first Monday in September (Labor Day), the second Monday in October (Columbus Day), November 11 (Veterans' Day/Armistice Day), the fourth Thursday in November (Thanksgiving Day), and December 25 (Christmas). Also, the Tuesday following the first Monday in November is Election Day and is a federal government holiday in presidential-election years (held every four years, in 2000 and next in 2004).

Legal Aid   Most foreign tourists will probably never become involved with the U.S. legal system. If you are stopped for a minor violation (for example, exceeding the speed limit while driving), never attempt to pay the fine directly to a police officer; this could be construed as attempted bribery, which is a serious crime. If you are involved in a traffic violation, do not get out of the car; stay seated and with your hands on the steering wheel until the officer approaches you. Pay fines by mail or directly into the hands of the clerk of the court. If you are accused of a more serious offense, say and do nothing before consulting a lawyer. Here the burden is on the state to prove a person's guilt beyond a reasonable doubt, and everyone has the right to remain silent, whether he or she is suspected of a crime or actually arrested. Once arrested, a person can make one telephone call to a party of his or her choice. Call your embassy or consulate.

Mail   Generally found at intersections, mailboxes are blue with a white eagle logo and carry the inscription U.S. MAIL. If your mail is addressed to a U.S. destination, don't forget to add the five-digit postal code (or zip code), after the two-letter abbreviation of the state to which the mail is addressed.

At press time, domestic postage rates were 20¢ for a postcard and 33¢ for a letter. For international mail, a first-class letter of up to one-half ounce costs 60¢ (46¢ to Canada and 40¢ to Mexico); a first-class postcard costs 50¢ (40¢ to Canada and 35¢ Mexico); and a preprinted postal aerogramme costs 50¢. Point your web browser to **www.usps.gov** for complete U.S. postal information, or call ☎ **800/275-8777** for information on the nearest post office. Most branches are open Monday to Friday from 8am to 5 or 6pm, and Saturday from 9am to 3pm.

Newspapers/Magazines   In addition to the *New York Times* and other city papers, many newsstands carry a selection of international newspapers and magazines. For nearly all major newspapers and magazines from around the world, head to **Universal News & Magazines,** 977 Eighth Ave., at 57th Street (☎ **212/459-0932**), or **Hotalings News Agency,** inside the Times Square Visitor Center at 1560 Broadway, between 46th and 47th streets (☎ **212/840-1868**).

Taxes   There is no value-added tax (VAT) or other indirect tax at the national level, but every state, county, and city has the right to levy its own local tax on all purchases, including hotel and restaurant checks, airline tickets, and so on. Sales tax is usually not included in the price tags on merchandise but is added at the cash register. Foreign visitors cannot get refunds on these sales taxes when they leave the country. In New York City, the sales tax is 8.25%, but it is not charged on groceries or clothing purchases under $110. The hotel tax is 13.25% plus $2 per room per night (including sales tax). The parking garage tax, added to already high basic fees, is 18.25%.

Telephone, Telegram & Fax   The telephone system in the United States is run by private corporations, so rates, especially for long-distance service and operator-assisted calls, can vary widely. Generally, hotel surcharges on long-distance and local calls are astronomical, so you're usually better off using a public pay telephone, which you'll find clearly marked in most public buildings and private establishments as well as in hotel lobbies and on the street. Many convenience stores and newsstands sell prepaid calling cards in denominations up to $50; these can be the least expensive way to call home. Many public phones at airports now accept American Express, MasterCard, and Visa credit cards. Local calls made from public pay phones usually cost 25¢ for the first five minutes, but sometimes it's 35¢. Pay phones do not accept pennies, and few will take anything larger than a quarter.

Most long-distance and international calls can be dialed directly from any phone. For **long-distance calls within the United States and to Canada,** dial 1 followed by the three-digit area code and the seven-digit number. For **other international calls,** dial 011 followed by the country code, city code, and the telephone number of the person you are calling. Some country and city codes are as follows: Australia 61, Melbourne 3, Sydney 2; Ireland 353, Dublin 1; New Zealand 64, Auckland 9, Wellington 4; United Kingdom 44, Belfast 232, Birmingham 21, Glasgow 41, London 71 or 81. If you're calling the United States from another country, the country code is 01.

For **reversed-charge, collect, operator-assisted,** and **person-to-person calls,** dial 0 (the number zero) followed by the area code and number you want; an operator will then come on the line, and you should specify that you are calling collect, or person-to-person, or both. If your operator-assisted call is international, ask for the overseas operator.

For **local and national directory assistance** ("information"), dial ☎ **411.**

Telegram services are provided primarily by Western Union. You can bring a telegram into the nearest Western Union office (there are hundreds across the country) or dictate it over the phone (☎ **800/325-6000;** www.westernunion.com). You can also telegraph money or have it telegraphed to you very quickly, but this service can cost as much as 15 to 20% of the amount sent.

Most hotels have **fax machines** available for guest use (be sure to ask about the charge to use it), and many hotel rooms even have in-room fax

Calls to area codes 800, 888, and 877 are toll-free. However, calls to numbers in area codes 700 and 900 (chat lines, bulletin boards, "dating" services, and so on) can be very expensive—usually a charge of 95¢ to $3 or more per minute, and they sometimes have minimum charges that can be $15 or more.

machines. Receiving faxes is usually free (always ask first if it matters, though), but a less expensive way to send faxes may be at stores such as Mail Boxes Etc., a national chain of packing service shops (look in the Yellow Pages under "Packing Services").

There are two kinds of telephone directories in the United States. The **White Pages** list private households and business subscribers in alphabetical order. The inside front cover lists emergency numbers for police, fire, ambulance, the poison-control center, crime-victims hotline, and so on. The first few pages tell you how to make long-distance and international calls, complete with country codes and area codes. Government numbers are usually printed on blue paper within the White Pages. Printed on yellow paper, the **Yellow Pages** list all local services, businesses, industries, and houses of worship according to activity with an index at the front or back. (Drugstores/pharmacies and restaurants are also listed by geographic location.) The Yellow Pages also include city plans or detailed area maps, postal zip codes, and public transportation routes. A useful online directory for finding phone numbers and addresses in New York and other U.S. cities is **www.yp.ameritech.net**.

Time The continental United States is divided into four time zones: eastern standard time (EST), the time zone New York is in, which is 5 hours behind Greenwich Mean Time (GMT); central standard time (CST); mountain standard time (MST); and Pacific standard time (PST). Alaska and Hawaii have their own zones. For example, noon in New York City (EST) is 11am in Chicago (CST), 10am in Denver (MST), 9am in Los Angeles (PST), 8am in Anchorage (AST), and 7am in Honolulu (HST).

Daylight saving time is in effect from 1am on the first Sunday in April through 1am the last Sunday in October, except in Arizona, Hawaii, part of Indiana, and Puerto Rico. Daylight saving time moves the clock 1 hour ahead of standard time.

For the correct local time in New York, dial ☎ 212/976-1616.

Tipping Tips are a very important part of certain workers' salaries, so it's necessary to leave appropriate gratuities. Unlike in most of Europe, tips aren't automatically added to restaurant and hotel bills. In restaurants, a tip to the waitperson of 15 to 20% of the total check is customary; in New York City, you can just double the 8.25% tax to figure the appropriate tip.

Other tipping guidelines: 15 to 20% of the fare to taxi drivers; 10 to 15% of the tab to bartenders; $1 to $2 per bag to bellhops; at least $1 per day to hotel maids; $1 per item to checkroom attendants; $1 to valet parking attendants; and 15 to 20% to hairdressers. Tipping theater ushers, gas station attendants, and cafeteria and fast-food restaurant employees isn't expected.

Toilets In general, you won't find public toilets or "rest rooms" on the streets in New York, but you can find them in hotel lobbies, bars, restaurants, museums, department stores, or railway and bus stations. See "Finding a Rest Room" under "Planning Your Outings" in chapter 3.

Index

See also Accommodations and Restaurant indexes below.

General Index

General Index

Accommodations Index

Restaurant Index

FROMMER'S® COMPLETE TRAVEL GUIDES

Alaska
Amsterdam
Arizona
Atlanta
Australia
Austria
Bahamas
Barcelona, Madrid &
   Seville
Beijing
Belgium, Holland &
   Luxembourg
Bermuda
Boston
British Columbia & the
   Canadian Rockies
Budapest & the Best of
   Hungary
California
Canada
Cancún, Cozumel &
   the Yucatán
Cape Cod, Nantucket &
   Martha's Vineyard
Caribbean
Caribbean Cruises & Ports
   of Call
Caribbean Ports of Call
Carolinas & Georgia
Chicago
China
Colorado
Costa Rica
Denmark
Denver, Boulder & Colorado
   Springs
England
Europe

European Cruises & Ports
   of Call
Florida
France
Germany
Greece
Greek Islands
Hawaii
Hong Kong
Honolulu, Waikiki & Oahu
Ireland
Israel
Italy
Jamaica
Japan
Las Vegas
London
Los Angeles
Maryland & Delaware
Maui
Mexico
Montana & Wyoming
Montréal & Québec City
Munich & the Bavarian
   Alps
Nashville & Memphis
Nepal
New England
New Mexico
New Orleans
New York City
New Zealand
Nova Scotia, New Brunswick
   & Prince Edward Island
Oregon
Paris
Philadelphia & the
   Amish Country

Portugal
Prague & the Best of the
   Czech Republic
Provence & the Riviera
Puerto Rico
Rome
San Antonio & Austin
San Diego
San Francisco
Santa Fe, Taos & Albuquerque
Scandinavia
Scotland
Seattle & Portland
Shanghai
Singapore & Malaysia
South Africa
Southeast Asia
South Florida
South Pacific
Spain
Sweden
Switzerland
Thailand
Tokyo
Toronto
Tuscany & Umbria
USA
Utah
Vancouver & Victoria
Vermont, New Hampshire
   & Maine
Vienna & the Danube Valley
Virgin Islands
Virginia
Walt Disney World &
   Orlando
Washington, D.C.
Washington State

FROMMER'S® DOLLAR-A-DAY GUIDES

Australia from $50 a Day
California from $60 a Day
Caribbean from $70 a Day
England from $70 a Day
Europe from $70 a Day

Florida from $70 a Day
Hawaii from $70 a Day
Ireland from $60 a Day
Italy from $70 a Day
London from $85 a Day

New York from $80 a Day
Paris from $80 a Day
San Francisco from $60 a Day
Washington, D.C.,
   from $70 a Day

FROMMER'S® PORTABLE GUIDES

Acapulco, Ixtapa &
   Zihuatanejo
Alaska Cruises & Ports of Call
Bahamas
Baja & Los Cabos
Berlin
California Wine Country
Charleston & Savannah
Chicago
Dublin

Hawaii: The Big Island
Las Vegas
London
Los Angeles
Maine Coast
Maui
Miami
New Orleans
New York City
Paris

Puerto Vallarta, Manzanillo
   & Guadalajara
San Diego
San Francisco
Sydney
Tampa & St. Petersburg
Venice
Washington, D.C.

FROMMER'S® NATIONAL PARK GUIDES

Family Vacations in the
   National Parks
Grand·Canyon

National Parks of the
   American West
Rocky Mountain

Yellowstone & Grand Teton
Yosemite & Sequoia/
   Kings Canyon
Zion & Bryce Canyon

FROMMER'S® MEMORABLE WALKS

Chicago
London

New York
Paris

San Francisco
Washington, D.C.

FROMMER'S® GREAT OUTDOOR GUIDES

New England
Northern California

Southern California & Baja
Southern New England

Washington & Oregon

FROMMER'S® BORN TO SHOP GUIDES

Born to Shop: France
Born to Shop: Italy

Born to Shop: London
Born to Shop: New York

Born to Shop: Paris

FROMMER'S® IRREVERENT GUIDES

Amsterdam
Boston
Chicago
Las Vegas

London
Los Angeles
Manhattan
New Orleans

Paris
San Francisco
Seattle & Portland
Vancouver

Walt Disney World
Washington, D.C.

FROMMER'S® BEST-LOVED DRIVING TOURS

America
Britain
California

Florida
France
Germany

Ireland
Italy
New England

Scotland
Spain
Western Europe

THE UNOFFICIAL GUIDES®

Bed & Breakfasts in
   California
Bed & Breakfasts in
   New England
Bed & Breakfasts in
   the Northwest
Bed & Breakfasts in
   Southeast
Beyond Disney
Branson, Missouri

California with Kids
Chicago
Cruises
Disneyland
Florida with Kids
Golf Vacations in the
   Eastern U.S.
The Great Smoky &
   Blue Ridge
   Mountains

Inside Disney
Hawaii
Las Vegas
London
Miami & the Keys
Mini Las Vegas
Mini-Mickey
New Orleans
New York City
Paris

San Francisco
Skiing in the West
Southeast with Kids
Walt Disney World
Walt Disney World
   for Grown-ups
Walt Disney World
   for Kids
Washington, D.C.

SPECIAL-INTEREST TITLES

Frommer's Britain's Best Bed & Breakfasts and
   Country Inns
Frommer's Britain's Best Bike Rides
The Civil War Trust's Official Guide
   to the Civil War Discovery Trail
Frommer's Caribbean Hideaways
Frommer's Adventure Guide to Central America
Frommer's Adventure Guide to South America
Frommer's Adventure Guide to Southeast Asia
Frommer's Food Lover's Companion to France
Frommer's Gay & Lesbian Europe
Frommer's Exploring America by RV
Hanging Out in Europe

Israel Past & Present
Mad Monks' Guide to California
Mad Monks' Guide to New York City
Frommer's The Moon
Frommer's New York City with Kids
The New York Times' Unforgettable
   Weekends
Places Rated Almanac
Retirement Places Rated
Frommer's Road Atlas Britain
Frommer's Road Atlas Europe
Frommer's Washington, D.C., with Kids
Frommer's What the Airlines Never Tell You